Essentials of
HEALTH INFORMATION MANAGEMENT

Principles & Practices

Essentials of
HEALTH INFORMATION MANAGEMENT

Principles & Practices

THIRD EDITION

Mary Jo Bowie, MS, BS, AAS, RHIA, RHIT
Consultant and Owner
Health Information Professional Services
Binghamton, New York
Associate Professor in Health Information
Management
Program Director
Mount Wachusett Community College
Gardner, Massachusetts

Michelle A. Green, MPS, RHIA, FAHIMA, CPC
SUNY Distinguished Teaching Professor
Department of Physical and Life Sciences
Alfred State College
Alfred, New York

CENGAGE
Learning·

Australia • Brazil • Japan • Korea • Mexico • Singapore • United Kingdom • United States

CENGAGE Learning®

Essentials of Health Information Management: Principles & Practices, Third Edition

Mary Jo Bowie, Michelle Green

SVP, GM Skills & Global Product Management: Dawn Gerrain

Product Manager: Jadin B. Kavanaugh

Senior Director, Development: Marah Bellegarde

Product Development Manager: Juliet Steiner

Senior Content Developer: Elisabeth F. Williams

Product Assistant: Mark Turner

Vice President, Marketing Services: Jennifer Ann Baker

Marketing Manager: Erica Glisson

Senior Production Director: Wendy Troeger

Production Director: Andrew Crouth

Senior Content Project Manager: Kara A. DiCaterino

Senior Art Director: Jack Pendleton

Cover image(s):

© Sergey Nivens/Shutterstock.com

For product information and technology assistance, contact us at
Cengage Learning Customer & Sales Support, 1-800-354-9706

For permission to use material from this text or product,
submit all requests online at **www.cengage.com/permissions.**
Further permissions questions can be e-mailed to
permissionrequest@cengage.com

Library of Congress Control Number: 2014959039

ISBN: 978-1-285-17726-7

Cengage Learning
20 Channel Center Street
Boston, MA 02210
USA

Cengage Learning is a leading provider of customized learning solutions with office locations around the globe, including Singapore, the United Kingdom, Australia, Mexico, Brazil, and Japan. Locate your local office at: **www.cengage.com/global**

Cengage Learning products are represented in Canada by Nelson Education, Ltd.

To learn more about Cengage Learning, visit **www.cengage.com**

Purchase any of our products at your local college store or at our preferred online store **www.cengagebrain.com**

Notice to the Reader

Publisher does not warrant or guarantee any of the products described herein or perform any independent analysis in connection with any of the product information contained herein. Publisher does not assume, and expressly disclaims, any obligation to obtain and include information other than that provided to it by the manufacturer. The reader is expressly warned to consider and adopt all safety precautions that might be indicated by the activities described herein and to avoid all potential hazards. By following the instructions contained herein, the reader willingly assumes all risks in connection with such instructions. The publisher makes no representations or warranties of any kind, including but not limited to, the warranties of fitness for particular purpose or merchantability, nor are any such representations implied with respect to the material set forth herein, and the publisher takes no responsibility with respect to such material. The publisher shall not be liable for any special, consequential, or exemplary damages resulting, in whole or part, from the readers' use of, or reliance upon, this material.

Printed in the United States of America
Print Number: 01   Print Year: 2015

Contents

List of Tables

Preface

INTRODUCTION

Managing health information is an important function of allied health professionals (e.g., cancer registrars, coders, health information administrators and technicians, medical assistants, medical office administrators, medical transcriptionists), and accurate management has become more exacting (e.g., due to changing federal regulations). Allied health professionals require thorough instruction in all aspects of health information management, including health care delivery systems, health information management professions, health care settings, the patient record (acute, outpatient, and alternate care settings) including the electronic health record, content of the patient record (standards and regulations), numbering and filing systems, record storage and circulation, indexes, registers, health data collection, legal aspects, and coding and reimbursement. *Essentials of Health Information Management,* third edition, provides the required information in a clear and comprehensive manner. Chapter content covers traditional record-keeping concepts covered in an introduction to health information management course, and concepts common to all types of health care facilities are included. Chapters also focus on differences associated with record-keeping practices in hospitals, ambulatory care facilities, and physicians' offices.

OBJECTIVES

The objectives of this text are to:

1. Introduce health information management concepts common to allied health professionals.
2. Describe characteristics of health care delivery and settings in the United States.
3. Delineate career opportunities for health information management professionals.
4. Describe types of patient records, including documentation issues associated with each.
5. Describe numbering and filing systems and record storage and circulation methods, including the electronic health record.
6. Explain indexes, registers, and health data collection.
7. Introduce legal aspects of health information management.
8. Provide an overview of coding and reimbursement issues.

This text is designed to be used by college and vocational school programs to train allied health professionals (e.g., cancer registrars, coders, health information administrators and technicians, medical assistants, medical office administrators, medical transcriptionists). It can also be used as an in-service training tool for new health care facility personnel and independent billing services, or individually by health information specialists.

NEW TO THE THIRD EDITION

- All chapters have been updated to include new information that relates to electronic health records and the transition from manual records to the electronic management of health information.
- Chapter 5 on electronic health records has been expanded to include new terminology relevant to electronic health record systems.
- Chapter 6 now includes numerous examples of electronic health records and systems.
- NEW! MindTap is a fully online, interactive learning experience built upon authoritative Cengage Learning content. MindTap combines readings, multimedia, activities, and assessments into a singular learning path, and elevates learning by providing real-world application to better engage students. MindTap includes an interactive eBook with highlighting and note-taking capability, self-quizzes, and learning activities such as image labeling, crossword puzzles, matching, multiple choice, flash cards, and more.

FEATURES OF THE TEXT

- Key terms and learning objectives at the beginning of each chapter help to organize the material. They can be used as a self-test for checking comprehension and mastery of the chapter. Key terms are bold-faced throughout each chapter and defined in the glossary to help students master the technical vocabulary associated with health information management.

- Exercises are located after major topics to provide students with an opportunity to apply concepts and skills immediately.
- Numerous examples are provided in each chapter to illustrate health information management concepts.
- End-of-chapter Internet links, summaries, study checklists, and reviews reinforce learning and identify topics requiring further study.
- Questions created for exercises and reviews serve as a self-test of chapter content. For questions written to prepare students for taking certification exams (e.g., RHIT, CCS, CPC), Cengage Learning distributes the following products created for this purpose:
  ○ Professional Review Guide for the RHIA and RHIT Examinations
  ○ Professional Review Guide for the CCA Examination
  ○ Professional Review Guide for the CCS and CCS-P Examinations

LEARNING PACKAGE FOR THE STUDENT

Student Lab Manual
ISBN 978-1-285-17735-9

The Student Lab Manual includes application-based assignments organized according to textbook chapters. These assignments reinforce learning and encourage skill building. While intended for all students, the student lab manual will be particularly appropriate preparation for health information management students who will complete a future professional practice experience in the health information department of a hospital.

The third edition of the lab manual features additional bonus activities using Neehr Perfect® VistA EHR software. A separate subscription is required. For more information on using Neehr Perfect® with the lab manual, please go to neehrperfect.com/Cengage for more information.

MindTap

MindTap is the first of its kind in an entirely new category: the Personal Learning Experience (PLE). This personalized program of digital products and services uses interactivity and customization to engage you, while offering a range of choice in content, platforms, devices, and learning tools. MindTap is device agnostic, meaning that it will work with any platform or learning management system and will be accessible anytime, anywhere: on desktops, laptops, tablets, mobile phones, and other internet-enabled devices. *Essentials of Health Information Management,* third edition, on MindTap includes:

- An interactive eBook with highlighting and note-taking functions, and more
- Case study scenarios with real-life examples and dilemmas to resolve
- Drag-and-drop exercises
- Flashcards for practicing chapter key terms
- Video scenarios to encourage critical thinking and application of concepts
- Computer-graded activities and exercises

Student Companion Website

Additional resources can be found online at www.cengagebrain.com. Search by author name, ISBN, or title to locate the online student companion for *Essentials of Health Information Management,* third edition. Resources include downloadable files to support the student lab manual and textbook, product updates, related links, and more. The student resources include Adobe PDF files of assignments that can be completed as forms and sent as an e-mail attachment to instructors for evaluation. (Go to www.adobe.com to download the latest version of Adobe Reader to fill in forms.) Save completed forms as electronic files using the naming convention required by your instructor.

TEACHING PACKAGE FOR THE INSTRUCTOR

Instructor Companion Website
ISBN 978-1-285-17732-8

The *Instructor Companion Website to Accompany Essentials of Health Information Management,* third edition, contains a variety of tools to help instructors successfully prepare lectures and teach within this subject area. This comprehensive package provides something for all instructors, from those teaching health information management for the first time to seasoned instructors who want something new. The following components of the website are free to adopters of the text:

- A downloadable, customizable *Instructor's Manual,* which consists of two parts, one for the text and one for the Student Lab Manual. Lesson plans, answers to chapter exercises and reviews, answers to chapter exams, and answers to Student Lab Manual assignments are included.

- A *Computerized Test Bank* with hundreds of questions and answers, for use in instructor-created quizzes and tests.
- Chapter slides created in PowerPoint® to use for in-class lecture material and as handouts for students.

MindTap

In the *Essentials of Health Information Management*, third edition MindTap platform, instructors customize the learning path by selecting Cengage Learning resources and adding their own content via apps that integrate the MindTap framework seamlessly with many learning management systems. The guided learning path demonstrates the relevance of basic principles in health information management, through engagement activities, quizzing, interactive exercises, and video activities, elevating the study by challenging students to apply concepts to practice. To learn more, visit www.cengage.com/mindtap.

ACKNOWLEDGMENTS

From Mary Jo Bowie:

To my husband, Bill, who always supports and encourages me in all that I do. To my daughter, Sarah, and daughter and son-in-law, Bethannie and Jesse, may you all grow strong in your faith.

To my parents for their support through all of my life.

To my dear friend, Michelle Green, your love for teaching will always be the driving force for each new edition of this book.

Reviewers

A special thank-you is extended to the reviewers who have provided recommendations and suggestions for improvement throughout the development of the third edition. Their experience and knowledge has been a valuable resource for the authors.

Carmen Bellos, RHIT
Director, HIT Program
National College
Madison, Tennessee

Valerie Brock, MBA, RHIA, CPC, CCP, CPAR
Assistant Professor
Tennessee State University
Nashville, Tennessee

Marie T. Conde, MPA, RHIA, CCS, FAHIMA
Program Director and Instructor
City College of San Francisco
San Francisco, California

Stephanie A. Donovan, MBA, RHIA
Program Manager and Assistant Professor, HIT/HIA
Peirce College
Philadelphia, Pennsylvania

Carolyn Eberly, MSHCM, RHIT
Program Director, HIT
Kaplan University-Hagerstown
Hagerstown, Maryland

Melissa H. Edenburn, RHIA
Associate Professor, HIT Program
McLennan Community College
Waco, Texas

Brenda K. Edwards, LPN, CPC, CPC-I, CEMC
Medical Support Careers Faculty
Minnesota State College-Southeast Technical
Winona, Minnesota

Carolyn Gaarder, RHIA, HIT
Program Director
Minnesota State Community and Technical College
Moorhead, Minnesota

Cheri Goretti, MA, MT (ASCP), CMA (AAMA)
Professor and Program Coordinator
Medical Assisting and Allied Health
Quinebaug Valley Community College
Danielson, Connecticut

Bonita R. Payne, RHIA
Instructor
National College of Business
Madison, Tennessee

Linda Pristelski, RHIT
Health Information Technology Instructor
Northeast Wisconsin Technical College
Green Bay, Wisconsin

Kelly Rinker, MA, CPHIMS, RHIA
Faculty
Regis University
Denver, Colorado

Ellen Shakespeare, MBA, RHIA
Program Coordinator
Raritan Valley Community College
North Branch, New Jersey

Amy K. Shay, BS, RHIT
Program Director
Health Information Management Program
Tidewater Community College
Virginia Beach, Virginia

Julia Steff, RHIA, CCS, CCS-P
Assistant Professor and Department Chair
Health Information Management and Medical
    Information Coder/Biller
Palm Beach State College
Lake Worth, Florida

Christina Thomas, BS, CPC, CMAA, CCMA, CBCS
Program Chair and Instructor
Florida Career College - Anthem College
Clearwater, Florida

Summer C. Tierno
MBC and MOA Program Director
Miller-Motte Technical College
Gulfport, Mississippi

TECHNICAL REVIEWERS

Kirsten M. Griffin, RHIT
Consultant, Type K Services
Binghamton, New York

Patricia Griffin, AAS, RHIT
Cengage Subject Matter Expert
Consultant
Binghamton, New York

Dana C. McWay, JD, RHIA
Saint Louis University
St. Louis, Missouri

Chapter 1

HEALTH CARE DELIVERY SYSTEMS

Chapter Outline

- Key Terms
- Objectives
- Introduction
- History of Medicine
- Health Care Delivery in the United States
- Continuum of Care
- Health Care Facility Ownership
- Health Care Facility Organization Structure and Operation
- Licensure, Regulation, and Accreditation
- Internet Links
- Summary
- Study Checklist
- Chapter Review

Key Terms

abstracting
accreditation
Accreditation Council for Graduate Medical Education (ACGME)
active
agenda
American Recovery and Reinvestment Act
associate
biometrics
board of directors
board of governors
board of trustees
bylaws
Centers for Medicare & Medicaid Services (CMS)
chief resident

Code of Federal Regulations (CFR)
coding
consulting
continuum of care
contract services
courtesy
Current Procedural Terminology (CPT)
deemed status
deeming authority
Deficit Reduction Act of 2005
Det Norske Veritas Healthcare, Inc. (DNV)
digital signature
disaster recovery plan
do not resuscitate (DNR)
electronic health record (EHR)

electronic signature
Emergency Medical Treatment and Labor Act (EMTALA)
Federal Register
for-profit
Genetic Information Nondiscrimination Act (GINA)
governing board
government-supported hospitals
HCPCS Level II (national) codes
Healthcare Integrity and Protection Data Bank (HIPDB)
Health Care Procedure Coding System (HCPCS)
health care proxy
Health Insurance Portability and Accountability Act (HIPAA)

Health Plan Employer Data and
   Information Set (HEDIS)
Hill-Burton Act
Hippocrates
Hippocratic Oath
honorary
hospital administration
hospital departments
hospitalists
Human Genome Project
incomplete record processing
intern
International Classification of
   Diseases, Ninth Revision,
   Clinical Modification (ICD-9-CM)
intranet
licensure
living will
Medicaid (Title 19)
medical staff
medical transcription
Medicare (Title 18)
Medicare Prescription Drug, Improvement, and Modernization
   Act of 2003 (MMA)

Medieval medicine
Middle Ages
minutes
modern medicine
National Practitioner Data
   Bank (NPDB)
not-for-profit
ORYX® initiative
paleopathology
papyrus
Patient Safety and Quality
   Improvement Act of 2005
Patient Self-Determination Act
Physician Quality Reporting
   Initiative (PQRI)
prehistoric medicine and ancient
   medicine
primary care
proprietary hospitals
public hospitals
public key cryptography
quality improvement
   organization (QIO)
quaternary care
record circulation

regulation
Renaissance medicine
resident
rules and regulations
secondary care
*Shared Visions—New
   Pathways*™
smart card
standards
State Children's Health Insurance
   Program (SCHIP)
state department of health
survey
Tax Equity and Fiscal
   Responsibility Act of 1982
   (TEFRA)
teaching hospitals
tertiary care
Title XXI of the Balanced Budget
   Act of 1997
triage
universal chart order
veterans
voluntary hospitals

Objectives

At the end of this chapter, the student should be able to:

- Define key terms
- Summarize the history of medicine and the delivery of health care in the United States
- List programs and services offered as part of the continuum of care
- Differentiate between for-profit and not-for-profit health care facility ownership

- Interpret the authority and responsibility associated with a health care facility's organizational structure
- Define and provide examples of licensure, regulation, and accreditation
- Differentiate among health care providers and their disciplines

INTRODUCTION

Health care delivery in the United States has been greatly impacted by escalating costs, resulting in medical necessity requirements (to justify acute care hospitalizations), review of appropriateness of admissions, and requirements for administration of quality and effective treatments. Patients routinely undergo preadmission testing (PAT) on an outpatient basis instead of being admitted as a hospital inpatient, and the performance of outpatient testing and surgical procedures has increased due to health care technological advances (e.g., laparoscopic surgeries). Health care consumers are better educated and demand higher-quality, more cost-effective health care; thus, the focus is on primary and preventive care.

HISTORY OF MEDICINE

Information about historical health care delivery practices comes primarily from the study of textual references, artistic illustrations, and the study of human remains (called paleopathology), which is probably the most reliable source because of less potential for written and artistic bias. While diagnoses and treatments associated with prehistoric and ancient medicine were mostly a product of ignorance and superstition, an occasional discovery actually worked. Health care delivery in the United States is based on beliefs about disease and health that evolved over past centuries.

Prehistoric medicine and ancient medicine (Table 1-1) were both characterized by the belief that illness was caused by the supernatural, an attempt to explain changes in body functions that were not understood (e.g., evil spirits were said to have invaded the body of the sick person).

TABLE 1-1 Prehistoric Medicine and Ancient Medicine

Period	Medical Practices
Prehistoric Medicine	• Belief that angry gods or evil spirits caused disease and tribal priests drove evil spirits from the body. • Skull fossils suggest that trephining, which involved using a stone instrument to cut a hole in the patient's skull, was performed to release evil spirits. • Plants may have been used to relieve pain, as evidenced by the use of willow bark to relieve pain. (Willow bark contains salicin, a substance related to salicylates used in making aspirin.)
Ancient Medicine	• World's first known physician Imhotep lived about 2650 BC. Imhotep was also the world's first acknowledged architect; he built Egypt's first pyramid. • Imhotep may have authored the ancient manuscript that was copied onto what became known as the Edwin Smith Papyrus, discovered by Egyptologist Edwin Smith. It contains descriptions of more than 90 anatomical terms and 48 injuries. It is one of the oldest known medical papyri. (**Papyrus** is a loose-textured, porous, white paper made from the papyrus water plant and used as a writing material.) • Following the decline of Egypt, the Greek physician **Hippocrates** (460–379 BC, known as the "father of medicine") was the first physician to consider medicine a science and art separate from the practice of religion. • **Hippocratic Oath** was adopted as an expression of early medical ethics and reflected high ideals. • Greek philosophers believed that the four elements of earth, air, water, and fire (cold, dry, moist, and hot) governed the universe, and harmony was achieved when there was balance among the four. Corresponding bodily fluids, or humors (blood, phlegm, yellow bile, and black bile) governed health, and illness and disease resulted from an imbalance among the four humors. • Roman physician Galen (129–200 AD) excised tumors and infected bone, and resectioned ribs and sternums. Appointed physician to the gladiators of his hometown of Pergamum early in his career, he gained anatomical insight treating fractures and brutal wounds. • Greek physician Antyllos performed and described new procedures, and he became an authority on aneurysms. He also left precise surgical directions as to the treatment of cataracts and fistulae of the bronchi and intestines. • Ancient Israelites made progress in preventive medicine from about 1200 to 600 BC by prohibiting the contamination of public wells and the eating of pork and other foods that might carry disease. They also required strict isolation of persons with gonorrhea, leprosy, and other contagious diseases. • Ancient Chinese developed traditional medical practices based on the belief that two life forces, yin and yang, flow through the human body. Disease results when the two forces are out of balance, and the Chinese use acupuncture (inserting needles into parts of the body) to control the flow of yin and yang. • Ancient India practiced medicine known as ayurveda, which stressed the prevention as well as treatment of illness. Indian surgeons also became successful at performing amputations and plastic surgery.

TABLE 1-2 Medieval Medicine

Period	Medical Practices
Medieval Medicine	• Rhazes, a Persian-born physician (864–930 AD), documented the first accurate descriptions of measles and smallpox. • Avicenna, an Arab physician (980–1037 AD), produced the *Canon of Medicine*, which summarized medical knowledge of the time and accurately described meningitis, tetanus, and many other diseases. • In Europe, a series of epidemics began with leprosy (500 AD) and culminated with the plague (1347 AD), which was carried by infected Crusaders and became known as the Black Death. Within six years, it killed 42 million people, a quarter of Europe's population. • The first hospitals were created in Baghdad, Cairo, and Damascus, and monastic orders built hospitals in the Near East to care for wounded Crusaders. • The first medical school was established in Salerno, Italy, and during the eleventh century, universities were founded in Bologna, Montpellier, Oxford, and Paris.

Medieval medicine (Table 1-2) developed during the **Middle Ages**, which were characterized by a lack of education except among nobility and the most wealthy. The most significant medical development was the construction of hospitals to care for the sick (e.g., for bubonic plague). Often managed by monks and nuns, the care of patients was based on charity rather than on scientific principles.

Renaissance medicine (Table 1-3), mostly associated with Europe, was characterized by a renewed interest in the arts, sciences, and philosophy. This was the beginning of modern medicine, based on education instead of spiritual beliefs.

Society had an impact on **modern medicine** (Table 1-4), which included the implementation of standards for sanitation, ventilation, hygiene, and nutrition. In addition, choosing health care as a profession became more acceptable, hospitals were reformed, and the training of physicians and nurses improved.

TABLE 1-3 Renaissance Medicine

Period	Medical Practices
Renaissance Medicine 1300 to 1600 AD	• Ambroise Paré (1509–1590 AD) became the greatest surgeon and surgical writer of the Renaissance when, after being rejected by medical schools, he was educated by the army on the battlefields. He saved thousands of lives by ending the use of burning oil to cleanse wounds and teaching the use of ligatures in amputations. • Laws against dissection were relaxed, and the first scientific studies of the human body began. Antonio Benivieni's autopsy observations were published in 1507, and Leonardo da Vinci, Michelangelo, and Albrecht Dürer participated in dissections. • Anatomist Andreas Vesalius revolutionized anatomy by writing *De Humani Corporis Fabrica*, which described and illustrated bones, muscles, blood vessels, nerves, and internal organs. • Syphilis was epidemic in the sixteenth century, the unfortunate result of the military on the move. • Girolamo Fracastoro (1483–1553 AD) was the first to identify the spread of syphilis to living organisms. In *De Contagione* he wrote about the revolutionary theory of the spread of infection by invisible germs and modes of disease transmission.

TABLE 1-4 Modern Medicine

Period	Medical Practices
Modern Medicine	• William Harvey proved the continuous circulation of the blood within a contained system; and Aselli discovered lymphatic vessels through experiments on animals, leading to a theory attributing cancer to lymph abnormalities. Lymphatic drainage became the key factor in developing more extensive surgical removal of cancer.
	• Dutch amateur scientist Anton van Leeuwenhoek began using a microscope to study organisms invisible to the naked eye (now called microorganisms, microbes, or germs). Leeuwenhoek discovered certain microbes that later became known as bacteria.
	• English physician Edward Jenner discovered a safe method of making people immune to smallpox; this was the first officially recorded vaccination. The success of the experiment initiated the science of immunology—the prevention of disease by building up resistance to it.
	• Louis Pasteur and Robert Koch firmly established the microbial, or germ, theory of disease. Pasteur proved that microbes are living organisms, that certain kinds of microbes cause disease, and that killing certain microbes stops the spread of specific diseases.
	• German physician Koch invented a method for determining which bacteria cause particular diseases. This method enabled him to identify the germ that causes anthrax—the first germ definitely linked to a particular disease.
	• By the end of the 1800s, researchers had discovered the kinds of bacteria and other microbes responsible for such infectious diseases as cholera, diphtheria, dysentery, gonorrhea, leprosy, malaria, plague pneumonia, tetanus, and tuberculosis.
	• In the 1840s, Americans Crawford Long and William T. G. Morton independently discovered that ether gas could safely be used to put patients to sleep during surgery. With an effective anesthetic, physicians could perform operations never before possible.
	• The scientific study of disease, called pathology, developed during the 1800s. German physician and scientist Rudolf Virchow believed the only way to understand the nature of disease was by close examination of the affected body cells. The development of much improved microscopes in the early 1800s made his studies possible.
	• Before the mid-1800s, hospitals paid little attention to cleanliness and surgeons operated in street clothes. Pasteur's early work on bacteria convinced an English surgeon named Joseph Lister that germs caused the death of many surgical patients. In 1865, Lister began using carbolic acid, a powerful disinfectant, to sterilize surgical wounds. But this method was later replaced by a more efficient technique known as aseptic surgery. This technique involved keeping germs away from surgical wounds in the first place instead of trying to kill germs already there. Surgeons began to wash thoroughly before an operation and to wear surgical gowns, rubber gloves, and masks. Steam was also introduced for physical sterilization (e.g., surgical instruments).
	• The discovery of x-rays by the German physicist Wilhelm Roentgen in 1895 enabled doctors to "see" inside the human body to diagnose illnesses and injuries. The discovery of radium by the French physicists Pierre and Marie Curie in 1898 provided a powerful weapon against cancer.

(Continues)

TABLE 1-4 Modern Medicine (*Continued*)

Period	Medical Practices
	• About 1910, German physician and chemist Paul Ehrlich introduced chemotherapy, which involved searching for chemicals to destroy the microbes responsible for particular diseases.
	• In 1928, the English bacteriologist Sir Alexander Fleming discovered the germ-killing power of a mold called Penicillium. In the early 1940s, a group of English scientists headed by Howard Florey isolated penicillin, a product of this mold. Penicillin thus became the first antibiotic.
	• In 1935, German doctor Gerhard Domagk discovered the ability of sulfa drugs to cure infections in animals, which led to the development of sulfa drugs to treat diseases in humans.
	• From 1940 through 1961, laboratory studies of prothrombin time, electrolytes, blood gases, and creatine phosphokinase (CPK) were introduced.
	• In 1955, the Salk polio vaccine was licensed.
	• During the 1960s and 1970s, the World Health Organization (WHO) conducted a vaccination program that virtually eliminated smallpox from the world.
	• In 1966, the International Smallpox Eradication program was established. Led by the U.S. Public Health Service, worldwide eradication of smallpox was accomplished in 1977.
	• In the 1970s, improvements in cardiac bypass and joint replacement surgery were made, and computed tomography and whole-body scanners were first used. Magnetic resonance imaging (MRI) was introduced in the 1980s.
	• In 1981, Acquired Immune Deficiency Syndrome (AIDS) and the Human Immunodeficiency Virus III (HIV) were identified. In 1984, the Public Health Service and French scientists identified the Human Immunodeficiency Virus. The National Organ Transplantation Act was signed into law. In 1985, the blood test used to detect HIV was licensed. By June 1990, 139,765 people in the United States had HIV/AIDS, with a 60 percent mortality rate. Also in 1990, the Ryan White Comprehensive AIDS Resource Emergency (CARE) Act began to provide support for communities to help people with AIDS.
	• In 1990, the **Human Genome Project** was established. This was a nationally coordinated effort to characterize all human genetic material by determining the complete sequence of the DNA in the human genome. In 2000, human genome sequencing was published.
	• In 1994, NIH-supported scientists discovered the genes responsible for many cases of hereditary colon cancer, inherited breast cancer, and the most common type of kidney cancer.
	• In 2006, the FDA approved the first vaccine for human papilloma virus (HPV). The vaccine is delivered in three injections over six months and protects against four strains of the virus that can lead to genital warts and cervical cancer.
	• Over the past decade, minimally invasive or robotic surgeries have expanded from gall bladder and gynecologic surgeries to include surgeries on the heart, intestinal organs, and cancer surgeries. The advantages of laparoscopic surgery over traditional "open" surgeries are smaller incisions, shorter recovery time and hospital stay, less scarring, and reduced blood loss.

HEALTH CARE DELIVERY IN THE UNITED STATES

The evolution of health care delivery in the United States (Table 1-5) began with crude folk remedies used by settlers who had to cope with epidemics, life-threatening weather, nutritional disorders, and starvation. Advances in health care delivery closely followed the changes in England and Europe, and hospitals were established in larger cities (e.g., Philadelphia, New York City, and Boston). As the population of the United States increased, there was a corresponding need for health care facilities and trained personnel. Because the increased number of schools and hospitals did not ensure quality, standards were later developed for hospitals and for the training of medical personnel. Health care delivery in the twentieth century is characterized by an emphasis on rising costs, the need for insurance, and the role of government in the payment for services (Figure 1-1). See Chapter 10 for extensive coverage of the United States health care reimbursement system.

TABLE 1-5 Evolution of Health Care Delivery in the United States

Year	Event
1751	The Pennsylvania Hospital founded by Benjamin Franklin and built in 1751 is the first United States hospital.
1765	Surgeon John Morgan organized a medical faculty at the University of Pennsylvania, thereby creating the United States' first medical school. It was based on a curriculum that combined instruction in the arts and the classics with practical knowledge necessary to make a living.
1798	The first Marine Hospital was funded to care for sailors. It was originally part of the Department of the Treasury because 20 cents per month was collected from seamen; later it became part of the Department of the Navy.
1847	The American Medical Association (AMA) was founded at the Academy of Natural Sciences in Philadelphia to elevate the standard of medical education in the United States. The AMA was reorganized in 1901 as a national organization of state and local associations, and membership increased from 8,000 physicians (1900) to 70,000 (1910), representing almost one-half of United States physicians. Partly as a result of the AMA's efforts, the first state licensing boards were set up in the late 1800s.
1862	President Lincoln appointed chemist Charles M. Wetherill to serve in the new Department of Agriculture, which became the Bureau of Chemistry, a forerunner to the Food and Drug Administration (FDA).
1872	The officers and employees of the Kansas Pacific Railroad in Denver, Colorado, started the Clara Hospital Association. Each contributed 50 cents per month toward its support.
1887	The federal government opened a one-room laboratory on Staten Island to conduct disease research, the forerunner to the National Institutes of Health (NIH).
1895	The National Medical Association (NMA) was created to represent African American physicians and health professionals in the United States.
1897	Osteopathic physicians founded the American Osteopathic Association (AOA) and adopted a "whole-person" approach to providing health care. The Doctor of Osteopathy (DO) particularly focuses on the musculoskeletal system, which reflects and influences conditions associated with other body systems.
1898	The Association of Hospital Superintendents was founded to facilitate discussion among hospital administrators, and in 1906 its name was officially changed to the American Hospital Association (AHA). The AHA currently represents almost 5,000 hospitals and health care networks to advance the health of individuals and communities and to lead, represent, and serve health care provider organizations that are accountable to the community and committed to health improvement.

(Continues)

TABLE 1-5 Evolution of Health Care Delivery in the United States (*Continued*)

Year	Event
1906	Congress passed the first Food and Drug Act, authorizing the government to monitor the purity of foods and the safety of medicines, now a responsibility of the FDA.
1910	The Carnegie Foundation for the Advancement of Teaching issued a report, *Medical Education in the United States and Canada,* which was prepared by United States educator Abraham Flexner. The *Flexner Report,* as it also came to be known, stated that only one of the 155 medical schools in the United States and Canada at that time provided an acceptable medical education. That school was the Johns Hopkins Medical School, founded in Baltimore in 1893.
1913	The American College of Surgeons (ACS) was founded to improve the quality of care for surgical patients by establishing standards for surgical education and practice. It adopted the "end-result system of hospital standardization" developed in 1910 by Ernest Codman, MD. Hospitals tracked patients long enough to determine whether treatment was effective; if treatment was ineffective, hospitals would attempt to determine how similar cases could be successfully treated in the future. *Note:* According to their website, the official abbreviation for the American College of Surgeons is ACS. Elsewhere, you might see the organization abbreviated as ACoS.
1917	The ACS developed the *Minimum Standard for Hospitals,* which was one page in length and contained five points.
1918	As part of its Hospital Standardization Program, the ACS performed on-site inspections of hospitals, with only 89 of 692 hospitals surveyed meeting requirements of the *Minimum Standard for Hospitals.* (The first standards manual, containing 18 pages, was printed in 1926; by 1950, the standard of care had improved with more than 3,200 hospitals achieving approval under the program.)
1926	General Motors established a group insurance plan contract with Metropolitan Life Insurance Company, which provided 180,000 employees with hospitalization and surgical benefits.
1929	The first Blue Cross plan was offered at Baylor University in Dallas, Texas, to guarantee school-teachers 21 days of hospital care for $6 a year. Other groups of employees in Dallas soon joined the plan, and Blue Cross began offering private health insurance coverage for hospital care in dozens of states. *Note:* Blue Cross usually covers the cost of hospital care.
1935	Congress passed the Social Security Act (SSA), which did not include disability coverage or medical benefits. It did include unemployment insurance, old-age assistance, aid to dependent children, and grants to states to provide various forms of medical care.
1939	The first Blue Shield plan was offered in California (based on a concept initiated at the turn of the century in which employers paid monthly fees to groups of physicians who provided health care services to Pacific Northwest lumber and mining camps). *Note:* Blue Shield usually covers the cost of physicians' services.
1946	The Communicable Disease Center (CDC) was established. It is the forerunner of the Centers for Disease Control and Prevention (also abbreviated CDC). The **Hill-Burton Act** (Hospital Survey and Construction Act) was passed and provided federal grants to modernize hospitals that had become obsolete due to lack of capital investment throughout the period of the Great Depression and World War II (1929 to 1945). In return for federal funds, facilities agreed to provide free or reduced-charge medical services to persons unable to pay. (The program has changed over time to address other types of infrastructure needs. It is managed by the Health Resources and Services Administration, located in the Department of Health and Human Services.)

(Continues)

TABLE 1-5 Evolution of Health Care Delivery in the United States (*Continued*)

Year	Event
1951	The Joint Commission on Accreditation of Hospitals (JCAH) was created as an independent, not-for-profit organization whose primary purpose is to provide voluntary accreditation. Its membership consisted of the American College of Physicians, the American Hospital Association, the American Medical Association, the Canadian Medical Association, and the American College of Surgeons. In 1987, the organization underwent a name change to become The Joint Commission on Accreditation of Healthcare Organizations, or JCAHO (pronounced jay' ko). In 2007, the organization underwent another name change, becoming The Joint Commission.
1952	The Hospital Standardization Program was transferred from the ACS to the JCAH (now The Joint Commission), which began accrediting hospitals in January of 1953 after publishing its *Standards for Hospital Accreditation.* (Hospitals were not charged for the accreditation process until 1964.)
1953	The Department of Health, Education, and Welfare (HEW) was created under President Eisenhower. (The cost of hospital care doubled in the 1950s.)
1961	The White House Conference on Aging was held, with many recommendations becoming law in the mid-1960s, including Medicare and Medicaid, Social Security reform, and the Older Americans Act that established the Administration on Aging and its counterpart, the State Units on Aging. The Community Health Services and Facilities Act of 1961 funded projects for testing and demonstrating new or improved services in nursing homes, home care services, and central information and referral centers, and provided additional personnel to serve the chronically ill and aged. It also funded the construction of nursing homes and the establishment of voluntary health planning agencies at local levels, resulting in community health centers to serve low-income regions.
1962	The Migrant Health Act was passed, providing medical and support services to migrant and seasonal farm workers and their families.
1964	The first *Surgeon General's Report on Smoking and Health* was released, becoming America's first widely publicized official recognition that cigarette smoking is a cause of cancer and other serious diseases.
1965	The Medicare and Medicaid programs were enacted as part of the Social Security Amendments of 1965 (SSA of 1965), making comprehensive health care available to millions of Americans. **Medicare (Title 18)** is for people 65 years of age or older, certain younger people with disabilities, and people with End-Stage Renal Disease (ESRD, which is permanent kidney failure treated with dialysis or a transplant). **Medicaid (Title 19)** is a joint federal and state program that helps with medical costs for some people with low incomes and limited resources. Medicaid programs vary from state to state, but most health care costs are covered for those who qualify for both Medicare and Medicaid. Provider-based utilization review was a condition of participation in Medicare, which helped assure medical necessity and quality of care. Amendments to the Dependents' Medical Care Act of 1956 created the *Civilian Health and Medical Program–Uniformed Services (CHAMPUS)*, which was designed as a benefit for dependents of personnel serving in the armed forces as well as uniformed branches of the Public Health Service and the National Oceanic and Atmospheric Administration. The program is now called *TRICARE*. The JCAH was granted **deemed status** by Congress as part of the SSA of 1965, which means JCAH-accredited hospitals have met or exceeded Conditions of Participation to participate in the Medicare and Medicaid programs. The Centers for Medicare & Medicaid Services (CMS) develop regulations to improve quality and protect the health and safety of beneficiaries, entitled *Conditions of Participation (CoP)* and *Conditions for Coverage (CfC)*. Health care organizations must meet these regulations to receive reimbursement from (participate in) the Medicare and Medicaid programs.

(Continues)

TABLE 1-5 Evolution of Health Care Delivery in the United States (*Continued*)

Year	Event
1970s	Health care costs escalated, partially due to unexpectedly high Medicare expenditures, rapid economic inflation, expansion of hospital expenses and profits, and changes in medical care including greater use of technology, medications, and conservative approaches to treatment.
1970	The National Health Service Corps was created to improve the health of people who live in communities without access to primary health care (or primary care), which is the patient's entry to the health care system in most non-emergency situations and encompasses preventive care, health maintenance, identification and management of common conditions, and coordination of consultations and referrals.
1971	The National Cancer Act of 1971 was signed into law, which amended the Public Health Service Act to more effectively carry out the national effort against cancer. This was part of President Nixon's "War on Cancer" and centralized research at the NIH.
1972	Social Security Amendments of 1972 strengthened the utilization review process through formation of Professional Standards Review Organizations (PSROs)—independent peer review organizations that monitored the appropriateness, quality, and outcome of the services provided to beneficiaries of the Medicare, Medicaid, and Maternal and Child Health Programs. (PSROs are now called Quality Improvement Organizations, or QIOs.) The federal Drug Abuse and Treatment Act of 1972 required that drug and alcohol abuse patient records be kept confidential and not subject to disclosure except as provided by law. This law applied to federally assisted alcohol or drug abuse programs that provide diagnosis, treatment, or referral for treatment of drug and/or alcohol abuse. *Note:* General medical care facilities are required to comply with the legislation *only* if they have an identified drug/alcohol abuse treatment unit or their personnel provide drug/alcohol diagnosis, treatment, or referral.
1973	The Veterans Healthcare Expansion Act of 1973 authorized Veterans Affairs (VA) to establish the *Civilian Health and Medical Program of the Department of Veterans Affairs* (*CHAMPVA*) to provide health care benefits for dependents of veterans rated as 100 percent permanently and totally disabled as a result of service-connected conditions, veterans who died as a result of service-connected conditions, and veterans who died on duty with less than 30 days of active service. The *Health Maintenance Organization Assistance Act of 1973* authorized federal grants and loans to private organizations that wished to develop *health maintenance organizations* (*HMOs*), which are responsible for providing health care services to subscribers in a given geographic area for a fixed fee.
1974	The Privacy Act of 1974 was implemented to (1) protect the privacy of individuals identified in information systems maintained by federal government hospitals (e.g., military hospitals) and (2) provide access to records concerning themselves. *Note:* While this law has no effect on records maintained by non-federal hospitals, effective April 14, 2003, the Health Insurance Portability and Accountability Act of 1996 (HIPAA) requires *all* health plans, health care clearinghouses, and health care providers who conduct electronic financial/administrative transactions (e.g., electronic billing) to comply with national patient privacy standards, which contain safeguards to protect the security and confidentiality of patient information.
1977	The Health Care Financing Administration (HCFA), now called the Centers for Medicare & Medicaid Services (CMS), was created separately from the Social Security Administration to manage Medicare and Medicaid. The Utilization Review Act of 1977 was implemented to facilitate ongoing assessment and management of health care services, requiring hospitals to conduct continued-stay reviews to determine the medical necessity and appropriateness of Medicare and Medicaid inpatient hospitalizations. Fraud and abuse legislation was also introduced.

(Continues)

TABLE 1-5 Evolution of Health Care Delivery in the United States (*Continued*)

Year	Event
1979	The Department of Education Organization Act was signed into law, providing for a separate Department of Education. Health, Education, and Welfare (HEW) officially became the Department of Health and Human Services (HHS) on May 4, 1980.
1982	The Peer Review Improvement Act of 1982 replaced PSROs with Peer Review Organizations (PROs), which were statewide utilization and quality control peer review organizations. (In 1985, PROs incorporated a focused second-opinion program, which referred certain cases for diagnostic and treatment verification.) The **Tax Equity and Fiscal Responsibility Act of 1982 (TEFRA)** established the first Medicare prospective payment system, which was implemented in 1983. Diagnosis-related groups (DRGs) required acute care hospitals to be reimbursed at a predetermined rate according to discharge diagnosis (instead of a per diem rate, which compensated hospitals retrospectively based on charges incurred for the total inpatient length of stay, usually 80 percent of charges). *Note:* Additional prospective payment systems were implemented in subsequent years for other health care settings. See Table 10-4 in Chapter 10.
1984	HCFA (now called CMS) required providers to use the *HCFA-1500* (now called the *CMS-1500*) to submit Medicare claims. The HCFA Common Procedure Coding System (HCPCS) (now called Health Care Procedure Coding System) was created, which included CPT, Level II (national), and Level III (local) codes. Commercial payers also adopted HCPCS coding and use of the HCFA-1500 claim.
1985	The Consolidated Omnibus Budget Reconciliation Act (COBRA) of 1985 allowed former employees, retirees, spouses, domestic partners, and eligible dependent children who lose coverage due to certain qualifying events the right to temporary continuation of health coverage at group rates. Benefits can continue for 18 or 36 months, depending on the qualifying event, and premiums are calculated at 102 percent of the total premium rate, payable by the enrollee on a monthly basis directly to the carrier. It also allowed HCFA (now CMS) to deny reimbursement for substandard health care services provided to Medicare and Medicaid patients. The **Emergency Medical Treatment and Labor Act (EMTALA)** (antidumping statute) addressed the problem of hospitals' failure to screen, treat, or appropriately transfer patients (patient dumping) by establishing criteria for the discharge and transfer of Medicare and Medicaid patients.
1986	The Omnibus Budget Reconciliation Act of 1986 (OBRA of 1986) required PROs to report cases of substandard care to licensing and certification agencies. The federal Health Care Quality Improvement Act of 1986 established the **National Practitioner Data Bank (NPDB)**, which contains information about practitioners' credentials, including previous medical malpractice payment and adverse action history. State licensing boards, hospitals, and other health care facilities access the NPDB to identify and discipline practitioners who engage in unprofessional behavior.
1987	The Nursing Home Reform Act (part of the Omnibus Budget Reconciliation Act of 1987) ensured that residents of nursing homes receive quality care, required the provision of certain services to each resident, and established a Residents' Bill of Rights. Nursing homes receive Medicaid and Medicare payments for long-term care of residents if they are certified by the state in which they reside to be in substantial compliance with the requirements of the Nursing Home Reform Act.
1988	The McKinney Act was signed into law, providing health care to the homeless.

(Continues)

TABLE 1-5 Evolution of Health Care Delivery in the United States (*Continued*)

Year	Event
1988	*Clinical Laboratory Improvement Act* (*CLIA*) legislation established quality standards for all laboratory testing to ensure the accuracy, reliability, and timeliness of patient test results regardless of where the test was performed. The *Medicare Catastrophic Coverage Act* mandated the reporting of ICD-9-CM diagnosis codes on Medicare claims; in subsequent years, private third-party payers adopted similar requirements for claims submission. *Note:* ICD-10-CM replaces the reporting of all ICD-9-CM diagnosis codes, and ICD-10-PCS replaces the reporting of ICD-9-CM inpatient procedure codes. CPT and HCPCS Level II codes continue to be reported for all outpatient procedures and services. All coding systems are discussed in Chapter 10 of this textbook.
1989	OBRA of 1989 created the Agency for Health Care Policy and Research (now called the Agency for Healthcare Research and Quality, or AHRQ), which conducts health services research for the Department of Health and Human Services (HHS) and complements the biomedical research mission of the National Institutes of Health (NIH). AHRQ develops outcomes measures of the quality of health care services.
1990	OBRA of 1990 required PROs to report adverse actions to state medical boards and licensing agencies. The **Patient Self-Determination Act** required consumers to be provided with informed consent, information about their right to make advance health care decisions (called advance directives), and information about state laws that impact legal choices in making health care decisions. The following are examples of advance directives that will be discussed in Chapter 6. • Do Not Resuscitate (DNR) Order • Durable Power of Attorney for Health Care • Health Care Proxy • Living Will • Organ or Tissue Donation
1991	The Workgroup on Electronic Data Interchange (WEDI) was created to reduce health care administrative costs through implementation of the electronic data interchange (EDI), which uses national standards to transmit data for reimbursement purposes. (ASC X12, the national standard, refers to the "Accredited Standards Committee X12" that is comprised of North American government and industry members who create EDI draft standards for submission to the American National Standards Institute, or ANSI). WEDI helped ensure passage of the Health Insurance Portability and Accountability Act (HIPAA) in 1996 and is a consultant to the Secretary of Health and Human Services for implementation of Administrative Simplification HIPAA legislation.
1993	The Vaccines for Children Program was established, providing free immunizations to all children in low-income families.
1995	The Social Security Administration became an independent agency on March 31, 1995.
1996	The **Health Insurance Portability and Accountability Act (HIPAA)** was passed. It mandates administrative simplification regulations that govern privacy, security, and electronic transactions standards for health care information. HIPAA also protects health insurance coverage for workers and their families when they change or lose their jobs. In addition, the **Healthcare Integrity and Protection Data Bank (HIPDB)** was created, which combats fraud and abuse in health insurance and health care delivery by alerting users to conduct a comprehensive review of a practitioner's, provider's, or supplier's past actions.
1997	The **State Children's Health Insurance Program (SCHIP)** (or **Title XXI of the Balanced Budget Act of 1997**) was established. It is a health insurance program for infants, children, and teens that covers health care services such as doctor visits, prescription medicines, and hospitalizations.

(Continues)

TABLE 1-5 Evolution of Health Care Delivery in the United States (*Continued*)

Year	Event
1999	The Ticket to Work and Work Incentives Improvement Act of 1999 was signed into law, making it possible for millions of Americans with disabilities to join the workforce without fear of losing their Medicaid and Medicare coverage. It also modernized the employment services system for people with disabilities. In addition, the initiative on combating bioterrorism was launched.
2000	The *Medicare, Medicaid, and SCHIP Benefits Improvement and Protection Act* (BIPA) requires implementation of a $400-billion prescription drug benefit, improved Medicare Advantage (formerly called Medicare+Choice) benefits, faster Medicare appeals decisions, and more. *Consumer-driven health plans* (*CDHPs*) are introduced as a way to encourage individuals to locate the best health care at the lowest possible price with the goal of holding down health care costs.
2001	The **Centers for Medicare & Medicaid Services (CMS)** was created, replacing the Health Care Financing Administration (HCFA). In addition, HHS responded to the nation's first bioterrorism attack, which was the delivery of anthrax through the mail.
2002	CMS announced that peer review organizations (PROs) will be known as **quality improvement organizations (QIOs)**, and that they will continue to perform quality control and utilization review of health care furnished to Medicare beneficiaries. Under the direction of CMS, the network of 53 quality improvement organizations is comprised of private contractors that work with consumers, physicians, hospitals, and other caregivers to refine care delivery systems to make sure patients get the right care at the right time, particularly among underserved populations. The program also safeguards the integrity of the Medicare trust fund by ensuring payment is made only for medically necessary services and by investigating beneficiary complaints about quality of care.
2002	The *employer identification number* (*EIN*), assigned by the Internal Revenue Service (IRS), is adopted by DHHS as the National Employer Identification Standard for use in health care transactions.
2003	The **Medicare Prescription Drug, Improvement, and Modernization Act of 2003 (MMA)** was implemented. This act: • Provides Medicare recipients with prescription drug savings and additional health care plan choices (other than traditional Medicare) • Modernizes Medicare by allowing private health plans to compete • Requires that Medicare Trustees analyze the combined fiscal status of the Medicare Trust Funds and warn Congress and the president when Medicare's general fund subsidy exceeds 45 percent The *Medicare Contracting Reform* (*MCR*) *initiative* was established to integrate the administration of Medicare Parts A and B fee-for-service benefits with new entities called Medicare administrative contractors (MACs). MACs replaced Medicare carriers, DMERCs, and fiscal intermediaries to improve and modernize the Medicare fee-for-service system and establish a competitive-bidding process for contracts.
2005	The **Deficit Reduction Act of 2005** created the Medicaid Integrity Program (MIP), which is a fraud and abuse detection program. The **Patient Safety and Quality Improvement Act of 2005** amends Title IX of the Public Health Service Act to provide for improved patient safety and reduced incidence of events adversely affecting patient safety. It encourages the reporting of health care mistakes to patient safety organizations by making the reports confidential and shielding them from use in civil and criminal proceedings. The Standard Unique Health Identifier for Health Care Providers, or *National Provider Identifier* (*NPI*), is implemented.
2006	The Tax Relief and Health Care Act (TRHCA) of 2006 authorized implementation of a **Physician Quality Reporting Initiative (PQRI)**, which established a financial incentive for eligible professionals who participate in a *voluntary* quality reporting program.

(Continues)

TABLE 1-5 Evolution of Health Care Delivery in the United States (*Continued*)

Year	Event
2008	The **Genetic Information Nondiscrimination Act (GINA)** prohibits group health plans and health insurance companies from denying coverage to a healthy individual or charging higher premiums based solely on a genetic predisposition to development of a disease in the future. It also bars employers from using genetic information when making hiring, firing, job placement, and promotion decisions. CMS grants *deeming authority* to Det Norske Veritas Healthcare, Inc. (DNV) as a national accreditation program for hospitals seeking to participate in the Medicare program. (Hospitals can pursue accreditation through DNV in addition to or as an alternative to The Joint Commission accreditation.)
2009	The **American Recovery and Reinvestment Act** authorized an expenditure of $1.5 billion for grants for construction, renovation and equipment, and the acquisition of health information technology systems. The Health Information Technology for Economic and Clinical Health Act (HITECH Act) (included in the American Recovery and Reinvestment Act of 2009) amended the Public Health Service Act to establish an Office of National Coordinator for Health Information Technology within HHS to improve health care quality, safety, and efficiency.
2010	The **Patient Protection and Affordable Care Act (PPACA)** focuses on private health insurance reform to provide better coverage for individuals with pre-existing conditions, improve prescription drug coverage under Medicare, and extend the life of the Medicare Trust fund by at least 12 years. Its goal is to provide quality affordable health care for Americans, improve the role of public programs, improve the quality and efficiency of health care, and improve public health. PPACA also amended the time period for filing Medicare fee-for-service (FFS) claims to one calendar year after the date of service. The Health Care and Education Reconciliation Act (HCERA) amended the PPACA to implement health care reform initiatives such as increasing tax credits to buy health care insurance, eliminating special deals provided to senators, closing the Medicare "donut hole," delaying taxes on "Cadillac" health care plans until 2018, implementing revenue changes (e.g., 10 percent tax on indoor tanning services effective 2010), and so on. HCERA also modified higher-education assistance provisions such as implementing student loan reform.
2011	The Investing in Innovations (i2) Initiative is designed to spur innovations in health information technology (health IT) by promoting research and development to enhance competitiveness in the United States. Examples of health IT competition topics include applications that allow an individual to securely and effectively share health information with members of his or her social network; generate results for patients, caregivers, and/or clinicians by providing them with access to rigorous and relevant information that can support real needs and immediate decisions; allow individuals to connect during natural disasters and other periods of emergency; and facilitate the exchange of health information while allowing individuals to customize the privacy allowances for their personal health records.

EXERCISE 1–1 History of Medicine and Health Care Delivery in the United States

Short Answer: Identify the significant historical event that occurred in each year.

1. 1847 _____

2. 1898 _____

3. 1913 _____

4. 1965 _____

5. 1985 _____

6. 1996 _____

7. 1997 _____

8. 2001 _____

9. 2002 _____

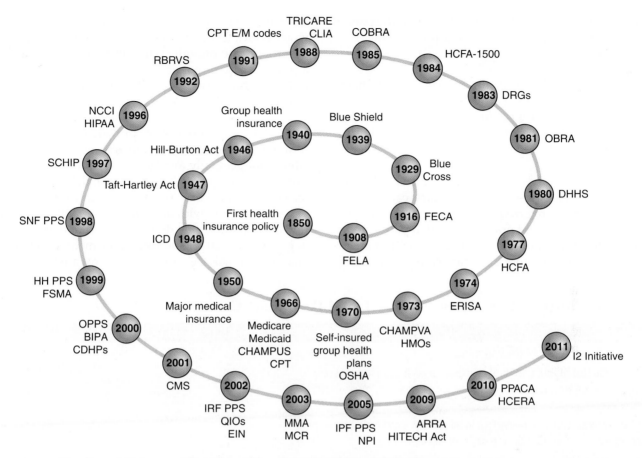

FIGURE 1-1 Timeline of Dates and Significant Events in Health Care Delivery

10. 2003 _____

11. 2003 _____

12. 2005 _____

13. 2006 _____

14. 2009 _____

15. 2011 _____

CONTINUUM OF CARE

A complete range of programs and services is called a continuum of care, with the *type of health care* indicating the *health care services provided*. The Joint Commission defines the continuum of care as "matching an individual's ongoing needs with the appropriate level and type of medical, psychological, health or social care or service." The continuum of care contains three levels: primary, secondary, and tertiary.

Primary care services include preventive and acute care, are referred to as the *point of first contact*, and are provided by a general practitioner or other

health professional (e.g., nurse practitioner) who has first contact with a patient seeking medical treatment, including general dental, ophthalmic, and pharmaceutical services. These services are usually provided in an office setting where the care is continuous (e.g., quarterly office visits for a chronic condition) and comprehensive (e.g., preventive and medical care). The primary care provider manages and coordinates the patient's care, including referring the patient to a consultant for a second opinion. Primary care services include the following:

- Annual physical examinations
- Early detection of disease
- Family planning
- Health education
- Immunizations
- Treatment of minor illnesses and injuries
- Vision and hearing screening

Secondary care services are provided by medical specialists or hospital staff members to a patient whose primary care was provided by a general practitioner who first diagnosed or treated the patient (the primary care provider refers the patient to the specialist).

> *Example* A family practitioner sees a patient with an unusual respiratory condition, provides primary care, and refers the patient to an internist who specializes in respiratory disorders; the internist then becomes the source of secondary care.

Note: In the United States, self-referral is often performed by patients seeking secondary care services (instead of being referred by a primary care provider). This is a very different practice from that performed in the United Kingdom and Canada, where all patients must first seek care from a primary care provider (e.g.,

emergency department physician, general practitioner) who decides whether to refer the patient to secondary or tertiary care providers. If a referral is not made by a primary care provider, the secondary care provider is not reimbursed by the nationally funded health care system.

Tertiary care services are provided by specialized hospitals equipped with diagnostic and treatment facilities not generally available at hospitals other than primary teaching hospitals or Level I, II, III, or IV trauma centers (Table 1-6). This level of service is also provided by doctors who are uniquely qualified to treat unusual disorders that do not respond to therapy that is generally available as secondary medical services. Stabilization services are provided by a tertiary care

TABLE 1-6 Tertiary Care—Level I, II, III, and IV Trauma Centers

Criteria	Level I	Level II	Level III	Level IV
Also called a regional trauma center	X			
Provides the highest level of comprehensive care for severely injured adult and pediatric patients with complex, multi-system trauma	X			
Has the capability of providing total patient care for every aspect of injury from prevention through rehabilitation	X			
Emergency physician, general surgeon, anesthesiologist, and nursing and ancillary personnel who can initiate immediate surgery are in-house and available to the patient upon arrival at the emergency department	X			
Broad range of sub-specialists are on-call and promptly available to provide consultation or care	X	X		
Provides care for severely injured adult and pediatric patients with complex trauma	X	X		
Physicians are Advanced Trauma Life Support (ATLS) trained and experienced in caring for traumatically injured patients; nurses and ancillary staff are in-house and immediately available to initiate resuscitative measures	X	X	X	X
Board-certified general surgeon and anesthesiologist are on-call and available to the patient		X	X	
Comprehensive diagnostic capabilities and supportive equipment are available	X	X		
Provides initial evaluation and stabilization, including surgical intervention, of severely injured adult or pediatric patients			X	
Provides comprehensive inpatient services to those patients who can be maintained in a stable or improving condition without specialized care			X	
Critically injured patients who require specialty care are transferred to a higher-level trauma system hospital in accordance with pre-established criteria			X	X

facility or a designated level IV trauma center when it is necessary to ensure, within reasonable medical probability, that no material deterioration of a patient's medical condition is likely to result from or occur during the transfer of the patient to a tertiary care facility.

The following facilities, procedures, and services are associated with tertiary care centers:

- Burn center treatment
- Cardiothoracic and vascular surgery
- Inpatient care for AIDS patients
- Magnetic resonance imaging (MRI)
- Neonatology level III unit services
- Neurosurgery
- Organ transplant
- Pediatric surgery
- Positron emission tomography (PET)
- Radiation oncology
- Services provided to a person with a high-risk pregnancy
- Services provided to a person with cancer
- State-designated trauma centers
- Trauma surgery

Quaternary care is considered an extension of "tertiary care" and includes advanced levels of medicine that are highly specialized, not widely used (e.g., experimental medicine), and very costly. Quaternary care is typically provided by tertiary care centers.

EXERCISE 1–2 Continuum of Care

True/False: Indicate whether each statement is True (T) or False (F).

_____ 1. Primary care services include patient immunizations and education.

_____ 2. Secondary care services include a patient being seen by a specialist because of angina.

_____ 3. Stabilization services are provided by a tertiary care facility to ensure that no material deterioration of a patient's medical condition occurs during the transfer to another facility.

_____ 4. Tertiary care services include a patient's annual history and physical.

_____ 5. The continuum of care contains two levels.

HEALTH CARE FACILITY OWNERSHIP

Hospital ownership is either for-profit (privately owned and excess income is distributed to share-holders and owners) or not-for-profit (excess income is reinvested in the facility) and categorized according to:

- Government (not-for-profit)
- Proprietary (for-profit)
- Voluntary (not-for-profit)

Government-supported hospitals (or public hospitals), representing about 25 percent of all health care facilities in the United States, are not-for-profit, supported by local, regional, or federal taxes, and operated by local, state, or federal governments.

Example 1
The Department of Veterans Affairs (VA) manages health care benefits for veterans (individuals who have served in the United States military), who are eligible to receive care at VA Medical Centers (VAMCs) located throughout the United States. The VA also operates ambulatory care and community-based outpatient clinics, nursing homes, domiciliaries, and comprehensive home-care programs.

Example 2
The Department of Defense establishes military treatment facilities for active personnel and their dependents.

Example 3
States own and operate behavioral health care facilities.

Example 4
Municipalities (cities) own and operate hospitals.

Proprietary hospitals represent about 15 percent of all health facilities in the United States, and they are for-profit and owned by corporations (e.g., Humana), partnerships (e.g., physicians), or private foundations (e.g., Tarpon Springs Hospital Foundation, Inc., which does business as Helen Ellis Memorial Hospital in Tarpon Springs, Florida). Corporations often own a chain of hospitals located in several states, and they may own nursing homes and other types of health care facilities as well.

Voluntary hospitals represent about 60 percent of all health care facilities in the United States, and they are not-for-profit. These hospitals are operated by religious or other voluntary groups (e.g., Shriners).

Teaching hospitals can be government (not-for-profit), proprietary (for-profit), or voluntary (nonprofit), and they are affiliated with a medical school. They include 24-hour access to physician care and the latest therapies; in addition to treating patients, they are training sites for physicians and other health professionals. Many of the physicians in a teaching hospital are interns and residents who work under the supervision of senior staff physicians. Historically, the term intern was used to designate a physician in the first year of graduate medical education (GME), which ordinarily immediately follows completion of the four-year medical curriculum. Since 1975, the Accreditation Council for Graduate Medical Education (ACGME) has not used the term *intern*, referring to individuals in their first year of GME as residents (although they still complete an internship). A resident is a physician who has completed an internship and is engaged in a program of training designed to increase his or her knowledge of the clinical disciplines of medicine, surgery, or any of the other special fields that provide advanced training in preparation for the practice of a specialty. A chief resident is a physician who is in his or her final year of residency (e.g., surgery) or in the year after the residency has been completed (e.g., pediatrics); the chief resident plays a significant administrative or teaching role in guiding new residents.

EXERCISE 1–3 Health Care Facility Ownership

Fill-in-the-Blank: Enter the appropriate term(s) to complete each statement.

1. A hospital that is affiliated with a medical school is called a _____.

2. A physician who has completed an internship and is engaged in a program of training designed to increase his or her knowledge of the clinical disciplines to prepare for a practice of specialty is called a(n) _____.

3. A hospital that is privately owned and distributes excess income to shareholders and owners is _____.

4. Public hospitals represent about 25 percent of all health care facilities in the United States and are also known as _____.

5. Voluntary hospitals are not-for-profit and represent about _____ percent of all health care facilities in the United States.

HEALTH CARE FACILITY ORGANIZATION STRUCTURE AND OPERATION

Most health care facilities utilize a *top-down format* so that authority and responsibility flow downward through a chain of command (Figure 1-2). Members of the organization include the following:

- Governing board
- Administration
- Medical staff
- Departments, services, and committees
- Contracted services

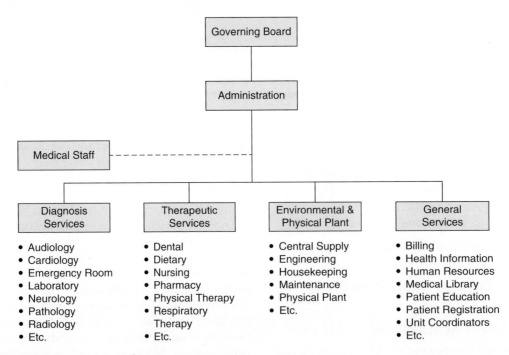

FIGURE 1-2 Hospital Organization Chart

Governing Board

The governing board (or board of trustees, board of governors, board of directors) serves without pay, and its membership is represented by professionals from the business community. It has ultimate legal authority and responsibility for the hospital's operation and is responsible for the quality of care administered to patients. The governing board is also responsible for:

- Hospital organization, management, control and operation, and for appointing the medical staff
- Abiding by the hospital's written constitution and bylaws, which clearly outline its organization, duties, responsibilities, and relationships with other members of the hospital team
- Conducting regular meetings (usually monthly) with minutes of meetings documented
- Hiring a competent administrator and delegating to that person the authority and responsibility for carrying out hospital policies
- Ensuring that competent, well-qualified personnel are employed in adequate numbers to carry out the functions of the hospital
- Providing a mechanism for assisting employees in addressing physical and mental health problems
- Maintaining standards of professional work in the hospital and requiring that the medical staff function competently

Administration

The hospital administration serves as liaison between the medical staff and governing board and is responsible for developing a strategic plan for supporting the mission and goals of the organization. In addition to the hospital administrator (Chief Executive Officer, or CEO), the following positions, which report to the CEO, may exist in the hospital organization:

- Chief Financial Officer (CFO), responsible for financial operations (e.g., accounting, billing, payroll)
- Chief Information Officer (CIO), responsible for information resources management (e.g., financial, administrative, and clinical)
- Chief Operating Officer (COO), responsible for overseeing specific departments (e.g., ancillary services)

Medical Staff

The medical staff consists of licensed physicians and other licensed providers as permitted by law (e.g., nurse practitioners and physician assistants) who are granted clinical privileges. The governing board delegates authority and responsibility to maintain proper standards of medical care and to provide well-defined patient care services to the medical staff. Licensed physicians include Doctors of Osteopathy (DO), Medical Doctors (MD), Doctors of Podiatric Medicine (DPM), and Doctors of Dental Surgery (DDS). The medical staff is organized into clinical departments according to medical specialty (Table 1-7), with a chairperson appointed to each department, and members serve on medical staff committees (Table 1-8) and hospital committees (Table 1-9). The types of medical specialties that a hospital has varies depending on the size of the facility.

TABLE 1-7 Medical Specialties

Medical Specialty	Description
Allergy & Immunology	Evaluation and treatment of immune system disorders (e.g., asthma, anaphylaxis, eczema, rhinitis, adverse reactions to drugs/foods/insect stings)
Anesthesiology	Assessment of patient risks for undergoing surgery, management of pain relief, monitoring of patients during and after surgery (postanesthesia recovery), and resuscitative care of patients with cardiac or respiratory emergencies (assessment of need for artificial ventilation)
Colon & Rectal Surgery	Diagnosis and medical/surgical treatment of diseases in the intestinal tract, colon, rectum, anal canal, perianal region, and related organs and tissues (e.g., liver, urinary, and female reproductive system)
Dermatology	Diagnosis and treatment of skin disorders (e.g., contact dermatitis, benign and malignant lesions or growths) and cosmetic disorders of the skin (e.g., scars)

(Continues)

TABLE 1-7 Medical Specialties (*Continued*)

Medical Specialty	Description
Family Practice	Management of an individual's or family's total health care, including geriatrics, gynecology, internal medicine, obstetrics, pediatrics, and psychiatry, with an emphasis on preventive and primary care
General Surgery	Management of conditions for which general surgery is warranted (e.g., appendectomy, tonsillectomy, hernia repair), including diagnosis and preoperative, intraoperative, and postoperative care to surgical patients
Gynecology	Diagnosis and treatment (including preventive management) of female reproductive and urinary system disorders
Internal Medicine	Management of common and complex illnesses of patients of all ages (e.g., cancer, infections, diseases of blood, digestive, heart, joints, kidneys, respiratory, and vascular systems). Primary care internal medicine includes disease prevention, mental health, substance abuse, and wellness. Subspecialties include: • Adolescent medicine • Cardiovascular medicine • Critical care medicine • Electrophysiology • Endocrinology • Gastroenterology • Geriatrics • Hematology • Immunology • Infectious disease • Nephrology • Oncology • Pulmonary medicine • Rheumatology • Sports medicine
Medical Genetics	Diagnosis and treatment of patients with genetically linked diseases
Neurology	Diagnosis and treatment of disorders of the nervous system
Obstetrics	Management of pregnancy, from prenatal to puerperium
Ophthalmology	Diagnosis and treatment of eye disorders
Orthopedics	Diagnosis and treatment of musculoskeletal disease and injury
Otorhinolaryngology	Diagnosis and treatment of ear, nose, and throat diseases
Plastic & Reconstructive Surgery	Surgery for the purpose of reconstructing, repairing, or restoring body structures
Psychiatry	Diagnosis and treatment of behavioral health diseases
Radiology	Diagnosis of diseases and injuries using radiologic methods (e.g., electromagnetic radiation, x-ray, radionuclides, and ultrasound). Treatment of diseases (e.g., cancer) using radiant energy (e.g., radiation oncologist)
Thoracic Surgery	Surgical management of disease within the chest (coronary artery disease, lung cancer)
Urology	Diagnosis and treatment of disorders of the genitourinary system and the adrenal gland

TABLE 1-8 Medical Staff Committees

Medical Staff Committee	Description
Credentials Committee	Reviews and verifies medical staff application data
Ethics Committee	Meets as needed in order to discuss ethical problems
Executive Committee	Acts on reports and recommendations from medical staff committees
Joint Conference Committee	Serves as liaison between governing body and administration

Note: Hospitalists are physicians who work in the hospital setting and treat patients who are receiving hospital-based care. They may or may not be considered hospital employees depending on the business arrangements that they make with the hospital.

The medical staff appointment procedure is performed every two years and follows these steps:

1. Physician completes application for clinical privileges
2. Medical staff coordinator conducts preliminary evaluation, verifying the applicant's:
   * Education (medical school)
   * Physical health status
   * Experience (internship and/or residency)
   * Request for medical staff category
   * References as to ethical character
   * Liability history (malpractice)
   * State licensure
   * Office of Professional Conduct report
   * Drug Enforcement Agency (DEA) license
   The medical staff coordinator also references the (1) National Practitioner Data Bank (NPDB), which contains reports on medical malpractice payments and adverse licensure actions, clinical privilege actions, and professional society membership actions; and (2) Healthcare Integrity and Protection Data Bank (HIPDB), which serves to alert users about a comprehensive review of a practitioner's, provider's, or supplier's past actions.
3. Medical Staff Credentials Committee reviews and verifies application and submits recommendation to Executive Committee
4. Medical Staff Department Chairperson reviews application
5. Executive Committee reviews application and recommendations, votes, and makes recommendation to Medical Staff
6. Medical Staff votes on application at its monthly meeting
7. Governing Board votes on application (approves or rejects application)

Medical staff membership categories include:

* Active (delivers most hospital medical services, performs significant organizational and administrative medical staff duties)
* Associate (advancement to active category is being considered)
* Consulting (includes highly qualified practitioners available as consultants when needed)
* Courtesy (admits an occasional patient to the hospital)
* Honorary (includes former members who are honored with emeritus status and other outstanding practitioners whom the medical staff wish to honor)

The medical staff creates and votes on bylaws (rules that delineate medical staff responsibilities) and rules and regulations (procedures based on federal and state regulations, and accreditation standards, which clarify bylaws).

Note: Hospital medical staffs used to be categorized as open or closed. Hospitals that had an open medical staff allowed any physician in the community to admit and treat inpatients. Hospitals with a closed medical staff required physicians to undergo the previous credentialing process. Open medical staffs proved to be a danger to patients when it was determined that individuals who were not actual physicians were admitting and treating inpatients. Thus, hospitals adopted the closed medical staff model. Interestingly, mention is rarely made of open versus closed medical staff models in medical literature—this is probably due to the closed model having become the standard.

Hospital Departments, Services, and Committees

Quality patient care delivery requires the coordinated effort of hospital departments, contract services, and hospital committees. Hospital departments (Table 1-10) include those that provide direct patient care as well as ancillary (e.g., clinical laboratory) and support services (e.g., health information department).

TABLE 1-9 Hospital Committees

Committee	Description and Functions
Disaster Control	Responsible for establishing a disaster plan, a requirement of state licensure and compliance with The Joint Commission standards. The committee assesses the facility's capability of responding to a disaster, including potential problem areas and other concerns. Membership includes representation from every department in the facility. (A **disaster recovery plan** ensures an appropriate response to internal and external disasters (e.g., explosion) that may affect hospital staff, patients, visitors, and the community. The plan identifies responsibilities of individuals and departments during the management of a disaster situation.)
Drug Utilization Review (or Pharmacy and Therapeutics)	Responsible for maintaining the formulary (updated list of medications and related information, representing the clinical judgment of physicians, pharmacists, and other experts in the diagnosis and/or treatment of disease and promotion of health), performing drug use evaluation, and developing policies and procedures regarding medications in all clinical areas
Education	An interdisciplinary committee that determines facility-wide education and training needs (e.g., disaster preparedness, new regulations, patient safety) and facilitates scheduling of in-service training for staff
Finance	Responsible for establishing guidelines and protocols for the management of funds within the facility
Forms	Reviews proposals for new patient record forms to ensure consistency with facility standards, reduces the number of patient record forms (wherever possible), consolidates patient information, enhances quality of documentation, and complies with regulatory agencies. Membership usually includes health information department management staff who meet with individuals submitting proposals.
Health Information	Responsible for ongoing review of patient records for timely completion and quality of documentation *Note:* In facilities where the information management department combines information technology services and health information management, an "information management team" meets to resolve issues related to (1) the impact of regulations (e.g., HIPAA) and information technology (e.g., electronic health record) on health care delivery; (2) problems regarding patient record documentation, including forms design; and (3) interdisciplinary record review (performed by separate teams comprising staff members and managers from all disciplines). Team membership usually includes the facility's CEO, CFO, director of patient care services, director of information management, quality/risk manager, and medical director.
Infection Control	Involved in prevention and correction of hospital-originated infections (nosocomial infections)
Quality Management	Concerned with quality of care provided to the patient
Risk Management	Responsible for coordinating and monitoring risk management activities, analyzing trends of incidents, and establishing priorities for dealing with high-risk areas. The goal is to ensure patient safety
Tissue Review	Responsible for reviewing preoperative and pathologic diagnosis to determine the medical necessity for surgery
Transfusion	Responsible for reviewing blood transfusion records to determine proper utilization
Utilization Management	Concerned with appropriate use of resources in providing patient care

TABLE 1-10 Hospital Departments

Department	Description
Admitting (Patient Registration)	• Registers emergency patients, inpatients, and outpatients • Obtains patient signature for consent to general medical treatment and release of information for insurance purposes • Provides patients with *advance directive* materials (e.g., living will, health care proxy, and do not resuscitate, or DNR) based on state regulations. Each state has different regulations that govern living wills, health care proxies and DNR orders. A **health care proxy** is a legal document in which the patient chooses another person to make treatment decisions in the event the patient becomes incapable of making these decisions. A **living will** contains the patient's instructions about the use of life-sustaining treatment. A **do not resuscitate (DNR)** order is documented in the patient's medical record by the physician. It instructs medical and nursing staff to not try to revive the patient if breathing or heartbeat stops.
Biomedical Engineering	• Maintains all clinical equipment used at the facility
Business Office (Finance Office)	• Accounting (prepares annual operating and capital budgets, and conducts annual facility audit) • Accounts payable (processes invoices for purchased services and products) • Patient accounts (processes patient bills and insurance claims) • Payroll (prepares and edits payroll)
Case Management (Discharge Planning)	• Initiates discharge planning process upon inpatient admission • Generates a discharge planning worksheet, which is used as an assessment tool to identify patients who may require post-hospital services on discharge • Discusses discharge plans with patients and their families on admission and during the hospital stay • Prepares a discharge plan to help determine home needs, assists in planning for needed medical equipment, helps in choosing a facility for care if the patient is unable to return home, and facilitates discharge to home or transfer to another facility
Central Sterilizing Service	• Processes the sterilization of surgical instruments and supplies
Chaplain	• Meets spiritual and religious needs of patients and families
Clinical Laboratory	• Conducts diagnostic tests ordered by physicians on samples of body fluids, body tissues, and body wastes • Information obtained from tests helps physicians diagnose illness, monitor treatment, and check general health. Results from tests are reported to physicians, who interpret them and explain them to patients • Directed by a pathologist, a physician employed by the hospital who has special training in clinical and laboratory sciences. Staffed by medical technologists, medical technicians, and assistants
Community Relations (Public Relations)	• Communicates special events, media concerns, and hospital publications to the public
Compliance	• Facility-wide program that monitors standards of conduct, offers educational programs, implements sanctions for noncompliance, and maintains a confidential integrity hotline to report concerns about possible legal and ethical violations
Durable Medical Equipment	• Provides patients with medical equipment to facilitate continuity of quality care from hospital to home, some facilities use a contracted service or refer patients to outside vendors to obtain equipment

(Continues)

TABLE 1-10 Hospital Departments (*Continued*)

Department	Description
Electroneurodiagnostic Testing	• Provides electroneurodiagnostic testing to patients with neurological diseases, including routine electroencephalogram (EEG), sleep deprived EEG, auditory evoked potential, visual evoked potential, and somatic sensory potential
Emergency Department	• Provides crisis care 24 hours per day after **triage** (organized method of identifying and treating patients according to urgency of care required)
Employee Assistance Program (EAP)	• Provides professional guidance to employees and family members when personal or work-related problems become difficult to manage
Employee Health Services	• Coordinates and monitors health-related activities for employees (employment screening physical, drug testing)
Environmental Services	• Provides general housekeeping services for the hospital, cleaning and disinfecting all patient and non-patient areas of the hospital • Disposes of regular and medical waste • Distributes linens throughout the facility • Provides general housekeeping services required for health safety and patient care
Health Information Management Services (Medical Records)	• Maintains complete inpatient, outpatient surgery, and emergency records in a confidential manner. Releases information only with patient's written authorization or with a court order • Transcribes medical dictation. Assembles, analyzes, codes, and abstracts patient records. Assigns standardized codes to diagnoses and procedures, which are used for statistical reports, strategic planning, mandatory reporting to state agencies, and insurance processing • Files, retrieves, and tracks patient records to assist physicians and nursing staff in providing patient care. Retrieves, stores, and processes cancer case data
Hospice Care	• Provides services to patients and families using an interdisciplinary team approach that includes the attending physician, nurses, social service counselors, home health aides, volunteers, and so on
Human Resources	• Conducts an orientation program to acclimate new employees to their work environment • Manages the employee benefit program (vacation time, health insurance) • Advertises employment opportunities and screens prospective employees
Information Systems	• Manages information resources and provides computing services to facility and medical staff
Legal Services	• Reviews policies (e.g., patient e-signature, web portal identification) and other documents (e.g., articulation agreements with college health information management academic programs) for hospital departments
Medical Education	• Coordinates the internship and residency programs
Medical Library	• Contains health care books, journals, and audio-visual materials, as well as Internet access to health care information • Is linked to public, private, and medical libraries nationwide through mail, phone, fax, and computer • Provides library services and resources to hospital and medical staff (and to patients when coordinated through nursing and medical staff)

(Continues)

TABLE 1-10 Hospital Departments (*Continued*)

Department	Description
Medical Staff	• Serves as liaison between the medical staff members and administration • Verifies physician credentials • Coordinates continuing medical education programs • Records minutes at committee meetings and physician functions
Nursing	• Provides 24-hour patient care to inpatients, outpatients, and emergency department patients
Nutrition and Food Service	• Manages production and service of meals for patients, staff, and visitors • Registered dietitians provide nutrition care for inpatients and clients in ambulatory settings
Occupational Therapy	• Serves patients who have experienced loss of function resulting from injury or disease
Operating Room Suite	• Includes operating rooms with scrub areas, equipment and instrument storage, dressing rooms, and recovery rooms
Patient Advocacy	• Serves as a representative for patients who issue recommendations or concern about the hospital to uphold care, ethics, moral, and operational standards
Patient Education	• Helps patients make informed decisions to better manage health care needs

Performance Improvement (PI)	• Facilitates desired outcomes by monitoring and evaluating the quality and appropriateness of patient care, measuring both process and outcome and conducting trend analyses, pursuing opportunities to improve patient care, ensuring high-quality care, and developing standards for monitoring quality of care
	• Six Sigma is a tool that was introduced to streamline processes and improve the quality of health care delivery. It involves a rigorous data-driven, decision-making process and uses a systematic five-phase, problem-solving process abbreviated as DMAIC (Define, Measure, Analyze, Improve, and Control)
	• Performance improvement in health care has evolved since its inception in the 1970s, and although the following are often used interchangeably with PI, each has a unique definition:
	  ○ *Quality Assurance (QA):* reviewing problems on a retrospective basis by performing medical audits, quality review studies, or focus review studies, which involved reviewing patient records according to pre-established criteria; the problem with QA was that it assumed that a certain level of error was normal (and therefore acceptable)
	  ○ *Continuous Quality Improvement (CQI):* replaced QA in the 1980s to provide an ongoing, proactive, data-driven *process* to assess ways to improve patient care; CQI is a tool that can be used to respond to identified problems, prevent problems, and improve upon the *status quo.* (Quality improvement [QI] has its origin in engineering, statistics, and management, and investigates the steps to be performed to make sure correct procedures are followed. PI has its origins in the behavioral sciences.)
	  ○ *Total Quality Management (TQM):* a management *philosophy* that emphasizes a commitment to excellence throughout the organization; implemented in combination with CQI
	  ○ *Quality Management (QM):* ensures patient access to quality health care by coordinating physician credentialing, clinical assessment activities, and utilization management functions; performance improvement is one aspect of QM

Pharmacy	• Supplies all medications administered to patients during hospitalizations • Pharmacists review physician medication orders, maintain and review individual patient medication profiles, and provide drug information to health care team members • Directed by a registered pharmacist who ensures safe and effective drug therapy in accordance with physicians' orders

(Continues)

TABLE 1-10 Hospital Departments (*Continued*)

Department	Description
Physical Therapy	• Uses physical agents of exercise, massage, and other modalities
Plant Operations and Maintenance	• Repairs and maintains non-medical equipment • Maintains building and grounds, and heating and cooling systems
Preadmission Testing (PAT)	• Patients visit PAT prior to elective admission (inpatient or outpatient surgery) to register with Admitting, undergo preoperative nursing assessment, and receive preanesthesia evaluation by an anesthesiologist • Phlebotomists draw blood samples for preoperative testing • Electrocardiograms and chest x-rays are performed if ordered • PAT results are documented in the patient's records and are available to the patient care team prior to the patient's admission
Purchasing	• Procures equipment, products, and services • Rents and leases equipment • Issues documents (e.g., purchase orders) that commit facility funds for future purchase of products and services

Radiation Oncology	• Provides radiation therapy for cancer patients, including:
	  ○ Clinical scoring of late effects (measures the amount of toxic radiation received)
	  ○ Radiation dosimetry (develops dose delivery mechanisms that minimize treatment of non-target tissue while optimizing tumor control)

Radiology	• Provides image-guided procedures for inpatients and outpatients, including:
	  ○ Computerized tomography (CT scan) in which the source of x-ray beams rotates around the patient, the beams are detected by sensors, and information from sensors is computer processed and displayed as an image on a video screen
	  ○ Magnetic resonance imaging (MRI), which uses a large magnet that surrounds the patient, along with radio frequencies and a computer, to produce images
	  ○ Mammography, a method for detecting early-stage breast abnormalities
	  ○ Nuclear medicine, which uses very small amounts of radioactive materials or radiopharmaceuticals to study organ function and structure and to treat disease (radiopharmaceuticals are substances that are attracted to specific organs, bones, or tissues)
	  ○ Positron emission tomography (PET), which measures radioactive tracers (e.g., radioactive glucose) injected into the body
	  ○ Radiography (x-rays), which detect disease or injury in the body when an image (x-ray film) is produced as the result of passing a small amount of radiation through the body to expose sensitive film on the other side
	  ○ Ultrasonography, which uses high-frequency sound waves to study parts of the body, including the heart and vessels, to generate an image of the area being studied
	• Directed by a radiologist, a physician employed by the hospital who has specialized training in radiology. Staffed by registered x-ray technicians.
	  Note: Patients who undergo a radiological procedure (x-ray, CT scan, mammogram, etc.) receive bills from both the facility and the radiologist (interpretation)

Recreation Therapy	• Restores, remediates, and rehabilitates patients to improve functioning and independence, as well as reduce or eliminate the effects of illness or disability
Rehabilitative Services	• *See* Occupational Therapy, Physical Therapy, and Speech and Language Pathology
Respiratory Therapy	• Supplies oxygen, breathing aids, prescribed inhalants, and other aids for patients with respiratory distress • Directed by a qualified therapist who follows physicians' orders

(*Continues*)

TABLE 1-10 Hospital Departments (*Continued*)

Department	Description
Respite Care	• Inpatient care provided to homebound hospice patients (AIDS, Alzheimer's, cancer) to provide primary caregivers with temporary relief from care
Risk Management	• Promotes delivery of quality health care and safety • Identifies and controls hazards and injuries, and protects the facility resources • Recipient of all incident reports • Risk manager works with the facility's insurance company and attorney when lawsuits are filed
Safety Management	• Provides patients, personnel, and visitors with a physical environment free of recognized hazards • Manages activities to reduce the risk of injuries
Social Services	• Assists patients and families in locating resources that are specific to their health care needs
Speech and Language Pathology	• Evaluates, diagnoses, plans, and provides therapy to patients with speech, language, and swallowing difficulties • Utilizes speech technologies to improve communication skills • Services are provided by licensed speech and language pathologists who are employed by (or may contract with) the hospital
Telemedicine	• Connects practitioners and patients through on-line consultation with specialists, live and interactive clinical and educational programs, and custom or Internet-based video streaming
Utilization Management	• Reviews and/or recommends admission for all levels of care. Monitors appropriate levels of care, assesses compliance with stated standards, and monitors utilization of patient care delivery resources • Works with case managers from insurance companies to determine whether an admission is appropriate and to agree on an appropriate length of stay • Follows Medicare conditions of participation with respect to admissions and transfers to lower levels of care
Volunteer	• Feeds and transports patients, delivers flowers and mail, staffs the gift shop, assists visitors at the information desk, and works as clerical and support staff

Hospitals contract with agencies and outside organizations to provide certain services, including health information management functions. Hospital committees (Table 1-9) are multidisciplinary, and composition consists of representation from hospital departments and the medical staff.

Successful Meetings

Hospital committees are central to a facility's activities and provide a forum during which decisions are made that impact the entire organization. Each committee must work as a team and be well structured and organized. Effective committee meetings are chaired by a person who is responsible for overseeing the committee and establishing an agenda for each meeting. Committee members must actively participate and be prepared to accept their roles and responsibilities during each meeting. The structure of a committee meeting can be formal or informal, and the purpose of the meeting will determine the structure.

Example Meetings conducted by the executive committee of the medical staff meeting will be formal, but a temporary committee that meets to plan the annual holiday party will be informal.

Prior to any meeting, the chairperson establishes an agenda, which is a listing of all items of business to be discussed. The chairperson and secretary are largely responsible for preparing the final meeting agenda, with the secretary responsible for circulating the agenda along with other documents to committee members prior to the meeting so members have time to review the items. It is common practice to arrange an agenda according to the following headings:

- Review of minutes of the previous meeting
- Old business (matters arising from the previous meeting)
- Member reports
- New business (items for decision, arranged in order of importance)
- Items for information or correspondence
- Other business (deals with items unknown to the chairperson when agenda was created but which are too urgent to table until the next meeting)
- List of documents circulated prior to the meeting
- Date, time, and location of next meeting

To document items discussed during meetings, the secretary records minutes, which are concise, accurate records of actions taken and decisions made during the meeting. The minutes should not contain lengthy accounts of discussions, but should serve as a summary of items discussed. The following information should be included when preparing committee minutes:

- Date, place, and time of the meeting
- Members present
- Members absent
- Guests present
- Items discussed
- Actions taken
- Time meeting was adjourned
- Location, time, and date of next meeting
- Secretary's name and signature

Note: A committee member who is assigned a task or volunteers for an assignment should be clearly indicated by name and responsibility accepted.

At more formal meetings during which legal business transpires, the minutes should also include:

- Decisions made
- Action required to implement decision
- Who will act to carry out the decision
- Any deadlines associated with the decision
- Full text of motions and amendments
- Names of proposer and seconder for each motion
- Results of votes, as announced by chairperson

When taking minutes, the secretary should document key items and statements to record "who says what," keeping each item separate under the headings outlined in the agenda. When recording minutes, members should be referred to by their full name (not by initials or first names), and abbreviations should not be used. Minutes should be an objective and impartial recording of the facts of the meeting without any editorial comments or opinions. Minutes should be prepared as soon as possible after the meeting is concluded, and the chairperson or another committee member should review them. Notes taken during the meeting should be kept until the following meeting. After the minutes have been approved by the committee at the next meeting, the chairperson should sign them.

Note: Minutes of a hospital (or medical staff) committee document facility and patient care issues, are considered confidential and privileged, and are protected from discovery (e.g., *subpoena duces tecum*) except in a legal action brought by a quality-management committee (e.g., to revoke a physician's license) or a legal proceeding alleging malpractice.

Health Information Department

The health information department is responsible for allowing appropriate access to patient information in support of clinical practice, health services, and medical research, while at the same time maintaining confidentiality of patient and provider data. Health information services (Figure 1-3) include:

- Department administration
- Cancer registry
- Coding and abstracting
- Image processing
- Incomplete record processing
- Medical transcription
- Record circulation
- Release of information processing

Department Administration

Health information department administrative functions are directed by registered health information administrators (RHIAs) and registered health information technicians (RHITs). They include (1) developing, monitoring, and improving systems related to the establishment, maintenance, control, and dissemination of medical records and related patient information; (2) planning activities of subordinate managers and staff to ensure continuous quality operation; and (3) participating in a variety of committee, team, and work group activities that monitor, establish policies

Health Information Department Basic Services

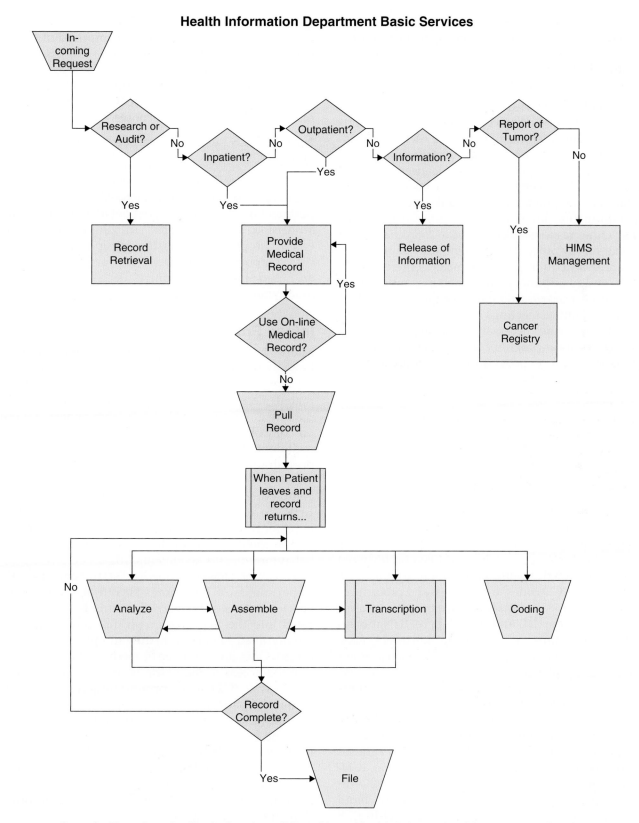

FIGURE 1-3 Sample Flowchart for Basic Services Offered by a Health Information Management Services Department (Permission to reuse granted by MCG Health, Inc)

and procedures for, and enhance the quality of patient care, education, financial, and management practices.

Cancer Registry

Cancer registry functions are performed by individuals who are credentialed as certified tumor registrars (CTRs) and include using computerized registry software to conduct lifetime follow-up on each cancer patient; electronically transmit data to state and national agencies (e.g., Georgia Center for Cancer Statistics, ACS National Cancer Data Base) for use at local, regional, state, and national levels; and generate reports and information for requesting entities (e.g., physicians). Other responsibilities include coordinating the national survey process through the ACS Commission on Cancer, scheduling weekly cancer conferences (in which multidisciplinary staff examine and discuss unique cancer cases), arranging monthly or bimonthly cancer committee meetings (multidisciplinary committee that provides necessary leadership to maintain an effective cancer program), generating statistics and graphs for the cancer program annual report, and participating in state and national professional association activities.

Note: Depending on the size of the facility, cancer registry might also be a stand-alone department with its own manager.

Coding and Abstracting

Coding involves assigning numeric and alphanumeric codes to diagnoses, procedures, and services; this function is usually performed by credentialed individuals (e.g., certified coding specialists, certified professional coders, registered health information technicians). Coders assign ICD codes to diagnoses and procedures for inpatient cases and diagnoses for outpatient cases. Coders also assign CPT and HCPCS Level II (National) codes to procedures and services for outpatient cases. *Current Procedural Terminology (CPT®)*, published annually by the American Medical Association, consists of five-digit codes assigned to ambulatory procedures and services. The International Classification of Diseases, Ninth Revision, Clinical Modification (ICD-9-CM) is used in the United States to collect information about diseases and injuries and to classify diagnoses and procedures. At the time of this publication, ICD-9-CM is in use; the implementation date for ICD-10-CM (International Classification of Diseases, Tenth Revision, Clinical Modification) and ICD-10-PCS (International Classification of Diseases, Tenth Revision, Procedural Coding System) is still under discussion. (ICD-10-CM and ICD-10-PCS are discussed in greater detail in Chapter 10.) The Health Care Procedure Coding System (HCPCS) is comprised of Level I (CPT) and Level II (national) codes. HCPCS Level II (national) codes, developed by the CMS, are used to classify report procedures and services. Codes are reported to third-party payers (e.g., insurance companies) for reimbursement purposes.

Note: HCPCS Level III (local) codes were discontinued in 2003.

Once the coding function is completed, abstracting of patient cases is performed to enter codes and other pertinent information (e.g., patient identification data, admission/discharge dates) utilizing computer software. The purpose of abstracting is to generate statistical reports and disease/procedure indexes, which are used for administrative decision-making and qualitymanagement purposes.

Image Processing

Many health information departments perform image processing to convert paper records to an electronic health record (EHR), which is an automated, accessible record that contains multimedia data (e.g., digital, scanned images, voice, video). To control access to the EHR and maintain patient confidentiality, only facility employees who have been granted *need-to-know status* are allowed to gain access to the EHR. Employees begin the process by completing an application requesting access to the EHR. To ensure the availability of information on an emergency basis, most facilities allow attending and resident physicians to access all but locked and behavioral health documents. (Behavioral health records can be viewed by medical staff members of the Departments of Behavioral Health and Emergency Services.) A security override feature is also incorporated into the EHR system so that physicians who are involved in current treatment episodes can gain access. Once an employee or medical staff member is granted access to the EHR, he or she receives training on system security, appropriate access to and utilization of patient information, password protection features, existence of audit trails and access monitoring, and consequences of inappropriate access and/or breach of patient confidentiality. Employees and medical staff members sign a statement indicating that they understand the confidential nature of patient information and the need to keep the information and their password secure.

Example According to SteamlineHealth, their Access-ANYware™ product provides enterprise access to a patient's document-based medical and financial records via a web-based technology. AccessANYware™ allows health care organizations to establish a private, secure intranet, which is a private network that utilizes Internet protocols and technology. Regardless of where they are located, users can immediately and simultaneously access any health care information across an intranet with complete security and audit trail.

Incomplete Record Processing

Incomplete record processing includes the assembly and analysis of discharged patient records. After a patient is discharged from a nursing unit, the record is retrieved and reports are assembled according to a hospital- and medical staff–approved order of assembly (Figure 1-4). Some facilities adopt a universal chart order, which means that the discharged patient record is organized in the same order as when the patient was on the nursing floor. This eliminates the time-consuming assembly task performed by the health information department.

Note: Inpatient reports are filed in reverse chronological date order within each section of the record. While discharged patient reports are usually assembled in chronological date order within each section of the record, some facilities maintain the reverse chronological date order to save assembly time and allow for inpatient-to-discharged-patient record review consistency.

Once assembled, the discharged patient record is analyzed for deficiencies, logged into an incomplete-record computer tracking system, and filed in the incomplete-record workroom. The health information department notifies medical and hospital staff about the status of incomplete records, and upon request the records are retrieved for medical and hospital staff to complete (e.g., sign transcribed reports, dictate missing reports). As incomplete records are completed, updates are made in the incomplete-record computer tracking system.

Medical Transcription

Medical transcription involves the accurate and timely transcription of dictated reports (e.g., history, physical examination, discharge summary). Once transcribed, printed reports are filed in the patient's record and the responsible provider reviews and signs them. For the EHR, transcribed reports are electronically routed to the patient's record for online review and electronic signature by the responsible provider.

An electronic signature encompasses all technology options available that can be used to authenticate a document. A digital signature is a type of electronic signature that uses public key cryptography, which attaches an alphanumeric number to a document that is unique to the document and to the person signing it. To begin the electronic signature process, a user authentication system requires log-in using a secure password; a smart card, a plastic card containing a small central processing unit, some memory, and a contact area that interacts with a smart-card reader; or biometrics, an identifier that measures a borrower's unique physical characteristics (e.g., fingerprints, hand or face geometry, retinal scan, or handwritten signature) or behavior and compares them to a stored digital template to authenticate the identity of the borrower. Once logged in, the user enters a code to electronically sign a document, and the computer system verifies the code, recording a date and time stamp.

Record Circulation

Record circulation includes the retrieval of patient records for the purpose of:

- Inpatient readmission (records are transported to nursing units)
- Scheduled and unscheduled outpatient clinic visits (records are transported to the clinics such as dermatology, orthopedics, and so on)
- Authorized quality-management studies (records remain in the health information department for review)
- Education and research (records remain in the health information department for review)

Records are requested by either calling the health information department or submitting a record request through an automated patient management system. Health information department staff retrieve the record, sign it out (either manually in a log book or electronically in a chart tracking system), and transport the record to the appropriate area of the facility. This topic is thoroughly discussed in Chapter 7.

Release of Information Processing

Written requests for release of information are reviewed for authenticity (e.g., appropriate authorization) and processed by health information department staff. Requests include those from patients, physicians and other health care providers, third-party payers, Social Security Disability, attorneys, and so on. (Release of information processing is thoroughly discussed in Chapter 9.)

Note: A smart card can also be used to store personal health information, as discussed in Chapter 8.

Section of Record	Organization of Reports within Section
Admission & Discharge	Face Sheet (or Admission/Discharge Record)
	Note: Consent for Medical Treatment, Authorization for Release of Information (to third-party payers), and Leave of Absence Authorization are usually found on reverse of Face Sheet.
	Authorization to Leave Against Medical Advice
	Request and Authorization for Transfer (to another health care facility)
	Advance Directive Checklist
	Discharge (or Death) Summary (or Clinical Résumé)
	Discharge Instructions Summary Sheet
	Anatomical Gift Form
Emergency & Transport	Emergency Department Record
	Ambulance Record
Medical Care & Treatment	History
	Physical Examination
	Consultation(s)
	Progress Notes
	Physician Orders
Operative Services	Consent to Operative Procedure
	Preanesthesia Evaluation
	Anesthesia Record
	Operative Report
	Recovery Room Record
	Postanesthesia Evaluation
	Pathology Report
	Cancer Staging Form (for AJCC TNM Staging) (if cancer case)
Diagnostic Tests	Clinical Laboratory
	Radiology
	Other ancillary reports (e.g., Echocardiography, EEG, EKG, EMG)
Rehabilitative Therapy	Audiology/Speech
	Occupational
	Physical
	Respiratory
Nursing	Medication Administration Record (MAR)
	Graphic Record
	Intake/Output Record
	Care Plan
	Clinical Care Pathway
	Assessments and Flowsheets
	Nurses' Notes

FIGURE 1-4 Sample of Discharged Patient Record Assembly Order (Reports are filed in chronological date order within each section.)

Contract Services

According to The Joint Commission, hospitals must ensure that contract staff are qualified, competent, and provide quality patient care. In addition, hospital medical staff must be involved in the selection of vendors and the approval of vendor contracts, especially for clinical services. The best way to ensure compliance is to inventory all contract services used by the hospital and include what each contractor does for the organization and which staff members are responsible for overseeing the vendor's work and employees.

Facilities use contract services for health information services (Table 1-11) in addition to general services such as housekeeping, medical waste disposal, and clinical services such as physical therapy, emergency care, and speech pathology. The purpose of contracting out these services is to improve quality (e.g., credentialed staff are employed by contractor) while containing costs (e.g., hospital doesn't have to pay benefits to contract employees).

EXERCISE 1–4 Health Care Facility Organization Structure and Operation

Short Answer I: Identify the medical specialty for each description.

_____ 1. Diagnosis and treatment of skin disorders

_____ 2. Management of pregnancy, from prenatal to puerperium

_____ 3. Diagnosis and treatment of eye disorders

TABLE 1-11 Contract Services for Health Information Management

Service	Description
Cancer Registry	Certified tumor registrars (CTRs) organize and assess cancer registry programs, assist in the preparation of an annual report, and perform the following technical functions: cancer case abstracting, patient care evaluation and research studies, follow-up for survival analysis, management of cancer data collection, and survey preparation/compliance with ACS standards
Coding	Credentialed coding staff provide outsourced coding support (e.g., for facilities experiencing coding staff shortages), perform coding compliance audits to determine the accuracy of codes and to ensure that Office of Inspector General (OIG) guidelines are met, review chargemasters for accuracy, and conduct reimbursement validation studies (e.g., to determine accuracy of DRG assignment)
Document Conversion	Companies that specialize in document-conversion procedures convert paper-based documents and data (e.g., scanning), automate data entry using optical character readers (OCR), publish records on the Internet, manage messaging systems, and provide storage solutions (including providing immediate access to information)
Master Patient Index (MPI) Duplication Review	Companies use software to identify, correct, and eliminate duplicate MPI records, increasing patient identification accuracy and patient care safety (e.g., patient records can be more quickly retrieved for patient care purposes)
Medical Transcription	Local and national medical transcription services provide Internet-based and pickup/delivery of medical transcription to health care facilities. Characteristics of services include quality, convenience, and accessibility (e.g., 24/7 availability).
Release of Information Processing	Use of an outside copy service to process release of information requests
Trauma Registry	Credentialed professionals create and maintain a registry of all trauma admissions and deaths in the emergency department due to trauma, recording data elements for each entry that become part of a national registry developed by the ACS. The registry used for education, prevention, quality improvement, and research activities

_____ 4. Surgical management of diseases with the chest

_____ 5. Diagnosis and treatment of musculo-skeletal disease/injury

Short Answer II: Identify the committee described.

_____ 6. Concerned with quality care provided to patients

_____ 7. Acts on reports and recommendations from medical staff committees

_____ 8. Reviews preoperative and pathologic diagnoses to determine the necessity of surgery

_____ 9. Serves as liaison between the governing body and administration

_____ 10. Meets to discuss ethical issues and problems

LICENSURE, REGULATION, AND ACCREDITATION

State laws require health care facilities and providers (e.g., physicians) to obtain licensure (a license to operate or practice medicine) before providing health care services to a patient population. A state department of health issues the license, which requires facilities and providers to comply with state laws and regulations. Licensed facilities and providers are required to comply with both general licensure regulations as well as those specific to services provided (e.g., home health care, long-term care).

A regulation is an interpretation of a law that is written by the responsible regulatory agency. For example, the Conditions of Participation (CoP) are regulations written by the CMS. Congress writes and passes an act, the President signs the act into law, and CMS interprets the law creating a regulation.

Federal and state laws are passed by legislative bodies (e.g., federal congress and state legislatures). These laws are then implemented as regulations. Federal regulations govern programs such as Medicare, Medicaid, TRICARE, and the Federal Employees Health Benefit Plans (FEHBP). State laws regulate insurance companies, patient record-keeping practices, and provider licensing. The _Code of Federal Regulations_ (CFR) is the codification of the general and permanent rules published in the _Federal Register_ by the executive departments and agencies of the federal government. It is divided into 50 titles that represent broad areas subject to federal regulation. Each volume of the CFR is updated once each calendar year and is issued on a quarterly basis. Each title is divided into chapters, which usually bear the name of the issuing agency. The _Federal Register_ is a legal newspaper published every business day by the National Archives and Records Administration (NARA). It is available in paper form, on microfiche, and online.

Accreditation is a voluntary process that a health care facility or organization (e.g., hospital) undergoes to demonstrate that it has met standards beyond those required by law. Accreditation organizations (Table 1-12) develop standards, which are measurements of a health care organization's level of performance in specific areas and are usually more rigorous than regulations. A survey (evaluation) process is conducted both off-site (e.g., hospital submits a self-study document for review) and on-site (at the hospital) to determine whether the facility complies with standards. When a facility undergoes accreditation, it communicates to the public that it is willing to go "above and beyond" what is required to offer the best quality health care possible.

Note: It is important to make a distinction between the terms _regulation_ and _accreditation_. Think of _regulation_ as being _required_ and _accreditation_ as being _voluntary_.

EXERCISE 1–5 Licensure, Regulation, and Accreditation

Matching: Enter a 1 if the abbreviation represents an accrediting agency and a 2 if it represents a regulatory agency.

_____ 1. AAAHC

_____ 2. AOA

_____ 3. CARF

_____ 4. CMS

_____ 5. CDC

Short Answer: Enter the meaning of each abbreviation.

6. AAAHC _____

7. AOA _____

8. CHAP _____

9. CMS _____

10. NCQA _____

TABLE 1-12 Accrediting Organizations

Accrediting Organization	Description
Accreditation Association for Ambulatory Health Care (AAAHC)	AAAHC was incorporated in 1979 as a multidisciplinary accreditation organization to focus exclusively on ambulatory health care. The *AAAHC Accreditation Handbook* for ambulatory care is revised annually, and over 1,400 organizations nationwide are accredited by the AAAHC. Core standards include rights of patients, governance, administration, quality of care, quality management and improvement, clinical records and health information, professional improvement, and facilities and environment. (AAAHC also surveys managed care organizations.)
American Osteopathic Association (AOA)	The AOA's Healthcare Facilities Accreditation Program (HFAP) was implemented in 1945, originally to make sure that osteopathic students received training in facilities that provided a high quality of patient care. AOA transferred administrative responsibility for the HFAP to the American Osteopathic Information Association (AOIA), founded in 1999. HFAP accreditation activities and decisions remain the responsibility of the AOA and its Bureau of Healthcare Facilities Accreditation (BHFA). The AOA received deeming authority to survey hospitals under the Medicare Conditions of Participation (CoP) and the Clinical Laboratory Improvement Amendments of 1988 (CLIA). **Deeming authority** means that an accrediting organization's standards have met or exceeded CMS's Conditions of Participation for Medicare certification, accredited facilities are eligible for reimbursement under Medicare and Medicaid, and CMS is less likely to conduct an on-site survey of its own.
Commission on Accreditation of Rehabilitation Facilities (CARF)	CARF was established in 1966 as an independent, not-for-profit accrediting organization for rehabilitation facilities. CARF "establishes customer-focused standards to help providers measure and improve the quality, value, and outcomes of their services." Types of rehabilitation facilities accredited include adult day services, assisted living, behavioral health, employment and community services, and medical rehabilitation.
Community Health Accreditation Program (CHAP)	Since 1965, CHAP has specialized in accrediting community-based health care organizations (e.g., home health, hospice, home medical equipment). CHAP has received deeming authority from CMS for home health, hospice, and home medical equipment (HME) agencies.
The Joint Commission	According to its corporate brochure, The Joint Commission (formerly Joint Commission on Accreditation of Health Care Organizations, JCAHO) has offered and maintained state-of-the-art accreditation programs for health care organizations since 1951 and provides organizations with standards, performance improvement tools, and an external evaluation of performance. The Joint Commission's approach to accreditation is patient centered and data driven. Surveyors observe actual experiences of a sample of patients as they interact with their health care team to evaluate the actual provision of care, and they examine specific high-risk components of the health care organization (e.g., medication management). • The Joint Commission was granted *deemed status* by the federal government, which means it is recognized by the CMS as an equivalent substitute for CMS inspections. State agencies (e.g., state departments of health) also rely on The Joint Commission to perform independent quality evaluations of health care organizations and programs (instead of states conducting their own inspections).

(Continues)

TABLE 1-12 Accrediting Organizations (*Continued*)

Accrediting Organization	Description
	• The Joint Commission's **ORYX®** initiative integrates outcomes and other performance measurement data into the accreditation process for quality improvement (QI) purposes. *Performance measures* guide the standards-based survey process by continuously monitoring actual performance and impacting continuous improvement in health care organizations. Accredited organizations submit core performance measurement data (or core measures) to The Joint Commission. The Joint Commission and CMS work together to standardize common measures called the *National Hospital Quality Measures.* • The Joint Commission's **Shared Visions—New Pathways**™ initiative changed the scoring and accreditation process, focusing on whether organizations are making improvements system-wide. The continuous survey process requires organizations to score *elements of performance* (to ensure safe, high-quality care, treatment, and services) to determine compliance with standards. • The Joint Commission implements a continuous (ongoing) survey process. It has developed a *Periodic Performance Review (PPR)* tool that helps organizations meet the continuous demand for accountability and is used for self-evaluation of an organization's compliance with standards. The Joint Commission's on-site survey process includes a *tracer methodology* evaluation process, during which surveyors use a patient's record as a "roadmap" to services provided; the services are assessed and evaluated to determine whether the organization is compliant with standards of providing care and services. • The Joint Commission's *National Patient Safety Goals* and random unannounced surveys help organizations focus on providing high-quality patient care. Organizations participate in the identification and voluntary reporting of *sentinel events* (unexpected incidents or occurrences that involve patient death or serious physical or psychological injury, or risk thereof) to facilitate evaluation and prevention.
National Committee for Quality Assurance (NCQA)	Private, not-for-profit organization established in 1989 to assess and report on the quality of managed care plans. Created the **Health Plan Employer Data and Information Set (HEDIS)**, which is the "tool used by health plans to collect data about the quality of care and service they provide."
National Commission on Correctional Health Care (NCCHC)	Correctional facilities that provide contracted or on-site health care services to inmates are eligible for NCCHC accreditation.
National Integrated Accreditation for Healthcare Organizations (NIAHO)	An alternative to other hospital accreditation organizations, the NIAHO is the accreditation program for **Det Norske Veritas Healthcare, Inc. (DNV)** that conducts surveys annually, integrating ISO 9001 with the Medicare *Conditions of Participation.* The NIAHO has been granted *deemed status* by the CMS. DNV Healthcare's hospital-accreditation program is unique in that it integrates the ISO 9001 standards (international quality standards that define minimum requirements for a quality-management system) and the Medicare hospital regulations (e.g., conditions for coverage, conditions of participation) *Note:* In 2010, DNV was selected as the investigative contractor by the federal government's Joint Investigation Team of the departments of the Interior and Homeland Security. DNV performed the forensic examination of the blowout preventer and lower marine riser package that was fitted to the Macondo well in the Gulf of Mexico, which was the site of the disastrous Deepwater Horizon oil spill.

Internet Links

Accreditation Association for Ambulatory Health Care
http://www.aaahc.org

Community Health Accreditation Program
http://www.chapinc.org

American College of Surgeons
http://www.facs.org

Det Norske Veritas (DNV)
http://dnvglhealthcare.com

American Hospital Association
http://www.aha.org

The Joint Commission
http://www.jointcommission.org

American Medical Association
http://www.ama-assn.org

National Committee for Quality Assurance
http://www.ncqa.org

American Osteopathic Association
http://www.osteopathic.org

National Commission on Correctional Health Care
http://www.ncchc.org

Centers for Medicare & Medicaid Services
http://www.cms.hhs.gov

National Practitioner Data Bank
http://www.npdb.hrsa.gov

Commission on Accreditation of Rehabilitation Facilities
http://www.carf.org

NCQA's Health Plan Report Card
http://reportcard.ncqa.org

SUMMARY

Information about historical health care delivery practices comes primarily from the study of textual references, artistic illustrations, and the study of human remains. While diagnoses and treatments associated with prehistoric and ancient medicine were mostly a product of ignorance and superstition, an occasional discovery actually worked. Health care delivery in the United States is based on beliefs about disease and health that evolved over the past centuries. A complete range of programs and services is called a *continuum of care*, with the *type of health care* indicating the *health care services provided*. The continuum of care contains three levels: primary, secondary, and tertiary. (Quaternary care is part of the tertiary level of care.) Hospital ownership is either *for-profit* or *not-for-profit* and categorized as government (not-for-profit), proprietary (for-profit), and voluntary (not-for-profit). Most health care facilities use a *top-down format* so that authority and responsibility flow downward through a chain of command. State laws require health care facilities to obtain licensure before providing health care services to a patient population. Licensed facilities are required to comply with general licensure regulations and those specific to services provided. A *regulation* is an interpretation of a law, and it is written by the responsible regulatory agency. *Accreditation* is a voluntary process that a health care facility or organization undergoes to demonstrate that it has met *standards*, which are usually more rigorous than regulations.

STUDY CHECKLIST

- Read the textbook chapter and highlight key concepts. (Use colored highlighter sparingly throughout the chapter.)
- Create an index card for each key term. (Write the key term on one side of the index card and the concept on the other. Learn the definition of each key term, and match the term to the concept.)
- Access chapter Internet links to learn more about concepts.
- Answer the chapter exercises and review questions, verifying answers with your instructor.
- Study content, view videos, and take practice tests online at www.CengageBrain.com.
- Complete lab manual assignments, verifying answers with your instructor.
- Form a study group with classmates to discuss chapter concepts in preparation for an exam.

CHAPTER REVIEW

True/False: Indicate whether each statement is true (T) or false (F).

_____ 1. Administrative simplification regulations that govern privacy, security, and electronic transactions standards for health care information were mandated by the Health Insurance Portability and Accountability Act.

_____ 2. Anton van Leeuwenhoek established the germ theory of disease.

_____ 3. Diagnosis-related groups required hospitals to be reimbursed a per diem amount.

_____ 4. Hippocrates was the first physician to consider medicine a science and art separate from the practice of religion.

_____ 5. Medicare, also known as Title 19, was established to provide comprehensive health care for people 65 years of age or older, certain younger people with disabilities, and people with End-Stage Renal Disease.

_____ 6. The American Medical Association was established in 1901 as a national organization of state and local associations.

_____ 7. The AMA developed the Minimum Standard for Hospitals to outline the protocol for on-site inspections of hospitals.

_____ 8. The Centers for Medicare & Medicaid Services (CMS) was previously known as the Health Care Financing Administration.

_____ 9. The primary purpose of The Joint Commission is to provide voluntary accreditation.

_____ 10. Tertiary care centers include services such as neurosurgery, radiation oncology, and pediatric surgery.

Multiple Choice: Select the most appropriate response.

11. Which is a characteristic of a governing board?
    a. It is also known as the medical staff.
    b. Its membership is represented by professionals from the community.
    c. It is responsible for administering care to patients.
    d. It reports directly to the medical staff and administration.

12. A patient is seen in the emergency department with glass in her eye. The attending emergency department physician feels it is necessary for the patient to be seen by a specialist. The specialist that most likely would see the patient would be from
    a. anesthesiology.
    b. dermatology.
    c. ophthalmology.
    d. urology.

13. The medical staff committee that reviews and verifies medical staff application data is the
    a. credentials committee.
    b. infection control committee.
    c. joint conference committee.
    d. tissue review committee.

14. Which of the following is a function of the admitting department?
    a. Register inpatients and outpatients.
    b. Provide patients with names of individuals who will sign an advance directive.
    c. Obtain patient signature for surgical consents.
    d. Document admission orders in the patient record.

15. Someone who is responsible for working with case managers of insurance companies to determine the appropriateness of admissions is employed in which hospital department?
    a. Admitting
    b. Community relations
    c. Nursing
    d. Utilization management

16. Health information management services include which of the following?
    a. Patient billing
    b. Coding and abstracting
    c. Patient registration
    d. Discharge planning

17. The assembly and analysis of discharged patient records is called
    a. abstracting.
    b. document conversion.
    c. image processing.
    d. incomplete-record processing.

18. The CPT coding book is published annually by the AMA to assign what type(s) of code?
    a. Diagnostic
    b. Diagnostic and procedure
    c. Procedures and durable medical equipment
    d. Procedures and services

19. A hospital committee that is responsible for analyzing trends of accidents and establishing priorities for dealing with high-risk areas is
    a. disaster control.
    b. risk management.
    c. safety management.
    d. utilization review.

20. United States health care delivery has been impacted by which of the following?
    a. Decreasing health care costs
    b. Absence of medical necessity requirements
    c. Review of appropriateness of admissions
    d. Lack of quality and effective treatments

Fill-in-the-Blank: Enter the appropriate term(s) to complete each statement below.

21. The private, not-for-profit organization established to assess and report on the quality of managed care plans is called the _____.

22. Health care consumers are _____ educated and demand higher _____ health care.

23. The implementation of standards for sanitation, ventilation, hygiene, and nutrition occurred during _____ medicine.

24. An oath that was adopted as an expression of early medical ethics is known as the _____.

25. In the Middle Ages, the care of patients was based on charity and was often managed by _____.

26. French physicists Pierre and Marie Curie, in 1898, discovered that _____ provided a powerful weapon against cancer.

27. Benjamin Franklin founded _____, the first United States hospital.

28. Services that include preventative and acute care and are provided by a general practitioner are known as _____ services.

29. A hospital that is privately owned and whose excess income is distributed to shareholders and owners is a _____ hospital.

30. Health care information can be released only with patient's _____ or by a _____.

Short Answer: Briefly respond to each question.

31. Define the term *multidisciplinary* as it relates to hospital committees, and list at least three hospital committees.

32. Describe the uses of diagnosis and procedure indexes.

33. Compare the terms *electronic signature* and *digital signature*.

34. Describe three contract services that a health information department would use.

35. Distinguish between the terms *regulation* and *accreditation*.

36. List the types of organizations that The Joint Commission accredits.

37. Explain the relationship between *abstracting* and the *generation of diagnosis and procedure indexes*.

38. Compare *primary care, secondary care,* and *tertiary/quaternary care* services. Include an example of each service.

39. Differentiate between a *proprietary* and a *voluntary* hospital.

40. Summarize the purposes of record circulation.

Chapter 2

HEALTH INFORMATION MANAGEMENT PROFESSIONALS

Key Terms

cancer registrar
case manager
Certified Documentation Improvement Practitioner (CDIP)
Certified Health Data Analyst (CHDA)
Certified Healthcare Technology Specialist (CHTS)
Certified in Healthcare Privacy and Security (CHPS)
Chief Information Officer (CIO)
Chief Knowledge Officer (CKO)
claims examiner

clinical documentation improvement (CDI) program
coding and reimbursement specialist
coding specialist
consultant
ethics
health information manager
health insurance specialist
health services manager
listserv
medical assistant
medical office administrator

medical office manager
medical staff coordinator
medical transcriptionist
privacy officer
professional practice experience
professional practice experience supervisor
quality manager
reciprocity
risk manager
tumor registrar
utilization manager
vendor salesperson

Objectives

At the end of this chapter, the student should be able to:

- Define key terms
- Differentiate among health information management career opportunities
- Identify professional associations available to health care professionals
- Name the benefits of completing an academic professional practice experience

INTRODUCTION

This chapter will focus on a variety of career opportunities in health care and health information management, the role of the professional practice experience (externship or internship), the importance of joining professional associations, the interpretation of professional codes of ethics, the impact of networking with other professionals, and the development of opportunities for professional advancement.

HEALTH INFORMATION MANAGEMENT CAREERS

Health information management combines a profession in health care with information technology. Employment opportunities are available in different types of health care settings as well as in a variety of positions within those settings. Depending on the academic program in which you are enrolled and your future health care professional aspirations, one or more of the career opportunities discussed in the following text will appeal to you. The discussion of each career contains an overview of job requirements as well as information about training, credentialing, and employment opportunities.

Cancer Registrar

Cancer registrars (or tumor registrars) collect cancer data from a variety of sources and report cancer statistics to government and health care agencies (e.g., state cancer registries). The primary responsibility of the cancer registrar is to ensure the timely, accurate, and complete collection and maintenance of cancer data. The cancer registrar enters information into a computer database, either manually or through database linkages and computer interfaces. They work closely with physicians, administrators, researchers, and health care planners to provide cancer program development support, ensure compliance with reporting standards, and serve as a valuable resource for cancer information.

Training

College-based cancer registry management programs typically include coursework in medical terminology, anatomy and physiology, health information management, computer information systems, health data collection, epidemiology, cancer registry management, and cancer case abstracting, coding, and staging. In addition to formal college courses, students are required to complete a professional practice experience that totals 160 unpaid hours. Once formal education has been achieved, continuing education is available in a variety of formats (e.g., daylong workshops, intensive, two-week training programs, and web-based training modules).

Credentials

Eligibility requirements for the Certified Tumor Registrar (CTR) credential include a combination of experience in the cancer registry profession and/or formal education. The National Cancer Registrars Association (NCRA) administers the CTR examination to mark achievement, foster professional pride, and provide national recognition in the recruitment and retention of registry personnel. Once certified, the NCRA requires CTRs to pay an annual continuing education maintenance fee and to submit proof of continuing education hours every two years (so that individuals remain up-to-date in the fields of oncology and cancer registry management).

Employment Opportunities

Job opportunities for cancer registrars exist in a variety of settings, including hospital-based, state, central, or regional cancer registries; consulting firms, for which travel is a requirement; and private and government agencies (e.g., American College of Surgeons, Centers for Disease Control). The National Program of Cancer Registries (NPCR), a product of the 1992 Cancer Registries Amendment Act, authorizes the Centers for Disease

Control and Prevention (CDC)—a federal government agency responsible for protecting the health and safety of people)—to provide funds to states and territories to improve existing cancer registries; to plan and implement registries where they do not exist; to develop model legislation and regulations for states to enhance the viability of registry operations; to set standards for data completeness, timeliness, and quality; to provide training for registry personnel; and to help establish a computerized reporting and data-processing system. As a result of the program, employment opportunities for cancer registrars have grown.

Coding and Reimbursement Specialist

A coding and reimbursement specialist (or coding specialist) acquires a working knowledge of CPT (Current Procedural Terminology) and ICD-9-CM (International Classification of Diseases, Ninth Revision, Clinical Modification) coding principles, governmental regulations, and third-party payer (e.g., insurance company) requirements to ensure that all diagnoses (conditions), services (e.g., office visit), and procedures (e.g., surgery, x-ray) documented in patient records are coded accurately for reimbursement, research, and statistical purposes. Coding is the assignment of numbers to diagnoses, services, and procedures, based on patient record documentation. Excellent interpersonal skills are also required of coding specialists, who must communicate with providers about documentation and compliance issues related to the appropriate assignment of diagnoses and procedure codes.

Note: At the time of the printing of this book, the timeline for implementation of ICD-10-CM/PCS is still under discussion.

Training

A variety of training methods are available to those interested in a coding and reimbursement specialist career. College-based programs include coursework in medical terminology, anatomy and physiology, health information management, pathophysiology, pharmacology, ICD-9-CM, CPT, and HCPCS Level II coding, and reimbursement procedures. In addition, most academic programs require students to complete an unpaid professional practice experience (e.g., 240 hours). Professional associations (e.g., American Health Information Management Association, AHIMA) offer noncredit-based coding training, usually as distance learning (e.g., Internet-based), and some health care facilities develop internal programs to retrain health professionals (e.g., nurses) who are interested in a career change.

Credentials

Three professional associations offer coding certification:

* American Academy of Professional Coders (AAPC)
* American College of Medical Coding Specialists (ACMCS)
* American Health Information Management Association (AHIMA)

AAPC credentials include the Certified Professional Coder (CPC), Certified Professional Coder–Hospital (CPC-H), and Apprentice status for each (CPC-A, CPC-H-A). The AAPC also offers the Certified Professional Coder–Payer (CPC-P) and a multitude of specialty credentials. ACMCS credentials include the Coding Specialist for Payors (CSP), Facility Coding Specialist (FCS), and Professional Coding Specialist (PCS). AHIMA's coding credentials include the Certified Coding Associate (CCA), Certified Coding Specialist (CCS), and Certified Coding Specialist–Physician-based (CCS-P).

The type of health care setting in which you seek employment will direct you to the proper credential. For example, inpatient coders usually obtain CCS certification, while physician office coders choose CCS-P or CPC certification. Those who have not met requirements for field experience as a coder can seek apprentice-level certification.

Employment Opportunities

Coding and reimbursement specialists can obtain employment in a variety of settings, including clinics, consulting firms, government agencies, hospitals, insurance companies, nursing facilities, home health agencies, hospices, and physician offices. Coding specialists also have the opportunity to work at home for employers who partner with an Internet-based application service provider (ASP). For example, eWebHealth.com is a third-party entity that manages and distributes eWebCoding software-based services and solutions to customers across a wide area network (WAN—computers that are far apart and are connected by telephone lines) from a central data center.

Chief Information Officer

A Chief Information Officer (CIO) is responsible for the overall technological direction of an organization and is increasingly becoming part of the executive team. To perform effectively, CIOs must be knowledgeable about the workings of the total organization. They propose budgets for projects and programs, make decisions about staff training and equipment purchases, and hire and assign computer specialists, information technology workers, and support personnel to carry out information-technology-related projects. CIOs manage the work of these employees, review their output, and establish administrative procedures and policies. CIOs also provide organizations with the vision to master information technology as a competitive tool.

Training

The formal education and experience required to become a CIO varies, but considerable experience is needed, along with a bachelor's and/or master's degree in information technology.

Credentials

The Institute of Certified Professional Managers offers the Certified Manager (CM) credential, which is earned by completing training and passing an exam. This certification is held by individuals at all experience levels, from those seeking to enter management careers to senior executives. Certification is not necessary for advancement but may be helpful in developing and demonstrating valuable management skills.

Employment Opportunities

Job opportunities for CIOs exist in a variety of settings. There is intense competition for these positions

due to their prestige and high pay, and because they attract many applicants.

Chief Knowledge Officer

In health care, a Chief Knowledge Officer (CKO) leads the development, management, and sharing of knowledge within a health care organization for the purpose of improving patient care and its day-to-day operations. The CKO manages the organization's intellectual capital and serves as the custodian of knowledge-management practices within the organization. The chief knowledge officer serves a broader role in an organization than does the chief information officer (who focuses on physical computer and network assets): he or she assists the organization in maximizing returns on investment in knowledge (e.g., people, processes, intellectual capital), exploits intangible assets (e.g., customer relationships), facilitates repeat successes, shares best practices, improves innovation, and prevents knowledge loss after organizational restructuring (Figure 2-1). CKO responsibilities include:

- Actively promoting the knowledge agenda within and beyond the company
- Collecting relevant data useful to the organization as knowledge

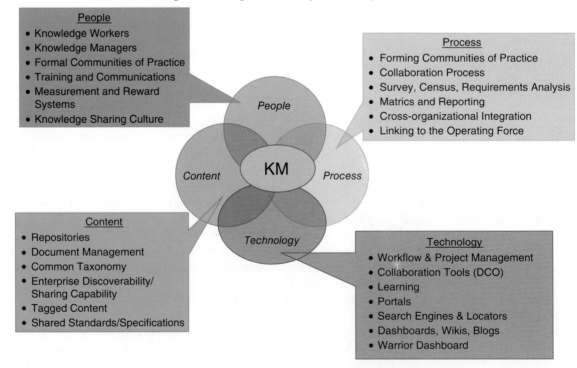

Using Knowledge ... to Prepare, Adapt and Win!

People
- Knowledge Workers
- Knowledge Managers
- Formal Communities of Practice
- Training and Communications
- Measurement and Reward Systems
- Knowledge Sharing Culture

Process
- Forming Communities of Practice
- Collaboration Process
- Survey, Census, Requirements Analysis
- Matrics and Reporting
- Cross-organizational Integration
- Linking to the Operating Force

Content
- Repositories
- Document Management
- Common Taxonomy
- Enterprise Discoverability/ Sharing Capability
- Tagged Content
- Shared Standards/Specifications

Technology
- Workflow & Project Management
- Collaboration Tools (DCO)
- Learning
- Portals
- Search Engines & Locators
- Dashboards, Wikis, Blogs
- Warrior Dashboard

FIGURE 2-1 **Knowledge Management in an Organization** (Source: http://www.tradoc.army.mil/)

- Developing an overall framework that guides knowledge management
- Facilitating communications, connections, and coordination
- Overseeing development of a knowledge infrastructure

Training

The formal education and experience required to become a chief knowledge officer varies, but considerable experience is needed, along with a bachelor's and/or master's degree in business management or a specialized discipline.

Credentials

Currently, there are no specific credentialing exams for a CKO. However, the characteristics of an individual who decides to pursue the position include the following: intelligent, life-long learner, organizational savvy, passion, patience, persistence, sensitivity, "thick skinned," and wise.

Employment Opportunities

Job opportunities for CKOs exist in a variety of settings. The individual most likely to be considered for such a position will possess general management characteristics (e.g., interpersonal communication skills, leadership skills) and specific characteristics (e.g., conceptual thinker who can develop "the big picture" and advocate for the knowledge agenda; has project/people management skills and excellent listening skills; is sensitive to the organization's obstacles and opportunities).

Health Information Managers

Each time patients receive health care, a record is generated to document the patient's current symptoms, medical history, results of examination, treatments rendered along with outcomes, ancillary report results (e.g., laboratory), diagnoses, and plans for treatment. This patient data is organized, analyzed, and maintained by health information managers to ensure the delivery of quality health care. According to the AHIMA, health information managers are considered experts in managing patient health information and medical records, administering computer information systems, and coding diagnoses and procedures for health care services provided to patients.

Training

A health information technician (HIT) earns an associate degree from a community, junior, or technical college. A health information administrator (HIA) earns a bachelor's degree from college or university. To be eligible to take the national certification exam offered by AHIMA, a person must graduate from a program accredited by the Commission on Accreditation of Health Informatics and Information Management (CAHIIM). In addition to general education, coursework includes medical terminology, anatomy, and physiology; legal aspects of health information; coding and abstraction of data; statistics; database management; quality improvement methods; and computer training. Students are also required to complete professional practices in the health information management departments of a variety of health care settings (e.g., acute, ambulatory, long-term, and mental health care).

Credentials

Most employers prefer to hire Registered Health Information Technicians (RHIT) or Registered Health Information Administrators (RHIA), who must pass a written credentialing examination offered by AHIMA. AHIMA requires credentialed individuals to pay an annual continuing education maintenance fee and to submit proof of continuing education hours every two years to ensure that individuals remain up-to-date in the field of health information management.

Employment Opportunities

Health information technicians and administrators can obtain employment in a variety of settings, including clinics, consulting firms, government agencies, hospitals, insurance companies, nursing facilities, home health agencies, hospices, and physician offices. Job titles for RHITs include health data analyst, insurance claims analyst, records technician specialist, clinical coding specialist, physician practice manager, and patient information coordinator. RHIA job titles include department director, system manager, data quality manager, information security officer, educator, and consultant.

As health information management professionals advance in their careers, they may choose to obtain additional certifications that designate them as having specific expertise in the field. AHIMA offers the following certifications.

Certified Health Data Analyst (CHDA)

The Certified Health Data Analyst (CHDA) credential, offered by AHIMA, allows an individual to demonstrate expertise in health data analysis. A health data analyst obtains employment in a variety of health care settings and data-warehousing companies conducting data analysis. Data-warehousing companies process data from various health care databases to create information that is used to conduct such activities as research data management and clinical trials management. The CHDA credential validates a person's ability to "acquire, manage, analyze, interpret, and transform data into accurate, consistent, and timely information, while balancing the "big-picture" strategic vision with day-to-day details." CHDA-credentialed professionals use their data-analysis skills to communicate with individuals and groups at multiple levels of the health care industry, both within facilities and with organizations external to health care facilities.

Candidates who sit for the CHDA examination must meet one of the following eligibility requirements:

- Associate's degree and minimum of five years of health care data experience
- Health care information management credential (RHIT) and minimum of three years of health care data experience
- Baccalaureate degree and a minimum of three years of health care data experience
- Health care information management credential (RHIA) and minimum of one year of health care data experience
- Master's or related degree (JD, MD, or PhD) and one year of health care data experience

Certified Documentation Improvement Practitioner (CDIP)

Accurate clinical documentation is essential to improve the quality of health care and achieve goals of health care organizations. Professionals earning the Certified Documentation Improvement Practitioner (CDIP) credential, from AHIMA, demonstrate knowledge and competency in ensuring that health record documentation captures the clinical information necessary to fully document patients' health care diagnoses and treatments.

The need for clinical documentation professionals has increased because of the implementation of electronic health records, the high complexity of documentation requirements relative to coding and billing, and the audits conducted by various health care organizations external to facilities.

A clinical documentation improvement practitioner is responsible for performing patient record reviews for the purpose of:

- Implementing documentation clarification and specificity processes (as part of the physician query process)
- Using and interpreting clinical documentation improvement statistics

- Conducting research and providing education to improve clinical documentation
- Ensuring compliance with initiatives that serve to improve of the quality of health care, which include:
  ○ Complying with fraud and abuse regulations
  ○ Enforcing privacy and security of patient information
  ○ Monitoring *health information exchange (HIE)*

The purpose of a clinical documentation improvement (CDI) program is to help health care facilities comply with government programs (e.g., RAC audits, ARRA/HITECH) and other initiatives (Joint Commission accreditation) with the goal of improving health care quality. As part of a CDI program, the CDIP initiates concurrent and retrospective reviews of patient records to identify conflicting, incomplete, or nonspecific provider documentation. Concurrent reviews are performed on patient care units (to access paper-based patient records) or remotely (to access electronic health records). The goal of the CDI program is to ensure that patient diagnoses and procedures are supported by ICD-9-CM (or ICD-10-CM/PCS) codes. A CDIP uses a physician query form (Figure 2-2) to communicate with physicians (and other health care providers) with the intended result of improving documentation, coding, reimbursement, and severity of illness (SOI) and risk of mortality (ROM) classifications. CDI programs are usually associated with acute health care facilities; however, they are also implemented on alternate health care settings (e.g., acute rehabilitation facilities, skilled nursing facilities, and physician practices).

The American Health Information Management Association offers the Certified Documentation Improvement Practitioner (CDIP) credential, which is earned by completing training and passing an exam. This certification is held by individuals at all experience levels, from those seeking to enter management careers to senior executives. Certification is not necessary for advancement but may be helpful in developing and demonstrating valuable management skills.

AHIMA requires that candidates who sit for the CDIP examination meet one of the following requirements:

- A RHIA, RHIT, CCS, CCS-P, RN, MD or DO and two years of experience in clinical documentation improvement
- An Associate's degree or higher and three years of experience in clinical documentation improvement (candidates must also have completed coursework in medical terminology and anatomy and physiology)

PHYSICIAN QUERY FORM

Patient Name: _____   Date: _____
Admission Date: _____   Coder: _____
Patient Number: _____   Email Address: _____
                                      Office Number: _____

Dear Dr. _____,

The diagnosis or procedure of _____ requires more specific information in order to assign the most accurate and complete code. The following information is documented in the _____.
_____
_____
_____
_____
_____

I have the following question(s) about this record:
_____
_____
_____
_____
_____

Please respond to this question in the space below, and if appropriate also document an amendment in the patient record:
_____
_____
_____
_____
_____

FIGURE 2-2 Sample Physician Query Form

Certified in Healthcare Privacy and Security (CHPS)

The **Certified in Healthcare Privacy and Security (CHPS)** credential, offered by AHIMA, demonstrates a professional's competency in health care data and information privacy and security issues. As health information documentation evolves from paper-based systems to electronic systems, privacy and security protection in all types of health care organizations has become increasingly complex. CHPS professionals organize and manage privacy and security programs within organizations to protect patient information.

Candidates for the CHPS examination must meet one of the following requirements to sit for the examination:

- Associate's degree and six years of experience in health care privacy or security management
- Health care information management credential (RHIT) and minimum of four years of experience in health care privacy or security management

- Baccalaureate degree and a minimum of four years of experience in health care privacy or security management
- Health care information management credential (RHIA) and minimum of two years of experience in health care privacy or security management
- Master's or related degree (JD, MD, or PhD) and two years of experience in health care privacy or security management

Certified Healthcare Technology Specialist (CHTS)

The United States Bureau of Labor Statistics estimates there will be a shortage of about 50,000 qualified health information technology professionals to meet the needs of hospitals and health care facilities expanding to the use electronic health information systems. The **Certified Healthcare Technology Specialist (CHTS)** competency exams allow professionals to demonstrate an understanding of technologies and procedures relevant to information technology in the health care industry.

AHIMA states that the CHTS exams will demonstrate the competency of health IT professionals to:

- Assess information workflows
- Select hardware and software that will be utilized in health care facilities
- Work with vendors
- Install and test information systems
- Diagnose information technology problems
- Train practice staff on systems

Health Insurance Specialist

A health insurance specialist (or claims examiner) reviews health-related claims to determine whether the costs are reasonable and medically necessary, based on the patient's diagnosis. This process involves verification of the claim against third-party payer guidelines to authorize appropriate payment or refer the claim to an investigator for a more thorough review. A health information manager can also perform medical billing, coding, record keeping, and other medical office administrative duties.

Training

Training and entry-level requirements vary widely for health insurance specialists; most third-party payers prefer to hire college or vocational school graduates and provide additional training on the job.

Credentials

While most health insurance specialists become certified through AHIMA or the AAPC, three other organizations offer specialty certifications.

The American Medical Billing Association (AMBA) was created to facilitate networking, share information and ideas, provide member support and publicly market professional services as a group. AMBA is targeted toward assisting small and home-based professional medical billers with similar needs, interests, and goals. AMBA offers the Certified Medical Reimbursement Specialist (CMRS) exam.

The International Claim Association (ICA) provides a program of education for its member life and health insurance companies, reinsurers, managed care companies, third-party administrators (TPAs), and Blue Cross and Blue Shield organizations worldwide. The ICA offers Associate, Life and Health Claims (ALHC) and the Fellow, Life and Health Claims (FLHC) examinations to claims examiners in the life and health insurance industries. According to the ICA, the ALHC and FLHC designations are awarded only upon successful completion of all required courses in both the introductory and ICA course segments. The ALHC program contains six courses designed to provide students with a thorough background in the administration of life and health insurance claims. The FLHC program provides advanced claims education by requiring additional courses.

The Medical Association of Billers (MAB) is an insurance claims organization that offers certification as a Certified Medical Billing Specialist (CMBS), Certified Medical Billing Specialist for Hospitals (CMBS-H), Certified Medical Billing Specialist-Chiropractic Assistants (CMBS-CA), and Certified Medical Billing Specialist–Instructor (CMBS-I). CMBSs must complete continuing education units (CEUs) each year to remain current.

Employment Opportunities

Health insurance specialists are employed by insurance companies, third-party administrators, and managed care companies. They are also employed in health care facilities, physician offices, and clinics. Home-based employment opportunities are also available for health insurance specialists who become self-employed or work for an organization that allows claims to be processed off-site.

Health Services Manager

Health services managers plan, direct, coordinate, and supervise the delivery of health care. They include specialists who direct clinical departments or services and generalists who manage an entire facility or system. Because of health care restructuring and refinancing, health services managers often deal with evolving integrated health care delivery systems (an arrangement between health care providers to offer comprehensive services as a single health care delivery system), technological innovations, complex regulations, and an increased focus on preventive care. They are also required to improve health care efficiency and quality.

Training

According to the Bureau of Labor Statistics, most general health services managers earn a master's degree in a related health services administration field, while a bachelor's degree is adequate for most entry-level positions in smaller facilities and at the departmental level within health care organizations. Clinical department heads usually require a degree in the appropriate field along with work experience (e.g., nursing department).

Credentials

Health services managers who become nursing home administrators are required by all states and the District of Columbia to have a bachelor's degree, pass a licensing examination, complete a state-approved training program, and pursue continuing education. The American College of Health Care Administrators (ACHCA) offers the Certified Nursing Home Administrator (CNHA) credential, which is endorsed by the National Association of Boards of Examiners for Long Term Care Administrators (NAB) as an option for state licensure reciprocity (credential is recognized by another entity). Many states currently recognize the ACHCA's CNHA program, and additional states are in the process of officially recognizing the CNHA program or are favorably considering the program as an option for reciprocity.

Note: A license is not required in other areas of medical and health services management.

Employment Opportunities

Hospitals employ a large number of health services managers. However, employment opportunities will also be available in clinics and other outpatient care settings (e.g., home health care).

Medical Assistant

Medical assistants perform routine administrative and clinical tasks to keep the offices and clinics of physicians, podiatrists, chiropractors, and optometrists running smoothly. (They should not be confused with physician assistants who examine, diagnose, and treat patients under the direct supervision of a physician.) Medical assistants who perform mainly administrative duties answer telephones, greet patients, update and file patient medical records, complete insurance claims, process correspondence, schedule appointments, arrange for hospital admission and laboratory services, and manage the office's billing and bookkeeping.

The clinical duties of a medical assistant vary according to state law and include taking medical histories and recording vital signs, explaining treatment procedures to patients, preparing patients for examination, and assisting the physician during the examination. Medical assistants also collect and prepare laboratory specimens or perform basic laboratory tests on the premises, dispose of contaminated supplies, and sterilize medical instruments. They instruct patients about medication and special diets, prepare and administer medications as directed by a physician (if allowed under state law), authorize drug refills as directed, telephone or fax prescriptions to a pharmacy, draw blood, prepare patients for X-rays, take electrocardiograms, remove sutures, and change dressings.

Training

A medical assistant earns an associate degree from a community, junior, or technical college or a vocational school. In addition to general education, students take anatomy, physiology, medical terminology, keyboarding, medical transcription, administrative and clinical medical assisting, accounting, and insurance processing. Students learn laboratory techniques, clinical and diagnostic procedures, pharmaceutical principles, medication administration, and first aid. They study office practices, patient relations, medical law, and ethics. Most programs require students to complete professional practice in physicians' offices or other health care facilities.

Credentials

A medical assistant becomes credentialed as a Certified Medical Assistant, abbreviated as CMA (AAMA), through the American Association of Medical Assistants (AAMA) or a Registered Medical Assistant (RMA) through the American Medical Technologists (AMT). The credentials are not mandatory in most states, and the federal government does not require a medical assistant to be credentialed. To be eligible to take the CMA exam, students must graduate from a medical assisting program accredited by either the Commission on Accreditation of Allied Health Education Programs (CAAHEP) or the Accrediting Bureau of Health Education Schools (ABHES). (Be sure to check the accreditation status of your academic program.) Students enrolled in programs not accredited by CAAHEP or ABHES, but whose college is accredited by an organization approved by the United States Department of Education, are eligible for RMA (AMT) certification.

Employment Opportunities

Medical assistants traditionally become employed in physician offices and clinics. Other employment opportunities include public and private hospitals as well as nursing and residential care facilities.

Medical Transcriptionist

Medical transcriptionists transcribe prerecorded dictation, creating medical reports (e.g., history, physical, discharge summary), correspondence, and other administrative material (e.g., committee minutes). They use a special headset to listen to dictation and a foot pedal to pause dictation as they key text into a personal computer (editing grammar as necessary). Before becoming a permanent part of the patient's record, the transcribed documents are forwarded to the dictator for review and signature, or correction.

Many medical transcriptionists work at home, and the Internet has transformed the procedure of receiving dictation and returning transcribed reports to clients for approval. (In the past, cassette tapes were delivered to medical transcriptionists.) An emerging trend is the implementation of speech recognition technology, which electronically translates sound into text and creates drafts of reports. Reports are then formatted; edited for mistakes in translation, punctuation, or grammar; and checked for consistency and possible medical errors. Transcriptionists working in specialized areas with more standard terminology, such as radiology or pathology are more likely to encounter speech recognition technology.

Training

Employers prefer to hire medical transcriptionists who have completed postsecondary training in medical transcription offered by many vocational schools, community colleges, and distance-learning programs. In addition to medical transcription practice coursework, students take anatomy, physiology, medical terminology, disease processes, pharmacology, medicolegal issues, keyboarding, and English grammar and punctuation. Most academic programs also require students to complete a professional practice in the medical transcription department of a health care facility.

Credentials

The Association for Healthcare Documentation Integrity (AHDI), formerly the American Association for Medical Transcription (AAMT), offers the Certified Medical Transcriptionist (CMT) credential to experienced professionals and the Registered Medical Transcriptionist (RMT) credential to those who do not qualify to take the CMT exam. The AHDI requires CMTs and RMTs to become recertified every three years.

Employment Opportunities

Medical transcriptionists are employed in a wide variety of health care settings such as hospitals, clinics, and physician offices. Home-based employment is also available for individuals who wish to become self-employed or work for a medical transcription service organization. The demand for transcription services is influenced by the need for electronic documentation that can be easily shared among providers, third-party payers, regulators, and consumers. Advancements in speech recognition technology will not adversely impact job opportunities for medical transcriptionists because of the need to amend patient records, edit documents from speech recognition systems, and identify discrepancies in medical reports.

Other Employment Opportunities in Health Information Management

As health care becomes an increasingly information-rich industry, many organizations are using HIM consultants to help meet information management needs. Consultant is a general term that can be applied to any number of individuals with a wide variety of educational backgrounds, knowledge, and skills. Health information management consultants specialize in coding, long-term care, information security, ambulatory care, and so on. They provide assistance (e.g., backlog coding projects), advice (e.g., coding validation studies to determine staff training needs), and information (e.g., credentialed person who consults for a long-term care facility). Because there is a shortage of credentialed HIM professionals, consultants are retained to provide advice and direction for the needs of organizations that do not have a permanent HIM professional on staff. Consultants typically will not work for any one organization on a full-time basis, but rather will work for a number of organizations at the same time.

A medical office manager (or medical office administrator) coordinates the communication, contract, data, financial, human resource, health information, insurance, marketing, and risk management operations of a provider's office. (Refer to Table 2-1 for detailed tasks associated with each area of office management.)

A medical office manager usually earns at least a certificate or an associate degree from a community, junior, or technical college. Academic programs are designed to provide students with practical and managerial skills required by medical practices. Some are associated with medical assistant programs, requiring students to study office practices, patient relations, medical law, and ethics. Most programs require students to complete professional practice in physicians' offices or other health care facilities. The Professional Association of Health Care Office Managers sponsors a Certified Medical Manager (CMM) credential, which is available to members who meet eligibility criteria.

Medical staff coordinators usually report directly to the health care facility's administrator. They are responsible for managing the medical staff office (e.g., attending medical staff meetings) and complying with medical staff bylaws (e.g., physician credentialing and recredentialing process) and accreditation and regulatory agencies. Educational opportunities include enrollment in the National Association for Medical Staff Services (NAMSS) Independent Study Program or at a community, junior, or technical college. The NAMSS sponsors two credentials: the Certified Professional in Medical Services Management (CPMSM) and the Certified Provider Credentialing Specialist (CPCS).

TABLE 2-1 Medical Office Management Responsibilities

Management Area	Associated Responsibilities
Communication	Conflict resolution (e.g., patients, office staff) Public speaking (e.g., staff training) Telephone (e.g., patients, sales representatives) Written communication (e.g., policies, procedures)
Contracts	Analysis and interpretation Development and negotiation
Data	Computer applications (e.g., database, spreadsheet, word processing) Interpretation of computer data Vendor systems (e.g., medical office management software) Software analysis and training
Financial	Accounts payable and receivable Budget—personnel and supplies/expenses Inventory control Payroll Purchasing
Human Resources	Benefits Interviewing, hiring, training, counseling, and terminating personnel Job descriptions Legislation Performance evaluation
Health Information	Legislation (e.g., retention laws, privacy, and security) Patient record management (e.g., storage, retrieval)
Insurance	Claims processing Coding Third-party payers
Marketing	Community referrals Medical practice products
Risk	Confidentiality Ethics Medical malpractice

Examination eligibility requirements are available from the NAMSS.

According to AHIMA, a **privacy officer** oversees all ongoing activities related to the development, implementation, maintenance of, and adherence to the organization's policies and procedures covering the privacy of, and access to, patient health information in compliance with federal and state laws and the health care organization's information privacy practices. Privacy officers have an appropriate educational background and work experience in legislation (laws) related to information privacy, access to records, and release of information. They are also knowledgeable about security

technologies and apply HIM principles to project and change management. Education as a health information technician or health information administrator plus appropriate experience in health care legislation will qualify you for a privacy officer position in a health care facility. AHIMA offers the Certified in Healthcare Privacy and Security (CHPS) credential, which is intended to represent advanced knowledge and competencies in health information privacy and security management.

A **quality manager** coordinates a health care facility's quality improvement program to ensure quality patient care, improve patient outcomes, confirm accreditation/regulatory compliance, and prepare for surveys. Quality managers have usually obtained appropriate work experience in a related field (e.g., director of health information) after first pursuing formal education (e.g., bachelor's degree in health information management). The National Association for Healthcare Quality (NAHQ) sponsors the Certified Professional in Healthcare Quality (CPHQ) credential. Eligibility requirements are available from the NAHQ.

A risk manager is responsible for gathering information and recommending settlements concerning professional and general liability incidents, claims, and lawsuits. They initially investigate and analyze actual and potential risks to the health care facility as well as review and investigate incident reports for the purpose of recommending appropriate corrective action. Educational requirements for a risk manager include a bachelor's degree and work experience in one or more of the following areas: patient care, public policy, health care administration, business administration, legal support, or insurance/claims investigation and settlement. The Global Risk Management Institute, Inc. (GRMI), a subsidiary of the Risk & Insurance Management Society, Inc. (RIMS), sponsors the Canadian Risk Management (CRM), Fellow in Risk Management (CRM), and RIMS Fellow (RF) designations.

A utilization manager (or case manager) is responsible for coordinating inpatient care to ensure the appropriate utilization of resources, delivery of health care services, and timely discharge or transfer. Utilization managers usually have a bachelor's degree (e.g., nursing, social work), professional licensure (e.g., RN), and clinical practice experience. Because some utilization managers must have extensive knowledge of coding and reimbursement systems, health information managers are also employed in these positions.

Note: Utilization managers work closely with physicians on a daily basis, and they are a logical choice to facilitate the *physician query* process. In this role, they serve as the liaison for coders (and physicians) by helping coders write appropriate queries and clarifying queries for physicians to ensure timely and complete responses.

The Certified Case Manager (CCM) credential is sponsored by the Commission for Case Manager Certification (CCMC), which is accredited by the National Commission for Certifying Agencies (NCCA). McKesson Corporation offers a Certified Professional in Healthcare Management (CPHM) credential, combining original certification programs in utilization review (CPUR) and utilization management (CPUM). The American Board of Quality Assurance and Utilization Review Physicians, Inc. (ABQAURP) offers the Certified in Health Care Quality and Management (CHCQM) credential.

Vendor salespersons manage a company's sales for a given territory, provide information about available consulting services, and demonstrate products to potential customers. Professional advancement opportunities usually exist within the organization, with promotion to marketing manager, customer manager, or corporate account manager. Computer vendor positions usually require a bachelor's degree level of education or higher and prior experience in health information management sales. Personal characteristics include the ability to be a team player and to manage critical issues.

Other employment settings for health information managers include attorney offices, government agencies (e.g., state departments of health, peer review organizations), information technology companies (e.g., Dell), the pharmaceutical industry (e.g., data collection/studies for new drug approval), research support (e.g., Centers for Disease Control), third-party payers (e.g., Blue Cross Blue Shield), and veterinary hospitals.

EXERCISE 2–1 Careers

Instructions: Research career information at the Bureau of Labor Statistics (BLS) website.

1. Enter http://www.bls.gov to access the BLS website.

2. Locate the section entitled Occupations. Click on OCCUPATIONAL OUTLOOK HANDBOOK.

3. Use the index to search for information regarding your future career (Health Information Technician, Medical Assistant, and so on).

4. Once you locate your career, click on its title.

5. Prepare a one-page, double-spaced summary of career information, including a description of the work, working conditions, employment, training, other qualifications and advancement, job outlook, and earnings. Include facts listed on the website.

PROFESSIONAL PRACTICE EXPERIENCE

The professional practice experience (PPE) (also called an externship or internship) benefits both the student and the facility that accepts the student for placement. Students receive on-the-job experience prior to graduation, which assists them in obtaining permanent employment, and facilities have the opportunity to participate in and improve the formal education process. Quite often, students who complete professional practices are later employed by the facility at which they completed the experience. Academic programs (e.g., health information management, medical assistant) are required to place students in professional practice experiences to comply with accreditation requirements; other programs that also require such experiences provide students with a value-added education. (Even if your academic program doesn't require you to complete a professional practice experience, you can arrange to volunteer in a health care facility so that you can benefit from actual work experience.)

Preparing for the Professional Practice

To provide the maximum benefit to students, professional practices are non-paid work experiences that are arranged by the academic program faculty. Students are usually told about the professional practice requirement in their first semester of study, and information about possible practice sites may be obtained at that time or during a later semester. The program director sends a letter (Figure 2-3) to the site, which introduces the student and details academic courses the student will have completed by the start of the professional

10 Main Street
Anywhere NY 10001
101.555.1111 (office) • 101.555.2222 (fax)

June 14, YYYY

Sandy Supervisor
Cancer Registry Department
Alfred Medical Center
100 Main St
Alfred NY 14802

Dear Sandy:

Thank you so much for accepting a student for professional practice. **Sally Smith, a student in the Cancer Registry Management Certificate Program,** will complete the 160 nonpaid hours of professional practice during Summer YYYY.

I have enclosed our standard articulation agreement so that you can have your administrative representative review, sign, and return it to me. I will then obtain our administrative representative's signature and mail a copy to you.

I have also enclosed the evaluation instrument that needs to be completed on the student at the conclusion of the professional practice experience.

If you have any questions or concerns, please contact me at 607.555.5487 (office) or 607.555.5488 (home). I appreciate your accepting a student for professional practice, and I look forward to working with you this year.

Sincerely,

P. J. Professor

P.J. Professor

Enclosure

FIGURE 2-3 Professional Practice Letter from PPE or Internship Coordinator to Health Care Facility or Physician's Office (Permission to reprint granted by Alfred State College)

AFFILIATION AGREEMENT

This Agreement is made by and between the _____ with its principal office located at _____ _____ (hereinafter referred to as "Affiliate") and the State College, with its principal office located at 10 Main St, Anywhere, New York 10001 (hereinafter referred to as "University").

WHEREAS, the University has undertaken an educational program in the discipline of <u>Health Information Technology</u>, and WHEREAS, the University and the Affiliate desire to have an association for the purpose of carrying out the said educational program in the discipline of <u>Health Information Technology/Medical Records</u>. NOW, THEREFORE, it is agreed that:

1. The University shall assume full responsibility for planning and executing the educational program in the discipline of <u>Health Information Technology</u> including programming, administration, curriculum content, faculty appointments, faculty administration and the requirements for matriculation, promotion and graduation and shall bear all costs and expenses in connection therewith. Attached as Exhibit B is a copy of the curriculum.

The University further agrees to coordinate the program with the Affiliate's designee.

2. The University shall be responsible for assigning students to the program for professional practice experience. However, the University shall notify the Affiliate one (1) month in advance of the planned schedule of student assignments to clinical duties including the dates, number of students and instructors. The schedule shall be subject to written approval by the Affiliate.

3. The University at its sole expense and cost shall provide faculty as may be required for the teaching and supervision of students assigned to the program for professional practice experience.

4. The University agrees that at all times students and faculty are subject to the supervision of the Affiliate administration, and the University shall inform both students and faculty that they must comply with all applicable rules and insofar as they may pertain to the activities of both while at the Affiliate's facility, and failure to comply shall constitute a cause for terminating such student's assignment to or faculty member's relationship with the Affiliate. The Affiliate will provide copies of all policies and procedures to the students and faculty members.

5. The University shall advise each student and faculty that he/she must provide the Affiliate, upon request, with a physician's statement that the student is free from any health impairment that may pose a risk of illness or injury to health center patients or interfere with the performance of his/her assigned duties. The following documentation is also required: (i) PPD (Mantoux) skin test for tuberculosis performed within one year, and a chest X-ray if positive; (ii) Td (Tetanus-diphtheria) booster within ten years; and (iii) proof of immunity against measles (Rubella) and German measles (Rubella); such proof is documentation of adequate immunization or serologic confirmation. The health information and documentation required by this paragraph shall be furnished, upon request, to the Affiliate with respect to each student prior to the assignment of such student for clinical experience. The health information and documentation required to be furnished for participating students shall also be furnished for any faculty.

6. The students and faculty shall respect the confidential nature of all documentation and information associated with the Affiliate, especially patient records.

FIGURE 2-4 Professional Practice Articulation Agreement (partial) (Permission to reprint granted by Alfred State College)

practice experience. Attached to the letter are the standard articulation agreement (Figure 2-4), which must be signed by an administrative representative of the site, and a student evaluation instrument (Figure 2-5) that delineates tasks to be accomplished by the student.

Creating a Professional Résumé and Preparing for an Interview

Students are often required to submit a professional résumé to the professional practice experience supervisor (the person to whom the student reports) and to schedule an interview prior to being accepted for placement. While this can be an intimidating process, it is excellent experience for the interview process you will undergo prior to obtaining permanent employment. Be sure to research the résumé writing and interview technique services available from your college's career services office. This office will review your résumé and provide you with interview tips. Some offices even videotape mock interviews for students.

To the Professional Practice Experience Supervisor: Circle the grade that corresponds to the student's skill level for each, and meet with the student to discuss the grades selected.

Instructions: Consider the following when selecting the score for each area:
- **productivity** (student completed appropriate volume of work)
- **application to work** (student demonstrated good evidence of independent study and motivation)
- **knowledge of HIM principles** (student applied HIM principles to practice in an appropriate manner)
- **decision-making** (student demonstrated good judgment in making decisions, which were accurate)
- **understanding of work flow** (student demonstrated an understanding of the task in relation to HIM department work flow)

Key to Selecting Skill Level: Student consistently performed:
A   well above average
B   above average
C   at an average level
D   below average
F   below the required level

Skill Area	Circle The Score That Corresponds To The Student's Skill Level For Each Area														
	A			B			C			D			F		
Attendance Student completed 240 hours of professional practice.	100														0
Promptness Student reported to the department on time each day; returned from breaks and lunch on time.	100	96	93	89	85	81	79	75	71	69	65	61	59	55	0
Professionalism Student dressed appropriately, was respectful to colleagues/superiors, accepted constructive criticism well, etc.	100	96	93	89	85	81	79	75	71	69	65	61	59	55	0
Communication Student asked appropriate questions, etc.	100	96	93	89	85	81	79	75	71	69	65	61	59	55	0
Initiative Student displays energy and motivation in starting and competing tasks.	100	96	93	89	85	81	79	75	71	69	65	61	59	55	0
Organization Student functions in a systematic and logical fashion.	100	96	93	89	85	81	79	75	71	69	65	61	59	55	0
Supervision Student was receptive to supervision, etc.	100	96	93	89	85	81	79	75	71	69	65	61	59	55	0

Skill Area	Circle The Score That Corresponds To The Student's Skill Level For Each Area														
	A			B			C			D			F		
ICD-9-CM Coding Student reviewed policy/procedure for ICD-9-CM coding of inpatient, outpatient, ED, etc. records; coded at least 50 discharged inpatient records, 50 outpatient records, and 50 ED records; used an encoder; etc.	100	96	93	89	85	81	79	75	71	69	65	61	59	55	0
CPT/HCPCS Coding Student reviewed policy/procedure for CPT/HCPCS coding of outpatient, ED, etc. records; coded at least 50 outpatient records and 50 ED records; used an encoder; etc.	100	96	93	89	85	81	79	75	71	69	65	61	59	55	0
Abstracting Student abstracted at least 50 records, using the HIM department's abstracting system; reviewed disease/operation/physician indices; used indices for data retrieval and research.	100	96	93	89	85	81	79	75	71	69	65	61	59	55	0

FIGURE 2-5 Student Evaluation Instrument (Permission to reprint granted by Alfred State College)

Student Responsibilities During the Professional Practice

The professional practice experience is on-the-job training even though it is non-paid, and you should expect to provide proof of immunizations (available from your physician), undergo a pre-employment physical examination, and participate in facility-wide and department-specific orientations. In addition, because of the focus on privacy and security of patient information, the facility will require you to sign a nondisclosure agreement (Figure 2-6), which is kept on file at your college and by the professional practice site.

Note: Breach of patient confidentiality can result in termination from the professional practice experience site, failure of the professional practice experience course, and even possible suspension and/or expulsion from your academic program. Be sure to check your academic program's requirements regarding this issue.

During the professional practice experience, you are expected to report to work according to the schedule established by your supervisor. If you cannot attend on a particular day or if you will arrive late, be sure to call in. (You will be required to make up any lost time.) Because this is a simulated job experience, you are also expected to be well groomed and to dress professionally. In addition, it is very important that you act interested in all aspects of the experience, develop good working relationships with coworkers, and react appropriately to criticism and direction. If any concerns arise during the experience, be sure to discuss them with your professional practice supervisor and/or instructor.

EMPLOYEE/SERVICE PROVIDER NON-DISCLOSURE AGREEMENT

Office Name:______________________ Date:__________

Address:______________________ Phone:__________

Employee/Service Provider Name:______________________

☐ Employee ☐ Service Provider Employed By:

____
Name

____
Street Address

____
City/State/Zip

I have been asked by______________ to reaffirm my commitment made at the time of my employment/assignment to protect the confidentiality of health information. I understand that ______________ reminds its employees, volunteers, and service providers of their confidentiality obligations on a periodic basis to help ensure compliance, due to the significance of this issue. By my signature below, I acknowledge that I agree to uphold, as a condition of my employment or as provider of service to______________, the confidentiality of protected health information.

______________ has a legal and ethical responsibility to safeguard the privacy of all patients and protect the confidentiality of their health information. In the course of my employment/assignment at ______________, I may have access to or come into possession of confidential patient information, even though I may not be directly involved in providing patient services.

I understand that such information must be maintained in the strictest of confidence. As a condition of my employment/assignment, I hereby agree, unless directed by my supervisor, that I will not at any time during or after my employment/assignment with ______________ disclose any patient information to any person whatsoever or permit any person whatsoever to examine or make copies of any patient reports or other documents prepared by me, or to which I have free access, or that may come into my possession, or under my control, or use patient information, other than as necessary in the course of my employment/assignment.

I understand that violation of this agreement could result in disciplinary action, up to and including termination and/or legal action.

SAMPLE

Employee's/Service Provider's Name (Printed): ______________ Date: __________

Employee's/Service Provider's Signature: ______________ SS # __________

Witness Name (Printed): ______________________

Witness Signature: ______________________

HIPAA Privacy Training Completed: ______No ______Yes (Date: ______________)

#25-8403 • 12/02 • BIBBERO SYSTEMS, INC • PETALUMA, CA TO REORDER FORMS: (800) BIBBERO (800 242-2376) OR FAX: (800) 242-9330 MFG IN U.S.A.

FIGURE 2-6 Non-Disclosure Agreement (Copyright © Courtesy of Bibbero Systems, Inc., Petaluma, CA. Phone: 800-242-2376; Fax: 800-242-9330; www.bibbero.com.)

Professional Code of Ethics

Ethics are judgments about what is right and wrong, and each professional association has a code of ethics that is to be followed by its membership. Even if you are not an active member in your professional as-sociation, you are expected to comply with the established ethics. (Professional codes of ethics can be found at your professional association's website.)

EXERCISE 2–2 Professional Practice Experience

1. Identify five health care facilities and/or offices that could serve as professional practice sites. Use the telephone book or search the Internet to locate facilities and/or offices in your area.

2. Contact each facility and/or office, and talk with the switchboard operator or office reception-ist to identify the name and phone number of the department manager or other professional to whom you would report during the profes-sional practice. Explain that you are a student in an academic program (identify the program), and that you are gathering preliminary information for an assignment. It is possible that you will be transferred to the department in which you would complete the professional practice.

Remember! You are not authorized to discuss the specifics of the professional practice placement. That is the responsibility of your college's professional prac-tice coordinator, who has performed this task hundreds of times and is in a position to provide specific infor-mation upon request. When students initiate conversa-tions about professional practices, it can be perceived as inappropriate and unauthorized. This can result in a site refusing to accept a student for placement.

Note: Because this assignment provides an excellent way to initiate contact with working professionals who can eventually help you obtain employment, be courteous, patient, and polite.

3. Generate a list of potential professional practice experience sites including the name of the facil-ity, mailing address, contact person in the HIM department, and the contact person's telephone number (including area code).

4. Submit the information to your instructor (or other individual identified by your instructor) using the format in Figure 2-7.

Student Name: _____

Mailing Address: _____

Telephone Number (Daytime): _____

Telephone Number (Evening): _____

Email Address: _____

Name of Academic Program: _____

Number/Name of Professional Practice Course: _____

Name of Facility or Office	Mailing Address	Contact Person	Telephone Number
(1)			
(2)			
(3)			
(4)			
(5)			

FIGURE 2-7 Professional Practice Experience Placement Form

JOIN YOUR PROFESSIONAL ASSOCIATION

Students are often able to join their professional association (Table 2-2) for a reduced membership fee and receive most of the same benefits as active members (who pay much more!). Benefits of joining your professional association include:

- Receiving publications (e.g., professional journals)
- Website access for members only
- Networking with members (professional practice and job placement)
- Reduced certification exam fees
- Eligibility for scholarships and grants

Attending professional conferences and meetings is one way to network with professionals. Another is to join a listserv, which is an Internet-based or email discussion forum that covers a variety of topics and issues (Table 2-3).

EXERCISE 2–3 Join Your Professional Association

1. Review Table 2-2 to identify the professional association for your health-related career.

2. Contact your professional association and request a student membership application. (Most application forms are available at the professional association's website. Refer to the Internet Links section of this chapter.)

3. Complete the application form and, if required, obtain your program director's signature.

4. Submit the application to the professional association with payment.

Note: Student membership fees are usually less than those for active members, but you receive many of the same benefits.

TABLE 2-2 Careers and Related Professional Associations

Career	Professional Associations
Cancer Registrar	National Cancer Registrars Association (NCRA)
Coding Specialist	American Academy of Professional Coders (AAPC) American College of Medical Coding Specialists (ACMCS) American Health Information Management Association (AHIMA)
Health Information Manager	American Health Information Management Association (AHIMA)
Health Insurance Specialist	American Medical Billing Association (AMBA) International Claim Association (ICA) Medical Association of Billers (MAB)
Health Services Manager	American College of Health Care Administrators (ACHCA)
Medical Assistant	American Association of Medical Assistants (AAMA) American Medical Technologists (AMT)
Medical Office Manager	Professional Association of Health Care Office Managers (PAHCOM)
Medical Staff Coordinator	National Association for Medical Staff Services (NAMSS)
Medical Transcriptionist	Association for Healthcare Documentation Integrity (AHDI)
Quality Manager	National Association for Healthcare Quality (NAHQ)
Risk Manager	Risk & Insurance Management Society, Inc. (RIMS)
Utilization Manager	Case Management Society of America (CMSA)

TABLE 2-3 Internet-Based Bulletin Boards and Discussion Forums (Listservs)

Type of List	Listserv Name	Website
AAPC Members	Forums	Go to http://www.aapc.com, click on the Account Login link, and click on the Forums link. To access the Forums link you must be a member of AAPC.
Coders	Discussion Groups	Go to http://coding911.com, and click on the "Discussion—Join" link.
AHIMA Members	Communities of Practice	Go to http://www.ahima.org, and log in. To access the Communities of Practice you must be a member of AHIMA.
Health Information Professionals	Advance Forum	Go to http://community.advanceweb.com, and click on the HIM Insider: Forums link, located below the "ADVANCE for Health Information Professionals" heading.
Medicare Part B Claims	PartB-L	Go to http://pbn.decisionhealth.com, click on the Communities tab, then ListServ. Click on a specific forum decision and join the forum discussion. "JOIN Part B-L" listserv link to join.

NOTE: Go to https://list.nih.gov, click on the Browse link to view a list of federal government listservs (e.g., HIPAA-REGS), and join those that interest you.

Internet Links

American Association of Medical Assistants (AAMA)
http://www.aama-ntl.org

American Academy of Professional Coders (AAPC)
http://www.aapc.com

American Association of Coding Specialists (AACS)
http://americanassoccodingspecialists.com

American Health Information Management Association (AHIMA)
http://www.ahima.org

Association for Healthcare Documentation Integrity (AHDI)
http://www.ahdionline.org

American Medical Billing Association (AMBA)
http://www.ambanet.net

American Medical Technologists (AMT)
http://www.americanmedtech.org

Bureau of Labor Statistics
http://www.bls.gov

National Cancer Registrars Association (NCRA)
http://www.ncra-usa.org

Professional Association of Health Care Office Management (PAHCOM)
http://www.pahcom.com

SUMMARY

Health information management combines a profession in health care with information technology, and employment opportunities are available in many types of health care settings. The professional practice experience provides students with on-the-job training prior to graduation and assists students in obtaining permanent employment. Students are usually able to join their professional association for a reduced membership fee and receive most of the same benefits as active members. The benefits of joining a professional association include receiving publications, logging in to websites reserved for members only, networking with members, paying reduced certification exam fees, and becoming eligible for scholarships and grants.

STUDY CHECKLIST

- Read the textbook chapter, and highlight key concepts. (Use colored highlighter sparingly throughout the chapter.)
- Create an index card for each key term. (Write the key term on one side of the index card and the concept on the other. Learn the definition of each key term, and match the term to the concept.)
- Access chapter Internet links to learn more about concepts.
- Answer the chapter Exercises and Review questions, verifying answers with your instructor.
- Study content, view videos, and take practice tests online at www.CengageBrain.com.
- Complete lab manual assignments, verifying answers with your instructor.
- Form a study group with classmates to discuss chapter concepts in preparation for an exam.

CHAPTER REVIEW

True/False: Indicate whether each statement is True (T) or False (F).

_____ 1. Once certified, a tumor registrar pays an annual fee to the NCRA and, therefore, does not have to participate in continuing education.

_____ 2. Coding and reimbursement specialists can obtain employment in a variety of health care settings.

_____ 3. A health information manager has a wider range of skills than a certified coder.

_____ 4. Registered health information technician job titles include data quality manager, information security officer, educator, and consultant.

_____ 5. Medical assistants examine, diagnose, and treat patients under the direct supervision of a physician.

Multiple Choice: Select the most appropriate response.

6. A health care professional who has the primary responsibility of ensuring the timely, accurate, and complete collection and maintenance of cancer data is known as a(n)
   a. cancer registrar.
   b. coder.
   c. health information manager.
   d. medical staff coordinator.

7. Two professional associations that offer certification in coding are
   a. AAPC and AHIMA.
   b. AHIMA and CDC.
   c. ICA and CDC.
   d. NCRA and AAPC.

8. Which is a benefit of joining a professional association?
   a. Guarantee of a grant or scholarship
   b. Joint membership with other associations
   c. Membership fee that is reduced for all
   d. Networking with professional members

9. Which professional is required to pass a licensing examination in all states and the District of Columbia?
   a. Chief executive officer
   b. Health information manager
   c. Information systems manager
   d. Nursing home administrator

10. Medical transcriptionists have unique skills that enable them to
    a. code diagnostic and procedural information.
    b. enter information into computerized data banks.
    c. keyboard prerecorded medical dictation.
    d. stage tumors according to SEER and TNM.

Fill-in-the-Blank: Enter the appropriate term(s) to complete each statement.

11. The assignment of numbers to diagnoses, services, and procedures based on patient record documentation is known as _____.

12. The Bureau of Labor Statistics states that employment for the health information management profession is expected to grow _____ for all occupations through 2022.

13. The insurance claims organization that offers certification as a Certified Medical Billing Specialist is the _____.

14. The American Association of Medical Assistants credentials medical assistants as _____, and the American Medical Technologists credentials medical assistants as _____.

15. Each professional association has a(n) _____, which are judgments about what is right or wrong.

Short Answer: Briefly respond to each question.

16. Sally Smith is interested in pursuing a career as a physician office coder. What is the most appropriate coding certification for her to obtain?

17. How has Internet-based technology allowed coding specialists to work at home?

18. According to the American Health Information Management Association, health information managers have specific areas of expertise. State the areas of expertise of health information managers.

19. What is the purpose of a professional practice experience?

20. Professional associations often allow students to join as student members. List the benefits to the student of doing so.

21. For each abbreviation, define the certification it denotes and briefly explain the credential.
    a. CHDA
    b. CDIP
    c. CHPS
    d. CHTS

Chapter 3

HEALTH CARE SETTINGS

Chapter Outline

- Key Terms
- Objectives
- Introduction
- Acute Care Facilities (Hospitals)
- Ambulatory and Outpatient Care Facilities
- Behavioral Health Care Facilities
- Home Care and Hospice Facilities
- Long-Term Care Facilities
- Federal, State, and Local Health Care Facilities
- Internet Links
- Summary
- Study Checklist
- Chapter Review

Key Terms

activities of daily living (ADL)
acute care facility (ACF)
acute (short-term) hospital
    classification
Administration for Children
    and Families (ACF)
Administration on Aging (AoA)
adult day care
Agency for Healthcare Research
    and Quality (AHRQ)
Agency for Toxic Substances
    and Disease Registry (ATSDR)
Alzheimer's treatment facilities
ambulatory care
ambulatory infusion center (AIC)
ambulatory patients
ambulatory surgery patient
ambulatory surgical center (ASC)

ancillary services
assisted-living facility (ALF)
bed count
bed size
behavioral health care hospital
Bureau of Prisons (BOP)
Centers for Disease Control
    and Prevention (CDC)
chemical dependency program
chemotherapy
clinical laboratory
clinic outpatient
continuing care retirement
    communities (CCRC)
correctional facilities
crisis service
critical access hospital (CAH)
curative care

day treatment program
dementia care facilities
developmentally disabled/mentally
    retarded facilities
diagnosis-related groups (DRGs)
drug therapy
durable medical equipment (DME)
emergency care center
emergency care patient
family practitioners
family support services
federal certification
federal medical centers (FMCs)
Food and Drug Administration (FDA)
general hospitals
Health Resources and Services
    Administration (HRSA)
heart and vascular center

home care

home infusion care

hospice care

hospital-owned physician practice

hydration therapy

imaging center

Indian Health Service (IHS)

industrial health clinic

infusion center

inpatients

intensive case management

intermediate care facility (ICF)

internal medicine physicians

long-term care

long-term care hospital (LTCH)

long-term hospital classification

Military Health System (MHS)

Military Medical Support Office (MMSO)

military treatment facility (MTF)

multi-hospital systems

multi-specialty group physician practices

National Commission on Correctional Health Care (NCCHC)

National Institutes of Health (NIH)

neighborhood health center

newborn patients

nursing facility (NF)

observation patients

outpatient care

outpatient clinic

outpatients

pain management

pain management center

palliative care

partial hospitalization program

pediatricians

personal care and support services

primary care center

public health department

Public Health Service (PHS)

referred outpatient

rehabilitation facility (outpatient)

rehabilitation hospitals (inpatient)

residential care facility (RCF)

residential treatment facility

respite care

satellite clinics

short-term (acute) hospital classification

single hospitals

single-specialty group physician practices

skilled care

skilled nursing facility (SNF)

solo physician practices

specialty hospitals

student health center

subacute care

Substance Abuse and Mental Health Services Administration (SAMHSA)

swing bed

Temporary Assistance to Needy Families (TANF)

therapeutic group home

total parenteral nutrition (TPN)

urgent care center

ventilator

Veterans Health Administration (VHA)

Veterans Integrated Service Network (VISN)

Objectives

At the end of this chapter, the student should be able to:

- Define key terms
- List and define hospital categories and identify types of hospital patients
- Differentiate among freestanding, hospital-based, and hospital-owned ambulatory care settings
- Distinguish among various types of behavioral health care facilities

- Detail services provided by home care and hospice agencies
- Explain the various types of care
- Describe federal, state, and local health care facilities

INTRODUCTION

Prior to 1983, when the inpatient prospective payment system (IPPS) was implemented as part of the Tax Equity and Fiscal Responsibility Act of 1982 (TEFRA), patients typically received health care services as hospital inpatients and stayed hospitalized until they were well enough to be discharged home. The IPPS uses diagnosis-related groups (DRGs) to classify inpatient hospital cases into groups that are expected to consume similar hospital resources. Medicare originally introduced this classification system to pay for inpatient hospital care, with other payers adopting this IPPS in subsequent years. Under DRGs, inpatients are discharged once the acute phase of illness has passed, and they are often transferred to other types of health care, such as outpatient care, skilled care facilities, rehabilitation hospitals, home health care, and so on. The transfer facilities provide an appropriate level of health care in a safe and cost-effective manner after the patient's attending physician (with the assistance of discharge planners, case managers, social workers, nurses, and others) has determined which facility is best by evaluating the patient's medical condition, special needs, and treatment goals.

ACUTE CARE FACILITIES (HOSPITALS)

An acute care facility (ACF) is a hospital that provides health care services to patients who have serious, sudden, or acute illnesses or injuries and/or who need certain surgeries. ACFs provide a full range of health care services, including ancillary services, emergency and critical care, surgery, obstetrics (labor and delivery), and so on. Ancillary services are diagnostic and therapeutic services provided to inpatients and outpatients (laboratory, physical therapy, and so on). Most hospital inpatient stays are short (less than 30 days), although some patients may stay for longer periods of time if it is medically necessary. Because each inpatient day is very expensive, a utilization or case manager closely monitors patient care to determine whether acute health care services are required.

Hospitals have an organized medical and professional staff, and inpatient beds are available 24 hours a day. The primary function of hospitals is to provide inpatient medical, nursing, and other health-related services to patients with surgical and nonsurgical conditions; they usually also provide some outpatient services. Hospitals are categorized as (1) single hospitals (hospital is self-contained and not part of a larger organization) and (2) multi-hospital systems (two or more hospitals owned, managed, or leased by a single organization; these may include acute, long-term, pediatric, rehabilitation, and/or psychiatric care facilities).

Another consideration when discussing hospital organization is to identify the *population served by a health care facility,* which means that health care is provided to specific groups of people. Some hospitals specialize in the treatment of children (e.g., pediatric hospitals) while others have special units (e.g., burn unit). The hospital bed size (or bed count) is the total number of inpatient beds for which the facility is licensed by the state; the hospital must be equipped and staffed to care for these patient admissions. The hospital's average length of stay (LOS) determines whether the hospital stay is classified as short-term or acute, with an average LOS of 4 to 5 days and a total LOS of less than 25 days, or long-term, with an average LOS of greater than 25 days.

> *Example* Patient was admitted April 5 and discharged on April 10. To calculate the LOS, count the day of admission but not the day of discharge. This patient's LOS is 5 days.

Hospitals are also categorized by the following types:

- Critical access hospitals (CAHs) are those located more than 35 miles from any other hospital or another CAH, or they are state certified as being a necessary provider of health care to area residents. Mileage criteria is reduced to 15 miles in areas where only secondary roads are available or in mountainous terrain. CAHs must provide emergency services 24 hours a day and maintain no more than 15 inpatient beds (except for swing-bed facilities, which can have up to 25 inpatient beds if no more than 15 are used at any one time for acute care). Inpatients are restricted to 96-hour stays, unless a longer period is required due to inclement weather or the development of another emergency condition. (Swing-bed criteria allow a rural hospital to admit a nonacute care patient.)
- General hospitals provide emergency care, perform general surgery, and admit patients for a range of problems from fractures to heart disease, based on licensing by the state.
- Specialty hospitals concentrate on a particular population of patients (e.g., children) or disease category (e.g., cancer).
- Rehabilitation hospitals (inpatient) admit patients who are diagnosed with trauma (e.g., car accident) or disease (e.g., stroke) and need to learn how to function.
- Behavioral health care hospitals specialize in treating individuals with mental health diagnoses.

Note: Hospitalists are physicians who spend most of their time in a hospital setting admitting patients to their inpatient services from local primary care providers. Long-term care hospitals (LTCHs) are categorized as long-term care.

Hospital patients are categorized as ambulatory patients (outpatients), ambulatory surgery patients (e.g., day surgery), emergency care patients, inpatients, newborn patients, observation care patients, and subacute care patients.

- Ambulatory patients (or outpatients) are treated and released the same day and do not stay overnight in the hospital. Their length of stay is a maximum of 23 hours, 59 minutes, and 59 seconds.
- Ambulatory surgery patients undergo certain procedures that can be performed on an outpatient basis, with the patient treated and released the same day. Their length of stay is a maximum of 23 hours, 59 minutes, and 59 seconds. If they require a longer stay, they must be admitted to the facility as an inpatient.

- **Emergency care patients** are treated for urgent problems (e.g., trauma) and are either released the same day or admitted to the hospital as inpatients.
- **Inpatients** stay overnight in the facility for 24 or more hours, and are provided with room and board and nursing services.
- **Newborn patients** receive infant care upon birth, and if necessary they receive neonatal intensive care either within the hospital or as the result of transfer to another hospital.
- According to the *Medicare Hospital Manual,* observation patients receive services furnished on a hospital's premises that are ordered by a physician or other authorized individual, including use of a bed and periodic monitoring by nursing or other staff, which are reasonable and necessary to evaluate an outpatient's condition or determine the need for a possible admission as an inpatient.
- **Subacute care** is provided in hospitals that provide specialized, long-term, acute care such as chemotherapy, injury rehabilitation, ventilator (breathing machine) support, wound care, and other types of health care services provided to seriously ill patients. These facilities can look like *mini-intensive care units,* and they usually do not offer the full range of health care services available in acute care facilities (e.g., emergency departments, obstetrics, and surgery). Subacute care costs much less than acute care, and patients are often transferred directly from an intensive care unit. Medicare will reimburse subacute care facilities if care provided is appropriate and medically necessary.

EXERCISE 3–1 Acute Care Facilities (Hospitals)

Fill-in-the-Blank: Enter the appropriate term(s) to complete each statement.

1. Hospitals are categorized as single or _____ systems.

2. The hospital bed count or _____ is the total number of inpatient beds for which the facility is licensed by the _____ .

3. The hospital's average length of stay is classified as _____ (or acute) or _____ .

AMBULATORY AND OUTPATIENT CARE FACILITIES

Ambulatory care (or outpatient care) allows patients to receive care in one day without the need for inpatient hospitalization. Care is provided in either a freestanding or hospital-based facility and includes the following (Table 3-1):

- Ambulatory surgical centers (freestanding)
- Hospital-based outpatient department (e.g., dialysis, physical therapy)
- Hospital-based emergency department, including observation services
- Hospital-based ambulatory surgery program
- Hospital-based partial hospitalization program
- Hospital-owned physician practice
- Hospital-owned satellite clinics
- Industrial health clinic
- Miniclinics located in retail stores
- Neighborhood health centers
- Physician offices
- Public health departments
- Satellite clinics
- Staff model health maintenance organizations
- Urgent care centers

EXERCISE 3–2 Ambulatory/Outpatient Care Facilities

True/False: Indicate whether each statement is True (T) or False (F).

_____ 1. Ambulatory infusion centers are freestanding centers that dispense and administer prescribed medications by continuous or intermittent infusion to ambulatory patients.

_____ 2. A freestanding facility that provides only radiographic and imaging services is called a partial hospitalization program.

_____ 3. A health care center that provides treatment to the economically disadvantaged in a family-centered atmosphere is known as a neighborhood health center.

_____ 4. Clinical laboratories are stand-alone laboratories that perform testing in microbiology, clinical chemistry, and toxicology.

_____ 5. Single-specialty group physician practices consist of three or more physicians who provide patients with one specific kind of care.

BEHAVIORAL HEALTH CARE FACILITIES

The behavioral health *continuum of care* (complete range of programs and services), under special licensing (e.g., mental health or psychiatric services), ranges from health care settings that are least restrictive

TABLE 3-1 Freestanding, Hospital-Based, and Hospital-Owned Ambulatory Facilities

Type of Facility	Name of Facility	Definition
Freestanding Centers and Facilities	Ambulatory surgical center (ASC)	Surgery is performed on an outpatient basis at a freestanding ambulatory surgical center. Patients arrive on the day of procedure, undergo surgery in an operating room, and recover under the care of nursing staff.
	Clinical laboratory	Stand-alone clinical laboratory performs testing in microbiology, clinical chemistry, and toxicology. The laboratory is directed by a pathologist, and testing is performed by certified, professional technologists and technicians.
	Heart and vascular center	Provides ambulatory cardiovascular services to include diagnosis and treatment, disease prevention, research, education, and cardiac rehabilitation. Diagnostic and treatment services include cardiac catheterization, Coumadin care, echocardiography, enhanced external counterpulsation (EECP), heart scans, pacemaker care, and percutaneous transluminal coronary angioplasty (PTCA).
	Imaging center	Freestanding facility that provides radiographic and other imaging services (MRI, PET, and so on) to ambulatory patients. Some centers also provide training and participate in national research projects.
	Industrial health clinic	Located in a business setting (e.g., factory), the emphasis is on employee health and safety.
	Infusion center (or ambulatory infusion center, AIC)	Freestanding center that dispenses and administers prescribed medications by continuous or intermittent infusion to ambulatory patients. Infusion is supervised by a licensed health care professional (e.g., registered nurse).
	Neighborhood health center	Health care is provided to the economically disadvantaged, and treatment is family-centered because illnesses may result indirectly from crowded living conditions, unsanitary facilities, and other socioeconomic factors. Family care team consisting of a physician, nurse, and social worker provides continuity of care to families.
	Pain management center	Specializes in treatment of acute and chronic pain syndromes using proven medications and procedures. Usually a multi-disciplinary approach is used, involving participating specialists such as physiatrists, psychiatrists, neurologists, neurosurgeons, internists, and physical and occupational therapists.
	Physician office	**Solo physician practices** do not have physician partners or employment affiliations with other practice organizations. **Single-specialty group physician practices** consist of two or more physicians who provide patients with one specific type of care (e.g., primary care). **Multi-specialty group physician practices** offer various types of medical specialty care in one organization, and they may be located in more than one location.
	Primary care center	Offers adult and family care medicine in internal medicine, pediatrics, and family practice. **Internal medicine physicians** specialize in the care of adults; **pediatricians** provide comprehensive services for infants, children, and adolescents; and **family practitioners** provide care for the entire family and focus on general medicine, obstetrics, pediatrics, and geriatrics.

(Continues)

TABLE 3-1 Freestanding, Hospital-Based, and Hospital-Owned Ambulatory Facilities (*Continued*)

Type of Facility	Name of Facility	Definition
Freestanding Centers and Facilities (*Continued*)	Public health department	Provides preventive medicine services such as well-baby clinics, which include immunizations and routine checkups. Public health programs are administered at federal, state, and local levels. States have the constitutional authority to oversee their own public health measures. Federal programs through the Department of Health and Human Services provide services and ensure that public health measures are in place. Many counties within states also have public health departments to deliver health care and monitor health care issues.
	Rehabilitation facility (outpatient)	Provides occupational, physical, and speech therapy to patients with orthopedic injuries, work-related injuries, sports-related injuries, and various neurological and neuromuscular conditions.
	Student health center	Provides health care to full- and part-time students who become ill or injured. Services usually include allergy injections, contraception and counseling, health education, immunizations, HIV testing, laboratory services, routine medications, primary care and preventive medicine, screening for sexually transmitted diseases (STDs), smoking cessation, and women's health care.
	Urgent care center (or emergency care center)	Immediate care is provided by an on-duty physician (usually salaried).Usually owned by private corporations in states where permitted (e.g., Humana) or nonprofit facilities (e.g., hospitals).
Hospital-Based Departments and Programs	Ambulatory surgery	Elective surgery is performed on patients who are admitted and discharged the same day (e.g., biopsy); both general and local anesthesia are administered; also called *short-stay* or *one-day surgery.*
	Outpatient department	**Clinic outpatient** receives scheduled diagnostic and therapeutic care (e.g., chemotherapy following an inpatient stay). **Referred outpatient** receives diagnostic (e.g., lab tests) or therapeutic care (e.g., physical therapy) because such care is unavailable in the primary care provider's office. Follow-up is done at the primary care provider's office.
	Emergency department	Immediate care is provided by an on-duty physician to patients who have sustained trauma or have urgent problems (e.g., heart attack).
	Partial hospitalization program	Program for hospital patients who regularly use the hospital facilities for a substantial number of either daytime or nighttime hours (e.g., behavioral health, geriatric, rehabilitative care).
Hospital-Owned Facilities	Hospital-owned physician practice	Hospital-owned practices are at least partially owned by the hospital, and the physicians participate in a compensation plan provided by the hospital.
	Satellite clinics	Ambulatory care centers that are established remotely from the hospital. Primary care is provided by an on-duty physician (usually salaried). *Example:* The Veterans Administration Palo Alto Health Care System, located in the western United States, is a 961-bed tertiary care facility with seven outpatient satellite clinics that serve patients scattered over hundreds of miles.

(e.g., outpatient weekly psychotherapy) to most restrictive (e.g., year-round residential treatment) and includes a variety of types of health care settings (Table 3-2).

EXERCISE 3–3 Behavioral Health Care Facilities

Fill-in-the-Blank: Enter the appropriate term(s) to complete each statement.

1. An intensive treatment program, known as a _____, is provided to patients who live in the community but come to the facility up to five days per week.

2. Treatment services for a _____ program can include detoxification, withdrawal management, and medical assessment.

3. In a _____ setting six to ten individuals are provided supervised housing and supportive services.

4. Crisis services provide for _____ crisis intervention and treatment.

5. Patients that need intensive and comprehensive psychiatric treatment on a long-term basis are treated in a _____ facility.

TABLE 3-2 Behavioral Health Care

Type of Health Care	Definition
Chemical Dependency Program	Provides 24-hour medically directed evaluation and withdrawal management in an acute care inpatient setting. Treatment services usually include detoxification (detox), withdrawal management, methadone detox, alcohol detox, opiate detox, oxycodone detox, chemical dependency, substance abuse, and individual needs and medical assessment.
Crisis Service	Provides short-term (usually fewer than 15 days) crisis intervention and treatment. Patients receive 24-hour-a-day supervision.
Day Treatment Program	Intensive treatment program provided to patients who live in the community but come to the facility up to five days per week.
Developmentally Disabled/ Mentally Retarded Facilities	Sometimes categorized as an intermediate care facility (ICF), these facilities provide residential care and day programming, including academic training, clinical and technical assistance, health care services, and diagnosis and evaluation of individuals with developmental disabilities.
Emergency Care Facilities	24-hour-a-day services for emergencies (e.g., hospital emergency department).
Family Support Services	Services are provided to assist families in caring for the patient (e.g., support groups).
Home Health Care	A team of specially trained staff visit the patient in the home to develop a treatment program, and care is provided in the home.
Hospital Treatment	Patients receive comprehensive psychiatric treatment on an inpatient basis in a hospital. Length of treatment varies.
Intensive Case Management	Specially trained individuals coordinate and/or provide mental health, financial, legal, and medical services to help the patient live successfully at home and in the community.
Outpatient Clinic	Patients receive follow-up mental health care, and visits are usually under one hour. The number of visits per week depends on the patient's needs.
Partial Hospitalization Program	Patients use the facility for a substantial number of either day-time or night-time hours.
Residential Treatment Facility	Seriously disturbed patients receive intensive and comprehensive psychiatric treatment on a long-term basis.
Respite Care	Care is provided by specially trained individuals at a setting other than the patient's home to offer relief and rest to primary caregivers.
Therapeutic Group Home	Six to 10 individuals are provided with supervised housing (may be linked with a day treatment program).

HOME CARE AND HOSPICE FACILITIES

Home care allows people who are seriously ill or dying to remain at home and receive treatment from nurses, social workers, therapists, and other licensed health care professionals who provide skilled care in the home. Skilled care includes services that are ordered by a physician and provided under the supervision of a registered nurse, or physical, occupational, or speech therapist. Skilled care services include:

- Assessment/monitoring of illnesses
- Intravenous (IV) and medication administration
- Insertion of catheters
- Tube feedings
- Wound care

Home health care also covers the use of durable medical equipment (DME), which includes the following:

- Canes
- Crutches
- IV supplies
- Hospital beds
- Ostomy supplies
- Oxygen
- Prostheses
- Walkers
- Wheelchairs

Another aspect of home care provided to individuals involves personal care and support services, which provide assistance in performing daily living activities such as bathing, dressing, grooming, going to the toilet, mealtime assistance, travel training, and accessing recreation services. Home infusion care is also provided by home health care agencies when intravenous administration of medication is medically appropriate for the patient's condition, and treatment is administered in the home instead of on an inpatient hospital basis. Examples of infusion therapy include:

- Chemotherapy: intravenous administration of chemical agents that have specific and toxic effects upon a disease-causing cell or organism
- Drug therapy: intravenous administration of other drugs including antibiotics, antivirals, and so on
- Hydration therapy: intravenous administration of fluids, electrolytes, and other additives
- Pain management: intravenous administration of narcotics and other drugs designed to relieve pain
- Total parenteral nutrition (TPN): administration of nutritional substances by peripheral or central intravenous infusion to patients who are either already malnourished or have the potential for developing malnutrition

Hospice care provides comprehensive medical and supportive social, emotional, and spiritual care to terminally ill patients and their families. The goal of hospice is palliative care (comfort management) rather than curative care (therapeutic). Most hospice care is provided in the home, but patients sometimes receive respite care, which offers relief and rest to primary caregivers. A trained worker or a trained volunteer comes into the home to provide care, community agencies host centers for respite care, or longer-term respite care is provided by hospitals and nursing facilities that offer short-term stays. Most hospice patients have cancer, although a growing number of hospice patients have end-stage heart, lung, kidney, neurological, or liver disease, HIV/AIDS, stroke, Alzheimer's disease, and other conditions. The hospice team consists of doctors, nurses, social workers, clergy, and volunteers who coordinate an individualized plan of care for each patient and family. Hospice care allows every person and family to participate fully in the final stages of life.

Note: Medicare will reimburse both home health care and hospice services.

EXERCISE 3–4 Home Care and Hospice

Short Answer: List two examples for each type of care.

1. Durable medical equipment

2. Personal care and support services

3. Infusion therapy

LONG-TERM CARE FACILITIES

Long-term care includes a range of nursing, social, and rehabilitative services for people who need ongoing assistance. Lengths of stay typically average greater than 30 days. While most residents of long-term care facilities are elderly, young people also need long-term care during an extended illness or after an accident. Long-term care facilities provide a range of services including custodial, intermediate, rehabilitative, and skilled nursing care.

Adult day care provides care and supervision in a structured environment to seniors with physical or mental limitations. Most are located in assisted-living facilities, churches, freestanding facilities, hospitals, or nursing facilities. Some centers specialize in caring for those with certain diseases, such as Alzheimer's disease. Adult day care staff members usually include an activity director, nurse, and social worker, as well as volunteers to run many activities.

An assisted-living facility (ALF) is a combination of housing and supportive services including personal care (e.g., bathing) and household management (e.g., meals) for seniors. Assisted-living residents pay monthly rent and additional fees for services they require. An ALF is not a nursing facility, and it is not designed for people who need serious medical care. An ALF is intended for adults who need some help with activities such as housecleaning, meals, bathing, dressing, or medication reminders, and would like the security of having assistance available on a 24-hour basis in a residential environment. While dementia care facilities and Alzheimer's treatment facilities have many of the same characteristics as assisted-living facilities, there is more extensive monitoring of residents and day-to-day care. Often, these facilities are associated with assisted-living facilities, usually as a separate building or unit; and the cost is higher than for assisted living (but lower than for nursing facility care).

Continuing care retirement communities (CCRC) provide different levels of care based on the residents' needs from independent living apartments to skilled nursing care in an affiliated nursing facility. Residents move from one setting to another based on their needs, but they continue to remain a part of their CCRC community. Many CCRCs require a large down payment prior to admission, and they bill on a monthly basis.

An intermediate care facility (ICF) provides developmentally disabled people with medical care and supervision, nursing services, occupational and physical therapies, activity programs, educational and recreational services, and psychological services. They also provide assistance with activities of daily living, including meals, housekeeping, and assistance with personal care and taking medications. ICFs are state licensed and federally certified, which allows them to receive reimbursement from Medicare and Medicaid. Licensure confirms that health care facilities meet minimum standards of service and quality in compliance with *state* law and regulations. Federal certification measures the ability of health care facilities to deliver care that is safe and adequate, in accordance with *federal* law and regulations.

A long-term care hospital (LTCH) is defined in Medicare law as a hospital that has an average inpatient length of stay greater than 25 days. These hospitals typically provide extended medical and rehabilitative care for patients who are clinically complex and may suffer from multiple acute or chronic conditions (comprehensive rehabilitation, cancer treatment, and so on).

A residential care facility (RCF) provides nonmedical custodial care, which can be provided in a single family residence, a retirement residence, or in any appropriate care facility including a nursing home. RCFs are not allowed to provide skilled services (injections, colostomy care, and so on), but they can provide assistance with activities of daily living (ADL), which include bathing, dressing, eating, toileting, walking, and so on. This type of care is called *custodial care* because there is no health care component, and the care may be provided by those without medical skills or training. (*Note:* Medicare does not pay for this level of care.)

A skilled nursing facility (SNF) (or nursing facility, NF) provides medically necessary care to inpatients on a daily basis that is performed by, or under the supervision of, skilled medical personnel. SNFs provide IV therapy, rehabilitation (physical therapy, speech therapy, and so on), and wound care services. Patients are often transferred from acute care facilities to the SNF if they need continuing medical care and are not well enough to return home, or if they cannot tolerate the requirements of a rehabilitation facility. After receiving care in the SNF, a patient may be transferred to a rehabilitation facility or home. Medicare pays for up to 100 days of skilled nursing care in an SNF during a benefit period, but there are special eligibility requirements.

A rehabilitation facility provides services to patients who have experienced a recent decline in function, often due to a stroke or a head or spinal cord injury. Intensive medical rehabilitation is provided by specially trained health care professionals. These facilities can be located in an acute care or nursing facility, or they can be freestanding. Patients must be willing and able to tolerate their rehabilitation treatment plan, and they must make progress to remain in this type of facility. Patients are transferred to rehabilitation care from acute care, post-acute care, skilled care, or from home.

EXERCISE 3–5 Long-Term Care

Short Answer: State the meaning of each abbreviation.

1. ALF

2. CCRC

3. ICF

4. RCF

5. SNF

FEDERAL, STATE, AND LOCAL HEALTH CARE FACILITIES

Federal, state, and local correctional facilities provide inmates with a secure housing environment that also offers vocational and educational advancement.

Medical, dental, and mental health care services are provided to inmates according to a standard of care imposed by court decisions, legislation, accepted correctional and health care standards, and departmental policies and procedures. Care is provided by qualified health care professionals who are licensed by the state, as follows:

- Primary health care is provided by nurses, physicians, dentists, and other staff at clinics located in each prison.
- Chronic disease management, dental care, vision care, health screening, and emergency care are provided on-site within the correctional facility.
- Inpatient acute care is provided at local hospitals, with medical, surgical, long-term, and psychiatric care provided by specialists at outpatient clinics located within a secure area of the hospital.

The federal Bureau of Prisons (BOP) provides necessary medical, dental, and mental health services to inmates by a professional staff and consistent with acceptable community standards. BOP institutions provide inmate ambulatory care, and federal medical centers (FMCs) provide major medical care.

Note: Go to http://www.usphs.gov, click on the Video Tours link, and click on each "View the video tour" link to preview services provided by federal medical centers.

In each institution, inmate sick call is conducted at least four days per week, with urgent care services available at all times. A physician is either on-site or available for 24-hour continuous duty to handle medical problems that may occur after normal working hours. If an inmate requires medical services that the health care staff cannot provide, the inmate is transferred to an outside community care provider or to one of the BOP's federal medical centers.

The BOP established a quality assessment and improvement (QA&I) program that includes the evaluation and assessment of significant medical events, trends, and patterns. The Health Services Division coordinates the BOP's Safety Program (Occupational Safety, Environmental Health, and Life Safety and Fire Protection), which ensures a safe, healthy environment for staff and inmates. Two methods for evaluating the quality of health care provided to inmates are assessments by the federal Health Services Division's (HSD) Office of Quality Management and by The Joint Commission.

Note: The mission of The Joint Commission is to improve the quality of health care provided to the public. The Joint Commission develops standards of quality in collaboration with health professionals and others and encourages health care organizations to meet or exceed the standards through accreditation and the teaching of quality improvement concepts. The Joint Commission's inspections certify that BOP facilities meet national health care standards.

The National Commission on Correctional Health Care (NCCHC) was established in the 1970s to provide an external peer review process for correctional institutions that wish to meet its nationally accepted *Standards for Health Services*. The areas covered by the *Standards* include:

- Facility governance and administration
- Health care services support
- Health promotion and disease prevention
- Health records
- Inmate care and treatment
- Maintaining a safe and healthy environment
- Medicolegal issues
- Personnel and training
- Special inmate needs and services

The Military Health System (MHS) administers health care for active members of the uniformed services (and their dependents) as provided by military treatment facilities (Figure 3-1) and networks of civilian health care professionals. A military treatment facility (MTF) is a clinic and/or hospital located on a United States military base, and the Military Medical Support Office (MMSO) coordinates civilian health care services when MTF services are unavailable.

The Veterans Health Administration (VHA), an agency in the Department of Veterans Affairs, provides medical, surgical, and rehabilitative care to veterans of the armed services.

The VHA created regional Veterans Integrated Service Networks (VISN), which administer and provide health care services at VA medical centers (VAMCs) and community-based outpatient clinics.

The Public Health Service (PHS) Commissioned Corps, one of seven Uniformed Services of the United States, provides highly trained and mobile health professionals who carry out programs to promote the nation's health, understand and prevent disease and injury, assure safe and effective drugs and medical devices, deliver health services to federal beneficiaries, and furnish health expertise in time of war or other national or international emergencies. The PHS Commissioned Corps is led by the surgeon general (who reports to the assistant secretary of health), and it coordinates the activities of the

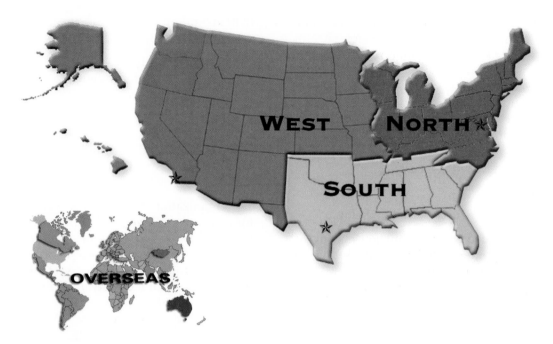

FIGURE 3-1 **Map of TRICARE Regions.** (Permission to reuse in accordance with www.tricare.mil Web site policy.)

following DHHS agencies, operating divisions, and programs:

- Administration for Children and Families (ACF) is responsible for programs that provide services and assistance to needy children and families, including Temporary Assistance to Needy Families (TANF), a state-federal welfare program.
- Administration on Aging (AoA) supports a nationwide aging network, providing services to the elderly to enable them to remain independent.
- Agency for Healthcare Research and Quality (AHRQ) supports research designed to improve the outcomes and quality of health care, reduce its costs, address patient safety and medical errors, and broaden access to effective services.
- Agency for Toxic Substances and Disease Registry (ATSDR) works with states and other federal agencies to prevent exposure to hazardous substances from waste sites.
- Centers for Disease Control and Prevention (CDC) provides a system of health surveillance to monitor and prevent outbreak of diseases.
- Centers for Medicare & Medicaid Services (CMS) administers Medicare, Medicaid, and the Children's Health Insurance Program (CHIP) and was formerly called the Health Care Financing Administration, or HCFA.
- Food and Drug Administration (FDA) assures the safety of foods and cosmetics, and the safety and

efficacy of pharmaceuticals, biological products, and medical devices.
- Health Resources and Services Administration (HRSA) provides health resources for medically underserved populations, works to build the health care workforce, maintains the National Health Service Corps, oversees the nation's organ transplantation system, works to decrease infant mortality and improve child health, and provides services to people with AIDS through the Ryan White CARE Act programs.
- Indian Health Service (IHS) supports a network of hospitals, health centers, school health centers, health stations, and urban Indian health centers to provide services to nearly 2 million American Indians and Alaska Natives of 557 federally recognized tribes.
- National Institutes of Health (NIH), with 27 separate institutes, is the world's premier medical research organization, supporting thousands of research projects nationwide for conditions such as Alzheimer's disease, diabetes, arthritis, heart ailments, and AIDS.
- Substance Abuse and Mental Health Services Administration (SAMHSA) works to improve the quality and availability of substance abuse prevention, addiction treatment, and mental health services.

State departments of health protect and promote health care through prevention, science, and the assurance of quality health care delivery. State departments of mental health operate mental health care facilities (or psychiatric centers) and regulate, certify, and oversee programs that are operated by local governments and nonprofit agencies. These programs include inpatient and outpatient programs, emergency, community support, residential, and family care programs.

EXERCISE 3–6 Federal, State, and Local Health Care Facilities

Short Answer: Complete each statement below.

1. Inmates are provided with a secure housing environment that also offers vocational and educational advancement in federal, state, and local _____.

2. The federal Bureau of Prisons (BOP) provides necessary medical, dental, and mental health services to inmates by a professional staff and consistent with acceptable community standards.

BOP institutions provide inmate ambulatory care, and _____ provide major medical care.

3. Health care for active members of the uniformed services (and their dependents) as provided by military treatment facilities and networks of civilian health care professionals is administered by the _____.

4. The Medicare, Medicaid, and Children's Health Insurance Program (CHIP) programs are administered by the _____.

5. The organization that provides health resources for medically underserved populations, works to build the health care workforce, maintains the National Health Service Corps, oversees the nation's organ transplantation system, works to decrease infant mortality and improve child health, and provides services to people with AIDS through the Ryan White CARE Act programs is called the _____.

Internet Links

Assisted Living
http://www.assistedlivinginfo.com

Nursing Home
http://www.seniorliving.net

State Health Agencies
http://www.statepublichealth.org

U.S. Government Official Web Portal
http://www.usa.gov

U.S. Department of Veterans Affairs
http://www.va.gov

SUMMARY

An acute care facility (ACF) provides health care services to patients who have serious, sudden, or acute illnesses or injuries and/or who need certain surgeries. They are categorized as single hospitals or multi-hospital systems as well as by type, such as general hospitals, specialty hospitals, rehabilitation hospitals, and behavioral health care hospitals. Hospital patients are categorized as outpatients, ambulatory surgery patients, emergency care patients, inpatients, newborn patients, observation care patients, and subacute care patients. Some hospitals establish satellite clinics.

Ambulatory care allows patients to receive care in one day without the need for inpatient hospitalization. Care is provided in either a freestanding or hospital-based facility. Behavioral health care ranges from settings that are least restrictive (e.g., outpatient

weekly psychotherapy) to most restrictive (e.g., year-round residential treatment) and includes a variety of types of health care settings. Home care allows people who are seriously ill or dying to remain at home and receive treatment, and it includes the use of durable medical equipment (DME), personal care and support services, and home infusion care. Hospice care provides comprehensive medical and supportive social, emotional, and spiritual care to terminally ill patients and their families. Long-term care facilities provide a range of services including custodial, intermediate, rehabilitative, and skilled nursing care. Managed care refers to the prepaid health care sector, which combines health care delivery with the financing of health care services as well as some forms of indemnity coverage that incorporate utilization management activities.

Federal, state, and local correctional facilities provide secure housing for inmates in an environment that also provides vocational and educational advancement. The Military Health System (MHS) administers health care for active members of the uniformed services provided by military treatment facilities and networks of civilian health care professionals. The Veterans Health Administration (VHA) provides medical, surgical, and rehabilitative care to veterans of the armed services. The Public Health Service (PHS) Commissioned Corps provides highly trained and mobile health professionals who carry out programs to promote the nation's health, understand and prevent disease and injury, assure safe and effective drugs and medical devices, deliver health services to federal beneficiaries, and furnish health expertise in time of war or other national or international emergencies.

State departments of health protect and promote health care through prevention, science, and the assurance of quality health care delivery. State departments of mental health operate mental health care facilities (or psychiatric centers) and regulate, certify, and oversee programs that are operated by local governments and nonprofit agencies.

STUDY CHECKLIST

- Read the textbook chapter, and highlight key concepts. (Use colored highlighter sparingly throughout the chapter.)
- Create an index card for each key term. (Write the key term on one side of the index card and the concept on the other. Learn the definition of each key term, and match the term to the concept.)
- Access chapter Internet links to learn more about concepts.
- Answer the chapter Exercises and Review questions, verifying answers with your instructor.
- Study content, view videos, and take practice tests online at www.CengageBrain.com.
- Complete lab manual assignments, verifying answers with your instructor.
- Form a study group with classmates to discuss chapter concepts in preparation for an exam.

CHAPTER REVIEW

True/False: Indicate whether each statement is True (T) or False (F).

_____ 1. Clinic outpatients receive scheduled diagnostic and therapeutic services.

_____ 2. Diagnosis-related groups classify inpatient and outpatient hospital cases into groups that are expected to consume similar hospital resources.

_____ 3. General hospitals admit patients for a range of problems from fractures to heart disease and provide emergency care and general surgery services.

_____ 4. Outpatient psychotherapy is considered the most restrictive type of behavioral health care service.

_____ 5. A cane or a walker is an example of durable medical equipment.

_____ 6. Critical access hospitals provide emergency services and maintain no more than 30 inpatient beds.

_____ 7. Swing beds allow rural hospitals to admit emergency patients.

Multiple Choice: Select the most appropriate response.

8. A patient who has a serious, sudden, or acute illness or injury would be treated in a(n)
   a. acute care facility.
   b. intermediate care facility.
   c. long-term care facility.
   d. skilled nursing facility.

9. Hospitals that provide specialized, long-term, acute care such as chemotherapy, wound care, or injury rehabilitation are known as _____ hospitals.
   a. general
   b. rehabilitation
   c. specialty
   d. subacute

10. The type of care that provides comprehensive medical and supportive social, emotional, and spiritual care to terminally ill patients and their families is known as _____ care.
    a. home
    b. hospice
    c. personal
    d. support

11. The abbreviation TPN is defined as
    a. total parenteral nutrition.
    b. temperature, pulse, and nutrition.
    c. total palliative nutrition.
    d. temporary parenteral nutrition.

12. A _____ is either on-site or available for 24-hour continuous duty to handle an inmate's medical problems that may occur after normal working hours.
    a. certified medical assistant
    b. physician
    c. prison guard
    d. warden

Fill-in-the-Blank: Enter the appropriate term(s) to complete each statement.

13. A hospital that admits patients who are diagnosed with trauma or disease and need to learn how to function again is a(n) _____.

14. Services that are ordered by a physician and are provided under the supervision of a registered nurse, or physical, occupational, or speech therapist, are known as _____.

15. The goal of hospice is _____ rather than _____.

16. Individuals with mental health diagnoses that require inpatient intervention are treated in _____ hospitals.

17. Internal medicine physicians specialize in the care of adults, while _____ provide services to infants, children, and adolescents.

Short Answer: Briefly respond to each question.

18. Explain the goal of hospice care, and list the types of services provided in hospice programs.

19. The federal Bureau of Prisons (BOP) provides health care to inmates. Describe the two methods for evaluating the quality of health care provided to inmates.

20. List and discuss the four types of hospitals covered in your textbook.

21. Sally Smith's 80-year-old mother, Mary, lives with her. Sally works fulltime in the day and also attends to Mary's needs. Sally still wants her mother to remain in her home with her; however, Mary can no longer be left alone while Sally is at work. Discuss the type of facility that would be able to offer assistance in this situation.

22. Define ancillary services and give three examples of this type of service.

Chapter 4

INTRODUCTION TO THE PATIENT RECORD

Key Terms

abbreviation list
addendum
administrative data
age of consent
age of majority
alternate care facilities
alternative storage method
amending the patient record
archived records
assessment (A)
ASTM E 1762–Standard Guide for Authentication of Healthcare-Information
audit trail
authentication
auto-authentication
chart deficiencies
chronological date order
clinical data

countersignature
database
deficiency slip
delinquent records
delinquent record rate
demographic data
diagnostic/management plans
digital archive
electronic health record (EHR)
hospital ambulatory care record
hospital inpatient record
hospital outpatient record
inactive records
incident report
independent database
information capture
initial plan
integrated record
magnetic degaussing

manual record
mHealth
microfilm
nursing assessment
objective (O)
off-site storage
patient education plans
patient record
patient's representative
physician office record
plan (P)
potentially compensable event (PCE)
preadmission testing (PAT)
primary sources
problem list
problem oriented medical record (POMR)
problem oriented record (POR)

provisional diagnosis
purge
record destruction methods
record retention schedule
remote storage
report generation
retention period
reverse chronological date order

secondary sources
sectionalized record
shadow record
signature legend
signature stamp
solo practitioner
source oriented record (SOR)
speech recognition software

statute of limitations
subjective (S)
telephone order (T.O.)
therapeutic plans
transfer note
voice order (V.O.)
voice recognition software

Objectives

At the end of this chapter, the student should be able to:

- Define the patient record, and explain its purpose
- Delineate provider responsibilities for the patient record
- Summarize the development of the patient record
- Distinguish among patient record formats
- Compare alternative storage methods to archived records
- Summarize patient record completion responsibilities

INTRODUCTION

The paper and electronic patient record has many purposes but only one goal—documentation of patient care. Hospital inpatient records have traditionally served as the documentation source and business record for patient care information; however, alternate care facilities that provide behavioral health, home health, hospice, outpatient, skilled nursing, and other forms of care also serve as a documentation source for patient care information. As an increased number of health care services continue to be provided on an outpatient and primary care basis, the importance and volume of this information are increasing. Regardless of the type of care provided, a health care facility's patient records contain similar content (e.g., consent forms) and format features (e.g., all records contain patient identification information).

DEFINITION AND PURPOSE OF THE PATIENT RECORD

A patient record serves as the business record for a patient encounter, contains documentation of all health care services provided to a patient, and is a repository of information that includes demographic data, as well as documentation to support diagnoses, justify treatment, and record treatment results. Fundamental types of data are present in a patient's record, whether that data is captured on paper or in an electronic medical record. The purpose of this chapter is to get you to think about the content of the patient record regardless of how the information is recorded. Since the health care industry is currently evolving from paper record systems to electronic medical records, we will discuss information that is found in the paper record and then address how this same information is found in electronic records. In order for HIM professionals to assist the health care industry with the transition from paper to electronic systems, the content of the record must be understood. Demographic data is patient identification information collected according to facility policy and includes the patient's name and other information such as date of birth, place of birth, mother's maiden name, social security number, and so on. In addition, the facility includes its name, mailing address, and telephone number on each page of the patient record because providers who receive copies of records may need to contact the facility for clarification about record content.

Note: Each page of the patient record should include the following identification information: name of the attending or primary care provider, patient's name, patient number, date of admission/visit, and name/address/telephone number of the facility. In an electronic health record the same demographic information is captured via various screens.

The Medical Record Institute (MRI) categorizes health care documentation as information capture and report generation.

Information capture is the process of recording representations of human thought, perceptions, or actions in documenting patient care, as well as device-generated information that is gathered and/or computed about a patient as part of health care. Typical means for information capture are handwriting, speaking, typing, touching a screen, or pointing and clicking on words, phrases, etc. Other means include videotaping, audio recordings, and image generation through x-rays, etc. Report generation, i.e., the construction of a health care document (paper or digital), consists of the formatting and/or structuring of captured information. It is the process of analyzing, organizing, and presenting recorded patient information for authentication and inclusion in the patient's health care record.

The MRI developed the following *Essential Principles of Healthcare Documentation*:

- Unique patient identification must be assured within and across health care documentation systems.
- Health care documentation must be accurate and consistent, complete, timely, interoperable across types of documentation systems, accessible at any time and at any place where patient care is needed, and auditable.
- Confidential and secure authentication and accountability must be provided.

Patient record reports are often generated through the process of medical transcription, which involves keyboarding medical information dictated by a provider into a system that stores dictation on tape or using computer media such as a hard drive or a disc. A medical transcriptionist listens to dictated information and keyboards the report. (Medical transcriptionists can be certified through the Association for Healthcare Documentation Integrity [AHDI], formerly the AAMT.) The provider reviews the report for accuracy, and it is (1) filed in the patient's paper-based medical record or (2) scanned or electronically inserted in the electronic health record. In addition to transcription, many providers use speech recognition software—also known as voice recognition software—to dictate reports and progress notes. Speech recognition software translates the spoken word into text. Sometimes this is called "talk to text." Speech recognition software is a component of some electronic health record systems; it also can be acquired as an add-on feature. Speech recognition expedites transcription and saves costs. The following reports are typically generated as a result of medical transcription or speech recognition technology:

- Admission history and physical examinations
- Operative reports
- Consultation reports
- Biopsychosocial reports
- Laboratory reports
- Radiology reports
- Nuclear and imaging studies
- Progress notes
- Autopsy reports
- Discharge summaries

Continuity of care includes documentation of patient care services so that others who treat the patient have a source of information on which to base additional care and treatment. According to The Joint Commission, the purpose of the record is to identify the patient; support and justify the patient's diagnosis, care, treatment, and services provided; document the course of treatment and results; and facilitate continuity of care among health care providers. The record also serves as a communication tool for physicians and other patient care professionals and assists in planning individual patient care and documenting a patient's illness and treatment.

Secondary purposes of the patient record do not relate directly to patient care and include:

- Evaluating quality of patient care
- Providing information to third-party payers (e.g., insurance company) for reimbursement
- Serving the interests of the patient, facility, and providers of care
- Providing data for use in clinical research, epidemiology studies, education, public policy making, facilities planning, and health care statistics

The patient record is also used as a personal or an impersonal source of information, depending on the user. When the user requests access to a specific patient record, this is considered a personal use of the patient record (e.g., third-party payer). When a user requests access to randomly selected patient records, this is considered an impersonal use of the patient record (e.g., quality management coordinator).

Ownership of the Patient Record

The medical record is the property of the provider, and as governed by federal and state laws, the patient has the right to access its contents for review (e.g., third-party payer reimbursement) and to request that inaccurate information be amended. (If the provider chooses not to amend the record, the patient can write a letter clarifying the information, which is then filed in the record.) This means that the provider owns the documents and maintains possession of original records according to federal regulations (e.g., Medicare Conditions of Participation) and state laws (e.g., New York State retention law). In addition, the provider has the option to maintain the record on its premises or at an appropriate off-site storage facility. Electronic health records (EHRs), also known as electronic medical records, and previously known as computer-based patient records (CPRs) include electronic and/or digital characters and signatures that are permanently stored using electronic media the records are viewed on a monitor or as a printout. The provider is responsible for retaining minimum data elements of authoritative original EHRs in the same manner as original paper records. Each facility designates their legal medical record as either electronic or paper-based.

Example Upon review of her patient record, Patty Patient notes that her physician documented multiple episodes of upper respiratory tract infections over the past five years. Patty recalls telling the physician that she had just two episodes in the last five years. Patty has the option of writing a letter to the facility to clarify the documentation and having the letter filed in her record.

Hospital Inpatient Record

The hospital inpatient record documents the care and treatment received by a patient admitted to the hospital. While the patient is in the hospital, the paper record is typically located at the nursing station. Some facilities locate the inpatient record in a locking-wall desk (Figure 4-1), and providers enter documentation at the patient's bedside. With the increased use of electronic health records, some facilities now have bedside terminals or a single computer on wheels. Typically, inpatient admissions average 6 to 8 days, which means that a typical record contains approximately 60 to 100 pages. While the content and size of the hospital inpatient record will vary according to the patient's diagnosis and treatment, all hospital inpatient records include similar content, including administrative and clinical data (Table 4-1). Administrative data includes demographic, socioeconomic, and financial information. Clinical data includes all patient health

FIGURE 4-1 Locking-Wall Desk Used at a Nursing Station (Permission to reprint granted by Ames Color-File.)

TABLE 4-1 Examples of Administrative and Clinical Data

Type of Data	Examples
Administrative Data	**Demographic**
	• Patient name
	• Patient address
	• Gender
	• Date of birth
	• Social security number
	• Telephone number
	Socioeconomic
	• Marital status
	• Race and ethnicity
	• Occupation
	• Place of employment
	Financial
	• Third-party payer
	• Insurance number
	• Secondary insurance
Clinical Data	
	• Consultation report
	• Discharge summary
	• History
	• Laboratory results
	• Medication administration records
	• Operative record
	• Pathology report
	• Physical examination
	• Progress notes
	• Radiology report
	• Medication lists
	• Problem lists
	• Radiological images

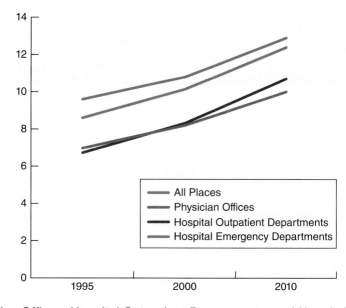

FIGURE 4-2 Visits to Physician Offices, Hospital Outpatient Departments, and Hospital Emergency Departments: United States, Selected Years, 1995–2010 (Data from: http://www.cdc.gov/nchs/hus/contents2013.htm#089)

information obtained throughout the treatment and care of the patient.

> *Example* Table 4-1 contains examples of administrative and clinical data.

Hospital Outpatient Record

The hospital outpatient record (or hospital ambulatory care record) documents services received by a patient who has not been admitted to the hospital overnight and includes ancillary services (e.g., lab tests, x-rays), emergency department services, and outpatient (or ambulatory) surgery. Since the early 1980s, outpatient services have steadily increased due to cost savings associated with providing health care on an ambulatory instead of an inpatient basis. This shift from inpatient to outpatient care has also resulted in hospital health information departments managing an increasing volume of outpatient information. The number of physician offices visits has also continued to grow (Figure 4-2).

Note: Federal regulations and The Joint Commission documentation standards for outpatient records are discussed in Chapter 7.

Physician Office Record

Patient health care services received in a physician's office are documented in the physician office record.

Registration data is collected on each patient prior to the patient being seen or at the time of the patient's first visit. Figure 4-3 is an example of a patient registration form. While the content and format of physician office records vary greatly from office to office, they include both administrative and clinical data. Generally, physicians who practice independently use a less structured office record, while those associated with a group practice use a more structured office record.

Alternate Care Settings

The content of alternate care records depends on the types of services delivered, accreditation standards, and state and federal regulations. There are similarities and differences among the various types of records, but all contain administrative and clinical data. The types of services delivered in the various alternate care settings determine the unique clinical data content of the patient record (Table 4-2).

> *Example* A home care record generated for a Medicare patient contains a *Home Health Certification and Plan of Care (CMS-485)* form (Figure 4-4), which certifies the patient's need for home health services. This form is unique to home care documentation (Figure 4-4).

College Clinic
4567 Broad Avenue
Woodland Hills, XY 12345-0001
TELEPHONE: (013) 486-9002
FAX (013) 487-8976

REGISTRATION
(PLEASE PRINT)

Account #: _006_   Today's Date: _9/21/YY_

PATIENT INFORMATION

Name _Wolford_ _Carey_ _S._   Soc. Sec # _404-78-6732_
         Last Name   First Name   Initial

Address _2164 Carlisle Drive_   Home Phone _(013) 488-8201_

City _Woodland Hills_   State _XY_   Zip _12345_

Single _X_ Married ___ Widowed ___ Separated ___ Divorced ___   Sex M ___ F _X_ Age ___ Birthdate _2/2/73_

Patient Employed by _United Travel Services_   Occupation _travel agent_

Business Address _20016 Bard Street Ste. A. Woodland Hills_   Business Phone _(013) UTR-AVEL_

By whom were you referred? _____

In case of emergency who should be notified? _Paige Wolford_   _mother_   Phone _(618) 964-2987_
                                              Name   Relation to Patient

PRIMARY INSURANCE

Insured/Subscriber _Wolford_ _Carey_ _S._
                    Last Name   First Name   Initial

Relation to Patient _self_   Birthdate _____   Soc. Sec. # _____

Address (if different from patient's) _same_   Phone _____

City _____   State _____   Zip _____

Person Responsible Employed by _____   Occupation _____

Business Address _____   Business Phone _____

Insurance Company _Blue Shield Physician Services_

Insurance Address _P.O. Box 7184   Big Lake XY 12345_

Insurance Identification Number _CED404 78 6732_   Group # _74980A   Plan 06_

ADDITIONAL INSURANCE

Is patient covered by additional insurance? ___ Yes _X_ No

Subscriber Name _N/A_   Relation to Patient _____   Birthdate _____

Address (if different from patient's) _____   Phone _____

City _____   State _____   Zip _____

Subscriber Employed by _____   Business Phone _____

Insurance Company _____   Soc. Sec. # _____

Insurance Address _____

Insurance Identification Number _____   Group# _____

ASSIGNMENT AND RELEASE

I, the undersigned, certify that I (or my dependent) have insurance coverage with _Blue Shield_
                                                                    Name of Insurance Company(ies)
and assign directly to Dr. _Cutis_ insurance benefits, if any, otherwise payable to me for services rendered. I understand that I am financially responsible for all charges whether or not paid by insurance. I hereby authorize the doctor to release all information necessary to secure the payment of benefits. I authorize the use of this signature on all insurance submissions.

Carey Wolford   _self_   _9/21/YY_
Responsible Party Signature   Relationship   Date

ORDER # 58-8426 • © 1996 BIBBERO SYSTEMS, INC • PETALUMA, CALIFORNIA • TO REORDER CALL TOLL FREE (800) 242-2376 OR FAX: (800) 242-9330

FIGURE 4-3 Paper Patient Registration Form (Reprinted with permission of Bibbero Systems, Inc., Petaluma, CA. 800242–2376.www.bibbero.com.)

TABLE 4-2 Alternate Care Clinical Data

Alternate Care Setting	Clinical Data
Ambulatory Care	Patient history Problem/diagnostic list Medication list Physical examination Progress notes Flow sheets (e.g., growth chart)
Behavioral Health	Behavioral health diagnoses Psychiatric and medical history Patient assessment

(Continues)

TABLE 4-2 Alternate Care Clinical Data (*Continued*)

Alternate Care Setting	Clinical Data
Behavioral Health (*Continued*)	Biopsychosocial assessments Patient treatment plan Medication administration record Documentation of therapy and treatment Progress notes Behavioral documentation Team/case conference notes Consultation notes Discharge summary Follow-up care report Aftercare plan
Clinical Laboratory (stand-alone)	Physician orders Testing results
Home Care	Certification Plan of care Case conference notes Physician orders Treatment documentation Progress notes Discharge summary
Long-Term Care	History (patient, social, and medical) Physical examination Nursing assessment Care plan Physician treatment orders Medication administration record Progress notes Interdisciplinary notes (e.g., medical, therapeutic, nursing) Ancillary reports (e.g., lab, x-ray) Consultation reports Psychological assessments Nutritional services Activities Social service notes Occupational therapy notes Physical therapy notes Speech therapy notes Discharge plan of care
Surgical Center (stand-alone)	Patient history Problem list Medication list Physical examination Progress notes Anesthesia record Pre- and post-anesthesia evaluation Operative record Pathology report Recovery room record Flow sheets (e.g., anesthesia flow sheet, pain scale)

Department of Health and Human Services
Centers for Medicare & Medicaid Services

Form Approved
OMB No. 0938-0357

HOME HEALTH CERTIFICATION AND PLAN OF CARE

1. Patient's HI Claim No.	2. Start of Care Date	3. Certification Period		4. Medical Record No.	5. Provider No.
		From:	To:		

6. Patient's Name and Address

7. Provider's Name, Address, and Telephone Number

8. Date of Birth	9. Sex ☐ M ☐ F	10. Medications: Dose/Frequency/Route (N)ew (C)hanged

11. ICD-9-CM	Principal Diagnosis	Date
12. ICD-9-CM	Surgical Procedure	Date
13. ICD-9-CM	Other Pertinent Diagnoses	Date

14. DME and Supplies

15. Safety Measures:

16. Nutritional Req.

17. Allergies:

18.A. Functional Limitations

1	☐ Amputation	5	☐ Paralysis	9	☐ Legally Blind
2	☐ Bowel/Bladder (Incontinence)	6	☐ Endurance	A	☐ Dyspnea with Minimal Exertion
3	☐ Contracture	7	☐ Ambulation	B	☐ Other (Specify)
4	☐ Hearing	8	☐ Speech		

18.B. Activities Permitted

1	☐ Complete Bedrest	6	☐ Partial Weight Bearing	A	☐ Wheelchair
2	☐ Bedrest BRP	7	☐ Independent at Home	B	☐ Walker
3	☐ Up As Tolerated	8	☐ Crutches	C	☐ No Restrictions
4	☐ Transfer Bed/Chair	9	☐ Cane	D	☐ Other (Specify)
5	☐ Exercises Prescribed				

19. Mental Status:

1	☐ Oriented	3	☐ Forgetful	5	☐ Disoriented	7	☐ Agitated
2	☐ Comatose	4	☐ Depressed	6	☐ Lethargic	8	☐ Other

20. Prognosis:

1	☐ Poor	2	☐ Guarded	3	☐ Fair	4	☐ Good	5	☐ Excellent

21. Orders for Discipline and Treatments (Specify Amount/Frequency/Duration)

22. Goals/Rehabilitation Potential/Discharge Plans

23. Nurse's Signature and Date of Verbal SOC Where Applicable:	25. Date HHA Received Signed POT

24. Physician's Name and Address	26. I certify/recertify that this patient is confined to his or her home and needs intermittent skilled nursing care, physical therapy and/or speech therapy, or continues to need occupational therapy. The patient is under my care, and I have authorized the services on this plan of care and will periodically review the plan.
27. Attending Physician's Signature and Date Signed	28. Anyone who misrepresents, falsifies, or conceals essential information required for payment of Federal funds may be subject to fine, imprisonment, or civil penalty under applicable Federal laws.

Form CMS-485 (C-3) (02-94) (Formerly HCFA-485) (Print Aligned)

FIGURE 4-4 Home Health Certification and Plan of Care (From Centers for Medicare & Medicaid Services, CMS.gov)

EXERCISE 4–1 Definition and Purpose of the Patient Record

Matching: Enter an "A" if the item is administrative data and a "C" if it is clinical data.

_____ 1. Laboratory report

_____ 2. Patient name

_____ 3. Patient's insurer

_____ 4. Vital signs

_____ 5. Progress note

_____ 6. Patient number

_____ 7. Hospital name and address

_____ 8. Problem list

_____ 9. Attending or primary care physician

_____ 10. Care plan

_____ 11. Allergies

_____ 12. Medications

_____ 13. Date of birth

_____ 14. Occupation

_____ 15. Anesthesia record

PROVIDER RESPONSIBILITIES

The Joint Commission standard RC.01.02.01 states that "only authorized individuals may make entries in the medical record." AHIMA recommends that "anyone documenting in the health record should be credentialed or have the authority and right to document as defined by the organization's policy. Individuals must be trained and competent in the fundamental documentation practices of the organization and legal documentation standards. All writers should be trained in and follow their organization's standards and policies for documentation."

Health care providers are responsible for documenting care, treatment, and services rendered to patients in a manner that complies with federal and state regulations as well as accreditation, professional practice, and legal standards. It is important to remember that services rendered *must* be documented to prove that care was provided and that good medical care is supported by patient record documentation. Thus, inadequate patient record documentation may indicate poor health care delivery; if services provided are not documented, continuity of care is compromised.

Note: Providers must remember the familiar phrase, "If it wasn't documented, it wasn't done." Because the patient record serves as a medicolegal document and the facility's business record, if a provider performs a service but doesn't document it the patient (or third-party payer) can refuse to pay for the service. In addition, because the patient record serves as an excellent defense of the quality of care administered to a patient, missing documentation can result in problems if the record needs to be admitted as evidence in a court of law.

Example A third-party payer routinely reviews inpatient claims to ensure that all services billed are documented in patient records. If reconciliation of the claim with the patient record results in the determination that documentation is missing, the payer can reduce payment of the amount billed on the claim. Sunny Valley Hospital submitted a claim that reported radiology and laboratory services for Pamela Wright. The total charges were $3,400, including a $120 charge for a cholesterol screening. The payer reviewed copies of patient records, determined that cholesterol screening documentation was missing, and disallowed the charge due to an unsubstantiated charge.

Authentication of Patient Record Entries

All patient record entries require authentication, which means an entry is signed by the author (e.g., provider). The *Federal Regulations/Interpretive Guidelines for Hospitals (482.24(c)(1)(i))*, published by the Centers for Medicare & Medicaid Services, specifies that only the *author* of an entry can authenticate that entry, thus establishing that the entry is accurate and has been verified by the author. Guidelines further state that "failure to disapprove an entry within a specific time period is *not* acceptable as authentication." The *Guidelines* also allow for authentication of patient record entries through an author-entered computer code.

Note: Auto-authentication involves a provider authenticating a dictated report prior to its transcription. This practice is not consistent with proper authentication procedures because providers must authenticate the document *after* it was transcribed. Each health care facility must select acceptable authentication method(s), which comply with federal, state, and/or third-party payer requirements. Methods include:

- Written signatures
- Countersignatures
- Initials
- Fax signatures
- Electronic signatures or computer key signatures
- Signature stamps

The Joint Commission standard RC.01.02.01 states that entries in the medical record are to be authenticated by the author, and only authorized individuals can make entries in the medical records.

Signature Requirements for Patient Records

As a minimum, the facility must require that providers sign with their first initial, last name, and title/credential or discipline. Stricter minimums can be adopted (e.g., provider's full name and title/credential), and if two providers have the same first initial and last name, both must use their full signatures. (*Note:* Medicare requires a legible identity for services provided and ordered but does not specify the method to be used, such as electronic, handwritten, or signature stamp.)

Countersignatures

As required by state law, the provider countersigning an entry must be qualified. A **countersignature** is a form of authentication by an individual in addition to the signature by the original author of an entry. The *Federal Regulations/Interpretive Guidelines for Hospitals (482.24(c)(1)(i))* require medical staff rules and regulations to identify types of documents *nonphysicians* may complete as well as entries that require countersignatures by a supervisory or attending medical staff member. The Joint Commission standard RC.01.02.01 also addresses countersignatures and states that a hospital must "define the types of entries in the medical record made by nonindependent practitioners that require countersigning."

> *Example* Dr. Jones is an unlicensed resident who performs and dictates a history and physical examination on Patty Patient, whose attending physician is Dr. Smith. Once Dr. Jones has signed the transcribed report, Dr. Smith must countersign it. Dr. Smith's countersignature indicates that he is supervising the care delivered to the patient by Dr. Jones.

Countersignatures are also required when nurses and other authorized personnel (e.g., pharmacists) document a telephone order taken from a physician. A **telephone order (T.O.)** is a verbal order taken over the telephone by a qualified professional (e.g., registered nurse) from a physician. Documenting telephone orders should be reserved for emergency situations when the physician is not available in the facility (e.g., patient becomes unstable at midnight). The qualified professional documents the order so that it can be carried out, and the responsible physician countersigns the order within the time period specified by the facility's medical staff bylaws in accordance with state regulations. A **voice order (V.O.)**, also known as a verbal order, is an order where the physician dictates an order in the presence of a responsible person. A V.O. is documented in emergencies only. The Joint Commission standards specify that hospitals must have a written policy to identify the staff members authorized to receive and record verbal orders. The standards further specify that the verbal order must include the "date and the names of individuals who gave, received, recorded and implemented the orders."

Note: Facilities usually require telephone orders to be authenticated by the responsible physician within 24 hours of documentation. The countersignature of telephone orders has become a somewhat controversial issue for health information departments because, upon review of discharged patient records, many telephone orders have not yet been countersigned by the responsible physician. As a result, some departments have discontinued their review of physician orders for countersignatures. If the responsible physician did not countersign the telephone order within the period of time specified by medical staff bylaws, countersigning *after discharge of the patient from the facility* appears improper.

Initials

A complete signature that matches initials used must be included on the same form or on a separate **signature legend**, a document maintained by the health information department to identify the author by full signature when initials are used to authenticate entries. Initials are typically used to authenticate entries on flow sheets (e.g., intake/outpatient record) and medication records.

Fax Signatures

Fax signatures can be accepted by facilities, as allowed by federal and state regulations. Fax signatures are generally acceptable unless expressly prohibited by state law. However, the Uniform Business Records as Evidence Act, which addresses admissibility of copies of records in court, states that when a document with a fax signature is included in the patient record, the document containing the original signature should be retrievable.

Electronic Signatures

Electronic signatures can be accepted by facilities, as allowed by federal and state regulations. An electronic signature is a generic term that refers to the various methods by which an electronic document can be authenticated. They include:

- Name typed at the end of an email message by the sender
- Digitized image of a handwritten signature that is inserted (or attached to) an electronic document
- Secret code or personal identification number PIN to identify the sender to the recipient
- Unique biometrics-based identifier (e.g., fingerprint, retinal scan)
- Digital signature, created using *public key cryptography* to authenticate a document or message. Public key cryptography uses an algorithm of two keys, one for creating the digital signature by transforming data into a seemingly unintelligible form and the other to verify a digital signature and return the message to its original form (Figure 4-5).

The American Society for Testing and Materials (ASTM) developed ASTM E 1762–Standard Guide for Authentication of Healthcare Information, which is intended to complement standards developed by other organizations (e.g., Health Level 7, or HL7) and define:

- A document structure for use by electronic signature mechanisms
- The characteristics of an electronic signature process
- Minimum requirements for different electronic signature mechanisms
- Signature attributes for use with electronic signature mechanisms
- Acceptable electronic signature mechanisms and technologies
- Minimum requirements for user identification, access control, and other security requirements for electronic signatures

- Technical details for all electronic signature mechanisms in sufficient detail to allow interoperability between systems supporting the same signature mechanism

Example Highland Hospital of Rochester, New York uses an electronic signature application (ESA) that assists providers in the timely completion of records. Some providers can avoid trips to the health information department entirely if all that is required to complete records is electronic signatures. A provider goes to the health information department to obtain an assigned identification number (also their dictation number) and a generic four-letter password, and to sign a confidentiality statement. A health information staff member shows the provider how to log in to the ESA software, at which time the provider changes his or her generic password to something of his or her own choice (alphabetic or numeric). Once a report has been transcribed, it appears in the provider's queue to review and "sign." The provider can edit the document online and electronically sign it by entering the ESA password. The report then prints in the transcription area and is placed on the patient's record. The provider a trip to the department because he or she can "sign" reports from his or her home or office by accessing the hospital's website.

Signature Stamps

Signature stamps (Figure 4-6) can be accepted by facilities as allowed by state and federal law. When signature stamps are authorized for use in a facility, the provider whose signature the stamp represents must sign a statement that she or he alone will use the stamp to authenticate documents. The statement

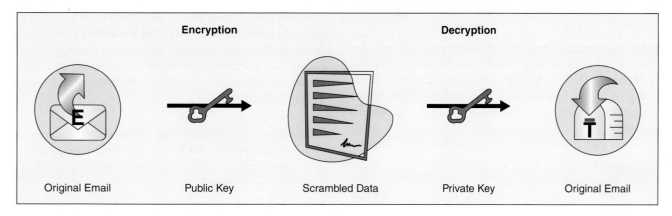

Encryption			Decryption	
Original Email	Public Key	Scrambled Data	Private Key	Original Email

FIGURE 4-5 Depiction of Public Key Cryptography

FIGURE 4-6 Signature Stamp (Permission to reprint granted by eRubberStamp.com.)

is maintained on file in the facility's administrative offices. The use of signature stamps should also be specified in the the hospital bylaws.

Providers who use a signature stamp should recognize that there is a potential for misuse or abuse because it is a much less secure method than other modes of signature identification (e.g., handwritten signature). Providers should check with their attorneys and malpractice insurers regarding the use of signature stamps.

Note: Medicare does not allow the use of signature stamps (or date stamps) on certificates of medical necessity (CMN) for durable medical equipment.

Abbreviations Used in the Patient Record

Every health care facility should establish a policy as to which abbreviations, acronyms, and symbols can be documented in the patient record. The facility should maintain an official abbreviation list, which includes medical staff–approved abbreviations, acronyms, and symbols (and their meanings) that can be documented in patient records. Figure 4-7 provides an example of an excerpt from an abbreviation list. When more than one meaning exists for an abbreviation, acronym, or symbol, the facility should prohibit its use.

Note: The Joint Commission standards do not explicitly require an approved list of abbreviations. Its National Patient Safety Goals prohibit the use of "dangerous" abbreviations, acronyms, and symbols in patient records because they could be misinterpreted.

Example 1
BMI means body mass index.

Example 2
D/C could mean discontinue *or* discharge (Figure 4-7).

Legibility of Patient Record Entries

All entries in the patient record must be legible, and if an entry is illegible it should be rewritten by its author. The rewritten entry should state "Clarified entry of (date)" and contain exactly the same information as the original entry; it should be documented on the next available line in the record (e.g., progress notes).

Note: Legibility of entries impacts patient care—if a nurse cannot read a physician's order, the order may be interpreted and carried out improperly. In addition, third-party payers may deny payment for services if documentation is illegible.

Timeliness of Patient Record Entries

Patient record entries should be documented as soon as possible after care is provided so as to increase accuracy of information recorded. Accrediting and licensing agencies require the timely completion of documentation, such as the Medicare Conditions of Participation (CoP) for hospitals that require a complete physical examination to be performed no more than 30 days prior to admission or within 24 hours after admission.

Example The CoP states that the report of physical examination must be placed in the patient record within 24 hours after admission. The Joint Commission requires the history and physical examination to be documented in the patient record within 24 hours of inpatient admission.

Example The primary counselor documents notes about the patient's therapy session immediately following therapy (instead of at the end of the day) to avoid the possibility of confusing similar patient therapy sessions.

The Joint Commission requires patient records to be completed 30 days after the patient is discharged, at which time they become delinquent records. To calculate the delinquent record rate, divide the total number of delinquent records by the number of discharges in the period.

Example As of September 30, 175 total delinquent records were on file. The facility discharged 510 patients during September. The delinquent record rate for September is 34 percent.

$$\frac{175}{510} = 0.343 \times 100 = 34 \text{ percent}$$

Sunny Valley Hospital Abbreviation List

NOTE: Go to http://www.jointcommission.org to obtain The Joint Commission's official "Do Not Use" list

Abbreviation	Meaning
abd	abdomen
Abd	abduction
ABR	auditory brain response
a.d.	before meals
ADL	activities of daily living
AM	morning
AP	anteroposterior
AROM	active range of motion
B/K	below knee
bid	twice a day
bili	bilirubin
BLE	bilateral lower Extremities
BM	bowel movement
BP	blood pressure
BUE	bilateral upper extremities
BW	birth weight
bx	biopsy
Cal	calorie
Caps: cap.	capsule
CT	computerized axial tomography
cath	catheter
CBC	complete blood count
CHD	congenital heart disease
CHF	congestive heart failure
c/o	complained of
CPR	cardio-pulmonary resuscitation
CV	cardiovascular
CVA	cardiovascular accident (stroke)
CXR	chest x-ray
D	distal
D&C	dilation & curettage
Ddx	differential diagnosis
DSD	dry sterile dressing
Dsg	dressing
DTP	diptheria-tetanus-pertussis
DTR	deep tendon reflexes
Dx	diagnosis
EEG	Electroencephalogram
e.g.	for example
EKG	electrocardiogram
ENT	ear, nose, and throat
EOM	extraocular movement
ER	emergency room
F	facial
FH	family history
freq	frequency
FUO	fever undetermined origin
Fx.	fracture
Gm	gram

FIGURE 4-7 Abbreviation List (*Continues*)

Abbreviation	Meaning
g/m	grand mal seizure
GT	gastrostomy tube
GU	genitourinary
GYN	gynecological
Hb	hemoglobin
H/O	history of
H&P	history and physical
h.s.	at bedtime
Ht	height
Hx	history
IC	Intracutaneous
ICU	intensive care unit
I&D	incision and drainage
Impress	impression
I&O	intake and output
IPJ	Interphalangeal joint
IV	intravenous
jt	joint
L	left
LA	local anesthetic
lab	laboratory
lat	lateral
L/S	lumbo-sacral
mand	mandible or mandibular
max	maxillary
mcg	microgram
MD	doctor of medicine
mg.	milligram
MI	myocardial infarction (heart attack)
ml.	milliliter
N_2O	nitrous oxide
NAD	nothing abnormal detected
NKA	no known allergies
NPEX	new patient exam
NPO	nothing by mouth
NT	nasotracheal
NWB	non weight bearing
OB	obstetrics
OR	operating room
OT	occupational therapy
P	pulse
PE	physical exam
PH	past history
p.m.	afternoon
PMH	past medical history
p.o.	orally; by mouth
PO	post operative
Post-op	postoperative
PRN	as needed
pt	patient
PT	physical therapy/therapist
PTA	physical therapy/assistant

FIGURE 4-7 Abbreviation List (*Continues*)

Abbreviation	Meaning
q	every
q.h.	every hour
qid	four times per day (every 6 hours)
R	right
Rad	radiation absorbed dose
RBC	red blood cell count
RDS	respiratory distress syndrome
RN	registered nurse
R/O	rule out
ROM	range of motion
Rx	prescription
S	supervision
SC	subcutaneous
SH	social history
SI	sensory integration
SR	suture removal
ST	speech therapy
STAT	immediately
T	temperature
T&A	tonsillectomy and adenoidectomy
TBI	traumatic brain injury
Temp	temporary
TM	tympanic membrane
TMD	temporomandibular joint dysfunction
TMJ	temporomandibular joint
t.i.d.	three times a day
TLR	tonic labyrinthine reflex
tx	treatment
u/a	urinalysis
URI	upper respiratory infection
UTI	urinary tract infection
VA	veteran's Administration
V.O.	verbal order
VS	vital signs
WB	weight bearing
WBC	white blood count
WD	well developed
WFL	within functional limits
WN	well nourished
WNL	within normal limits
w/o	without
X	times
Y/O	years old
Yr	year
↑	increase
↓	decrease
2	secondary
>	greater than
<	less than

FIGURE 4-7 Abbreviation List

Amending the Patient Record

It is occasionally necessary to correct documentation in the patient record (Figure 4-8), which is called amending the patient record. The only person authorized to correct an entry is the author of the original entry. To amend an entry in a manual patient record system, the provider should:

- Draw a single line through the incorrect information, making sure that the original entry remains legible.
- Date, specify time, and sign the corrected entry.
- Document a reason for the error in a location as close to the original documentation as possible (e.g., "entry made in error" or "entry made in wrong chart").
- Enter the correct information as close to the original information as possible. If the length of information to be newly entered prohibits this, enter the correct information in the next available space in the record, and reference the original entry.

Note: Providers who edit transcribed reports prior to authentication must also follow a version of the previous procedure. If the provider re-dictates a report after the original report has been filed in the record, the original report must be maintained along with the re-dictated report. The provider should draw a single line across each page of the original report, write "re-dictated," document a reason for re-dictation, and date, specify time, and sign the "re-dictated" notation. When the re-dictated original report is placed on the record, the provider should review and sign it.

Electronic health record system errors will be corrected in a number of different ways, depending on the type of information that needs to be corrected. The basic principles for correcting documentation errors should be followed, and the electronic health record system should store both the original *and* corrected entry as well as a record of who documented each entry. The date, time, and authentication of the person making the correction should be maintained, as well as the reason for the change. Most electronic health record systems will create a list of all changes made to patient documentation in the form of an audit trail, a technical control created by an electronic health record system that consists of a listing of all transactions and activities that occurred. The listing also contains the date, time, and user who performed the transaction.

11/17	Patient tolerated diet well. VSS.	11/17	Patient tolerated diet well. VSS.
	Afeb. Pt. remains improved since		Afeb. Pt. remains improved since
	a.m. No purulent drainage. K Lee MD		a.m. No purulent drainage. K Lee MD
11/18	Pt essentially no changes. VSS.	11/18	Pt essentially no changes. VSS.
	Afeb. Pt tolerated diet well. Continue		Afeb. Pt tolerated diet well. Continue
	current meds. K Lee MD		current meds. K Lee MD
11/18	~~Pt stable & responding well to antibiotics.~~		
	~~Would keep on cleocin. I would ask gyn~~		
	~~to consult RE: ovarian cyst.~~ 11/19 8:00 Error.		
	Written in wrong patient's chart. E. Lang, MD		
Correct Method		**Incorrect Method**	

FIGURE 4-8 Amending the Patient Record

The Health Insurance Portability and Accountability Act (HIPAA) Privacy Rule gives an individual the right to "have a covered entity that is a health care provider amend (or correct) protected health information (PHI) about him or her in designated record sets . . . for as long as the covered entity maintains the information." The covered entity can deny the request for amendment or correction if the entry was not created by the covered entity, is not part of the designated record set, or is accurate and complete.

Note: If the covered entity denies the request to amend or correct the record, the individual can submit a written statement disagreeing with the denial. In addition, an individual can submit a written statement clarifying information that is believed to be inaccurate and request that the statement be made an unofficial part of the patient's record.

Note: HIPAA was passed in 1996 and mandated administrative simplification regulations that govern privacy, security, and electronic transactions standards for health care information. HIPAA also protects health insurance coverage for workers and their families when they change or lose their jobs.

It may be necessary for a provider to amend an entry by adding an addendum to the record to *clarify* (avoid incorrect interpretation of information), add additional information about previous documentation, or enter a *late entry* (out of sequence). The purpose of the addendum is to provide additional information, *not to change documentation,* and the addendum should be documented as soon after the original entry as possible. When it is necessary to amend a record, the provider should:

- Document the word "addendum", "clarification", or "late entry," depending on circumstances, at the beginning of the new entry.
- Document the current date and time as well as the date and time of the original entry as a reference.
- Authenticate the addendum (or late entry).
- State the reason for documenting the addendum, and provide any supporting information that provides clarification.
- Enter the current date and time. Do not try to make it appear as if the entry was made on a previous date or at a different time.

Note: If routine review of patient records (e.g., random monthly review, audit) reveals missing information on ancillary and nursing records (e.g., lab reports, graphic charts, medication records) and hospital staff fill in missing information as the result of audit, this is considered "falsification of the record" or "tampering with the record" and is illegal. Policies and procedures for amending patient records and documenting late entries are established by facilities to allow for total recall of the patient care situation (e.g., no later than by the end of a nursing shift). It is acceptable for health information departments to routinely review records upon discharge of the patient from the facility to identify documentation deficiencies and arrange for providers and hospital staff to complete records within a timely fashion (e.g., within 15 days after discharge of the patient).

EXERCISE 4–2 Provider Responsibilities

Fill-in-the-Blank: Enter the appropriate term(s) to complete each statement.

1. The *Federal Regulations/Interpretive Guidelines for Hospitals* specifies that only the _____ of an entry can authenticate the entry, which indicates that the entry is _____ and has been verified by the author.

2. A digitized image of a handwritten signature that is inserted in (or attached to) an electronic document is a type of _____ that allows for authentication of a document.

3. A form of authentication by an individual, in addition to the signature by the original author of an entry, is known as a(n) _____.

4. Health care facilities select various acceptable authentication method(s), which comply with federal, state, and/or third-party payer requirements including _____, countersignatures, _____, fax signatures, electronic signatures, and signature stamps.

5. Since the patient record serves as a medicolegal document, providers must always remember the familiar phrase, "If it wasn't _____, it wasn't _____."

6. The following progress note contains an error. Instead of right abdominal pain, the note should state "left upper abdominal pain." Correct the entry using proper procedures.

Date/Time	Progress Note
1/02/YYYY 3:00 p.m.	Patient complains of right abdominal pain. The patient has requested that her physician be called for pain medication.

7. The Joint Commission standards specify that only _____ individuals can make entries in the medical record.

8. The Joint Commission has established a list of _____ abbreviations, acronyms, and symbols that are prohibited for use in patients records.

9. A technical control created by an electronic health record system that lists all transactions and activities is known as a(n) _____.

10. A verbal order is also called a(n) _____.

DEVELOPMENT OF THE PATIENT RECORD

Patient records are developed from many sources—inpatient record creation might actually begin prior to admission because preadmission testing was performed. Preadmission testing (PAT) incorporates patient registration, testing, and other services into one visit prior to inpatient admission (or scheduled outpatient surgery), and the results are incorporated into the patient's record. PAT is ordered by the patient's physician to provide timely medical data, which facilitates treatment and reduces inpatient lengths of stay. Preadmission testing usually includes the following:

- Chest x-ray
- Electrocardiogram (EKG)
- Laboratory testing (e.g., blood typing, urinalysis)

Other services may include:

- Anesthesia screening and pre-anesthesia evaluation
- Coordination of ancillary services
- Discharge planning
- Health history screening
- Patient teaching by a registered nurse

Ancillary services are diagnostic and therapeutic services provided by a health care facility, including dental care, diagnostic and pathological laboratory services, discharge planning, infection control, multilingual services, nutrition, patient education, pharmacy, physical therapy, radiology, respiratory therapy, social services, and so on.

Inpatient Record: Admission to Discharge

The inpatient record is generated in the facility's admissions office unless the patient is admitted through the emergency department (ED). Preadmission testing (PAT) information is incorporated into the patient record to combine it with demographic data.

Remember! Demographic data includes the patient's name, address, home telephone number, place of employment, and social security number.

Demographic data is typically documented on the face sheet (or admission/discharge record) of a manual patient record or on the admission screen of an electronic health record. (The face sheet is discussed in detail in Chapter 7.) The admissions office also enters the patient's provisional diagnosis (or working, tentative, admission, preliminary diagnosis), which is obtained from the attending physician and is the diagnosis upon which patient care is based.

At the time of admission, the patient or patient's representative, the person who has legal responsibility for the patient, signs an admission consent form to document consent to treatment. This general consent to treatment is usually located on the reverse of the face sheet (or admission/discharge record). While HIPAA no longer requires covered entities such as health care facilities to obtain admission consent, most facilities continue to obtain it. Specific consents for surgery and/or diagnostic and therapeutic procedures are obtained by the facility during inpatient hospitalization using special consent forms (discussed in Chapter 7). If a patient is unable to sign and no one else is designated to sign on behalf of the patient, the procedure for obtaining a signature to consent should follow state laws (e.g., one MD and two witnesses).

Upon completion of the admission process, the patient is transported to the nursing unit, where admission information is reviewed with the patient and a nursing assessment is completed. A nursing assessment documents the patient's history, current medications, and vital signs on a variety of nursing forms, including nurses' notes, graphic charts, and so on. Nursing staff are also responsible for carrying out admission physician orders that contain instructions (e.g., diet, medications) documented by the physician or medical staff approved provider, such as a nurse practitioner or physician assistant.

The attending physician is responsible for performing an admission history and physical examination on the patient, which is either handwritten or dictated/transcribed depending on medical staff rules and regulations. All providers involved in patient care record progress notes to document a narrative account of a plan of care and the patient's response to treatment. If diagnostic or surgical procedures are completed, the provider who performs the procedure is responsible for documenting an operative record of the procedure performed and operative findings. As the patient undergoes testing and therapy provided by ancillary service departments, reports and notes are documented in the patient record. Reports generated throughout the patient's stay are discussed in detail in Chapter 7.

Example The attending physician orders a chest x-ray on an inpatient, who undergoes the test in the radiology department. The radiologist interprets the x-ray and dictates a report, which is transcribed and placed in the patient record. The attending physician reviews the report and bases treatment decisions on its findings. His review of the chest x-ray report and treatment decisions are documented in the progress notes.

When a patient is discharged from the facility, the attending physician dictates a discharge summary to document the care provided to the patient during the inpatient hospitalization and includes the reason for hospitalization, the course of treatment, and the patient's condition at discharge. (The discharge summary is discussed in detail in Chapter 7.) Other departments such as nursing, social services, and physical therapy also document notes and summaries of care provided to patients. In addition, upon discharge from the facility, instructions are discussed with and provided to the patient. These include directions about post-discharge care (e.g., diet) and follow-up (e.g., recheck in provider's office).

Date Order of Patient Record Reports

All reports documented in the patient record must be organized during inpatient hospitalization and upon discharge. Each facility determines the organization of reports in the record and establishes a policy to define the proper order of the record. While most facilities organize the record according to reverse chronological date order during inpatient hospitalization, they reverse the order to chronological date order upon discharge of the patient. Organizing inpatient records according to reverse chronological date order means that the most current document is filed first in a section of the record.

Example Progress notes dated 7/3 are filed on top of notes for 7/2, allowing the most current information to be viewed first as you read from the front to the back of the record.

Discharged patient records are typically organized in chronological date order, with the oldest information filed first in a section. The order of reports is in strict date order, allowing the record to read like a diary.

Note: Some facilities organize reports in the same order for both inpatient and discharged patient records; this is called the *universal chart order.* The universal chart order saves time in processing discharged patient records because reorganizing reports is unnecessary—the record remains in the same reverse chronological date order at discharge as during inpatient hospitalization.

Outpatient Record: Handling Repeat Visits

In the outpatient setting, records are more frequently retrieved because of the frequency of patient visits. Each time an outpatient receives a service such as an x-ray, the record must be retrieved and sent to the outpatient department. Because patients usually receive more frequent outpatient care, these records are retrieved more frequently than inpatient records.

Physician Office Record: Continuity of Care

The main purpose of the physician office record is to provide documentation to assist in the continuity of patient care, and the development of the office record varies. Office records for a solo practitioner, a physician who practices alone, are typically not as structured as records created for group practices. A group practice contains more than one provider who uses the record; therefore, the record must be maintained in a consistent fashion to facilitate use by all providers. As with the outpatient record, office records are accessed frequently due to patients undergoing annual physicals, acute treatment, visits for prescription reills, and so on.

Note: As the size of a group practice increases, the need for record management also increases. Large group practices may even contain health information departments that function in a manner similar to those in hospitals.

EXERCISE 4–3 Development of the Patient Record

Short Answer: Briefly respond to each question.

1. What are the benefits of using universal chart order?

2. What is the impact of preadmission testing on inpatient length of stay?
3. List three examples of preadmission tests.
4. Discuss nursing admission documentation requirements.
5. Explain the purpose of a discharge summary.

PATIENT RECORD FORMATS

Many facilities and physician offices maintain patient records in a paper format known as a **manual record**. A variety of formats are used to maintain manual records, including the source oriented record (SOR), problem oriented record (POR), and integrated record. Automated record systems include the EHR, electronic medical record (EMR), and optical disk imaging. The use of wireless technology to enable health care professionals to make better-quality decisions, while reducing the cost of care and improving convenience to caregivers, is referred to as **mHealth**. For example, a patient's telemetry results can be conveniently viewed on a wireless personal computer, allowing the provider to quickly update physician orders.

Primary and Secondary Sources of Information

Records that document patient care provided by health care professionals are considered **primary sources** of patient information (e.g., original patient records, x-rays, scans, EKGs, and other documents of clinical findings). **Secondary sources** of patient information contain data abstracted (selected) from primary sources of patient information (e.g., indexes and registers, committee minutes, incident reports). (Indexes and registers are discussed in Chapter 9.) An **incident report** (Figure 4-9) collects information about a **potentially compensable event (PCE)**, which is an accident or medical error that results in personal injury or loss of property. Incident reports are generated on patients and visitors, and they provide a summary of the PCE in the event that the patient (or visitor) files a lawsuit. Because court dates for lawsuits are routinely scheduled months and years after

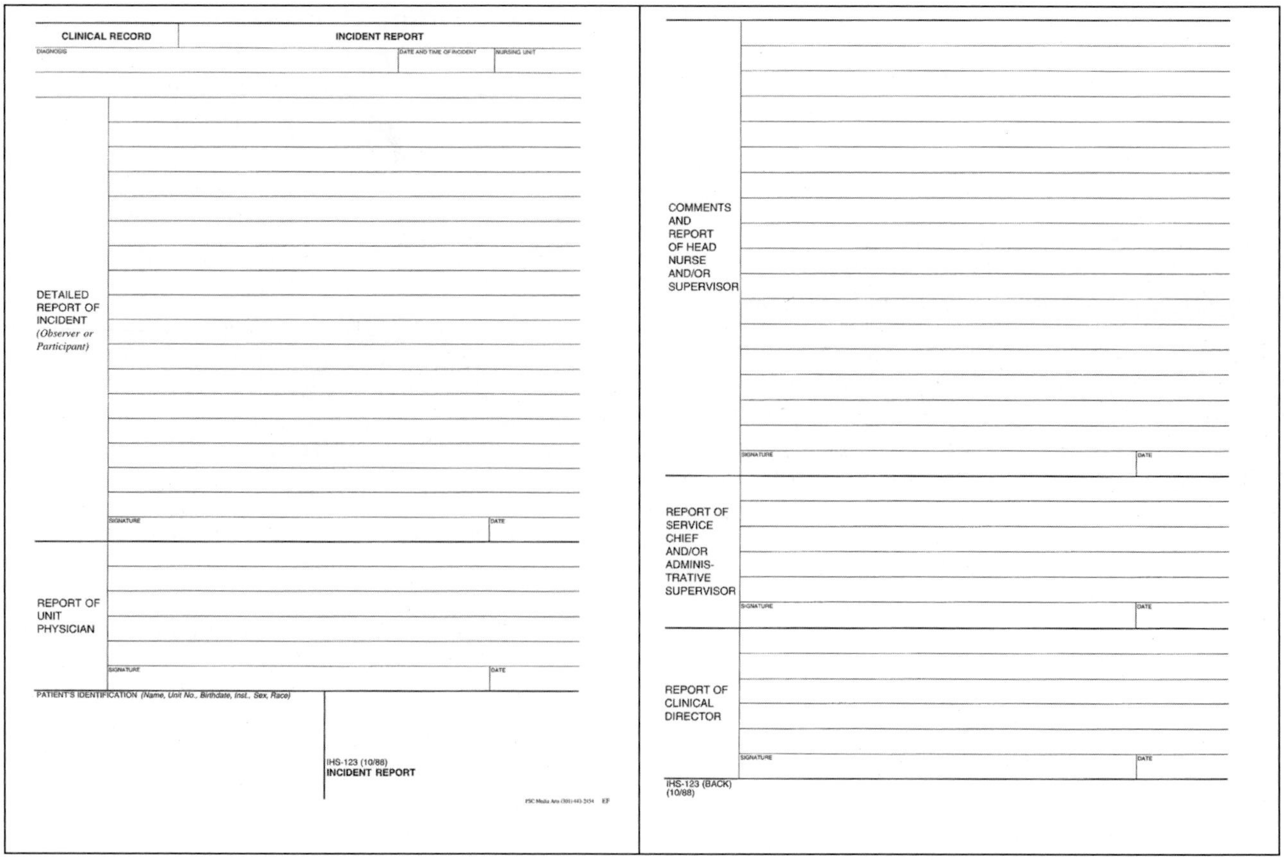
CLINICAL RECORD | INCIDENT REPORT
DIAGNOSIS | DATE AND TIME OF INCIDENT | NURSING UNIT

DETAILED REPORT OF INCIDENT *(Observer or Participant)*

SIGNATURE | DATE

REPORT OF UNIT PHYSICIAN

SIGNATURE | DATE

PATIENT'S IDENTIFICATION (Name, Unit No., Birthdate, Inst., Sex, Race)

IHS-123 (10/88)
INCIDENT REPORT

COMMENTS AND REPORT OF HEAD NURSE AND/OR SUPERVISOR

SIGNATURE | DATE

REPORT OF SERVICE CHIEF AND/OR ADMINISTRATIVE SUPERVISOR

SIGNATURE | DATE

REPORT OF CLINICAL DIRECTOR

SIGNATURE | DATE

IHS-123 (BACK) (10/88)

FIGURE 4-9 Incident Report (From USDHHS, Indian Health Service, www.ihs.gov.)

the PCE, the incident report allows those involved in the lawsuit to refresh their memories about the PCE.

INCIDENT REPORTS ARE NEVER FILED IN THE PATIENT RECORD

Note: When an incident occurs (e.g., a patient falls out of bed and breaks her hip), document the facts in the progress notes. *Do not* enter a note in the patient record that an incident report has been completed. *Do not* refer to the incident report when charting in the patient record. *Do not* file the incident report in the patient record. Incident reports are filed with the facility's risk management office, and they are considered a secondary source of patient information. Thus, they are *not* subject to disclosure (release) when patient records are subpoenaed or requested (e.g., by an attorney) upon patient authorization. Incident reports are *never* filed in the patient's record, which would result in their release upon subpoena or patient authorized request. Attorneys for the health care facility are allowed access to incident reports to properly prepare a defense.

> *Example 1:*
> A nurse administers the wrong medication to a patient. The nurse documents an incident report of this PCE and files it with the facility's risk manager.

> *Example 2:*
> A visitor slips and falls on a wet floor, even though the wet floor was well marked. A health care provider documents this PCE and files it with the facility's risk manager.

Note: The easiest way to remember the difference between primary and secondary sources of patient information is to consider the original patient record (and x-ray films and scans) a primary source of information and everything else a secondary source.

Source Oriented Record (SOR)

A traditional patient record format known as the source oriented record (SOR) maintains reports according to source of documentation. This means that all documents generated by the nursing staff are located in a nursing section of the record, radiology reports in a radiology section, and physician-generated documents (e.g., physician orders, progress notes) in the medical section. Each source of data in the inpatient record has a labeled section. This format is also known as the sectionalized record because it is subdivided into sections.

Many facilities use this format because it is easy to locate documents. For example, if a physician needs to reference a recent lab report, it can easily be found in the laboratory section of the record. However, if a physician wanted to reference all information about a particular diagnosis being treated or treatment given on a particular day, many different sections of the record would be consulted.

Problem Oriented Record (POR)

Lawrence Weed developed the problem oriented medical record (POMR), now called the problem oriented record (POR), in the 1960s to improve organization of the patient record. The problem oriented record (POR) or problem oriented medical record (POMR) shown in Figure 4-10 is a more systematic method of documentation consisting of four components:

- Database
- Problem list
- Initial plan
- Progress notes

The database contains a minimum set of data to be collected on every patient, such as chief complaint; present conditions and diagnoses; social data; past, personal, medical, and social history; review of systems; physical examination; and baseline laboratory data. The database serves as an overview of patient information. The problem list acts as a table of contents for the patient record because it is filed at the beginning of the record and contains a list of the patient's problems. Each problem is numbered, which helps to index documentation throughout the record. Problems include anything that requires diagnostic review or health care intervention and management, such as past and present social, medical, psychiatric, economic, financial, and demographic issues. Symptoms, specific diagnoses, abnormal findings, and physiologic findings are all considered problems and would be included on a problem list. Once a problem has been placed on the problem list, it remains on the list even if resolved (date of resolution is documented on the problem list). As new problems are identified, the list is updated by adding the new problem and assigning it a number. The strategy for management of the patient's care is outlined in the initial plan, which describes actions that will be taken to learn more about the patient's condition and to treat and educate the patient, according to three categories:

- Diagnostic/management plans—plans to learn more about the patient's condition and management of the condition

DATABASE

Medium-sized black-and-white spotted dog admitted ambulatory. Appears anxious. Vital signs include BP 120/80 left foreleg; pulse 100 per minute left front paw; respirations 36 per minute; nose is warm and dry.

CHIEF COMPLAINT: Can't eat.

HISTORY: No previous hospitalizations; born at home.

ALLERGIES: Cats, smoke.

VACCINATIONS: Rabies.

OCCUPATION: Mascot, Engine Co. #6 (delusions of grandeur).

EDUCATION: Obedience school drop-out.

HOBBIES: Baseball, collecting bones.

HOME: One room, unheated.

FAMILY: Whereabouts of siblings unknown; number of children unknown.

TYPICAL DAY: Very busy; spends day playing with firemen, sleeping, going for walks, and riding in fire truck.

PERSONAL HABITS: Sparky eats one meal per day, likes canned foods and cereals, dislikes vegetables.

FOOD ALLERGIES: Fish.

Sleeping habits include frequent naps; sleeps soundly. Hygiene: bathes once per month. Elimination: occasionally eats grass as a laxative (sometimes needs treatment for worms); voids frequently in small amounts, nocturia, housebroken.

PROBLEM LIST

DATE	PROBLEM #	PROBLEM DESCRIPTION	DATE RESOLVED
7/1/YYYY	1	Anorexia	
7/1/YYYY	2	Missing teeth	
7/1/YYYY	3	Unheated house	
7/1/YYYY	4	Delusions	
7/1/YYYY	5	Allergy (cats)	
7/1/YYYY	6	Allergy (smoke)	
7/1/YYYY	7	Pruritus (fleas)	

SOAP PROGRESS NOTE

7/1/YYYY

#2 Missing Teeth

S: Lost three teeth last week while playing baseball; doesn't remember where teeth went.

O: One incisor and one canine missing from upper jaw; one canine missing from lower jaw; sockets healing well.

A: Teeth could have been swallowed, accounting for opaque objects on X-ray film.

P: Diagnostic: discuss missing teeth with attending physician. Therapeutic: continue saline rinse. Educational: explain importance of dental hygiene and use of glove to catch baseball.

INITIAL PLAN

DATE	PROBLEM #	MEDICAL PLANS	NURSING PLANS
7/2/YYYY	7	DX: check for fleas	DX: observe for fleas; observe frequency of itching and areas of scratching
		RX: calamine lotion	RX: apply calamine lotion to affected areas of skin
		ED: pruritus	ED: communicate importance of *not* scratching

FIGURE 4-10 Problem Oriented Record (POR)

- Therapeutic plans—specific medications, goals, procedures, therapies, and treatments used to treat the patient
- Patient education plans—plans to educate the patient about conditions for which the patient is being treated

In a POR, each patient is assigned one or more problems and notes are documented for each problem using the SOAP structure:

- Subjective (S)—patient's statement about how she feels, including symptomatic information (e.g., headache)
- Objective (O)—observations about the patient, such as physical findings or lab or x-ray results (e.g., chest x-ray negative)
- Assessment (A)—judgment, opinion, or evaluation made by the health care provider (e.g., acute migraine)
- Plan (P)—diagnostic, therapeutic, and educational plans to resolve the problems (e.g., patient to take Tylenol as needed for pain)

The discharge summary is documented in the progress note section of the POR to summarize the patient's care, treatment, response to care, and condition on discharge—documentation of all problems is included. A transfer note is documented when a patient is being transferred to another facility; it summarizes the reason for admission, current diagnoses and medical information, and reason for transfer.

Integrated Record

The integrated record format usually arranges reports in strict chronological date order (record could also be arranged in reverse date order). This format allows for observation of how the patient is progressing according to test results and how the patient responds to treatment based on test results. Most hospitals integrate physician and ancillary (e.g., physical therapy) progress notes only, requiring progress note entries to be clearly identified by discipline. The discipline should be identified (e.g., dietary) at the beginning of each progress note.

Chief Complaint, History, Examination, Details, Drugs/Dosages, Assessment, and Return Visit (CHEDDAR)

Another documentation format is CHEDDAR, which is an acronym for:

Chief Complaint: The problem that the patient presents with is recorded in the first section of the note. This is recorded in the patient's own words and reports subjective information presented by the patient.

History: This section records the patient's prior personal medical, family, and social history.

Examination: Objective physical examination findings are recorded in this section. Includes both physical and cognitive findings.

Details: The details of the problems and complaints are recorded in this section.

Drugs/Dosages: This section includes a comprehensive list of all current medications and over-the-counter drugs, as well as any vitamins, herbal supplements, and illicit substances. Dosages and frequency are also recorded.

Assessment: This section records the diagnosis(es), tests ordered, and treatment.

Return Visit: If applicable, this section will record when a return visit should occur.

The CHEDDAR format encourages the provider to document in a very comprehensive and structured fashion, which can lead to enhanced patient information.

History Physical Impression Plan (HPIP)

This system is similar to a SOAP note. The acronym HPIP stands for:

History: Subjective information presented by the patient.

Physical: Objective information obtained by the completion of a physical examination.

Impression: Assessment and diagnosis(es) after completion of the physical.

Plan: Provider's treatment plan.

As with the SOAP and CHEDDAR formats, the HPIP format also provides for a logical organization of patient information. By using a structured format, providers are less likely to omit or fail to document valuable patient information.

Example Documentation on the same patient according to integrated, POR, and SOR formats.

Integrated Record

Progress notes

4/15/YYYY
8 a.m.

CC: Chest pain. Anxious.
Exam: BP 130/80. Pulse 85. Respirations 20. Temperature 98.6°. Lungs clear. Heart regular. Abdomen nontender.
Current medications: Paxil 40 mg daily.
Possible severe panic attack.
Rule out myocardial infarction.
Plan: Chest x-ray. EKG. Total CPK. Total LDH. Consult with Dr. Miller, psychiatrist.

4/15/YYYY
noon.

No chest pain. Patient is calmer. Feels slightly anxious.
Exam: BP 130/75. Pulse 80. Respirations 20. Temperature 98.6°.
Chest x-ray: negative.
EKG: negative.
Total CPK 45.
Total LDH 100.

4/15/YYYY
7 p.m.

Patient resting comfortably. No chest pain.
Exam: BP 130/75. Pulse 80. Respirations 20. Temperature 98.6°.

4/16/YYYY
6:30 a.m.

Patient slept well. No chest pain. Less anxiety today.
Exam: BP 120/70. Pulse 75. Respirations 20. Temperature 98.6°.
Discharge home. Follow-up in Dr. Miller's office in one week.

Problem Oriented Record

Problem 1: Acute bronchitis

4/15/YYYY
8 a.m.

S: Chest pain.
O: BP 130/80. Pulse 85. Respirations 20. Temperature 98.6°. Lungs clear. Heart regular. Abdomen nontender.
A: Rule out myocardial infarction.
P: Chest x-ray. EKG. Total CPK. Total LDH.

4/15/YYYY
noon

S: No chest pain.
O: BP 130/75. Pulse 80. Respirations 20. Temperature 98.6°.
A: Chest x-ray: negative. EKG: negative. Total CPK 45. Total LDH 100.
A: Not applicable.
P: Keep overnight for observation.

4/16/YYYY
6:30 a.m.

S: Patient slept well. No chest pain.
O: Exam: BP 120/70. Pulse 75. Respirations 20. Temperature 98.6°.
A: Panic attack.
P: Discharge home. Follow-up at office in one week.

Problem 2: Anxiety

4/15/YYYY
8 a.m.

S: Anxious
O: BP 130/80. Pulse 85. Respirations 20. Temperature 98.6°. Lungs clear. Heart regular. Abdomen nontender.
A: Possible severe panic attack.
P: Alprazolam 0.25 mg t.i.d. Consult with Dr. Miller, psychiatrist.

4/15/YYYY
noon

S: Patient calmer. Still anxious
O: Exam: BP 130/75. Pulse 80. Respirations 20. Temperature 98.6°. EKG: negative.
A: Possible severe panic attack.
P: Continue monitoring.

4/15/YYYY
7 p.m.

S: Patient resting comfortably.
O: Exam: BP 130/75. Pulse 80. Respirations 20. Temperature 98.6°.
A: Possible severe panic attack.
P: Continue monitoring.

4/16/YYYY
6:30 a.m.

S: Patient slept well. Less anxiety today.
O: BP 120/70. Pulse 75. Respirations 20. Temperature 98.6°.
A: Panic attack.
P: Discharge home. Follow-up in Dr. Miller's office in one week. Xanax 0.25 mg t.i.d.

Source Oriented Record

Progress notes

4/15/YYYY
8 a.m.

CC: Chest pain. Anxious.
Exam: BP 130/80. Pulse 85. Respirations 20. Temperature 98.6°. Lungs clear. Heart regular. Abdomen nontender.
Current medications: None.
Possible severe panic attack.
Rule out myocardial infarction.
Plan: Chest x-ray. EKG. Total CPK. Total LDH. Consult with Dr. Miller, psychiatrist.

4/15/YYYY
noon.

No chest pain. Patient is calmer. Feels slightly anxious.
Exam: BP 130/75. Pulse 80. Respirations 20. Temperature 98.6°.
EKG: negative.

4/15/YYYY
7 p.m.

Patient resting comfortably. No chest pain.
Exam: BP 130/75. Pulse 80. Respirations 20. Temperature 98.6°.

4/16/YYYY
6:30 a.m.

Patient slept well. No chest pain. Less anxiety today.
Exam: BP 120/70. Pulse 75. Respirations 20. Temperature 98.6°.
Discharge home. Follow-up in Dr. Miller's office in one week.
Xanax 0.25 mg t.i.d.

Laboratory tests

| 4/15/YYYY | Total CPK 45. |
| 4/15/YYYY | Total LDH 100. |

x-rays

| 4/15/YYYY | Chest x-ray: negative. |

EKGs

| 4/15/YYYY | EKG: negative. |

TABLE 4-3 Advantages and Disadvantages of Record Formats

Format	Advantage	Disadvantage
Source Oriented Record (*SOR*)	• Files same source documents together • Easy to locate information from same source	• Difficult to follow one diagnosis • Creates many sections in record • Filing reports is time-consuming
Problem Oriented Record (POR)	• Links all documentation to a specific problem • Facilitates patient treatment and education • Provides high degree of organization	• Requires training • Filing of reports is time-consuming • Data associated with more than one problem must be documented several times
Integrated Record	• Easy to use • All information on an episode of care is filed together • Less time-consuming to file reports	• Difficult to compare information from same discipline • Difficult to retrieve information from same discipline
Chief Complaint, History, Examination, Details, Drugs/Dosages, Assessment, and Return Visit (CHEDDAR)	• Provides organization of information • Encourages greater detail in history and exam documentation	• Requires training
History Physical Impression Plan (HPIP)	• Provides a structured format • Easy to locate information	• Requires training

EXERCISE 4–4 Patient Record Formats

Fill-in-the-Blank: Enter the appropriate term(s) to complete each statement below.

1. The _____ consists for four components: a database, problem list, initial plan, and progress note.

2. The table of contents of a problem oriented record is known as the _____.

3. Indexes and registers are considered _____ sources of patient information.

4. A record format that divides the record into sections is known as _____.

5. In the POR system, the _____ format is used for progress notes.

The advantages and disadvantages of different record formats are summarized in Table 4-3.

ARCHIVED RECORDS

Records placed in storage and rarely accessed are called archived records (or inactive records). Those stored in paper format create the need for a large filing area; therefore, each facility should develop policies that indicate the length of time a facility will maintain an archived record. This time period is called a retention period and is based on federal and state laws.

A digital archive is a storage solution that consolidates electronic records (e.g., audio, emails, scanned documents and images, video) on a computer server for management and retrieval. The digital archive can be created and managed on the facility's internal computer system, or it can be outsourced to a company that creates and manages access to digital archives on computer servers using an Internet-based interface.

Shadow Records and Independent Databases

A shadow record is a paper record that contains copies of original records and is maintained separately from the primary record. An independent database contains clinical information created by researchers, typically in academic medical centers. Facilities that use shadow records and independent databases must establish policies to identify reasons for use, secure maintenance, and for HIPAA purposes, reasons for exclusion/inclusion in the facility's designated record set.

Example 1:
A patient is treated by the physical therapy department on an outpatient basis, and for each treatment an original

record is generated. The original record is forwarded to the health information department, and a copy of the record (shadow record) is maintained for the convenience of physical therapists who provide continuous outpatient treatment. Documentation about current treatment is filed in the original record, *not* the shadow record.

Example 2:
According to SecurityFocus.com, a sophisticated hacker downloaded 4,000 computerized admissions records of a university medical center's heart patients. It was only after a reporter sent the university medical center a copy of one of the downloaded records that the university realized their security system had been breached.

Note: An electronic health record system that makes information available to health professionals at any time would be an alternative to creating shadow records. To control access to independent databases, facilities should develop a security evaluation program (e.g., National Institute of Standards and Technology Special Publication 800-37, "Guide for the Security Certification and Accreditation of Federal Information Technology Systems").

Record Retention Laws

Depending on where the health care provider offers health care services, federal and state laws may prescribe minimum periods that records must be retained. While providers and facilities often retain records longer than required (e.g., for educational and research purposes), they must consider the impact of record storage costs. As a result, many providers opt to purge (remove inactive records from the file system) and convert paper-based records to microfilm or optical disk. Others adopt electronic health record systems that allow them to retain records indefinitely. (Keeping records indefinitely presents a different problem: It is possible that records not used for patient care could be used improperly for other purposes.)

The Medicare Conditions of Participation (CoP) requires hospitals, long-term care facilities, specialized providers, and home health agencies to retain medical records for a period of no less than five (5) years. (Medicare does not specify a retention period for ambulatory surgical services, health maintenance organizations or other capitated/prepaid plans, or hospices.) The Occupational Safety and Health Administration (OSHA) requires records of employees who have worked for longer than one year to

be retained 30 years. The Public Health Services Act Immunization Program and National Childhood Vaccine Injury Act specifies a 10-year retention period. State record retention laws vary. Some establish time frames based on a statute of limitations, which is the time period during which a person may bring forth a lawsuit. Record retention is also impacted by state laws that govern the age of consent (or age of majority), which means facilities must retain records for a time period (e.g., 18 years) in addition to the retention law. Accreditation organizations (e.g., The Joint Commission) do not mandate record retention schedules, but the American Hospital Association (AHA) recommends a five-year retention period and AHIMA recommends that operative indices be retained for a minimum of 10 years and the operating room register permanently.

Example New York State requires that hospital records be retained for a period of six years from the date of discharge or three years after the patient's age of majority (18 years). North Carolina requires hospitals to maintain medical records for a minimum of 11 years following the discharge of an adult; for a minor, the record must be retained until the patient's 30th birthday.

Facility Retention Policy Considerations

Each health care facility must establish a record retention schedule for patient information. This schedule outlines the information that will be maintained, the time period for retention, and the manner in which information will be stored. Records can be stored on paper, microfilm, magnetic tape, optical disk, or as part of an electronic (or computer) system.

When developing a record retention schedule, consider the following:

- Accreditation agency recommendations
- Federal retention laws
- Legal requirements
- Need for continuing patient care
- Research/educational uses
- State retention laws

Alternative Storage Methods

Many facilities must store more records than they physically can accommodate. The HIM department must then decide how to store the records using an alternative storage method, such as off-site storage, microfilm, or optical imaging.

Off-Site or Remote Storage

Off-site storage (or **remote storage**) is used to store records at a location separate from the facility. It is common for the off-site storage area to be part of a company that stores various types of records in addition to patient records (e.g., banking records).

> *Example* Military patient records accessibility became a huge problem due to "misplacing" of records. The management of medical records during Desert Storm resulted in those records being viewed as more items that needed cleaning before they could be brought back to the United States. Military personnel deployed to create and maintain medical records were not always trained in record-keeping practices. Although they knew how to admit and discharge a patient and file reports in a folder, they didn't know how to properly "retire" a military medical record, which involved removing records that were 3 to 5 years old from active shelves and sending them to a St. Louis military storage facility. Prior to sending the records to the St. Louis facility, the records had to be reviewed to determine compliance with The Joint Commission documentation standards. If the records were found to be deficient upon review by the St. Louis facility, they were returned for correction.

Note: All "retired" medical records were assigned an accession number by the St. Louis storage facility to facilitate access to medical records; however, when returned to the unit for correction, some records were lost.

When off-site storage is selected, be sure to negotiate a contract that considers accessibility of records at the storage facility as well as policies and procedures for safeguarding patient records. Other considerations include:

- *Cost:* Cost of services should be stated in the contract; determine cost according to number of records stored, amount of storage space required, or type of record stored; be sure to specify the cost of retrieving records if needed, including any additional charges for immediate delivery of a record.
- *Storage:* Records must be stored in a locked, secure area that is accessible to authorized personnel only; the contract should specify whether records are to be stored in boxes (Figure 4-11) or in open or closed shelving units.
- *Transportation of records:* Records should be transported by trained personnel in a fashion that ensures

FIGURE 4-11 Records Stored in Boxes (Permission to reprint granted by Ames Color-File.)

timely delivery; the contract should specify whether records will be transported in a vehicle owned by the company, by courier, or by another method.

- *Security:* The vendor should outline training procedures for employees as well as policies and procedures for safeguarding the security of records in storage.
- *Access to records:* The contract should state how frequently records will be delivered to the facility and outline procedures for requesting records; the hours that records can be requested should also be stated.

An important issue to remember is that the records will no longer be under the direct control of the facility; however, the facility must ensure that records are secure and accessible. To conform to the 2013 HIPAA Omnibus Rule, facilities must have vendors sign a Business Associates Agreement to attest to storing the protected health information in a secure fashion.

Microfilm

Microfilm is a photographic process that records the original paper record on film, with the film image

TABLE 4-4 Microfilm Storage Methods

Film Storage Method	Description
Aperture Card	Punched card onto which frames of a microfilmed document are mounted.
Cartridge Film	Roll film that is stored in a plastic cartridge for protection and holds multiple patient records.
Jacket Film	Individual images stored in 4 × 6 inch plastic sleeves, which contain multiple rows per page. Each jacket typically stores one patient record. Sometimes, more than one sleeve is needed per record.
Microfiche Film	A 4 × 6 Mylar film sheet that stores microfilm images directly onto the sheet. Each sheet typically stores the record of one patient.
Reel Film	Plastic reel of continuous film strip that holds thousands of images of multiple patient records.
Roll Film	Continuous strip of film that holds thousands of images of multiple patient records. (Roll film is often stored on a plastic reel.)

appearing similar to a photograph negative. (The paper record is prepared according to the same method used for scanning, discussed in Chapter 5.) Once microfilmed, film media is organized for storage (Table 4-4, Figure 4-12).

After the film is assembled according to one of these methods, its quality is reviewed by comparing the original record to the microfilm (to ensure that all pages of the record have been microfilmed properly). After the comparison determines that the microfilm quality is acceptable, the original paper record can be destroyed.

Note: To view and/or print microfilmed records, a microfilm reader/printer is used (Figure 4-13).

Optical Disk Imaging

Optical disk imaging systems (discussed in Chapter 5) are capable of scanning a paper-based record, converting it to images stored in an electronic format, storing the images on optical disk, and rapidly retrieving the image.

Record Destruction Methods

Paper-based records should be destroyed in a manner consistent with established policies and procedures, after the legal retention period (e.g., federal, state), and after microfilming or using optical imaging to store records. Each facility establishes a record destruction policy. When records are destroyed, a certificate of record destruction (Figure 4-14) is maintained by the facility, which documents the date of destruction, method of destruction, signature of the person supervising the destruction process, listing of destroyed records, dates records were disposed of, and a statement that records were destroyed in the normal course of business. The certificate of record destruction should be permanently maintained by the facility, as it may need to be referenced for court actions and legal proceedings.

Records must be destroyed so that they cannot be re-created. Record destruction methods for paper records usually include dissolving records in acid, incineration (burning), pulping or pulverizing (crushing

FIGURE 4-12 Types of Microfilm Products (Permission to reprint granted by elmageData Corp.)

into powder), or shredding. AHIMA recommends that automated records be destroyed using magnetic degaussing, which alters magnetic fields on a computer medium. Electronic records can also be destroyed by overwriting data, a process during which original data is covered with multiple patterns of data. Microfilm is usually destroyed using chemical recycling processes.

Note: When destroying computerized data, it is also necessary to destroy backup information maintained by the facility.

Disposition of Patient Records Following Facility Closure

The integrity and confidentiality of patient records must be maintained when a facility or medical

FIGURE 4-13 Microfilm Reader/Printer (Permission to reprint granted by eImageData Corp.)

Alfred State Medical Center
100 Main Street
Alfred, NY 12345-0000

Certificate of Record Destruction

Record Series	Dates of Records	Method of Destruction	Retention
Inpatient records	1/1/YYYY to 12/31/YYYY	Shredding	7 years
Emergency department records	1/1/YYYY to 12/31/YYYY	Shredding	7 years
Outpatient records	1/1/YYYY to 12/31/YYYY	Shredding	7 years
Date of Destruction: 12/31/YYYY			

The above records were destroyed in the normal course of business.

This destruction was authorized by:

Melissa A. Manager

Melissa Manager
Records Management Officer
Date 12/31/YYYY

This destruction was certified by:

Peter Thomson

Peter Thomson
Health Information File Area Supervisor
Date 12/31/YYYY

Sandy Slocum

Health Information Manager
Date 12/31/YYYY

FIGURE 4-14 Certificate of Record Destruction

practice closes. It is the responsibility of the closing entity to ensure that records are handled according to federal and state statutes and professional organization guidelines. Facility or practice closure is addressed in state statutes, and this information can typically be obtained from state departments of health.

In some states, records from the closed entity are stored in a state archive or by the state department of health. This would most likely happen when the closure occurs without a sale of the facility or medical practice.

Example Hospital Licensure Rules of the Indiana State Board of Health require a facility to transfer medical records to a local public health department or public hospital in the same geographic area. The statute further requires that if records cannot be transferred to a public hospital or local health department, they should be sent to the Indiana Board of Health.

When a facility or medical practice is sold to another health care entity, the patient records are considered part of the sale. The new owner becomes responsible for maintaining the patient records. When a facility is closed, patients must be notified (e.g., newspaper announcement and/or letters mailed to former patients) of the following:

- Date of closure
- New location of records
- How to access records following closure
- Proper procedure for accessing records (e.g., written request for information required)

Example In Maryland, state statute requires patient notification using the United States Postal Service (USPS) *and* publication of a notice in the local newspaper. This affords patients an opportunity to obtain a copy of their record. *This is a common practice even if there is no specific state statute that addresses this issue.*

EXERCISE 4–5 Archived Records

True/False: Indicate whether each statment is True (T) or False (F).

_____ 1. Individual providers and facilities determine minimum periods that records must be retained.

_____ 2. Off-site storage is used to house records at a location separate from the facility.

_____ 3. The time period during which a person may initiate a lawsuit is called the retention period.

_____ 4. Patient record retention is impacted by state laws that govern the age of majority in addition to state record retention laws.

_____ 5. A shadow record is maintained according to the same record retention guidelines established for original records.

PATIENT RECORD COMPLETION RESPONSIBILITIES

Responsibility for completing the patient record resides with the governing body, facility administration, attending physician, other health care professionals, and the health information department. Each has specific responsibilities that are outlined in the facility's policies and procedures.

Governing Body and Facility Administration

The governing body is responsible for ensuring that each patient receives high-quality medical care and that the care is documented as part of a complete and accurate patient record. The facility administration is responsible for ensuring that the medical staff adopts rules and regulations that provide for the maintenance of complete patient records in a timely fashion. Administration is also responsible for enforcing these policies.

Attending Physician and Other Health Care Professionals

The major responsibility for an adequate patient record rests with the attending physician. The Joint Commission accreditation standards and Medicare Conditions of Participation (CoP) address issues of patient record keeping by the physician.

Example 1
The Joint Commission standards state that the physician must complete a discharge summary that contains the reason for hospitalization, significant findings, procedures performed and treatment rendered, the patient's condition at discharge, and instructions to the patient and family.

Example 2
Medicare CoP require that a physician complete a history and physical examination of the patient within 24 hours after admission or no more than 30 days before admission, and that the report shall be on the chart within 24 hours after admission. In addition, when the history and physical is recorded with the 30 days prior to admission, there must be a medical record entry

documenting an examination for any changes in the patient's condition, and this must be documented in the medical record within 24 hours after admission.

Role of the Health Information Department

The health information manager is responsible for educating physicians and other health care providers regarding proper documentation policies. Health information department staff members assist in the design of patient record systems to facilitate sound medical record documentation practices and perform record completion tasks to ensure compliance with facility policies and state and federal regulations (Table 4-5).

Following the completion of record assembly and analysis, providers are notified of documentation deficiencies that need to be completed. The health information department notifies providers about incomplete and delinquent charts using a variety of formats, including:

- Mailing a letter or postcard to the provider offices
- Inserting a letter or postcard into the provider mailboxes at the facility
- Calling and/or emailing providers about record deficiencies

When providers receive notification, they come to the health information department to complete deficient records.

To facilitate completion of record deficiencies, a deficiency slip is completed by the analysis clerk and attached to the patient record. Incomplete records are then filed in the incomplete record file area according to:

- Name of provider (commonly called doctors' boxes)
- Patient record number

Filing incomplete records by patient number allows more than one provider to access the same record to complete deficiencies. When incomplete records are filed according to provider names, more than one provider cannot work on the same incomplete record. This means that if other providers need to complete deficiencies in the same record, the record cannot be easily retrieved for that purpose. In fact, filing incomplete records according to provider name delays the completion process.

After incomplete records that contain deficiencies have been completed by health care providers, records are reanalyzed to ensure that all deficiencies have been corrected. (Some facilities call this process "check-forperm" or "record recheck.") Once all deficiencies have been completed, the record is stored in the permanent file area.

Note: The Joint Commission and Medicare require that records be completed within 30 days after discharge of a patient from the facility. After 30 days, incomplete records are considered delinquent, and facilities establish policies that serve to motivate providers to complete records on a timely basis. For example, providers with delinquent records have admitting and surgical privileges suspended until records are completed. (However, it is frustrating for health information departments that such a policy is rarely enforced because of the impact on reimbursement to the facility.)

TABLE 4-5 Record Completion Tasks

Task	Description
Record Assembly	Process of organizing discharged patient record according to accepted chart order and preparing it for storage.
Quantitative Analysis	Review of patient record for completeness (e.g., presence of dictated reports, written progress notes, authentications), including identification of chart deficiencies which include missing reports and other documentation and missing signatures. A deficiency slip (Figure 4-15) is used to record chart deficiencies that are flagged in the record (Figure 4-16).
Qualitative Analysis	Review of patient record for inconsistencies that may identify incomplete or inaccurate documentation, including review of final diagnoses or procedures on the face sheet.
Concurrent Analysis	Review of patient record during inpatient hospitalization to ensure quality of care through quality patient documentation.
Statistical Analysis	Abstracting data from the patient record for clinical or administrative decision making.

		DEFICIENCY SLIP	
PATIENT NAME _____		MR # _____	ADMISSION DATE _____
INSTRUCTIONS: Review the patient record, and circle the deficiency identified.			

Name of Report	Attending Physician:_____	Other Physician: _____	Other Physician: _____
Discharge Summary	Dictate Sign		
History & Physical Exam	Dictate Sign		
Consultation Report		Dictate Sign	Dictate Sign
Admission Progress Note	Document Date Sign		
Daily Progress Notes	Document Date Sign	Document Date Sign	Document Date Sign
Discharge Progress Note	Document Date Sign		
Doctors Orders	Document Date Sign	Document Date Sign	Document Date Sign
Discharge Order	Document Date Sign		
Operative Report	Dictate Sign	Dictate Sign	Dictate Sign
Other:	Document Dictate Date Sign	Document Dictate Date Sign	Document Dictate Date Sign
Other:	Document Dictate Date Sign	Document Dictate Date Sign	Document Dictate Date Sign

FIGURE 4-15 Deficiency Slip

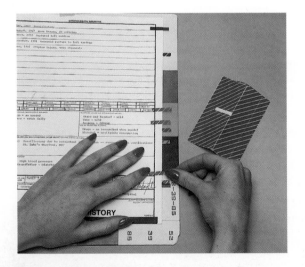

FIGURE 4-16 Flags Used to Mark Deficient Pages in Records (Permission to reprint granted by Ames Color-File.)

Automated chart completion management software can assist health information departments in managing retrospective analysis of discharged patient records by generating:

- Deficiency reports (lists of physicians who have incomplete records to complete, along with patient record numbers and deficiencies associated with each record)
- Suspension letters (mailed to physicians who have delinquent records to be completed; delinquent status is established by the facility)
- Customized reports (used to satisfy accreditation self-study requirements) (Figure 4-17). To review the Hospital Medical Record Statistics Form designed by The Joint Commission visit: http://www.jointcommission.org and search on Hospital Medical Record Statistics Form.

Software also allows file clerks to retrieve incomplete chart data using a computer and to print lists used to retrieve incomplete records for physician completion.

Example Dr. Damrad entered the health information department and asked that his incomplete records be retrieved so he could work on them. The file clerk accessed the list of Dr. Damrad's incomplete records using the automated chart completion management software, printed a list of records to be completed, and retrieved them from the incomplete file system. Once completed, the clerk reanalyzed the records to ensure they were complete and cleared each record in the automated chart completion management software. If other physicians needed to complete deficiencies, the records

were refiled in the incomplete record system. If complete, the records were filed in the permanent file system.

EXERCISE 4–6 Patient Record Completion Responsibilities

Fill-in-the-Blank: Enter the appropriate term(s) to complete each statement.

1. The review of patient records during inpatient hospitalization to ensure quality of care through quality patient documentation is known as _____.

2. The health information manager is responsible for educating _____ and other health care pro-viders regarding proper _____ policies.

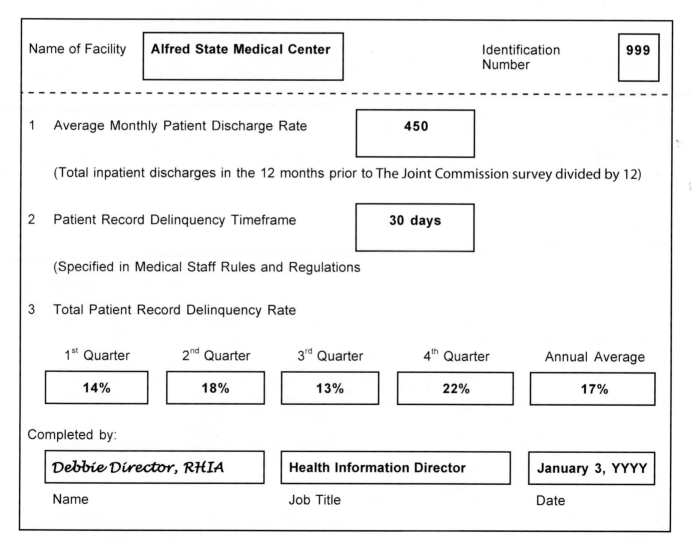

| Name of Facility | **Alfred State Medical Center** | Identification Number | **999** |

| 1 | Average Monthly Patient Discharge Rate | **450** |

(Total inpatient discharges in the 12 months prior to The Joint Commission survey divided by 12)

| 2 | Patient Record Delinquency Timeframe | **30 days** |

(Specified in Medical Staff Rules and Regulations

3 Total Patient Record Delinquency Rate

1st Quarter	2nd Quarter	3rd Quarter	4th Quarter	Annual Average
14%	**18%**	**13%**	**22%**	**17%**

Completed by:

Debbie Director, RHIA	**Health Information Director**	**January 3, YYYY**
Name	Job Title	Date

FIGURE 4-17 The Joint Commission Hospital Patient Records Statistics Form

3. The identification of _____ or missing reports occurs through the process known as _____ or the review of patient records for completeness.

4. Record assembly is the process of organizing _____ according to accepted chart order and preparing it for _____.

5. Medicare CoP require that a physician complete a physical examination of the patient within _____ hours after admission or no more than _____ days before admission, and that the report shall be on the chart within _____ hours after admission.

Internet Links

Go to **http://ww.ahima.org**, and search to locate the following Practice Briefs:

- Authentication of Health Record Entries
- Best Practices in Medical Record Documentation and Completion
- Definition of the Health Record for Legal Purposes
- Destruction of Patient Health Information
- Electronic Signatures
- Managing Health Information in Facility Mergers and Acquisitions
- Protecting Patient Information after a Facility Closure
- Retention of Health Information
- Storage Media for Health Information
- Verbal/Telephone Order Authentication and Time Frames

Go to **http://www.HealthIT.gov** to locate resources on health IT initiatives and electronic health records.

Review medical documentation issues from the American Academy of Family Physicians at **http://www.aafp.org** by clicking on Family Practice Management.

The *Code of Federal Regulations* can be found at **http:// www.federalregister.gov/**. Sign up for My FR, where sections of the Federal Register can be saved.

Go to **http://www.ironmountain.com** to check out a record storage and management company that provides record storage, off-site data protection, secure shredding, and digital services.

The Joint Commission publishes information about the official "Do Not Use" list at **http:// www.jointcommission.org**, search on "Do Not Use List."

Safesite, Inc. explains their off-site record management services at **http://www.safesite.cc**.

Go to **http://www.bibbero.com** to view samples of patient record forms.

SUMMARY

A patient record contains administrative and clinical data. Administrative data includes demographics and socioeconomic and financial information. Clinical data includes all patient health information.

Records are defined as hospital inpatient records, hospital outpatient records, physician office records, and alternate care records. The primary purpose of a patient record is to document patient care delivered and to assist in the care of the patient, Authentication of both manual and computerized record entries is required by state and federal laws.

Facilities develop policies and procedures that address the use of abbreviations, legibility of records, countersignatures, and timeliness of documenting entries, correcting errors, and amending patient records. Using the same filing order for active and discharged records is known as the universal chart order.

Patient record formats include manual and computerized formats. Manual formats include source oriented, problem oriented, and integrated. Progress notes in the problem oriented record are organized into four components: subjective, objective, assessment, and plan.

Retention policies are developed to establish a schedule for retention of patient information. Alternative storage methods include off-site storage, microfilm, and optical imaging. Patient record completion responsibilities are shared by the governing board, administration, physicians, health care providers, and the HIM staff.

STUDY CHECKLIST

- Read the textbook chapter and highlight key concepts. (Use colored highlighter sparingly throughout the chapter.)

- Create an index card for each key term. (Write the key term on one side of the index card and the concept on the other. Learn the definition of each key term, and match the term to the concept.)
- Access chapter Internet links to learn more about concepts.
- Answer the chapter exercises and review questions, verifying answers with your instructor.
- Study content, view videos, and take practice tests online at www.CengageBrain.com.
- Complete lab manual assignments, verifying answers with your instructor.
- Form a study group with classmates to discuss chapter concepts in preparation for an exam.

CASE STUDY

As part of the health information management committee at Sunny Valley Hospital, you have been asked to review abbreviations used in medical documents filed in the patient record.

1. Review the medical documents (below) to determine if abbreviations used are on the hospital's abbreviation list or on The Joint Commission's Official "Do Not Use" list. Refer to Figure 4–7, which represents Sunny Valley Hospital's abbreviation list, and go to http://www.jointcommission.org to locate the official "Do Not Use" list.

2. Identify abbreviations used in the documents (below) that are not located on Sunny Valley Hospital's abbreviation list. Also, identify any abbreviations used that are found on The Joint Commission's official "Do Not Use" list.

3. Prepare a one-page summary of your findings, discussing the importance of establishing a facility policy and procedure on the appropriate use of abbreviations.

MEDICAL DOCUMENTS TO REVIEW

Progress Note

Patient: John Smith   Record#: 019238

2/15/XX

S—John was admitted on 2/13/XX because of a fractured pelvis. He also has a history of arteriosclerotic dementia.

O—He is alert, disoriented. Vital signs: BP-162/102, P-76, R-18, W-133. Lungs—good inspiratory effort, no adventitious sounds.

Heart—regular rhythm with systolic murmur unchanged. The nurse stated that his BP is high. I am increasing his ACE inhibitor because of elevated blood pressure.

A—Arteriosclerotic dementia, IHD with dysrhythmia, depression

P—Monitor BP and follow up in the morning.

Brian Jones, MD

Progress Note

Patient: Samantha Woods   record #: 229991

2/15/XX

S—Samantha is being admitted because of uncontrolled diabetes. She had a left CVA with right-sided hemiparesis one year ago.

O—She is alert, oriented. Vital signs: BP-118/64, P-88, R-20, W-238. Lungs—clear, no adventitious sounds, good bilateral air entry.

Heart—regular rhythm with systolic murmur unchanged. She does not ambulate but can transfer.

Her blood sugar levels are elevated, and I am adjusting her insulin. A referral is being sent to a registered dietician to monitor her food intake. Blood pressures are slightly elevated.

A—Diabetes mellitus, insulin dependent, uncontrolled, and HT.

P—Continue to monitor blood sugar levels and refer to registered dietician; increase the morning insulin.

Julia Gymastro, MD

HISTORY AND PHYSICAL

Patient: Susan Smith   record # 495867

2/15/XX

A year ago, Susan was admitted after fracturing her left hip. She underwent rehab and was able to return home. She does have dementia as well as heart disease and glaucoma. She is being admitted today because she is complaining of chest pain that radiates down her left arm. CBC and additional lab work has been ordered, results pending. She also has quite a few problems with muscle spasms in her legs, and she was given a very low dose of Robaxin, which has proved to be helpful.

Review of systems noncontributory secondary to dementia.

General status reveals an alert person. Vital signs: BP-153/77, P-87, R-28, W-122. She is 5'2''.

HEENT—head normocephalic.

Eyes—corneas clear, conjunctivae pale pink, sclerae nonicteric. Pupils react to light.

Neck—supple, carotids without bruit, no lymphadenopathy or thyromegaly.

Lungs—clear to auscultation, no wheezes, rhonchi, or rales.

Heart—regular rhythm without murmur, rubs, heaves, or gallops. Distal pulses palpable bilaterally. No cyanosis, clubbing, or edema.

Breasts—no masses palpated.

Abdomen—soft, nontender, nondistended. Bowel sounds active.

Rectal—no stool obtained for guaiac testing.

Musculoskeletal—functional range of motion of her joints including the left hip. She transfers and walks independently with the use of a walker.

Neurological—cranial nerves 2–12 grossly intact bilaterally. She is alert and oriented to person. She follows finger to nose exercise test. No Babinski. Reflexes physiologic.

Plan of care for admission

1. For her chest pain request cardiac consult.

2. For her muscle spasms, continue medications daily, monitor effectiveness.

3. For her hypertension, continue to monitor blood pressure and adjust medications as indicated. Review following cardiac consult.

Francis Urster, MD

CHAPTER REVIEW

True/False: Indicate whether each statement is true (T) or false (F).

_____ 1. Archived records are also called active records.

_____ 2. Behavioral health records include a behavioral health diagnosis, treatment plan, and psychiatric and medical history.

_____ 3. Clinical data includes patient financial information.

_____ 4. Telephone orders do not require countersignatures if the nurse taking the order records the name of the ordering physician.

_____ 5. When correcting a documentation error, the author of the original entry should make the correction.

_____ 6. The abbreviation list should be approved by the medical staff.

_____ 7. A history and physical report is an example of administrative data.

_____ 8. Over the last decade, there has been an increase in the number of ambulatory visits.

Fill-in-the-Blank: Enter the appropriate term to complete each statement.

9. An abbreviation list contains acceptable explanations of meanings as _____ and _____.

10. A note that is added to the record after an original note has been documented is called a(n) _____.

11. A preliminary diagnosis is called a provisional diagnosis, a working diagnosis, an admission diagnosis, or a(n) _____ diagnosis.

12. When a patient is discharged, the _____ is responsible for documenting the discharge summary.

13. Indexes, registers, and committee minutes are considered _____ of patient information.

14. A document maintained by the health information department to identify the author by full signature when initials are used to authenticate entries is known as a(n) _____.

15. A discharge summary is an example of _____ data.

Multiple Choice: Select the most appropriate response.

16. Which is not a component of the problem oriented record?
   a. Database
   b. Problem list
   c. Progress note
   d. Table of contents

17. The judgment, opinion, or evaluation made by a health care professional is documented in which section of a SOAP progress note?
    a. Assessment
    b. Objective
    c. Plan
    d. Subjective

18. When the order of the record reads like a diary, the forms are said to be filed in a(n)
    a. chronological date order.
    b. discharged record order.
    c. integrated format.
    d. reverse chronological date order.

19. Which is a disadvantage of the problem oriented record?
    a. Difficulty following one diagnosis throughout the documentation
    b. Filing of forms is time-consuming
    c. Poor degree of organization in the documentation
    d. Retrieval of information is difficult

20. Which type of microfilm storage uses Mylar film?
    a. Cartridge
    b. Jackets
    c. Microfiche
    d. Roll film

Short Answer: Briefly respond to each question.

21. Discuss when countersignatures are needed in a patient's record.

22. Outline the procedure for correcting an error in a patient's record.

23. Briefly discuss the flow of inpatient records from admission to discharge.

24. Describe the format of the source oriented record.

25. Discuss two secondary purposes of the patient record.

Chapter 5

ELECTRONIC HEALTH RECORDS

Key Terms

application software
bar code reader
bar codes
bar code scanner
character
central processing unit (CPU)
clinical data repository
computer-based patient record (CPR)
computerized medical records
data
document imaging
electronic medical record (EMR)
field
file

hardware
health data
health information
health information exchange (HIE)
Health Information Technology for Economic and Clinical Health Act (HITECH)
Health Level Seven (HL7)
indexed
information
input device
longitudinal patient record
meaningful use
networking equipment
operating software

optical disk imaging
output device
patient monitoring system
patient portal
personal health record (PHR)
record
record transitional template
regional health information organization (RHIO)
registration-admission-discharge-transfer system (RADT)
scanner
software
storage device (memory device)

Objectives

At the end of this chapter, the student should be able to:

- Define key terms
- Distinguish between computerized patient records, electronic patient records, and electronic health records
- Discuss electronic record implementation issues

- Define and discuss the importance of regional health information organizations
- Identify the administrative and clinical applications found in electronic health records

INTRODUCTION

The health information profession is being transformed from a paper environment to a virtual electronic world. Health information professionals have unique patient information management skills that will assist facilities in making the transition to electronic health record including meeting the demands of the Centers for Medicare and Medicaid's meaningful use programs. However, in order for HIM professionals to understand the expanding role of technology in health care, an understanding of computer terminology is necessary.

OVERVIEW OF COMPUTER TERMS

A basic understanding of computer terms is needed to understand the complex electronic health record systems in use today. Hardware and software are the basic components of computer systems. Hardware includes the physical equipment, or machinery, that is used by the system. In a broad definition it includes the central processing unit, storage devices, input and output devices, and networking equipment. Think of hardware as the parts of the system that you can actually touch. Hardware includes:

- Central processing unit—The central processing unit (CPU) controls the processing of information throughout the system and includes the control unit, arithmetic/logic unit, and primary storage unit.
- Input and output devices—Input devices allow users to enter information into the computer system. Examples of input devices include the keyboard, the mouse, scanners, microphones, and cameras. Output devices allow users to print or display information produced by a computer system. Examples of output devices include printers and computer screens.

- Storage devices—Storage devices (memory devices) hold data during processing or for later retrieval and use. Examples of storage devices include computer chips, CDs, DVDs, hard drives, and magnetic tape.
- Networking equipment—Organizations may develop more complex computer systems known as information systems. These are automated systems connected via a network to run various applications within an organization. Networking equipment includes the wires, modems, routers, and cables that are used to connect the system.

Besides hardware, computers also need software, programs that are used to operate the computer and perform functions. There are two types of software:

- Operating software consists of a set of computer programs that control the hardware and interfaces with the application software.
- Application software consists of computer programs that allow the user to perform a particular task or function. Examples are billing and coding software, document imaging, and patient-registration applications. These will be discussed in various chapters within this textbook.

Advances in hardware and software development have a profound impact on the manner in which the health care industry incorporates technology into the health care environment. As consumers demand more access to their health information, health care professionals are required to manage health information in a technologically advanced environment. For example, consumers now communicate with providers using mobile health applications on smartphones and other devices, thus requiring the health care industry to determine how this technology can be used in light of health information security regulations. Before we can discuss the challenges of today, we must understand the evolution of electronic health records.

EVOLUTION OF ELECTRONIC HEALTH RECORDS

From the 1960s to the present, many terms have been used to describe automated medical record systems. The terms have changed due to the advancement of technology and because automated systems have evolved from single computer applications to a combination of numerous systems that are networked together.

In the period 1970–1980, the term computerized medical records was used to describe early medical record automation efforts that focused on the development of alerts, medication administration records, provider orders communication, and notes. Automation was primarily used in the following types of systems: patient registration, finance, laboratory, radiology, pharmacy, nursing, and respiratory therapy. During the 1970s, most computerized medical records were developed in university settings for use that was tailored to the needs of the developing entity; therefore, these early systems could not be easily implemented at other facilities.

Throughout the 1980s, the development of automated systems was slow, but the vision of electronic record systems was a goal of the health care industry. The Institute of Medicine (IOM), in 1991, released a report, "The Computer-based Patient Record: An Essential Technology for Health Care." The vision from this report was to develop automated systems that would provide a longitudinal patient record. A longitudinal patient record contains records from different episodes of care, providers, and facilities that are linked to form a view, over time, of a patient's health care encounters.

The IOM concluded that this could be accomplished through a computer-based patient record (CPR). The term CPR was used to describe a broader view of the patient record than was present in the 1980s.

The CPR is multidisciplinary and multienterprise, (Figure 5-1), and it has the ability to link patient information at different locations according to a unique patient identifier. Although this is the primary advantage of CPR systems, there are also many other advantages of automated records systems. Refer to Table 5-1 for a comparison of manual and automated record systems. A CPR also provides access to complete and accurate health problems, status, and treatment data; and it contains alerts (e.g., drug interaction) and reminders (e.g., prescription renewal notice) for health care providers. According to the IOM's 1991 report, electronic records should support the following:

- Physician access to patient information
- New and past test results in multiple-care settings
- Computerized order entry
- Computerized decision-support systems to prevent adverse drug interactions and improve compliance with best practices
- Secure electronic communication among providers and patients
- Patient access to records, disease management tools, and health information resources
- Computerized administration processes such as scheduling systems
- Standards-based electronic data storage
- Reporting for patient safety and disease surveillance efforts

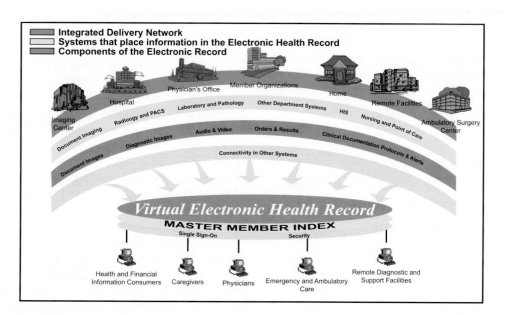

FIGURE 5-1 Virtual Electronic Health Record (Permission to reprint granted by Cerner DHT, Inc.)

TABLE 5-1 Advantages and Disadvantages of Manual and Automated Record Systems

Type of System	Advantages	Disadvantages
Manual	• Low start-up costs • Training of staff is simple • Requires less technically trained staff • Paper records are available because there is no downtime	• Retrieval of information is not easily customized • Hand-written information can be illegible • Difficult to abstract information • Undocumented services are not usually discovered until discharge analysis of record occurs
Automated	• Improves access to patient information • Multiple users can access patient information simultaneously and remotely • Eliminates paper record storage • Improves readability of patient information • Timely capture of data • Views of patient record can be customized by users • Updates of information can easily occur • Retrieval of customized information • Enhanced security of patient information • Reduces administrative costs	• Increased start-up costs • Selection and development of system is time-consuming • Staff training is time-consuming and can be expensive • Technical staff need to maintain system • User resistance can occur

A second edition of the report was released in 1997, which further validated the need for the development of automated medical record systems.

As automated systems developed throughout the 1990s, dictation, transcription, and document imaging functions were merged with CPR functions. Document imaging and optical disk imaging provided an alternative to traditional microfilm or remote storage systems as patient records were converted to an electronic image and saved on servers or optical disks. Optical disk imaging uses laser technology to create the image. A scanner is used to capture paper record images onto electronic storage media. Capturing images electronically allows rapid, automated retrieval of records occurs.

Scanning of Documents

Document scanning affords health care facilities the ability to move away from paper-based medical record systems toward the development of an electronic health record. Prior to scanning, the paper record is "prepped" for scanning by:

- Removing all staples, paper clips, or fasteners from documents.
- Ensuring that the patient's name and medical record number appear on each page. If the

document is two sided, the patient's name and medical record number must appear on both sides of the document.
- Repairing any pages that have tears. If tears on pages are present, the page should be repaired, and then a copy of the page should be used as the scan document. Pages with tears can jam the scanning equipment.

After preparation of the documents, the paper is inserted into a scanner. Document imaging systems now index the scanned forms to aid in data retrieval. Each scanned page is indexed, which means it is identified according to a unique identification number, which is commonly the patient's medical record number. Because of document indexing, all documents for the same patient do not have to be scanned at the same time. The complete patient record can be retrieved because each page has been indexed. Many facilities now use bar coding as part of the scanning process. Bar codes are machine-generated identification codes that can be used on paper documents. When the document is scanned, an input device, known as a bar code reader or bar code scanner, reads the bar code and identifies the document as belonging to a specific patient. Therefore, the bar codes allow for the indexing of the documents that are being scanned.

After the pages are scanned, the quality of the scanned document should be verified prior to the destruction of the original document. Many facilities have two quality reviews of the scanned documents. The first review is completed by the person scanning the document, the second by another staff member.

Continued Evolution of Electronic Records

The next step in the evolution of electronic records includes the merging of data from different data systems into one centralized database known as a clinical data repository, which provides easy access to data in electronic or printed form. The term electronic medical record (EMR) was used in the late 1990s to describe systems that were based on imaging and the merging of data from various stand-alone systems. The terms "computerized patient records" and "electronic medical records" were used interchangeably. During this period of time, many vendors developed electronic medical record systems for use in ambulatory care and, primarily, physician offices. Many inpatient facilities were also using electronic medical record systems, but there was limited networking between the inpatient and ambulatory worlds.

In his 2004 State of the Union Address, President George W. Bush supported the use of electronic health records (EHRs) to improve care and reduce medical mistakes and costs. President Bush issued an executive order to establish the position of the National Coordinator for Health Information Technology within the Office of the Secretary of HHS. This position was created for the primary purpose of aiding the secretary of HHS in achieving the president's goal. In February 2009, Congress enacted the American Recovery and Reinvestment Act, which included an estimated net investment of $19 billion for health information technology, including the development of technologies to enhance the advancement of electronic health records.

The term "electronic health record" is used by the IOM and Health Level Seven (HL7) in the development of standards that relate to the exchange of clinical health information. Health Level Seven (HL7) is a standards-development organization that develops EHR standards under the direction of the U.S. Department of Health and Human Services. The standards outline the process for the exchange of health information and provide a nationwide interoperability plan with common parameters to be used for electronic data and record exchange.

From 2002 to 2009, the National Alliance for Health Information Technology (NAHIT) promoted health IT

initiatives. NAHIT consisted of health care providers, payers, and other industry organizations that were stakeholders in the development of IT systems in health care. NAHIT accomplished many initiatives that had an impact on the advancement of IT in health care in the United States. NAHIT worked with the Office of the National Coordinator for Health IT to define the terms electronic medical record and electronic health record. The definitions established by NAHIT are as follows:

- An electronic medical record is "an electronic record of health-related information on an individual that can be created, gathered, managed and consulted by authorized clinicians and staff within one health care organization."
- An electronic health record is "an electronic record of health-related information on an individual that conforms to nationally recognized interoperability standards and that can be created, managed, and consulted by authorized clinicians and staff across more than one health care organization."

One noticeable difference in the definitions is that the electronic health record encompasses the transmission of health information that is standardized and shared between health care organizations.

As electronic health record systems advance, we are seeing the emergence of the health information exchange (HIE). The term health information exchange is now being used to describe the transmission of standardized health information between health care professionals to other professionals and patients. This is further discussed later in this chapter.

Another term that is used is "personal health record (PHR)," an electronic or paper medical record maintained and updated by an individual for his or her own personal use. A PHR is not meant to replace the medical information that a health care provider would maintain on the patient. The PHR is managed and controlled by the individual. To learn more about personal health records, or to establish one for yourself, visit http://www.myPHR.com.

EXERCISE 5–1 Evolution of Electronic Health Records

Fill-in-the-Blank: Enter the appropriate terms(s) to complete each statement.

1. Merging the data from different data systems into one centralized database is known as a _____.

2. A _____ contains records from different episodes of care, providers, and facilities that are

linked to form a view, over time, of a patient's health care encounters.

3. An electronic or paper medical record maintained and updated by an individual for his or her own personal use is known as a _____.

4. The standards for the exchange of health information were being developed by _____.

5. An _____ device allows users to enter information into the computer system.

ELECTRONIC HEALTH RECORD SYSTEMS

No two facilities have the same electronic health record system. Electronic health record systems that are used in various facilities today are combinations of various systems that integrate medical documentation needs into an electronic format. During their careers, health information administrators may work worked with numerous facilities to implement electronic health record systems in a variety of types of health care organizations. Each implementation will be a unique journey based on the information needs, budget, existing automated systems, and other factors.

Transition from Paper Records to Electronic Health Records

Facilities transitioning to electronic health records are at various stages. Many facilities use a hybrid records, a part paper, part electronic record. This is considered as a transitional state until a true electronic health record can be realized. In a hybrid system, some documents remain on paper while other parts of the record are electronic. One of the most important issues when managing a hybrid record is the facility's definition of its legal record. It should be noted that state law is the primary basis for the definition of the legal patient record.

Issues Impacting the Electronic Legal Health Record

Facilities need to clearly define their legal record to be able to respond to various requests for a patient's entire record. The content of the legal record must be defined in facility policy, and standards for maintaining the security and integrity of the record need to be clearly defined. In a hybrid record system, part of the record will be retrieved manually, while the remaining part will be housed in the automated system. It is essential that all aspects of the record—regardless of the media used to store the record—be addressed in facility policy.

As facilities transition from paper to electronic formats, it is most helpful to develop a document that delineates the various sources of the component parts of the patient's record. Figure 5-2 illustrates this type of document known as a record transitional template. As the facility moves down the path to a full electronic format, the document should be modified to reflect the current state of the record. For example, in Figure 5-2, it should be noted that at Sunny Valley Hospital the Nursing Intake is currently in paper format. If the facility were to develop this form in an electronic format, the record transitional template would be modified to document this change.

Another issue that should be addressed in facility policy is document completion and the time period in which documents can be changed before they become part of the legal record. Facilities need to establish policies that address the management of different versions of electronic documentation.

Example Sunny Valley Hospital has an electronic health record that includes electronic progress notes. After seeing the patient, the clinical staff documents the progress of the patient in an electronic note. The note is considered in draft format and needs to be final saved by the clinician entering the note. If the clinician is called away from the computer prior to completion, the system will automatically lock down the note after 3 minutes. Since the document was not final saved by the clinician, the note can be completed and edited. However, if the note is final saved it cannot be edited.

There is more than one manner in which documents are final saved in electronic systems. It is important for HIM professionals to identify the manner in which documents are final saved and to develop policies that facilitate a complete and accurate record. Organizations need to establish policies that delineate the acceptable time period for a document to remain in draft format. After a document is final saved, it must not be altered. If the document needs to be changed after it has been final saved, the correction needs to occur following the procedure for record correction, late entry, or amendment. Policies that govern corrections, late entries, and amendments to patient records need to be established based on the functionality of the electronic health record. When subsequent corrections are made, the original entry will remain with the corrected version.

Typically, the HIM staff is responsible for ensuring that all entries are authenticated and final saved. As per The Joint Commission standards, inpatient hospital records must be completed within 30 days after discharge

Paper Document Name and Number	Location	Format
Inpatient Face Sheet- MR 001	Patient registration screen	Electronic
Authorization for Consent to Treatment- MR 002	Section 1 of paper record	Paper
Nursing In-Take- MRN 001	Section 2 of paper record	Paper
Laboratory Reports- MRL 001- 124	Laboratory report screen 1–55	Electronic
Radiology Reports- MRR- 001- 023	Radiology report screen 1–20	Electronic
Medication	Medication order screen – 1	Electronic
Medication Administration Record- MRN-027	Medication administration screen – 1	Electronic
Admission History and Physical- MRP-002	Section 2 of paper record	Paper
Operative Report- MRP-003	Section 3 of paper record	Paper
Discharge Summary- MRP-004	Section 4 of paper record	Paper
Nursing Progress Notes- MRN 002	Nursing bedside screen 1–58	Electronic
Preanesthesia Evaluation- MRA- 001	Section 4 of paper record	Paper
Recovery Room Record- MRA- 002	Surgery recovery screen	Electronic
Postanesthesia Evaluation- MRA- 003	Section 4 of paper record	Paper
Pathology Report- MRN 125- 135	Laboratory report screen 56–75	Electronic
Ancillary Reports- MRAR- 1-94	Section 4 of paper record	Paper
Physical Therapy Report- MRPT- 001-035	Physical therapy screens 1–21	Electronic
Occupational Therapy Report- MROT-001- 021	Occupational therapy screens 1–16	Electronic
Graphic Reports- MRN- 039- 55	Graphic report generator screens	Electronic

All reports in paper record are filed in chronological date order within each section.

FIGURE 5-2 Sunny Valley Hospital Record Transitional Template

regardless of the storage media of the record. In a paper system the documents are reviewed manually, whereas in an electronic system reports can be generated to identify documents that are not final saved. This demonstrates how the role of HIM professionals has changed with the adoption of electronic records. In the electronic environment, HIM professionals do not have to manually complete a task; instead, they have to monitor the task to ensure completion by clinicians.

Another issue that must be considered when transitioning to EHRs is how the record will look when it is printed from its electronic format. One of the greatest challenges facing HIM professionals today is how to print the entire electronic record when needed. HIM and IT professionals need to work cooperatively to develop a hard copy of the electronic record.

REGIONAL HEALTH INFORMATION ORGANIZATION

With an increasing number of health care facilities developing electronic health record systems, the networking of electronic information between facilities has become a reality by the establishment of regional health information organizations (RHIOs). A regional health information organization is an electronic network of patient medical information gathered from multiple health care organizations in a geographical region. The goal of the RHIO is to allow health care providers the opportunity to access patient information that was generated at other facilities, thus allowing for health information exchange (HIE). RHIOs allow access to multiple types of patient information such as lab reports, test results, encounter information, and so on, regardless of where the patient might have been seen.

The first step in the establishment of a RHIO is for a group of stakeholders to come together to establish the need for the RHIO and to articulate the vision. Although each stakeholder gains different benefits, successful RHIOs are developed through the collaborative efforts of the following stakeholders:

- Hospitals—Benefits for hospitals include reduced administrative costs, improved patient care, reduced admission times, improved testing result delivery, and a reduction in medical errors due to increased availability of clinical patient information.

- Physicians—Rapid access to patient information occurs when providers use a RHIO. The provider can easily access information that was generated at various levels of care, thus streamlining access to timely information.
- Patients—The benefits for patients include comprehensive documentation of medical information, improved coordination of care, and improved patient safety.
- Health plans and insurers—Administrative savings occur when health plans and insurers participate in a RHIO because they can more efficiently access medical records. A reduction in duplicate testing also helps to reduce costs.
- Public/governmental health agencies—Participation by this type of stakeholder has been limited at this time; however, there is an increased ability to monitor public health issues through the use of aggregate data.

As RHIOs are established, a number of patient information security issues that must be addressed. One of the most important issues is the need to establish a HIPAA-compliant notice of privacy practices (NPP), which will address the exchange of information via the RHIO. The RHIO participants will have to determine if a separate NPP will be used or if all RHIO participants will use an NPP designed by the RHIO. Many states now have policies on the written consent of the patient in a RHIO.

> *Example* In New York State, a patient must sign an approved NYS Department of Health (DOH) consent form, which will allow the RHIO to exchange patient information for treatment purposes when patients are seen at different health systems and medical facilities that participate in the RHIO.

The development of RHIOs has mostly occurred by private and nonprofit organizations coming together. With the passage of the American Recovery Reinvestment Act of 2009, Public Law 111-5, health information exchange will be enhanced through funding mechanisms and national efforts to develop nationwide health information exchange.

Impact of the American Recovery and Reinvestment Act

The American Recovery and Reinvestment act was signed into law on February 17, 2009. The impact of this act on health information technology will be a major force in moving the U.S. health care system into the electronic record environment. There are numerous sections within ARRA. The Health Information Technology for Economic and Clinical Health Act (HITECH) section provides incentives through the Medicare and Medicaid EHR Incentive program. Professionals, hospitals, and critical access hospitals (CAHs) will receive financial incentives when they are "meaningfully using" EHRs by meeting CMS "meaningful use" objectives. For example, eligible professionals can receive up to $44,000 through the Medicare EHR Incentive Program, and up to $63,750 through the Medicaid EHR Incentive Program. The Medicaid EHR Incentive Program is managed by individual states. State programs must receive approval from CMS prior to program implementation.

The meaningful use criteria are defined in stages. Each stage includes objectives that are specific to eligible professionals, hospitals, or CAHs. CMS maintains extensive information on this program. To view additional information, visit http://www.cms.gov. Areas that the act will further impact include:

- The advancement of health information exchange (HIE)
- New privacy regulations for both HIPAA and non-HIPAA entities
- HIM workforce opportunities that will expand the opportunities for professionals

As the ARRA is being implemented, many components of the act are evolving. For the most current information on topics that relate to ARRA, visit the AHIMA website: http://www.ahima.org.

COMPONENTS OF ELECTRONIC HEALTH RECORD SYSTEMS USED IN HEALTH CARE

As stated earlier in this chapter, there are numerous electronic health record systems used in facilities. Regardless of the system used, the goal is the same: to collect, analyze, process, display, and retrieve health care data and information.

In any system, the collection of data must occur. Data is defined as raw facts that are not interpreted or processed, such as numbers, letters, images, symbols, and sounds. Data is described and organized in a hierarchy that begins with the smallest piece of data, known as a character. A character is a lowercase or an uppercase letter, numeric digit, or special character. A group of characters forms a field, while a collection of related fields forms a record. A collection of related records is a file. Examples of a character and field are illustrated in Figure 5-3, a screen that is used at the

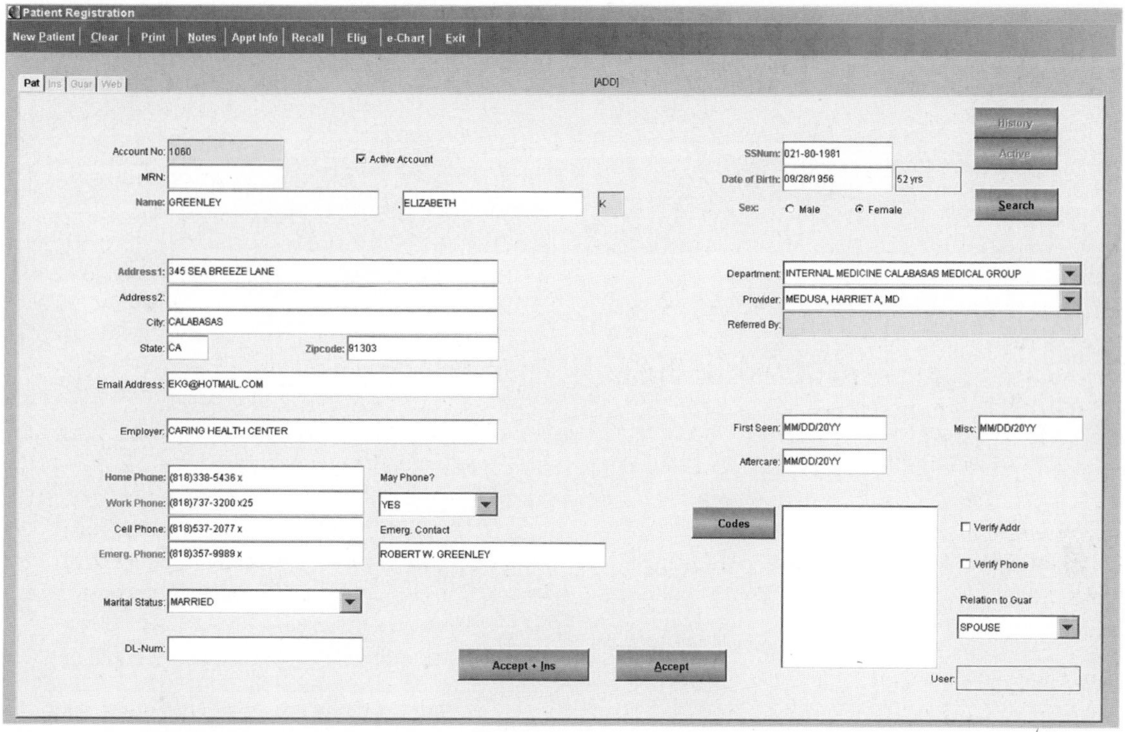

FIGURE 5-3 Patient Registration Screen (Reprinted with permission of PracticeOne.)

time of patient registration. The following areas on the screen represent a field:

Account No, MRN, Name, Address1, Address2. The following represent characters:

The individual digits of the account number: 1, 0, 6, 0.

After data has been collected, it is given meaning and is useful for decision making. Data then becomes information.

Example The numbers 120/80 are a form of data, but when we define the numbers as a patient's blood pressure reading they become information.

The blood pressure reading also represents health data. Health data is comprised of health facts that are collected about a patient or group of patients and that describe a health issue. If a facility has collected the blood pressure readings on all patients on the coronary care unit, this would represent health data that relates to this group of patients. If the blood pressure readings were analyzed and given meaning, health information would be generated. Health information is defined as health data that has been given meaning and has been processed or organized in a manner that is useful for decision making. For example, if

the blood pressures of the coronary care unit patients were all found to be high, this information would be clinically relevant and would be used in the medical decision-making process.

Administrative and Clinical Electronic Health Record Applications

There are two major components of all electronic health record systems: administrative applications and clinical applications. Administrative applications include patient scheduling, admission/registration, business/financial functions, and other management applications. Clinical applications include the collection, storage, and display of clinical information.

One basic function found in all systems is the collection of patient demographic and insurance information. The accuracy of the data collected during the patient registration process is essential. This data is entered into screens that are part of a registration-admission-discharge-transfer system (RADT). The application creates a centralized database of patient demographic information and has replaced the paper master patient index in the virtual world. Figures 5-3 and 5-4 illustrate patient intake screens that collect patient demographic and insurance information.

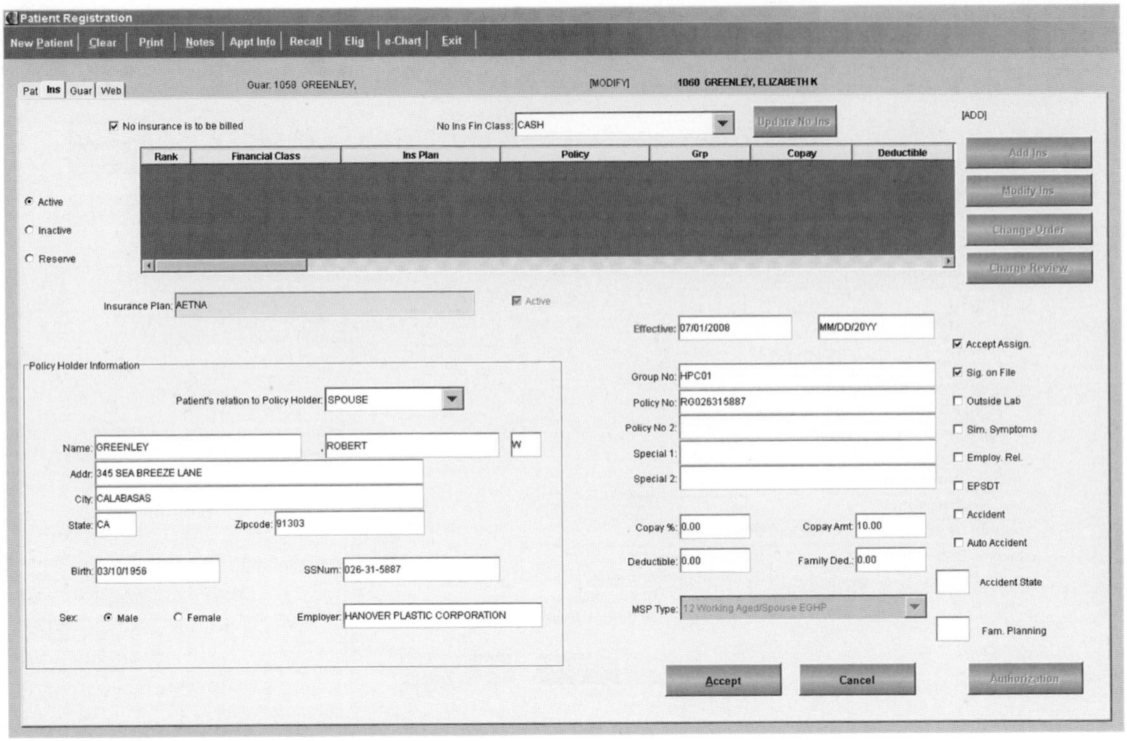

FIGURE 5-4 Patient Registration Insurance Screen (Reprinted with permission of PracticeOne.)

The value of any electronic record system is dependent on the clinical applications that exist within the system. For the purpose of this textbook, various types of clinical applications can be summarized as follows:

- Patient monitoring systems—A patient monitoring system includes systems that collect, monitor, and record patient physiological data. For example, patients' vital signs are monitored in intensive care units via patient monitoring systems. These systems allow for the continuous monitoring and collection of vital signs. Alerts will occur if the patient's vital signs are abnormal.

- Pharmacy applications—Pharmacy applications automate various aspects of the processing of patient medications. The following functions can be included in pharmacy applications: order entry, identification of drug interactions, pharmacist review, medical label printing, and pharmacy administrative reports such as inventory control and drug usage.

- Laboratory applications—Automation of laboratory functions includes the processing of laboratory orders and the management of the laboratory functions. The basic functions include the ordering

of tests, the reporting of test results, and report generation. Many laboratory applications provide test results to providers via electronic health information exchange. This function allows the provider to view test results from remote locations.

- Radiology applications—The functions of radiology applications include the ordering of tests, the creation of radiological images, reporting of test results, and various administrative functions. With the shortage of radiologists, systems have been developed that allow radiological images to be taken at a facility and reviewed by a radiologist at another location. The reports are then electronically generated and can be accessed by the ordering facility.

- Nursing applications—Numerous nursing applications are used to support both the clinical and administrative nursing functions. Automated clinical functions include the development of nursing intake assessments, documentation of nursing care, ongoing assessments of patients, medication administrative records, and various other charting functions. Many administrative nursing activities are also embedded in electronic nursing applications and vary depending on the functionality of the system. Nursing management applications can

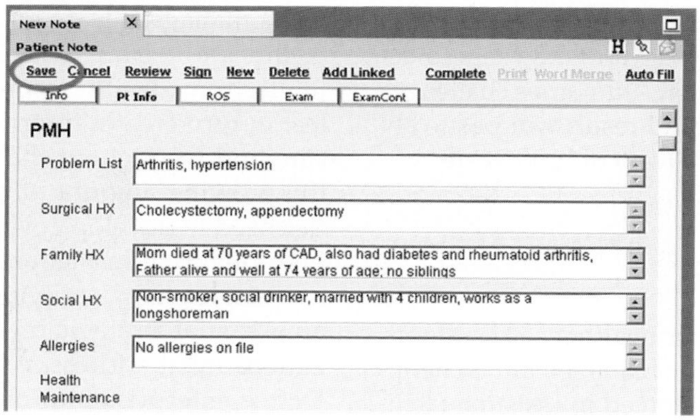

FIGURE 5-5 Past Medical History Screen (Reprinted with permission of PracticeOne.)

include reports on late dosing of medications, infection rates, nursing response times, assessments on the quality of nursing services, and personnel resource management.

- Medical documentation applications—Medical documentation applications include a multitude of charting functions including progress note documentation, medication and diagnostic profiles, treatment planning, and the tracking of patient vital signs to name a few. Figure 5-5 illustrates a screen that is used to collect a past medical history on a patient. Figure 5-6 illustrates a screen that is used to collect information recorded at the time of a patient exam.
- Patient access application—This application can be considered both a clinical and administrative application. Some electronic health record systems allow patients to communicate with their health care provider via a patient portal, a special application that provides patients with secure access to their electronic health information and patient-provider communication tools. Typically, patients can view

online medical records and financial account information, schedule appointments, and communicate with providers via an encrypted email system. Facilities may limit the medical information that a patient can view online. Although the patient has the legal right to access and to have a copy of his or her medical record, it would not be in the patient's best interest to view all medical information without having a provider present. For example, imagine what it would be like to be a patient reading the results of a lab test stating that cancer was detected. Additional features of patient portals can include health and fitness information, and requests for prescription renewals.

To see examples of patient portals, visit https://mygeisinger.geisinger.org or www.eclinicalworks.com.

Health information professionals must have a basic understanding of the various applications that exist to be an active participant in the selection of electronic

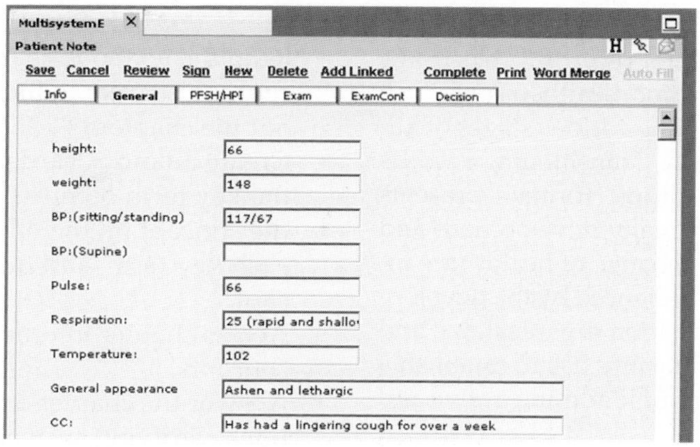

FIGURE 5-6 Patient Exam Screen (Reprinted with permission of PracticeOne.)

record systems. Transitioning to electronic record systems is an evolving process that can take years to accomplish within an organization. Numerous challenges will have to be met, but the end result will positively impact patient care and the delivery of health care.

BEYOND HEALTH DATA AND HEALTH INFORMATION

As more facilities use electronic health record systems, the world of health information management is changing. HIM professionals are involved in assisting facilities with the use of data that is now at one's fingertips because of advances in technology. This data is used within facilities and is also shared via health information exchanges. In order for data—and the information that comes from data—to be useful, the data has to be managed. Data governance must occur within facilities to ensure that only quality data is recorded in electronic health record systems. The data we collect in turn creates information that is used in patient care and throughout the health care industry. Given the growing amount of data and information, facilities need to develop governance processes that ensure high-quality information. In 2013, AHIMA published a strategic plan identifying information governance as an essential strategic process that health care organizations must address. AHIMA's plan stated that "effective enterprise information management in health care requires governance of both data and information to improve health care." Governance has become a critical function as the health care industry uses ever more data and information to make clinical, financial, and administrative decisions.

Internet Links

To review AHIMA resources on electronic record topics, visit **http://www.ahima.org**. On the home page, click on **HIM** Body of Knowledge. On the left side of the page there is a listing of folders. The E-health and E-HIM/EHR folders contain numerous resources that pertain to electronic record topics. Visit the home page of Computer Professionals for Social Responsibility a **http://cpsr.org**, and search the term "medical records." Numerous articles will then display.

The Office of the National Coordinator for Health Information Technology provides counsel to the secretary of HHS and departmental leadership for the development and nationwide implementation of an interoperable health information technology infrastructure. To obtain information on this office, visit **http://www.hhs.gov**.

To learn more about RHIOs, log on to **http://www.grrhio.org**. This is the home page for the Rochester Regional Health Information Organization, which was developed by and for doctors, hospital systems, health insurers, and privacy officers in the nine-county Greater Rochester New York area.

Visit **http://www.ehidc.org** for the latest updates on national eHealth initiatives.

SUMMARY

The terms "computerized patient records," "electronic patient records," and "electronic health records" all have unique meanings and define various stages of automated health record systems. Transitioning records from a paper format to electronic formats presents the health care industry with many development and implementation issues. The exchange of health care information will continue to be enhanced by the development of regional health information organizations and other federal initiatives. Each facility has to establish a plan for the integration of electronic administrative and clinical applications.

STUDY CHECKLIST

- Read the textbook chapter and highlight key concepts. (Use colored highlighter sparingly throughout the chapter.)
- Create an index card for each key term. (Write the key term on one side of the index card and the concept on the other. Learn the definition of each key term, and match the term to the concept.)
- Access chapter Internet links to learn more about concepts.
- Answer the chapter exercises and review questions, verifying answers with your instructor.

- Study content, view videos, and take practice tests online at www.CengageBrain.com.
- Complete the lab manual assignments verifying answers with your instructor.
- Form a study group with classmates to discuss chapter concepts in preparation for an exam.

CASE STUDY

Assume that you are the health information management director of Sunny Valley Hospital. Currently, the medical record system is a paper-based system. The CEO of the facility would like to explore the selection and implementation of an electronic health record. The CEO has determined that a planning team needs to explore electronic record systems and has asked you to respond to the following questions:

1. What disciplines should be represented on the planning team?

2. Do you feel that you could act as the chairperson for the planning team? Explain your answer.

3. What questions/issues need to be a part of the initial investigation of the selection and implementation of an EHR?

CHAPTER REVIEW

True/False: Indicate whether each statement is true (T) or false (F).

_____ 1. According to the IOM's 1991 study, the health care industry's development of automated systems was fast paced.

_____ 2. A patient monitoring system includes systems that collect patient demographic information.

_____ 3. Electronic health records will improve care and reduce medical mistakes and costs.

_____ 4. Per The Joint Commission standards, inpatient hospital records must be completed within 30 days after discharge for paper records and within 20 days for electronic records.

_____ 5. The benefits of electronic health data exchange for patients include comprehensive documentation of medical information, improved coordination of care, and improved patient safety.

Multiple Choice: Select the most appropriate response.

6. Which of the following is not an administrative application of an electronic record system?
   a. admission/registration
   b. business/financial functions
   c. patient scheduling
   d. pathology reports

7. In the period 1970–1980, the term _____ was used to describe early medical record automation attempts.
   a. computerized medical record
   b. electronic medical record
   c. longitudinal health record
   d. personal health record

8. Which term was used starting in the late 1990s to describe systems that were based on imaging and the merging of data from various stand-alone systems?
   a. computerized medical record
   b. electronic medical record
   c. longitudinal health record
   d. personal health record

9. An electronic or paper medical record maintained and updated by individuals for their own personal use is known as a(n)
   a. computerized medical record.
   b. electronic medical record.
   c. longitudinal health record.
   d. personal health record.

10. A system that collects, monitors, and records patient physiological data is known as a(n)
    a. nursing clinical application.
    b. patient monitoring system.
    c. physiological application.
    d. electronic monitoring system.

11. Which of the following is not a benefit of the establishment of a RHIO for patients?
    a. comprehensive documentation of medical information
    b. decreased waiting time to see providers
    c. improved coordination of care
    d. improved patient safety

12. Sunny Valley Hospital has purchased an application that includes the following functions: order entry, identification of drug interactions, medical label printing, and administrative reports such as drug usage. This type of application is known as a(n)
    a. drug application.
    b. medical documentation application.
    c. pharmacy application.
    d. order-entry application.

13. Raw facts that are not interpreted or processed, such as numbers, letters, images, symbols, and sounds, are referred to as
    a. characters.
    b. data.
    c. information.
    d. fields.

14. A group of characters form a _____.
    a. field
    b. file
    c. record
    d. screen

15. Records that are part paper and part electronic are known as
    a. computerized medical records.
    b. hybrid records.
    c. longitudinal records.
    d. personal health records.

Short Answer: Briefly respond to each question.

16. Compare and contrast the advantages and disadvantages of paper and automated record systems.

17. Outline the steps that should be taken to prepare documents for scanning.

18. Discuss how health information professionals can contribute to the transition to electronic record systems.

19. Summarize the impact of electronic health information exchange on the quality of patient care.

20. List and discuss three electronic clinical applications.

Chapter 6

PATIENT RECORD DOCUMENTATION GUIDELINES: INPATIENT, OUTPATIENT, AND PHYSICIAN OFFICE

Key Terms

addressograph machine
admission/discharge record
admission note
admitting diagnosis
advance directive
advance directive notification form
against medical advice (AMA)
alias
ambulance report
ambulatory record
ancillary reports
ancillary service visit
anesthesia record
antepartum record
anti-dumping legislation
APGAR score
attestation statement
automatic stop order
autopsy

autopsy report
bedside terminal system
birth certificate
birth history
case management note
certificate of birth
certificate of death
chief complaint (cc)
clinical data
clinical résumé
comorbidities
complications
conditions of admission
consent to admission
consultation
consultation report
death certificate
dietary progress note
differential diagnosis

discharge note
discharge order
discharge summary
doctors orders
DRG creep
durable power of attorney
emergency record
encounter
encounter form
face sheet
facility identification
family history
fee slip
final diagnosis
first-listed diagnosis
follow-up progress note
forms committee
graphic sheet
health care proxy

history
history of present illness (HPI)
informed consent
integrated progress notes
interval history
labor and delivery record
licensed practitioner
macroscopic
maximizing codes
medication administration
   record (MAR)
necropsy
necropsy report
neonatal record
newborn identification
newborn physical examination
newborn progress notes
nonlicensed practitioner
nurses notes
nursing care plan
nursing discharge summary
nursing documentation
obstetrical record
occasion of service
operative record

outpatient visit
past history
pathology report
patient identification
patient property form
patient record documentation
   committee
physical examination
physician office records
physician orders
postanesthesia care unit (PACU)
   record
postanesthesia evaluation note
postmortem report
postoperative note
postpartum record
preanesthesia evaluation note
prenatal record
preoperative note
principal diagnosis
principal procedure
progress notes
read and verified (RAV)
recovery room record
rehabilitation therapy progress note

respiratory therapy progress note
review of systems (ROS)
routine order
secondary diagnoses
secondary procedures
short stay
short stay record
social history
standing order
stop order
superbill
telephone order (T.O.)
telephone order call back policy
tissue report
transfer order
Uniform Ambulatory Care Data Set
   (UACDS)
Uniform Hospital Discharge
   Data Set (UHDDS)
upcoding
verbal order
voice order (V.O.)
written order

Objectives

At the end of this chapter, the student should be able to:

- Define key terms
- Explain general documentation issues that impact all patient records
- Differentiate between administrative and clinical data collected on patients

- List the contents of inpatient, outpatient, and physician office records
- Detail forms design and control requirements, including the role of the forms committee

INTRODUCTION

Health care providers (hospitals, physician offices, and so on) are responsible for maintaining a record for each patient who receives health care services. If accredited, the provider must comply with standards that impact patient record keeping (e.g., The Joint Commission). In addition, federal and state laws and regulations (e.g., Medicare Conditions of Participation (COP)) provide guidance about patient record content requirements (inpatient, outpatient, and so on). To appropriately comply with accreditation standards and federal and state laws and regulations, most facilities establish a forms design and control procedure along with a forms committee to manage the process.

As health care organizations advance from paper-based to electronic medical records, bear in mind that the content of the record remains the same however it is stored. HIM professionals play a critical role in assisting with this transition from paper to electronic systems. This chapter discusses medical record content and provides examples of many medical record forms. The data contained on these forms must also be captured in electronic health records. I tell my students that, for most of us, it is easier to visualize a paper record than an electronic health record. So, as you read through this chapter, concentrate on the types of data that are placed on the forms, not on the format.

Note: For content of alternate care patient records (e.g., home health care, hospice care, long-term care), refer to Cengage Learning's *Comparative Records for Health Information Management* by Ann Peden.

GENERAL DOCUMENTATION ISSUES

The Joint Commission standards require that the patient record contain patient-specific information appropriate to the care, treatment, and services provided. Patient records contain clinical/case information (e.g., documentation of emergency services provided prior to inpatient admission), demographic information (e.g., patient name, gender), and other information (e.g., advanced directive). Medicare Conditions of Participation (CoP) require each hospital to establish a medical record service that has administrative responsibility for medical records, and the hospital must maintain a medical record for each inpatient and outpatient. Medical records must be accurately written, promptly completed, properly filed, properly retained, and accessible. The hospital must use a system of author identification and record maintenance that ensures the integrity of the authentication and protects the security of all record entries. The medical record must contain information to justify admission and continued hospitalization, support the diagnosis, and describe the patient's progress and response to medications and services. All entries must be legible and complete, and must be authenticated and dated promptly by the person (identified by name and discipline) who is responsible for ordering, providing, or evaluating the service furnished. The author of each entry must be identified and must authenticate his or her entry—authentication may include signatures, written initials, or computer entry. Medical records must be retained in their original or legally reproduced form for a period of at least 5 years, and the hospital must have a system of coding and indexing medical records to allow for timely retrieval by diagnosis and procedure to support medical care evaluation studies. The hospital must have a procedure for ensuring the confidentiality of patient records. Information from or copies of records may be released only to authorized individuals, and the hospital must ensure that unauthorized individuals cannot gain access to or alter patient records. Original medical records must be released by the hospital only in accordance with federal or state laws, court orders, or subpoenas.

The patient record is a valuable tool that documents care and treatment of the patient. It is essential that every report in the patient record contain **patient identification**, which consists of the patient's name and some other piece of identifying information such as medical record number or date of birth. Every report in the patient record and every screen in an electronic health record (EHR) must include the patient's name and medical record number. In addition, for paper-based reports that are printed on both sides of a sheet of paper, patient identification must be included on both sides. Paper-based documents that contain multiple pages (e.g., computer-generated lab reports) must include patient identification information on all pages.

Note: Some patients insist on the use of an **alias**, which is an assumed name, during their encounter. The patient might be a movie star or sports figure; receiving health care services under an alias affords privacy (e.g., protection from the press). The name that the patient provides is accepted as the official name, and the true name can be entered in the master patient index as an AKA (also known as). However, the true name is not entered in the patient record or in the billing files. Patients who choose to use an alias should be informed that their insurance company probably will not reimburse the facility for care provided, and the patient will be responsible for payment. In addition, use of an alias can adversely impact continuity of care.

> *Example* A pregnant patient was admitted to the hospital and signed in under an alias. Her baby was delivered, and the baby's last name was entered on the record using the alias. The patient explained that an order of protection had been issued because her spouse was abusive and she didn't want him to know that she had been admitted to deliver the baby. Upon discharge, she and the baby traveled to a safe house.

It is common for health care facilities to print the attending/primary care physician's name and the date of admission/visit on each form using an **addressograph machine** (Figure 6-1), which imprints patient identification information on each report. A plastic card that looks similar to a credit card is created for each patient and placed in the addressograph machine to make an impression on the report. Using an addressograph also allows forms to be imprinted prior to patient admission, creating the record ahead of time. (Some facilities print computer-generated labels, which are affixed to blank forms.) Addressograph imprints and computer-generated labels should be in the same location on each report (e.g., upper-right corner).

Facility identification, including the name of the facility, mailing address, and a telephone number, must also be included on each report in the record so

FIGURE 6-1 Addressograph Machine and Plastic Card (Permission to reprint granted by Addressograph.com.)

that an individual or health care facility in receipt of copies of the record can contact the facility for clarification of record content.

Dating and Timing Patient Record Entries

For a record to be admissible in a court of law according to Uniform Rules of Evidence, all patient record entries must be dated (month, date, and year, such as mmddyyyy) and timed (e.g., military time, such as 0400). Providers are responsible for documenting entries as soon as possible after the care and treatment of a patient, and predated and postdated entries are *not* allowed. (Refer to the discussion of addendums in Chapter 4 for clarification on how providers should amend an entry.)

Note: When nurses summarize patient care at the end of a shift, documentation should include the actual date and time the entry was made in the record.

Content of the Patient Record

Because patient record content serves as a medicolegal defense, providers should adhere to guidelines (Table 6-1) that ensure quality documentation.

EXERCISE 6–1 General Documentation Issues

True/False: Indicate whether each statement is true (T) or false (F).

_____ 1. Every report in the patient record must contain patient identification, which consists of the patient's name and some other piece of identifying information such as medical record number and date of birth.

_____ 2. Facility identification includes the name of the facility, mailing address, and a telephone number, all of which are included on each report in the record so that an individual or health care facility in receipt of copies of the record can contact the facility for clarification of record content.

_____ 3. Providers are encouraged to document all patient record entries after the patient has been discharged.

_____ 4. When documenting on preprinted forms it is acceptable to leave a blank field.

HOSPITAL INPATIENT RECORD—ADMINISTRATIVE DATA

As defined in Chapter 4, *administrative data* includes demographic, socioeconomic, and financial information, which is gathered upon admission of the patient to the facility and documented on the inpatient face sheet (or admission/discharge record). Some facilities gather this information prior to admission through a telephone interview. The following reports comprise administrative data:

- Face sheet (or admission/discharge record)
- Advance directives
- Informed consent
- Patient property form
- Birth certificate (copy)
- Death certificate (copy)

Face Sheet

The Joint Commission standards do not specifically require a face sheet, but it does require that all medical records contain identification data. The Joint Commission requires completion of the medical record within 30 days following patient discharge. Medicare CoP requires a final diagnosis with completion of medical records within 30 days following patient discharge.

Both the paper-based and computer-generated face sheet (or admission/discharge record) (Figures 6-2A and 6-2B) contain patient identification or demographic, financial data, and clinical information (Table 6-2). Within some electronic record-keeping systems, a hard copy document is not printed.

TABLE 6-1 Patient Record Documentation Guidelines

Guideline	Description
Authentication	• Entries should be documented and signed (authenticated) by the author.
Change in Patient's Condition	• If the patient's condition changes (e.g., worsens) or a significant patient care issue develops (e.g., patient falls out of bed and breaks hip), documentation must reflect this as well as indicate follow-through.
Communication with Others	• Any communication provided to the patient's family (e.g., discharge requirements) or physician (e.g., change of condition on night shift) should be properly documented.
Completeness	• Significant information related to the patient's care and treatment should be documented (e.g., patient condition, response to care, treatment course, and any deviation from standard treatment/reason). • All fields on preprinted forms should be completed (e.g., flow sheets). For information not entered, document N/A for not applicable. • If an original entry is incomplete, the provider should amend the entry (e.g., document in the next blank space in the record and refer to the date of the original entry). • If documentation is reported by exception (e.g., only when a specific behavior occurs), the form should indicate these charting instructions.
Consistency	• Document current observations, outcomes, and progress. • Entries should be consistent with documentation in the record (e.g., flow charts). • If documentation is contradictory, an explanation should be included.
Continuous Documentation	• Providers should not skip lines or leave blanks when documenting in the patient record. • Do not generate a new form (e.g., progress note sheet) until the previous form is filled. • If a new form is started, the provider should cross out any remaining space on the previous form. (An entry documented out of order should be added as a late entry.) • Blank space on a form raises the question that the record may have been falsified (e.g., blank page inserted or pages out of order because the provider backdated an entry).

Objective Documentation	• State facts about patient care and treatment, and avoid documenting opinions.
	    Incorrect: Patient is peculiar.
	    Correct: Patient exhibits odd behavior.

Referencing Other Patients	• If other patient(s) are referenced in the record, do not document their name(s). Reference their patient number(s) instead.
Permanency	• Documentation entries in the patient record are considered permanent, and policies and procedures should be established to prevent falsification of and tampering with the record.
Physical Characteristics	• Select white paper with permanent black printing (e.g., laser, not inkjet printer) to ensure readability of paper-based records. • Require providers to enter documentation using permanent black ink. • Plain paper (not thermal paper) faxes are best if filed in the patient record. • File original documents in the patient record, not photocopies. • Avoid using labels on reports because they can detach from the report.

Specificity	• Be sure to document specific information about patient care and treatment. Avoid vague entries.
	    Incorrect: Eye exam is normal.
	    Correct: Eye exam reveals pupils equal, round, and reactive to light.

Alfred State Medical Center

100 Main St, Alfred NY 14802

(101) 555-1111

Inpatient Face Sheet

Patient Name and Address						Gender		Race	Birth Date	Patient No.

						Maiden Name		Employer		Occupation

Home Telephone Number: (   )   −

Admission Date	Time	Room	Discharge Date	Time	Length of Stay		Employer Telephone Number
					days ( ) −		

Guarantor Name and Address	Next of Kin Name and Address

Guarantor Telephone No.	Relationship to Patient	Next of Kin Telephone Number	Relationship to Patient
( ) −		( ) −	

Primary Payer	Primary Payer Policy No.	Secondary Payer	Secondary Payer Policy No.

Admitting Physician	Service	Admit Type	Room Number/Bed

Attending Physician	Admitting Diagnosis

Diagnoses and Procedures ICD Codes

Principal Diagnosis	

Secondary Diagnoses	

Principal Procedure	

Secondary Procedures	

Signature of Attending Physician:

FIGURE 6-2A Paper-Based Patient Record Face Sheet

ABC Hospital
1000 Inpatient Lane
Hospital City, New York 12345

FACE SHEET

PATIENT RECORD NUMBER: 23345670	TYPE OF ADMISSION: Inpatient	6/08/YYYY	13:40

NAME/ADDRESS:
Sam Jones
123 Wood Street
Endwell, NY 13456

AGE: 085Y   SEX: M   RACE: W
REL: SRC: 7   ROOM/BED: MD 220 1

ATTENDING DOCTOR: Best, Sarah
REFERRING DOCTOR: Great, Beth

NEAREST RELATIVE:
Sandy Jones (daughter)
45 Brook Street
Liberty, PA 56789
(607) 123-3456

EMPLOYER NAME:
Retired

MARITAL STATUS
Widowed

EMERGENCY CONTACT:
Sandy Jones (daughter)
45 Brook Street
Liberty, PA 56789
(607) 123-3456

GUARANTOR #: 1123   GUARANTOR EMPLOYER: R

ADMITTING DIAGNOSIS: Dyspnea. Dehydration.

INS # 1: Medicare   PLAN: 10
SUBSCRIBER: Sam Jones
ID #: 098586389T

INS # 2: Mutual of Omaha   PLAN: 20
SUBSCRIBER: Sam Jones
ID #: 67890TNH

COMMENTS: POWER OF ATTORNEY: None   ADVANCE DIRECTIVE: On file

---

CONSULTANT:
Fenton, Sean

DISCHARGE: 6/12/YYYY   10:30

CONDITION AT DISCHARGE: Improved

ATTENDING PHYSICIAN
Keen, Abby

Abby Keen	*06/12/YYYY*
SIGNATURE	DATE

FIGURE 6-2B Computer-Generated Face Sheet

Figure 6-2C represents a screen from an electronic system that contains data typically found on a printed face sheet. When a paper document is not printed, this information can be viewed in the electronic system. The face sheet is usually filed as the first page of the patient record because it is frequently referenced. Upon admission to the facility, the attending physician establishes an admitting diagnosis that is entered on the face sheet by the admitting department staff. The admitting diagnosis (or provisional diagnosis) is the condition or disease for which the patient is seeking treatment. The admitting diagnosis is often not the patient's final diagnosis, which is the diagnosis determined after evaluation and documented by the attending physician upon discharge of the patient from the facility.

Note: Financial data is collected from the patient upon admission and submitted to third-party for reimbursement purposes.

The Uniform Hospital Discharge Data Set (UHDDS) is the minimum core data set collected on individual hospital discharges for the Medicare and Medicaid programs. Much of this information is located on the

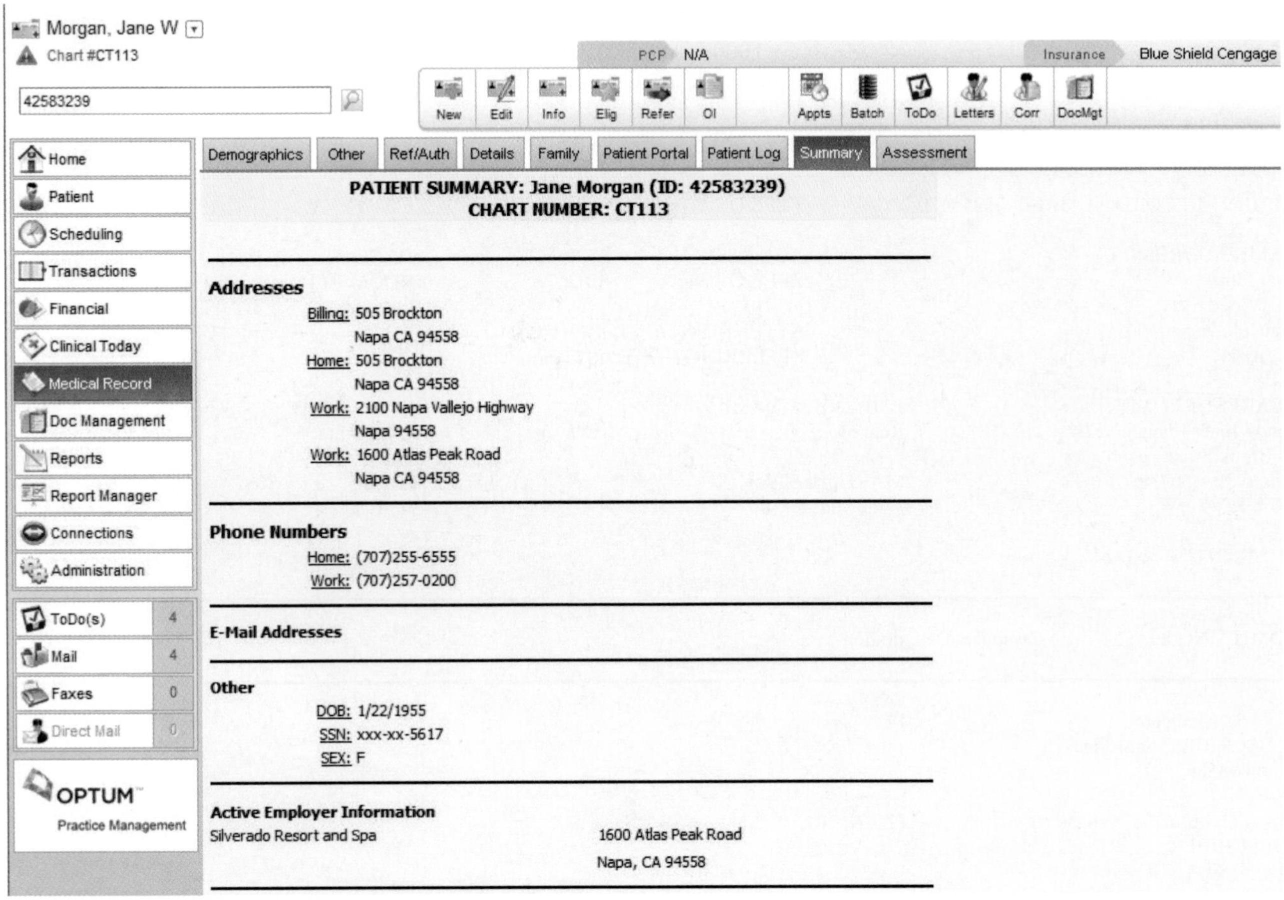

FIGURE 6-2C Electronic System Screen Shot (Courtesy of Optum™ PM and Physician EMR)

face sheet. The official data set consists of the following items:

- Personal Identification/Unique Identifier
- Date of Birth
- Gender
- Race and Ethnicity
- Residence
- Health Care Facility Identification Number
- Admission Date and Type of Admission
- Discharge Date
- Attending Physician Identification
- Surgeon Identification
- Principal Diagnosis
- Other Diagnoses
- Principal Procedure and Dates
- Other Procedures and Dates
- Disposition of Patient at Discharge
- Expected Payer for Most of This Bill
- Total Charges

In early 2003, the National Committee on Vital and Health Statistics (NCVHS) recommended that the following be collected as the standard data set for persons seen in both ambulatory and inpatient settings, unless otherwise specified:

- Personal/Unique Identifier
- Date of Birth
- Gender
- Race and Ethnicity
- Residence
- Living/Residential Arrangement
- Marital Status
- Self-Reported Health Status
- Functional Status
- Years of Schooling
- Patient's Relationship to Subscriber/Person Eligible for Entitlement
- Current or Most Recent Occupation/Industry
- Type of Encounter
- Admission Date (inpatient)

TABLE 6-2 Face Sheet—Sections and Content

Section	Content
Identification (or demographic) Data	• Complete name • Mailing address • Phone number • Date and place of birth, and age • Patient record number • Patient account number • Gender • Race and ethnicity • Marital status • Admission and discharge date and time* • Type of admission (e.g., elective, emergency) • Next-of-kin name and address • Next-of-kin contact information • Employer name, address, and phone number • Admitting and/or referring physician • Hospital name, address, and phone number

Financial Data	• Third-party payer
	  ○ Name
	  ○ Address
	  ○ Phone number
	  ○ Policy number
	  ○ Group name and/or number
	• Insured (or guarantor)**
	  ○ Name
	  ○ Date of birth
	  ○ Gender
	  ○ Relationship to patient (e.g., self, spouse)
	  ○ Name and address of employer
	• Secondary and/or supplemental payer information (all information collected for primary payer is also collected for secondary and/or supplemental payers)

Clinical Information	• Admitting (or provisional or working) diagnosis • Principal diagnosis • Secondary diagnoses (e.g., comorbidities and/or complications) • Principal procedure • Secondary procedure(s) • Condition of patient at discharge • Authentication by attending physician • ICD-9-CM (or ICD-10-CM/PCS) or CPT/HCPCS Level II codes

*Military time is usually reported on the face sheet (e.g., 3:00 p.m. is 1500).

**This is primary payer information.

- Discharge Date (inpatient)
- Date of Encounter (ambulatory and physician services)
- Facility Identification
- Type of Facility/Place of Encounter
- Provider Identification (ambulatory)
- Attending Physician Identification (inpatient)
- Operating Physician Identification (inpatient)
- Provider Specialty
- Principal Diagnosis (inpatient)
- First-Listed Diagnosis (ambulatory)
- Other Diagnoses (inpatient)
- Qualifier for Other Diagnoses (inpatient)
- Patient's Stated Reason for Visit or Chief Complaint (ambulatory)
- Physician's Tentative Diagnosis (ambulatory)
- Diagnosis Chiefly Responsible for Services Provided (ambulatory)
- Other Diagnoses (ambulatory)
- External Cause of Injury
- Birth Weight of Newborn (inpatient)
- Principal Procedure (inpatient)
- Other Procedures (inpatient)
- Dates of Procedures (inpatient)
- Services (ambulatory)
- Medications Prescribed
- Medications Dispensed (pharmacy)
- Disposition of Patient (inpatient)
- Disposition (ambulatory)
- Patient's Expected Sources of Payment
- Injury Related to Employment
- Total Billed Charges

Note: Terms in parentheses indicate items collected for those settings only. The NHVCS also provides specifications as to data to be collected for each item (e.g., patient/unique identifier involves collection of patient's last name, first name, middle initial, suffix, and a numerical identifier).

The identification and financial sections of the face sheet are completed by the admitting (or patient registration) clerk upon patient admission to the facility (or prior to admission as part of the preadmission registration process). Third-party payer information is classified as financial data and is obtained from the patient at the time of admission. If a patient has more than one insurance plan, the admitting clerk will determine which insurance plan is primary, secondary, and/or supplemental. This process is important for billing purposes so that information is appropriately entered on the face sheet. The admitting clerk enters the patient's admitting diagnosis (obtained from the

admitting physician), and the attending physician documents the following:

- **Principal diagnosis** (condition established after study to be chiefly responsible for occasioning the admission of the patient to the hospital for care)

  Example Patient admitted with chest pain. EKG is negative. Chest x-ray reveals hiatal hernia. *Principal diagnosis* is hiatal hernia.

- **Secondary diagnoses** (additional conditions for which the patient received treatment and/or impacted the inpatient care), including:
  - **Comorbidities** (pre-existing condition that will, because of its presence with a specific principal diagnosis, cause an increase in the patient's length of stay by at least one day in 75 percent of the cases)

  Example Patient is admitted for acute asthmatic bronchitis and also treated for uncontrolled hypertension during the admission. *Comorbidity* is hypertension.

Note: To code a comorbidity, the pre-existing condition must be treated during inpatient hospitalization *or* the provider must document how the pre-existing condition impacted inpatient care.

- **Complications** (additional diagnoses that describe conditions arising *after* the beginning of hospital observation and treatment and that modify the course of the patient's illness or the medical care required; they prolong the patient's length of stay by at least one day in 75 percent of the cases)

  Example Patient is admitted for viral pneumonia and develops a staph infection during the stay. The infection is treated with antibiotics. *Complication* is "staph infection."

- **Principal procedure** (procedure performed for definitive or therapeutic reasons, rather than diagnostic purposes, or to treat a complication, or that procedure which is most closely related to the principal diagnosis)

  Example Patient is admitted with a fracture of the right tibia for which a reduction of the tibia was performed. While hospitalized, patient developed appendicitis and underwent an appendectomy. *Principal diagnosis* is fracture, right tibia. *Secondary diagnosis* is appendicitis. *Principal procedure* is open reduction, fracture, right tibia. *Secondary procedure* is appendectomy.

- Secondary procedures (additional procedures performed during inpatient admission)

    Example The patient is admitted for myocardial infarction and undergoes EKG and cardiac catheterization within 24 hours of admission. On day 2 of admission, the patient undergoes coronary artery bypass graft (CABG, pronounced "cabbage") surgery. *Principal procedure* is CABG. *Secondary procedure* is cardiac catheterization. (Most hospitals do not code an inpatient EKG.)

Health information personnel with the title of "coder" assign numerical and alphanumerical codes (ICD-9-CM, ICD-10, CPT, and HCPCS codes) to all diagnoses and procedures. These codes are recorded on the face sheet and in the facility's abstracting system. (Some facilities allow coders to enter diagnoses/procedures from the discharge summary onto the face sheet or to code directly from the discharge summary if the face sheet does not contain diagnoses/procedures. If, upon review of the record, coders determine that additional diagnoses/procedures should be coded, they contact the responsible physician for clarification.) (Abstracting is discussed in Chapter 8.)

Prior to 1995, the Health Care Financing Administration (HCFA, now called Centers for Medicare and Medicaid Services, CMS) required physicians to sign an attestation statement, which verified diagnoses and procedures documented and coded at discharge. Medicare originally required the statement because, when the diagnosis-related groups' prospective payment system was implemented in 1983, there was concern that physicians would document diagnoses and procedures that resulted in higher payment for a facility (also known as upcoding, maximizing codes, or DRG creep). In 1995, the attestation requirement was discontinued. At the same time, some hospitals also eliminated the requirement that physicians document diagnoses/procedures on the face sheet since this information is routinely documented as part of the dictated/transcribed discharge summary. Hospitals now establish facility policy regarding documentation of diagnoses and procedures upon discharge of patients.

Advance Directives

The *Patient Self Determination Act (PSDA) of 1990* required that all health care facilities notify patients age 18 and over that they have the right to have an *advance directive* (e.g., health care proxy, living will, medical power of attorney) placed in their record. Facilities must inform patients, in writing, of state laws regarding advance directives and facility policies

regarding implementation of advance directives. Upon admission, an advance directive notification form (Figure 6-3) is signed by the patient to document that the patient has been notified of his or her right to have an advance directive. The patient record must document whether the individual has executed an advance directive (Table 6-3), which is a legal document in which patients provide instructions as to how they want to be treated in the event they become very ill and there is no reasonable hope for recovery. The written instructions direct a health care provider regarding a patient's preferences for care *before* the need for medical treatment.

Note: State laws regarding advance directives vary greatly.

    Example Anne, who lives in the state of Washington, writes a living will allowed by law, which documents her requests in the event that she is diagnosed with a terminal condition or is permanently unconscious. She relocates to New York State and gives a copy of her living will to her new health care provider. The provider informs her that living wills are not legal in New York State; however, she can designate a health care proxy.

Informed Consent

The Joint Commission standards require that a patient consent to treatment and that the record contain evidence of consent. The Joint Commission states that evidence of appropriate informed consent is to be documented in the patient record. The facility's medical staff and governing board are required to develop policies with regard to informed consent. In addition, the patient record must contain "evidence of informed consent for procedures and treatments for which it is required by the policy on informed consent." Medicare CoP state that all records must contain written patient consent for treatment and procedures specified by the medical staff, or by federal or state law. In addition, patient records must include documentation of "properly executed informed consent forms for procedures and treatments specified by the medical staff, or by federal or state law if applicable, to require written patient consent."

Informed consent is the process of advising a patient about treatment options and, depending on state laws, the provider may be obligated to disclose the patient's diagnosis, proposed treatment/surgery, reason for the treatment/surgery, possible complications, likelihood of success, alternative treatment options, and risks if the patient does not undergo treatment/surgery.

Addressograph

ADVANCE DIRECTIVE ADMISSION
FORM & CHECKLIST

Your answers to the following questions will assist your Physician and the Medical Center to respect your wishes regarding your medical care. This information will become a part of your patient record.

		YES	NO	PATIENT'S INITIALS
1.	Have you been provided with a copy of the information called "Patient Rights Regarding Health Care Decisions"?			
2.	Have you prepared a "Living Will"? If yes, please provide a copy for your patient record.			
3.	Have you prepared a "Health Care Proxy"? If yes, please provide a copy for your patient record.			
4.	Have you prepared a Durable Power of Attorney for Health Care? If yes, please provide a copy for your patient record.			
5.	Have you provided this facility with an Advance Directive on a prior admission and is it still in effect? If yes, Admitting Office will contact Health Information Department to obtain a copy for your current patient record.			

6.	Do you wish to execute a Living Will, Health Care Proxy, and/or Durable Power of Attorney? If yes, Admitting Office will notify:
	  a. Physician
	  b. Social Service
	  c. Volunteer Service			

ADMITTING OFFICE STAFF: Enter a checkmark when each step has been completed.

1. _____ Verify the above questions where answered and actions taken where required.

2. _____ If the "Patient Rights" information was provided to someone other than the patient, state reason:

   _____

   _____   _____
   Name of Individual Receiving Information   Relationship to Patient

3. _____ If information was provided in a language other than English, specify language and method below.

   _____

4. _____ Verify patient was advised on how to obtain additional information on Advance Directives.

5. _____ Verify the Patient/Family Member/Legal Representative was asked to provide the Medical Center with a copy of the Advance Directive, which will be retained in the patient record.

6. _____ File this form in the patient record, and give a copy to the patient.

_____
Name of Patient or Name of Individual giving information, if different from Patient

_____   _____
Signature of Patient   Date

_____   _____
Signature of Medical Center Representative   Date

ALFRED STATE MEDICAL CENTER ■ 100 MAIN ST, ALFRED NY 14802 ■ (607) 555-1234

FIGURE 6-3 Advance Directive Admission Form and Checklist

TABLE 6-3 Advance Directives—Types and Descriptions

Advance Directive	Description
Do Not Resuscitate (DNR) Order (Figure 6-4)	• Instructs medical professionals not to perform cardiopulmonary resuscitation (CPR), which means that doctors, nurses, and emergency medical personnel will not attempt emergency CPR if the patient's breathing or heartbeat stops. • DNR orders are written for patients in a hospital or nursing home, or for patients at home. Hospital DNR orders tell the medical staff not to revive the patient if cardiac arrest occurs. If the patient is in a nursing home or at home, a DNR order instructs the staff and emergency medical personnel not to perform emergency resuscitation and not to transfer the patient to a hospital for CPR. • An adult patient may consent to a DNR order through a *health care proxy*, which allows patients to appoint someone to make decisions about CPR and other treatments if they are unable to decide for themselves.
Living Will (Figure 6-5)	• Legal document in which patients state the kind of health care they do or do not want under certain circumstances. • Written document that informs a health care provider of a patient's desires regarding life-sustaining treatment.
Health Care Proxy (or **durable power of attorney**) (Figure 6-6)	• Legal document in which patients name someone close to them to make decisions about health care in the event they become incapacitated.
Organ or **Tissue Donation** (Figure 6-7)	• Individuals indicate their intent to donate organ(s) and/or tissue. • Persons under 18 years of age must have a parent's or guardian's consent. • Medical suitability for donation is determined at the time of death. • Indicate intent to be an organ and tissue donor on your driver's license, and inform family members of your intention.

Do Not Resuscitate (DNR) Consent

I, _____,**do not authorize resuscitation in the event of cardiac or respiratory arrest**. I understand that this order remains in effect until revoked by me. I acknowledge that cardiopulmonary resuscitation (CPR) will not be performed if breathing or heartbeat stops. I understand this decision will **not** prevent me from obtaining other emergency care by emergency medical services personnel and/or care directed by a physician prior to my death. I understand I may revoke this DNR consent at any time by destroying this consent form.

_____   _____
Patient or Legal Representative Signature   Date

_____
Address of Patient

_____   _____
Attending Physician Signature   Date

_____
Address of Attending Physician

_____   _____
Witness Signature   Date

_____
Address of Witness

FIGURE 6-4 Do Not Resuscitate (DNR) Advance Directive Consent Form

---

LIVING WILL DECLARATION

My name is _____ and my address is _____. If I am determined by my attending physician to be in a terminal condition or a persistent vegetative state, and I am no longer able to make or communicate decisions regarding my medical treatment, then I direct my attending physician to withhold or withdraw all life-sustaining treatment that is not necessary for my comfort or to alleviate pain; and if there is any conflict at that time between this document and any other document I may have signed previously then this document shall control.

_____   _____   _____
My Signature   Date   Date of Birth

WITNESSES' SIGNATURES

The above named _____, in my presence, voluntarily signed this writing or directed another to sign this writing on his/her behalf.

_____   _____   _____
Witness Signature   Date   Witness Address

_____   _____   _____
Witness Signature   Date   Witness Address

FIGURE 6-5 Living Will (Reprinted according to CMS Web reuse policy.)

Informed consent should be carefully documented whenever applicable. An informed consent entry should include an explanation of the risks and benefits of a treatment or procedure, alternatives to the treatment or procedure, and evidence that the patient or appropriate legal surrogate understands and consents to undergo the treatment or procedure.

Consent to Admission

Upon admission the patient may be asked to sign a consent to admission (or conditions of admission), which is a generalized consent that documents a patient's consent to receive medical treatment at the facility. (Figure 6-8A represents a paper consent, while Figure 6-8B represents a consent that would appear in an electronic health record).

Note: The Health Insurance Portability and Accountability Act (HIPAA) privacy rule specifies that facilities are no longer required to consent to admission, but most still obtain the patient's signed consent. (HIPAA mandates administrative simplification regulations that govern privacy, security, and electronic transactions standards for health care information.)

Consent to Release Information

Patient authorization to release information for reimbursement (Figure 6-9) is routinely obtained as part of the consent to admission. Releases of information for other purposes require the patient's authorized consent to release information.

Note: The HIPAA privacy rule specifies that facilities are no longer required to consent to release information for the purpose of reimbursement, research, and education, but most still obtain the patient's signed consent.

Special Consents

Health care facilities require separate consents such as a consent to surgery (Figure 6-10) and for diagnostic, therapeutic, and surgical procedures. Prior to the patient undergoing medical or surgical treatment, it is required that written consent be obtained from the patient or representative, which indicates that the patient acknowledges informed consent as to the nature of treatment, risks, complications, alternative forms of treatment available, and the consequences of the treatment or procedure. The surgeon (or other provider, such as radiologist) will discuss the procedure to be

---

Health Care Proxy

I, _____, hereby appoint _____
(name)

_____
(home address and telephone number)

as my health care agent to make any and all health care decisions for me, except to the extent that I state otherwise. This proxy shall take effect only when and if I become unable to make my own health care decisions.

Unless I revoke it or state an expiration date or circumstances under which it will expire, this proxy shall remain in effect indefinitely. This proxy shall expire _____.
(specify date and/or conditions)

I direct my health care agent to make health care decisions according to my wishes and limitations, as he or she knows or as stated below. I direct my health care agent to make health care decisions in accordance with the following limitations and/or instructions:

_____
(state wishes or limitations above)

Identification

Name _____

Signature _____   Date _____

Address _____

Statement by Witnesses

(Witnesses must be 18 years of age or older and cannot be the health care agent.)

I declare that the person who signed this document is personally known to me and appears to be of sound mind and acting of his or her own free will. He or she signed (or asked another to sign for him or her) this document in my presence.

Name of Witness #1   _____

Signature of Witness #1 _____   Date _____

Address of Witness #1   _____

Name of Witness #2   _____

Signature of Witness #2 _____   Date _____

Address of Witness #2   _____

FIGURE 6-6 Health Care Proxy (or Durable Power of Attorney)

performed with the patient. Patients sign special consents, which include the following elements:

- Patient identification
- Proposed care, treatment, and services
- Potential benefits, risks, and side effects, including likelihood of patient achieving goals, and any potential problems that might occur during recuperation
- Reasonable alternatives to proposed care, treatment, and services

- Circumstances under which information about patient must be disclosed or reported (e.g., reportable diseases such as HIV, TB, viral meningitis)
- Signature of person qualified to give consent and date
- Name of surgeon performing procedure
- Physician/surgeon signature (per facility policy)
- Witness signature and date

Organ/Tissue Donor Card

I wish to donate my organs and tissues. I wish to give:

❑ any needed organs and tissues

❑ only the following organs and tissues:

_____

_____

Donor Signature _____

Date _____

Witness _____

Witness _____

FIGURE 6-7 Organ/Tissue Donation Card (Reprinted according to OrganDonor.gov Web reuse policy.)

Patient Property Form

The patient property form (Figure 6-11) records items patients bring with them to the hospital. Figure 6-11A represents a paper-based patient property form while figure 6-11B represents a patient property form contained in an electronic health record. This form is completed and signed by a hospital staff member and also signed by the patient. It is important for the staff member to complete this form correctly as some patients may claim that they arrived at the hospital with items they do not actually possess.

Certificate of Birth

The certificate of birth (or birth certificate) (Figure 6-12) is a record of birth information about the newborn patient and the parents. It identifies medical information regarding the pregnancy and birth of the newborn. The National Center for Heath Statistics (NCHS) developed a standard certificate of birth, which states can adopt for their use. Birth certificate information is submitted to state departments of health or offices of vital statistics (or records, depending on state title), usually within 10 days of birth. State policies and procedures for birth certificates vary. Some states require electronic submission of birth certificate information. Other states do not require electronic submission because they require that a physician sign the certificate. Birth certificate contents include:

- Infant's and parents' demographic information
- Parents' occupation, education, ethnicity, race
- Pregnancy information
- Medical risk factors, complications, and/or abnormal conditions of newborn

Note: Some states do not allow a copy of the birth certificate to be filed in the patient record. However, they usually allow the worksheet used to collect birth certificate data to be filed in the record.

CONSENT TO ADMISSION

I, _____ , hereby consent to admission to the Alfred State Medical Center and I further consent to such routine hospital care, diagnostic procedures, and medical treatment which the medical and professional staff of the Alfred State Medical Center may deem necessary or advisable. I authorize the use of medical information obtained about me as specified above and the disclosure of such information to my referring physician(s). This form has been fully explained to me, and I understand its contents. I further understand that no guarantees have been made to me as to the results of treatments or examinations done at the Alfred State Medical Center.

_____   _____
Signature of Patient   Date

_____   _____
Signature of Parent/Legal Guardian for Minor   Date

_____
Relationship to Minor

_____   _____
WITNESS: Alfred State Medical Center Staff Member   Date

FIGURE 6-8A Consent to Admission

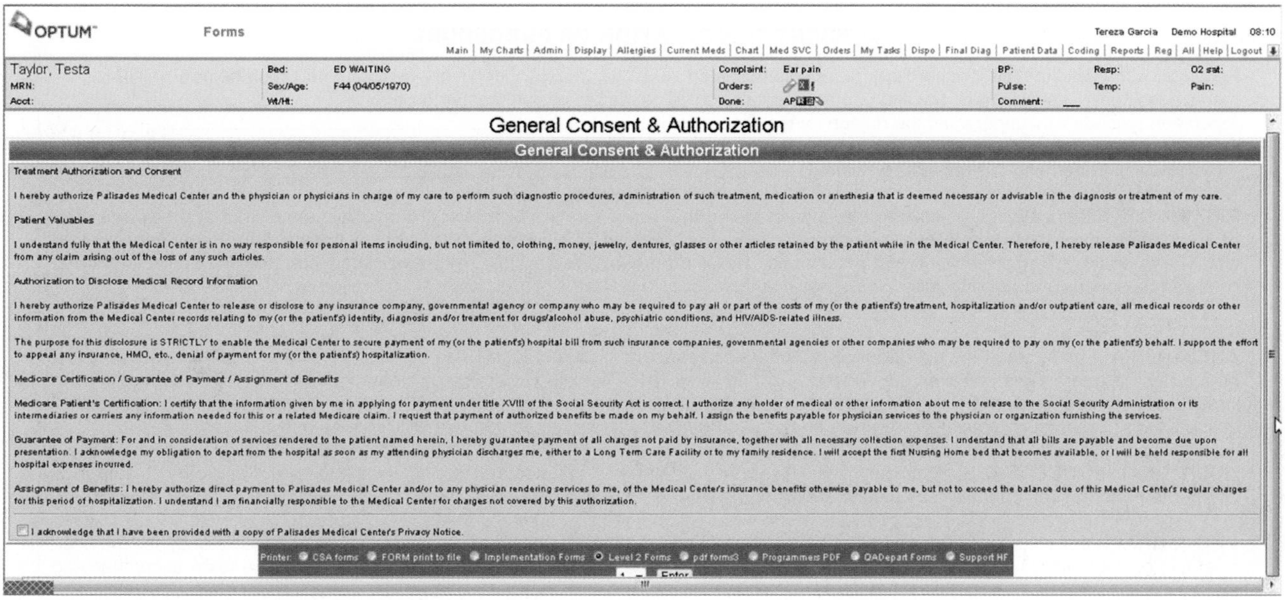

OPTUM™ Forms

Tereza Garcia Demo Hospital 08:10

Main | My Charts | Admin | Display | Allergies | Current Meds | Chart | Med SVC | Orders | My Tasks | Dispo | Final Diag | Patient Data | Coding | Reports | Reg | All | Help | Logout

Taylor, Testa
MRN:
Acct:

Bed: ED WAITING
Sex/Age: F44 (04/05/1970)
Wt/Ht:

Complaint: Ear pain
Orders:
Done: AP

BP: Resp: O2 sat:
Pulse: Temp: Pain:
Comment:

General Consent & Authorization

General Consent & Authorization

Treatment Authorization and Consent

I hereby authorize Palisades Medical Center and the physician or physicians in charge of my care to perform such diagnostic procedures, administration of such treatment, medication or anesthesia that is deemed necessary or advisable in the diagnosis or treatment of my care.

Patient Valuables

I understand fully that the Medical Center is in no way responsible for personal items including, but not limited to, clothing, money, jewelry, dentures, glasses or other articles retained by the patient while in the Medical Center. Therefore, I hereby release Palisades Medical Center from any claim arising out of the loss of any such articles.

Authorization to Disclose Medical Record Information

I hereby authorize Palisades Medical Center to release or disclose to any insurance company, governmental agency or company who may be required to pay all or part of the costs of my (or the patient's) treatment, hospitalization and/or outpatient care, all medical records or other information from the Medical Center records relating to my (or the patient's) identity, diagnosis and/or treatment for drugs/alcohol abuse, psychiatric conditions, and HIV/AIDS-related illness.

The purpose for this disclosure is STRICTLY to enable the Medical Center to secure payment of my (or the patient's) hospital bill from such insurance companies, governmental agencies or other companies who may be required to pay on my (or the patient's) behalf. I support the effort to appeal any insurance, HMO, etc., denial of payment for my (or the patient's) hospitalization.

Medicare Certification / Guarantee of Payment / Assignment of Benefits

Medicare Patient's Certification: I certify that the information given by me in applying for payment under title XVIII of the Social Security Act is correct. I authorize any holder of medical or other information about me to release to the Social Security Administration or its intermediaries or carriers any information needed for this or a related Medicare claim. I request that payment of authorized benefits be made on my behalf. I assign the benefits payable for physician services to the physician or organization furnishing the services.

Guarantee of Payment: For and in consideration of services rendered to the patient named herein, I hereby guarantee payment of all charges not paid by insurance, together with all necessary collection expenses. I understand that all bills are payable and become due upon presentation. I acknowledge my obligation to depart from the hospital as soon as my attending physician discharges me, either to a Long Term Care Facility or to my family residence. I will accept the first Nursing Home bed that becomes available, or I will be held responsible for all hospital expenses incurred.

Assignment of Benefits: I hereby authorize direct payment to Palisades Medical Center and/or to any physician rendering services to me, of the Medical Center's insurance benefits otherwise payable to me, but not to exceed the balance due of this Medical Center's regular charges for this period of hospitalization. I understand I am financially responsible to the Medical Center for charges not covered by this authorization.

☐ I acknowledge that I have been provided with a copy of Palisades Medical Center's Privacy Notice.

Printer: CSA forms FORM print to file Implementation Forms Level 2 Forms pdf forms3 Programmers PDF QADepart Forms Support HF

Enter

FIGURE 6-8B Electronic General Admission Form (Courtesy of Optum™ PM and Physician EMR)

AUTHORIZATION TO RELEASE INFORMATION FOR REIMBURSEMENT PURPOSES

In order to permit reimbursement, upon request, the Alfred State Medical Center (ASMC) may disclose such treatment information pertaining to my hospitalization to any corporation, organization, or agent thereof, which is, or may be liable under contract to the ASMC or to me, or to any of my family members or other person, for payment of all or part of the ASMC's charges for services rendered to me (e.g., the patient's health insurance carrier). I understand that the purpose of any release of information is to facilitate reimbursement for services rendered. In addition, in the event that my health insurance program includes utilization review of services provided during this admission, I authorize ASCM to release information as is necessary to permit the review. This authorization will expire once the reimbursement for services rendered is complete.

Signature of Patient	Date
Signature of Parent/Legal Guardian for Minor	Date
Relationship to Minor	
WITNESS: Alfred State Medical Center Staff Member	Date

FIGURE 6-9 Authorization to Release Information for Reimbursement Purposes

---

CONSENT TO OPERATION OR PROCEDURE

I _____ (patient or guardian), hereby authorize Dr. _____ or his/her designee and such other physicians, medical residents, physicians-in-training or other persons as are needed to assist him/her to perform _____ (operation/procedure). I understand the reason for the procedure is _____ .

Alternatives to performing this procedure include _____ .

RISKS: This authorization is given with the understanding that any operation or procedure involves some risks and hazards. The more common risks include infection, bleeding (including severe loss of blood requiring a blood transfusion), nerve injury, blood clots, heart attack, allergic reactions and pneumonia. These are not all the possible risks associated with this procedure, but these risks can be serious and possibly fatal. *Some significant and substantial risks of this particular operation or procedure include* _____
_____ .

ANESTHESIA: I understand the act of delivering intravenous sedation and analgesia has benefits of relief and protection from pain, but carries no guarantees. Intravenous sedation also involves risks including infection or bleeding from needle sticks, damage to vessels and nerves (including paralysis), pneumonia, seizures, heart attack, stroke, adverse reaction (allergic reaction) and death. I consent to the use of such anesthetics as may be considered necessary by the person responsible for these services.

ADDITIONAL PROCEDURES: If my physician discovers a different, unsuspected condition at the time of surgery, I authorize him/her to perform such treatment, as he/she deems necessary.

PHOTOGRAPHY: I consent to the photographing of operations performed, including appropriate portions of my body for medical, scientific or educational purposes, providing my identity is not revealed by the pictures or by the descriptive texts accompanying them.

TISSUE DISPOSAL: I consent to the examination and disposal by hospital authorities of any tissues or body parts that may be removed.

SOCIAL SECURITY NUMBER: I authorize the disclosure of my social security number to the manufacturer of a medical device implanted during this procedure and for which tracking is required by the FDA under the Safe Medical Device Act.

Documenting the social security number (SSN) in a consent form links documentation to a patient. The use of the SSN as a patient identifier has been discontinued in most facilities.

BLOOD TRANSFUSIONS: It has been explained to me that I may need a blood transfusion to promote recovery, stabilize my condition or save my life. I understand in general what a transfusion is, the procedures that will be used and that there is a small but definite risk of potentially serious infectious disease transmission and/or other reactions, including, but not limited to, hepatitis, acquired immune deficiency syndrome (AIDS), fever, chills, hives, the destruction of transfused cells, immunization, bacterial infections or rarely death. I understand steps to safeguard the blood supply include: volunteer donations, donor questioning about health history/risk factors and testing blood, although no process or testing is 100% reliable. My physician will decide the amount and type of blood product needed based on my particular needs. Options/alternatives to receiving blood from the community supply for elective transfusions include autologous donation (pre-donation of my own blood), directed donation (blood donated by my family/ friends), autotransfusion (my own blood lost during surgery, processed and reinfused). Benefits/risks of transfusion and the consequences of refusal that include seriously jeopardizing my health or resulting in death have been explained to me by my physician.

_____ (initials) I consent to a blood transfusion if my physician determines it is needed.
_____ (initials) I **DO NOT** consent to a blood transfusion and I assume all risks and hazards that may occur due to this refusal to consent.

NO GUARANTEE: I understand that no guarantee or assurance has been made as to the results of the procedure and it may not cure the condition.

PATIENT'S CONSENT: I have read and fully understand this consent form. I understand I should not sign this form if all items, including my questions, have not been explained or answered to my satisfaction, or if I do not understand any of the terms or words contained in this consent form. I understand that I can withdraw this consent to the operation/procedure at any time before the beginning of the procedure/operation. Do NOT sign unless you have read and thoroughly understand this form.

_____   _____   _____
Patient/Responsible Party Signature (state relationship)   Date/Time   Witness Signature

PHYSICIAN DECLARATION: I have explained to the patient/patient's representative the procedure/operation and the risks, benefits, recuperation and alternatives (including the probable or likely consequences if no treatment is pursued). I have answered all of the patient's questions and to the best of my knowledge, I believe the patient has been adequately informed.

_____
Physician Signature

FIGURE 6-10 Consent to Surgery

Addressograph

PATIENT PROPERTY RECORD

I understand that while the facility will be responsible for items deposited in the safe, I must be responsible for all items retained by me at the bedside. (Dentures kept at the bedside will be labeled, but the facility cannot assure responsibility for them.) I also recognize that the hospital cannot be held responsible for items brought in to me after this form has been completed and signed.

Signature of Patient   Date

Signature of Witness   Date

I have no money or valuables that I wish to deposit for safekeeping. I do not hold the facility responsible for any other money or valuables that I am retaining or will have brought in to me. I have been advised that it is recommended that I retain no more than $5.00 at the bedside.

Signature of Patient   Date

Signature of Witness   Date

I have deposited valuables in the facility safe. The envelope number is _____.

Signature of Patient   Date

Signature of Person Accepting Property   Date

I understand that medications I have brought to the facility will be handled as recommended by my physician. This may include storage, disposal, or administration.

Signature of Patient   Date

Signature of Witness   Date

ALFRED STATE MEDICAL CENTER ■ 100 MAIN ST, ALFRED NY 14802 ■ (607) 555-1234

FIGURE 6-11A Patient Property Record

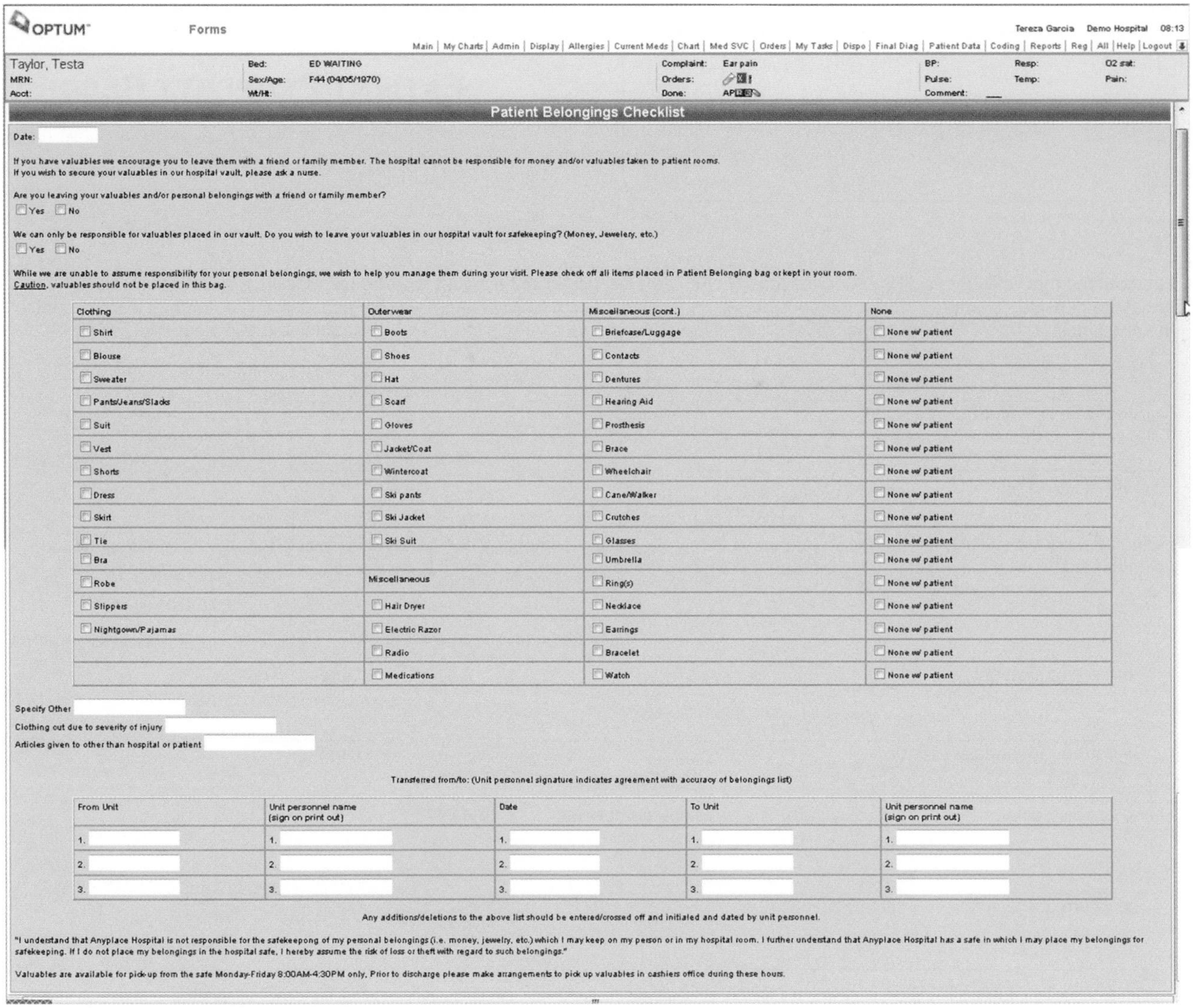

OPTUM Forms

Tereza Garcia Demo Hospital 08:13

Main | My Charts | Admin | Display | Allergies | Current Meds | Chart | Med SVC | Orders | My Tasks | Dispo | Final Diag | Patient Data | Coding | Reports | Reg | All | Help | Logout

Taylor, Testa
MRN:
Acct:

Bed: ED WAITING
Sex/Age: F44 (04/05/1970)
Wt/Ht:

Complaint: Ear pain
Orders:
Done: AP

BP: Resp: O2 sat:
Pulse: Temp: Pain:
Comment:

Patient Belongings Checklist

Date:

If you have valuables we encourage you to leave them with a friend or family member. The hospital cannot be responsible for money and/or valuables taken to patient rooms.
If you wish to secure your valuables in our hospital vault, please ask a nurse.

Are you leaving your valuables and/or personal belongings with a friend or family member?
☐ Yes ☐ No

We can only be responsible for valuables placed in our vault. Do you wish to leave your valuables in our hospital vault for safekeeping? (Money, Jewelery, etc.)
☐ Yes ☐ No

While we are unable to assume responsibility for your personal belongings, we wish to help you manage them during your visit. Please check off all items placed in Patient Belonging bag or kept in your room.
Caution, valuables should not be placed in this bag.

Clothing	Outerwear	Miscellaneous (cont.)	None
☐ Shirt	☐ Boots	☐ Briefcase/Luggage	☐ None w/ patient
☐ Blouse	☐ Shoes	☐ Contacts	☐ None w/ patient
☐ Sweater	☐ Hat	☐ Dentures	☐ None w/ patient
☐ Pants/Jeans/Slacks	☐ Scarf	☐ Hearing Aid	☐ None w/ patient
☐ Suit	☐ Gloves	☐ Prosthesis	☐ None w/ patient
☐ Vest	☐ Jacket/Coat	☐ Brace	☐ None w/ patient
☐ Shorts	☐ Wintercoat	☐ Wheelchair	☐ None w/ patient
☐ Dress	☐ Ski pants	☐ Cane/Walker	☐ None w/ patient
☐ Skirt	☐ Ski Jacket	☐ Crutches	☐ None w/ patient
☐ Tie	☐ Ski Suit	☐ Glasses	☐ None w/ patient
☐ Bra		☐ Umbrella	☐ None w/ patient
☐ Robe	Miscellaneous	☐ Ring(s)	☐ None w/ patient
☐ Slippers	☐ Hair Dryer	☐ Necklace	☐ None w/ patient
☐ Nightgown/Pajamas	☐ Electric Razor	☐ Earrings	☐ None w/ patient
	☐ Radio	☐ Bracelet	☐ None w/ patient
	☐ Medications	☐ Watch	☐ None w/ patient

Specify Other
Clothing cut due to severity of injury
Articles given to other than hospital or patient

Transferred from/to: (Unit personnel signature indicates agreement with accuracy of belongings list)

From Unit	Unit personnel name (sign on print out)	Date	To Unit	Unit personnel name (sign on print out)
1.	1.	1.	1.	1.
2.	2.	2.	2.	2.
3.	3.	3.	3.	3.

Any additions/deletions to the above list should be entered/crossed off and initialed and dated by unit personnel.

"I understand that Anyplace Hospital is not responsible for the safekeepong of my personal belongings (i.e. money, jewelry, etc.) which I may keep on my person or in my hospital room. I further understand that Anyplace Hospital has a safe in which I may place my belongings for safekeeping. If I do not place my belongings in the hospital safe, I hereby assume the risk of loss or theft with regard to such belongings."

Valuables are available for pick-up from the safe Monday-Friday 8:00AM-4:30PM only, Prior to discharge please make arrangements to pick up valuables in cashiers office during these hours.

FIGURE 6-11B Electronic Patient Property Record (Courtesy of Optum™ PM and Physician EMR)

Certificate of Death

The certificate of death (or death certificate) (Figure 6-13) contains a record of information regarding the decedent, his or her family, cause of death, and the disposition of the body. The NCHS also developed a standard certificate of death, which states can adopt for their use. The death certificate, signed by a physician, is filed with the state department of health's office of vital statistics (or records, depending on the title of the state agency), usually within five days. While each state develops its own death certificate, in general it contains the following information:

- Name of deceased
- Deceased's date and place of birth
- Usual residence of deceased at time of death
- Cause of death
- Deceased's place of burial
- Names and birth places of both parents
- Name of informant (usually a relative)
- Name of doctor
- Method and place of disposition of body
- Signature of funeral director
- Signature of certifying physician

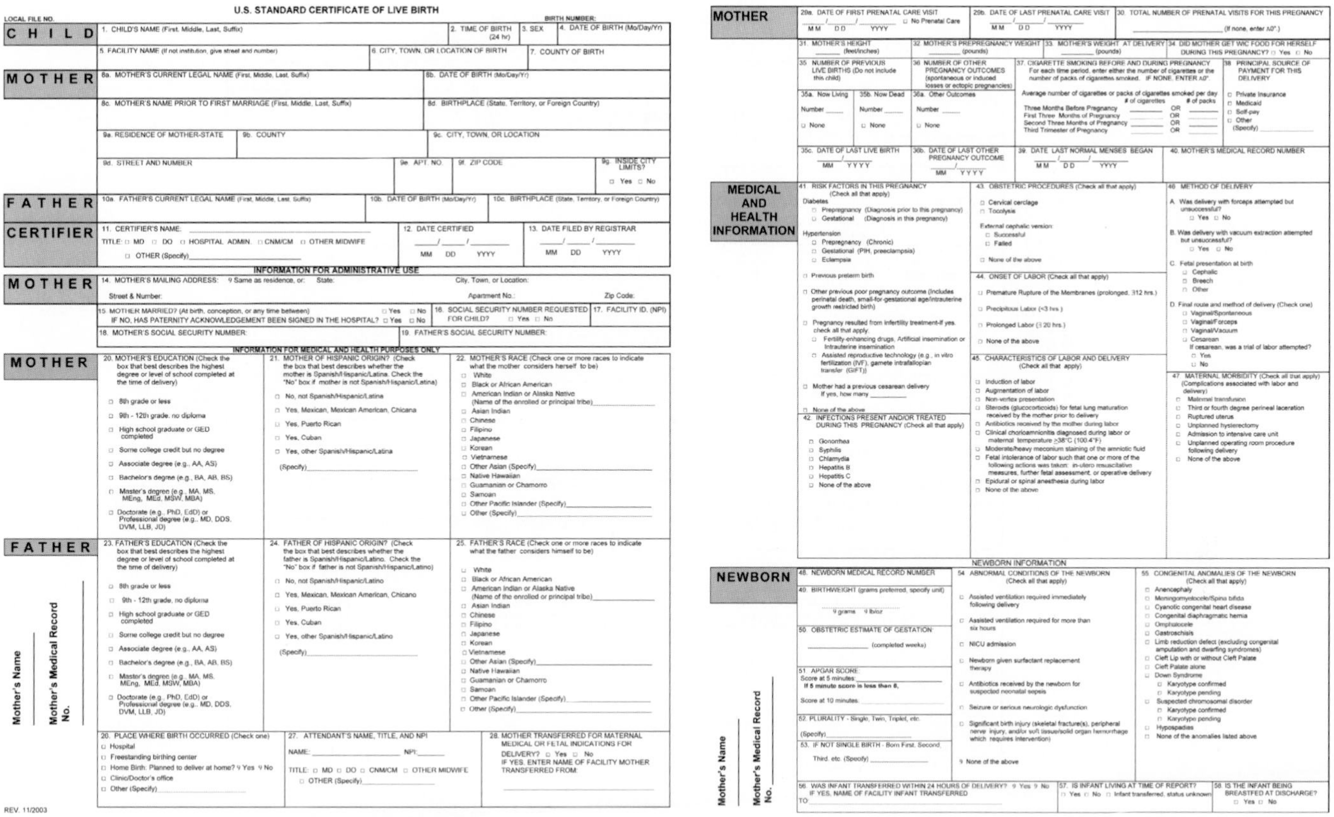
U.S. STANDARD CERTIFICATE OF LIVE BIRTH

LOCAL FILE NO. BIRTH NUMBER:

CHILD: 1. CHILD'S NAME (First, Middle, Last, Suffix); 2. TIME OF BIRTH (24 hr); 3. SEX; 4. DATE OF BIRTH (Mo/Day/Yr); 5. FACILITY NAME (If not institution, give street and number); 6. CITY, TOWN, OR LOCATION OF BIRTH; 7. COUNTY OF BIRTH

MOTHER: 8a. MOTHER'S CURRENT LEGAL NAME (First, Middle, Last, Suffix); 8b. DATE OF BIRTH (Mo/Day/Yr); 8c. MOTHER'S NAME PRIOR TO FIRST MARRIAGE (First, Middle, Last, Suffix); 8d. BIRTHPLACE (State, Territory, or Foreign Country); 9a. RESIDENCE OF MOTHER-STATE; 9b. COUNTY; 9c. CITY, TOWN, OR LOCATION; 9d. STREET AND NUMBER; 9e. APT. NO.; 9f. ZIP CODE; 9g. INSIDE CITY LIMITS? □ Yes □ No

FATHER: 10a. FATHER'S CURRENT LEGAL NAME (First, Middle, Last, Suffix); 10b. DATE OF BIRTH (Mo/Day/Yr); 10c. BIRTHPLACE (State, Territory, or Foreign Country)

CERTIFIER: 11. CERTIFIER'S NAME; TITLE: □ MD □ DO □ HOSPITAL ADMIN. □ CNM/CM □ OTHER MIDWIFE □ OTHER (Specify); 12. DATE CERTIFIED; 13. DATE FILED BY REGISTRAR

INFORMATION FOR ADMINISTRATIVE USE

MOTHER: 14. MOTHER'S MAILING ADDRESS; 15. MOTHER MARRIED? (At birth, conception, or any time between) □ Yes □ No; IF NO, HAS PATERNITY ACKNOWLEDGEMENT BEEN SIGNED IN THE HOSPITAL? □ Yes □ No; 16. SOCIAL SECURITY NUMBER REQUESTED FOR CHILD? □ Yes □ No; 17. FACILITY ID. (NPI); 18. MOTHER'S SOCIAL SECURITY NUMBER; 19. FATHER'S SOCIAL SECURITY NUMBER

INFORMATION FOR MEDICAL AND HEALTH PURPOSES ONLY

MOTHER: 20. MOTHER'S EDUCATION; 21. MOTHER OF HISPANIC ORIGIN?; 22. MOTHER'S RACE

FATHER: 23. FATHER'S EDUCATION; 24. FATHER OF HISPANIC ORIGIN?; 25. FATHER'S RACE

26. PLACE WHERE BIRTH OCCURRED; 27. ATTENDANT'S NAME, TITLE, AND NPI; 28. MOTHER TRANSFERRED FOR MATERNAL MEDICAL OR FETAL INDICATIONS FOR DELIVERY?

MOTHER: 29a. DATE OF FIRST PRENATAL CARE VISIT; 29b. DATE OF LAST PRENATAL CARE VISIT; 30. TOTAL NUMBER OF PRENATAL VISITS FOR THIS PREGNANCY; 31. MOTHER'S HEIGHT; 32. MOTHER'S PREPREGNANCY WEIGHT; 33. MOTHER'S WEIGHT AT DELIVERY; 34. DID MOTHER GET WIC FOOD FOR HERSELF DURING THIS PREGNANCY?; 35. NUMBER OF PREVIOUS LIVE BIRTHS; 36. NUMBER OF OTHER PREGNANCY OUTCOMES; 37. CIGARETTE SMOKING BEFORE AND DURING PREGNANCY; 38. PRINCIPAL SOURCE OF PAYMENT FOR THIS DELIVERY; 39. DATE LAST NORMAL MENSES BEGAN; 40. MOTHER'S MEDICAL RECORD NUMBER

MEDICAL AND HEALTH INFORMATION: 41. RISK FACTORS IN THIS PREGNANCY; 42. INFECTIONS PRESENT AND/OR TREATED DURING THIS PREGNANCY; 43. OBSTETRIC PROCEDURES; 44. ONSET OF LABOR; 45. CHARACTERISTICS OF LABOR AND DELIVERY; 46. METHOD OF DELIVERY; 47. MATERNAL MORBIDITY

NEWBORN INFORMATION

NEWBORN: 48. NEWBORN MEDICAL RECORD NUMBER; 49. BIRTHWEIGHT; 50. OBSTETRIC ESTIMATE OF GESTATION; 51. APGAR SCORE; 52. PLURALITY; 53. IF NOT SINGLE BIRTH; 54. ABNORMAL CONDITIONS OF THE NEWBORN; 55. CONGENITAL ANOMALIES OF THE NEWBORN; 56. WAS INFANT TRANSFERRED WITHIN 24 HOURS OF DELIVERY?; 57. IS INFANT LIVING AT TIME OF REPORT?; 58. IS THE INFANT BEING BREASTFED AT DISCHARGE?

Mother's Name; Mother's Medical Record No.

REV. 11/2003

FIGURE 6-12 Standard Birth Certificate (Department of Health and Human Services, hhs.gov.)

EXERCISE 6–2 Hospital Inpatient Record—Administrative Data

Matching: For each data element, state whether it represents clinical (C), financial (F), or patient identification (I).

____ 1. First-listed diagnosis

____ 2. Patient name

____ 3. Insurance policy number

____ 4. Patient medical record number

____ 5. Admitting diagnosis

____ 6. Patient address

True/False: Indicate whether each statement is true (T) or false (F).

____ 7. A health care proxy is a legal document a patient uses to name someone to make health care decisions in the event the patient becomes incapacitated.

____ 8. A death certificate, signed by a physician, is filed with the NCHS, usually within five days.

____ 9. The identification and financial sections of the face sheet are completed by the admitting nurse when the patient arrives on the nursing unit.

____ 10. The NCHS has developed a standard certificate of birth that states must adopt for their use.

____ 11. Upon admission, all patient records must contain documentation as to whether an individual has executed an advance directive.

HOSPITAL INPATIENT RECORD—CLINICAL DATA

Clinical data includes all health care information obtained about a patient's care and treatment, which is documented on numerous forms in the patient record. For inpatients, the first clinical data item is the admitting diagnosis that is entered on the face sheet. Sometimes, a patient is admitted through the emergency department (ED), and the first clinical data item is the chief complaint recorded as part of the ED record.

U.S. STANDARD CERTIFICATE OF DEATH

LOCAL FILE NO.   STATE FILE NO.

NAME OF DECEDENT
For use by physician or institution

To Be Completed/Verified By: FUNERAL DIRECTOR

1. DECEDENT'S LEGAL NAME (Include AKA's if any) (First, Middle, Last) | 2. SEX | 3. SOCIAL SECURITY NUMBER

4a. AGE-Last Birthday (Years) | 4b. UNDER 1 YEAR — Months / Days | 4c. UNDER 1 DAY — Hours / Minutes | 5. DATE OF BIRTH (Mo/Day/Yr) | 6. BIRTHPLACE (City and State or Foreign Country)

7a. RESIDENCE-STATE | 7b. COUNTY | 7c. CITY OR TOWN

7d. STREET AND NUMBER | 7e. APT. NO. | 7f. ZIP CODE | 7g. INSIDE CITY LIMITS? Yes No

8. EVER IN US ARMED FORCES? Yes No | 9. MARITAL STATUS AT TIME OF DEATH — Married / Married, but separated / Widowed / Divorced / Never Married / Unknown | 10. SURVIVING SPOUSE'S NAME (If wife, give name prior to first marriage)

11. FATHER'S NAME (First, Middle, Last) | 12. MOTHER'S NAME PRIOR TO FIRST MARRIAGE (First, Middle, Last)

13a. INFORMANT'S NAME | 13b. RELATIONSHIP TO DECEDENT | 13c. MAILING ADDRESS (Street and Number, City, State, Zip Code)

14. PLACE OF DEATH (Check only one: see instructions)

IF DEATH OCCURRED IN A HOSPITAL: Inpatient / Emergency Room/Outpatient / Dead on Arrival | IF DEATH OCCURRED SOMEWHERE OTHER THAN A HOSPITAL: Hospice facility / Nursing home/Long term care facility / Decedent's home / Other (Specify):

15. FACILITY NAME (If not institution, give street & number) | 16. CITY OR TOWN, STATE, AND ZIP CODE | 17. COUNTY OF DEATH

18. METHOD OF DISPOSITION: Burial / Cremation / Donation / Entombment / Removal from State / Other (Specify): | 19. PLACE OF DISPOSITION (Name of cemetery, crematory, other place)

20. LOCATION-CITY, TOWN, AND STATE | 21. NAME AND COMPLETE ADDRESS OF FUNERAL FACILITY

22. SIGNATURE OF FUNERAL SERVICE LICENSEE OR OTHER AGENT | 23. LICENSE NUMBER (Of Licensee)

ITEMS 24-28 MUST BE COMPLETED BY PERSON WHO PRONOUNCES OR CERTIFIES DEATH | 24. DATE PRONOUNCED DEAD (Mo/Day/Yr) | 25. TIME PRONOUNCED DEAD

26. SIGNATURE OF PERSON PRONOUNCING DEATH (Only when applicable) | 27. LICENSE NUMBER | 28. DATE SIGNED (Mo/Day/Yr)

29. ACTUAL OR PRESUMED DATE OF DEATH (Mo/Day/Yr) (Spell Month) | 30. ACTUAL OR PRESUMED TIME OF DEATH | 31. WAS MEDICAL EXAMINER OR CORONER CONTACTED? Yes No

To Be Completed By: MEDICAL CERTIFIER

CAUSE OF DEATH (See instructions and examples) | Approximate interval: Onset to death

32. PART I. Enter the chain of events–diseases, injuries, or complications–that directly caused the death. DO NOT enter terminal events such as cardiac arrest, respiratory arrest, or ventricular fibrillation without showing the etiology. DO NOT ABBREVIATE. Enter only one cause on a line. Add additional lines if necessary.

IMMEDIATE CAUSE (Final disease or condition ------> resulting in death)   a._____
Due to (or as a consequence of):

Sequentially list conditions, if any, leading to the cause listed on line a. Enter the UNDERLYING CAUSE (disease or injury that initiated the events resulting in death) LAST   b._____
Due to (or as a consequence of):

c._____
Due to (or as a consequence of):

d._____

PART II. Enter other significant conditions contributing to death but not resulting in the underlying cause given in PART I. | 33. WAS AN AUTOPSY PERFORMED? Yes No | 34. WERE AUTOPSY FINDINGS AVAILABLE TO COMPLETE THE CAUSE OF DEATH? Yes No

35. DID TOBACCO USE CONTRIBUTE TO DEATH? Yes / Probably / No / Unknown | 36. IF FEMALE: Not pregnant within past year / Pregnant at time of death / Not pregnant, but pregnant within 42 days of death / Not pregnant, but pregnant 43 days to 1 year before death / Unknown if pregnant within the past year | 37. MANNER OF DEATH: Natural / Homicide / Accident / Pending Investigation / Suicide / Could not be determined

38. DATE OF INJURY (Mo/Day/Yr) (Spell Month) | 39. TIME OF INJURY | 40. PLACE OF INJURY (e.g., Decedent's home; construction site; restaurant; wooded area) | 41. INJURY AT WORK? Yes No

42. LOCATION OF INJURY: State: | City or Town: | Street & Number: | Apartment No.: | Zip Code:

43. DESCRIBE HOW INJURY OCCURRED: | 44. IF TRANSPORTATION INJURY, SPECIFY: Driver/Operator / Passenger / Pedestrian / Other (Specify)

45. CERTIFIER (Check only one):

Certifying physician-To the best of my knowledge, death occurred due to the cause(s) and manner stated.
Pronouncing & Certifying physician-To the best of my knowledge, death occurred at the time, date, and place, and due to the cause(s) and manner stated.
Medical Examiner/Coroner-On the basis of examination, and/or investigation, in my opinion, death occurred at the time, date, and place, and due to the cause(s) and manner stated.

Signature of certifier:_____

46. NAME, ADDRESS, AND ZIP CODE OF PERSON COMPLETING CAUSE OF DEATH (Item 32)

47. TITLE OF CERTIFIER | 48. LICENSE NUMBER | 49. DATE CERTIFIED (Mo/Day/Yr) | 50. FOR REGISTRAR ONLY- DATE FILED (Mo/Day/Yr)

To Be Completed By: FUNERAL DIRECTOR

51. DECEDENT'S EDUCATION-Check the box that best describes the highest degree or level of school completed at the time of death.

8th grade or less
9th - 12th grade; no diploma
High school graduate or GED completed
Some college credit, but no degree
Associate degree (e.g., AA, AS)
Bachelor's degree (e.g., BA, AB, BS)
Master's degree (e.g., MA, MS, MEng, MEd, MSW, MBA)
Doctorate (e.g., PhD, EdD) or Professional degree (e.g., MD, DDS, DVM, LLB, JD)

52. DECEDENT OF HISPANIC ORIGIN? Check the box that best describes whether the decedent is Spanish/Hispanic/Latino. Check the "No" box if decedent is not Spanish/Hispanic/Latino.

No, not Spanish/Hispanic/Latino
Yes, Mexican, Mexican American, Chicano
Yes, Puerto Rican
Yes, Cuban
Yes, other Spanish/Hispanic/Latino (Specify) _____

53. DECEDENT'S RACE (Check one or more races to indicate what the decedent considered himself or herself to be)

White
Black or African American
American Indian or Alaska Native (Name of the enrolled or principal tribe) _____
Asian Indian
Chinese
Filipino
Japanese
Korean
Vietnamese
Other Asian (Specify) _____
Native Hawaiian
Guamanian or Chamorro
Samoan
Other Pacific Islander (Specify) _____
Other (Specify) _____

54. DECEDENT'S USUAL OCCUPATION (Indicate type of work done during most of working life. DO NOT USE RETIRED).

55. KIND OF BUSINESS/INDUSTRY

FIGURE 6-13 Standard Death Certificate (Department of Health and Human Services, hhs.gov.)

Emergency Record

The Joint Commission standards outline the following documentation requirements in the emergency department record: time and means of arrival, whether the patient left against medical advice (AMA), and conclusion at termination of treatment, including final disposition, condition at discharge, and instructions for follow-up. The Joint Commission standards require that pertinent inpatient and ambulatory care patient records (including emergency records) be made available upon request by the attending physician or other authorized individuals. The emergency record is to be authenticated by the practitioner responsible for its clinical accuracy. To ensure continuity of care, The Joint Commission standards also state that a copy of the emergency record should be sent to the provider who administers follow-up care (if authorized by the patient or legal representative).

The emergency record (Figure 6-14A) documents the evaluation and treatment of patients seen in the facility's emergency department (ED) for immediate treatment urgent medical conditions or traumatic injuries. The record includes documentation of the immediate assessment and treatment of patients, reason for the patient's disposition (whether admitted, discharged, or transferred), and a copy of the discharge instructions provided to the patient (Figure 6-14B). Some patients are transported to the ED via ambulance, and an ambulance report is generated by emergency medical technicians (EMTs) to document clinical information such as vital signs, level of consciousness, appearance of the patient, and so on. Figure 6-15A represents a paper-based ambulance report while Figure 6-15B represents a screen from an electronic health record that would capture similar information. A copy of the ambulance report is placed on the ED record. (The original ambulance report is the property of the ambulance company.)

Anti-dumping legislation (Emergency Medical Treatment and Labor Act, EMTALA) prevents facilities licensed to provide emergency services from transferring patients who are unable to pay to other institutions, and it requires that a patient's condition must be stabilized prior to transfer (unless the patient requests transfer).

Example 1
A woman in active labor cannot be transferred to another facility due to inability to pay for care.

Example 2
If permanent disability or death would result from delayed treatment, a patient cannot be transferred to another facility due to inability to pay.

Contents of an emergency record include:

- Patient identification
- Time and means of arrival at the emergency department

Example Patient transported via ambulance.

- Pertinent history of illness or injury

Example Patient pulled Foley catheter out at nursing home. He was unable to void the next morning and started running a very high fever (105 degrees). He was brought to the ED for evaluation.

- Physical findings, including vital signs

Example Skin warm and moist. Fever of 104.9 degrees at present. Color pale. Pulse 112. Respirations 32. BP 110/50.

- Emergency care provided prior to arrival

Example Patient received IV D5NSS 200 mL/hr. Kefzol 1 gram IV stat.

- Diagnostic and therapeutic orders

Example Chest x-rays. CBC. Foley catheter insertion. Urinalysis. Electrolytes. BUN.

- Clinical observations, including results of treatment

Example Foley catheter insertion attempted, which failed. Consult with Dr. Bellinger, who was able to insert Foley without significant difficulty. Dr. Bellinger evaluated the patient and did not feel further treatment was necessary.

- Reports of procedures, tests, and results

Example Chest x-ray negative. CBC revealed WBC 10.6, Hgb 12.3, Hct 36.3. UA revealed 3+ WBC and 3+ gram-negative rods. Blood chemistry test revealed bilirubin (direct) 1.1, bilirubin (total) 1.8, and albumin 5.6. BUN negative.

- Diagnostic impression

Example Diagnosis: Urinary tract infection.

- Conclusion at termination of evaluation/treatment, including final disposition, patient's condition, instructions given to the patient, and physician's signature

Example Patient admitted to hospital for treatment (Kefzol 1 gram every 6 hours).

Alfred State Medical Center
Emergency Department Record

PATIENT NAME		M.R. #

BIRTH DATE	MARITAL STATUS	GENDER	RACE

DATE	TIME IN	LOG #	PATIENT ADDRESS: STREET, CITY, STATE, ZIP CODE	HOME PHONE #

NEXT OF KIN	NEXT OF KIN ADDRESS: STREET, CITY, STATE, ZIP CODE	NEXT OF KIN PHONE #

REFERRING PHYSICIAN	PRIMARY PAYER	POLICY #	SECONDARY PAYER	POLICY 3

ACCIDENT DATE & TIME	PRIMARY PHYSICIAN	PRIMARY PHYSICIAN PHONE #	LAST ED VISIT/LOG #	LAST HOSPITAL DISCHARGE

BP	P	R	T: PO/TM/R	WT	FAMILY ☐ PRESENT ☐ EN ROUTE ☐ UNKNOWN	MEANS OF ARRIVAL

CHIEF COMPLAINT:

☐ CARDIAC MONITOR
☐ GLUCOSE _____
☐ NG/OG _____
☐ FOLEY _____
☐ O2 SAT @ _____
☐ O2 @ _____
☐ IV ☐ SALINE LOCK
☐ IV FLUID _____

ASSESSED NEEDS:

NUTRITION	Y N
SUBST ABUSE	Y N
SAFETY	Y N
VALUES/BELIEFS	Y N
PAIN	Y N
DAILY FUNCITON	Y N
SOCIAL WORKER	Y N

LAB TESTS
☐ WBC
☐ HGB
☐ HCT
☐ PLTS
☐ DIFF
☐ GLU
☐ NA
☐ K
☐ CL
☐ CO2
☐ BUN
☐ CR
☐ MG
☐ PHOS
☐ CK-MB
☐ TROPONIN
☐ AMY
☐ BILI
☐ LIPASE
☐ LFTs
☐ PT / PTT
☐ INR
☐ HCG URINE
☐ ETOH
☐ TRAUMA LAB
☐ T & S
☐ T&C x ____ UNITS
☐ pH
☐ PCO2
☐ PO2
☐ UA SENT / SAVED
☐ C&S: URINE/BLOOD
☐ _____
☐ _____
☐ _____
☐ ECG

ALLERGIES: ☐ DENIES   CURRENT MEDICATIONS: ☐ DENIES   PAST MEDICAL HX:

LMP: LAST TETANUS: IMMUNIZATIONS:

MEDICATIONS / DIAGNOSTIC / TREATMENT ORDERS

TIME	ORDER	ORDERED BY	TIME / GIVEN BY

TETANUS (TD) 0.5 ml   IM   SITE:
MANUF: LOT #:   EXP. DATE:

X-RAYS ORDERED
☐ CHEST
☐ ABDOMEN
☐ WRIST L / R
☐ HAND L / R
☐ FOOT L / R
☐ ANKLE L / R
☐ HIP/PELVIS L / R
☐ CT HEAD
☐ CT ABDOMEN
☐ C-SPINE ☐ L-SPINE
☐ T-SPINE
☐ TRAUMA SERIES
☐ ULTRASOUND
☐ OTHER _____

DISCHARGE DIAGNOSES & PLAN

1.
2.
3.

ECG & X-RAY RESULTS:

PRIMARY PHYSICIAN NAME	☐ FOLLOW-UP	☐ CONTACTED	TIME OF DISCHARGE

DISPOSITION	☐ HOME	☐ JAIL	☐ NSG FAC	☐ AMA	CONDITION ON DISCHARGE:	☐ IMPROVED ☐ STABLE
TRANSFER	☐ HOSPITAL	☐ REHAB	☐ PSYCH			☐ GUARDED ☐ EXPIRED

☐ CONSULT SERVICE	CONSULTING PHYSICIAN	TIME CALLED	TIME ARRIVED
☐ ADMIT SERVICE	MONITOR ☐ YES ☐ NO	ADMITTING PHYSICIAN	INPATIENT UNIT	TIME ADMISSION PROCESSED

NURSE PRACTITIONER	EMERGENCY DEPARTMENT PHYSICIAN

FIGURE 6-14A Emergency Department Record

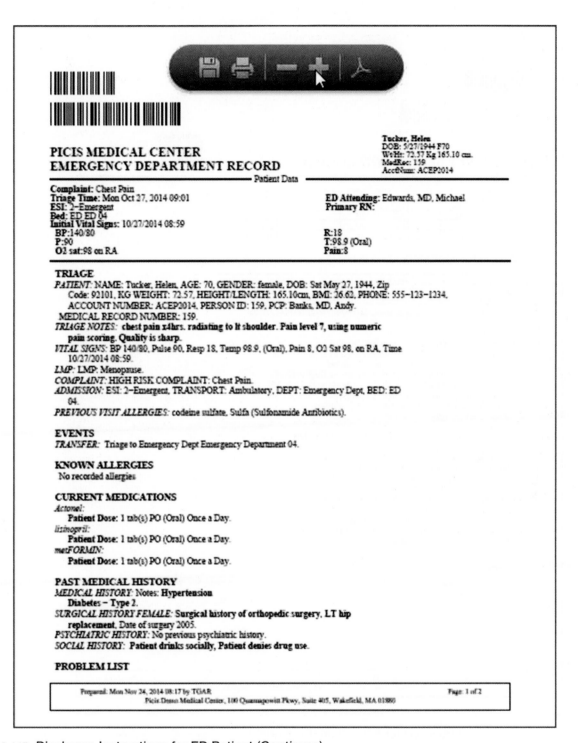

PICIS MEDICAL CENTER
EMERGENCY DEPARTMENT RECORD

Tucker, Helen
DOB: 5/27/1944 F70
Wt/Ht: 72.57 Kg 165.10 cm.
MedRec: 159
Acc#Num: ACEP2014

─────────────────── Patient Data ───────────────────

Complaint: Chest Pain
Triage Time: Mon Oct 27, 2014 09:01
ESI: 2–Emergent
Bed: ED ED 04
Initial Vital Signs: 10/27/2014 08:59
  BP:140/80
  P:90
  O2 sat:98 on RA

ED Attending: Edwards, MD, Michael
Primary RN:

R:18
T:98.9 (Oral)
Pain:8

TRIAGE
PATIENT: NAME: Tucker, Helen, AGE: 70, GENDER: female, DOB: Sat May 27, 1944, Zip
  Code: 92101, KG WEIGHT: 72.57, HEIGHT/LENGTH: 165.10cm, BMI: 26.62, PHONE: 555–123–1234,
  ACCOUNT NUMBER: ACEP2014, PERSON ID: 159, PCP: Banks, MD, Andy.
  MEDICAL RECORD NUMBER: 159.
TRIAGE NOTES: chest pain x4hrs. radiating to lt shoulder. Pain level 7, using numeric
  pain scoring. Quality is sharp.
VITAL SIGNS: BP 140/80, Pulse 90, Resp 18, Temp 98.9, (Oral), Pain 8, O2 Sat 98, on RA, Time
  10/27/2014 08:59.
LMP: LMP: Menopause.
COMPLAINT: HIGH RISK COMPLAINT: Chest Pain.
ADMISSION: ESI: 2–Emergent, TRANSPORT: Ambulatory, DEPT: Emergency Dept, BED: ED
  04.
PREVIOUS VISIT ALLERGIES: codeine sulfate, Sulfa (Sulfonamide Antibiotics).

EVENTS
TRANSFER: Triage to Emergency Dept Emergency Department 04.

KNOWN ALLERGIES
  No recorded allergies

CURRENT MEDICATIONS
Actonel:
  Patient Dose: 1 tab(s) PO (Oral) Once a Day.
lisinopril:
  Patient Dose: 1 tab(s) PO (Oral) Once a Day.
metFORMIN:
  Patient Dose: 1 tab(s) PO (Oral) Once a Day.

PAST MEDICAL HISTORY
MEDICAL HISTORY: Notes: Hypertension
  Diabetes – Type 2.
SURGICAL HISTORY FEMALE: Surgical history of orthopedic surgery, LT hip
  replacement, Date of surgery 2005.
PSYCHIATRIC HISTORY: No previous psychiatric history.
SOCIAL HISTORY: Patient drinks socially, Patient denies drug use.

PROBLEM LIST

FIGURE 6-14B Discharge Instructions for ED Patient (*Continues*)   (Courtesy of Optum™ PM and Physician EMR)

PICIS MEDICAL CENTER
EMERGENCY DEPARTMENT RECORD

Tucker, Helen
DOB: 5/27/1944 F70
WtHt: 72.57 Kg 165.10 cm.
MedRec: 159
AcctNum: ACEP2014

Problem Name	Status	Date Diagnosed	Date Resolved	Confirm Status
DMII wo cmp nt st uncntr		Tue Jan 20, 2000		Unconfirmed
Depressive disorder NEC		Wed Feb 01, 2012		Unconfirmed
Hypertension NOS		Mon Oct 11, 2004		Unconfirmed
OSTEOPOROSIS		Mon Feb 09, 2009		Unconfirmed

MEDICATION ADMINISTRATION SUMMARY

Drug Name	Dose Ordered	Route	Status	Time
*nitroglycerin sublingual	0.4 mg	Sublingual	Ordered	09:09 10/27/2014
sodium chloride 0.9 % intravenous	150 mL/hr	Intravenous Fluid	Ordered	09:09 10/27/2014

*Additional information available in notes. Detailed record available in Medication Service section.

ORDERS

Call Cardiologist: Ordered for: Edwards, MD, Michael
    Status: Done by: Edwards, MD, Michael – Mon Oct 27, 2014 09:10.
Cardiac Monitor:* Ordered for: Edwards, MD, Michael
    Status: Done by: Edwards, MD, Michael – Mon Oct 27, 2014 09:10.
CBC, AUTOMATED (PLATELET & DIFF):* Ordered for: Edwards, MD, Michael
    Status: Done by: System – Mon Oct 27, 2014 09:10.
CHEST PORTABLE:* Ordered for: Edwards, MD, Michael
    Status: Done by: System – Mon Oct 27, 2014 09:08
    Reason: Chest Pain.
CPK MB QUANTITATIVE:* Ordered for: Edwards, MD, Michael
    Status: Done by: System – Mon Oct 27, 2014 09:10.
FULL EKG–ED ONLY:* Ordered for: Edwards, MD, Michael
    Status: Done by: System – Mon Oct 27, 2014 09:10.
IV Saline Lock:* Ordered for: Edwards, MD, Michael
    Status: Done by: Edwards, MD, Michael – Mon Oct 27, 2014 09:10.
METABOLIC PANEL, BASIC:* Ordered for: Edwards, MD, Michael
    Status: Done by: System – Mon Oct 27, 2014 09:10.
Oxygen >>:* Ordered for: Edwards, MD, Michael
    Status: Done by: Edwards, MD, Michael – Mon Oct 27, 2014 09:10.
TROPONIN–I:* Ordered for: Edwards, MD, Michael
    Status: Done by: System – Mon Oct 27, 2014 09:10.

Key:
   CHOW=Chelchowski, MD, Tom MEDW=Edwards, MD, Michael TC=Chelchowski, RN, Tom

Prepared: Mon Nov 24, 2014 08:17 by TGAR
Picis Demo Medical Center, 100 Quannapowitt Pkwy, Suite 405, Wakefield, MA 01880

Page: 2 of 2

FIGURE 6-14B Discharge Instructions for ED Patient (*Continued*) (Courtesy of Optum™ PM and Physician EMR)

- Evidence of a patient leaving against medical advice (e.g., signed AMA form and physician documentation in progress notes)

Note: An appropriate filing system must be established for storage of emergency records and, when appropriate, emergency records are to be combined with inpatient and outpatient records.

Discharge Summary

The Joint Commission standards require that the discharge summary be completed by the attending physician to facilitate continuity of care. A final progress note can be documented instead of a discharge summary *if* a patient is treated for minor problems or interventions, as defined by the medical staff (short stay). When a patient

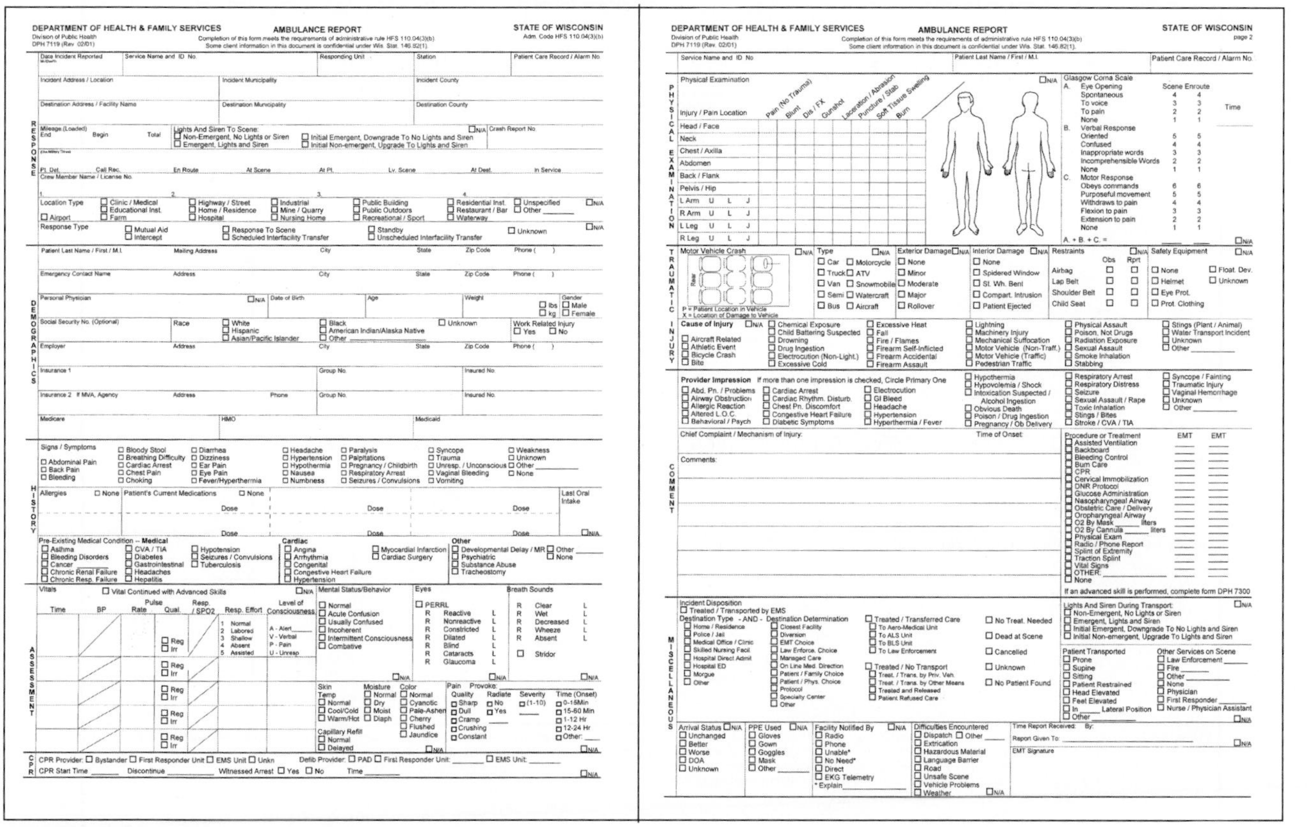

FIGURE 6-15A Ambulance Report (Reproduced with permission from the State of Wisconsin, Department of Health and Family Service Division of Public Health.)

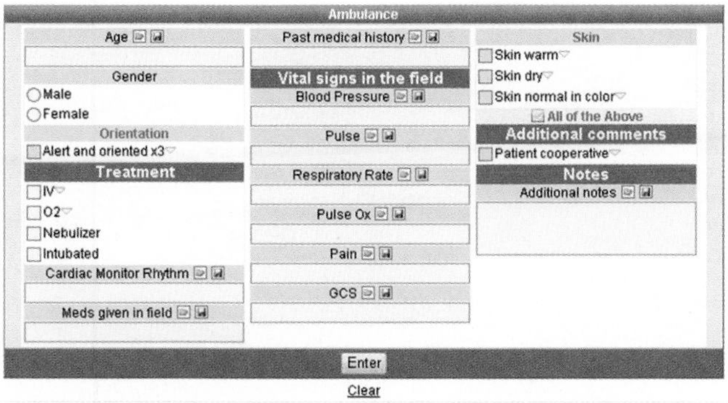

FIGURE 6-15B Electronic Ambulance Report (Courtesy of Optum™ PM and Physician EMR)

is transferred to a different level of care within the same hospital, the discharge summary is called a *transfer summary*, which can be documented in the progress notes if the same practitioner continues to provide care. The Joint Commission also requires that "the use of approved discharge criteria to determine the patient's readiness for discharge" (e.g., decreased dependency on oxygen, discharge planning, transition of patient from intravenous to oral medications) be documented in the record.

(Many facilities use utilization management criteria such as McKesson Interqual products for this purpose. Facilities also develop criteria used to discharge patients from specialty units [e.g., intensive care unit] and departments [e.g., anesthesia department].) Medicare CoP state that all records must document a discharge summary including the outcome of hospitalization, disposition of the case, and follow-up provisions.

The discharge summary (or clinical résumé) (Figure 6-16) provides information for continuity of care and facilitates medical staff committee review; it can also be used to respond to requests from authorized individuals or agencies (e.g., a copy of the discharge summary will suffice instead of the entire patient record). Figure 6-16A represents a paper discharge summary while Figure 6-16B represents a printed discharge summary from a electronic health record. The discharge summary documents the patient's hospitalization, including reason(s) for hospitalization; procedures performed; care, treatment, and services provided; patient's condition at discharge; and information provided to the patient and family.

PATIENT'S NAME *(Last, first, middle initials)*	AGE	SEX	RACE	PATIENT NUMBER	CLAIM NO. C-	NAME OF FACILITY

DIAGNOSES: *(List in numerical order: first the primary diagnosis. The primary diagnosis is defined as that diagnosis, condition, or situation responsible for the major part of the patient's length of stay (DXLS). Then, in order of clinical importance, list other diagnoses which were treated during this episode of care, observed for possible medical intervention or known to have impacted the patient's length of stay. Prefix the DXLS with an alpha character "X." DO NOT INCLUDE DIAGNOSES ESTABLISHED ONLY BY AUTOPSY IN THIS SECTION. DO NOT ABBREVIATE DIAGNOSES.)*

DIAGNOSTIC CODE

PERTINENT CLINICAL DIAGNOSES NOTED BUT NOT TREATED AND WHICH DID NOT IMPACT UPON THIS EPISODE OF CARE *(Include autopsy diagnoses not listed as clinical above):*

OPERATION/PROCEDURES PERFORMED DURING THIS EPISODE OF CARE: DATE **OPERATION/PROCEDURES CODE**

SUMMARY *(Brief statement should include, if applicable, history, pertinent physical findings, provisional diagnosis, course in hospital, treatment given; condition at release; date patient is capable of returning to full employment, period of convalescence, if required; recommendations for followup treatment including date of first VA outpatient visit, where applicable, medications furnished at release, any specific instructions given to the patient and/or family, including diet, physical activity limitations, competency opinion when required, rehabilitation potential; and, name of Nursing Home or other receiving facility, if known)*

ADMISSION DATE	DISCHARGE DATE	TYPE OF RELEASE	INPATIENT DAYS	ABSENCE DAYS	WARD NO.	SIGNATURE PHYSICIAN/ DENTIST	SIGNATURE OF APPROVING PHYSICAN/DENTIST

VA FORM
MAY 1985 **10-1000**   EXISTING STOCK OF VA FORM 10-1000, SEP 1983, WILL BE USED.   **DISCHARGE SUMMARY (INPATIENT CARE)**

FIGURE 6-16A Discharge Summary (Permission to reprint in accordance with va.gov Web reuse policy.)

PICIS MEDICAL CENTER
DISCHARGE SUMMARY

Bock, Alfred
DOB: 9/9/1945 M69
Wt/Ht: 99.79 Kg 185.42 cm.
MedRec: afred1
AcctNum: 7654

————————————— Patient Data —————————————

Complaint: Shortness of Breath
Triage Time: Mon Oct 27, 2014 08:50
ESI: 2-Emergent
Bed: ED ED 02
Initial Vital Signs: 10/27/2014 08:49
  BP:110/50 (Standing)
  P:90
  O2 sat:97 on 2L

ED Attending: Chelchowski, MD, Tom
Primary RN: Hendrian, RN, Carol

R:30
T:99 (Oral)
Pain:1

DIAGNOSIS (Tue Oct 28, 2014 14:53 CHOW)
FINAL: PRIMARY: sob.

KNOWN ALLERGIES
codeine sulfate: Severity: 1234567, Source: Patient, – Entered brand: CODEine Tab —
  Nausea

CURRENT MEDICATIONS (08:58 CHRN)
Lasix:
  Patient Dose: 20 mg PO (Oral) Once a Day.
multivitamin:
  Patient Dose: 1 tab(s) PO (Oral) Once a Day.

MEDICATION ADMINISTRATION SUMMARY

Drug Name	Dose Ordered	Route	Status	Time
Nitro-Bid transdermal	1 in.	Transdermal	Ordered	09:07 10/27/2014

Detailed record available in Medication Service section.

Key:
  CHOW=Chelchowski, MD, Tom CHRN=Hendrian, RN, Carol

FIGURE 6-16B Electronic Discharge Summary (Courtesy of Optum™ PM and Physician EMR)

The discharge summary must fully and accurately describe the patient's condition at the time of discharge, patient education when applicable, including instructions for self-care, and that the patient/responsible party demonstrated an understanding of the self-care regimen. Contents of a discharge summary include:

- Patient and facility identification
- Admission and discharge dates
- Reason for hospitalization (brief clinical statement of chief complaint and history of present illness)

Example Patient was admitted with long-term ulcer on dorsum of left foot that has not improved, and in fact is getting worse. He was given intensive medication as an outpatient, but the foot became more swollen and red. and he is admitted at this time for more intensive therapy.

- Principal/secondary diagnoses and principal/secondary procedures, including results and dates (all relevant diagnoses and operative procedures should be recorded using acceptable disease and operative terminology that includes topography and etiology as appropriate)

Example
Principal diagnosis: Cellulitis and gangrene, left foot and lower leg.
Comorbidities: Diabetes mellitus, insulin dependent, controlled. *Staphylococcus aureus* coagulase-positive septicemia. Urinary retention.
Principal procedure: Amputation, left leg, above knee.
Secondary procedures: Suprapubic cystostomy with permanent suprapubic drainage.

- Significant findings, including pertinent laboratory, x-ray, and pathological findings—negative results may be as pertinent as positive

Example Blood culture revealed *Staphylococcus aureus* coagulase-positive septicemia. EKG revealed left bundle branch block and myocardial changes similar to previous tracings. Chest x-ray showed no active pulmonary disease, and heart was normal size. Lower-leg specimen showed severe atherosclerosis with focal thrombosis. Gangrene of the foot with extensive dissection of acute inflammatory exudates into the lower leg between the fascial planes. Sugars came under good control. Urinalysis showed evidence of the bleeding and minimal infection.

- Treatment provided (medical and surgical), and patient's response to treatment, including any complications and consultations

Example Patient was placed on insulin to control new onset of diabetes. His diabetes is well controlled with insulin, but his bladder condition did not improve. He underwent suprapubic cystostomy, and following this began to improve. His temperature finally dropped to a reasonable level, and he is eating well. He remains uncommunicative, as he has been for several years. He was treated with IV vancomycin and following surgery placed on gentamicin and IV vibramycin.

- Condition on discharge, as stated in specific measurable terms relative to condition on admission, avoiding use of vague terms such as *improved* (in addition, presence and status of drains, wounds, and sutures should be noted)

Example Patient's medications were effective in controlling his infection. He is transferred to the nursing facility for continued care. His leg stump sutures will be removed as able, probably in about two weeks.

- Instructions to patient and/or family (relative to physical activity, medication, diet, and follow-up care)

Example Patient will continue his insulin dosage and be followed at the nursing facility as necessary. Discharge instructions, including medications, diet, physical activities, and plans for follow-up care, were discussed with the primary care nurse at the nursing facility.

- Authentication by attending physician

History and Physical Examination

The Joint Commission standards and Medicare CoP state that the history and physical examination must be performed and documented in the patient record within 24 hours after admission (including weekends and holidays). If a history and physical examination (H&PE) was completed within 30 days prior to admission and reviewed and updated, it can be placed on the record within 24 hours after admission. This means the patient must either have undergone no changes subsequent to the original examination *or* the changes must be documented upon admission. When the history and physical cannot be placed on the record within the required time frame due to a transcription delay, the physician can document a handwritten note containing pertinent findings, (e.g., enough information to manage and guide patient care). If a patient is scheduled for surgery prior to these deadlines, a complete history and physical must be documented.

Usually the history and physical examination is prepared as one handwritten or transcribed report, which assists the physician in establishing a diagnosis on which to base treatment and serves as a reference for future illnesses. The history (Figure 6-17A) documents the patient's chief complaint, HPI, past/family/social history (PFSH), and review of systems (Table 6-4). In an electronic health record, this information, because of its length, is recorded on various screens. Figure 6-17B shows an electronic health record screen that is used to record a review of systems for a patient. Note that the review of systems is part of the patient history. The individual responsible for documenting the history should obtain the information directly from the patient and should document only the facts regarding the patient's case. The source of the history should also be documented,

especially when the individual providing the information is someone other than the patient.

Note: Although the history might be documented by someone other than the attending physician (e.g., intern or resident), the attending physician is responsible for authenticating the report generated.

An interval history documents a patient's history of present illness and any pertinent changes and physical findings that occurred *since a previous inpatient admission if the patient is readmitted within 30 days after discharge for the same condition.*

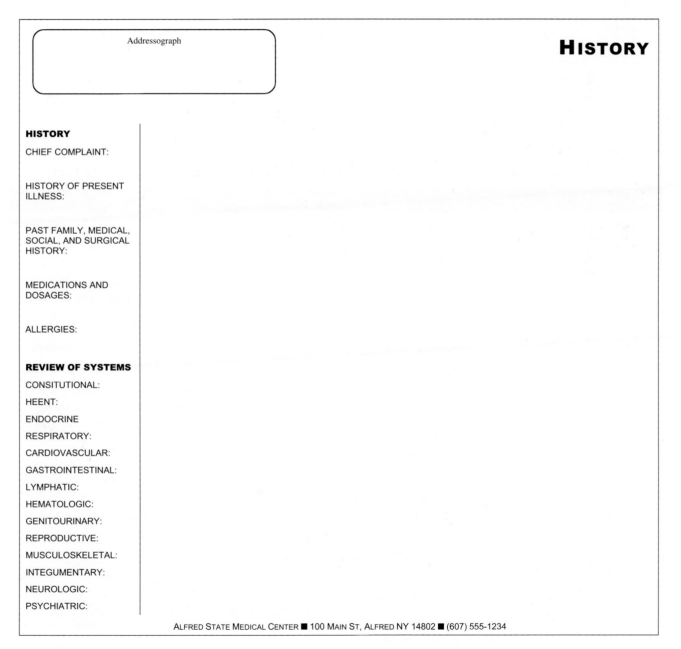

FIGURE 6-17A History Report

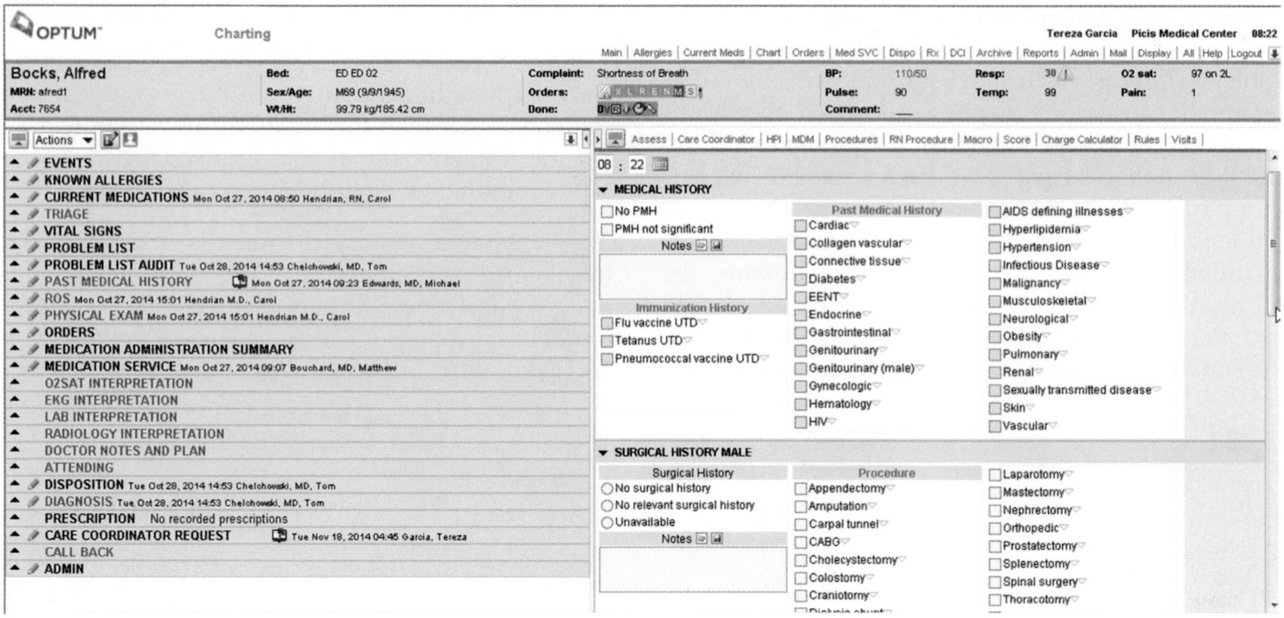

FIGURE 6-17B Review of Systems Screen in an Electronic Health Record (Courtesy of Optum™ PM and Physician EMR)

TABLE 6-4 Description and Documentation Examples for Elements of Patient History

Element	Description
Chief complaint (CC)	Patient's description of medical condition, stated in the patient's own words. *Example:* Chief complaint: "My knee gives out and knee hurts when I walk." (Patient is scheduled for arthroscopy, knee.)
History of present illness (HPI)	Chronological description of patient's present condition from time of onset to present. HPI should include location, quality, severity, and duration of the condition, and associated signs and symptoms. *Example:* HPI: Patient presents for arthroscopy, left knee. Probable torn cartilage. Knee is very bruised. Patient complains of pain, which started one week ago. Patient denies injury.
Past history	Summary of past illnesses, operations, injuries, treatments, and known allergies. *Example:* Past history: Reveals a healthy individual who has been hospitalized in the past x3 for childbirth; the patient has NKA, no history of diseases, and is not currently on any medications. *Note:* NKA means no known allergies.
Family history	A review of the medical events in the patient's family, including diseases that may be hereditary or present a risk to the patient. *Example:* Family history: Patient states that father died at age 51 of heart disease, and mother is living and well.
Social history	An age-appropriate review of past and current activities such as daily routine, dietary habits, exercise routine, marital status, occupation, sleeping patterns, smoking, use of alcohol and other drugs, sexual activities, and so on. *Example:* Social history: Patient has history of marijuana use as a teenager and currently drinks alcohol socially; previous history of smoking cigarettes (quit three years ago).

(Continues)

TABLE 6-4 Description and Documentation Examples for Elements of Patient History (*Continued*)

Element	Description
Medications	A listing of current medications and dosages. *Example:* Medications: Zocor 40 mg daily.
Review of systems (ROS)	Inventory by systems to document subjective symptoms stated by the patient. Provides an opportunity to gather information that the patient may have forgotten to mention or that may have seemed unimportant. *Note:* Providers should not document *negative* or *normal* in response to ROS items. Instead, they should document a statement relative to the item. *Example:* Respiratory: The patient denies shortness of breath.
	The ROS includes: • General • Cardiovascular • Skin • Gastrointestinal • Head • Genitourinary • Eyes • Musculoskeletal • Ears • Neurological • Nose • Endocrine • Mouth • Psychological • Throat • Hematologic/lymphatic • Breasts • Allergic/immunologic • Respiratory

The original history and physical examination must also be made available to the attending physician (e.g., a copy filed on the current inpatient chart or the previous discharged patient record available on the unit).

Example Patient is discharged from the hospital with the diagnosis of acute asthmatic bronchitis. Within 30 days, the patient is readmitted for the same condition. In this situation, it would be appropriate for the attending physician to document an interval note that specifies the patient's present complaint, pertinent changes, and physical findings since the last admission.

After the history is completed, the physician performs a physical examination (Figure 6-18A represents a paper-based physical examination report while Figure 6-18B represents a screen in an electronic health record that is used to record a patient's physical examination.), which is an assessment of the patient's body systems (Table 6-5), to assist in determining a diagnosis, documenting a *provisional diagnosis,* and which may include differential diagnoses. A differential diagnosis indicates that several diagnoses are being considered as possible. The physician also summarizes results of pre-admission testing (PAT) (e.g., blood tests, urinalysis, ECG, x-rays). PAT results are filed in the patient's record.

Example Patient is admitted to the hospital with complaints of severe pain in the pelvic region. The physician documents the following differential diagnoses: Possible endometriosis. Possible adhesions.

Note: While the HP&E is the responsibility of the attending physician, it is appropriate for *house staff* to perform it and dictate the report. The house staff member signs the report, and the attending physician reviews the report to be sure it is completed. The attending physician is responsible for documenting additional pertinent findings and authenticating the report.

Consultation Report

The Joint Commission standards state that medical records shall contain documentation of consultation reports.

A consultation (Figure 6-19) is the provision of health care services by a consulting physician whose opinion or advice is requested by another physician. (Once a patient is admitted to the hospital, the attending physician is responsible for requesting consultations.) A consultation report, documented by the consultant, includes the consultant's opinion and findings based on a physical examination and review of patient records.

Andrus/Clini-Rec
BIBBERO SYSTEMS, INC.

COMPREHENSIVE
PHYSICAL EXAMINATION
MALE OR FEMALE
NEW OR ESTABLISHED PATIENT
CPT # 99201 - 99215

(For Office Use Only)

TODAY'S DATE _____

NAME _____ AGE _____ YRS. OLD DATE OF BIRTH _____

C O N F I D E N T I A L

Key: [O] Neg. Findings [+] Positive Findings [X] Omitted [✔] See Notes/CIRCLE WORDS OF IMPORTANCE & EXPLAIN

1 GEN. APPEARANCE	[ ]	Apparent Age/Nutrition/Development/Mental & Emotional Status/Gait/Posture/Distress/Speech –
2 HEAD / SCALP	[ ]	Size/Shape/Tender over Sinuses/Hair/Alopecia/Eruption/Masses/Bruit –
3 EYES	[ ]	Conjunct/Sclerae/Cornea/Pupils/EOM's/Arcus/Ptosis/Fundi/Tension/Eyelids/Pallor/Light/Bruit –
4 EARS	[ ]	Ext. Canal/TM's/Perforation/Discharge/Tophi/Hearing Problem/Weber/Rinne –
5 NOSE / SINUSES	[ ]	Septum/Obstruction/Turbinates/Discharge –
6 MOUTH / THROAT	[ ]	Odor/Lips/Tongue/Tonsils/Teeth/Dentures/Gums/Pharynx –
7 NECK	[ ]	Adenopathy/Thyroid/Carotids/Trachea/Veins/Masses/Spine/Motion/Bruit –
8 BACK	[ ]	Kyphosis/Scoliosis/Lordosis/Mobility/CVA/Bone/Tenderness –
9 THORAX	[ ]	Symmetry/Movement/Contour/Tender –
10 BREASTS	[ ]	Size/Size-Consistency/Nipples/Areolar/Palpable Mass/Discharge/Tenderness/Nodes/Scars –
11 HEART	[ ]	Rate/Rhythm/Apical Impulse/Thrills/Quality of Sound/Intensity/Splitting/Extra Sounds/Murmurs –
12 CHEST / LUNGS	[ ]	Excursion/Dullness or Hyperresonance to Percussion/Quality of Breath Sounds/Rales/Wheezing/Rhonchi/Diaphragm/Rubs/Bruit –
13 ABDOMEN	[ ]	Bowel Sounds/Appearance/Liver/Spleen/Masses/Hernias/Murmurs/Contour/Tenderness/Bruit/Inguinal Nodes –
14 GROIN	[ ]	Hernia/Inguinal Nodes/Femoral Pulses –
15 MALE GENITALIA	[ ]	Penis/Testes/Scrotum Epididymis/Varicocele/Scars/Discharge –
16 FEMALE GENITALIA	[ ]	Vulva/Vagina/Cervix/Uterus/Adnexa/Rectocele/Cystocele/Bartholin Gland/Urethra/Discharge – PAP Smear (if done ✔) [ ]
17 EXTREMITIES	[ ]	Deformity/Clubbing/Cyanosis/Edema/Nails/Peripheral Pulses/Calf Tenderness/Joints for Swelling/ROM –
18 SKIN	[ ]	Color/Birthmarks/Scars/Texture/Rash/Eczema/Ulcers –
19 NEUROLOGICAL	[ ]	DTR's/Babinski/Cranial Nerves/Motor Abnormalities/Tremor/Paralysis/Sensory Exam – (touch, pin prick, vibration)/Coordination/Romberg –
20 MUSCULAR SYSTEM	[ ]	Strength/Wasting/Development –
21 RECTAL EXAM	[ ]	Sphincter Tone/Hemorrhoids/Fissures/Masses/Prostate/Stool Guaiac (if done ✔) ☐ Pos ☐ Neg –

Impression: [ ] Check If Normal Physical Examination
Summary: _____

Signature _____ Date _____

ORDER # 19-744-2 • 1982 BIBBERO SYSTEMS, INC. • PETALUMA, CA.TO REORDER CALL TOLL FREE: (800) BIBBERO (800-242-2376) OR FAX (800) 242-9330   Mfg. In U.S.A.   (Rev. 4/96)

FIGURE 6-18A Physical Examination Report (*Continues*) (Copyright © Courtesy of Bibbero Systems, Inc., Petaluma, CA. Phone: 800-242-2376; Fax: 800-242-9330; www.bibbero.com.)

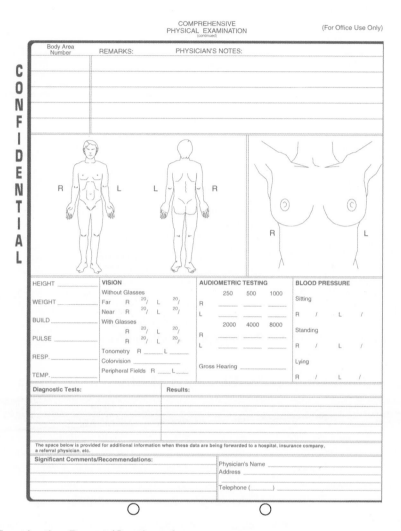

COMPREHENSIVE PHYSICAL EXAMINATION (continued)

(For Office Use Only)

CONFIDENTIAL

Body Area Number	REMARKS: PHYSICIAN'S NOTES:

HEIGHT	VISION	AUDIOMETRIC TESTING	BLOOD PRESSURE
WEIGHT	Without Glasses Far R 20/ L 20/ Near R 20/ L 20/	250 500 1000 R L	Sitting R / L /
BUILD PULSE	With Glasses R 20/ L 20/ R 20/ L 20/	2000 4000 8000 R L	Standing R / L /
RESP. TEMP.	Tonometry R ____ L ____ Colorvision ____ Peripheral Fields R ____ L ____	Gross Hearing ____	Lying R / L /

Diagnostic Tests:	Results:

The space below is provided for additional information when these data are being forwarded to a hospital, insurance company, a referral physician, etc.

Significant Comments/Recommendations:	Physician's Name Address Telephone ( )

FIGURE 6-18A Physical Examination Report (*Continued*) (Copyright © Courtesy of Bibbero Systems, Inc., Petaluma, CA. Phone: 800-242-2376; Fax: 800-242-9330; www.bibbero.com.)

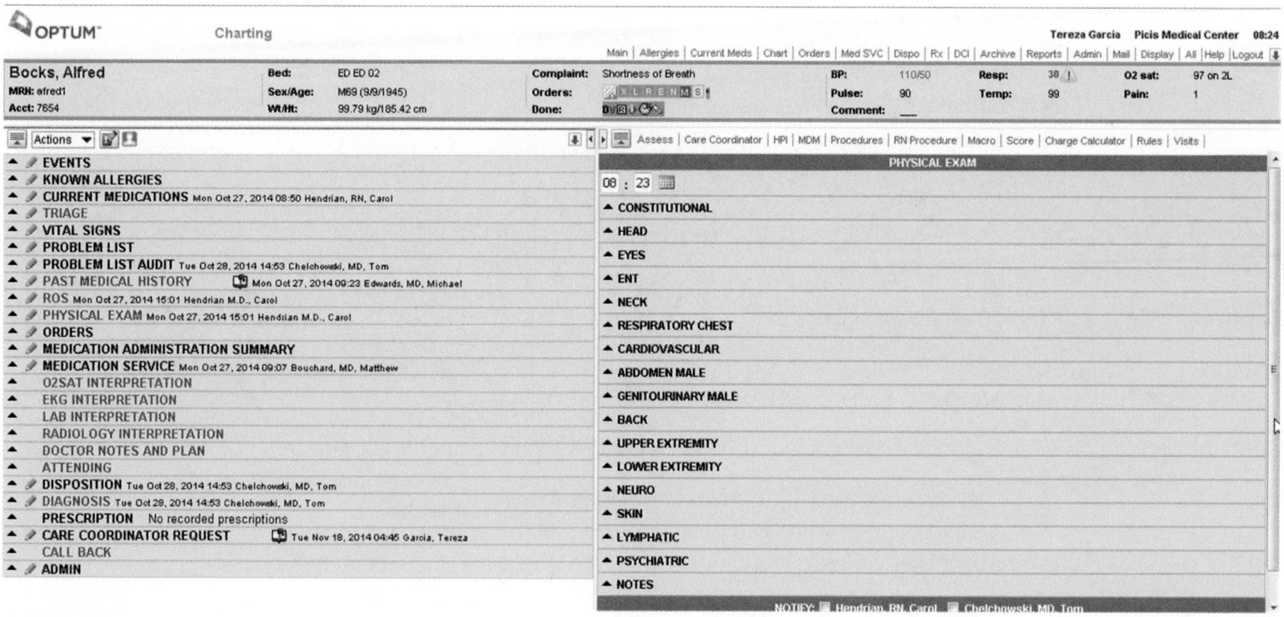

FIGURE 6-18B Electronic History and Physical Exam Report (*Continues*) (Courtesy of Optum™ PM and Physician EMR)

FIGURE 6-18B Electronic History and Physical Exam Report (*Continued*) (Courtesy of Optum™ PM and Physician EMR)

TABLE 6-5 Documentation Examples for Elements of Physical Examination

Element	Example
General survey	Reveals well-developed, somewhat obese, elderly, white male in severe distress with severe substernal discomfort and pain in upper arms. Conscious. Alert. Appears to be stated age. No deformity. Patient cannot sit or stand still because he is in such agony. Gait affected only by pain; otherwise it is normal. Carriage normal. Age 67. Sex male. Height 5′11″. Weight 188 lbs. Temperature 98.0°F orally. Pulse 56 and regular. Blood pressure 150/104.
Skin	Reveals pale, cool, moist surface with no cyanosis or jaundice. No eruption. No tumors.
Head	Hair, scalp, skull within normal limits. Facies anxious.
Eyes	Pupils round, regular, equal. Pupils react normally to light and accommodation. Extraocular muscles intact. Corneae, sclerae, conjunctivae clear. Fields intact. Ophthalmoscopic examination reveals fundi discs to be well outlined.
Ears	Examination reveals grossly intact hearing. No lateralization. External canals and ears, and left membrana tympanica clear. No tumor.
Nose and sinuses	Inspection reveals grossly intact sense of smell. No deformity. No tenderness. Septum benign. Only residual mucus in both nostrils. No tumor. Sinuses within normal limits.
Mouth	Mouth edentulous. Lips, gums, buccal mucosa, and tongue within normal limits.
Throat	Examination reveals posterior oropharynx and tonsils to be very red and inflamed. Palate and uvula benign. Larynx not visualized.
Neck	Reveals cervical structures to be supple with no masses, scars, or abnormal glands or pulsations.
Chest	Chest inspection reveals it to have normal expansion. Thorax observation reveals it to be somewhat obese but with normal shape and symmetry without swellings or tumors or significant lymphadenopathy. Respiratory motions normal. Palpable tactile fremitus physiologically normal.

(Continues)

TABLE 6-5 Documentation Examples for Elements of Physical Examination (*Continued*)

Element	Example
Breasts	Felt to be symmetrical and without masses or tenderness. Nipples normal. No axillary lymphadenopathy.
Lungs	Investigation reveals lungs clear on inspection, palpation, percussion, and auscultation.
Heart	Examination reveals heart to be indicated as normal since the area of cardiac dullness is normal in size, shape, and location. Heart rate slow. Rhythm regular. No accentuation of A2 and P2.
Abdomen	Appearance is slightly obese with no striae. Has a well-healed herniorrhaphy scar on the right inguinal area. No tenderness, guarding, rigidity, or rebound phenomena. No abnormal abdominal masses palpable. No organomegaly. No distention. No herniae. Bowel sounds are normal.
Genitalia	Reveals male type and circumcised penis. Scrotum, testes, and epididymides appear to be normal in size, shape, and color, without skin lesions or tumors.
Rectal	Inspection proves sphincter tone good. Lumen clear. Hemorrhoids, internal and external, found on examination.
Extremities	Examination reveals no loss of motor function of the extremities or back. Patient can sit, stand, squat, and walk although it causes excruciating pain in the substernal chest area. Patient advised to avoid doing these things. No evidence of injury. No paralysis. Patient squirms and moves constantly in his agony. He cannot sit long nor can he stand in one position. Extremities exam reveals them to be intact. Shoulder girdle inspection reveals no tenderness, muscle spasms, or abnormality or motion. No crepitation. Examination of the back reveals a slight infected and tender pilonidal cyst over the sacrum. No deformity or limitation of motion of the back noted. No other tenderness. Arms, hands, legs, and feet investigation reveals no deformity, fracture, dislocations, injury, tremors, atrophic muscles, swelling, tenderness, muscle spasms, or abnormality of motion.
Lymphatics	System check reveals lymph glands to be normal throughout.
Blood Vessels	Investigation reveals veins to be normal. Arteries are arteriosclerotic and all peripheral pulses are palpable and undiminished.
Neurological	System review reveals the patient generally conscious, cooperative, mentally alert, and reasonably intelligent, although he seems to be somewhat confused. Cranial nerves intact. Superficial and deep tendon reflexes intact and equal bilaterally. No pathological reflexes. No abnormality of the sensory perception, or the associated movements, or the autonomic or endocrine systems felt to be due to neurological disorder.
Impression	Acute myocardial infarction. Essential hypertension. Arteriosclerosis. Pilonidal cyst with mild infection. Internal and external hemorrhoids.

The attending physician generally requests a consulting physician (e.g., specialist) to provide evaluation and, possibly, treatment of a patient. Occasionally, a general surgeon will request a general practitioner to evaluate a patient prior to surgery to determine medical risks, if any. To initiate a consultation, the attending physician:

- Documents a physician order requesting consultation with a particular doctor
- Documents a progress note that outlines the reason for consultation
- Contacts the consulting physician to discuss the patient's case and to agree to the consultant's role in patient care, if any

Note: The consulting physician may participate in patient care with the attending physician or even take over patient care and become the patient's attending physician.

CONSULTATION REQUEST and REPORT FORM

Patient's Name	Age

To: Dr.

From: Dr.

Patient Location:

Type of Consultation Desired   ☐ Consultation Only

☐ Consultation and Follow Jointly

☐ Accept in Transfer

Referring Diagnoses:

Reason for Consultation:

Signature: Date: Time:

Consultation Report:

Signature: Date: Time:

3 Part Form   Top Copy - Consultation Request & Report to be Returned
2nd Copy - Consulting Dr.'s Copy   3rd Copy - Requisition Control Copy

ORDER #26-7116   ANDRUS CLINI-REC   CHART ORGANIZING SYSTEMS · 1976 BIBBERO SYSTEMS, INC. · PETALUMA, CA
TO REORDER CALL TOLL FREE: (800) BIBBERO (800-242-2376) OR FAX (800) 242-9330   Mfg In U.S.A.

FIGURE 6-19 Consultation Report (Copyright © Courtesy of Bibbero Systems, Inc., Petaluma, CA. Phone: 800-242-2376; Fax: 800-242-9330; www.bibbero.com.)

As part of the consultation process, the consulting physician:

- Reviews the patient's record
- Examines the patient
- Documents pertinent findings
- Provides recommendations and/or opinions

Physician Orders

The Joint Commission standards require medical records to contain diagnostic and therapeutic orders and verbal orders (e.g., telephone orders) to be authenticated by the responsible physician within a time frame specified by the facility (based on state laws, if applicable). The Joint Commission added a standard that each medication ordered be supported by a documented diagnosis, condition, or indication-for-use. Facilities may require physicians to document either the indication for usage, such as a diagnosis, for each medication ordered. This standard also serves to facilitate patient safety because it is less likely that a medication will be misinterpreted as written (e.g., physician mistakenly documents "Paclitaxel for anxiety," nurse questions the order, and physician amends it documenting "Paxil for anxiety"). Medicare CoP state that all physician order entries must be legible, complete, authenticated (name and discipline), dated, and timed promptly by the prescribing practitioner in electronic or written form. If permitted by facility bylaws (policies), it is also acceptable for another practitioner responsible for the care of the patient to authenticate the order, even if the order did not originate with that practitioner.

Physician orders (or doctor's orders) (Table 6-6) (Figure 6-20 A represents a form used for a paper physician order while Figure 6-20C represents a screen that is used in an electronic health record to enter physician orders.) direct the diagnostic and therapeutic patient care activities (e.g., medications and dosages, frequency of dressing changes). They should be:

- Clear and complete
- Legible, if handwritten
- Dated and timed
- Authenticated by the responsible physician

Computerized physician order entry (CPOE) uses a computer network to communicate physician (and other qualified provider) instructions for patient care to the health care facility staff (e.g., nurses, physical therapists, consulting physicians) and the departments (e.g., pharmacy, laboratory, radiology) responsible for carrying out the orders. CPOE improves patient safety by eliminating the need for nursing, unit clerk, or ancillary staff to transcribe handwritten or verbal orders.

Note: Think of physician orders as prescriptions for care while an individual is an inpatient. When a patient visits the physician in the office, the doctor often "prescribes" a medication or lab test. In the hospital, the physician documents numerous such "prescriptions" as physician orders.

Example Adam is treated in the ED due to trauma sustained from an automobile accident. The ED physician evaluates Adam and starts immediate treatment due to severity of injuries. He dictates a series of orders to the registered nurse, who records them in the patient's ED record. The ED physician authenticates the verbal order after Adam is transferred to the intensive care unit.

TABLE 6-6 Physician Orders

Type of Order	Description
Discharge order	The final physician order documented to release a patient from a facility.
	Note: Patients who sign themselves out of a facility do so **against medical advice (AMA)** and sign a release from responsibility for discharge that includes the following language:
	I hereby request my discharge from this hospital against the advice of its medical staff. It has been explained to me that my present condition is such as to require further hospitalization and that I leave the hospital at my own risk. I hereby release the hospital and its staff from all responsibility for any consequences of this act.
	Note: The Joint Commission requires facilities to implement medication reconciliation procedures as a patient safety measure. Reconciling medications across the continuum of care involves obtaining a medication history from the patient, prescribing medications based upon review of the medication history, and comparing prescribed admission medications to those on the medication history, resolving any discrepancies. The medication reconciliation process continues upon discharge and transfer of the patient, and the complete list of patient medications is shared with the next provider of patient care and the patient's primary care physician.

(Continues)

TABLE 6-6 Physician Orders (*Continued*)

Type of Order	Description
Routine order	Physician orders preapproved by the medical staff, which are preprinted and placed on a patient's record (e.g., standard admitting orders for a surgical patient, discharge orders following surgery).
Standing order (Figure 6-20B)	Physician orders by the medical staff (preprinted and placed on the patient's record), which direct the continual administration of specific activities (e.g., medications) for a specific period of time as a part of diagnostic or therapeutic care.
Stop order (or automatic stop order)	As a patient safety mechanism, state law mandates—and in the absence of state law, facilities decide the circumstances preapproved standing physician orders are automatically discontinued (stopped), requiring the physician to document a new order (e.g., 72 hours after narcotics are ordered, they are automatically stopped).
Telephone order (T.O.)	A verbal order dictated via telephone to an authorized facility staff member. Facilities should establish a **telephone order call back policy**, which requires the authorized staff member to read back and verify what the physician dictated to ensure that the order is entered accurately. To document that the policy was followed, the staff member enters the abbreviation **RAV (read and verified)** below the telephone order and then signs the order. *Note:* Avoid using the abbreviation P.O. (phone order) because it is also an abbreviation for the Latin phrase *per os*, which means "by mouth."
Transfer order	A physician order documented to transfer a patient from one facility to another.
Verbal order	Orders dictated to an authorized facility staff member (e.g., registered nurse, pharmacist, physical therapist) because the responsible physician is unable to personally document the order. *Note:* Medical staff rules and regulations contain the qualifications of staff members authorized to record verbal orders.
Voice order (V.O.)	A verbal order dictated to an authorized facility staff member by the responsible physician who also happens to be present. *Note:* Medical staff rules and regulations must stipulate when voice orders are allowed (e.g., emergency situations only, such as when the emergency department physician has made a chest incision and inserted both hands to massage the patient's heart to restartit).
Written order	Orders that are handwritten in a paper-based record or entered into an electronic health record by the responsible physician.

		Addressograph		**PHYSICIAN ORDERS**

Date	Time	Orders		Nurse's Initials

HIM501/01-03

COPIES: White-Record
Yellow-Pharmacy

ALFRED STATE MEDICAL CENTER ■ 100 MAIN ST, ALFRED NY 14802 ■ (607) 555-1234

FIGURE 6-20A Physician Orders

PHYSICIAN'S STANDING ORDERS

1. PASSES: To Include therapeutic leaves; Individualized activities, school and programming; off campus consultations, including appointments and follow-up visits with physicians in clinic; and other diagnostic studies done off campus; and other purposes approved by the attending physician.

2. ROUTINE TREATMENT FOR WOUND CARE AND INJURIES:
    1. Superficial wounds: Clean with saline twice a day and apply antibiotic ointment (Neosporin or bacltracin) until healed.
    2. Ice pack as needed.
    3. For sutures: Clean with saline twice a day and apply antibiotic ointment and remove sutures in 7 days, unless otherwise ordered.

3. FEVER/PAIN:
    For fever greater than 100.5° F, rectally (99.5° oral, 98.5° axillary), or above, and/or for pain give:
    1. Tylenol 10 mg/kg up to 650 mg q. 4 h. as needed or
    2. Tylenol Suppository 325 mg per rectum for clients weighing less than 45 pounds and 650 mg per rectum for clients weighing more than 45 pounds q. 4 h. as needed.

    For fever not relieved by Tylenol within 1 hour:
    May give Ibuprofen 10 mg/kg up to 800 mg q. 6 h. PRN.

    For temperature of 103° F rectally (102° oral, 101° axillary) or above:
    3. Use a cooling blanket.
    4. Give tepid sponge bath and Tylenol/ibuprofen as noted above.
    5. CBC with differential on A shift closest to occurrence of fever.
    6. Check complete set of vital signs and notify M.D.

4. HYPOTHERMIA: (temp less than 96° rectal, 95° oral, 94° axillary)
    1. Put socks and cap on client.
    2. Wrap client up with a regular blanket.
    3. If temperature does not respond, put on heating blanket.

5. NAUSEA AND VOMITING: (New Onset)
    1. Check for fecal impaction.
    2. If positive, follow orders for impaction. If negative, and after vomiting two times, give Phenergan Suppository 25 mg, 1 whole one for clients over 45 pounds, $\frac{1}{2}$ for clients under 45 pounds.

    NAME:_____ CASE NUMBER:_____

FIGURE 6-20B Physician's Standing Orders (*Continues*)

6. DIARRHIA: (New Onset)
   1. Hold any laxatives or prune juice for 48 hrs.
   2. Imodium 2 mg p.o. after 3rd loose stool. May repeat once within an hour.

7. SEIZURES:
   After 2nd grand mal seizure:
   1. Check for impaction.
   2. Give Ativan 2 mg IM for clients weighing greater than 50 pounds or 1 mg. IM for clients weighing less than 50 pounds.
   3. Check complete set of vitals and notify M.D. if seizures are not resolved.
   4. If impaction was positive, follow orders for impaction.

8. IMPACTION:
   1. Give one Dulcolax or bisacodyl suppository per rectum.
   2. May manually disimpact as needed.

9. CONSTIPATION:
   1. Give MOM 30 mL by mouth or PEG.

10. MOUTH INJURIES:
    1. Glyoxide application three times a day for 5 days.
    2. Refer to the physician or dentist as needed.

11. RUNNY NOSE: Nalex-A:
    1. Age greater than 12, give 1 tablet or 2 teaspoons three times a day x 5 days, or
    2. Age less than 12, give 1 teaspoon or $\frac{1}{2}$ tablet three times a day x 5 days with first and last dose being at least 12 hours apart and middle dose being at least 4 hours from first and last. (e.g., 7am, 4pm, 8pm, or 8am, 12am, 8pm)

    OR

    Rondec:
    1. Age greater than 6, give 1 tablet or 1 teaspoon three times a day x 5 days, or
    2. Age less than 6, give 1/2 tsp. of the liquid three times a day x 5 days with first and last dose being at least 12 hours apart and middle dose being at least 4 hours from first and last. (e.g., 7am, 4pm, 8pm, or 8am, 12am, 8pm)

NAME:_____ CASE NUMBER:_____

FIGURE 6-20B Physician's Standing Orders (*Continues*)

12.   FOR RED EYES WITH DRAINAGE/CONJUNCTIVITIS: Bacitracin or Neosporin Ophthalmologic ointment three times a day for 5 days with first and last dose being at least 12 hours apart.

13.   DIAPER RASH: A & D ointment as needed and with every diaper change.

14.   PURULENT EAR DRAINAGE:C ortisporin Otic Suspension or Cortaine-B,4 drops in affected ear four times a day for 7 days.D o not use if there is a known tympanic membrane perforation or PE Tubes.

15.   COUGH:
    1.   For clients 12 and above, give Robitussin DM 3 teaspoons four times a day for 7 days.
    2.   For clients 12 and under, give 2 teaspoons of Robitussin DM four times a day for 7 days.

16.   EAR WAX REMOVAL:(Do not use if there is a known tympanic membrane perforation or PE Tubes.)
    1.   Cerumenex 3 or 4 drops in affected ear at 8 PM and repeat again at 8 AM the next morning.
    2.   Or, for more stubborn cerumen: Cerumenex 3 to 4 drops in affected ear three times a day for 5 days.
    3.   Then irrigate with warm water after the Cerumenex treatment.

17.   FINGER STICK GLUCOSE: Do a finger stick glucose for signs and symptoms of hypoglycemia or hyperglycemia (nausea, diaphoresis, shakiness, decreased level of consciousness).
    1.   If glucose is less than 70, give juice and sugar or Instaglucose and recheck in 15 minutes. If still less than 70, continue with juice and sugar or Instaglucose, check complete set of vitals and notify M.D.
    2.   If glucose is greater than 400, check complete set of vitals and notify M.D.

18.   ROUTINE MEDICATION ORDERS THAT RUN OUT ON THE WEEKENDS OR HOLIDAYS:C ontinue same medications and dosages until the next working day.

19.   For any acute illness or change in status, check a complete set of vitals (Blood pressure, Temperature, Pulse, Respirations) and notify M.D.

DO NOT GIVE ANY OF THE ABOVE MEDICATIONS IF ALLERGIC. ANY SPECIFIC ORDERS ON ANY CLIENT SUPERCEDES THESE STANDING ORDERS.

_____

Physician   Date   Nurse   Date

NAME:_____ CASE NUMBER:_____

FIGURE 6-20B Physician's Standing Orders (*Continued*)

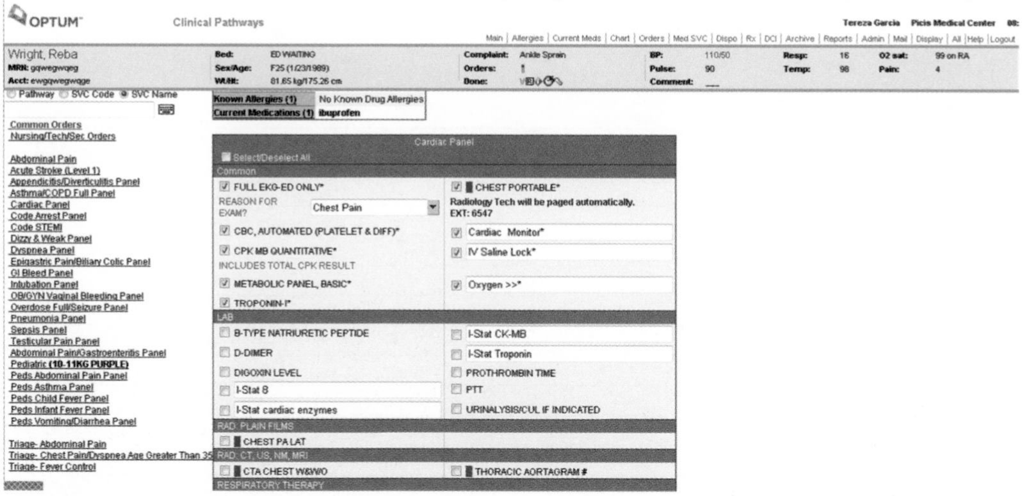

FIGURE 6-20C Electronic Physician Orders (Courtesy of Optum™ PM and Physician EMR)

Progress Notes

Progress notes contain statements related to the course of the patient's illness, response to treatment, and status at discharge. Figure 6-21A represents a paper-based progress note while Figure 6-21B represents the screens used to collect a doctor's progress note for a patient in an electronic health record. They also facilitate health care team members' communication by providing a chronological picture and analysis of the patient's clinical course—they document continuity of care, which is crucial to quality care. As a minimum, progress notes should include an admission note, follow-up notes, and a discharge note (Table 6-7); the frequency of documenting progress notes is based on the patient's condition (e.g., once per day to three or more times per day). Progress notes are usually organized in the record according to discipline (e.g., each discipline, such as physical therapy, has its own section of progress notes). Some facilities adopt integrated progress notes, which means organizing all progress notes documented by physicians, nurses, physical therapists, occupational therapists, and other professional staff members in the same section of the record. Integrated progress notes allow the patient's course of treatment to be easily followed by presenting a chronological "picture" of patient information. Facilities also allow physicians and other staff to dictate progress notes, which are later transcribed by medical transcriptionists and placed on the patient's record. While convenient for physicians and others, a delay in transcribing dictated notes could delay patient care. Facilities that allow the dictation of progress notes should adopt electronic authentication procedures to avoid placing another document on the patient's record that requires signatures.

Note: Progress notes must be documented in a timely, accurate, and legible manner. There is no standard or regulation that specifies how often notes are to be documented *except* that they are to be documented as the patient's condition warrants. This means that a patient admitted to an intensive care unit will have proportionately more progress notes documented on the chart than a patient admitted for an uncomplicated, elective surgery.

PROGRESS NOTES

Patient Name _____ Date of Birth: ___ / ___ / ___ Age _____
LAST   FIRST   MIDDLE

Prob. No. or Letter	* Physician Notes Start Here	** Nurse's Notes Start Here	Diagnosis

* PHYSICIAN START NOTES AT LEFT MARGIN, NEXT TO PROBLEM NO. COLUMN
** NURSE NOTES BEGIN AT INDENTED SHADED COLUMN

PAGE #_____

PROGRESS NOTES

BIBBERO SYSTEMS, INC., PETALUMA, CA

TO REORDER CALL TOLL FREE: (800) BIBBERO (800 242-2376)
FORM # 26-7216

FIGURE 6-21A Progress Notes (Permission to reprint granted by Bibbero Systems, Inc, (800) 242-2376 www.bibbero.com.)

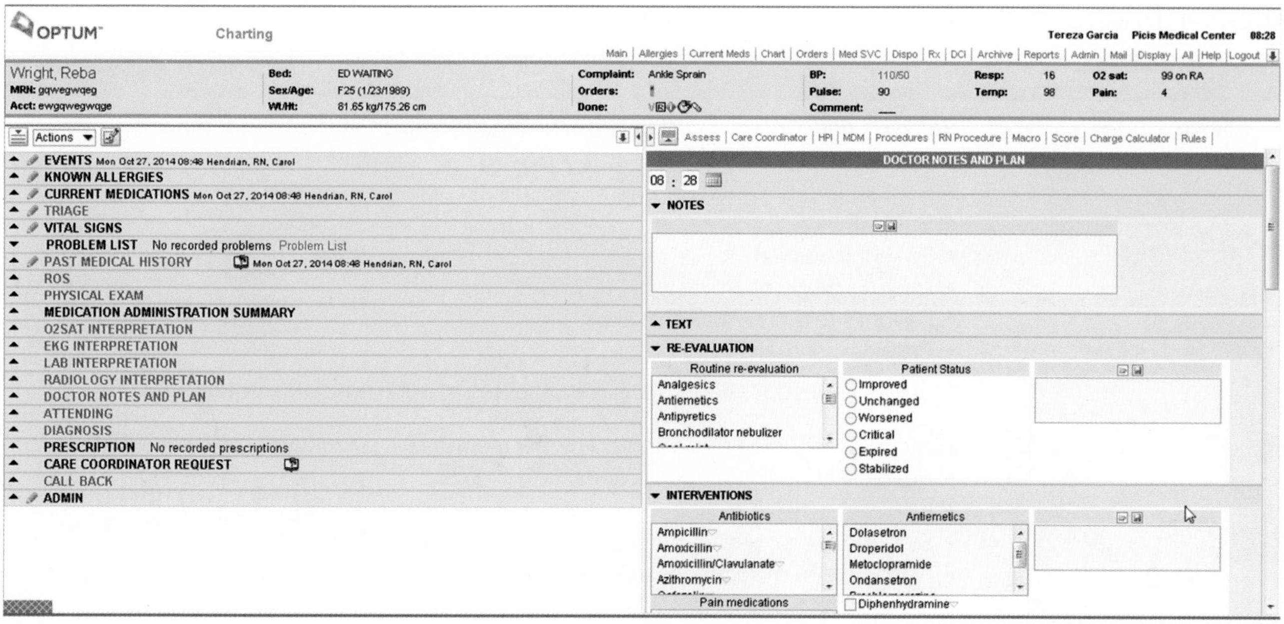

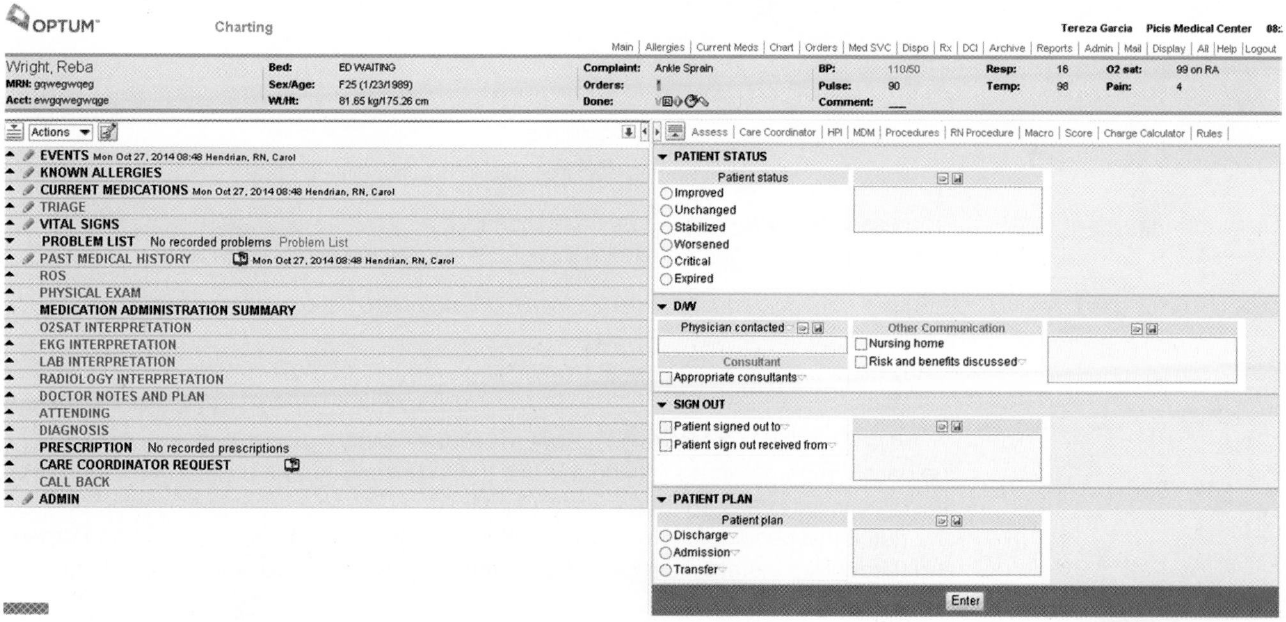

FIGURE 6-21B **Electronic Doctor's Notes** (Courtesy of Optum™ PM and Physician EMR)

TABLE 6-7 Progress Notes

Type of Progress Note	Definition
Admission note	Progress note *documented by the attending physician* at the time of patient admission, which includes: • Reason for admission, including description of patient's condition • Brief HPI • Patient care plan • Method/mode of arrival (e.g., ambulance) • Patient's response to admission • Physical assessment *Note:* The admission note is documented in addition to the dictated H&PE.
Follow-up progress note	Daily progress notes *documented by the responsible physicians,* which include: • Patient's condition • Findings on examination • Significant changes in condition and/or diagnosis • Response to medications administered (e.g., effectiveness of pain medications) • Response to clinical treatment • Abnormal test findings • Treatment plan related to each of the above
Discharge note	Final progress note *documented by the attending physician,* which includes: • Patient's discharge destination (e.g., home) • Discharge medications • Activity level allowed • Follow-up plan (e.g., office appointment) *Note:* The discharge note is documented in addition to a dictated discharge summary.
Case management note	Progress note *documented by a case manager,* which outlines a discharge plan that includes case management/social services provided and patient education.
Dietary progress note	Progress note *documented by the dietitian (or authorized designee),* which includes: • Patient's dietary needs • Any dietary observations made by staff (e.g., amount of meal consumed, food likes/dislikes). *Note:* The Joint Commission standards require dietary orders to be documented in the patient record prior to serving the diet to the patient. After a physician order is written, dietetic services can be provided to patients. AOA requirements state that "food and nutritional needs of the patient should be met in accordance with physician orders and recognized dietary practices." The nutritional care of the patient is to be documented in the patient record.
Rehabilitation therapy progress note	Progress notes *documented by various rehabilitation therapists* (e.g., occupational therapy, physical therapy, psychology, speech/audiotherapy, and so on), which demonstrate the patient's progress (or lack thereof) toward established therapy goals. The Joint Commission standards require the following to be documented in the patient record: • Reason for referral to rehabilitation care • Summary of patient's clinical condition • Goals of treatment and treatment plan • Treatment and progress records (including ongoing assessments) • Assessment of physical rehabilitation achievement and estimates of further rehabilitation potential (documented at least monthly for outpatient care)

(Continues)

TABLE 6-7 Progress Notes (*Continued*)

Type of Progress Note	Definition
Respiratory therapy progress note	Respiratory therapy progress notes *documented by respiratory therapists,* which include therapy administered, machines used, medication(s) added to machines, type of therapy, dates/times of administration, specifications of the prescription, effects of therapy including any adverse reactions, and reassessment of duration/frequency of respiratory therapy. Patients discharged from the hospital on respiratory therapy should be provided with instructions as to pulmonary care (e.g., indications for therapy, dosage of medications, complications of misuse, safety, maintenance of equipment, frequency/use of machine settings, postural drainage, and therapeutic percussion). Examples of respiratory therapy include: • Aerosol, humidification, and therapeutic gas administration • Mechanical ventilatory and oxygenated support • Coughing and breathing exercises • Bronchopulmonary drainage • Therapeutic percussion and vibration • Pulmonary function testing • Blood gas analysis • Cardiopulmonary resuscitation *Note:* The Joint Commission standards and Medicare CoP state that the attending physician is responsible for documenting a physician's order for respiratory care services, including type, frequency and duration of treatment, type and dose of medication, type of dilutant, and oxygen concentration.
Preanesthesia evaluation note	A progress note documented by any individual qualified to administer anesthesia (not just the individual who administered anesthesia to the patient) prior to the induction of anesthesia, which includes evidence of: • Patient interview to verify past and present medical and drug history and previous anesthesia experience(s) • Evaluation of the patient's physical status • Review of the results of relevant diagnostic studies (EKG, pulmonary function tests, cardiac stress tests, laboratory, imaging) • Discussion of preanesthesia medications and choice of anesthesia to be administered (e.g., general, spinal, or other regional anesthesia) • Surgical and/or obstetrical procedure to be performed • Potential anesthetic problems (e.g., smoking) and risks
Postanesthesia evaluation note	A progress note documented by any individual qualified to administer anesthesia (not just the individual who administered the anesthesia), which includes: • Patient's general condition following surgery • Description of presence/absence of anesthesia-related complications and/or postoperative abnormalities • Blood pressure, pulse, presence/absence of swallowing reflex and cyanosis *Note:* A written order releasing the patient from the recovery room must also be authenticated by the physician responsible for release (e.g., surgeon or anesthesiologist).
Preoperative note	A progress note *documented by the surgeon* prior to surgery, which summarizes the patient's condition and documents a preoperative diagnosis.
Postoperative note	A progress note *documented by the surgeon* after surgery, which documents the patient's vital signs and level of consciousness; any medications, including intravenous fluids, administered blood, blood products, and blood components; and any unanticipated events or complications (including blood transfusion reactions) and the management of those events. *Note:* The surgeon documents the postoperative note in addition to a dictated operative record.

In addition to being dated, timed, and authenticated, progress notes must document that adequate treatment was rendered to justifythe patient's length of stay; thus, progress notes indicate that a patient's care required intervention by a physician and professional personnel.

Example 1
Sarah has a postoperative temperature of 101 and is vomiting. The nursing staff monitors her condition continually and documents multiple progress notes (e.g., nurses notes) for each shift, including date, time, and authentication for each note.

Example 2
2/3/YYYY 1300 Patient admitted with severe pain in upper arms and a constricting, squeezing feeling in the substernal area that feels like indigestion and gas and was not relieved by soda.

> Tony Tierney, M.D.

Example 3
2/24/YYYY Less weak. Walking without instability or pain.

> Patricia Smart, M.D.

2/25/YYYY Patient very much improved. To start patient walking more.

> Patricia Smart, M.D.

2/25/YYYY Very upset and unable to rest all night due to his demented and very noisy roommate.

> Patricia Smart, M.D.

2/27/YYYY Patient states he feels good. Clear to decrease Valium to 5 mg. Slept last night without a sleeping capsule.

> Patricia Smart, M.D.

Anesthesia Record

The Joint Commission standards require documentation of a preanesthesia or presedation assessment and monitoring of the patient during administration of moderate or deep sedation or anesthesia. The patient's physiological status is assessed immediately after recovery from moderate or deep sedation or anesthesia. Medicare CoP require documentation of a preanesthesia evaluation note by an individual qualified to administer anesthesia within 48 hours prior to surgery. Medicare CoP also require that an intraoperative anesthesia record be maintained. A postanesthesia evaluation is also to be documented by the individual who administered the anesthesia no later than 48 hours after surgery, and in accordance with state law and medical staff policies and procedures.

In addition to preoperative and postoperative anesthesia progress notes (discussed previously), an anesthesia record (Figure 6-22A) documented by the individual qualified to administer anesthesia is required when a patient receives an anesthetic other than a local anesthetic, to document patient monitoring during administration of anesthetic agents and other activities related to the surgical episode. The anesthesia record, pre- and postanesthesia progress notes (Figure 6-22B), and recovery room record (discussed below) provide complete documentation of the administration of preoperative medications, anesthetic agents administered during operative procedures, evaluation of the patient pre- and postoperatively, and recovery of the patient from anesthesia during the immediate postoperative period.

Note: Preanesthesia and postanesthesia evaluation progress notes are sometimes documented on a special form located on the reverse side of the anesthesia record. This helps anesthesiologists ensure that no documentation elements are forgotten.

Contents of the anesthesia record include:

- Preanesthesia medication administered, including time, dosage, and effect on patient
- Appraisal of any changes in the patient's condition (since preanesthesia evaluation)
- Anesthesia agent administered, including amount, technique(s) used, effect on patient, and duration
- Patient's vital signs (e.g., temperature, pulse, blood pressure)
- Any blood loss
- Transfusions administered, including dosage and duration
- IV fluids administered, including dosage and duration
- Patient's condition throughout surgery, including pertinent or unusual events during induction of, maintenance of, and emergence from anesthesia
- Authentication by the individual qualified to administer anesthesia (e.g., certified registered nurse anesthetist, anesthesiologist)

Operative Record

The Joint Commission standards require the surgeon to document the following *prior to* performing surgery: history, physical examination, laboratory and x-ray examinations, and preoperative diagnosis. Authentication is the responsibility of the individual caring for the patient. All diagnostic and therapeutic procedures are to be documented in the patient record. According to The Joint Commission, an operative or other high-risk procedure report is to be written or dictated *upon completion of the operative or other high-risk procedure and before the patient is transferred to the next level of care.* If the practitioner performing the operation or high-risk procedure accompanies the patient from the operating room to the next unit or area of care, the report can be written or dictated in the new unit or area of care.

ANESTHESIA RECORD

Addressograph

PROCEDURE(S):		ANESTHESIA	START	STOP
SURGEON(S):		PROCEDURE		
DATE OF SURGERY:		ROOM TIME	IN	OUT

PRE-PROCEDURE

- ❏ Patient Identified ❏ ID band verified
- ❏ Patient questioned ❏ Chart reviewed
- ❏ Consent form signed
- ❏ Patient reassessed prior to anesthesia (ready to proceed)
- ❏ Peri-operative pain management discussed with patient/guardian (plan of care completed)

Pre-Anesthetic State:
- ❏ Awake ❏ Anxious ❏ Calm
- ❏ Lethargic ❏ Uncooperative
- ❏ Unresponsive
- ❏ Other: _____
- ❏ Anesthesia machine #5626984 checked
- ❏ Secured with safety belt
- ❏ Arm secured on board ❏ Left ❏ Right

MONITORS/EQUIPMENT

- ❏ Stethoscope ❏ Precordial
- ❏ Suprasternal ❏ Esoph
- ❏ Non-invasive B/P ❏ V-lead ECG
- ❏ Continuous ECG ❏ ST Analysis
- ❏ Pulse oximeter ❏ End tidal CO_2
- ❏ Nerve stimulator: ❏ Ulnar ❏ Tibial ❏ Facial
- ❏ Oxygen monitor ❏ Cell Saver
- ❏ ET agent analyzer ❏ B/S ❏ TEE
- ❏ Fluid/Blood warmer ❏ Temp: _____
- ❏ BIS ❏ ICS
- ❏ NG/OG tube ❏ FHT monitor
- ❏ Foley catheter ❏ EEG
- ❏ Airway humidifier
- ❏ Evoked potential: ❏ SSEP ❏ BAEP ❏ MEP
- ❏ Arterial line _____ ❏ CVP _____

ANESTHETIC TECHNIQUES

GA Induction: ❏ IV ❏ Pre-O $_2$ ❏ RSI ❏ PR
❏ Cricoid pressure ❏ Inhalation ❏ IM
GA Maintenance: ❏ TIVA ❏ Inhalation
❏ Inhalation/IV ❏ GA/Regional Comb.

Regional:
Epidural : ❏ Thoracic ❏ Lumbar ❏ Caudal
❏ Femoral ❏ Auxiliary ❏ Interscalene
❏ CSE ❏ Bier ❏ SAB ❏ Ankle
❏ Continuous Spinal ❏ Cervical Plexus

Regional Techniques:
- ❏ Position _____ ❏ See Remarks
- ❏ Site _____ ❏ Prep _____
- ❏ LA _____ ❏ Needle _____
- ❏ Additive _____ ❏ Narcotic _____
- ❏ Test dose Rx _____

AIRWAY MANAGEMENT

- ❏ Oral ETT ❏ LTA ❏ RAE
- ❏ Nasal ETT ❏ LMA # _____
- ❏ Stylet ❏ LMA Fastrach # _____
- ❏ DVL ❏ LMA ProSeal # _____
- ❏ EMG ETT ❏ Bougie
- ❏ Armored ETT ❏ LIS
- ❏ Breath sounds = bilateral
- ❏ Cuffed – min occ pres with ❏ air ❏ NS
- ❏ Uncuffed – leaks at _____ cm H_2O
- ❏ Oral airway ❏ Nasal airway ❏ Bite block
Circuit: ❏ Circle system ❏ NRB ❏ Bain
- ❏ Via tracheotomy/stoma ❏ Mask case
- ❏ Nasal cannula ❏ Simple O_2 mask
- Nebulizer: _____
- Nerve Block(s): _____

TIME: 15 30 45 | 15 30 45 | 15 30 45 | 15 30 45 | 15 30 45

AGENTS
- ❏ Des ❏ Iso ❏ Sevo ❏ Halo (%)
- Air (L/min)
- ☑ Oxygen (L/min)
- ☑ N_2O (L/min)
- ☑ Forane (%)
- ☑ Anectine (mg)
- ☑ Pentothal (mg)

FLUIDS
- Urine
- EBL
- Gastric

MONITORS
- ☑ ECG
- ☑ % Oxygen Inspired (FIO_2)
- ☑ End Tidal CO_2
- ☑ Temp: ❏ C ☑ F
- ☑ BP Monitor

PERI-OP MEDS
200 180 160 140 120 100 80 60 40 20 10

VENT
- Tidal Volume (ml)
- Respiratory Rate
- Peak Pressure (cm H_2O)
- ❏ PEEP ❏ CPAP (cm H_2O)

TOTALS

SYMBOLS

▼ ▲
BP cuff pressure

⊥
Arterial line pressure

×
Mean arterial pressure

●
Pulse

○
Spontaneous Respirations

∅
Assisted Respirations

T
Tourniquet

Time of Delivery:
_____
_____

Gender: ❏ M ❏ F

Apgars: _____ / _____

Position:	Surgeon	
	Assistant	
	Scrub Nurse	
	Circulating Nurse	
	Signature of Anesthesiologist or C.R.N.A.	

ALFRED STATE MEDICAL CENTER ■ 100 MAIN ST, ALFRED NY 14802 ■ (607) 555-1234

FIGURE 6-22A Anesthesia Report (Permission to reprint granted by www.anesthesia-nursing.com.)

PRE- AND POSTANESTHESIA EVALUATION RECORD

Addressograph

PREANESTHESIA EVALUATION

HISTORY TAKEN FROM:	❏Patient	❏Parent/ Guardian	❏Significant Other	❏Chart	❏Poor Historian	❏Language Barrier

PROPOSED PROCEDURE:

AGE	GENDER ❏Male ❏Female	HEIGHT	WEIGHT	BLOOD PRESSURE	PULSE	RESPIRATIONS	TEMPERATURE	O2 SAT %

PREVIOUS ANESTHESIA:	❏None
PREVIOUS SURGERY:	❏None
CURRENT MEDICATIONS:	❏None
FAMILY HX – ANES. PROBLEMS:	❏None
ALLERGIES	❏None

AIRWAY (Enter X in appropriate boxes)	❏MP1 ❏MP2 ❏MP3 ❏MP4	❏Unrestricted neck ROM	❏T-M distance = _____
	❏Obesity ❏↓ neck ROM	❏History of difficult airway	❏Short muscular neck
	❏Teeth poor repair ❏Teeth chipped/loose	❏Edentulous	❏Facial hair

BODY SYSTEM	COMMENTS	DIAGNOSTIC STUDIES
RESPIRATORY	❏WNL Tobacco Use: ❏Yes ❏No ❏Quit _____ Packs/Day for ____ Years	ECG CHEST X-RAY Pulmonary Studies
CARDIOVASCULAR	❏WNL Pre-procedure Cardiac Assessment:	LABORATORY STUDIES PT/PTT/INR: T&S / T&C:
GASTROINTESTINAL	❏WNL Ethanol Use: ❏Yes ❏No ❏Quit Frequency _____ ❏History of Ethanol abuse	HCG: LMP: UA:
		OTHER DIAGNOSTIC TESTS
MUSCULOSKELETAL	❏WNL	PLANNED ANESTHESIA/MONITORS
GENITOURINARY	❏WNL	
OTHER	❏WNL	PREANESTHESIA MEDICATION
PREGNANCY	❏WNL ❏AROM ❏SROM ❏Pitocin Drip ❏Induction ❏MgDrip Weeks Gestation: ____ G: ____ P: ____ EDC: _____	
		SIGNATURE OF ANESTHESIOLOGIST OR C.R.N.A.

POSTANESTHESIA EVALUATION

CONTROLLED MEDICATIONS

Location	Time	B/P	O₂ Sat	Pulse	Respirations	Temperature	Medication	Used	Destroyed	Returned

❏Awake ❏Mask O₂ ❏Somnolent ❏Unarousable ❏Oral/nasal airway
❏Stable ❏NC O₂ ❏Unstable ❏T-Piece ❏Intubated ❏Ventilator
❏Regional – dermatome level: _____ ❏Continuous epidural analgesia
❏Direct admit to hospital room ❏No anesthesia related complications noted
❏See notes for anesthesia related concerns ❏Satisfactory postanesthesia/analgesia recovery

SIGNATURE OF ANESTHESIOLOGIST OR C.R.N.A.

ALFRED STATE MEDICAL CENTER ■ 100 MAIN ST, ALFRED NY 14802 ■ (607) 555-1234

FIGURE 6-22B Pre- and Postanesthesia Evaluation Record (Permission to reprint granted by www.anesthesia-nursing.com.)

When a full operative or other high-risk procedure report cannot be entered immediately into the patient's medical record after the operation or procedure, a progress note is to be written in the patient record before the patient is transferred to the next level of care. The full report is written or dictated within a timeframe established by the hospital. The progress note must include the name of the primary surgeon, assistant surgeon(s), procedure performed, description of operative findings, estimated blood loss, specimens removed, and postoperative diagnosis. Medicare CoP require a complete H&PE to be documented in the patient's record prior to surgery—If the report is not available in the patient's record, the responsible physician must document a statement to that effect along with a complete admission note.

Note: The patient record often contains a comprehensive operative progress note documented by the surgeon *as well as* a transcribed operative record—both are authenticated by the responsible surgeon. Also, do not confuse pre- and postoperative evaluations documented by the surgeon with pre- and postanesthesia evaluations documented by the anesthesiologist. These are often documented in the progress notes and are authenticated by the responsible physician (surgeon or anesthesiologist). Some hospitals create special forms to facilitate documentation of these evaluations.

The operative record (Figure 6-23) describes gross findings, organs examined (visually or palpated), and techniques associated with the performance of surgery. It is to be dictated or handwritten immediately following the operation and authenticated by the responsible surgeon.

Documentation elements include:

- Principal participants (e.g., surgeon, assistant surgeon, anesthesiologist)
- Pre- and postoperative diagnoses
- Surgical procedure performed
- Anesthesia administered
- Detailed evidence that surgically acceptable techniques were used
- Indications for surgery
- Condition of the patient (pre-, intra-, and postoperatively)
- Detailed description of the operative procedure performed (e.g., surgical techniques), including organs explored
- Description of operative findings, unique elements in the course of procedures performed, any unusual events that occurred during the procedure, any estimated blood loss, and any specimens removed
- Description of other procedures performed during operative episode

- Documentation of ligatures, sutures, number of packs, drains, and sponges used

Note: Postoperative documentation includes the discharge of the patient from the postsedation or postanesthesia care area (e.g., recovery room), which is documented by the practitioner responsible (e.g., anesthesiologist); use of approved criteria to determine patient readiness for discharge; and the name of the practitioner responsible for discharge.

OPPS Major and Minor Procedures

For outpatient prospective payment system (OPPS) purposes, the CMS categorizes procedure codes as major or minor procedures, assigning status indicators to each procedure code to differentiate them. A *major procedure* (e.g., carpal tunnel repair, cervical diskectomy, lumbar fusion) includes surgery that may require a hospital stay; it usually takes a longer time and is riskier than a minor procedure. (Anesthesia is usually required for major surgery and includes the administration of general, local, or regional anesthesia.) A *minor procedure* includes minimally invasive diagnostic tests and treatments (e.g., trigger point injection, administration of an epidural, insertion of a pain pump). The CMS has developed the following guidelines:

- Endoscopies are classified as a distinct group, regardless of duration.
- Minor procedures are usually performed in less than 5 minutes.
- Major procedures are usually performed in 5 minutes or more.

Pathology Report

The Joint Commission standards require documentation of an authenticated, dated report or examination as performed by pathology and clinical laboratory services. The pathologist is responsible for documenting a descriptive diagnostic report of gross specimens received and of autopsies performed.

The pathology report (or tissue report) (Figure 6-24) assists in the diagnosis and treatment of patients by documenting the analysis of tissue removed surgically or diagnostically (e.g., biopsy), or that was expelled by the patient (e.g., products of conception). A *tissue examination request* is submitted to the pathologist along with the specimen and a *clinical diagnosis*. The pathologist performs macroscopic (gross) and microscopic examination of tissue and documents a report.

Addressograph

OPERATIVE RECORD

Patient Number	Room/Bed
Patient Name (Last, First, MI)	Date of Procedure
Name of Attending Physician	Time Started	Time Ended
Patient DOB	Gender	Service

Surgeon: Assistant:

Anesthetist: Anesthetic:

Preoperative Diagnosis:

Postoperative Diagnosis:

Procedure(s) Performed:

Complications:

Operative Findings:

Dictation Date_____

Transcription Date_____

Signed _____

Form 4107, OCT 03

ALFRED STATE MEDICAL CENTER ■ 100 MAIN ST, ALFRED NY 14802 ■ (607) 555-1234

FIGURE 6-23 Operative Report

Addressograph

PATHOLOGY REPORT

Clinical History/Preoperative Diagnosis: ◄——

Patient's diagnosis prior to review of tissue by pathologist.

EXAMPLE: Breast mass. Right breast lumpectomy performed.

Specimen(s) Obtained: ◄——

Specimen received by pathologist as a result of the procedure (e.g., breast tissue).

EXAMPLE: Single piece of fibrofatty tissue received in formalin.

Gross Description: ◄——

Pathologist views specimen without a microscope and describes size (after measuring it) and appearance (after feeling it).

EXAMPLE: Fibrofatty tissue is 2 x 3 x 3 cm. A central mass is palpable.

Microscopic Description: ◄——

Pathologist views specimen using a microscope and describes tissue.

EXAMPLE: Tissue reveals infiltrating ductal carcinoma. Tumor contains irregular nests of infiltrating cells with minimal gland formation. Surgical margins are clear.

Pathologic Diagnosis: ◄——

Pathologist documents grade, histology, and stage.

Grade: nature of cells and their aggressiveness.
Histology: type of cancer found and arrangement of cells.
Stage: size of cancer and extent to which it has spread.

EXAMPLE: Poorly differentiated infiltrating ductal carcinoma, Grade III, Stage II.

ALFRED STATE MEDICAL CENTER ■ 100 MAIN ST, ALFRED NY 14802 ■ (607) 555-1234

FIGURE 6-24 Pathology Report (Permission to reprint granted by TheDoctorsDoctor.com.)

The pathology report is filed in the patient record as soon as completed, usually within 24 hours. Contents of the pathology report include:

- Date of examination
- Clinical diagnosis
- Tissue examined
- Pathologic diagnosis
- Macroscopic (or gross) examination
- Microscopic examination
- Authentication by pathologist

Note: During a frozen section procedure (e.g., for suspected cancer), rapid microscopic analysis of a specimen is performed. Tissue removed is evaluated by the pathologist during the operative episode to allow a positive margin to be corrected prior to surgical closure and reconstruction. A final pathology report is issued after all tissue removed during the procedure has been analyzed.

Post Anesthesia Care Unit (PACU) Record

The Joint Commission standards also require the patient's postoperative status to be evaluated immediately after the procedure and/or administration of moderate or deep sedation or anesthesia. The patient must also be evaluated upon admission to and discharge from the postanesthesia recovery area, as follows: record of postoperative vital signs and level of consciousness medications (including intravenous fluids) and blood and blood components administered; IV fluids and drugs administered, including blood and blood products; any unusual events or complications, including blood transfusion reactions; and the management of those events. A qualified licensed independent practitioner discharges the patient from the recovery area or from the hospital according to criteria approved by clinical leaders.

After the completion of surgery, patients are taken to the recovery room, where the anesthesiologist and recovery room nurse are responsible for documenting a postanesthesia care unit (PACU) record (or recovery room record) (Figure 6-25), which delineates care administered to the patient from the time of arrival until the patient is moved to a nursing unit or discharged home. Elements of the recovery room record include:

- Patient's general condition upon arrival in recovery room
- Postoperative/postanesthesia care given
- Patient's level of consciousness upon entering and leaving the recovery room
- Description of presence/absence of anesthesia-related complications and/or postoperative

abnormalities (may be documented in progress notes)
- Monitoring of patient vital signs, including blood pressure, pulse, and presence/absence of swallowing reflex and cyanosis
- Documentation of infusions, surgical dressings, tubes, catheters, and drains
- Written order releasing patient from recovery room (authenticated by physician responsible for release) documented in the physician orders
- Documentation of transfer to nursing unit or discharge home

Note: The recovery room record is dated, timed, and authenticated by the responsible physician (anesthesiologist) or certified registered nurse anesthetist (CRNA).

Ancillary Reports

The Joint Commission standards require patient records to include reports of pathology and clinical laboratory examinations, radiology and nuclear medicine examinations or treatment, anesthesia records, and any other diagnostic or therapeutic procedures. Requests for ancillary testing must include the study requested and appropriate clinical data to aid in the performance of the procedures requested.

Ancillary reports (Table 6-8) are documented by such departments as laboratory, radiology (or x-ray), nuclear medicine, and so on; they assist physicians in diagnosis and treatment of patients. The responsible physician must document requests for ancillary testing to be performed in the physician orders, and the patient record must include documentation of ancillary report results as well as a treatment plan.

All ancillary reports should be filed in the patient's records as soon as an interpretation has been made (usually within 24 hours).

Nursing Documentation

The Joint Commission standards require documentation of a nursing assessment, nutritional screening, and a functional screening within 24 hours after inpatient admission.

Nursing documentation (Table 6-9) plays a crucial role in patient care because the majority of care delivered to inpatients is performed by nursing staff, including registered nurses (RN), licensed practical nurses (LPN), and certified nurses' aides (CNA). Upon admission to the hospital, a nursing assessment is documented to obtain the patient's history and evaluate vital signs.

Addressograph

POST ANESTHESIA CARE UNIT RECORD

	0	15	30	45	60	15	30	45	60
230									
220									
210									
200									
190									
180									
170									
160									
150									
140									
130									
120									
110									
100									
90									
80									
70									
60									
50									
40									
30									
20									
10									
0									

DATE: _____ TIME: _____

OPERATION: _____

ANESTHESIA: _____

AIRWAY: _____

O $_2$ USED: ❏ YES ❏ NO

ROUTE: _____

TIME	MEDICATIONS	SITE

INTAKE	AMOUNT
TOTAL	

OUTPUT	AMOUNT
CATHETER	
LEVINE	
HEMOVAC	
TOTAL	

DISCHARGE STATUS

ROOM: _____ TIME: _____

CONDITION: _____

TRANSFERRED BY _____

R.R. NURSE: _____

PREOP VISIT: _____

POSTOP VISIT: _____

Postanesthesia Recovery Score		Adm	30 min	1 hr	2 hr	Disch
Moves 4 extremities voluntarily or on command (2) Moves 2 extremities voluntarily or on command (1) Moves 0 extremities voluntarily or on command (0)	Activity					
Able to deep breathe and cough freely (2) Dyspnea or limited breathing (1) Apneic (0)	Respiration					
BP 20% of preanesthetic level BP + 20% of preanesthetic level BP + 50% of preanesthetic level	Circulation					
Fully awake (2) Arouseable on calling (1) Not responding (0)	Consciousness					
Pink (2) Pale, dusky, blotchy, jaundiced, other (1) Cyanotic (0)	Color					

COMMENTS & OBSERVATIONS:

_____

SIGNATURE OF RECOVERY ROOM NURSE

ALFRED STATE MEDICAL CENTER ■ 100 MAIN ST, ALFRED NY 14802 ■ (607) 555-1234

FIGURE 6-25 Postanesthesia Care Unit (PACU) Record

This information is used to create a nursing care plan, which records nursing diagnoses and interventions. Nursing staff is also responsible for recording vital signs, administration of medication, observations and progress during the patient's inpatient hospitalization, and a discharge plan. This information is documented on various forms, including nurses notes, graphic sheets, medication sheets, and so on.

TABLE 6-8 Ancillary Reports

Type of Ancillary Report	Description
Laboratory (Figure 6-26A represents a paper-based laboratory report while figure 6-26B represents a screen used in an electronic health record to document laboratory information.)	Clinical laboratory reports document name, date and time of lab test, results, time specimen was logged into the lab, time the results were determined, reference section (that contains normal ranges for lab values), and initials of the laboratory technician. Examples include: • Blood chemistry (e.g., blood glucose level, WBC, CBC, urinalysis, culture and sensitivity) • Therapeutic drug assay (e.g., drug level in blood) • Blood gases (e.g., oxygen saturation) • Cardiac enzymes • Blood types • Blood factor (Rh) • Genetic testing
Radiology (Figure 6-27A represents a paper-based radiology report, figure 6-27B represents an electronic radiology report, and figure 6-27C represents a chest x-ray electronic image that appears in an electronic health record.)	Radiology (or imaging) reports document a description of the image, techniques used, narrative report of findings, diagnosis or impression, and authentication by the radiologist. Examples include: • X-rays (radiology) • CAT scans • Nuclear medicine • Ultrasound • MRI • Xerography • PET scans • Thermography *Note:* Obtain signed patient consent prior to performing deep x-ray therapy, radioactive isotope treatment, or special diagnostic procedures.
Electrocardiogram (EKG or ECG) (Figure 6-27D)	EKG report includes the following: • Printout of graphic tracing of electrical changes in heart muscle, commonly called the EKG strip, and date and time of EKG (or ECG) test • Physician's interpretation of the tracing • Authentication by physician
Electroencephalogram (EEG) (Figure 6-27E)	EEG report includes the following: • Graphic printout of measurement of electrical activity of the brain and date and time of EEG test • Physician's interpretation of graphics • Authentication by physician
Electromyogram (EMG) (Figure 6-27F)	EMG report includes the following: • Graphic printout of measurement of skeletal muscle activity and date and time of EMG test • Physician's interpretation of graphics • Authentication by physician
Transfusion record (Figure 6-27G)	Blood transfusion records contain documentation of the complete and accurate description of the requisition for blood, date and time of transfusion, report of crossmatching (compatibility tests), blood type and Rh, report of administration of blood, donor's identification number, and notation of any transfusion reactions.

Addressograph

LABORATORY REPORT

DATE SPECIMEN COLLECTED: **DATE SPECIMEN RECEIVED:**

TEST	RESULT	FLAG	REFERENCE
Glucose			82-115 mg/dl
BUN			8-25 mg/dl
Creatinine			0.9-1.4 mg/dl
Sodium			135-145 mmol/L
Potassium			3.6-5.0 mmol/L
Chloride			99-110 mmol/L
CO2			21-31 mmol/L
Calcium			8.6-10.2 mg/dl
WBC			4.5-11.0 thous/UL
RBC			5.2-5.4 mill/UL
HGB			11.7-16.1 g/dl
HCT			35.0-47.0 %
Platelets			140-400 thous/UL
PT			11.0-13.0 seconds

End of Report

ALFRED STATE MEDICAL CENTER ■ 100 MAIN ST, ALFRED NY 14802 ■ (607) 555-1234

FIGURE 6-26A Laboratory Report

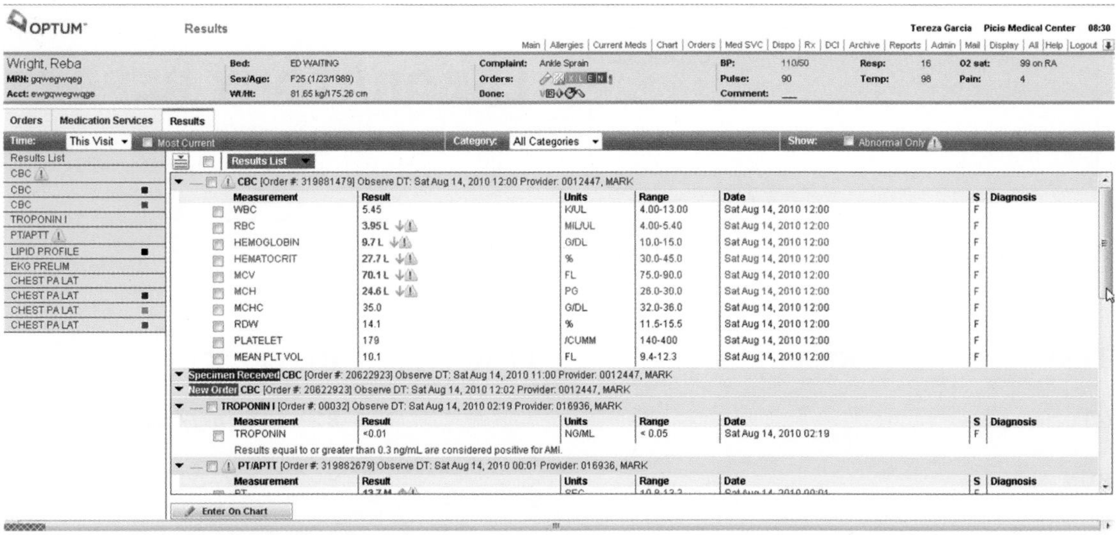

FIGURE 6-26B Electronic Lab Report (Courtesy of Optum™ PM and Physician EMR)

Addressograph

RADIOLOGY REPORT

Clinical History/Indications:

Exam:

Date of Exam:

Reason for Exam:

Findings:

Impression:

Recommendation:

_____
Signature of Radiologist

ALFRED STATE MEDICAL CENTER ■ 100 MAIN ST, ALFRED NY 14802 ■ (607) 555-1234

FIGURE 6-27A Radiology Report (or Diagnostic Imaging Report)

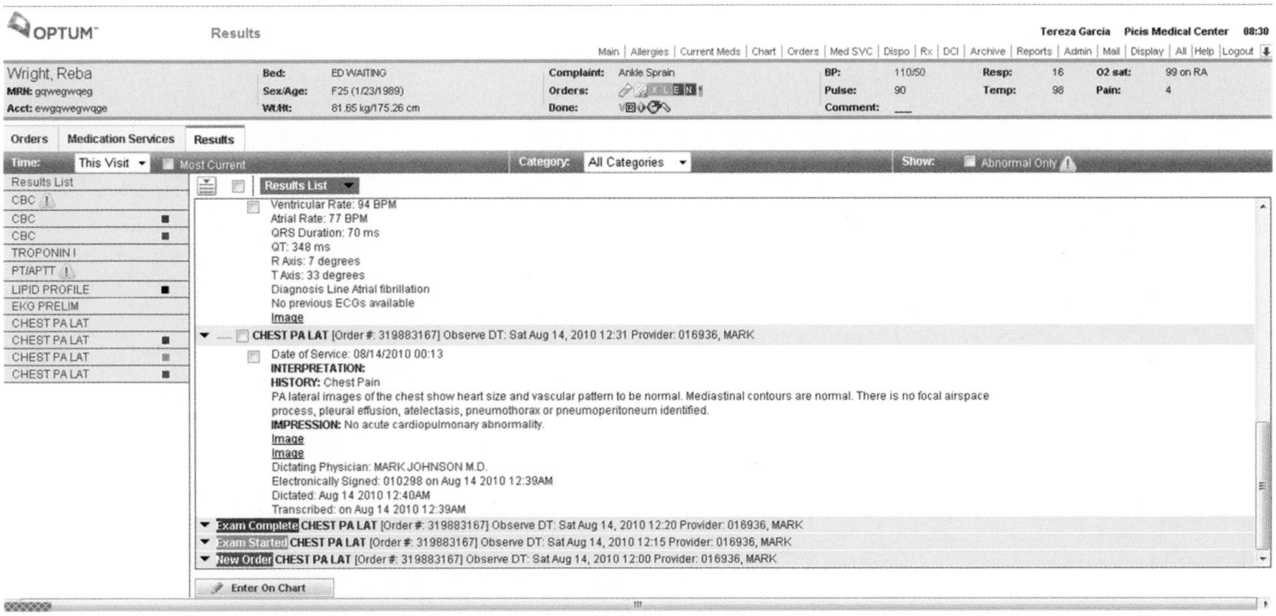

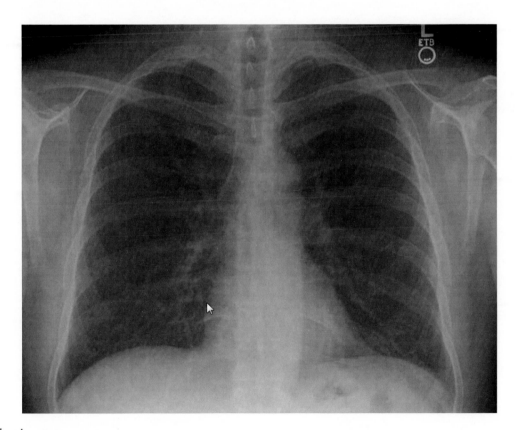

FIGURE 6-27B Electronic Radiology Report (Courtesy of Optum™ PM and Physician EMR)

FIG 6-27C Chest x-ray (Courtesy of Optum™ PM and Physician EMR)

ELECTROCARDIOGRAPH REQUEST

PREV. ECG   YES ☐   NO ☐   AMB. ☐   BED. ☐   EMERG. ☐   DIG. ☐   QUIN. ☐   AGE   SEX   B.P.   DATE

CLIN. DIAG.:   ORDERED BY

                                                                                                                            M.D.

ELECTROCARDIOGRAPH REPORT

RHYTHM: SINUS ☐ OTHER	RATES:	INTERVALS:	AXIS:
	ATR. VENTR.	P-R QRS QTc	+ ° _ °

DESCRIPTION: LIMB LEADS	PRECORDIAL LEADS
P	
QRS	
S-T	
T.U.	

PATIENT IDENTIFICATION	INTERPRETATION

DATE _____ INTERPRETED BY_____ M.D.

12-01 PRINTED IN U.S.A. 009

FIGURE 6-27D Electrocardiogram (EKG) Report (Copyright © Courtesy of Bibbero Systems, Inc., Petaluma, CA. Phone: 800-242-2376; Fax: 800-242-9330; www.bibbero.com.)

```
┌─────────────────────────────────────────────────────────────┐
│  ╭──────────────────────╮                                    │
│  │   Addressograph      │      ELECTROENCEPHALOGRAM REPORT    │
│  │                      │                                    │
│  ╰──────────────────────╯                                    │
│                                                               │
│  Age of Patient:                      EEG #:                  │
│                                                               │
│  History:                                                     │
│                                                               │
│  Medications:                                                 │
│                                                               │
│  Conditions of the Recording:                                 │
│                                                               │
│  Analysis and Description of EEG Pattern:                     │
│                                                               │
│                                                               │
│  Impression:                                                  │
│                                                               │
│                                      _____       │
│                                      Signature of Physician    │
│       ALFRED STATE MEDICAL CENTER ■ 100 MAIN ST, ALFRED  NY 14802 ■ (607) 555-1234 │
└─────────────────────────────────────────────────────────────┘
```

FIGURE 6-27E Electroencephalogram (EEG) Report

Special Reports

Records of obstetric and neonatal patients contain unique forms. The obstetrical record is the mother's record and contains an antepartum record, labor and delivery record, and postpartum record. The neonatal record (Figure 6-29) is the newborn's record and contains a birth history, newborn identification, physical examination, and progress notes.

The obstetrical record consists of the following reports:

- Antepartum record (or prenatal record): Started in the physician's office, it includes health history of the mother, family and social history, pregnancy risk factors, care during pregnancy including tests performed, medications administered, and so on. A summary of this information is also documented in the hospital patient record or a copy is filed at the birthing facility by the 36th week of pregnancy.
- Labor and delivery record: Records progress of the mother from time of admission through time of delivery. Information includes time of onset of contractions, severity of contractions, medications administered, patient and fetal vital signs, and progression of labor.
- Postpartum record: Documents information concerning the mother's condition after delivery.

Contents of neonatal record include:

- Birth history: Documents summary of pregnancy, labor and delivery, and newborn's condition at birth.

Addressograph

ELECTROMYOGRAM REPORT

Neurological and Electrodiagnostic Consultation:

Past History:

Social History

Neurological Examination:

Electromyographic Study:

Nerve Conduction Velocity Test:

Sensory Results:

Late Responses:

Summary:

Impression:

Recommendations:

_____
Signature of Physician

ALFRED STATE MEDICAL CENTER ■ 100 MAIN ST, ALFRED NY 14802 ■ (607) 555-1234

FIGURE 6-27F Electromyogram (EMG) Report

- **Newborn identification:** Immediately following birth, footprints and fingerprints of the newborn are created, and a wrist or ankle band is placed on the newborn (with an identical band placed on the mother); within 12 hours of birth, an identification form is also used to document information about the newborn and mother.
- **Newborn physical examination:** An assessment of the newborn's condition immediately after birth, including time and date of birth, vital signs, birth weight and length, head and chest measurements, general appearance, and physical findings is completed.
- **Newborn progress notes:** Documents information gathered by nurses in the nursery and includes vital signs, skin color, intake and output, weight, medications and treatments, and observations.

BLOOD TRANSFUSION RECORD

Addressograph

Blood Results

Date:	Date:	Date:	Date:
Hb	Hb	Hb	Hb
Platelets	Platelets	Platelets	Platelets
WBC	WBC	WBC	WBC
Neutrophils	Neutrophils	Neutrophils	Neutrophils

Blood Component Transfusion Record

History of reaction to blood products: ❑ No ❑ Not known ❑ Yes; specify reaction: ❑ Hyperpyrexia ❑ Other _____

Special blood products required: ❑ No ❑ Yes; specify _____

Allergies: _____

Date Administered	Blood Component	Units	Duration	Signature	Serial No.	T, P, BP at start of each unit	Start time	Volume	T, P, BP at 15 minutes	End time

Drug	Dose	Route	Frequency	Signature	Date/time administered	Administered by
Hydrocortisone						
Piriton						

If a reaction occurs:	Name of physician informed: _____	
	Was the laboratory informed?	❑ Yes ❑ No
	Was a transfusion reaction form completed?	❑ Yes ❑ No

ALFRED STATE MEDICAL CENTER ■ 100 MAIN ST, ALFRED NY 14802 ■ (607) 555-1234

FIGURE 6-27G Blood Transfusion Report

TABLE 6-9 Nursing Documentation

Nursing Documentation	Description
Nursing care plan (Figure 6-28A)	Documents nursing interventions to be used to care for the patient. *Note:* Nursing care plans are not usually filed in the permanent patient record.
Nurses' notes (Figure 6-28B)	Documents daily observation about patients, including an initial history of the patient, patient's reactions to treatments, and treatments rendered.
Nursing discharge summary (Figure 6-28C)	Documents patient discharge plans and instructions.
Graphic sheet (Figure 6-28D represents a paper-based vital signs graphic sheet while Figure 6-28E represents a screen used to record vital signs in an electronic health record.)	Documents patient's vital signs (e.g., temperature, pulse, respiration, blood pressure) using a graph for easy interpretation of data.
Medication administration record (MAR) (Figure 6-28F represents a paper-based MAR while Figure 6-28G represents a screen used in an electronic health record to record a medication administration summary.)	Documents medications administered, date and time of administration, name of drug, dosage, route of administration (e.g., orally, topically, by injection, or infusion), and initials of nurse administering medication. *Note:* Patient reactions to drugs are documented in nurses notes.
Bedside terminal system	Computer system located at the patient's bedside, used to automate nursing documentation. Patient information can be entered, stored, retrieved, and displayed.

Note: The APGAR score measures the baby's appearance (A) (e.g., skin color), pulse (P), grimace (G) (e.g., irritability), activity (A) (e.g., muscle tone and motion), and respirations (R) on a scale of 1 to 10, with up to 2 points assigned for each measurement and 10 being the maximum score. An APGAR score is documented in the newborn record (and in some states as part of the birth certificate) as an indication of infant health; it also helps direct medical personnel in determining whether intervention is necessary (e.g., oxygen therapy). (Although named for pediatrician Virginia Apgar, the letters also serve as a memory aid.) The APGAR score is usually measured at 1 minute and 5 minutes after birth, but may be recorded for up to 10 or 15 minutes if the infant is being resuscitated.

	Addressograph				**NURSING CARE PLAN**

Date/Initials	Nursing Diagnosis	Nursing Intervention	Outcome Evaluation	Projected Date/Initials

IHS-80-1 (Rev. 3/89)
Part 2

EF

FIGURE 6-28A Nursing Care Plan (Reprinted according to IHS.gov Web reuse policy.)

			Addressograph		**NURSES NOTES**

DATE	TIME	NOTES	SIGNATURE

ALFRED STATE MEDICAL CENTER ■ 100 MAIN ST, ALFRED NY 14802 ■ (607) 555-1234

FIGURE 6-28B Nurses' Notes

NURSING DISCHARGE SUMMARY

Addressograph

Date/Time	Discharge to: ❏Home ❏Other: _____	Mode: ❏Ambulatory ❏Other: _____	Accompanied by:

Activity

Specify limitations _____

Diet

❏No dietary restrictions   ❏Special diet _____

Medications   ❏ No medications

Name of Medication	Dosage	Frequency of Administration	Special Instructions

Treatment/Care

Instructions: _____

Equipment/Supplies: _____

Follow-up

You are scheduled to see Dr. _____ on _____ at _____ .

Date   Time

Patient's Conditions:

_____

Signature of Registered Nurse

ALFRED STATE MEDICAL CENTER ■ 100 MAIN ST, ALFRED NY 14802 ■ (607) 555-1234

FIGURE 6-28C Nursing Discharge Summary

IHS-350 (REV. 01/89)

VITAL SIGNS RECORD

MONTH	HOSPITAL DAY													
YEAR 19	DAY OF MONTH													
19	HOUR													

PULSE (○)	TEMP. F (●)													TEMP. C
140	105°													
130	104°													40°
120	103°													
110	102°													38.9°
100	101°													
90	100°													37.8°
80	99°													
	98.6°													37°
70	98°													
60	97°													36.4°
50	96°													

(Centigrade Equivalents, for Reference only)

RESPIRATION RECORD														
BLOOD PRESSURE	AM													
	PM													
HEIGHT WEIGHT														
DIET														
BATH														
STOOLS														

URINE	TIME OF DAY	SUGAR	ACE-TONE	SUGAR	ACE-TONE	SUGAR	ACE-TONE	SUGAR	ACE-TONE	SUGAR	ACE-TONE	SUGAR	ACE-TONE	SUGAR	ACE-TONE
	AM														
	AM														
	PM														
	PM														

PATIENT'S IDENTIFICATION (For typed or written entries give: Name___last, first, middle; hospital or medical facility)

RECORD OF TEMPERATURE, PULSE & RESPIRATION AND ACTIVITIES OF DAILY LIVING (EXCEPTION TO SF-511)

FIGURE 6-28D Vital Signs Record Graphic Sheet (Reprinted according to IHS.gov Web reuse policy.)

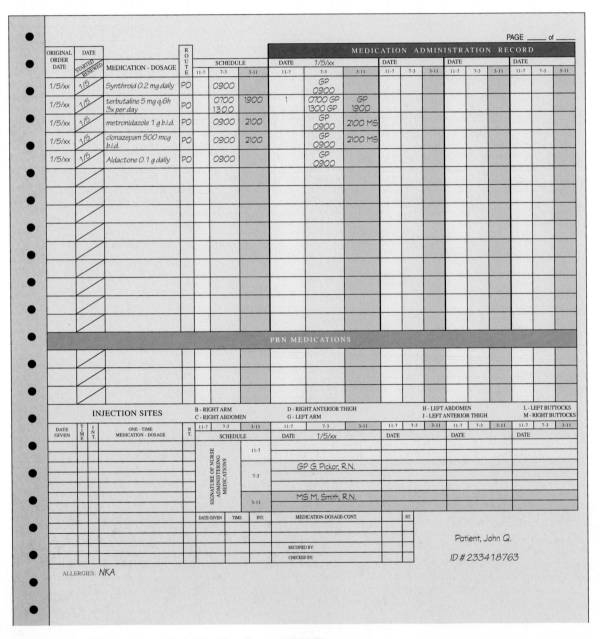

FIGURE 6-28E Electronic Vital Signs (Courtesy of Optum™ PM and Physician EMR)

FIGURE 6-28F Medication Administration Record (MAR)

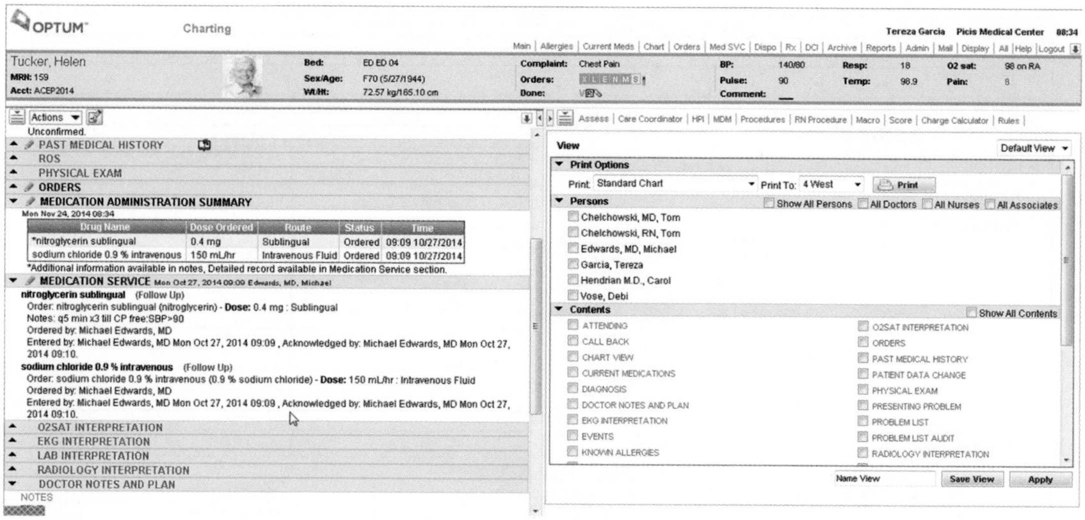

FIGURE 6-28G Electronic MAR Screen (Courtesy of Optum™ PM and Physician EMR)

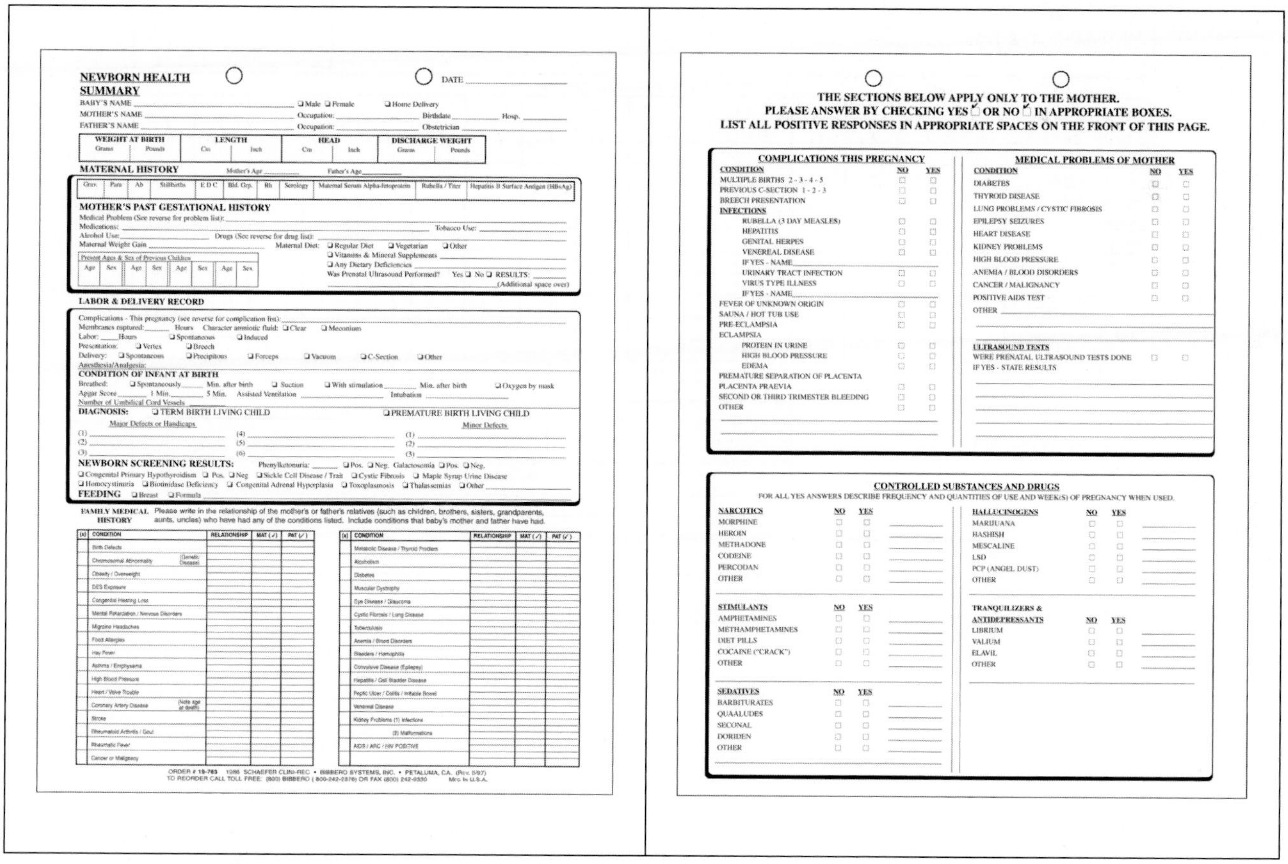

NEWBORN HEALTH SUMMARY

DATE ______

BABY'S NAME ______ ❑ Male ❑ Female ❑ Home Delivery

MOTHER'S NAME ______ Occupation: ______ Birthdate ______ Hosp. ______

FATHER'S NAME ______ Occupation: ______ Obstetrician ______

WEIGHT AT BIRTH		LENGTH		HEAD		DISCHARGE WEIGHT	
Grams	Pounds	Cm	Inch	Cm	Inch	Grams	Pounds

MATERNAL HISTORY Mother's Age ______ Father's Age ______

Grav.	Para	Ab	Stillbirths	E D C	Bld. Grp.	Rh	Serology	Maternal Serum Alpha-fetoprotein	Rubella / Titer	Hepatitis B Surface Antigen (HBsAg)

MOTHER'S PAST GESTATIONAL HISTORY

Medical Problem (See reverse for problem list): ______

Medications: ______ Tobacco Use: ______

Alcohol Use: ______ Drugs (See reverse for drug list): ______

Maternal Weight Gain ______ Maternal Diet: ❑ Regular Diet ❑ Vegetarian ❑ Other

❑ Vitamins & Mineral Supplements ______

❑ Any Dietary Deficiencies ______

Was Prenatal Ultrasound Performed? Yes ❑ No ❑ RESULTS: ______ (Additional space over)

Present Ages & Sex of Previous Children							
Age	Sex	Age	Sex	Age	Sex	Age	Sex

LABOR & DELIVERY RECORD

Complications - This pregnancy (see reverse for complication list): ______

Membranes ruptured: ______ Hours Character amniotic fluid: ❑ Clear ❑ Meconium

Labor: ____ Hours ❑ Spontaneous ❑ Induced

Presentation: ❑ Vertex ❑ Breech

Delivery: ❑ Spontaneous ❑ Precipitous ❑ Forceps ❑ Vacuum ❑ C-Section ❑ Other

Anesthesia/Analgesia: ______

CONDITION OF INFANT AT BIRTH

Breathed: ❑ Spontaneously ______ Min. after birth ❑ Suction ❑ With stimulation ______ Min. after birth ❑ Oxygen by mask

Apgar Score ______ 1 Min. ______ 5 Min. Assisted Ventilation ______ Intubation ______

Number of Umbilical Cord Vessels ______

DIAGNOSIS: ❑ TERM BIRTH LIVING CHILD ❑ PREMATURE BIRTH LIVING CHILD

Major Defects or Handicaps: (1) ______ (2) ______ (3) ______ (4) ______ (5) ______ (6) ______

Minor Defects: (1) ______ (2) ______ (3) ______

NEWBORN SCREENING RESULTS: Phenylketonuria: ______ ❑ Pos. ❑ Neg. Galactosemia ❑ Pos. ❑ Neg.

❑ Congenital Primary Hypothyroidism ❑ Pos. ❑ Neg ❑ Sickle Cell Disease / Trait ❑ Cystic Fibrosis ❑ Maple Syrup Urine Disease

❑ Homocystinuria ❑ Biotinidase Deficiency ❑ Congenital Adrenal Hyperplasia ❑ Toxoplasmosis ❑ Thalassemias ❑ Other ______

FEEDING ❑ Breast ❑ Formula ______

FAMILY MEDICAL HISTORY Please write in the relationship of the mother's or father's relatives (such as children, brothers, sisters, grandparents, aunts, uncles) who have had any of the conditions listed. Include conditions that baby's mother and father have had.

(x)	CONDITION	RELATIONSHIP	MAT (✓)	PAT (✓)
	Birth Defects			
	Chromosomal Abnormality (Genetic Disease)			
	Obesity / Overweight			
	DES Exposure			
	Congenital Hearing Loss			
	Mental Retardation / Nervous Disorders			
	Migraine Headaches			
	Food Allergies			
	Hay Fever			
	Asthma / Emphysema			
	High Blood Pressure			
	Heart / Valve Trouble			
	Coronary Artery Disease (Note age at death)			
	Stroke			
	Rheumatoid Arthritis / Gout			
	Rheumatic Fever			
	Cancer or Malignancy			

(x)	CONDITION	RELATIONSHIP	MAT (✓)	PAT (✓)
	Metabolic Disease / Thyroid Problem			
	Alcoholism			
	Diabetes			
	Muscular Dystrophy			
	Eye Disease / Glaucoma			
	Cystic Fibrosis / Lung Disease			
	Tuberculosis			
	Anemia / Blood Disorders			
	Bleeders / Hemophilia			
	Convulsive Disease (Epilepsy)			
	Hepatitis / Gall Bladder Disease			
	Peptic Ulcer / Colitis / Irritable Bowel			
	Venereal Disease			
	Kidney Problems (1) Infections			
	(2) Malformations			
	AIDS / ARC / HIV POSITIVE			

ORDER # 19-783 1986 SCHAEFER CLIN-REC • BIBBERO SYSTEMS, INC. • PETALUMA, CA. (Rev. 5/97)
TO REORDER CALL TOLL FREE: (800) BIBBERO (800-242-2376) OR FAX (800) 242-9330 Mfg. in U.S.A.

THE SECTIONS BELOW APPLY ONLY TO THE MOTHER.
PLEASE ANSWER BY CHECKING YES ☐ OR NO ☐ IN APPROPRIATE BOXES.
LIST ALL POSITIVE RESPONSES IN APPROPRIATE SPACES ON THE FRONT OF THIS PAGE.

COMPLICATIONS THIS PREGNANCY

CONDITION	NO	YES
MULTIPLE BIRTHS 2 - 3 - 4 - 5	☐	☐
PREVIOUS C-SECTION 1 - 2 - 3	☐	☐
BREECH PRESENTATION	☐	☐
INFECTIONS		
RUBELLA (3 DAY MEASLES)	☐	☐
HEPATITIS	☐	☐
GENITAL HERPES	☐	☐
VENEREAL DISEASE	☐	☐
IF YES - NAME ______		
URINARY TRACT INFECTION	☐	☐
VIRUS TYPE ILLNESS	☐	☐
IF YES - NAME ______		
FEVER OF UNKNOWN ORIGIN	☐	☐
SAUNA / HOT TUB USE	☐	☐
PRE-ECLAMPSIA	☐	☐
ECLAMPSIA		
PROTEIN IN URINE	☐	☐
HIGH BLOOD PRESSURE	☐	☐
EDEMA	☐	☐
PREMATURE SEPARATION OF PLACENTA		
PLACENTA PRAEVIA	☐	☐
SECOND OR THIRD TRIMESTER BLEEDING	☐	☐
OTHER	☐	☐

MEDICAL PROBLEMS OF MOTHER

CONDITION	NO	YES
DIABETES	☐	☐
THYROID DISEASE	☐	☐
LUNG PROBLEMS / CYSTIC FIBROSIS	☐	☐
EPILEPSY SEIZURES	☐	☐
HEART DISEASE	☐	☐
KIDNEY PROBLEMS	☐	☐
HIGH BLOOD PRESSURE	☐	☐
ANEMIA / BLOOD DISORDERS	☐	☐
CANCER / MALIGNANCY	☐	☐
POSITIVE AIDS TEST	☐	☐
OTHER ______		

ULTRASOUND TESTS

	NO	YES
WERE PRENATAL ULTRASOUND TESTS DONE	☐	☐
IF YES - STATE RESULTS ______		

CONTROLLED SUBSTANCES AND DRUGS

FOR ALL YES ANSWERS DESCRIBE FREQUENCY AND QUANTITIES OF USE AND WEEK(S) OF PREGNANCY WHEN USED.

NARCOTICS	NO	YES	
MORPHINE	☐	☐	______
HEROIN	☐	☐	______
METHADONE	☐	☐	______
CODEINE	☐	☐	______
PERCODAN	☐	☐	______
OTHER	☐	☐	______

STIMULANTS	NO	YES	
AMPHETAMINES	☐	☐	______
METHAMPHETAMINES	☐	☐	______
DIET PILLS	☐	☐	______
COCAINE ("CRACK")	☐	☐	______
OTHER	☐	☐	______

SEDATIVES	NO	YES	
BARBITURATES	☐	☐	______
QUAALUDES	☐	☐	______
SECONAL	☐	☐	______
DORIDEN	☐	☐	______
OTHER	☐	☐	______

HALLUCINOGENS	NO	YES	
MARIJUANA	☐	☐	______
HASHISH	☐	☐	______
MESCALINE	☐	☐	______
LSD	☐	☐	______
PCP (ANGEL DUST)	☐	☐	______
OTHER	☐	☐	______

TRANQUILIZERS & ANTIDEPRESSANTS	NO	YES	
LIBRIUM	☐	☐	______
VALIUM	☐	☐	______
ELAVIL	☐	☐	______
OTHER	☐	☐	______

FIGURE 6-29A Neonatal Record (Permission to reprint granted by Bibbero Systems, Inc, (800) 242-2376 www.bibbero.com.)

MEDICAL RECORD -- PRENATAL AND PREGNANCY

Patient's Name	Age	Race/Tribe	Father of Baby	Age

Address/Location	Home Phone	Work Phone

Pregnancy History: Grav: Para: Term: Premature: Ab's: Living: Stillbirth Neonatal Death:

GESTATIONAL AGE ASSESSMENTS:

1. Menstrual History: LNMP:_____ Certain?_____
2. Use of BCP's Yes:_____ No:_____ Last Taken?_____
3. Clinical Evaluation
   Pregnancy Test:
      Date _____ Gestation by LMP _____ wks
   First Uterine Size Estimate:
      Date _____ Gestation by LMP _____ wks
      Size by Examination _____ wks
   Uterus at Umbilicus
      Date _____ Gestation by LMP _____ wks
   Quickening:
      Date _____ Gestation by LMP _____ wks
   FHT First Heard by Doppler:
      Date _____ Gestation by LMP _____ wks
   FHT First Heard by Fetoscope:
      Date _____ Gestation by LMP _____ wks
   Ultrasound Scan:
      Date _____ Gestational Age _____ Sonar EDC _____
      Date _____ Gestational Age _____ Sonar EDC _____
4. Predicted EDC _____
   Reliability: Poor _____, Good _____, Excellent _____

LABORATORY FINDINGS

INITIAL LAB SCREEN			ADDITIONAL LAB DATA		
DATE	TEST	RESULT	DATE	TEST	RESULT
	Hct/Hgb				
	Type & Rh				
	Antibodies				
	Serology				
	Rubella				
	UA: Micro				
	C&S				
	Pap				
	G.C.				
	Diabetes Screen				
	PPD				

PRENATAL RISK ASSESSMENT

REPRODUCTIVE HISTORY		ASSOCIATED CONDITIONS		PRESENT PREGNANCY	
Age Under 16 or Over 35	1____	Chronic Renal Disease	2____	Bleeding: Less than 20 wks	1____
Parity 0 or Over 5	1____	Diabetes: Gestational	2____	After 20 wks	1-3____
Habitual Abortion	1____	Class B or Higher	3____	Anemia: Hematocrit < 34	1____
Infertility	1____	Cardiac Disease	1-3____	Prolonged Pregnancy > 42 wks	3____
P P Hem, Manual Removal	1____	Major Gyn Surgery, Cone Bx.	2____	Hypertension, Preeclampsia	2-3____
Previous Baby > 9 lbs. (4050 gms)	1____		1-3____	Premature Rupt. Membranes	3____
< 5½ lbs. (2500 gms)	2____		1-3____	Polyhdramnios	2____
Prev. Toxemia, Hypertension	1____		1-3____	Small for Dates	3____
Previous Cesarean Section	3____	Cigarette Smoking	1____	Multiple Pregnancy	3____
Pre. Stillbirth or N N D	3____	Alcohol Use	1-2____	Breech > 36 weeks	3____
Prolonged Labor (> 30 Hrs.)		Teratogen/Drug Exposure		Rh Negative. Sensitized?	1-3____
or Difficult Delivery	1____		1-2____	Genital Herpes, active	3____
	1____	Significant Social Problem		Excessive or inadeq. wt. gain	1-2____
			1-2____		1-3____

Low Risk = Score 0-2   Medium Risk = Score 3-6   Extreme Risk = Score 7

OBSTETRIC PROGNOSIS
AND
MANAGEMENT PLAN FOR
AT RISK CONDITIONS

L & D Tour: _____
Referrals: _____

PRENATAL FLOW RECORD

Date														
Est. wks. gest. D/S														
WT. (Pre Preg)														
Blood Pressure														
Fundal Height														
Position														
Station														
Fetal Heart: FS-DOP														
Edema														
UA: Prot/Gluc/Acet														
Rick Reassessment														
Provider Initials														

Patient's Identification	Signature Code: Initials	Signature & Title

Other Information

IHS-800-1 (PAGE 1)
REV. 01/89

FIGURE 6-29B Antepartum (or Prenatal) Record (Reprinted according to IHS.gov Web reuse policy.)

LABOR FLOW RECORD

RECORD ALL EXAMINATIONS SERIALLY FROM ADMISSION TO DELIVERY: PLEASE INITIAL AND INDICATE PROGRESS NOTE BY ✓

DATE & TIME	Blood Pr. Temp. Pulse	F.H.R.		Contractions		Vaginal Exam.			Observations: (Bleeding; Amn. fluid color, etc.) Procedures: (Block, Amniotomy, etc.)	Drugs - Fluids		Initials	See Progress Note
		Rate	? EFM	Freq.	Qual.	Eff.	Dil.	Sta.		Agent & Rt.	Amount		

PATIENT'S IDENTIFICATION

Signature Code / Initials	Signature and Title

IHS-800-3
1/89

FIGURE 6-29C Labor Record (Reprinted according to IHS.gov Web reuse policy.)

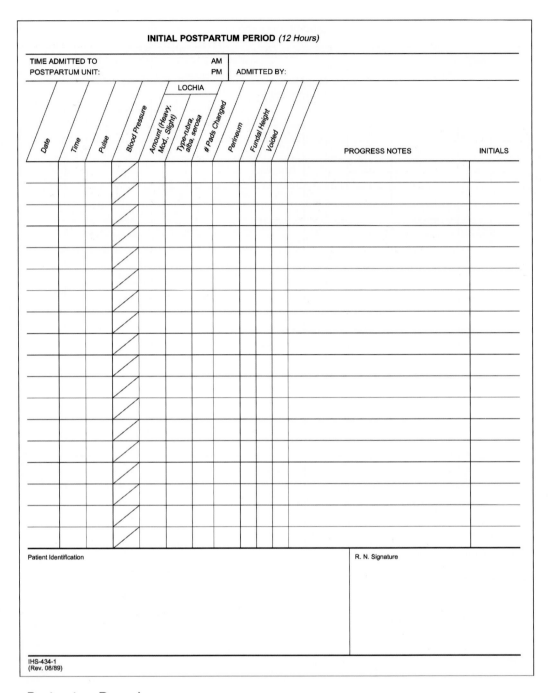

INITIAL POSTPARTUM PERIOD *(12 Hours)*

Date	Time	Pulse	Blood Pressure	Amount (Heavy, Mod., Slight)	Type-rubra, alba, serosa	# Pads Changed	Perineum	Fundal Height	Voided		PROGRESS NOTES	INITIALS

IHS-434-1
(Rev. 08/89)

FIGURE 6-29D Postpartum Record (Reprinted according to IHS.gov Web reuse policy.)

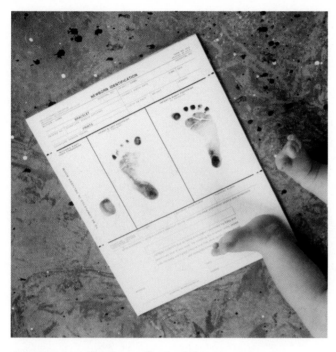

FIGURE 6-29E Newborn Footprints (Permission to reprint granted by Precision Dynamics Corporation. Web site: PDCorp.com.)

Autopsy Report

Medicare CoP state that the medical staff should attempt to obtain autopsies in all cases of unusual deaths and to pursue medicolegal and educational interest. In addition, the mechanism for documenting permission to perform an autopsy must be defined, and there must be a system for notifying the medical staff—and specifically the attending practitioner—when an autopsy is being performed.

An autopsy (or necropsy) (Figure 6-30) is an examination of a body after death. It includes the macroscopic and microscopic examination of vital organs and tissue specimens to assist in determining a cause of death and the character or extent of changes produced by disease. Prior to performing an autopsy, consent must be obtained from the legal next-of-kin of the deceased, and the signed consent becomes part of the permanent patient record (unless it is a coroner's case, based on state law). In addition, documentation that an autopsy was performed is to be entered in the patient record (e.g., progress notes), and the record is considered incomplete until the autopsy report is filed. Elements of an autopsy report (necropsy report or postmortem report) include:

- Summary of patient's clinical history, including diseases, surgical history, and treatment
- Detailed results of the macroscopic and microscopic findings, including external appearance of the body and internal examination by body system
- Contributing factors that led to death

- Clinical-pathologic correlation (e.g., medical conclusion of patient's disease process)
- Authentication by pathologist

Note: An autopsy is completed for suspicious deaths and in the event of an untimely death. (State laws govern when autopsies are mandated.)

Typically, an autopsy is required for the following circumstances:

- Any case where there is medical/legal necessity
- Cause of death is not related to treatment
- Dead on arrival to ED or dying in ED (without previous diagnosis or before definitive diagnosis)
- Occult hemorrhage
- Pneumonia (no microbiologic diagnosis)
- Sudden infant death
- Trauma (internal)
- Pediatric and perinatal deaths
- Deaths that occur in the operating room and/or during a procedure

EXERCISE 6–3 Hospital Inpatient Record—Clinical Data

Fill-in-the-Blank: Enter the appropriate term(s) to complete each of the following statements.

1. A discharge summary, also known as a _____, documents the patient's hospitalization, including reason(s) for hospitalization, _____, and condition at discharge.

2. The _____ documents the patient's chief complaint, _____, past/family/social history, and review of systems.

3. If a patient is readmitted within _____ days after discharge for the same condition, a(n) _____ can be completed to document the patient's history of the present illness and any pertinent changes and physical findings that occurred since the previous admission.

4. Diagnostic and therapeutic patient care activities, such as medications and dosages, and completion of a chest x-ray, are initiated by _____, also known as _____.

5. Preprinted physician orders, known as _____ or _____ orders, are preapproved by the medical staff and placed on a patient's record, usually at the time of admission.

6. A(n) _____ is generated by emergency medical technicians to document clinical information such as vital signs, level of consciousness, appearance of the patient, and so on when a patient is transported via ambulance to the emergency department.

Addressograph

REPORT OF AUTOPSY

CASE #:   AGE: RACE: GENDER:

DATE OF DEATH: DATE OF AUTOPSY:

MANNER OF DEATH:

IMMEDIATE CAUSE OF DEATH:

FINAL ANATOMIC DIAGNOSES:

PROTOCOL

EXTERNAL EXAMINATION

EVIDENT OF TREATMENT

EVIDENCE OF INJURY

INTERNAL EXAMINATION

    CAVITIES

    CARDIOVASCULAR SYSTEM

    RESPIRATORY SYSTEM

    CENTRAL NERVOUS SYSTEM

    URINARY SYSTEM

    GENITAL SYSTEM

    HEPATOBILIARY SYSTEM

    GASTROINTESTINAL TRACT

    LYMPHOPROLIFERATIVE SYSTEM

    MUSCULOSKELETAL SYSTEM

    MISCELLANEOUS

BRAIN AFTER FIXATION

MICROSCOPIC DESCRIPTION

LABORATORY DATA

DRUG SCREEN RESULTS

DRUG QUANTITATION RESULTS

SIGNATURE OF PATHOLOGIST

ALFRED STATE MEDICAL CENTER ■ 100 MAIN ST, ALFRED NY 14802 ■ (607) 555-1234

FIGURE 6-30 Autopsy Report

7. A consulting physician, as part of the consultation process, is responsible for reviewing the patient's record, _____, documenting pertinent findings, and providing _____ and/or opinions to the referring physician.

8. Some facilities adopt _____, which means all progress notes documented by physicians, nurses, physical therapists, occupational therapists, and other professional staff members are organized in the _____ of the record.

9. The anesthesia record, pre- and postanesthesia _____, and _____ record provide complete documentation of the administration of

medications and anesthetic agents administered during the pre- and postoperative time and during surgery.

10. The gross findings, organs examined (visually or palpated), and techniques associated with the performance of surgery are documented in the _____ .

11. The _____ assists in the diagnosis and treatment of patients by documenting the analysis of tissue removed surgically or diagnostically, or expelled by the patient.

12. Reports produced by the laboratory, radiology, and nuclear medicine departments are known as _____ .

13. Nursing diagnoses and interventions are documented on a _____ .

14. The _____ documents information concerning the mother's condition after delivery.

15. An examination of a body after death, which includes the _____ and microscopic examination of vital organs and tissue specimens to assist in determining a cause of death and the character or extent of changes produced by disease, is an _____ .

HOSPITAL OUTPATIENT RECORD

The Joint Commission standards state that by the third visit, the patient record of a patient who receives continuing ambulatory services (e.g., physical therapy services) must contain a summary list that documents significant diagnosis and conditions, significant operative and invasive procedures, adverse or allergic drug reactions, and current and long-term medications (including over-the-counter medications and herbal remedies). (This summary list must be updated on subsequent visits.) Medicare CoP categorize outpatient care as *optional hospital services*.

Outpatient care is defined as medical or surgical care that does not include an overnight hospital stay (and not longer than 23 hours, 59 minutes, 59 seconds). Hospital outpatient services usually include diagnostic, therapeutic (surgical and nonsurgical), and rehabilitation services. (For reimbursement purposes, Medicare categorizes emergency room services as hospital outpatient care.) The provision of medical supplies (e.g., splints) and ancillary tests (e.g., lab) billed by the hospital are also

included as outpatient care. Hospital outpatient records (or ambulatory records) include a patient registration form similar to the inpatient face sheet, and depending on the complexity of outpatient services provided, additional reports can include ancillary reports, progress notes, physician orders, operative reports, pathology reports, nursing documentation, and so on. In addition, some hospital outpatient departments use a short stay record (Figure 6-31), which allows providers to record the history, physical examination, progress notes, physician orders, and nursing documentation on one double-sided form.

Example 1
Sam undergoes a laparoscopic cholecystectomy on an outpatient basis. Sam's patient record will consist of a patient registration form, H&PE report, operative report, anesthesia record, recovery room record, pathology report, and so on.

Example 2
Omar undergoes an outpatient x-ray of his left wrist. His outpatient record consists of only a patient registration form, a physician order form, and the x-ray report.

The Uniform Ambulatory Care Data Set (UACDS) is the minimum core data set collected on Medicare and Medicaid outpatients. The goal of collecting standardized UACDS data is to improve data comparison in ambulatory and outpatient settings. Current UACDS data elements include the following:

• Patient (person receiving health care services)

  Example VA medical centers collect patient's name, date of birth, social security number (SSN) (to confirm eligibility), and so on.

• Date and time of encounter or ancillary service (actual date and time encounter or service occurred, usually collected from appointment scheduling software)

Note: An outpatient visit is the visit of a patient on one calendar day to one or more hospital departments for the purpose of receiving outpatient health care services (e.g., encounter or ancillary service visit). An encounter is a professional contact between a patient and a provider who delivers services or is professionally responsible for services delivered to a patient. An encounter is *not* the same as an ancillary service visit

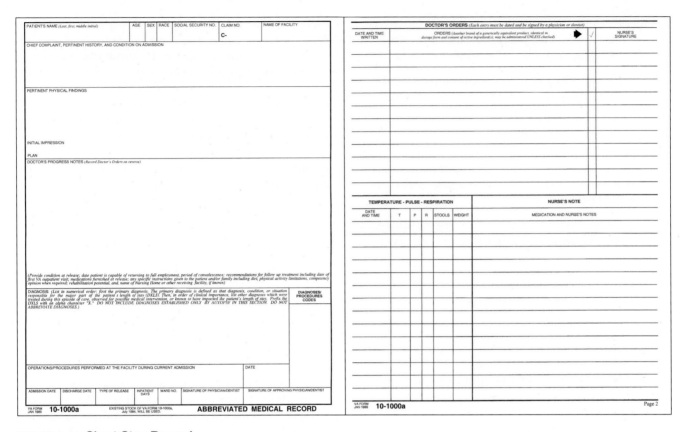

FIGURE 6-31 **Short Stay Record** (Reprinted according to www.vha.gov Web Reuse Policy.)

(or occasion of service), which is the appearance of an outpatient to a hospital department to receive an ordered service, test, or procedure. Ancillary services do *not* include exercise of independent medical judgment in diagnosing, evaluating, and/or treating conditions; an ancillary service is usually the result of an encounter.

Example 1
Laboratory tests or x-ray procedures are ordered as part of an encounter. A patient may undergo multiple ancillary services during one outpatient visit.

Example 2
A telephone contact between a physician and a patient is *considered* an encounter if the telephone contact includes the appropriate elements of a face-to-face encounter (e.g., history and medical decision making).

- Practitioner (e.g., physician, nurse practitioner, physician's assistant)

Note: Practitioners are categorized as licensed and nonlicensed. A licensed practitioner is required to have a public license/certification to deliver care to patients (e.g., MD, RN), and a practitioner can *also* be a provider. A *provider* is a business entity that furnishes health care to consumers or a professionally licensed practitioner authorized to operate a health care delivery facility (e.g., VA medical centers). A nonlicensed practitioner does not have a public license/certification and is supervised by a licensed/certified professional in the delivery of care to patients (e.g., physical therapy assistant).

- Place of service (location where service was provided to outpatient)
- Active problem(s) (purpose of outpatient visit, which is the diagnosis treated and coded according to ICD-9-CM)

Note: When more than one active problem or diagnosis is identified for an encounter, the practitioner must determine the first-listed diagnosis (reason the patient sought treatment during that encounter). The first-listed diagnosis reflects the current, most significant reason for services provided or procedures performed. When coding pre-existing conditions, make certain the diagnosis code reflects the current reason for medical management. Chronic diseases may be coded as long as treated, but if the patient presents and a condition other than the chronic problem is treated, code only the new condition.

Also, never code a diagnosis that is no longer applicable; if the disease or condition has been successfully treated and no longer exists, it is not billable and should not be coded or reported.

• Services or procedures provided (services provided or procedures performed by the practitioner, which are coded according to CPT and HCPCS Level II)

EXERCISE 6–4 Hospital Outpatient Records

True/False: Indicate whether each statement is true (T) or false (F).

_____ 1. The Joint Commission standards require that by no earlier than the fourth ambulatory visit the patient record of a patient who receives continuing ambulatory services must contain a summary list that documents the significant diagnosis and conditions, procedures, drug allergies, and medications.

_____ 2. Inpatient care is defined as medical or surgical care that does not include an overnight hospital stay.

_____ 3. The summary list for outpatient records needs to be updated on all subsequent visits.

_____ 4. Medicare CoP categorize outpatient care as *optional hospital services.*

_____ 5. Medicare categorizes ED services as hospital outpatient care for reimbursement purposes.

Fill-in-the-Blank: Enter the term that completes each statement.

6. The minimum core data set collected on Medicare and Medicaid outpatients is the _____ .

7. A professional contact between a patient and a provider who delivers services or is professionally responsible for services delivered to a patient is known as a(n) _____ .

8. A practitioner must determine the _____ , or the reason the patient sought treatment, when more than one active problem or diagnosis is identified for an encounter.

9. Ancillary service visits and encounters are considered types of _____ , in which a patient receives outpatient health care services on one calendar day in one or more hospital departments.

10. An outpatient visit to a hospital department to receive an ordered service, test, or procedure is known as an ancillary service visit or a(n) _____ .

PHYSICIAN OFFICE RECORD

The content and organization of physician office records varies greatly depending on the size of the office, ownership, and whether the practice is accredited. As a minimum, physician office records (Table 6-10) should contain patient registration information, a problem list, a medication record, progress notes (including patient's history and physical examination), and results of ancillary reports. When office surgery is performed, the provider documents a report of surgery in the record.

TABLE 6-10 Physician Office Reports

Physician Office Report	Description
Patient registration form (Figure 6-32A)	Documents demographic, administrative, and financial data.
Problem list (Figures 6-32B.1 and 6-32B.2)	Documents diseases, conditions, allergies, and procedures.
Medication list (Figure 6-32C)	Documents medications, dosage, associated diagnosis, and ordering physician.
Progress notes (Figure 6-32D)	Documents the initial history and physical examination and all subsequent visits.
Ancillary reports (Figure 6-32E)	Documents reports of ancillary testing completed in the office or by outside labs, including hospital labs.
Immunization record (Figure 6-32F)	Documents immunizations (vaccines) administered.
Growth and development chart (Figure 6-32G and Figure 6-32H)	Documents height and weight, which is used to monitor growth patterns.

○   ○

Insurance cards copied ❑   **Patient Registration**   Account # : _____
Date: _____   **Information**   Insurance # : _____
                                                                                 Co-Payment: $ _____
                                          Please PRINT AND complete ALL sections below!

Is your condition a result of a work injury? YES NO   An auto accident? YES NO   Date of injury: _____

PATIENT'S PERSONAL INFORMATION Marital Status: ❑ Single ❑ Married ❑ Divorced ❑ Widowed   Sex: ❑ Male   ❑ Female
Name:_____
             last name   *first name*   *initial*
Street address: _____ (Apt # _____) City: _____ State: _____ Zip: _____
Home phone: (___) _____ Work phone: (___) _____
Date of Birth: _____ / _____ / _____ Driver's License: (State & Number) _____
         month   *day*   *year*
Employer / Name of School _____ ❑ Full Time ❑ Part Time
Spouse's Name: _____ _____ _____ Spouse's Work phone: (___) _____
         last name   *first name*   *initial*
How do you wish to be addressed? _____ Social Security # _____ - _____ - _____

PATIENT'S / RESPONSIBLE PARTY INFORMATION
Responsible party: _____ Date of Birth: _____
Relationship to Patient: ❑ Self ❑ Spouse ❑ Other _____ Social Security # _____ - _____ - _____
Responsible party's home phone: (____) _____ Work phone: (____) _____
    Address: _____ (Apt # _____) City: _____ State: _____ Zip: _____
Employer's name: _____ Phone number: (____) _____
    Address: _____ City: _____ State: _____ Zip: _____
    Your occupation: _____
Spouse's Employer's name: _____ Spouse's Work phone: (___) _____
    Address: _____ City: _____ State: _____ Zip: _____

PATIENT'S INSURANCE INFORMATION Please present insurance cards to receptionist.
PRIMARY insurance company's name: _____
Insurance address: _____ City: _____ State: _____ Zip: _____
Name of insured: _____ Date of Birth: _____ Relationship to insured: ❑ Self ❑ Spouse / ❑ Other ❑ Child
Insurance ID number: _____ Group number: _____
SECONDARY insurance company's name: _____
Insurance address: _____ City: _____ State: _____ Zip: _____
Name of insured: _____ Date of Birth: _____ Relationship to insured: ❑ Self ❑ Spouse / ❑ Other ❑ Child
Insurance ID number: _____ Group number: _____
Check if appropriate: ❑ Medigap policy ❑ Retiree coverage

PATIENT'S REFERRAL INFORMATION   (please circle one)
Referred by: _____ If referred by a friend, may we thank her or him? YES NO
Name(s) of other physician(s) who care for you: _____
_____

EMERGENCY CONTACT
Name of person not living with you: _____ Relationship: _____
Address: _____ City: _____ State: _____ Zip: _____
Phone number (home): (_____) _____ Phone number (work): (_____) _____

Assignment of Benefits • Financial Agreement
I hereby give lifetime authorization for payment of insurance benefits to be made directly to _____ , and any assisting
physicians, for services rendered. I understand that I am financially responsible for all charges whether or not they are covered by insurance. In the event
of default, I agree to pay all costs of collection, and reasonable attorney's fees. I hereby authorize this healthcare provider to release all information nec-
essary to secure the payment of benefits.
I further agree that a photocopy of this agreement shall be as valid as the original.
Date: _____ Your Signature: _____
Method of Payment: ❑ Cash ❑ Check ❑ Credit Card
FORM # 58-8424 • BIBBERO SYSTEMS, INC. • PETALUMA, CA. • TO ORDER CALL TOLL FREE : 800-BIBBERO (800-242-2376) • FAX (800) 242-9330   7/94

PATIENT REGISTRATION

FIGURE 6-32A Patient Registration Form (Permission to reprint granted by Bibbero Systems, Inc, (800) 242-2376 www.bibbero.com.)

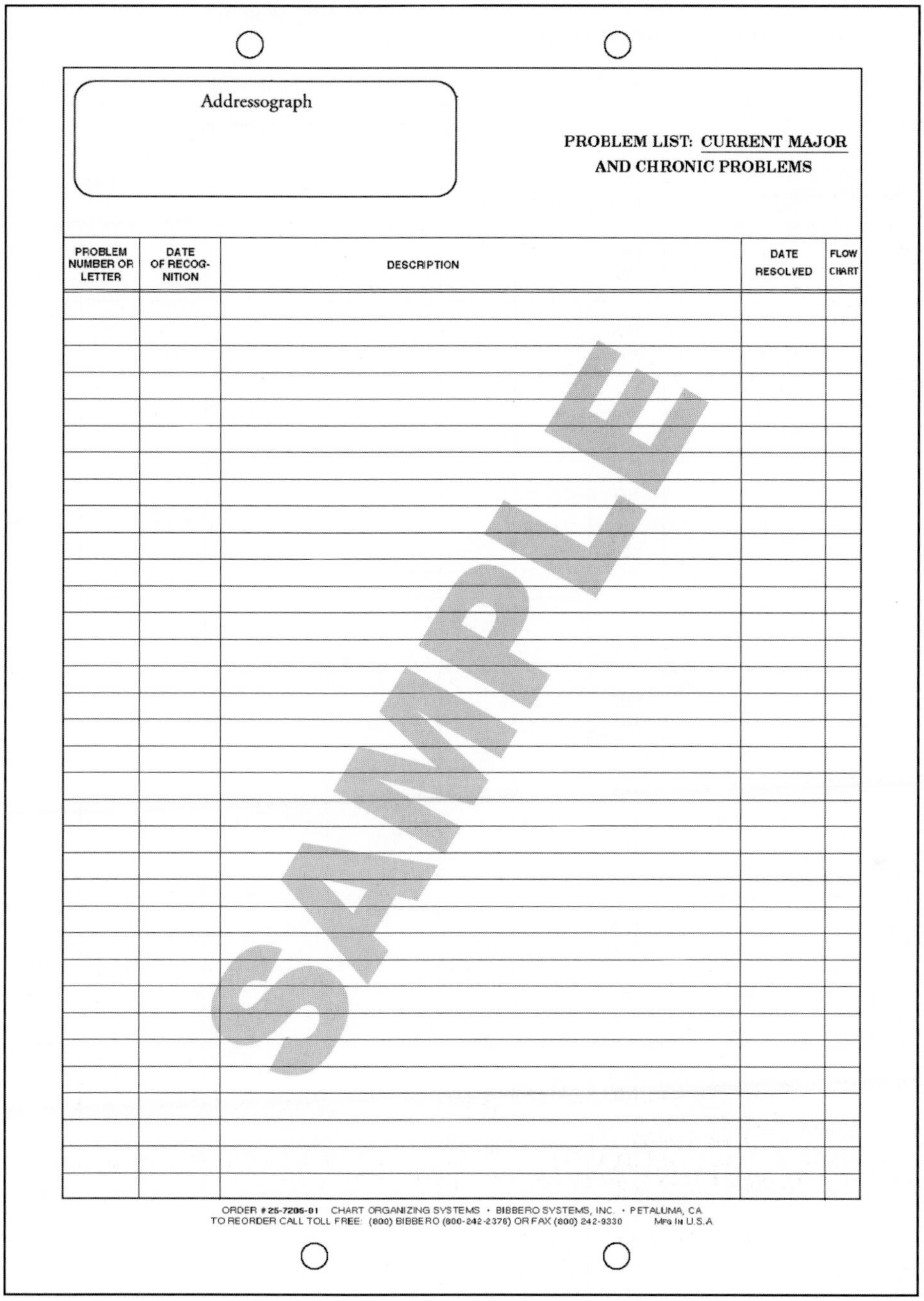

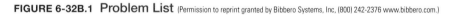

FIGURE 6-32B.1 Problem List (Permission to reprint granted by Bibbero Systems, Inc, (800) 242-2376 www.bibbero.com.)

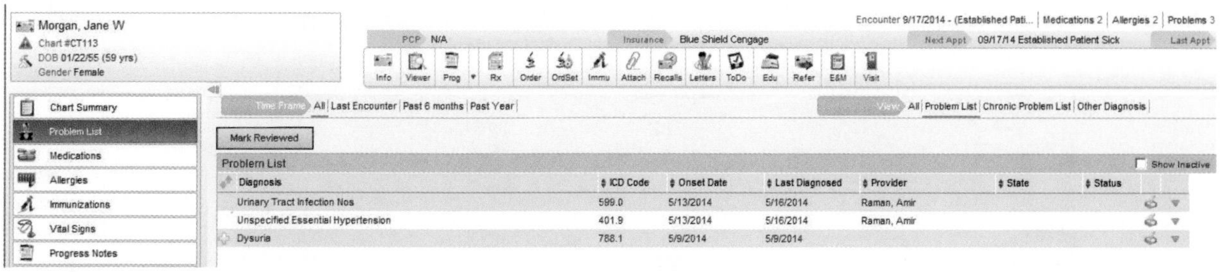

FIGURE 6-32B.2 Electronic Health Record Problem List (Courtesy of Optum™ PM and Physician EMR)

MEDICATIONS AND THERAPEUTIC MODALITIES			ALLERGIES-DRUG REACTIONS:					
PATIENT				**PHONE NO:**				
PHARMACY / THERAPIST				**PHONE NO:**				
Problem Number or Letter	MEDICATION / SIGNATURE / AMOUNT DISPENSED	NURSE TO REFILL	DATE		REFILLS / DATE / STRENGTH / INITIALS			
			Start	Stop				
			YES NO						
			YES NO						
			YES NO						
			YES NO						
			YES NO						
			YES NO						
			YES NO						
			YES NO						
			YES NO						
			YES NO						
			YES NO						
			YES NO						
			YES NO						
			YES NO						
			YES NO						
			YES NO						

ORDER # **25-7202-01**   CHART ORGANIZING SYSTEMS • © 1976 BIBBERO SYSTEMS, INC. • PETALUMA, CA.
TO REORDER CALL TOLL FREE: (800) BIBBERO (800-242-2376) OR FAX (800) 242-9330   M FG IN U.S.A.

FIGURE 6-32C Physician Office Medication List (Copyright © Courtesy of Bibbero Systems, Inc., Petaluma, CA., Phone: 800-242-2376; Fax: 800-242-9330; www.bibbero.com.)

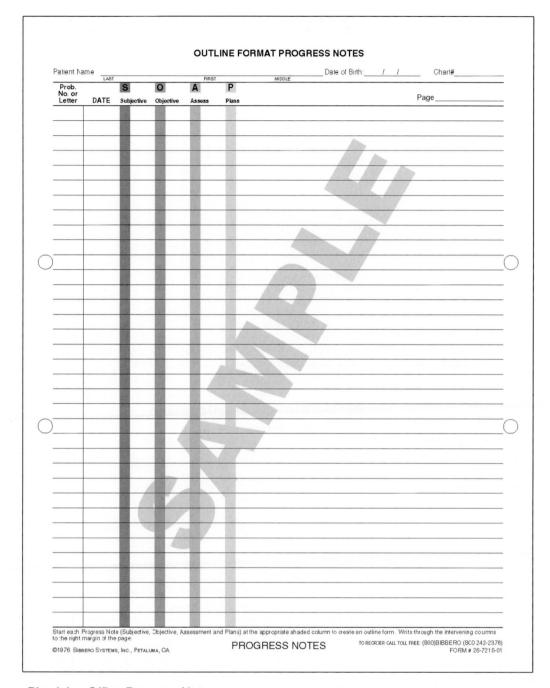

FIGURE 6-32D Physician Office Progress Notes (Permission to reprint granted by Bibbero Systems, Inc, (800) 242-2376 www.bibbero.com.)

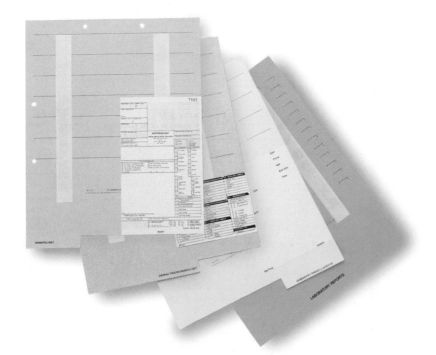

FIGURE 6-32E Ancillary Report Forms (Permission to reprint granted by Bibbero Systems, Inc, (800) 242-2376 www.bibbero.com.)

ALFRED STATE MEDICAL CENTER

PATIENT IMMUNIZATION RECORD

PATIENT LAST NAME _____

PATIENT FIRST NAME _____

PATIENT DATE OF BIRTH _____

PARENT/GUARDIAN _____

VACCINE	ADMINISTRATION DATE	PATIENT AGE (YR, MO)	ADMINISTRATION SITE	VACCINE MANUFACTURER	VACCINE LOT NUMBER	PATIENT EDUCATION	NURSE INITIALS
DTP1							
DTP2							
DTP3							
DTP/DTaP4							
DTP/DTaP5							
DT							
DTP/Hib1							
DTP/Hib2							
DTP/Hib3							
DTP/Hib4							
Td							
OPV/IPV1							
OPV/IPV2							
OPV/IPV3							
OPV/IPV4							
MMR1							
MMR2							
Hib1							
Hib2							
Hib3							
Hib4							
HepB1							
HepB2							
HepB3							

FIGURE 6-32F Immunization Record

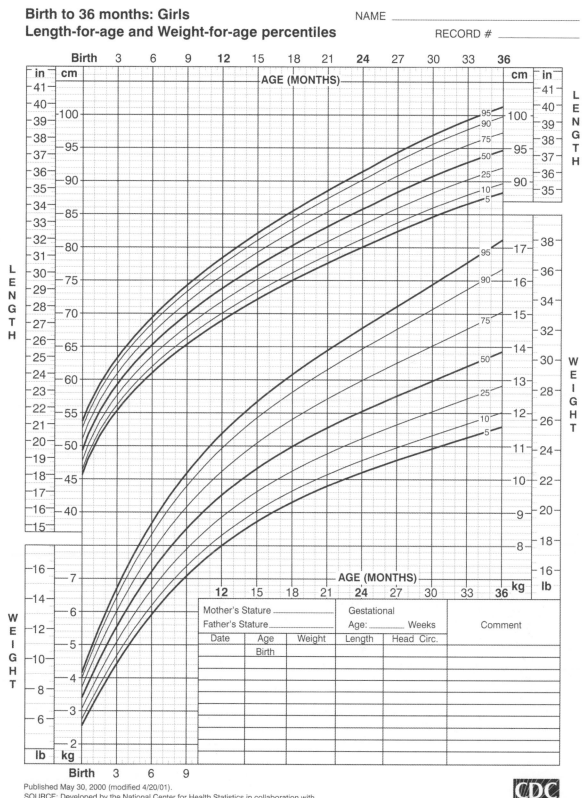

Birth to 36 months: Girls
Length-for-age and Weight-for-age percentiles

NAME

RECORD #

Published May 30, 2000 (modified 4/20/01).
SOURCE: Developed by the National Center for Health Statistics in collaboration with
the National Center for Chronic Disease Prevention and Health Promotion (2000).
http://www.cdc.gov/growthcharts

CDC
SAFER • HEALTHIER • PEOPLE™

FIGURE 6-32G Length and Weight Record (Reprinted from cms.gov)

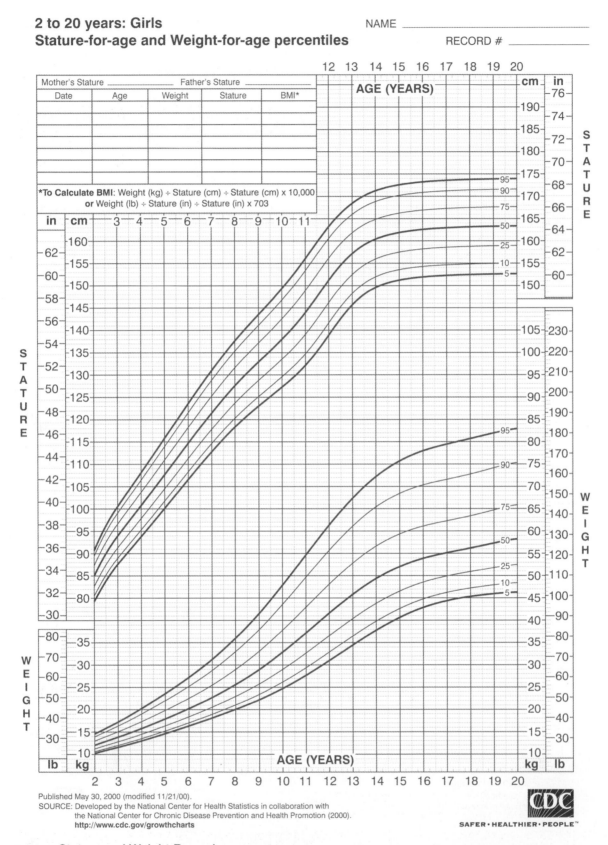

2 to 20 years: Girls
Stature-for-age and Weight-for-age percentiles

NAME _____

RECORD # _____

FIGURE 6-32H Stature and Weight Record (Reprinted from cms.gov)

An encounter form (superbill or fee slip) (Figure 6-33) is commonly used in physician offices to capture charges generated during an office visit and consists of a single page that contains a list of common services provided in the office. This form is initiated when the patient registers at the front desk and is completed by providers as the patient receives care. Diagnostic codes are reported for

ENCOUNTER FORM

Tel: (101) 555-1111
Fax: (101) 555-2222

Kim Donaldson, M.D.
INTERNAL MEDICINE
101 Main Street, Suite A
Alfred NY 14802

EIN: 11-9876543
NPI: 1234567890

OFFICE VISITS	NEW	EST
☐ Level I	99201	99211
☐ Level II	99202	99212
☐ Level III	99203	99213
☐ Level IV	99204	99214
☐ Level V	99205	99215

OFFICE CONSULTS (NEW or EST)	
☐ Level I	99214
☐ Level II	99242
☐ Level III	99243
☐ Level IV	99244
☐ Level V	99245

OFFICE PROCEDURES	
☐ EKG with interpretation	93000
☐ Oximetry with interpretation	94760
LABORATORY TESTS	
☐ Blood, occult (feces)	82270
☐ Skin test, Tb, intradermal (PPD)	86580
☐	
☐	
☐	
☐	
☐	
☐	

INJECTIONS	
☐ Influenza virus vaccine	90656
☐ Admin of Influenza vaccine	G0008
☐ Pneumococcal vaccine	90732
☐ Admin of pneumococcal vaccine	G0009
☐ Hepatitis B vaccine	90746
☐ Admin of Hepatitis B vaccine	G0010
☐ Tetanus toxoid vaccine	90703
☐ Immunization administration	90471
☐	
☐	

DIAGNOSIS

☐ Anemia, iron deficiency	280.9 (D50.9)	☐ Ventricular flutter	427.42 (I49.02)	☐	
☐ Anemia, protein deficiency	281.4 (D53.0)	☐	————	☐	
☐ Anxiety state, unspecified	300.00 (F41.9)	☐	————	☐	
☐ Appendicitis	541 (K37)	☐		☐	
☐ Chest pain	786.50 (R07.9)	☐		☐	
☐ Cholecystitis, acute	575.0 (K81.0)	☐		☐	
☐ Dizziness	780.4 (R42)	☐		☐	
☐ Epistaxis	784.7 (R04.0)	☐		☐	
☐ Fever	780.60 (R50.9)	☐		☐	
☐ Loss of weight	783.21 (R63.4)	☐		☐	
☐ Obsessive-compulsive Disorder	300.3 (F42)	☐		☐	
☐ Palpitations	785.1 (R00.2)	☐		☐	
☐ Peritioneal abscess	567.22 (K65.1)	☐		☐	
☐ Syncope & collapse	780.2 (R55)	☐		☐	
☐ Ventricular fibrillation	427.41 (I49.01)	☐		☐	

PATIENT IDENTIFICATION		FINANCIAL TRANSACTION DATA	
PATIENT NAME:		INVOICE NO.	
PATIENT NUMBER:		ACCOUNT NO.	
DATE OF BIRTH:		TOTAL FOR SERVICE:	$
ENCOUNTER DATE		AMOUNT RECEIVED:	$
DATE OF SERVICE:	/ /	PAID BY:	☐ Cash ☐ Check ☐ Credit Card
RETURN VISIT DATE			
DATE OF RETURN VISIT:	/ /	CASHIER'S INITIALS:	

FIGURE 6-33 Encounter Form

payment using ICD-9-CM codes. In the near future ICD-10-CM codes will be reported. ICD-10-CM codes are more detailed, so encounter forms will not contain enough space to list all codes utilized by providers. Therefore, additional codes will have to be added during the encounter or at the time of discharge. Note that Figure 6-33 contains both ICD-9-CM and ICD-10-CM codes for illustrative purposes. Once ICD-10-CM is implemented, ICD-9-CM codes will be removed from encounter forms.

Example Polly presents to the office registration desk and the medical assistant generates an encounter form, which is attached to the cover of her patient record. Polly is an established patient who is being monitored for anemia, and Dr. Healthy orders blood tests and performs an examination. Using the encounter form, the doctor selects the proper code for the level of exam completed. After the medical assistant completes the *venipuncture* (drawing of blood) procedure, she selects the code on the encounter form. The completed encounter form is returned to the registration desk, where the patient is scheduled for a follow-up visit. The medical assistant will use the completed encounter form to generate the patient's bill and insurance claim, which is submitted to the third-party payer. (The blood specimen will be delivered to the hospital lab later that afternoon, where the blood test will be performed. The hospital billing department will generate a bill and claim for charges.)

EXERCISE 6–5 Physician Office Record

Matching: Match the term with its description.

_____ 1. Ancillary reports

_____ 2. Medication list

_____ 3. Progress notes

_____ 4. Patient registration form

_____ 5. Problem list

A. Documents initial history, physical examination, and all subsequent visits

B. Documents diseases, conditions, allergies, and procedures

C. Documents medications, dosage, associated diagnosis, and ordering physician

D. Documents reports of ancillary testing completed in the office or by outside labs, including hospital labs

E. Documents demographic, administrative, and financial data

FORMS CONTROL AND DESIGN

In a record system, it is imperative that each facility designate a person who is responsible for the control and design of all forms adopted for use in the patient record. This is usually the responsibility of the health information department, and in some facilities a forms committee (or patient record documentation committee) is established to oversee this process and to approve forms used in the record. The role of a forms committee is to scrutinize each proposed form to:

- Facilitate efficient use of the patient record (e.g., consolidation of forms, elimination of duplication of information throughout the record)
- Ensure that documentation collected on forms complies with accrediting, regulatory, and reimbursement organizations
- Enhance quality of documentation in the patient medical record
- Streamline the forms approval process

When designing a form, the following functional characteristics must be considered:

- Determine the purpose of the form.
  - Prior to designing the form, outline the purpose, use, and users of the form.
  - Make sure that the new form will not duplicate information that is already contained on another form.
- Keep the form simple.
  - The simpler the form design, the easier it will be to use.
- Include basic information.
  - All forms should contain the title of the form, form number, original date of form, revision date, and patient identification section.
  - Patient identification must be included on all reports (front and back), and it should be in the same general location on all forms.
- Include preprinted instructions.
  - Instructions for completion of the form should be printed on the form (e.g., reverse of the form).
- Plan spacing on the form.
  - Consider the type size and margins of the form.
  - If handwritten information is going to be entered on the form, make sure that there is sufficient space.
- Use color coding for various sections of the record.
  - Consider using a different color border on forms for each discipline.
  - Select a color of ink, usually black, that will photocopy easily.

- Allow for uniformity in size, content, and appearance.
  - All headings on the various forms should have a standard format.
  - Standardize the size and appearance of individual forms.
- Consider paper requirements.
  - Consider the weight and quality of paper used.
  - Reports that are accessed frequently (e.g., face sheet) should be printed on a heavier weight of paper so they can withstand frequent use.
- Prepare a draft of the form for review by the forms committee.

- Pilot the form for trial use (e.g., 30 days) on one nursing unit.
  - Revisions can be made if necessary.
- Consider adopting ready-to-use forms, which can be cheaper to purchase.
- Consider printing patient identification when form is generated (for patient safety purposes)

Some facilities require that proposed forms be accompanied by a completed application form (e.g., Application for New or Revised Patient Record Form) (Figure 6-34).

APPLICATION FOR A NEW OR REVISED PATIENT RECORD FORM

TO: Forms Committee

FROM: _____   Office Number: _____

DATE: _____

SUBJECT Application for approval of a new or revised patient record form

❐ New Form ❐ Revised Form (Form # _____) (**Attach copy of current and revised forms**)

Contact person for revisions/questions? _____

Title of Form: _____

Brief description of purpose of form: _____

Department that will use the form: _____

Estimated duration of use: ❐ Less than 1 year ❐ 1-5 years ❐ Indefinite

Number of NCR (no carbon required) copies to be attached to the form: _____

List of departments to which NCR copies will be distributed: _____

Storage location for form: _____

Is form designed for multidisciplinary use? ❐ Yes ❐ No

Explain: _____

What other forms currently in use document the same content? _____

Reserved for Forms Committee Use:

Forms Subcommittee Action: ❐ Form approved ❐ Form denied ❐ Deferred: _____
                                                                                    (date)

FIGURE 6-34 Application for a New or Revised Patient Record Form

EXERCISE 6–6 Forms Control and Design

True/False: Indicate whether each statement is true (T) or false (F).

_____ 1. One role of a forms committee is to review each proposed form to streamline the forms approval process.

_____ 2. In a paper-based record system, each department should designate a person who is responsible for the control and design of all forms adopted by the department for use in the patient record.

_____ 3. The person designing the form should make sure that the new form will not duplicate information that is already contained on another form.

_____ 4. It is usually the responsibility of administration to oversee the forms process and to approve forms used in the record.

_____ 5. Documents that are used frequently should be printed on a heavier weight paper so they can withstand frequent use.

Internet Links

Bibbero Systems
Go to **http://www.bibbero.com** to view ready-to-use forms.

Medicare Conditions of Participation
Go to **http://www.cms.hhs.gov**, click on REGULATIONS & GUIDANCE, Under the heading Legislation click on

CONDITIONS FOR COVERAGE (CFCS) & CONDITIONS OF PARTICIPATION (COPS), and click on HOSPITALS.

The Joint Commission
http://www.jointcommission.org

SUMMARY

The patient record includes documentation about care and treatment provided to patients. Each report and every screen in an electronic health record must include the patient's name and identification number as well as the health care facility's name, address, and telephone number. Health care facilities often use an addressograph machine to imprint provider and patient identification information on each report of a paper-based record. Under Uniform Rules of Evidence, each patient record entry must be dated and timed. Providers are responsible for adhering to patient record documentation guidelines.

The hospital inpatient record includes administrative data (e.g., demographic, financial, socioeconomic), which is gathered upon admission of the patient to the facility. Reports that comprise administration data include the face sheet (or admission/discharge record), advance directives, informed consent, patient property form, birth certificate (copy), and death certificate (copy). Also included in the hospital inpatient record is clinical data, which includes all health care information obtained about a patient's care and treatment that is documented on numerous forms in the patient record (e.g., admitting diagnosis entered on face sheet). When a patient is admitted to the hospital through the ED, the first clinical data item is the chief complaint documented as part of the ED record. Other clinical data documents include the discharge summary, history and physical examination, consultation, progress notes, nurses' notes, and so on.

The hospital outpatient record (or ambulatory record) documents diagnostic, therapeutic (surgical and nonsurgical), and rehabilitation services. Some hospitals use a short stay record to document ambulatory surgery cases. The physician office record contains patient registration information, a problem list, a medication record, progress notes (including patient's history and physical examination), results of ancillary reports, and reports of office surgery (if performed). An encounter form (superbill or fee slip), used to capture charges generated during an office visit, is initiated when the patient registers at the front desk and is completed by providers as the patient receives care.

Forms design and control are usually designated to a health information management professional who is responsible for oversight of all forms adopted for use in the patient record. Most facilities establish a forms committee (or patient record committee) to oversee this process and to approve forms used in the record.

STUDY CHECKLIST

- Read the textbook chapter and highlight key concepts. (Use colored highlighter sparingly throughout the chapter.)
- Create an index card for each key term. (Write the key term on one side of the index card and the concept on the other. Learn the definition of each key term, and match the term to the concept.)
- Access chapter Internet links to learn more about concepts.
- Answer the chapter exercises and review questions, verifying answers with your instructor.
- Complete lab manual assignments, verifying answers with your instructor.
- Form a study group with classmates to discuss chapter concepts in preparation for an exam.

CHAPTER REVIEW

Fill-in-the-Blank: Enter the appropriate term(s) to complete each of the following statements.

1. A graph used to record the patient's vital signs is called a _____.

2. The _____ record contains an antepartum record, labor and delivery record, and postpartum record.

3. The anesthesia record documents the monitoring of the patient during the administration of the _____.

4. The operative report contains both the _____ and _____ diagnoses.

5. The _____ aids in the diagnosis and treatment of the patient by documenting the pathologist's analysis of tissue.

Multiple Choice: Select the most appropriate response.

6. The first-listed diagnosis and procedure is _____ data.
   a. administrative
   b. clinical
   c. financial
   d. identification

7. Written instruction given by a patient to a health care provider outlining the patient's preference for care before the need for treatment is known as a(n)
   a. advance directive.
   b. consent to admission.
   c. consent for surgery.
   d. health care proxy.

8. A document that provides a summary of a patient's hospitalization is a(n)
   a. clinical résumé.
   b. history.
   c. operative report.
   d. physical examination report.

9. A chronological description of the patient's present condition from the time of onset to the present is a
   a. history of the present illness.
   b. medical history.
   c. review of systems.
   d. social history.

10. Preprinted orders that are placed on a patient's record (e.g., upon admission) are called
    a. discharge orders.
    b. phone orders.
    c. routine orders.
    d. stop orders.

11. The completion of an H&PE is the responsibility of the
    a. attending physician.
    b. nurse.
    c. surgeon.
    d. therapist.

12. A tissue report is also known as a
    a. pathology report.
    b. postanesthesia report.
    c. postoperative report.
    d. specimen report.

13. A report documenting blood chemistry, blood gases, and blood type is a
    a. blood report.
    b. drug record.
    c. laboratory report.
    d. pathology report.

14. All patient information obtained through treatment and care of the patient is called
    a. administrative data.
    b. clinical data.
    c. demographic data.
    d. financial data.

15. A review of the medical events in the patient's family, including disease which may be hereditary or present a risk to the patient, is part of the
    a. admission information.
    b. family history.
    c. medical information.
    d. social history.

True/False: Indicate whether each statement is true (T) or false (F).

_____ 16. A review of systems is a chronological description of the patient's present condition.

_____ 17. The Joint Commission requires that a discharge summary be completed by the attending physician to facilitate continuity of patient care.

_____ 18. The admitting diagnosis is also called a principal diagnosis.

_____ 19. The Patient Self Determination Act required that all patients age 21 and over have the right to have an advance directive placed in their record.

_____ 20. The final order that is written to release a patient from a hospital is known as a discharge order.

Chapter 7

NUMBERING & FILING SYSTEMS AND RECORD STORAGE & CIRCULATION

Chapter Outline

Key Terms

alphabetic filing system
automated chart tracking system
bar coding
binders
centralized filing system
charge-out system
chart tracking system
circulation system
color coding
combination centralized/
    decentralized filing system
compressible files
computers
consecutive numeric filing
conveyor belt

decentralized filing system
dumbwaiter
emergency requisition
envelopes
facsimile machines
family numbering
fax
file folders
filing controls
given name
jackets
lateral file
loose filing
middle-digit filing
mirrored processing

movable files
natural or man-made disaster
    record destruction corroboration
    process
non-routine requisition
numbering systems
numeric filing
open-shelf file
outguide
periodic audit of file area
planned requisition
pneumatic tube
power filing machines
primary memory
primary storage

pseudonumber
requisition form
reverse numeric filing
secondary device
secondary storage

serial numbering system
serial-unit numbering
social security numbering
Soundex
straight numeric filing

surname
terminal-digit filing
unit numbering system
vertical file
visible file

Objectives

At the end of this chapter, the student should be able to:

- Define key terms
- Explain the differences between serial, unit, and serial-unit numbering systems, and organize records according to these numbering systems
- Name, define, and organize records according to alphabetic and numeric filing systems
- Cite advantages and disadvantages of the use of alphabetic and numeric filing systems
- Explain the rules of, and arrange records for, alphabetic, straight numerical, terminal-digit, and middle-digit filing purposes

- Compare the types of filing equipment used to store file folders, and calculate storage needs
- Discuss the components of a file folder including color-coding, fastener position, preprinted material, and scoring and reinforcement
- Explain the procedure for organizing and managing loose filing
- Describe circulation systems that are used to transport patient records
- Identify security measures that occur to safeguard patient records and information from theft, fire, and water damage

INTRODUCTION

The patient record documents a patient's past medical history, services rendered (e.g., to diagnose conditions), and procedures performed (e.g., to treat problems). Many large health care facilities (e.g., hospitals) have automated their numbering/filing and record storage/circulation systems for paper-based medical records. However, a number of health care organizations (e.g., clinics, physician offices, veterinary offices/hospitals) continue to implement manual systems for their numbering/filing and record storage/circulation systems when paper-based medical records are used. A well-organized numbering and filing system is essential to the effective storage and retrieval of patient records. In addition to facilitating continuity of patient care among health care providers, the patient record supports services and procedures provided to patients (e.g., third-party reimbursement) and defends health care providers accused of medical malpractice. All of these activities require that patient records be easily accessible and retrieved in a timely fashion.

Note: For additional resources on filing and numbering systems, refer to Cengage Learning's *Medical Filing* by Theresa Claeys and *Office Filing Procedures* by Joseph S. Fosegan and Mary Lea Ginn. The information

within this chapter reviews concepts that are essential to manage paper-based medical record systems. As the industry transitions from paper-based systems to electronic health records, it is essential that there is an understanding of the concepts that relate to paper-based systems so that the information contained in these records can be transitioned to electronic systems.

NUMBERING SYSTEMS

Most health care providers organize patient records according to one of three numbering systems, which identify and file patient records according to preassigned numbers:

- Serial
- Unit
- Serial-Unit

Each type of numbering system has advantages and disadvantages (Table 7-1). Regardless of the numbering system selected, providers assign new patient numbers chronologically as the patient is admitted or readmitted to the facility (except for the unit system, where patients retain the original number assigned), and the facility maintains a master patient index used

TABLE 7-1 Advantages and Disadvantages of Numbering Systems

Numbering System	Advantages	Disadvantages
Serial	• Computer software is not needed to track assignment of patient numbers	• Patient records are filed in different locations in the filing system • Multiple locations must be accessed to retrieve patient records
Unit	• Patient records are filed in one location in the filing system • Patient is assigned same number for each subsequent admission • Patient records can be easily retrieved and refiled • System is cost effective because just one file folder per patient is needed	• Computer software must be purchased to manage unit numbering system • Folders can become thick and cumbersome • Multiple folders may be needed to house all records for one patient (and they should be labeled as Vol. I of II, and so on)
Serial-Unit	• Computer software is not needed to track assignment of patient numbers • Patient is assigned new number for subsequent visits, and previous records are brought forward to the new number • Patient records are filed in one location in the filing system • Patient records can be easily retrieved and refiled	• Previous folders must remain in file system with a note providing new patient number information • Folders can become thick and cumbersome, and multiple folders may be needed to house all records for one patient

to locate a patient's record. (Details about the master patient index are discussed in Chapter 8.)

Note: Providers (e.g., physician office) that do not adopt a numbering system file records alphabetically according to patient name.

Serial Numbering System

In a serial numbering system, each time the patient is registered (e.g., inpatient admission, outpatient/emergency department encounter) a new patient number is assigned by the provider and a new patient record is created. Thus, a patient who has had multiple admissions to the facility also has multiple patient numbers, and patient records are filed in multiple locations in the permanent file system. The serial numbering system is usually selected by facilities that do not use computerized admission /discharge/transfer (ADT) software; without ADT software, the facility has no efficient way to retrieve previously assigned numbers. (ADT software is discussed in Chapter 8.)

Example Polly Moore is scheduled for inpatient surgery on September 10. Prior to surgery, she is to undergo preadmission testing (PAT) on September 8. Polly is registered by the outpatient department on September 8 and is assigned patient record number 123456. On September 10, she is registered as an inpatient and is assigned patient record number 124566. She is discharged on September 13, and returns for outpatient physical therapy on September 15, when she is assigned patient record number 125678. Polly has three different patient record numbers that must be maintained by the health information department, and she also has three patient records that are filed in three different locations in the permanent storage system.

Remember! A serial numbering system generates patient records that are each filed in their own folder. This means that patient records must be retrieved from multiple locations in the filing system when previous records are requested by a physician (to facilitate continuity of patient care). Since the records are filed in multiple areas, the time needed to retrieve records increases.

Unit Numbering

The Joint Commission states that facilities should establish a system that tracks all patient records (e.g., inpatient, outpatient, and emergency records) and makes them available when patient presents for care.

In a unit numbering system, the patient is assigned a patient number the first time he or she is registered (e.g., inpatient admission, outpatient/emergency department encounter), and the patient is reassigned that same number for all subsequent admissions and encounters. Facilities that adopt the unit numbering system use admission/discharge/transfer software to manage patient number assignment, and all patient records are filed in one folder (as a unit) in the file system. If the patient has multiple admissions/encounters requiring multiple volumes, they are labeled and secured together.

Example Scott Trahan was born at Merry Hospital in 1995 and was assigned patient number 234567. When admitted to the hospital at age 9 for an appendectomy, he is reassigned patient number 234567, and this record is filed in the original folder created for his birth record. In a paper-based record system, the birth record is either still in hard copy form or it has been microfilmed or scanned into an optical imaging system for future reference (according to federal and state retention laws). In an automated record system, the new record is linked to any previous record(s).

Note: Two variations of the unit numbering system include social security numbering and family numbering.

Social Security Numbering

With social security numbering, a patient's social security number (SSN) is assigned as his or her patient number. This system is used in Veterans Affairs medical centers (VAMCs) because each veteran has an SSN, and the Social Security Administration (SSA) assists VAMCs in locating social security numbers as needed. Adopting social security numbering for other patient populations may not be practical because the facility must assign a pseudonumber to any patient who does not have an SSN. To assign a pseudonumber, use the following number chart and follow the procedure below.

abc	1	jkl	4	stu	7
def	2	mno	5	vwx	8
ghi	3	pqr	6	yz	9

Note: If the patient has no middle initial, assign 0.

Note: The pseudonumber uses the same format as the social security number: 000-00-0000.

1. Using the chart above, assign a number to the first letter of the patient's first, middle, and last name.

   Example

   Sally A. Fields = 712-
   Mary Jackson = 504-

2. Use the patient's date of birth to assign the remaining six digits, as follows: two-digit month, day, and year. (Enter a 0 before one-digit months and days.)

   Example

   September 10, 1994 = 09-1094
   March 8, 1908 = 03-0808

   Example Lee Choi (DOB: April 3, 1985) is a foreign exchange student living in Florida for three months who sought care at the local hospital emergency room. His pseudonumber is 401-04-0385.

Assigning social security numbers as patient numbers raises the following concerns:

- *Privacy.* Because social security numbers are used for other purposes (financial, public records, and so on), it is possible that unauthorized users could obtain a patient's social security number and access health information. The potential for identity theft also increases.
- *Length of the number.* Nine digits make it difficult to file the record.
- *Multiple social security numbers.* Some patients have been assigned more than one SSN.
- *Duplicate pseudonumbers.* The same pseudonumber could be assigned to more than one patient.

Family Numbering

In family numbering, each household is assigned a unique patient number, and each family member is assigned a two-digit modifier number that serves as a prefix to the patient number.

01	head of household (either father or mother)
02	spouse
03	first-born child
04	second-born child
05	third-born child
06	and so on

Thus, health information for the entire household is filed together according to the family number.

Example The Healthy family receives care at Riverside Primary Care and is assigned patient number 123456. John Healthy is considered head of the household, so his number is 01-123456. Mary Healthy, his wife, is assigned 02-123456. July Healthy, their first-born, is assigned 03-123456.

The family number system is often used by health care facilities that treat entire families (e.g., primary care clinics, neighborhood health centers, health maintenance organizations, family counseling centers) because it provides an easy way to track health information on an entire family, even if the family members have different last names. In addition, all family records can be retrieved quickly because the information is filed in one folder. The major disadvantage of this system occurs when the family composition changes (e.g., divorce, remarriage, children marry). When change occurs, the patient number must be changed and the original number cross-referenced to the new number.

Example Cindy and Martin Lee (and their child, Sandy) are assigned patient number 147852. Family numbers include 01-147852 (Martin), 02-147852 (Cindy), and 03-147852 (child). The couple divorce. Cindy is awarded custody of Sandy, and as head of her new household patient number 321654 is assigned (01-321654 for Cindy, and 03-321654 for Sandy). Later, when Sandy graduates college, becomes employed, and seeks health care, she is assigned her own patient number: 01-365969.

Serial-Unit Numbering

In serial-unit numbering, patients receive a new number each time they are registered by the facility, and records from a previous admission or encounter are reassigned the new number. This results in all patient records being filed in the most current folder in one location. The folders that contained previous patient records remain in the file, and a note identifying the new number is inserted into the folder. Thus, serial-unit numbering is actually a blend of both the serial and unit numbering systems.

Example Cindy Crane was admitted on January 20 and assigned patient number 345678. Four years later, she returned for an outpatient visit and was assigned number 446789. The patient record filed in the folder labeled 345678 is reassigned patient number 446789 and filed in the new folder; the folder labeled 345678 remains in the filing system with a note indicating that the new patient number is 446789.

EXERCISE 7–1 Numbering Systems

Matching: Identify the numbering system used for each situation.

a. Serial

b. Unit

c. Serial-unit

d. Unit—family numbering

e. Unit—Social Security numbering

_____ 1. William Wood is admitted for surgery on February 2 and assigned patient number 567890. On March 5, he returns for outpatient testing and is assigned patient number 678900. Records for the two encounters are contained in separate folders in two different locations in the file area.

_____ 2. Mary Adams and her three children receive care from Brookside Clinic, where the health information department retrieves one record that contains patient information on Mary and her three children.

_____ 3. Annie Smith is brought into the emergency department following a motor vehicle accident and assigned patient number 123456. She is discharged home, and three days later she returns for further evaluation. She is reassigned patient number 123456.

_____ 4. Perry Parks receives care at the local hospital and is assigned a patient number based on the letters of his name and his date of birth because he does not have a social security number.

_____ 5. Larry Allen registers for outpatient care on March 30 and is assigned patient number 363258. He returns on December 10, and is assigned patient number 456898. Records for both encounters are filed in a folder labeled 456898.

FILING SYSTEMS

Two systems are used to file patient records. These systems are

- Alphabetic
- Numeric

The patient identifier for an alphabetic filing system consists of alphabetic characters (e.g., patient's last name, first name, and middle initial), while the identifier for a numeric filing system contains numbers (e.g., patient's social security number, hospital patient number).

Note: A numeric filing system requires health care facilities to first adopt a numbering system.

Alphabetic Filing System

In an alphabetic filing system, the patient's last name, first name, and middle initial are used to file records (when no numbering system is selected for use by the facility) and master patient index cards (when a numbering system is used by the facility).

Example Primary Care Clinic uses an alphabetic filing system to file patient records.

Smith, Mary
Smith, Tara
Smith, William
Tokos, Marie
Tokos, Nicholas

There are no universally accepted rules for filing alphabetic records, but a facility can establish a policy and procedure based on Association of Records Managers and Administrators (ARMA) guidelines entitled *Simplified Filing Standard Rules and Specific Filing Guidelines.*

1. Arrange patient names according to the alphabet, beginning with the surname (or last name), given name (or first name) or initial, and middle name or initial.

Note: If patients use an initial instead of their given name, file according to the initial.

Example

Smith, Mary Elizabeth
Smith, W. Edward
Smith, William E.
Smith, William Edward
Smith, William Kenneth

2. Disregard all punctuation, and close up the letters or words and file them as one unit.

Example

Dresserby, Timothy
Dresser-Recktenwald, Wendy
Dresserton, Cynthia

3. Prefixes included as part of the patient's last name are filed alphabetically (e.g., D', de, De, L', La, Mac, Mc, Van, Von).

Hint: File prefixes as you would other alphabetic characters.

Example

Lack, Kaye
La Comb, James

Lacomis, Gary
L'Amoreaux, Lynn
Langone, Robert

Note: Some facilities file all "Mac" and "Mc" prefix names together.

Example

MacDonald, Peter
McDonald, Petra
MacDonald, Timothy
McDonald, Velda

4. Professional and religious titles and suffixes are often filed according to a variety of methods, and the facility must select a consistent method.

Hint: The simplest method is to disregard the title. However, per the note below, suffixes such as Jr. and Sr. or II and III can be helpful when filing identical names. File Sr. before Jr., and II before III.

Note: If two patients have identical names, file according to date of birth (oldest to youngest). If two patients have identical names and dates of birth, file alphabetically according to address in the following order: city name, state name, complete street name, and street number.

Example The list of patient names with titles and suffixes in column one is filed in alphabetical order in column two.

Patient names with titles/suffixes	Alphabetic filing of patient names
Sister Mary Alice Smith	Johns, Thomas
Dr. Mark Sounds	Robin, Jules
Rev. Thomas Johns	Robinson, Julianne
John Simpson, III	Simpson, John II
Ms. Jules Robin	Simpson, John III
John Simpson, II	Smith, Mary Alice
Mrs. Julianne Robinson	Sounds, Mark

Advantages and Disadvantages of Alphabetic Filing System

The alphabetic filing system has the following advantages:

- It is easy to learn.
- Staff members can be quickly trained.
- It does not require a master patient index.
- Record retrieval can be performed quickly.

Disadvantages of an alphabetic filing system include:

- Patient names must be spelled correctly or the entire system will fail.
- Misspelled patient names result in misfiling of records.
- Files do not expand at an even rate, causing reorganization of shelves. Typically about half of the filing space will store files that start with the letters B, C, H, M, S, and W.

Example Shelves that house patient records starting with the letter T will contain many more records than those that contain records starting with letters X, Y, and Z because more patients' last names begin with T than with X, Y, and Z. As a result, when planning the layout of shelving, more space must be allotted for records of patients with names that begin with certain letters.

- When a patient's name changes, the patient record must be filed in a different location and a cross-reference created.
- Record security is compromised because unauthorized persons can easily locate records and gain access to patient information.

Soundex

Soundex is a phonetic indexing system allowing surnames (last names) that sound alike but are spelled differently to be filed together. The system was developed so that a surname could be located easily even though it might have been filed under various spellings. Soundex has been adopted by the U.S. Census Bureau to organize census data and by health care facilities to organize master patient index (MPI) cards in communities with large populations of foreign-sounding names. It is also incorporated into computerized master patient name software. Soundex allows MPI cards to be filed according to sound rather than spelling of the patient's surname (last name); surnames that sound alike but are spelled differently are filed together (e.g., Choi, Chai, Choy).

Note: Soundex was formulated by the federal government with the Remington Rand Corporation in the 1930s under President Roosevelt's Works Project Administration. When nearly all census data was collected by individuals who walked from door to door, it was discovered that many census takers spelled surnames phonetically (e.g., one might spell Smith as "Smith," another might spell it as "Smyth," and still another "Smythe").

A four-character phonetic code containing a letter and three digits (e.g., G-123) is created using letters from the patient's surname (*except* a, e, i, o, u, w, h, y), and the alphabet is reduced to six key letters and their equivalents.

Key Letters	Code Number	Equivalents
b	1	pfv
c	2	skgjqxz
d	3	t
l	4	none
m	5	n
r	6	none

Rules to follow when assigning phonetic codes include:

1. Assign the first letter of the patient's last name as the first character.

Example
Bowie = B
Green = G

2. Do *not* assign a code number to the first letter of the patient's last name.
3. Assign just one code number when two or more key letters or their equivalents occur together.

Example 1
The "bb" in Babbots is coded once, to create phonetic code B-132. (Assign 1 to "bb," 3 to "t," and 2 to "s.")

Example 2
The "ck" in Serbacki is coded once, to create phonetic code S-612. (Assign 6 to "r," 1 to "b," and 2 to "ck.")

Note: Refer to the above chart to assign the code numbers.

4. Assign just one code number when two or more key letters or their equivalents are separated by h or w.

Example 1
The "skwsk" in Serbskwski is coded once, to create phonetic code S-612. (Assign 6 to "r," 1 to "b," and 2 to "skwsk.")

Example 2
The "shs" in Torbshsa is coded once, to create T-612. (Assign 6 to "r," 1 to "b," and 2 to "shs.")

5. Add zeroes to the phonetic code if a name contains less than three key letters or their equivalents.

Example 1

Day   D-000

Once you assign D as the first character of the phonetic code, there are no remaining key letters or their equivalents to which to assign codes. Therefore, add zeroes to the phonetic code to complete it.

Example 2

Jackson   J-250

Assign J as the first character of the phonetic code, and then assign 2 to the "cks" and 5 to the "n." This creates an incomplete phonetic code to which you add a zero.

6. Disregard remaining letters once the four-character code is created.

Example

Bartholomew   B-634

Assign 6 to "r," 3 to "t," and 4 to "l." Do not assign numbers to the remaining letters.

7. Assign separate code numbers when a repeated key letter or its equivalent is separated by a, e, i, o, u, or y.

Example 1

Delaler   D-446

Because the first and second "l" in Delaley are separated by the vowel "a," assign 4 twice and 6 to "r."

Example 2

Tatytial   T-334

Because the second and third "t" in Tatytia are separated by the letter "y," assign 3 twice and 4 to "l."

Once phonetic codes are assigned to each patient's surname, the codes are arranged alphabetically according to given name.

Example 1

Minnie Dwyer (D-600) is filed before Sam Dwyer (D-600).

Example 2

Linda Tatatia (T-330) is filed after Annie Tatatia (T-330).

Numeric Filing

A numeric filing methodology uses a number to file patient records. Patients are assigned a health record number, and the records are organized according to that number. Three types of numeric filing methodologies are commonly used: straight numeric, terminal digit, and middle digit. Numeric filing is most commonly used in facilities that have a large patient population and therefore a large number of records to organize.

Straight Numeric Filing

In straight numeric filing (or consecutive numeric filing), records are filed in strict chronologic order according to patient number, from lowest to highest.

Example

111234
111235
111236
111237
111238

Advantages and Disadvantages of Straight Numeric Filing

Straight numeric filing has the following advantages:

- Office staff can be easily and quickly trained.
- Patient records are more secure because unauthorized personnel cannot retrieve a record according to name (a patient number must be known).
- Retrieval of consecutive records for research or purging (for inactive storage) can easily be done.
- Files can be easily expanded to add additional file space at the end of files.

Straight numeric filing has the following disadvantages:

- Office staff must consider all digits of the number when filing, resulting in transposition of digits and misfiled records.
- Misfiles increase as the number of digits increases (the more digits, the greater the chance of error).
- Work flow problems arise because activity in the file area focuses on that section with the highest consecutive numbers (e.g., most recent patient records will be filed in that section).
- Work space is restricted when more than one staff member files records because they usually must file in the same section.

Terminal-Digit Filing

Terminal-digit filing (or reverse numeric filing) is commonly used in health care facilities that assign six-digit (or longer) patient numbers because the number can be easily subdivided into three parts: primary, secondary, and tertiary digits. (Some facilities use more than six digits in the patient number, such as VAMCs that use the SSN and file records according to terminal digit.) In a six-digit (or longer) patient number, a hyphen separates each part of the number, and terminal-digit numbers are read from right to left:

- Primary digits are located at the end of the patient number.
- Secondary digits are located in the middle of the patient number.
- Tertiary digits are located at the beginning of the patient number, and records are filed in straight numeric order according to its tertiary digits.

Example

Patient number 13-50-05 is organized as:

13	50	05
Tertiary	Secondary	Primary

The clerk reads the primary number (05) first and goes to that section of the file system. Then the secondary number (50) is read, and the clerk locates that subsection of the file system. Finally, the tertiary number (13) is read, and the clerk inserts the record into that file location.

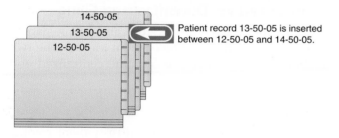

Patient record 13-50-05 is inserted between 12-50-05 and 14-50-05.

The terminal-digit file system is typically divided into 100 primary sections (00 to 99) and 100 secondary sections (00 to 99). Once the clerk locates the primary and secondary sections for a patient number, the record is filed in straight numeric order according to the tertiary digit.

Note: Tertiary digits can be of unlimited length.

Example 1

99-99-99 is followed by 100-99-99
999-99-99 is followed by 1000-99-99
9999-99-99 is followed by 10000-99-99

Example 2

To file record number 45-60-90, the clerk follows this procedure:

1. Identify primary digits (90), and take the record to primary section 90.
2. Identify secondary digits (60), and locate that secondary section within primary section 90. (It is located between secondary sections 59 and 61.)
3. Identify the tertiary digits (45). Within secondary section 60, file the record in straight numeric order between records 44-60-90 and 46-60-90.

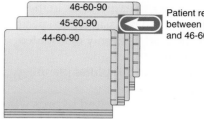

Patient record 45-60-90 is inserted between patient number 44-60-90 and 46-60-90.

Example 3

Sequence of records in a terminal-digit file.

Primary Section 00	Primary Section 01	Primary Section 10
80-99-00	01-10-01	23-34-10
81-99-00	02-10-01	24-34-10
82-99-00	03-10-01	25-34-10
83-99-00	04-10-01	26-34-10

VAMCs use terminal-digit filing, which is divided into three groups, to organize patient records according to Social Security number.

- The last two digits are primary.
- The next to the last two digits are secondary.
- The remaining five digits are tertiary and filed in straight numeric order within the secondary section of the filing system.

Example

SSN 790-22-3753

79022	37	53
Tertiary	Secondary	Primary

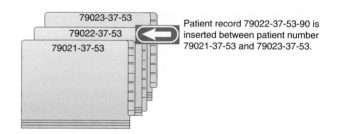

Patient record 79022-37-53-90 is inserted between patient number 79021-37-53 and 79023-37-53.

Advantages and Disadvantages of the Terminal-Digit Filing System

The terminal-digit filing system has the following advantages:

- It provides a high degree of record security as compared with other filing systems because unauthorized persons cannot easily locate files.
- Files expand evenly as new records are added because records are distributed throughout the 100 primary sections.

- More than one file clerk can easily work in the file area because clerks can be assigned to specific primary sections; the work is evenly distributed, eliminating congestion.
- Even distribution of records simplifies planning for file equipment.
- Large gaps in files will not occur, and records will be shifted infrequently.
- Misfiles are reduced because clerks are concerned with just two digits at a time when filing.
- Transposition of digits occurs less frequently, also resulting in decreased misfiles.
- Inactive records can be easily retrieved as new records are added to each section.

The terminal-digit filing system has the following disadvantages:

- Training time for staff is lengthier as compared with other filling methods, although clerks usually master terminal-digit filing in one day or less.
- Initially, more space and equipment will be needed to organize the file area. The file area must be well organized from the beginning to include room for even expansion of files.

Middle-Digit Filing

Middle-digit filing, a variation of terminal-digit filing, assigns the middle digits as primary, digits on the left as secondary, and digits on the right as tertiary.

Example 1
Patient number 13-50-05 is organized as:

13	50	05
Secondary	Primary	Tertiary

The clerk reads the primary number (50) first and goes to that section of the file system. Then the secondary number (13) is read, and the clerk locates that subsection of the file system. Finally, the tertiary number (05) is read, and the clerk inserts the record into that file location.

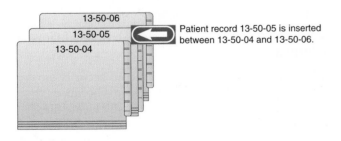

Patient record 13-50-05 is inserted between 13-50-04 and 13-50-06.

Example 2
Sequence of records in a middle-digit file.

39-18-09
39-18-10
39-18-11
01-19-10
01-19-11
01-19-12

Advantages and Disadvantages of the Middle-Digit Filing System

The middle-digit filing system has the same advantages and disadvantages as terminal-digit filing. In addition, it has the following disadvantage:

- Patient numbers should be limited to six digits to easily divide the number into primary, secondary, and tertiary digits.

Organization of Patient Records: Centralized vs. Decentralized Filing

Health care facilities must store and retain patient records so that they can be easily retrieved. The two methods for organizing records are centralized and decentralized.

Centralized Filing

A centralized filing system organizes patient records in one central location under the control of the facility's health information department.

Advantages of centralized filing include:

- Responsibility for record keeping is easily identified.
- Effective use of equipment, supplies, space, and personnel is made.
- All information about a patient is organized in one location.
- Consistent services are provided to all users.
- There is improved security.

Disadvantages of centralized filing include:

- Records may be too remote from staff for adequate patient care.
- It can result in increased personal filing systems (e.g., emergency department stores copy of records to facilitate rapid retrieval).
- It requires additional staff to handle filing and retrieval of records.
- It requires investment in more efficient filing equipment and/or automation.

Note: Using multipart forms to document outpatient and emergency room care allows the original record to be centralized in the health information department and copies to be maintained in the patient care area. This allows the patient care area to quickly reference patient information when patients return for follow-up care. Another option is to allow outpatient departments that provide continuous care for a specified period (e.g., physical therapy, radiation therapy) to forward all documentation to the health information department after treatment is concluded. The documentation is filed in the unit record at that time.

Decentralized Filing

A **decentralized filing system** organizes patient records throughout the facility in patient care areas under the control of the department that creates and uses them.

Advantages of decentralized filing include:

- Records are located near providers that create and use them.
- No "extra" space is needed in the health information department to store files.
- Providers control filing and retrieval of patient information.

Case Example

The military uses a combination of serial and unit numbering (with family numbering thrown in), but it's *not* the serial-unit numbering system described in this chapter. Each patient is assigned a new number upon admission (or visit), but records are filed in terminal-digit order according to a unit number based on the sponsor's (military service personnel) social security number. Each family member is assigned a family member prefix (FMP), ranging from 01–99 (e.g., 01 for sponsor's oldest child . . . 20 for the sponsor . . . 30–39 for sponsor's spouse(s) . . . 40 for sponsor's mother . . . 99 for civilian emergency not otherwise specified). Up to 19 children, 10 spouses (but not all at one time), and various categories of civilians and foreign military can be assigned an FMP. Advantages of this filing method include ease in retrieving records when families move from one location to another and when a physician wants to review all of one family's records. Also, the SSN is easy for the family to remember—they need to know it for anything else they do on the military base. Problems can occur with this filing method when stepchildren and new spouses are registered. Careful education of the family and staff is necessary.

> *Example* If a soldier marries someone whose children are older than his own, clerks who don't know the family situation can become confused and may try to erroneously change FMPs.

One military health information staff member personally encountered conflict with a woman who was the third spouse of a soldier—her FMP should have been 32, but someone mistakenly changed her number to FMP 30, thinking she was the only spouse. Apparently her husband had not told her he was previously married (and by law she could not be told by a military clerk). Problems arose when a clerk accessed the Defense Enrollment Eligibility Reporting System (DEERS) eligibility screen according to FMP 30 and displayed the name of the first wife—the clerk called the spouse by the first wife's name. After about the sixth visit to the military facility, the spouse stated that she was tired of being called by someone else's name, which triggered an audit of the account to correct the FMP (as well as an in-service to remind clerks not to change FMPs).

Other difficulties occur when a family member (e.g., widowed, divorced) marries another service person. The record under the first spouse's SSN is supposed to be transferred to the new spouse, but this does not always occur and can cause continuity of care problems (especially when the patient is undergoing cancer treatment). Attention to detail is an important skill; when the admitting clerk knows that the sponsor has changed, the two records can be merged so that the same record will appear in the computer with input of either sponsor's number.

The military also creates SSN pseudonumbers (called pseudosocials) differently than what is discussed in this chapter. Their reasoning is that the pseudonumber created according to the previous procedure may actually be a sponsor's SSN, and it's impossible to tell that it is "fake." If the sponsor (or a dependent) seeks treatment, he or she cannot be registered because his or her number is already in use as a pseudonumber. If these people can't register, they can't make appointments or receive ancillary

(Continues)

Case Example, continued

services (e.g., lab, x-ray). The military begins all pseudonumbers with 800 series numbers (no SSN starts with 800 series numbers), followed by the year of birth, followed by the month/day of birth.

> *Example* Theresa Saville was born February 21, 1969. Her pseudosocial is 800-69-0221.

Note: If a pseudosocial number is already in use, the facility assigns 801 as the first three digits, and so on. If the birth date is unknown (e.g., unconscious patient), the military assigns January 1, 1900 (e.g., 800000101). This acts as a trigger to remind a clerk to obtain the actual date of birth as soon as it is available.

Disadvantages of decentralized filing include:

- Confusion can occur regarding where patient information can be found.
- "Fragmented" documentation can result because information related to patient care is filed in multiple locations.
- Providers may not know how to properly maintain patient records.
- Lack of uniformity or consistency exists in record keeping and storage results.

Note: Even when a facility adopts the unit record for inpatient care, if other records are stored remotely from the health information department, decentralized filing is being used. In addition, when a facility's satellite clinics store their own records, the facility has adopted decentralized filing.

Combination System

The solution may be to structure a facility's record-keeping system using a combination centralized/decentralized filing system, which establishes the health information department manager as responsible for facility records management. This individual manages the record storage plan (e.g., security) and ensures that established procedures (forms design, order of the record, and so on) are followed. The most important consideration is that the facility must select a record-keeping method that best serves patient care needs.

EXERCISE 7–2 Filing Systems

1. Sequence the following names in alphabetical order.

    _____ Mr. John Franco

    _____ Steven John Smith

    _____ Geraldine Daven

    _____ Marie DeAngelo

    _____ Steven James Smith

    _____ Pamela LaBelle

    _____ Mary Alice Kane

    _____ Andrew Bittner

    _____ Andrew C. Bittner

    _____ William James DeBella

    _____ Patricia Francis Leska

    _____ Sister Theresa Mary Kane

2. Sequence the following numbers in straight numeric order.

    _____ 456123   _____ 789456   _____ 456124

    _____ 561238   _____ 456128   _____ 561240

    _____ 561237   _____ 789457   _____ 789459

    _____ 789450   _____ 456130   _____ 562140

3. Assign phonetic codes to the following surnames.
    a. Miller _____
    b. Brown _____
    c. Sczerbacki _____
    d. Dalton _____
    e. Paryron _____

4. Arrange the following numbers in terminal-digit order.

    _____ 30-50-06   _____ 30-40-94   _____ 88-39-20

    _____ 11-30-20   _____ 84-39-20   _____ 10-31-20

    _____ 54-40-94   _____ 01-01-04   _____ 12-40-96

    _____ 40-50-96   _____ 34-50-06   _____ 89-45-20

5. Arrange the following numbers in middle-digit order.

    _____ 30-50-06   _____ 30-40-94   _____ 88-39-20

    _____ 11-30-20   _____ 84-39-20   _____ 10-31-20

    _____ 54-40-94   _____ 01-01-04   _____ 12-40-96

    _____ 40-50-96   _____ 34-50-06   _____ 89-45-20

6. Explain the difference between centralized and decentralized filing systems.

FILING EQUIPMENT

Paper-based patient records require filing equipment for storage purposes, and the selection process must consider the location of files, number of records to be filed, length of time records will be stored, and type (Table 7-2) and cost of filing equipment.

TABLE 7-2 Types of Filing Equipment

Filing Equipment	Image	Description
Open-shelf file	 (Reprinted with permission of Bibbero Systems, Inc., Petaluma, CA. 800 242–2376. www.bibbero.com.)	Six- to eight-shelf unit, which resembles a book-shelf, provides twice as much filing space as a standard drawer file cabinet and requires less than 10 percent additional floor space. (If eight-shelf unit is purchased, clerks will need to use a step stool to access records on top shelves.) End-tab folders are housed in open-shelf file systems.
Lateral file	 (Reprinted with permission of Bibbero Systems, Inc., Petaluma, CA. 800 242–2376. www.bibbero.com.)	Two-to eight-shelf unit with retractable doors (and lock system if desired). (Bibbero Systems, Inc., offers Stak-n-Lock™ modular shelf filing by Datum, which allows a department to expand the filing system as filing needs increase.) Top-tab folders are housed in lateral file systems.
Movable (or compressible) file	 (Reprinted with permission of Bibbero Systems, Inc., Petaluma, CA. 800 242–2376. www.bibbero.com.)	Movable files include both manual and power types. Manual movable files are mounted on tracks that are secured to the floor and are moved by using a handle or crank. Power movable files are motorized systems that move when the file clerk presses a button. End-tab folders are housed in movable file systems.

(Continues)

TABLE 7-2 Types of Filing Equipment (*Continued*)

Filing Equipment	Image	Description
Power filing machines	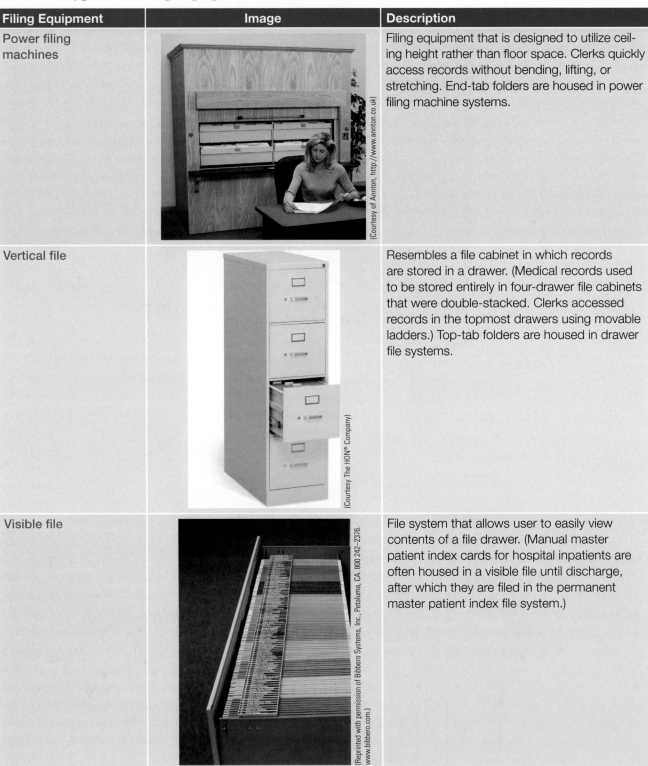 (Courtesy of Anmton, http://www.anmton.co.uk)	Filing equipment that is designed to utilize ceiling height rather than floor space. Clerks quickly access records without bending, lifting, or stretching. End-tab folders are housed in power filing machine systems.
Vertical file	(Courtesy The HON® Company)	Resembles a file cabinet in which records are stored in a drawer. (Medical records used to be stored entirely in four-drawer file cabinets that were double-stacked. Clerks accessed records in the topmost drawers using movable ladders.) Top-tab folders are housed in drawer file systems.
Visible file	(Reprinted with permission of Bibbero Systems, Inc., Petaluma, CA. 800 242-2376. www.bibbero.com.)	File system that allows user to easily view contents of a file drawer. (Manual master patient index cards for hospital inpatients are often housed in a visible file until discharge, after which they are filed in the permanent master patient index file system.)

Note: End-tab folders are used for open-shelf filing, and top-tab folders are used in lateral drawers or file cabinets.

Calculating Record Storage Needs

Before purchasing filing equipment, the filing space needed to house patient records must be calculated using the following procedure:

1. Determine the current linear filing inches used to store records.
2. Project linear filing inches needed for the time period during which records will be stored (e.g., if paper-based records are stored for five years, estimate the number of linear inches needed for the five-year period).
3. Calculate the linear filing inches provided by the shelving unit(s).
4. Convert linear filing inches to the number of shelving units to be purchased.

Example The number of linear filing inches storing current patient records is 1,600 and, during a projected five-year period, 700 additional filing inches will be needed for expansion. The shelving unit has five shelves with 40 inches of storage on each shelf (5 × 40 = 200 linear inches unit).

1. 1,600 + 700 = 2,300 linear filing inches
2. 2,300 ÷ 200 = 11.5 shelving units
3. Round up to 12 shelving units (because you can't purchase 11½ units)

Note: Filing equipment salespersons are helpful in assisting with calculations to determine filing needs. Don't hesitate to seek their assistance, but be sure to double-check their calculations!

EXERCISE 7–3 Filing Equipment

Matching: Match the filing system with its definition.

_____ 1. Shelving unit that resembles a bookshelf and uses end-tab folders.

_____ 2. Shelving that resembles a file cabinet.

_____ 3. Shelving that contains retractable doors and uses top-tab folders.

_____ 4. Units that are operated with a handle or crank.

a. drawer file
b. lateral file
c. movable file
d. open-shelf file
e. power filing machines

Short Answer: Briefly respond to the following.

5. Calculate the record storage needs, given the following information. The number of linear filing inches storing current patient records is 10,500, and during a projected five-year period 5,450 additional filing inches will be needed for expansion. The open-shelf filing unit has eight shelves, and each shelf measures 36 inches.

FILE FOLDERS

To protect the paper-based patient record, reports are housed in binders, file folders, and jackets (or envelopes). Inpatient binders (Figure 7-1) store records for hospital patients who are currently receiving care. File folders (Figure 7-2) store paper-based records and are color-coded, durable, come in a variety of sizes and weights, and can be customized by vendors. Jackets (or envelopes) (Figure 7-3) store x-rays and other over-sized materials; they are open at the top and closed on three sides. (Some physician offices also store patient records in envelopes, but they are cumbersome to use.)

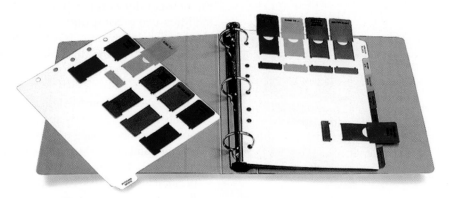

FIGURE 7-1 Inpatient Ringbinder Chartholder (Permission to reprint granted by Ames Color-File.)

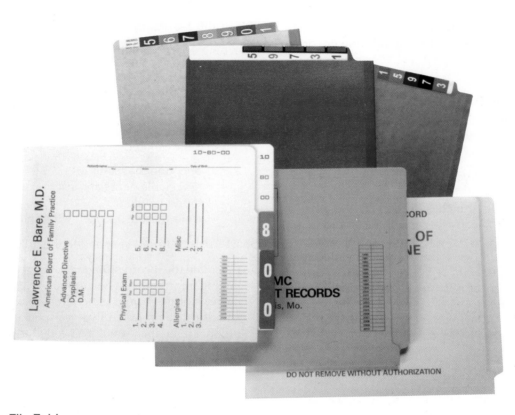

FIGURE 7-2 **File Folders** (Reprinted with permission of Bibbero Systems, Inc., Petaluma, CA. 800 242–2376. www.bibbero.com.)

When selecting file folders, the following should be considered:

- Color coding
- Fastener position
- Preprinted information
- Scoring and reinforcement

Color Coding

Color coding is the assignment of color to primary (and, in some cases, secondary) patient numbers or

FIGURE 7-3 **Jackets (or Envelopes) that House X-rays**
(Reprinted with permission of Bibbero Systems, Inc., Petaluma, CA. 800 242–2376. www.bibbero.com.)

letters used for filing patient records. Color bars are placed on the sides/edges of file folders (Figure 7-4) so that, when filed, all records with the same primary (and secondary) numbers have the same color pattern. This allows misfiles to be easily identified.

There are variations to color coding, and the most common approach is to assign color codes to the two-digit primary number used for filing. Ten different colors correspond to digits 0 to 9 (Table 7-3), and two bars of color are placed on the file folder to represent the primary numbers. More detailed color coding of secondary and tertiary digits is also done. Some facilities use a computer tracking system to monitor record circulation and have folders preprinted with bar coding (Figure 7-5), which looks like a UPC scanning code.

Example Alfred State Medical Center uses terminal-digit numbering to file records and color codes just the primary number. Using the color pattern from Table 7-3, patient number 46-59-01 will be color-coded orange (0) over red (1). Because color bars are placed in the same position on all folders, when the folder is inserted into the shelving unit it will appear with all other folders that have orange over red bars.

FIGURE 7-4 Color-Coded Folders (Reprinted with permission of Bibbero Systems, Inc., Petaluma, CA. 800 242–2376. www.bibbero.com.)

TABLE 7-3 Color Coding

Number	Color Bar
0	Orange
1	Red
2	Yellow
3	Purple
4	Light green
5	Light blue
6	Dark blue
7	Dark green
8	Pink
9	Brown

In addition to color coding the patient number on the folder label, some facilities purchase color-coded file folders to differentiate among types of services received by patients. Tabs are also added that indicate the year that the file was created. By adding the year tabs, the files can be easily identified and records can be pulled or thinned to facilitate record destruction.

Example Alfred State Rehabilitation Center assigns different colors to the types of patients who receive services. Physical therapy patients are assigned blue folders, occupational therapy patients green folders, speech therapy patients orange folders, and multi-service patients purple folders. The patient number is preprinted on the folder, and the primary number is color coded according to Table 7-3.

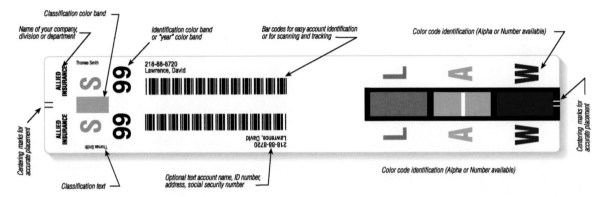

FIGURE 7-5 **Bar Code and Other Identification Information Preprinted on Label** (Reprinted with permission of Bibbero Systems, Inc., Petaluma, CA. 800 242–2376. www.bibbero.com.)

Fastener Position

To prevent reports from becoming separated from the record, all pages are secured to the file folder with adhesive strip, embedded, heat-bonded, or DocuClip fastener (Figure 7-6). Standard positions (Figure 7-7) for fasteners include the top or sides of the file folder. Vendors will customize folders and install a fastener in multiple positions if requested.

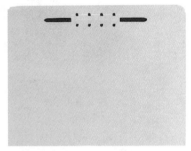

A. Adhesive strip   B. DocuClip   C. Heat-bonded   D. Machine-embedded

FIGURE 7-6 **File Folder Fasteners: A. Adhesive Strip; B. DocuClip; C. Heat-bonded; D. Machine-embedded** (Reprinted with permission of Bibbero Systems, Inc., Petaluma, CA. 800 242–2376. www.bibbero.com.)

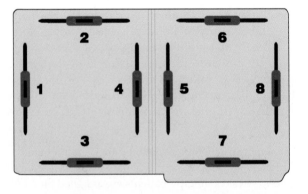
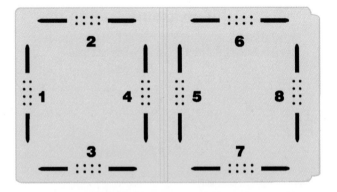

A. End-tab folder for shelf filing   B. Top-tab folder for drawer filing

FIGURE 7-7 **Fastener Positions: A. End-tab Folder for Shelf Filing; B. Top-tab Folder for Drawer Filing** (Reprinted with permission of Bibbero Systems, Inc., Petaluma, CA. 800 242–2376. www.bibbero.com.)

Preprinted Information

Preprinted information (Figure 7-2) on the outside of the file folder should, at a minimum, include an area for the patient's name and number and the facility's name and address. Other information that can be custom preprinted on folders includes:

- Allergy alerts (e.g., medications)
- Activity legend (e.g., year patient was treated, which assists in record purging)
- Confidentiality statement (e.g., alerts users that patient information is confidential and cannot be removed from the facility without proper authority)

Information can even be included on the inside of the folder (Figure 7-8), and facilities can have folders custom-designed and printed by many vendors.

Reinforcing, Rounding, and Scoring File Folders

Reinforcing a folder (end and top tabs) provides extra rigidity so a higher-point stock folder doesn't have to be purchased, and it makes folders more durable. Some folders are also reinforced along the spine. (*Single ply* means the top or end tab of the folder is not reinforced.) The *point stock* measures the thickness of the paper used to make the folder; the higher the point, the thicker the folder (e.g., 14-point stock is extra-heavy 200-pound manila tag paper). *Rounding* of side

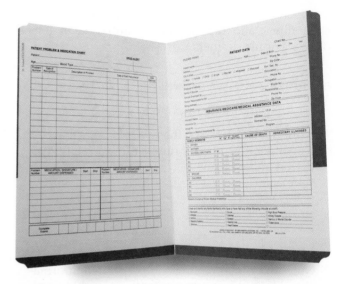

FIGURE 7-8 Preprinted Information Inside Folder. (Reprinted with permission of Bibbero Systems, Inc., Petaluma, CA. 800 242–2376. www.bibbero.com.)

and top tabs is done to prevent crushing folders when filed. The tab contains information needed to file the folder (e.g., patient number or patient name), and if color coding is used the tab also contains color bars. *Scoring* is done by embossing a crisp line on the edge of the folder so it can be folded to expand its capacity. Refer to Figure 7-9 to view reinforcing, rounding, and scoring features.

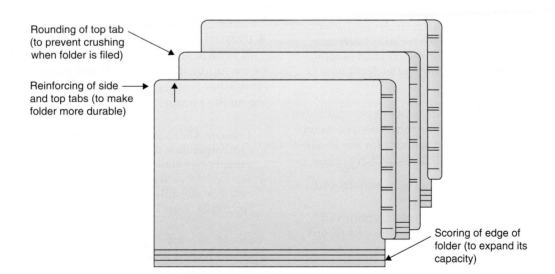

Rounding of top tab
(to prevent crushing
when folder is filed)

Reinforcing of side
and top tabs (to make
folder more durable)

Scoring of edge of
folder (to expand its
capacity)

FIGURE 7-9 Reinforcing, Rounding, and Scoring File Folders

Remember! End-tab folders are used for open-shelf filing, and top-tab folders are used in lateral drawers or file cabinets.

EXERCISE 7–4 File Folders

Short Answer: Briefly respond to each.

1. Using Table 7-3, assign the two color bars that correspond to the primary number for each terminal-digit number below.
   - 45-79-80 _____
   - 99-39-57 _____
   - 67-40-46 _____
   - 83-92-84 _____
   - 59-02-31 _____

2. Other than color coding and preprinted information, identify two other items that should be considered when selecting file folders. _____

3. What is the term for the assignment of color to primary patient numbers or letters used to file patient records? _____

4. All pages of the patient record should be secured to the file folder with a fastener. Identify the four types. _____

5. Identify the term used to measure a folder's weight (durability). _____

FILING CONTROLS

The Joint Commission standards state that a hospital must be able to retrieve all parts of the patient record (e.g., previous hospital admissions, outpatient services, and emergency department services) when the patient is admitted or is seen for ambulatory or emergency care. Medicare CoP requires that hospitals establish systems that allow for timely retrieval of patient information.

Health information departments must establish a charge-out system to control the movement of records in and out of the file area and account for the location of each record removed. Facilities establish policies to:

- Identify authorized personnel who may requisition a record from the file area
- Indicate how long the record may be removed
- Establish a procedure for the transfer of a record from one patient care area to another

Facilities also establish policies and procedures to address patient record maintenance and management issues, and only health information department and facility staff trained to use the file system are authorized

FIGURE 7-10 File Guides. (Permission to reprint granted by Ames Color-File.)

to file and retrieve records. Although standards and regulations do not specify *methods* for record management, all organizations are required to implement systems to effectively manage and control records. In addition, filing controls are established to ensure accurate filing and timely retrieval of patient records, including:

- Chart tracking system (manual or computerized)
- File guides (Figure 7-10)
- Periodic audit of file system

Chart Tracking System

A chart tracking system controls the release and return of patient records and uses record requisition forms to retrieve and track requests for patient records. Two types of requisitions typically occur:

1. Planned
2. Non-routine (or emergency)

A planned requisition is the request of a patient record for a scheduled service (e.g., routine outpatient follow-up visit). The health information department establishes a schedule for such requisitions, depending on the number of requests received each day.

Example Alfred State Medical Center is a large health care corporation that includes an acute care hospital, primary care clinics, a nursing facility, and outpatient services. All patient records are stored in a centralized area. For scheduled visits, departments must requisition records 24 hours in advance.

A non-routine (or emergency) requisition occurs when a patient record is needed for an unscheduled service such as an emergency department visit. Such requests are commonly made via telephone, and the health information department immediately retrieves and delivers the record to the requesting department.

Alfred State Medical Center
Requisition Form

Date Requested | Patient Record No. | Patient Name (Last, First, MI)

Requested by | Telephone Ext. | Location

Reason for request

This patient record must be returned within 48 hours.

FM180-HIM-R-06/03mag

ORIGINAL   Attach original to requested record.

COPY 2   Insert copy 2 in outguide.

COPY 3   File copy 3 in chart tracking file box.

FIGURE 7-11 Requisition Form

Manual chart tracking systems use paper requisition forms (Figure 7-11), which are submitted to the health information department to retrieve the record and track its return. Typically the form consists of an original (filed in the chart tracking index box) and two copies (one is attached to the patient record that is delivered to the requestor, and another is inserted into an outguide). An outguide (Figure 7-12) replaces the

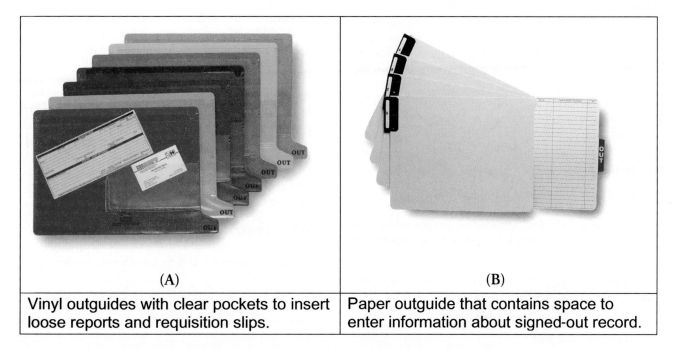

(A)	(B)
Vinyl outguides with clear pockets to insert loose reports and requisition slips.	Paper outguide that contains space to enter information about signed-out record.

FIGURE 7-12 Outguides: A. Vinyl Outguides with Clear Pockets to Insert Loose Reports and Requisition Slips; B. Paper Outguide that Contains Space to Enter Information about Signed-out Record (Reprinted with permission of Bibbero Systems, Inc., Petaluma, CA. 800 242–2376. www.bibbero.com.)

record in the file area to indicate it has been removed and to identify its current location. Vinyl outguides come in a variety of colors and usually contain two clear plastic pockets—a small one into which a copy of the requisition form can be inserted and a larger one for reports that need to be inserted into the record upon its return. Outguides are also made of heavy stock (e.g., cardboard), which allow the following information to be entered:

- Patient name
- Patient number
- Date of removal
- Current location of record
- Requestor's name or signature

Both types of outguides contain the word "out" on the end tab (open shelving) or top tab (drawer shelving).

Automated chart tracking systems (Figure 7-13) allow providers to request records using a computer, and the health information department clerk references a computer screen to process all requests. This facilitates tracking of patient record movement throughout the facility and eliminates the need to manually track records using requisition slips. Patient records usually contain a bar code, which the clerk scans to display patient information on a computer screen. The record is then "signed out" by entering the name and location of the requesting party. When the record is returned to the health information department, the chart tracking software is updated. Outguides may be used in conjunction with computerized chart tracking systems to indicate "at a glance" that a record has been removed from the file area.

Remember! To maintain control of the file area, an outguide must be inserted each time a record is removed from the area!

Periodic Audit of File Area

To ensure that all records removed from the file area are returned in a timely fashion, a periodic audit of file area must be conducted. Depending on the size of the facility, the audit is completed on a daily, weekly, or monthly basis.

Note: The more frequent the periodic audit, the better chance of locating lost patient records.

The file area should be reviewed for misfiles and records that have not been returned within the time period specified by hospital policy. (While records should be returned to the file area according to hospital policy, quality management or research studies may require that records may not be returned for weeks or even months.) If folders are color coded in the file area, misfiles can be quickly and easily identified. Outguides also prove beneficial in locating records that have been removed and are unreturned. (Sometimes outguides remain in the file area after the records have been refiled. Be sure to remove any outguides that should not be in the file area.)

Computerized chart tracking systems can assist in the period audit of the file area. The system is capable of producing a report that lists all patient records that have not been returned to the department. File clerks can then attempt to locate those records. Periodic audits are more frequently performed using computerized chart tracking systems because of the ability to print reports on demand. A manual chart tracking system requires a file clerk to search the file area for outguides and reconcile requisition slips with outstanding records.

EXERCISE 7–5 Filing Controls

Fill-in-the-Blank: Enter the appropriate term(s) to complete each statement below.

1. To control the movement of records into and out of the file area *and* to account for the location of each record, health information departments establish _____ systems.

2. A common policy and procedure established by HIM departments to address patient record maintenance and management issues is that only staff _____ to use the file system are permitted to file and retrieve records.

3. The request of a patient record for a scheduled service is called a _____ requisition.

4. When a record is removed from the file area, a(n) _____ replaces the record to indicate it has been removed and to identify its current location.

5. A system capable of generating a report that lists all patient records not returned to the department is a computerized _____ system.

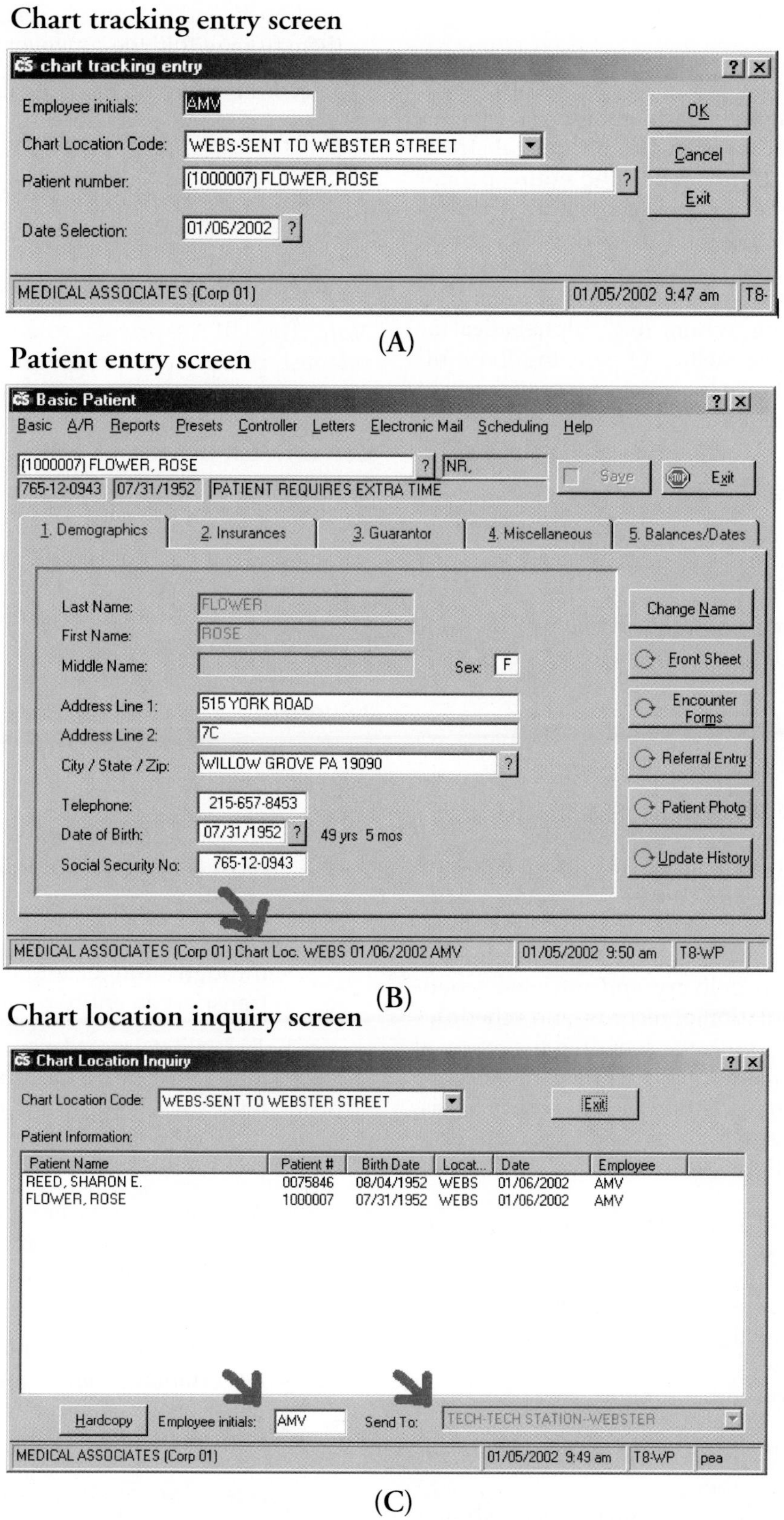

Chart tracking entry screen

(A)

Patient entry screen

(B)

Chart location inquiry screen

(C)

FIGURE 7-13 Chart Tracking Software Screens: A. Chart Tracking Entry Screen; B. Patient Entry Screen; C. Chart Location Inquiry Screen (Permission to reprint granted by Software Expressions, Inc.)

LOOSE FILING

After completion of patient services (e.g., inpatient, outpatient, emergency department), the record is sent to the health information department for chart assembly, incomplete chart processing, coding and abstracting, and permanent filing. While the entire patient record *should* be received at this time, individual reports that must be filed in the patient record are often received after discharge. This loose filing should be immediately added to the patient record or organized according to the filing system (e.g., alphabetical or numerical) used by the facility. Organizing loose filing in this manner allows for quick access to a report that is needed but is not found in the patient record.

EXERCISE 7–6 Loose Filing

Short Answer: Briefly respond to each.

1. Define "loose filing."

2. Discuss the advantages and disadvantages of the methods used by HIM managers to meet the challenge of loose filing.

CIRCULATION SYSTEMS

A circulation system transports records from one location in the facility to another (as well as to locations outside of the facility). The most common circulation system is a messenger who hand-carries records from the health information department to the requesting department. Health information departments establish delivery and retrieval schedules to facilitate circulation of records, and schedules are often coordinated with the schedule for retrieval of paper-based requisition slips. (When records are requisitioned on a non-routine or emergency basis, the requesting department often sends personnel to the health information department to retrieve the record.)

Mechanical circulation system devices used to transport records include:

- Pneumatic tube. Transports a single record in a tube through a tunnel (e.g., device used by bank drive-thru windows). It is often difficult to transport an entire record because tubes are not large enough.
- Dumbwaiter. Small elevator that transports records from one floor to another.
- Conveyor belt. Similar to a pneumatic tube, except it uses a belt instead of a tube and records are clipped to the belt for transport from one area to another. The problem with this system is that records become

unclipped, and personnel must manually retrieve them from within the conveyor belt routing system.

Record circulation has been enhanced through:

- Facsimile (or fax) machines transmit a document's image via telephone lines. Fax transmission allows for rapid transport of the record from one area to another. It is important to ensure that the fax machine is located in a secure area if patient information is transported in this fashion.

Note: The HIPAA privacy rule requires that facilities establish policies and procedures when fax transmissions are used to transport patient information. A good precaution to take when faxing patient information is to call the receiving site both before and after the fax is sent to confirm that a responsible person will receive the fax and confirm receipt.

- Computers allow for rapid circulation of patient information. Access to all patient information contained in the automated record is possible for authorized users via an intranet and/or the Internet.

EXERCISE 7–7 Circulation Systems

True/False: Indicate whether each statement is true (T) or false (F).

_____ 1. A chart tracking system is used to transport records from one location in the facility to another.

_____ 2. A pneumatic tube transports patient records through a tunnel, and it can be difficult to transport an entire record.

_____ 3. To facilitate record circulation, health information departments establish delivery and retrieval schedules and often coordinate these with the schedule for retrieval of paper-based requisition slips.

_____ 4. A dumbwaiter is similar to a pneumatic tube except that records are clipped to a belt (instead of placed in a tube) for transport from one area to another.

_____ 5. The HIPAA privacy rule requires that facilities establish policies and procedures for using fax transmissions to transport patient information.

SECURITY OF HEALTH INFORMATION

All patient information must be secured in a locked file or in a locked room, which is accessed by authorized staff members only. Records should be stored

Case Example

The Many Faces of Loose Reporting Filing (Permission to reprint granted by Opus Communications.)

A *Medical Records Briefing* benchmarking survey on filing productivity proves that there is no cookie-cutter approach to handling loose reports. That's because different-sized departments have different needs, and no two hospitals are run alike. Suffice to say, there are perhaps as many methods to file loose reports as there are health information management departments. Here are a few ways HIM managers have met the challenges to get the job done.

Filing on night shifts

Doris Shady, RHIT, supervisor of medical records at 339-bed Presbyterian Intercommunity Hospital in Whittier, CA California, has found that it makes sense for filing to be done on afternoon shifts. "The p.m. shift [3 p.m. to 11 p.m.] has more access to the medical records in the department because only three people are on duty as opposed to 20 or so in the morning," she explains. Besides filing, clerks on the late shift also pull charts for patient care and pull incomplete records for physicians. Shady has a hunch why her afternoon clerks are so productive. "The phone rings much less in the afternoon," she says, "and that's nice. Especially when one of the clerks is in the archives for two-and-a-half hours."

Using a point person

Lorrie Johnson, supervisor of outpatient records at 312-bed Robert Packer Hospital in Sayre, Pennsylvania, believes that the key to staying on top of the 2,000 or more loose reports that come to her department daily is a "sorter/receptionist" who sorts inpatient from outpatient materials for the file clerks. This full-time employee is the "drop-off point for anything that comes into the department—including mail," says Johnson. Because there are minimal inpatient materials to file, inpatient and outpatient materials are sorted differently. The sorter separates inpatient materials into one category and brings them to the incomplete room. The sorter separates the considerably larger stack of outpatient materials into different categories such as EKGs and clinic notes. This way, if staff need to access them before they are filed, they can limit their search to the appropriate pile.

Cutting steps

Joy Jones, CAMH, medical records director at 200-bed Mercy Hospital in Portland, Maine, has found that putting loose reports in the front pocket of charts instead of punching holes and inserting them inside the record saves time. "This way, if the information is needed for patient care, it is still available in the front folder, but we save the time of inserting it up front," she says. As a result, miscellaneous reports are consistently filed by the end of every week. If the information is eventually needed, staff—at that point—take the time to properly insert it. But Jones notes that about 75% of charts don't get pulled again for patient care. "When the charts are microfilmed, they all get filmed appropriately and if they go to storage, it doesn't matter anyway."

Taking a shift

Marilyn Wells, RHIA, director of medical records at 65-bed McDowell Hospital in Marion, North Carolina, has three "medical record analysts," full-time employees whose primary responsibilities are filing, chart analysis, and "everything else." Since filing is the least popular responsibility, analysts decided, on their own, to take weekly shifts. "I don't think any of them get excited about filing but they all know it has to be done. It gets done, and we have minimal problems," says Wells. "And I think because the job switches every week, they kind of encourage each other to finish up because nobody wants to have to put away the leftovers," she adds.

in file units that protect them from fire and water damage. It is common for the record room to contain fire walls and/or fire doors that prevent a fire from spreading from one area to another. The file area should also have a sprinkler system in place in case of fire. Records should have an enclosed top shelf to help protect them from water damage in the event of sprinkler system malfunction. There should be 18 to 20 inches of clearance between the top shelf and the ceiling. (Local fire codes dictate the clearance needed between the ceiling and the shelves as well the space required between file rows). The file area should also contain a fire extinguisher and a fire pull switch, and staff must be trained in the use of each.

Records must be protected from water damage due to malfunctioning sprinkler systems or flooding. Records should not be stored on the floor, as this presents a safety hazard to staff members and records could be damaged in the event of flooding. Records that are maintained in closed files are more protected from water damage than are records located on open-shelf units.

Patient information must also be protected from theft; only authorized personnel should have access to the file area. If a health information staff member is not available in the file area to retrieve a record, the area must be secured. If the file area is locked, only those authorized to access the area should have a key. When the file area is not staffed (e.g., evenings, nights, weekends), procedures must be established to allow limited access to records. Usually a nursing supervisor will be provided with a key to the file area and assigned responsibility for retrieving patient records if needed. File areas can also be secured by using authorized swipe cards (similar to those used for hotel rooms).

Patient information located in patient areas (e.g., nursing units) must be evaluated for protection against loss from fire, water, and theft.

Note: HIPAA regulations require that all patient information areas be analyzed to determine the potential for breaches of patient privacy and information security.

Computerized health information also needs to be protected from loss due to fire, water, or theft. It is common to create a backup file of all computerized patient information and to store the backup file off site (at a location other than the facility). In the event of loss, the backup can be used to re-create patient information.

Facilities must also establish policies and procedures to address portable computer security (laptops, cell phones, tablets, and so on). The risk of theft increases when someone can simply "walk off" with a laptop, resulting in stolen patient information. Health care facilities must establish appropriate controls to address this issue by:

- Establishing policies and procedures that address portable technology
- Educating and training users of portable technology about facility policies and the potential for theft and loss of patient information
- Using appropriate encryption and password security
- Purging information from portable computers when the computer is assigned to a new user

Record Destruction by Natural or Man-made Disasters

When a health care facility asserts that a natural or man-made disaster destroyed paper-based or electronic patient records, guidelines established by the CMS are followed to corroborate. The natural or man-made disaster record destruction corroboration process confirms allegations that patient records were destroyed during a natural or man-made disaster through:

- *Qualification* (submitted attestation statement is reviewed by CMS to determine whether the event qualifies as a natural or man-made disaster).
- *Accuracy* (CMS confirms accuracy of the attestation).

Upon confirmation of the corroboration process that a natural or man-made disaster destroyed patient records, the health care facility is not held liable for lost records that are requested by CMS.

Remember! Preventing tampering or defacement of patient information is equally important. Facilities must establish controls to prevent providers from altering record entries after the fact. Paper entries must be corrected according to facility policy (e.g., do not remove pages). Automated record systems must also include mechanisms to ensure that patient information remains unaltered (e.g., use of "write once, read many" software).

Electronic Storage Technology

Throughout this chapter, concepts that relate to the physical storage of paper-based records have been discussed. An electronic record system stores the same data found in the paper record. Electronic record systems allow for large volumes of data to be stored and accessed. It is the goal of all electronic systems to have real-time access. This allows for immediate access to vital patient information however this requires systems to store increasingly larger amounts of data.

Data can be stored on various devices. Stand-alone desktop computers and laptops all have a built-in microchip to store data and information. This is known as primary storage or primary memory. Secondary storage, also known as auxiliary, external, or permanent storage, stores data on storage devices or servers. Storing data on these devices allows multiple users to access the data. The physical equipment that stores data and programs is called secondary devices. Various types of secondary storage devices were discussed in Chapter 5 of this textbook.

As more patient information systems go paperless and allow real-time access of data, it is essential that all systems have an entire back-up of the information

Case Example

Developing an Information Security Policy, David Sobel (Permission to reprint granted by David Sobel)

David Sobel, president of Confidentiality Matters, Inc., specializes in providing comprehensive information security services to health care organizations. He previously wrote an article for *Partner Pointers* highlighting steps health care providers should take to protect patient care information. In the article that follows, he discusses the importance of following an information security policy:

Every health care organization—regardless of its level of computerization—needs to have a comprehensive information security policy. A policy defines an organization's commitment to confidentiality for its patients, members of the community and its employees. It provides a blueprint for defining standards and procedures. And it establishes a standard of care with respect to the handling of its confidential informational resources. In this second of three articles dealing with computers and confidentiality, I will discuss some issues to consider when developing an information security policy in a physician office practice.

To begin this process, an organization's executive leadership should appoint a confidentiality committee and charge this committee with the task of developing a comprehensive information security policy. While practices differ in their organizational structures, I would suggest that the following areas be represented on such a committee:

- Physicians
- Nurses
- Practice manager
- Office personnel

As the drafters begin their task, they should first define what information is confidential and who will have access to these informational resources. This includes patients' medical records, as well as information pertaining to employees, finance and physicians. Besides covering the topic of access to and disclosure of general health care information, how will you restrict access to the records of abused and neglected children? Moreover, under what conditions will restricted records be released to others?

Second, a policy should address access administration. Who will define directories or menus? Who will create and delete unique Logon Ids? And, who will provide assistance to users when they forget their passwords or require assistance in signing on and accessing applications? The key issue in an access administration is to ensure that each user has access on a need-to-know basis, i.e., access which is necessary to perform his or her responsibilities.

Third, a comprehensive policy should address educational awareness. Specifically, will you orient new employees to the importance of confidentiality? Will you have annual in-service programs on the importance of confidentiality? And, who will conduct these programs? No policy should gather dust. To be effective, it must be communicated and understood by physicians and staff.

Fourth, a policy should cover sanctions. Staff need to know that there is a price to pay for breaching patient confidentiality. While sanctions should correspond to your personnel policies, employees need to understand that their employment may be terminated for breaching confidentiality.

Fifth, every policy should have specific policy protocols on the following:

- E-mail and the user of the Internet
- Facsimile Transmissions
- Electronic Signatures
- Cellular Telephones
- PC Software
- Virus Protection
- Internet Home Page

Each of these areas presents organizations with risks and potential liabilities. Therefore, it is advisable to define and communicate to staff your organization's protocols when using these technologies.

Sixth, a policy should cover safeguarding confidential documents. How will you safeguard confidential documents? Specifically, how will you safeguard documents from cleaning crews who provide housekeeping services in the evening? Additionally, how will you store documents? And how will you dispose of confidential documents? Regarding the latter, if you contract with a recycling company, will you require a confidentiality clause in your contract?

Finally, who will administer the policy and program? In physician office practices, the Office or Practice Manager may be the ideal person to assume these responsibilities. Basically, this person would be

(Continues)

Case Example, continued

responsible for enforcing the policy, orienting new staff and conducting annual awareness programs.

When the Confidentiality Committee is satisfied that they have written a good first draft, they should circulate the draft and solicit revision suggestions from other members of the practice. Once these suggestions are incorporated into a revised policy, the policy should be reviewed again. Providing there are no further revisions, it should be submitted to the President or Chief Executive Officer of the practice for his or her signature. When it is signed, it should be communicated to employees and guest users. At this time it might be appropriate to have all employees sign new confidentiality agreements.

Having a strong information security policy and program accomplishes two important goals:

* protects the confidentiality rights of patients
* serves to reduce your organizational risks and potential liabilities.

Moreover, it enables a practice to maintain the public trust at a time when the public has serious concerns about the privacy of their medical information.

processing and data stored on secondary devices. In many systems mirrored processing occurs. **Mirrored processing** is the simultaneous entry and storage of data into a primary and secondary server. If the primary server fails, the secondary server acts as the system back-up. Some health care organizations also have a third server to provide an additional backup. It is also best practice to have the backup servers physically located at a different location from the first server, therefore if there is a disaster that impacts one location the another server could possibly not be impacted.

Health information professionals need to be actively involved in record storage issues that relate to electronic systems. Patient information—in any type of system, paper or electronic—stills needs to be maintained according to regulations that govern record retention and security of health information.

EXERCISE 7–8 Security of Health Information

True/False: Indicate whether each statement is true (T) or false (F).

_____ 1. File units that protect records from fire automatically protect them from water damage.

_____ 2. State laws require sprinkler systems in all health information file areas.

_____ 3. Open-shelf filing units that contain an enclosed top shelf help protect records from water damage in the event of sprinkler system malfunction.

_____ 4. Only authorized personnel should have access to the file area.

_____ 5. It is easier to protect computerized health information than paper-based records.

Internet Links

Go to **http://www.adldata.com**, and click on MEDICAL RECORDS to view various solutions for both paper-based and electronic medical record systems.

Go to **http://www.bibbero.com** and order file folder samples to assist you in better understanding concepts presented in this chapter.

Go to **http://www.filingtoday.com** and click on the headings to view information about file folders, alphabetic and numeric filing systems, and shelving and storage systems.

Go to **http://www.searchforancestors.com** and click on TOOLS and SOUNDEX CALCULATOR to enter your last name and convert it to Soundex (phonetic code).

Go to **http://www.3m.com** and click on your location and then products to read more about automated chart tracking software.

SUMMARY

Patient record numbers are assigned according to serial, unit, or serial-unit numbering systems, and records are filed according to alphabetic or numeric filing systems. File storage is either centralized or decentralized, and the health care facility selects filing equipment that meets their needs. Filing equipment and folders are selected to enhance record storage and retrieval. File controls include chart tracking and periodic audit of the file area. Health care facilities are responsible for implementing security policies and procedures for paper-based and electronic health records.

STUDY CHECKLIST

- Read the textbook chapter and highlight key concepts. (Use colored highlighter sparingly throughout the chapter.)
- Create an index card for each key term. (Write the key term on one side of the index card and the concept on the other. Learn the definition of each key term, and match the term to the concept.)
- Access chapter Internet links to learn more about concepts.
- Answer the chapter exercises and review questions, verifying answers with your instructor.
- Study content, view videos, and take practice tests online at www.CengageBrain.com.
- Complete lab manual assignments, verifying answers with your instructor.
- Form a study group with classmates to discuss chapter concepts in preparation for an exam.

CHAPTER REVIEW

True/False: Indicate whether each statement is true (T) or false (F).

_____ 1. Alphabetic filing is difficult to learn, and staff training is time-consuming.

_____ 2. Record security is enhanced by using a numeric filing system.

_____ 3. Another term for consecutive numeric filing is numeric filing.

_____ 4. In decentralized filing, records are filed in more than more location.

_____ 5. A requisition slip should contain, at a minimum, the patient name and record number, the requesting party, and the date that the record was requested.

Fill-in-the-Blank: Enter the appropriate term(s) to complete each statement.

6. The assignment of color bars to the primary numbers or letters used for filing is known as _____.

7. The use of a single location for all file storage is known as _____.

8. Records are filed in exact chronological order according to a patient identification number with the _____ system.

9. When a social security numbering system is used, a _____ is issued to a patient who does not have a social security number.

10. To protect pages in the patient record, they are stored in _____, binders, or _____.

11. Because of the safety hazard to staff and possible damage in the event of flooding, records should not be stored on the _____.

12. In case of fire, the file area should contain a(n) _____.

13. To protect records from possible water damage, they should be maintained in _____ files.

14. To protect patient information from theft, only _____ staff who should have access to the file area.

15. There should be _____ inches of clearance between the top shelf and the ceiling in the file area.

Short Answer: Briefly respond to each.

16. Sequence the numbers in straight number order.
____ 10-40-99   ____ 39-83-01   ____ 14-83-06
____ 11-40-98   ____ 90-17-54   ____ 39-84-01
____ 56-83-06   ____ 11-39-98   ____ 23-01-54
____ 15-84-06   ____ 12-40-98   ____ 24-01-54

17. Sequence the numbers in terminal-digit order.
____ 10-40-99   ____ 39-83-01   ____ 14-83-06
____ 11-40-98   ____ 90-17-54   ____ 39-84-01
____ 56-83-06   ____ 11-39-98   ____ 23-01-54
____ 15-84-06   ____ 12-40-98   ____ 24-01-54

18. Sequence the numbers in middle-digit order.
____ 10-40-99   ____ 39-83-01   ____ 14-83-06
____ 11-40-98   ____ 90-17-54   ____ 39-84-01
____ 56-83-06   ____ 11-39-98   ____ 23-01-54
____ 15-84-06   ____ 12-40-98   ____ 24-01-54

19. Assign phonetic codes to the following surnames.
a. Sanderson   _____
b. Fulsom   _____
c. Kczowski   _____
d. Mulholland   _____
e. Dresser-Rey   _____

20. Discuss the purposes of using outguides and performing periodic audits of the file area.

Chapter 8

INDEXES, REGISTERS, AND HEALTH DATA COLLECTION

Key Terms

admission/discharge/transfer (ADT) system
admission register
aggregate data
arithmetic mean
automated case abstracting systems
automated MPI
average daily census
average length of stay
bar graph
batched
case abstracting
case mix analysis
case report forms
comparative data
computer interface
continuous quality improvement (CQI)
daily census count

daily inpatient census
data accessibility
data accuracy
data analysis
data application
data collection
data comprehensiveness
data consistency
data currency
data definition
data dictionary
data granularity
data integrity
data mining
data precision
data relevancy
data reliability
data set
data timeliness
data validity

data warehousing
death register
descriptive statistics
discharge data statistics
discharge register
disease index
index
length of stay (LOS) data
line diagram
magnetic stripe card
manual case abstracting systems
manual master patient index (MPI)
master patient index (MPI)
master person index (MPI)
National Center for Health Statistics (NCHS)
online analytical processing (OLAP) servers
patient-centric data
physician index

pie chart
procedure index
register

registry
relational database
run chart

total length of stay
transformed-based data
vital statistics

Objectives

At the end of this chapter, the student should be able to:

- Define key terms
- Identify indexes, registers, and registries maintained by health care facilities and state and federal agencies
- Explain the uses of indexes, registers, and registries

- Determine case abstracting requirements for patient records
- Discuss the characteristics of health data collection

INTRODUCTION

Indexes, registers, and registries allow health information to be maintained and retrieved by health care facilities for the purpose of education, planning, research, and so on. According to *The American Heritage® Dictionary of the English Language*, an index "serves to guide, point out, or otherwise facilitate reference, especially an alphabetized list of names, places, and subjects treated in a printed work, giving the page or pages on which each item is mentioned." A common use is to locate a term in the index of a textbook and refer to the page number indicated. In health care, a master patient index is maintained, which allows for the retrieval of patient demographic information and the medical record number so the patient's record can be retrieved.

The same source defines register as "a formal or official recording of items, names, or actions." You may be familiar with church registers that record births, baptisms, marriages, deaths, and burials. Health care facilities also maintain registers to record admissions, discharges, births, deaths, operations, and other events. Registers are organized in chronological order, contain patient data, and are used for reference or control purposes. When used as a reference, they provide information about workload (e.g., number of births). As a control function, registers track patient data (e.g., number control log, which contains numbers assigned to patients). A registry is an organized system for the collection, storage, retrieval, analysis, and dissemination of information on individuals who have either a particular disease, a condition (e.g., a

risk factor) that predisposes them to the occurrence of a health-related event, or prior exposure to substances or circumstances known or suspected to cause adverse health effects (e.g., official record book, such as a death register).

Indexes and registers can be automated or manual. Automated indexes and registers are computerized, which allows information to be easily and quickly retrieved for administrative planning, data collection, patient care management, quality of patient care, and the study of diseases and their outcomes. Manual indexes and registers require the posting information to ledger cards and log books by hand, resulting in a cumbersome process when information retrieval becomes necessary.

Note: Indexes, registers, and registries are considered *secondary sources of patient information.* (Primary and secondary sources of information are discussed in Chapter 4.)

INDEXES

Health care facilities generally maintain the following indexes:

- Master patient index (MPI)
- Disease index
- Procedure index
- Physician index

Master Patient Index

A master patient index (MPI), sometimes called a master person index (MPI), links a patient's medical record number with common identification data elements (e.g., patient's complete name, date of birth, gender, mother's maiden name, and social security number). Because most health care facilities house patient records according to a medical record number, the MPI becomes the key to locating paper-based records in the health information department file system. Thus, the MPI is retained permanently because it serves as the "key" to finding the patient's record. It can be automated or manual.

Note: Physician offices often do not assign medical record numbers, which means an MPI is unnecessary because records are filed alphabetically according to patient's last name, first name, and middle initial.

An automated MPI is a computerized database of identification information about patients who have received health care services from a facility. An admission/discharge/transfer (ADT) system is used to input patient registration information (Figure 8-1), which results in the creation of an automated MPI database that allows for the storage and retrieval of the information. ADT software has the capability of generating standard reports for administrative and departmental purposes, including:

- Admission logs or register (list of patients admitted)
- Bed utilization reports (facility occupancy rates)
- Current charges reports (expected accounts receivable)
- Daily census summaries (current inpatients)
- Daily discharge logs or registers (list of patients discharged and transferred to other facilities)
- Patient profiles (based on patient demographics, diagnoses/procedures, and so on)
- Transfer reports (patients transferred to units within the facility)
- User-defined reports (based on user-defined criteria)

A manual master patient index (MPI) (Figure 8-2) requires the typing or manual posting of patient identification information on preprinted index cards, and limited information can be retrieved. MPI cards are housed in a vertical file (discussed in Chapter 7), with one card generated for each patient. When patients return to the facility, the MPI card is retrieved

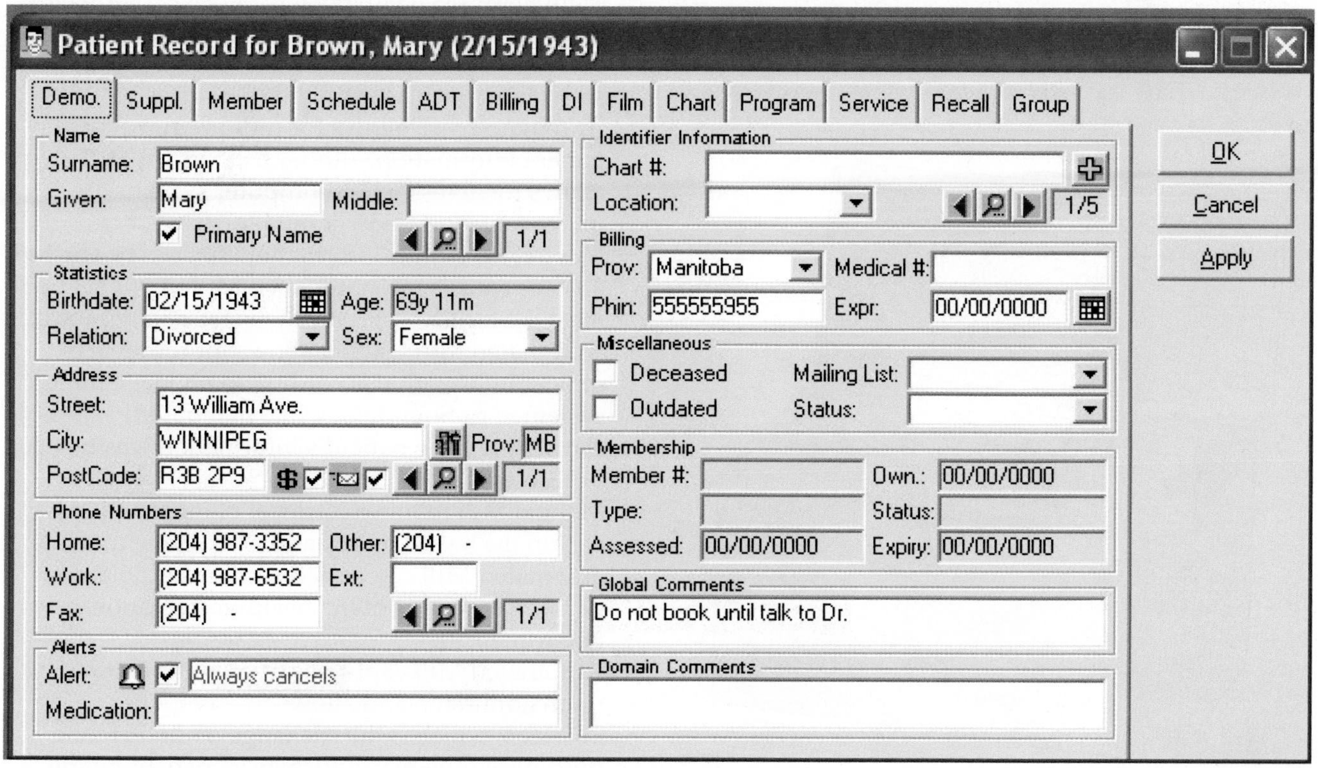

FIGURE 8-1 ADT Software Data Entry Screen (Permission to republish granted by Rise Health Systems.)

LAST NAME	FIRST NAME	MIDDLE NAME	GENDER	AGE	RACE	PATIENT NO.
Doe	John	James	Male	39	C	123456

ADDRESS	BIRTH DATE	MONTH	DAY	YEAR
123 Main St, Hometown, NY 12345-1234		05	05	1975

MOTHER'S MAIDEN NAME	PLACE OF BIRTH	SOCIAL SECURITY NUMBER (SSN)
Pasquale	Elmira, NY	123-45-6789

ADMISSION DATE	DISCHARGE DATE	PROVIDER	TYPE	DISCHARGE STATUS
05-05-2009	05-10-2009	Smith, James	IP	Home
06-10-2009		Lambert, Sandra	ED	Home
07-15-2010		Carmichael, John	OP	Home

FIGURE 8-2 Master Patient Index Card

and reviewed to verify demographic information and update the card with new admission information. File guides (Figure 8-3) help users quickly locate MPI cards and file folders by dividing the filing system into smaller subdivisions.

FIGURE 8-3 Alphabetic File Guides

Advantages and disadvantages of automated and manual MPI systems include:

- Manual MPI is relatively inexpensive to purchase as compared with automated MPI, which requires initial purchase of computer equipment and software as well as software upgrades.
- Automated MPI allows for rapid retrieval of patient information, although a manual MPI allows for access when computer systems are unavailable (e.g., power outage).
- Manual MPI limits information that can be entered on each card, while automated MPI can be set up to meet the facility's specifications for data retrieval.
- Automated MPI usually allows for retrieval of patient information according to phonetic filing system (e.g., Soundex), while manual MPI cards can be lost if the patient's information was typed or recorded incorrectly.
- Manual MPI requires retrieval of information within the health information department, while automated MPI can be accessed by authorized personnel outside of the health information department.
- Automated MPI captures patient information upon admission and allows for computer interface, which is the exchange of data among multiple software products (e.g., patient billing, case abstracting).

Facilities that convert to an automated MPI system usually enter manual MPI data into the automated system instead of retaining the manual MPI as a separate system. Once the conversion is complete and the health information department has verified that information entered into the automated MPI is accurate, the manual MPI system can be destroyed (e.g., shredded). It is recommended that the manual MPI be maintained for at least six months after a conversion so that inaccurate information can be corrected if necessary.

Identification information entered into an MPI typically includes the following, sometimes referred to as demographic information:

- Patient name (last name, first name, middle initial)
- Address (street, city, state, zip code)
- Social security number (SSN)
- Date of birth (using mmddyyyy format)
- Admission/discharge (or transfer) dates (using mmddyyyy format)
- Medical record number (assigned by the facility)
- Name of facility and/or provider (when multiple facilities/providers are associated with the network)
- Type of care received (inpatient, outpatient, emergency, provider office)

MPI systems can also capture diagnosis/procedure descriptions for each date of service if the facility determines that this information should be collected. Additional information entered may include race/ethnicity as well as the mother's maiden name and place of birth, which serves as identifying information for the purpose of verifying a patient (e.g., patients with common first and last names). When patients receive care at a number of facilities within a health care network (e.g., privately owned health care system), the need to maintain current demographic data and synchronize that data is crucial. The MPI allows the health care network to uniquely identify a patient and allows providers to retrieve clinical information from wherever the patient has received care.

Purpose of the Master Patient Index

The master patient index (MPI) is used administratively, for continuity of care or continuum of care, and externally. Administratively, the MPI serves as a "customer database" for the health care organization and allows for the production of a variety of reports that can be used as business planning and marketing tools. For continuity of care or continuum of care, the MPI assists in determining whether a patient has been previously treated by a health care facility. This alerts the provider to request previous patient records to be sent to the inpatient unit, emergency department, outpatient clinic, and other departments. The review of previous records allows the provider to most appropriately treat the patient. Externally, the MPI allows the facility to link patient services received outside of the organization with community-wide ancillary services (e.g., services provided by a stand-alone laboratory). As a result, the facility avoids providing duplicate services to patients, improves provider productivity (e.g., by making computerized test results available), and increases the possibility of detecting government medical program fraud or abuse.

Example of Administrative Use The public relations (PR) department has been requested to perform an analysis of its health care facility's target patient care market. The PR department submits a request to information services to generate a zip code distribution report of patients treated by the facility during the past five years. This report can be analyzed to determine additional markets that the facility should target for advertising purposes.

Example of Continuity of Care A patient comes to the emergency department (ED) complaining of severe headaches. The emergency physician instructs the ED clerk to determine whether the patient has previously been treated. The ED clerk obtains the patient's previous records, and upon review the ED physician notes that the patient underwent a head x-ray one week ago. Thus, the physician selects a diagnostic workup and treatment modality that does not duplicate previous care provided.

Example of External Use The board of directors of a health care facility based in an urban area researches whether building a satellite facility in the suburbs of a major city is justified. In addition to a zip code distribution report of patients treated by the facility, the board should also review reports that contain data including patient age, diagnoses, procedures, and so on.

Avoiding Duplicate Records

It is important to avoid the creation of duplicate records. Information should be entered into the MPI by one department that has control over the assignment of medical record numbers. Usually the admissions department generates or updates the MPI record for each patient in cooperation with the facility's health information department. Specialized consultants (Figure 8-4) can analyze a facility's MPI data and conduct on-site

FIGURE 8-4 Duplicate Records Can Turn into a Big Problem! (Permission to reprint granted by The MediBase Group, Inc.)

assessments to identify duplication issues and problems related to patient identification, including:

- Analysis of the MPI file to identify duplicate medical record numbers
- Evaluation of patient identification issues, including review of administrative policies and existing procedures as well as risk assessment associated with duplicate record problems
- Summary information regarding MPI data integrity, description of patient identification issues, and recommendations for solutions and cost-benefit justification.

Often, problems with duplicate MPI records occur when health care facilities merge: The MPIs are also merged, creating duplicate patient entries, medical record numbers, and so on. It is crucial to establish a merger plan to avoid the duplication of MPI records, and it is equally important to audit (or "clean") the MPI using a variety of mechanisms from the simple (e.g., perform a manual alphabetic search to identify duplicate patient files) to the complex (e.g., use sophisticated software to correct duplicates, overlaps, and other errors in the MPI).

Caution! Don't confuse a master patient index card with a smart card (Figure 8-5), which is a portable,

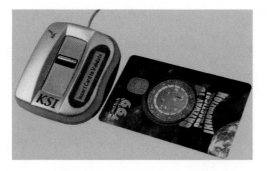

FIGURE 8-5 **Smart Card with Validation Device** (Permission to reprint granted by Kinetic Sciences, Inc.)

updatable card used to store personal identification, medical history, and insurance information (or as a security device, as discussed in Chapter 1). It has its own microprocessing chip and can store thousands more bits of information than a magnetic stripe card, although the smart card requires a special card-reading device. A magnetic stripe card (Figure 8-6) is similar to a plastic credit card that contains an electromagnetic surface capable of holding a small amount of information.

Disease, Procedure, and Physician Indexes

Note: Health information departments in acute care facilities no longer have disease, procedure, and physician indexes generated by the Information Technology (IT) department. Instead, the HIM director (or designee) works with an IT staff member to create needed reports by communicating data elements that comprise such a report.

Disease, procedure, and physician indexes contain data abstracted (selected) from patient records and entered into a computerized database from which the respective index is generated. The disease index (Figure 8-7) is organized according to ICD-9-CM disease codes. The procedure index (Figure 8-8) is organized according to ICD-9-CM and/or CPT/HCPCS procedure/service codes. The physician index (Figure 8-9) is organized according to numbers assigned by the facility to physicians who treat inpatients and outpatients. Elements routinely entered into the database include the following:

- Demographic information (age, ethnicity, gender, inpatient admission/discharge or outpatient treatment date, and zip code)
- Financial information (third-party payer type and total charges)
- Medical information (attending physician, consulting physician, surgeon, medical service classification (e.g., obstetrics), disease and/or procedure/service code(s), date(s) of surgery, and type of anesthesia)

Indexes are used to complete applications for accreditation prior to survey (e.g., The Joint Commission), documents required by licensing and regulatory agencies (e.g., CMS), medical and statistical reports (e.g., New York's Statewide Planning and Research Cooperative System or SPARCS), and facility-wide quality review studies of patient care.

EXERCISE 8–1 Indexes

Short Answer: Briefly respond to each question.

1. State the purpose of a disease index.

2. The master patient index is organized according to _____ so that patient records can be easily retrieved.

3. The director of medical education wants to determine the average length of time it takes a particular surgeon to perform surgery. Which index would best allow access to the surgeon's cases for the purpose of this study?

4. Identify the types of codes entered in a procedure index.

5. State the advantages and disadvantages of an automated MPI and a manual MPI.

6. What term describes a computer system used to input patient registration information?

7. What term describes the exchange of data among multiple software products?

8. Why is it important to manage duplicate records when two facilities merge?

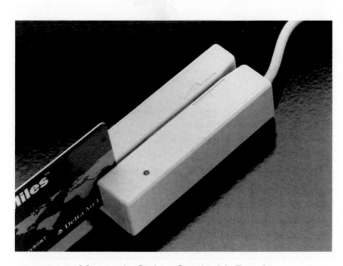

FIGURE 8-6 **Magnetic Stripe Card with Reader** (Permission to reprint granted by Scan Technology, Inc., http://www.scantechnology.com.)

```
┌─────────────────────────────────────────────────────────────────────────────┐
│                                                                               │
│                    Alfred State Medical Center                                │
│                          Disease Index                                        │
│                                                                               │
│  Reporting Period      0801YYYY–0801YYYY            Date Prepared  08-02-YYYY  │
│                                                                               │
│                                                       Page   1 of 5           │
│                                                                               │
│                                                                               │
│  Primary Dx   Other Diagnoses   Attending Dr   Age   Gender   Payer  Patient #│
│                                                                               │
│  HUMAN IMMUNODEFICIENCY VIRUS [HIV] DISEASE                                    │
│  042          112.0             138            24    M        BC      236248  │
│                                                                               │
│  042          136.3             024            35    M        BC      123456  │
│                                                                               │
│  042          176.0             036            42    F        BC      213654  │
│                                                                               │
│  ACUTE POLIOMYELITIS                                                           │
│  045          250.00            236            80    M        MC      236954  │
│                                                                               │
│  045          401.9             235            60    F        MD      562159  │
│                                                                               │
│  045          496               138            34    F        WC      236268  │
│                                                                               │
└─────────────────────────────────────────────────────────────────────────────┘
```

FIGURE 8-7 Disease Index (Note: Codes in this index contain ICD-9-CM codes.)

```
┌─────────────────────────────────────────────────────────────────────────────┐
│                                                                               │
│                    Alfred State Medical Center                                │
│                                                                               │
│                          Procedure Index                                      │
│                                                                               │
│  Reporting Period      0301YYYY–0301YYYY            Date Prepared  03-02-YYYY  │
│                                                                               │
│                                                       Page   1 of 5           │
│                                                                               │
│                                                                               │
│  Primary Px   Other Procedures   Attending Dr   Age   Gender   Payer  Patient#│
│                                                                               │
│  CLOSED BIOPSY OF BRAIN                                                        │
│  01.13                           248            42    F        01      562359 │
│                                                                               │
│  CRANIOTOMY NOS                                                                │
│  01.24                           235            56    F        03      231587 │
│                                                                               │
│  01.24                           326            27    M        02      239854 │
│                                                                               │
│  01.24                           236            08    F        05      562198 │
│                                                                               │
│  01.24                           236            88    M        05      615789 │
│                                                                               │
│  DEBRIDEMENT OF SKULL NOS                                                      │
│  01.25                           326            43    M        03      653218 │
│                                                                               │
└─────────────────────────────────────────────────────────────────────────────┘
```

FIGURE 8-8 Procedure Index (Note: Codes in this index contain ICD-9-CM codes.)

```
┌─────────────────────────────────────────────────────────────────────────────┐
│                     Alfred State Medical Center                               │
│                                                                               │
│                          Physician Index                                      │
│                                                                               │
│  Reporting Period    0101YYYY—0101YYYY            Date Prepared  01-02-YYYY    │
│                                                                               │
│                                                        Page  1 of 5           │
│                                                                               │
│  Attending Dr   Patient #   Age   Gender   Payer   Admission  Discharge  LOS  Dx │
│                                                                               │
│  JAMES SMITH, M.D.                                                            │
│      024          123456     35     M       BC     1228YYYY   0101YYYY    4   042 │
│                                                                               │
│      024          213654     42     F       BC     1229YYYY   0101YYYY    3   042 │
│                                                                               │
│      024          236248     24     M       BC     1229YYYY   0101YYYY    3   042 │
│                                                                               │
│  JANE THOMSON, M.D.                                                           │
│      025          236268     34     F       WC     1229YYYY   0101YYYY    3   045 │
│                                                                               │
│      025          562159     60     F       MD     1230YYYY   0101YYYY    2   045 │
│                                                                               │
│      025          236954     80     M       MC     1231YYYY   0101YYYY    1   045 │
└─────────────────────────────────────────────────────────────────────────────┘
```

FIGURE 8-9 Physician Index (Note: Codes in this index contain ICD-9-CM codes.)

REGISTERS AND REGISTRIES

Registers and registries contain information about a disease (e.g., cancer) or event (e.g., birth) and are maintained by individual health care facilities, federal and state government agencies (e.g., DOH, local law enforcement), and private organizations (e.g., American Hospital Association). Case report forms (Figure 8-10) are submitted by health care facilities (e.g., health information department) and providers to report data to sponsoring agencies, facilities, and organizations.

Remember! A *register* is a collection of information, such as a hospital's admission/discharge register, while a *registry* is a structured system for collecting and maintaining information about a defined population so that analyses and reviews can be performed. Use a register to verify information (e.g., adoption, birth, death, divorce, marriage) and a registry to collect (and sort) data and perform statistical analysis and study (e.g., cure for cancer). An admission register, usually maintained by the admissions office, is organized by admission date; contents include patient's name, patient number, admitting physician, admission date, admission diagnosis, and room number. A discharge register, usually maintained by the health information department, is organized according to discharge date;

contents include the patient's name, patient number, attending physician, admission date, discharge date, disposition, and service (e.g., medical, surgical, obstetrics, and so on). The discharge register is used by the health information department to account for records of patients discharged on a particular date to ensure that all have been processed (assembled, analyzed, coded, and abstracted). A death register, usually maintained by the health information department, is organized according to date of death; contents include patient's name, patient number, attending physician, admission date, date of death, and service (e.g., medical, surgical, obstetrics).

Facilities and providers are required to submit information to federal and state agencies for inclusion in registries, and the information is used for disease study (e.g., etiology, prognosis, cures) and to generate statistical reports (e.g., statewide hospital mortality, or death, rates). In public health and medicine, there are many uses for the information collected in registries, such as:

1. Estimating the magnitude of a problem

Example Registries of blind persons help determine the extent of blindness within a population that is due to preventable or treatable conditions (e.g., cataracts).

Data Reporting Form

To be used in conjunction with the Birth Defects Registry Data Reporting Manual

NOTICE: Information on this form is confidential and exempt from the provisions of section 119.07(1). Reporting of notifiable congenital anomalies is mandatory pursuant to section 381.0031, Chapter 405, and Rules 64D-3.002 and 64D-3.027. The data will be used for birth defects prevention, research, and epidemiologic investigations with the goals of reducing morbidity and mortality. It is not a violation of the confidential relationship between practitioner and patient to report data on this form.

Return Completed Forms by Mail or FAX to:

Birth Defects Registry
P.O. Box 100
Anywhere, US 12345-1234
101-555-1333 (Fax)

Direct Questions to the:

Birth Defects Registry Hotline
101-555-1300

Licensed Physician and Hospital Information

a) First and Last Name of Licensed Physician: _____

b) License Number: __ __ - __ __ __ __ __ __ __

c) Specialty: _____

d) Physician's Phone No.: __ __ __ - __ __ __ - __ __ __ __

e) Date Form Completed: __ __ / __ __ / __ __ __ __

f) Street Address: _____

g) City: _____

h) Zip Code: __ __ __ __ __ - __ __ __ __

i) Birth Facility Number: _____

j) Treatment Hospital Number(s): _____

 (Facility numbers for items i) and j) can be found in the Data Reporting Manual.)

k) First and Last Name of Person Completing Form: _____

l) Phone No. of Person Completing Form: __ __ __ - __ __ __ - __ __ __ __

Mother Information

m) First, Maiden, and Last Name: _____

n) Date of Birth: __ __ / __ __ / __ __ __ __

o) SSN: __ __ __ - __ __ - __ __ __ __

For Birth Defects Registry Office Use Only:

Date Received: __ __ / __ __ / __ __ __ __

Date Keyed: __ __ / __ __ / __ __ __ __

Keyer: _____

LB FD Certificate Number: _____

DH 4118, 10/08 Page 2 of 2

Infant or Fetus Information

p) First and Last Name: _____

(Complete for live births and fetal deaths if known.)

q) SSN: __ __ __ - __ __ - __ __ __ __

r) Medical Record Number: _____

s) Date of Birth: __ __ / __ __ / __ __ __ __

t) Date of Death: __ __ / __ __ / __ __ __ __

(Complete only for a live birth.)

(Complete only if infant was live born and subsequently deceased.)

FIGURE 8-10 Birth Defects Registry Case Reporting Form

2. Determining the incidence of disease

Example Cancer registries calculate tumor-specific cancer rates—information that can be used for investigating suspected cancer clusters.

3. Examining trends of disease over time

Example Cancer registry data has documented rapid increases in the occurrence among women of lung cancer, the most frequent cause of cancer in this group.

4. Assessing service delivery and identifying groups at high risk

Example Immunization registries document the extent of vaccine coverage within a community and identify groups with suboptimal coverage who are at increased risk for disease outbreak and transmission.

5. Documenting types of patients served by a health provider

Example Hospitals often establish several registries to collect data about their patient population (e.g., cancer registry, trauma registry, and so on).

6. Conducting research

Example Cancer registries track patient survival analysis and rates.

7. Serving as a source of potential donors

Example The National Bone Marrow Registry maintains information on individuals willing to serve as bone marrow donors if a suitable recipient is identified.

8. Serving as a source of potential participants in clinical trials

Example Commercial services register persons with certain medical conditions who wish to be considered for enrollment in clinical trials.

Characteristics of Registers and Registries

Registers and registries represent a secondary source of patient information, which provides facilities, providers, and public health officials with information needed to assess and monitor the health of a given population.

Note: State and federal legislation mandates the reporting of data to public health surveillance systems.

This data is called reportable diseases (e.g., communicable diseases) and reportable events (e.g., gunshot wounds).

The characteristics that distinguish registries from other sources of data include:

- Focus on a particular disease (e.g., hemophilia), group of similar diseases (e.g., cancer), or specific exposure (e.g., toxin such as PCB found at hazardous waste sites)
- Collection of data on individuals from multiple sources (e.g., physician records, hospital summaries, pathology reports, vital statistics)
- Active ascertaining of cases by reviewing likely sources for referrals (e.g., examining hospital discharge records for evidence of birth defects)
- Follow-up investigation and data collection on persons enrolled in the registry (determining the status of cancer registrants by examining vital records)
- High cost (actively seeking and linking data from multiple sources over time is expensive)

Vital Statistics

Vital statistics are compiled for events, which include births, deaths, fetal deaths, marriages, and divorces. The National Center for Health Statistics (NCHS) is the federal agency responsible for maintaining official vital statistics, while registration of vital events (e.g., births) is a state function. To facilitate uniform registration of events, the NCHS prepares standard certificates, which can be modified by individual states. When a birth or death occurs, a certificate is filed in the local (e.g., county) vital statistics office, which maintains a record and sends the original certificate to the state office of vital statistics. The state forwards vital statistic information to the NCHS, which publishes statistical reports (e.g., "Vital Statistics of the United States").

Note: Birth certificates are often completed and submitted by hospital health information departments, and death certificates (including fetal death certificates) are usually initiated by hospital nursing staff and/or the patient's attending physician and then completed and submitted by funeral homes.

Operation of Registers and Registries

Registers and registries (Table 8-1) are operated by a variety of entities, including:

- Federal government agencies (e.g., Center for Disease Control's Agency for Toxic Substances and Disease Registry maintains the National Exposure Registry)

TABLE 8-1 Partial List of Registers and Registries Maintained in the United States

Register/Registry	Sponsor	Description
Adoption Information Registry	State agencies	• Helps adoptees obtain available non-identifying information about birth parents • Enables the reunion of registered adoptees with birth parents and biological siblings • Provides a place for birth parents to file medical information updates that may be shared with registered adoptees
Alzheimer Registry	State agencies	• Collects data to evaluate prevalence of Alzheimer's disease and related disorders • Provides non-identifying information and data for policy planning purposes and to support research
Birth Defects Registry	State agencies	• Maintains statewide surveillance for collecting information on birth defect incidence • Monitors annual trends in birth defect occurrence and mortality • Conducts research studies to identify genetic and environmental risk factors for birth defects • Promotes educational activities for the prevention of birth defects
Birth Defects Registry, Congenital Anomaly Register (CAR), or Congenital Malformations Registry (CMR)	Health care facilities and state agencies	• Repository for case reports on children diagnosed before age 2 who have suspected or confirmed congenital anomalies, which are structural, functional, or biochemical abnormalities determined genetically or induced during gestation and not due to birthing events • Facilities and state agencies identify ICD codes to use for case reporting *Note:* Minor anomalies may be excluded from reporting (e.g., inguinal hernias, skin tags)
Cancer Registry	Health care facilities, groups of health care facilities (that form central registries), and state and federal agencies	• Collects information about all cancers diagnosed (except basal and squamous cell carcinoma of the skin and carcinoma in situ of the cervix, unless required by the registry) • Develops strategies and policies for cancer prevention, treatment, and control • Allows researchers to analyze geographic, ethnic, occupational, and other differences to identify cancer risk factors
Cardiac Registry	Health care facilities	• Captures cardiac surgery information as a research tool for assessing cardiac patient outcomes and pinpointing how patient care can improve
Immunization Registries	Federal and state agencies, such as the National Committee on Health and Vital Statistics (NCHVS), the statutory public advisory body to the Secretary of HHS	• Computerized systems that consolidate vaccination histories as provided by individual health care providers

(Continues)

TABLE 8-1 Partial List of Registers and Registries Maintained in the United States (*Continued*)

Register/Registry	Sponsor	Description
Implant Registries (or Medical Devices Registries)	Various organizations, depending on type of implant (e.g., National Breast Implant Registry, National Joint Registry, and so on)	• Tracks successful implants and assesses failures through retrieval analysis • Improves patient care through improvement of implants • Monitors device performance in vivo (inside the body) to permit early corrective therapy *Note:* Medical implant devices have a minimum life span of three months, penetrate and have a physiologic interaction with living tissue, and can be retrieved.
Inpatient Discharge Database	State and federal agencies	• Contains hospital inpatient discharge data • Collected to study patterns and trends in the availability, use, and charges for inpatient services • Consists of core data elements, as defined by state and federal agencies (e.g., Uniform Hospital Discharge Data Set, UHDDS)
Insulin-Dependent Diabetes Mellitus Registries	National Institutes of Health (NIH)	• Determine incidence of IDDM in defined populations • Identifies persons for subsequent enrollment in case-control studies and other research projects
Metropolitan Atlanta Congenital Defects Program	Centers for Disease Control and Prevention (CDC)	• Monitors occurrence of serious malformations in Atlanta metropolitan area • Tracks changes in trends and unusual patterns that may suggest avoidable risk factors • Maintains a case registry for epidemiologic and genetic studies
National Exposure Registry	CDC Agency for Toxic Substances and Disease Registries (ATSDR)	• Identifies, enrolls, and monitors persons who may have been exposed to a hazardous environmental substance
National Registry of Cardiopulmonary Resuscitation (NRCPR)	Sponsored by American Hospital Association and managed by Digital Innovation, Inc.	• Collects and analyzes in-hospital resuscitation data • Allows health care facilities to evaluate equipment, resources, and training, and to improve practices
National Registry of Myocardial Infarction (NRMI)		• Examines trends in treatment, length of hospital stay, mortality, and variations among specific patient populations
Organ (or Tissue) Donor Registry	Organizations (e.g., The Living Bank), State agencies	• Computerized database that documents an individual's plan to be an organ donor *Note:* Donors should inform family and friends of organ donor plans because enrollment cards and signing the reverse of driver's licenses are not legallybinding documents.
Rare Disease Registries (e.g., Li-Fraumeni Syndrome International Registry, Bloom's Syndrome Registry)	National Organization for Rare Disorders	• Collect clinical and genetic data • Provide referrals to genetic counseling and other services • Conduct ongoing research

(Continues)

TABLE 8-1 Partial List of Registers and Registries Maintained in the United States (*Continued*)

Register/Registry	Sponsor	Description
Surveillance, Epidemiology, and End Results (SEER) Program	National Cancer Institute (NCI)	• Collects cancer data on a routine basis from designated population-based cancer registries in nine areas of the United States
National Trauma Data Bank	American College of Surgeons (ACoS)	• Improves quality of patient care • Provides established information system for evaluation of injury care and preparedness • Develops injury scoring and outcome measures • Provides data for clinical benchmarking, process improvement, and patient safety
United States Eye Injury Registry (USEIR)	Helen Keller Eye Research Foundation	• Provides prospective, population-based, epidemiologic data to improve the prevention and control of eye injuries
Vital Records	Health care facilities, and county and state agencies	• Records births, deaths, fetal deaths, induced abortions, teen pregnancies, and teen suicides • Files certificates for births, deaths, divorces, and marriages • Collects mortality (death), fetal death (e.g., weight of 350 grams or more or, if weight is unknown, of 20 completed weeks gestation or more), and natality (birth) data; prepares reports • Distributes certificates to eligible persons (e.g., in NYS, birth certificates are distributed to person named on birth certificate; parent of person named on birth certificate—requesting parent's name must be on birth certificate; spouse, child, or other persons by order of a New York State Court) *Note:* No birth or death certificate is issued for induced abortions. Fetal death definition varies state to state.

- Individual and groups of hospitals (e.g., registry of persons diagnosed with primary pulmonary hypertension, assembled by researchers to understand the risk factors and causes of this rare medical condition)
- Nonprofit organizations (e.g., United States Eye Injury Registry)
- Private groups (e.g., transplant registries, registries that examine use of drugs during pregnancy)
- State government agencies (e.g., departments of health maintain registries of persons diagnosed with sexually transmitted diseases such as gonorrhea)
- Universities (e.g., Surveillance, Epidemiology, and End Results (SEER), cancer registries, supported by funds from the federal government)

Note: Reportable diseases and events are discussed in Chapter 9.

EXERCISE 8–2 Registers

Short Answer: Briefly respond to the following.

1. Identify a government agency that requires the reporting of information about diseases or events.
   _____

2. What is the name of the form used to submit reportable data to sponsoring agencies? _____

3. What is the difference between a register and a registry? _____

4. What are the uses for information collected in registries? _____

5. Do registers and registries represent a primary or secondary source of patient information? Explain.
   _____

6. Provide two examples of vital statistics. _____

7. Name the federal agency responsible for maintaining official vital statistics. _____

8. Identify three registers/registries, and name the sponsor and a brief description of each. _____

CASE ABSTRACTING

Case abstracting is an automated or manual process performed by health information department staff (e.g., abstractor) to collect patient information to determine prospective payment system (PPS) status, generate indexes (e.g., disease index), and report data to quality improvement organizations and state and federal agencies. Automated case abstracting systems allow health care facilities to:

- Calculate PPS reimbursement (e.g., diagnostic-related groups, DRGs)
- Create and maintain patient abstracts (Figure 8-11) within the software system
- Generate case abstract statistics (e.g., error reports)
- Generate reports and statistics for case mix analysis (study of types of patients treated by the facility)
- Generate special reports according to user-defined criteria

- Review patient charges concurrently (while patient is being treated)
- Submit mandatory reporting data to appropriate state and federal agencies

Example MEDITECH software offers a registration, medical records, and billing/accounts receivable application that allows for data capture and reporting of patient and financial data. The application also offers coding of inpatient and outpatient cases using ICD-9, ICD-10-CM, CPT, and HCPCS Level II (national) codes and modifiers, connectivity to other encoding products via HL7 compliant interface, customer-defined edit checks to guarantee all necessary fields of information are completed before finalizing an abstract, the ability to combine abstracting information for all patient classes in one abstracting (ABS) database, queries that can be utilized to display information from other applications, standard fields that can accept APG and APC information via encoding interfaces, and CPT modifiers that can be entered or captured through an encoding interface.

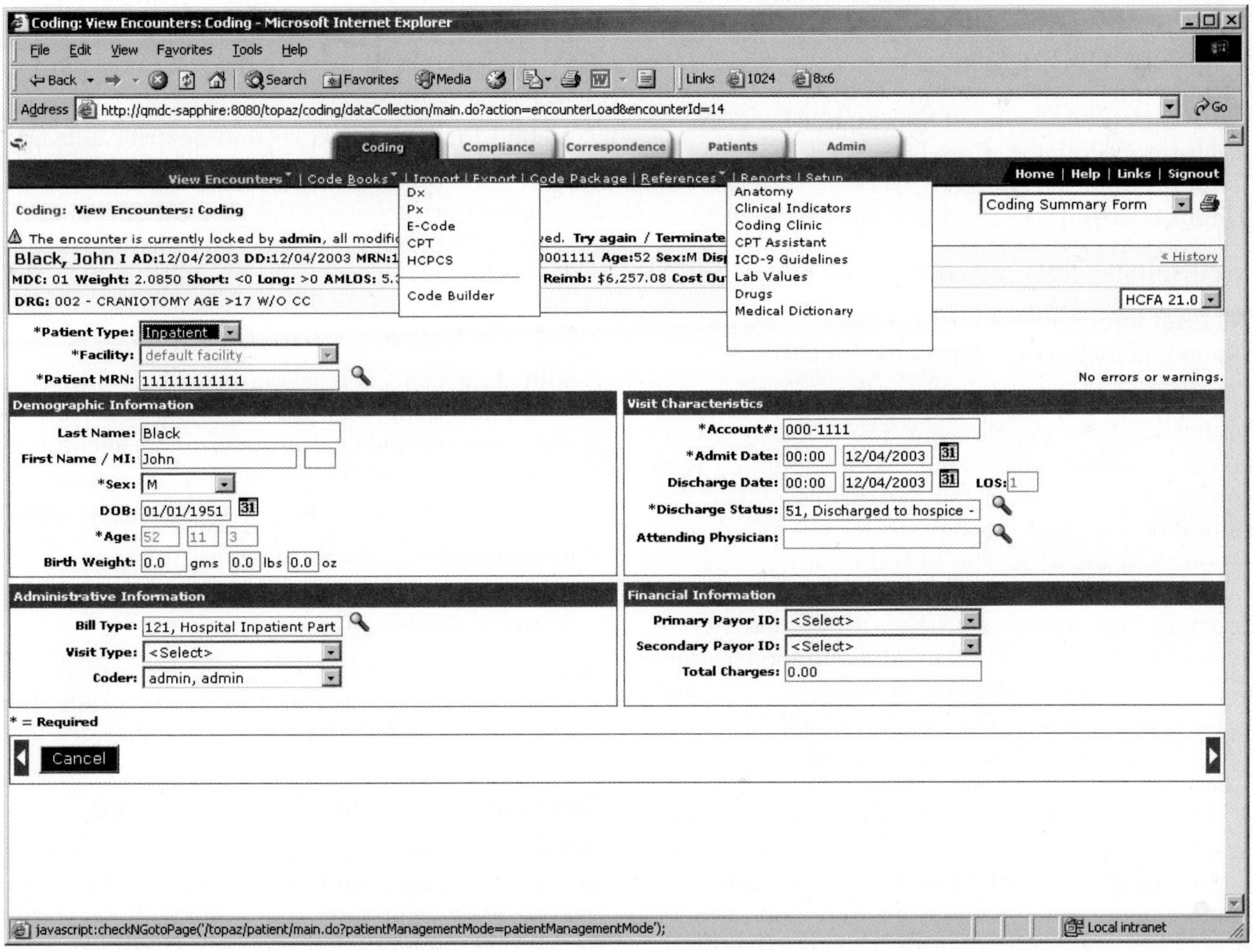

FIGURE 8-11 Automated Case Abstracting Data Entry Screen (Permission to reprint granted by QuadraMed.)

Manual case abstracting systems require health information department staff to enter patient data on a case abstract form (Figure 8-12A is for use with ICD-9-CM codes. Figure 8-12B is for use with ICD-10-CM codes.) and submit batched (predetermined groups) forms to a vendor for data entry and report generation. While hospital health information departments no longer routinely manually abstract patient cases, smaller facilities (e.g., home health agencies) may elect to implement a manual case abstracting system.

Before the case abstracting process can begin, a standard method for collecting and reporting individual data elements must be established (so data can be easily compared). This is called a data set. In addition, the organization should develop a data dictionary, which is a collection of data element definitions (Table 8-2). The data set (Table 8-3) used for collection and reporting purposes depends on patient type and includes the following:

- Data Elements for Emergency Department Systems (DEEDS)
- Essential Medical Data Set (EMDS)
- Health Plan Employer Data and Information Set (HEDIS®)
- Minimum Data Set (MDS)
- National Cancer Data Base (NCDB)
- Outcome and Assessment Information Set (OASIS)
- Uniform Ambulatory Care Data Set (UACDS)
- Uniform Clinical Data Set (UCDS)
- Uniform Hospital Discharge Data Set (UHDDS)

Two other data sets are associated with health care:

- Medical Information Bureau (MIB)
- National Practitioner Data Bank (NPDB)

The MIB is a clearinghouse of medical and avocation information about people who apply for insurance. When an insurance underwriter has an applicant with a condition considered significant to his or her risk classification (e.g., high blood pressure), this information is reported to the MIB. The MIB does *not* receive the applicant's entire medical record; the MIB record contains information that serves as an alert for an underwriter to review the background of an applicant more closely. MIB records include medical conditions (e.g., height and weight, blood pressure, ECG readings, and laboratory test results if considered significant to health or longevity) and nonmedical information that might affect insurability (e.g., adverse driving record, participation in hazardous sports, or aviation activity). MIB, Inc., is the not-for-profit sponsoring association of United States and Canadian life insurance companies whose goal is to protect insurers, policyholders, and applicants from insurance fraud.

The NPDB was legislated by the Health Care Quality and Improvement Act of 1986 due to an increasing occurrence of medical malpractice litigation and the need to improve the quality of medical care. The NPDB contains information about practitioners who engage in unprofessional behavior, and its purpose is to restrict the ability of incompetent physicians, dentists, and other health care practitioners to move to another state without disclosure or discovery of previous medical malpractice payment and adverse action (e.g., exclusion from Medicare and Medicaid participation) history. When a practitioner applies for health care privileges, the medical staff coordinator (and/or credentials committee) can contact the NPDB to inquire about the practitioner's licensure, medical malpractice payment history, professional society memberships, and record of clinical privileges.

EXERCISE 8–3 Case Abstracting

Short Answer: Briefly respond to the following.

1. Define case abstracting. _____
2. Discuss the importance of case abstracting as related to case mix analysis. _____
3. List the advantages and disadvantages of automated and manual abstracting systems. _____
4. What is the significance of the term "batched" case abstracts? _____
5. Define "data set," and list and describe at least three data sets. _____
6. What is the purpose of the Medical Information Bureau (MIB) and the National Practitioner Data Bank (NPDB)? _____

HEALTH DATA COLLECTION

Health data collection is performed by health care facilities for administrative planning and to report statistics to state and federal government agencies (and other organizations). This section of the chapter introduces the following health data collection concepts:

- Descriptive health care statistics
- Data quality
- Hospital-based statistics

Note: For in-depth study of health care statistics, consider purchasing Cengage Learning's *Basic Allied Health Statistics & Analysis,* 3rd edition, by Gerda Koch.

Descriptive Health Care Statistics

Health information managers are responsible for collecting, reporting, and retrieving *descriptive health care statistics,* which are used internally by facilities to describe the types and numbers of patients treated (patient population). Descriptive statistics summarize a set of data using charts, graphs, and tables.

ALFRED STATE MEDICAL CENTER ACUTE CARE (INPATIENT) CASE ABSTRACT

01 Hospital Number 9 9 9

02 Patient Date of Birth Month Day Year (YYYY)

03 Patient Gender
1 Male
2 Female
3 Other
4 Unknown

04A Race
1 American Indian/Eskimo/Aleut
2 Asian or Pacific Islander
3 Black
4 White
5 Other
6 Unknown

04B Ethnicity
1 Spanish origin/Hispanic
2 Non-Spanish origin/Non-Hispanic
3 Unknown

05A Living Arrangement
1 Alone
2 With spouse
3 With children
4 With parent or guardian
5 With relative other than spouse
6 With nonrelatives
7 Unknown

05B Marital Status
1 Married
2 Single
3 Divorced
4 Separated
5 Unknown

06 Patient Number

07 Admission Date and Hour Month Day Year (YYYY)
Military Time

08 Type of Admission
1 Scheduled
2 Unscheduled

09 Discharge Date and Time Month Day Year (YYYY)
Military Time

10 Attending Physician Number

11 Operating Physician Number

12 Principal Diagnosis Code ICD Code

16 Birth Weight of Neonate Kilograms

Date Abstract Completed Month Day Year (YYYY)

13 Other Diagnosis Code(s)

14 Qualifiers for Other Diagnoses
1 Onset preceded hospital admission
2 Onset followed hospital admission
3 Uncertain whether onset preceded or followed hospital admission

ICD Code (×7)

17 Procedures, Dates, and Operating Physician UPIN
Month Day Year (YYYY) UPIN (×7 rows)

15 External Cause of Injury Codes
ICD E-code (×5)

18 Disposition
1 Discharged to home
2 Discharged to acute care hospital
3 Discharged to nursing facility
4 Discharged home to be under the care of a home health service (including hospice)
5 Discharged to other health care facility
6 Left against medical advice (AMA)
7 Alive, other
8 Died

19 Patient's Expected Payment Source
1 Blue Cross/Blue Shield
2 Other commercial insurance
3 Other liability insurance
4 Medicare
5 Medicaid
6 Workers' Compensation
7 Self-insured employer plan
8 Health maintenance organization (HMO)
9 TRICARE
10 CHAMPVA
11 Other government payer
12 Self-pay
13 No charge (e.g., charity, special research, teaching)
14 Other

20 Total Charges $

FIGURE 8-12A Manual Case Abstracting Form for Use with ICD-9-CM Codes (Based on California Office of Statewide Health Planning and Development.)

ALFRED STATE MEDICAL CENTER ACUTE CARE (INPATIENT) CASE ABSTRACT

01 Hospital Number

02 Patient Date of Birth

Month   Day   Year (YYYY)

03 Patient Gender

1 Male
2 Female
3 Other
4 Unknown

04A Race

1 American Indian/Eskimo/Aleut
2 Asian or Pacific Islander
3 Black
4 White
5 Other
6 Unknown

04B Ethnicity

1 Spanish origin/Hispanic
2 Non-Spanish origin/Non-Hispanic
3 Unknown

05A Living Arrangement

1 Alone
2 With spouse
3 With children
4 With parent or guardian
5 With relative other than spouse
6 With nonrelatives
7 Unknown

05B Marital Status

1 Married
2 Single
3 Divorced
4 Separated
5 Unknown

06 Patient Number

07 Admission Date and Hour

Month   Day   Year (YYYY)

Military Time

08 Type of Admission

1 Scheduled
2 Unscheduled

09 Discharge Date and Time

Month   Day   Year (YYYY)

Military Time

10 Attending Physician Number

11 Operating Physician Number

12 Principal Diagnosis Code

ICD Code

16 Birth Weight of Neonate

Kilograms

Date Abstract Completed

Month   Day   Year (YYYY)

13 Other Diagnosis Code(s)

14 Qualifiers for Other Diagnoses

1 Onset preceded hospital admission
2 Onset followed hospital admission
3 Uncertain whether onset preceded or followed hospital admission

ICD Code

ICD Code

ICD Code

ICD Code

ICD Code

ICD Code

17 Procedures, Dates, and Operating Physician UPIN

Month   Day   Year (YYYY)   UPIN

Month   Day   Year (YYYY)   UPIN

Month   Day   Year (YYYY)   UPIN

Month   Day   Year (YYYY)   UPIN

Month   Day   Year (YYYY)   UPIN

Month   Day   Year (YYYY)   UPIN

Month   Day   Year (YYYY)   UPIN

15 External Cause of Injury Codes

18 Disposition

1 Discharged to home
2 Discharged to acute care hospital
3 Discharged to nursing facility
4 Discharged home to be under the care of a home health service (including hospice)
5 Discharged to other health care facility
6 Left against medical advice (AMA)
7 Alive, other
8 Died

19 Patient's Expected Payment Source

1 Blue Cross/Blue Shield
2 Other commercial insurance
3 Other liability insurance
4 Medicare
5 Medicaid
6 Workers' Compensation
7 Self-insured employer plan
8 Health maintenance organization (HMO)

9 TRICARE
10 CHAMPVA
11 Other government payer
12 Self-pay
13 No charge (e.g., charity, special research, teaching)
14 Other

20 Total Charges

$

FIGURE 8-12B Manual Case Abstracting Form for Use with ICD-10-CM Codes (Based on California Office of Statewide Health Planning and Development.)

TABLE 8-2 Portion of Data Dictionary Containing Elements and Definitions

Data Element	Definition
Account #	Nine-digit number assigned upon patient admission. Patient receives a new account number upon each admission (or visit) to the facility.
Patient Record #	Medical record number assigned to the patient upon his or her first admission (or visit) to the facility. The patient retains the same patient record number for all subsequent admissions (or visits).
Zip Code	Five-digit number that identifies a specific geographic delivery area. The patient's home address zip code is collected.
Diagnosis Code #	*International Classification of Diseases,* 9th Revision, Clinical Modification (ICD-9-CM) codes for patient's conditions, diagnoses, and problems are collected.
Procedure Code #	Current Procedural Terminology (CPT) and Healthcare Common Procedure Coding System (HCPCS) Level II codes for patient procedures and services are collected.

TABLE 8-3 Data Sets

Data Set	Health Care Setting	Purpose
Data Elements for Emergency Department Systems (DEEDS)	Providers responsible for maintaining record systems in 24-hour, hospital-based emergency departments (EDs) throughout the United States (participation is voluntary)	• Develops uniform data-element specifications for describing single emergency department patient encounters • Maintained by CDC
Essential Medical Data Set (EMDS)	Health care facilities that provide emergency services (participation is voluntary)	• Facilitates exchange of critical past medical history information among health care providers • Improves management of critical health care information in ED settings by identifying, defining, and standardizing data elements • Complements DEEDS • Formerly known as the Essential Emergency Data Set (EEDS) • Maintained by the National Information Infrastructure Health Information Network Program (NII-HIN), sponsored by the Defense Advanced Research Projects Agency of the United States government
Health Plan Employer Data and Information Set (HEDIS®)	Managed care organizations (MCOs) (participation is voluntary)	• Standardized performance measures used to compare performance of managed health care plans • Maintained by National Committee for Quality Assurance (NCQA)
Minimum Data Set (MDS)	Long-term care facilities (LTCFs) (participation is mandatory for LTCFs that participate in Medicare and Medicaid)	• Core set of screening elements for comprehensive assessment of LTCF residents; used to create resident assessment protocols (RAPs) • Resident Assessment and Validation and Entry (RAVEN) data-entry system is used • Standardizes communication about resident problems and conditions • Facilitates quality monitoring and improvement • Maintained by CMS

(Continues)

TABLE 8-3 Data Sets (*Continued*)

Data Set	Health Care Setting	Purpose
National Cancer Data Base (NCDB)	Acute care facility (hospital) cancer registries (participation is required for cancer registries accredited by the American College of Surgeons' Commission on Cancer, ACoS COC)	• Nationwide oncology (study of cancer) outcomes database • Assesses patterns of care and outcomes relative to national norms • Maintained by ACoS
Outcome and Assessment Information Set (OASIS)	Home health agencies (HHAs) (participation is mandatory for HHAs that participate in Medicare and Medicaid)	• Core set of comprehensive assessment for adult home care patients • Home Assessment and Validation and Entry (HAVEN) data-entry software is used • Measures patient outcomes for outcome-based quality improvement (OBQI) • Patient assessment and care planning, and internal HHA performance improvement • Agency-level case mix reports that contain aggregate statistics on various patient characteristics such as demographic, health, or functional status at start of care • Maintained by CMS
The Joint Commission ORYX® Initiative	The Joint Commission-accredited health care facilities (participation is required of facilities accredited by)	• Program developed by The Joint Commission that integrates outcomes and other performance measurement data into the accreditation process • Requires accredited facilities to track and submit clinical performance measures as part of accreditation process • Two measurement sets include core performance measures (specific indicators related to disease or process of care; e.g., acute myocardial infarction, or AMI) and non-core measures (general indicators; e.g., mortality rate for AMI patients) • Maintained by The Joint Commission
Uniform Ambulatory Care Data Set (UACDS)	Ambulatory care facilities (ACFs) (participation is mandatory for ACFs that participate in Medicare and Medicaid)	• Standard data set for ambulatory health records • Goal is to improve data comparison for ambulatory and outpatient care settings • Maintained by CMS
Uniform Clinical Data Set (UCDS)	Quality Improvement Organizations (QIOs) (participation is mandatory for hospitals that participate in Medicare and Medicaid)	• Initiative that involves collection of approximately 1,800 data elements that describe patient demographic characteristics, clinical history, clinical findings, and therapeutic intervention • Data is obtained from medical records of Medicare beneficiaries • Maintained by CMS
Uniform Hospital Discharge Data Set (UHDDS)	Acute care facilities (hospitals) (participation is mandatory for hospitals that participate in Medicare and Medicaid)	• Sponsored by National Center for Health Statistics (NCHS) • Standard for collecting data for Medicare and Medicaid programs • Maintained by CMS

Health care data is reported to state and federal agencies, and those agencies quantify the data (e.g., health care illnesses, activities, births, and deaths for specific periods of time) and release summary descriptive statistics. Regardless of the type of health care statistics collected, their primary purpose is to provide factual numerical information that can be used for decision making. Health care data is classified into the following categories:

- **Aggregate data** is based on performance, utilization, and resource management.
- **Comparative data** is used for health services outcomes measurement and research.
- **Patient-centric data** is directly related to patients.
- **Transformed-based data** is used for clinical and management decisions, support, and planning.

Example Sunny Valley Medical Center's health information department collects statistics (Table 8-4) to prepare an annual repqort for the board of directors. This report is used to make decisions that impact hospital operations.

Calculating health care statistics is a responsibility of the health information department, and while most statistics are collected using automated computer systems, it is important to understand how the statistics are calculated so accuracy can be verified. It is common for facilities to generate monthly and annual reports that describe the number of patients treated and the types of services delivered. In addition to reporting the number of patients treated, facilities will also calculate rates and percentages of deaths, autopsies, infections, and so on.

Example Sunny Valley Medical Center collects statistics for the birthing unit. The information below is interpreted

as 130 total newborns, of whom three died. Of the 130 total newborns, 25 were premature newborns. The three newborn deaths were premature newborns.

Type of Patient	No. of Patients	No. of Deaths
Newborn	130	3
Premature newborn	25	3

The health information department calculates the *newborn death rate* as

$$\frac{\text{Number of newborn deaths}}{\text{Number of newborn patients}} \times 100$$

or,

$$\frac{3}{130} \times 100 = 2.3\% \text{ newborn death rate}$$

The health information department calculates the *premature newborn death rate* as

$$\frac{\text{Number of premature newborn deaths}}{\text{Number of premature newborn patients}} \times 100$$

or,

$$\frac{3}{25} \times 100 = 12\%$$

Sunny Valley Medical Center has a newborn death rate of just 2.3 percent, but the premature newborn death rate is 12 percent. (*Note:* The non-premature newborn death rate is 0 percent.)

TABLE 8-4 Sunny Valley Medical Center Annual Report Statistics

Hospital Statistics	YTD Total	Previous Year
Total Patient Discharges	55,322	45,211
Newborns	3,452	3,432
Children (< age 18)	6,236	6,198
Adults	45,634	35,581
Average Length of Stay	5.6	6.2
Newborns	1.2	1.1
Children (< age 18)	7.8	8.1
Adults	6.5	6.8
Daily Census of Hospital Patients (154 beds)	152	151
Newborns (10 bassinets)	8.9	8.7
Children (< age 18) (22 beds)	21.4	21.8
Adults (122 beds)	119	116
Inpatient Surgical Procedures Performed	3,695	3,457
Newborns	54	67
Children (< age 18)	104	96
Adults	3,537	3,294
Outpatient Surgical Procedures Performed	3,984	3,024
Newborns	47	35
Children (< age 18)	957	844
Adults	2,980	2,145

Health information managers review statistics to ensure that calculations are accurate and interpret (or explain) statistical rates. Health care professionals analyze and use statistics in the treatment and prevention of diseases (e.g., cancer data), and analysis of statistics is enhanced when statistics are presented in a visual format. Various presentation techniques and tools (e.g., bar graphs, pie charts, line diagrams, and so on) help give meaning to statistics.

Example Data can be displayed using a variety of visual presentation tools.

- Bar graph displays data along an X-axis and a Y-axis.
- Pie chart displays component parts of data as it relates to the whole.
- Line diagram (or run chart) displays data over a period of time.

Bar Graph

The bar graph in Figure 8-13 has three sets of bars: motor vehicle traffic deaths, firearm suicides, and firearm homicides. Each set of bars includes five bars that show the percent distribution of injury deaths by external cause and body region of injury.

Pie Chart

The pie chart in Figure 8-13 shows the percent distribution of injury deaths by intent of injury.

Line Diagram

The line diagram (or line chart) in Figure 8-13 contains four lines that display age-adjusted death rates by intent (all injury, unintentional injury, suicide, and homicide).

Data Quality

Health care statistics are useful only if developed from quality data. The phrase "garbage in, garbage out" that is associated with computer data also applies to health care information. If inaccurate data is entered into a computer system, then incorrect information will be retrieved. This is also true of manual data systems. Inaccurate and incorrect data can result in serious and harmful errors being made, especially if the error involves patient health information. General data quality characteristics include:

- Data integrity. Data has integrity if it is accurate, complete, consistent, up-to-date, and the same no matter where the data is recorded.
- Data reliability. Data is reliable if it is consistent throughout all systems in which it is stored, processed, and/or retrieved.
- Data validity. Data is valid if it conforms to an expected range of values.

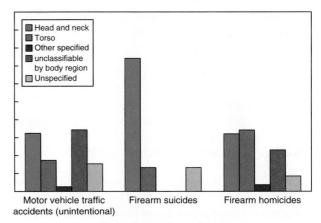

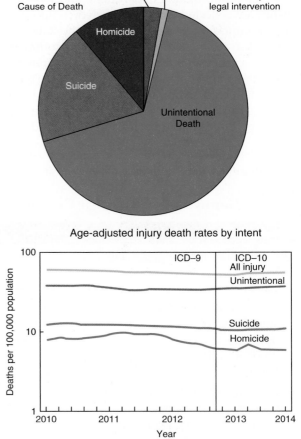

FIGURE 8-13 Sample Visual Statistics

Example Nancy Nurse is responsible for monitoring and recording patients' weight gain or loss on a unit that treats patients with eating disorders. She weighs each patient, records the information on a small notepad, and enters the information into each patient's record. When she enters the information in the patient records, she mistakenly reverses the weights for patient A and patient B (who both reside in room 404). Patient A's weight is recorded as 105, and patient B's weight as 95. Because the patients' physicians use weight data to prescribe treatment, this incorrect information will adversely impact development of the patients' treatment plans, and patients may receive incorrect treatment.

Health care data must be monitored to ensure that it is of the highest quality possible. AHIMA developed a data quality management model that outlines the characteristics of data quality achieved by managing data application, collection, warehousing, and analysis. These four areas of data quality management are defined by AHIMA as follows:

- Data application—purpose for which the data are collected
- Data collection—processes by which data elements are accumulated
- Data warehousing—processes and systems used to archive data and data journals
- Data analysis—process of translating data into information utilized for an application

Continuous quality improvement (CQI) plays a role in data quality for the organization and should include data application, collection, warehousing, and analysis. According to N. O. Graham's *Quality in Health Care* (1995), continuous quality improvement (CQI) is "an approach to quality management that builds upon traditional quality assurance methods by emphasizing the organization and systems; focuses on 'process' rather than the individual; recognizes both internal and external 'customers'; and promotes the need for objective data to analyze and improve processes." The characteristics of ensuring data quality include:

- Data accessibility—ease with which data can be obtained
- Data accuracy—error free and correct
- Data comprehensiveness—presence of all required data elements in the patient record
- Data consistency—reliability of data regardless of the way in which data are stored, displayed, or processed
- Data definition (defined meanings and values of all elements so all present and future users understand the data) (*Note:* Facilities create a data dictionary to facilitate this process.)
- Data granularity (definition of each attribute and value of data at the correct level of detail)
- Data precision (accurate data collection by defining expected data values)
- Data relevancy—(compilation of data that is valuable for the performance of a process or activity)
- Data timeliness (or data currency)—(collection of up-to-date data and availability to the user within a reasonable amount of time)

Data mining uses software to search for patterns and trends and to produce data content relationships. According to *Healthcare Informatics*, data mining allows an organization "to acquire, store, analyze and compare data across many parts of the enterprise, by many individuals." Organizations traditionally retain relational databases, which have a limited, two-dimensional structure that does not allow for complete trend analysis. Online analytical processing (OLAP) servers store data in multiple dimensions and facilitate trend analysis and forecasting, allowing health care organizations to make informed, proactive decisions.

Hospital-Based Statistics

All hospitals compile statistics regarding admission, discharge, and length of stay of patients, which are used to analyze and monitor operations. Hospital statistics provide a benchmark upon which decisions are made to operate and manage the facility. Health information professionals play a vital role in collecting and verifying the statistics generated by facilities. Even though most hospitals have automated the statistical process, HIM professionals are responsible for overseeing the process.

Note: A *brief* overview of hospital-based statistics is presented in this chapter. Comprehensive coverage of health care statistics can be found in Cengage Learning's *Basic Allied Health Statistics & Analysis*, by Gerda Koch, 4th edition.

Admission Data

Admission data are collected by facilities on a daily basis and commonly include:

- Daily census count—number of inpatients present at census taking (*Note:* Census-taking time is usually midnight.)
- Daily inpatient census—official count of inpatients present at midnight, which is calculated each day
- Average daily census—average number of inpatients treated during a given time period such as weekly, monthly, or annually (*Note:* An average is also known as an arithmetic mean.)

Example The average daily census is used by hospital administration to plan for needed hospital services. The formula is

$$\frac{\text{Total number of inpatients for a given period}}{\text{Total number of days in the period}}$$

or,

$$\frac{634}{30} = 21.13$$

The hospital admitted 634 patients during June. There are 30 days in June. After calculating the average daily census, it is determined that an average 21 patients were treated in the facility each day during the month of June.

Note: To easily determine the number of days in a month, remember the rhyme, *Thirty days has September, April, June, and November. All the rest have thirty-one, except for February alone, and it has twenty-eight days time, but in leap years February has twenty-nine.* Or, use the knuckles of your closed fist. Each knuckle month (e.g., January, March) has 31 days. Months falling between knuckles (e.g., September, November have 30 days). February still has 28 days, or 29 if it is a leap year.

Length of Stay Data

Facilities calculate **length of stay (LOS)** data, which represents the number of calendar days that a patient was an inpatient. The **total length of stay** for all discharged patients is calculated for a given time period. Facilities also calculate the **average length of stay** by dividing the total LOS by the number of patients discharged.

Example Sunny Valley Medical Center calculates the total LOS for the following six patients as follows:

Patient	LOS
James, H	7
Jones, B	5
Smith, M	9
Tyler, W	2
West, A	5
White, T	3
Total LOS	31

Example Sunny Valley Medical Center calculates the average length of stay for June as:

$$\frac{\text{Total length of stay for June}}{\text{Total number of discharges, including deaths for June}}$$

or,

$$\frac{412}{98} = 4.2 \text{ days}$$

In June, the hospital had a total of 412 days length of stay, and there were 98 discharges (including deaths). This means that each inpatient stay averaged 4.2 days. (If fewer patients had been discharged, the LOS would have increased. If more patients had been discharged, the LOS would have decreased.)

Discharge Data

Health care facilities calculate **discharge data statistics** (e.g., death rate, infection rate, and so on) to measure health status and outcomes, health care utilization, and access to health care. (Discharge data statistics are often reported to federal and state agencies.) To easily remember how to calculate discharge rates, *divide the number of times something happened by the number of times something **could** have happened.*

Example The hospital-acquired infection (or nosocomial infection) rate for June is calculated as

$$\frac{\text{Number of nosocomial infections for June}}{\text{Number of hospital discharges for June}} \times 100$$

or,

$$\frac{5}{98} = 0.0510 \times 100 = 5.1\%$$

In June, five patients out of 98 discharges acquired hospital-based (or nosocomial) infections. This means that the hospital has a 5.1 percent hospital-acquired infection rate for the month of June.

Hospitals use discharge data for planning and report this information to agencies outside of the facility (e.g., state health departments, federal public health agencies).

Note: The National Center for Health Statistics, a department in the Centers for Disease Control and Prevention, is responsible for maintaining health statistics at the federal level.

EXERCISE 8–4 Health Data Collection

Short Answer: Briefly respond to the following.

_____ 1. What is the purpose of descriptive health care statistics?

_____ 2. What are the three general data characteristics? Explain each.

_____ 3. What four areas of data quality management does AHIMA define? Explain each.

_____ 4. What role does CQI play in data quality?

_____ 5. How do you ensure data quality?

_____ 6. What three areas are associated with hospital-based statistics? Give an example of each.

Internet Links

Go to **http://www.ahima.org** and search on the following to find a wealth of information on these topics.

- *Data Quality*
- *Data Quality Management Model*
- *Data Collection*
- *Maintenance of Master Patient Index*

Go to **http://www.cdc.gov/nchs** to learn more about the NCHS and its National Vital Statistics System.

Visit the Medical Information Bureau (MIB) at **http://www.mib.com** and the National Practitioner Data Bank (NPDB) at **http://www.npdb-hipdb.com**.

SUMMARY

Indexes and registries allow health information to be maintained and retrieved by health care facilities for the purpose of education, planning, research, and other informational purposes. A master patient index (MPI), disease index, procedure index, and physician index are commonly maintained by facilities. Registries contain information about a disease or an event and are maintained by individual health care facilities, federal and state government agencies, and private organizations. The National Center for Health Statistics (NCHS) is the federal agency responsible for maintaining official vital statistics, while registration of vital events is a state function.

Case abstracting is an automated or manual process performed by health information department staff to collect patient information to determine prospective payment system (PPS) status, generate indexes, and report data to quality improvement organizations and state and federal agencies. Health data collection is performed by health care facilities for administrative planning and to report statistics to state and federal government agencies and other organizations.

STUDY CHECKLIST

- Read the textbook chapter and highlight key concepts. (Use colored highlighter sparingly throughout the chapter.)
- Create an index card for each key term. (Write the key term on one side of the index card and the concept on the other. Learn the definition of each key term, and match the term to the concept.)
- Access chapter Internet links to learn more about concepts.
- Answer the chapter exercises and review questions, verifying answers with your instructor.
- Study content, view videos, and take practice tests online at www.CengageBrain.com.
- Complete lab manual assignments, verifying answers with your instructor.
- Form a study group with classmates to discuss chapter concepts in preparation for an exam.

CHAPTER REVIEW

Multiple Choice: Select the most appropriate response.

1. Indexing allows for
   a. computer interfacing of data with other software systems.
   b. health information to be maintained and retrieved for education and research.
   c. patient records to be quickly retrieved when a patient is readmitted.
   d. automation of case abstracting, which results in cost and time savings.

2. Health care facilities maintain a master patient index (MPI)
   a. according to state retention laws.
   b. permanently.

3. Disease, procedure, and physician indexes are generated as the result of case
   a. abstracting.
   b. indexing.
   c. mix analysis.
   d. reporting.

4. The master patient index (MPI) links a patient's medical record number with
   a. common identification data elements.
   b. disease and procedure indexes.
   c. hospital-assigned physician numbers.
   d. vital statistics reporting agencies.

5. An admission/discharge/transfer system interfaces with an automated MPI to
   a. input patient registration information.
   b. conduct facility case mix analysis.
   c. report diseases/events to state agencies.
   d. generate case report forms.

6. Which is an example of an MPI's continuity of care (or continuum of care) use?
   a. Attending physician contacts the health information department to request old records on a readmitted patient
   b. Hospital administrator requests a report to determine whether a nursing unit should be reopened
   c. Public relations director requests a review of statistical mortality report of patients for the last year
   d. State department of health requests access to patient records to perform a drug utilization study

7. It is important to avoid the creation of duplicate MPI records, which means
   a. a consulting firm that specializes in MPI duplication should be hired to restructure the system.
   b. both an automated and manual master patient index should be maintained to avoid problems with duplicate records.
   c. the state does not allow health care facilities that are located in the same community to merge.
   d. information should be entered by the department that has control over the assignment of medical record numbers.

8. Disease, procedure, and physician indexes contain data abstracted (selected) from
   a. computerized databases.
   b. data sets.
   c. patient records.
   d. registers and registries.

9. Case report forms are used by health care providers to report data to
   a. sponsoring agencies.
   b. facilities.
   c. organizations.
   d. all of these.

10. Registers and registries are _____ sources of patient information.
    a. primary
    b. secondary

11. The NCHS responsible for maintaining official vital statistics is a _____ agency.
    a. federal
    b. state

12. Case abstracting is an automated or manual process performed by a health information department staff to collect patient information.
    a. True
    b. False

13. A discharge register is maintained by the admission department and is organized by date of admission.
    a. True
    b. False

14. A standard method for collecting and reporting individual elements is called a data
    a. dictionary.
    b. register.
    c. registry.
    d. set.

15. Registers and registries contain information about a disease or event and are maintained by
    a. federal and state governmental agencies.
    b. individual health care facilities.
    c. private organizations.
    d. all of these.

Matching I: Match the term with its description.
    a. Data integrity
    b. Data reliability
    c. Data validity

16. Data conforms to an expected range of values.

17. Data is the same no matter where the data is recorded.

18. Data is consistent throughout all systems.

Matching II: Match the term with its description.
    a. Data analysis
    b. Data application
    c. Data collection
    d. Data warehousing

19. Purpose for which the data are collected

20. Processes by which data elements are accumulated

21. Processes and systems used to archive data and data journals

22. Process of translating data into information utilized for an application

Matching III: Match the term with its description.
    a. Average daily census
    b. Daily census count
    c. Daily inpatient census

23. Number of inpatients present at census taking

24. Official count of inpatients present at midnight

25. Arithmetic mean of inpatients treated during a given period

Chapter 9

LEGAL ASPECTS OF HEALTH INFORMATION MANAGEMENT

Chapter Outline

- Key Terms
- Objectives
- Introduction
- Legal and Regulatory Terminology
- Maintaining the Patient Record in the Normal Course of Business
- Confidentiality of Information and HIPAA Privacy and Security Provisions
- Legislation That Impacts Health Information Management
- Release of Protected Health Information
- Internet Links
- Summary
- Study Checklist
- Chapter Review

Key Terms

administrative law
assault
battery
breach of confidentiality
burden of proof
call-back method
case law
civil law
Clinical Laboratory Improvements Amendments of 1988 (CLIA)
common law
confidentiality
contempt of court
contracts
coroner
court order
covered entities
criminal law

decrypt
defendant
de-identification of protected health information (PHI)
deposition
digital
disclosed
discovery
electronic protected health information (EPHI)
emancipated minor
encrypt
HIPAA standards for privacy of individually identifiable health information
impeach
interrogatory
law

malpractice insurance
medical examiner
medical liability insurance
medical malpractice
negligence
Occupational Safety & Health Administration (OSHA)
patient safety organizations (PSOs)
plaintiff
privacy
privacy rule
privileged communication
protected health information (PHI)
public law
qualified protective order
release of information log
res gestae
res ipsa loquitur

res judicata	sources of law	*subpoena ad testificandum*
respondeat superior	*stare decisis*	*subpoena duces tecum*
root cause analysis	statute	torts
security	statute of limitations	treatment, payment, and health
security rule	statutory law	care operations (TPO)

Objectives

At the end of this chapter, the student should be able to:

- Define key terms
- Identify and define health information legal and regulatory terminology
- Maintain the patient record in the normal course of business
- Maintain confidentiality of protected health information (PHI)

- Comply with HIPAA privacy and security provisions
- Interpret legislation that impacts health information management
- Appropriatly release protected health information

INTRODUCTION

> Whatsoever things I see or hear concerning the life of men, in my attendance on the sick or even apart therefrom, which ought not be noised abroad, I will keep silence thereon, counting such things to be as sacred secrets.
>
> *Oath of Hippocrates, 4th century, BC*

This chapter discusses legal aspects of health information management (HIM) covered as part of an introductory course in health care academic programs such as coding and reimbursement, health information administration, health information technology, medical assistant, medical billing, medical office administration, medical secretary, medical transcription, and so on. For comprehensive coverage (e.g., taught as a separate course), refer to Cengage Learning's *Legal and Ethical Aspects of Health Information Management*, 4th edition, by Dana C. McWay.

The following topics are covered in this chapter: legal and regulatory terminology Health Insurance Portability and Accountability Act of 1996 (HIPAA) privacy and security issues, release of information processing, reportable conditions and events, and the use of specialized health information (e.g., HIV). Additional information about HIPAA can be found in Cengage Learning's *HIPAA for Health Care Professionals*, by Carole Krager and Dan Krager. The following legal aspects of HIM are discussed elsewhere in this textbook:

- *Chapter 1:* Ethics
- *Chapter 2:* Accreditation, regulation, and physician credentialing
- *Chapter 4:* Amending record entries, authentication of record entries, computer-based patient record

(CPR), destruction of records, facility closure (e.g., handling patient records), incident reports, legibility of record entries, ownership of the patient record, patient record completion responsibilities, potentially compensable event (PCE), provider documentation requirements (e.g., amending the record, correcting errors), record retention laws, and timeliness of record entries
- *Chapter 6:* Advanced directives, consent forms, content of the patient record (e.g., The Joint Commission standards, Medicare conditions of participation), and informed consent
- *Chapter 7:* Security of patient information
- *Chapter 10:* Health care reimbursement legislation

LEGAL AND REGULATORY TERMINOLOGY

A law (or statute) is a rule of conduct passed by a legislative body (e.g., Congress) that is enforced by the government and results in penalties when violated.

- Civil law deals with the legal rights and relationships of private individuals and includes:
  - Torts (any wrongful acts for which a civil suit can be brought)
  - Contracts (binding agreements between two or more parties)
- Public law deals with relationships between individuals and government and includes:
  - Criminal law (crimes and their punishments)
  - *Regulations* (published rules that interpret laws)

The individual who initiates a civil complaint and has the burden of proof (responsibility for proving harm) is called the plaintiff. (There is no plaintiff in criminal law). The defendant is the individual against whom the complaint is brought. Usually a civil case is initiated when the plaintiff's attorney *files a complaint* with the appropriate court and has a summons issued and served on the defendant. The defendant's attorney files a response with the court.

Discovery is the legal process lawyers use to obtain information about all aspects of a case. Its goal is to find information that will help prepare a case for trial or settlement. An interrogatory is a form of discovery that includes a list of written questions that must be answered by the party served (either defendant or plaintiff); that party must swear, under oath, that the answers provided are accurate to the best of his or her knowledge. Answers to interrogatories are sometimes used during a trial to impeach a party, which means that if an answer to a trial question is different from that given to the same question in interrogatory format, the judge could doubt the party's honesty. Because answers to interrogatories are prepared as a formal, written document prepared by a lawyer, there is more control over how responses are delivered (as compared with being asked the same question during a deposition). As a result, depositions are sometimes preferred over interrogatories for discovery of certain types of information. A deposition is a form of discovery used to learn answers to certain questions, obtain a sworn statement from the deponent, observe a witness's behavior and ability to testify, and discover weaknesses and strengths in each party's case.

The health care industry is involved most often in civil cases and less often in criminal cases. However, because government is increasing its focus on investigations into and prosecutions for health care fraud and refusing to treat patients based on financial status, the number of criminal cases in the health care industry is also on the rise. The types of civil legal actions that most typically affect the health care industry are torts and contracts. Many claims founded in tort and contract law are resolved without appearing in court.

Sources of Law

In addition to the Constitution of the United States and individual state constitutions, sources of law include:

- Administrative law
- Case law (or common law)
- Statutory law

Administrative law includes regulations created by administrative agencies of government. *Regulations*

interpret how a law is to be enforced, and they are generally much more detailed than the law on which they are based. Federal regulations are issued as the *Code of Federal Regulations* (CFR), which is subdivided into 50 titles containing numerous chapters, parts, and sections (Figure 9-1).

Example The Centers for Medicare and Medicaid Services (CMS) is the federal administrative agency responsible for creating regulations to implement HIPAA legislation. Privacy regulations were published in the *Federal Register,* Volume 65, Number 250, Part II 45, Code of Federal Regulations (CFR), Parts 160 and 164—Standards for Privacy of Individually Identifiable Health Information. The regulation that clarifies which businesses must comply with the privacy rule is as follows:

160.102 Applicability

Applies to health plan, health plan clearinghouse, health care provider who transmits any health information in electronic form in connection with a transaction covered by this subchapter.

Case law (or common law) is based on judicial decisions and precedent rather than on statutes. Sometimes case law applies only to situations where the facts of a new case exactly match the facts of the case that was previously decided. In other cases, the court makes a decision on a general principle that may apply to many situations. Case law principles also include the following:

- *Res gestae.* Latin for "things done," which means that hearsay statements made during an incident are admissible as evidence.
- *Res ipsa loquitur.* Latin for "the thing speaks for itself," which means that something is self-evident (e.g., surgical instrument left in patient's abdominal cavity).
- *Res judicata.* Latin for "the thing is decided," which means that the final judgment of a competent court is conclusive; it prevents a plaintiff from suing on a claim that has already been decided, and it prevents a defendant from raising any new defense to defeat enforcement of an earlier judgment.
- *Respondeat superior.* Latin for "let the master answer," which means that an employer is responsible for the legal consequences of an employee's actions.
- *Stare decisis.* Latin for "to stand by things decided," which means it is a doctrine of precedent and courts adhere to the previous ruling.
- *Subpoena ad testificandum.* (Figure 9-2) A court order that requires an individual to appear in court to testify. A court order is a written command

Chapter IV—Centers for Medicare and Medicaid Services, Department of Health and Human Services (Parts 400-499)

SUBCHAPTER A—GENERAL PROVISIONS

400 Introduction; definitions.

401 General administrative requirements.

403 Special programs and projects.

SUBCHAPTER B—MEDICARE PROGRAM

405 Federal health insurance for the aged and disabled.

406 Hospital insurance eligibility and entitlement.

407 Supplementary medical insurance (SMI) enrollment and entitlement.

408 Premiums for supplementary medical insurance.

409 Hospital insurance benefits.

410 Supplementary medical insurance (SMI) benefits.

411 Exclusions from Medicare and limitations on Medicare payment.

412 Prospective payment systems for inpatient hospital services.

413 Principles of reasonable cost reimbursement; payment for ESRD services ...

414 Payment for Part B medical and other health services.

415 Services furnished by physicians in providers, supervising physicians in teaching settings ...

416 Ambulatory surgical services.

417 Health maintenance organizations, competitive medical plans, and health care prepayment plans.

418 Hospice care.

420 Program integrity: Medicare.

421 Intermediaries and carriers.

424 Conditions for Medicare payment.

SUBCHAPTER C—MEDICAL ASSISTANCE PROGRAMS

430 Grants to States for medical assistance programs.

431 State organization and general administration.

432 State personnel administration.

433 State fiscal administration.

434 Contracts.

435 Eligibility in the States, District of Columbia, the Northern Mariana Islands, and American Samoa.

436 Eligibility in Guam, Puerto Rico, and the Virgin Islands.

440 Services: General provisions.

441 Services: Requirements and limits applicable to specific services.

442 Standards for payment to nursing facilities and intermediate care facilities for the mentally retarded.

447 Payments for services.

455 Program integrity: Medicaid.

456 Utilization control.

SUBCHAPTER D—PEER REVIEW ORGANIZATIONS

462 Peer review organizations.

466 Utilization and quality control review.

473 Reconsiderations and appeals.

476 Acquisition, protection, and disclosure of peer review information.

SUBCHAPTER E—STANDARDS AND CERTIFICATION

482 Conditions of participation for hospitals.

483 Requirements for States and long-term care facilities.

484 Conditions of participation: home health agencies.

485 Conditions of participation: providers of specialized services.

486 Conditions for coverage of specialized services furnished by suppliers.

488 Survey and certification procedures.

489 Provider agreements and supplier approval.

491 Certification of certain health facilities.

493 Laboratory requirements.

494 Conditions for coverage of particular services.

498 Appeals procedures for determinations that affect participation in the Medicare program ...

FIGURE 9-1 Partial List of Code of Federal Regulations (CFR) Titles, Chapters, Subchapters, and Parts

```
ADAM ATTORNEY
15 MAIN STREET
ALBANY NY 00000
PHONE:  (518) 555-1234
```

> Notice the title of this subpoena.

BEFORE THE DEPARTMENT OF HEALTH, STATE OF NEW YORK

JOHN DOE,	)	
Petitioner,	)	**_SUBPOENA AD TESTIFICANDUM_**
	)	
vs.	)	
	)	
RICHARD ROE, M.D.	)	
Respondent.	)	Case No. ____NY-123456789____
	)	

```
TO:    Richard Roe, M.D.
       000 Medical Plaza
       Anytown, U.S.A.  84100

       RE:    John Doe
       Date of Birth:  8/28/55
```

> Notice the language pertaining to appearance in court.

YOU ARE COMMANDED to appear at the County Courthouse, 15 Main Street, Room 14A, Albany NY 00000 on or before (June 5th, YYYY), pertaining to the above-referenced individual who has requested the Division of Professional Licensing to conduct a prelitigation panel review of a claim of medical malpractice.

DATED this _fifth_ day of _May_ YYYY.

```
                          DEPARTMENT OF HEALTH

                          By:    Petra Lyons

                          Petra Lyons, Regulatory & Compliance Officer
                          Division of Professional Licensing
```

FIGURE 9-2 *Subpoena ad Testificandum*

or direction ordered by a court or judge. Failure to obey a subpoena constitutes contempt of court, which is punishable by fine or imprisonment.

• *Subpoena duces tecum.* (Figure 9-3) A written command or direction, signed by the clerk of court, ordering an individual to appear in court with documents (e.g., medical records).

Note: Individual states govern the release of psychiatric records. For example, in New York State, a court order (signed by a judge) for psychiatric records must be obtained instead of a *subpoena duces tecum* (except when the patient signs an authorization to release protected health information).

Example Dorrence Kenneth DARLING, II, Appellee, v. CHARLESTON COMMUNITY MEMORIAL HOSPITAL, Appellant. No. 38790. Supreme Court of Illinois. Sept. 29, 1965.

This action was brought against the hospital to recover damages for allegedly negligent medical and hospital treatment which necessitated below the knee amputation of his right leg. The jury returned a verdict against the hospital in the sum of $150,000. This amount was reduced by $40,000, the amount of the settlement with the doctor. The judgment in favor of the plaintiff in the sum of $110,000 was affirmed on appeal by the Appellate Court for the Fourth District, which granted a certificate of importance.

ADAM ATTORNEY
15 MAIN STREET
ALBANY NY 00000
PHONE: (518) 555-1234

> Notice the title of this subpoena.

BEFORE THE DEPARTMENT OF HEALTH, STATE OF NEW YORK

JOHN DOE,   )
Petitioner,   )   ***SUBPOENA DUCES TECUM***
)
vs.   )
)
RICHARD ROE, M.D.   )
Respondent.   )   Case No. _____ NY-123456789 _____
)

TO: Richard Roe, M.D.
      000 Medical Plaza
      Anytown, U.S.A. 84100

> Notice the language requiring production of a complete copy of medical records.

      RE: John Doe
      Date of Birth: 8/28/55

YOU ARE COMMANDED to produce at the County Courthouse, 15 Main Street, Room 14A, Albany NY 00000 on June 5th, YYYY at 9 A.M., a complete copy of your medical records, pertaining to the above-referenced individual who has requested the Division of Professional Licensing to conduct a prelitigation panel review of a claim of medical malpractice. **Attendance is not required if records are timely forwarded to the indicated address.**

DATED this _fifth_ day of _May_ YYYY.

> Notice this statement, which indicates that records can be mailed or delivered to the attorney instead of an appearance in court with records.

DEPARTMENT OF HEALTH

By: *Petra Lyons*

Petra Lyons, Regulatory & Compliance Officer
Division of Professional Licensing

FIGURE 9-3 *Subpoena Duces Tecum*

On November 5, 1960, the plaintiff, who was 18 years old, broke his leg while playing in a college football game. He was taken to the emergency department at the defendant hospital where Dr. Alexander, who was on emergency call that day, treated him. Dr. Alexander, with the assistance of hospital personnel, applied traction and placed the leg in a plaster cast. A heat cradle was applied to dry the cast. Not long after the application of the cast plaintiff was in great pain and his toes, which protruded from the cast, became swollen and dark in color. They eventually became cold and insensitive. On the evening of November 6, Dr. Alexander "notched" the cast around the toes, and on the afternoon of the next day he cut the cast approximately three inches up from the foot. On November 8 he split the sides of the cast with a Stryker saw; in the course of cutting the cast the plaintiff's leg was cut on both sides. Blood and other seepage were observed by the nurses and others, and there was a stench in the room, which one witness said was the worst he had smelled since World War II. The plaintiff remained in Charleston Hospital until November 19, when he was transferred to Barnes Hospital in St. Louis and placed under the care of Dr. Fred Reynolds, head of orthopedic surgery at Washington University School of Medicine and Barnes Hospital. Dr. Reynolds found that the fractured leg contained a considerable amount of dead tissue, which in his opinion resulted from interference with the circulation of blood in the limb caused by swelling or hemorrhaging of the leg against the construction of the cast. Dr. Reynolds performed several operations in a futile attempt to save the leg but ultimately it had to be amputated eight inches below the knee.

Statutory law is passed by a legislative body (e.g., Congress), and it can be amended, repealed, or expanded by the legislative body. A statute of limitations refers to the time period after which a lawsuit cannot be filed. Such statutes vary from state to state, and the statute of limitations for medical malpractice cases varies from one to three years. Medical malpractice results when a health care provider acts in an improper or negligent manner and the patient's result is injury, damage, or loss. The *American Heritage® Dictionary of the English Language* defines negligence as the "failure to exercise the degree of care considered reasonable under the circumstances, resulting in an unintended injury to another party" (e.g., misdiagnosis, error in performing a surgical procedure, failure to recognize and treat complications, failure to obtain informed consent from a patient for treatment performed). Providers purchase medical liability (or malpractice) insurance, which pays a lawsuit's covered damages (settlement amount) and defense costs (e.g., lawyer fees).

Example The Health Insurance Portability and Accountability Act of 1996 (HIPAA) is a federal law passed by Congress that amended "the Internal Revenue Code of 1986 to improve portability and continuity of health insurance coverage in the group and individual markets, to combat waste, fraud, and abuse in health insurance and health care delivery, to promote the use of medical savings accounts, to improve access to long-term care services and coverage, to simplify the administration of health insurance, and for other purposes."

EXERCISE 9-1 Legal and Regulatory Terminology

True/False: Indicate whether each statement is true (T) or false (F).

_____ 1. Public law includes both federal regulations and criminal law.

_____ 2. The health care industry is most often involved in criminal cases.

_____ 3. Statutory law is based on precedent and judicial decisions.

_____ 4. *Stare decisis* is Latin for "let the master answer."

_____ 5. The defendant is the individual who initiates a civil complaint.

MAINTAINING THE PATIENT RECORD IN THE NORMAL COURSE OF BUSINESS

The medical record is a legal business record that must be maintained according to accreditation standards (e.g., The Joint Commission), legal principles (e.g., federal and state laws), professional practice standards (e.g., AHIMA practice briefs that provide guidelines for record-keeping issues), and regulations (e.g., medical conditions of participation). While laws, regulations, and standards originally applied to the maintenance of paper records, they also apply to electronic (or computer-based) records that are usually legally acceptable as long as they are properly created and maintained in the normal course of business.

Note: Standards will vary depending on applicable case law, state laws, and type of health care setting.

Currently, no state has enacted a comprehensive law that systematically deals with all issues raised by the computerization of records, although some states have enacted legislation that expressly recognizes the validity of the electronic health record (EHR). Other states have indirectly recognized the validity of EHRs by passing laws that standardize electronic authentication, recognize the right of providers to create and maintain medical records in electronic form, and require that computer systems have certain characteristics such as the capacity to prevent subsequent alterations or to protect the security of records. HIPAA legislation also does not attempt to formulate standards for electronic records, although it directs regulatory authorities to devise appropriate rules for the transmission of data.

Although medical record documentation is technically considered hearsay, most states have adopted the Federal Rules of Evidence 803(6) and the Uniform Business Records as Evidence Act, which excepts records maintained in the regular course of business as an exception to the hearsay rule. For a medical record to be considered admissible as evidence, it must be:

- Created by a person within the business who has knowledge of the acts, conditions, diagnoses, events, or opinions documented
- Documented in the normal course of business
- Generated at or near the time of patient care
- Maintained in the regular course of business

EHRs are also admissible if they meet the four principles above *and* meet the following *Comprehensive*

Guide to Electronic Health Records guidelines that demonstrate accuracy and trustworthiness:

- Type of computer used is accepted as standard and efficient equipment
- Method of operation to create electronic medical record is recorded
- Method and circumstances of preparing the record include sources of information on which the record is based, procedures for entering information into and retrieving information from the computer, controls and checks used, and tests performed to ensure the accuracy and reliability of the record
- Information documented in the EHR has not been altered in any way

Other safeguards that can help ensure the admissibility of the EHR include:

- Maintaining records at an off-site backup storage system in case the on-site system is damaged or destroyed
- Using an imaging system to copy documents that contain signatures
- Ensuring that records, once in electronic form, cannot be altered
- Safeguarding the confidentiality of records and preventing access by unauthorized persons
- Allowing authentication of record entries via electronic signature keys
- Implementing procedures for system maintenance

EXERCISE 9–2 Maintaining the Patient Record in the Normal Course of Business

Fill-in-the-Blank: Enter the term that most appropriately completes the statement.

1. From a legal standpoint, medical record documentation is officially considered _____. However, most states have adopted the Federal Rules of Evidence 803(6) and the _____ as Evidence Act as an exception.

2. Laws, regulations, and standards originally applied to maintenance of records, but now also apply to _____ records.

3. HIPAA legislation directs regulatory authorities to devise appropriate rules for the _____ of data.

4. Standards that govern medical records will vary depending on application case law, type of health care setting, and _____.

5. A safeguard that can help ensure the admissibility of the EHR in court is _____.

CONFIDENTIALITY OF INFORMATION AND HIPAA PRIVACY AND SECURITY PROVISIONS

Any information communicated by a patient to a health care provider is considered privileged communication, which means it is private. Patients have the right to confidentiality, which is the process of keeping privileged communication secret and means that information cannot be disclosed without the patient's authorization. (Exceptions include information released via *subpoena duces tecum* and according to statutory reporting requirements, discussed later in this chapter.) A breach of confidentiality occurs when patient information is disclosed (or released) to other(s) who do not have a right to access the information. In this situation, the disclosing provider failed to obtain patient authorization to release privileged communication; this results in violation of federal law (HIPAA). According to HIPAA privacy and security provisions:

- Patients have the right to an expectation of privacy regarding their privileged communication, which means information cannot be disclosed without their authorization.
- Security safeguards must be implemented to ensure that facilities, equipment, and patient information are safe from damage, loss, tampering, theft, or unauthorized access.

The Health Information Technology for Economic and Clinical Health Act of 2009 (HITECH Act) imposes data breach notification requirements for unauthorized uses and disclosures of *unsecured protected health information (PHI)*, which essentially means *unencrypted PHI*. The HITECH Act requires that patients be notified about any unsecured breach, and HHS must be notified if a breach impacts 500 patients or more; the local media may also need to be notified about breaches that impact 500 patients or more. (The HITECH Act is part of the American Recovery and Reinvestment Act of 2009.)

Note: If security policies and procedures are *not* established and enforced, concerns might be raised about the security of patient information during legal proceedings. This could result in questioning the integrity of the medical record.

Health Insurance Portability and Accountability Act of 1996

Example 1
A patient entered the health information department and requested a copy of the results of a brain scan that she had undergone in the emergency department the night before. The patient signed the release of information

authorization form, and when the record was retrieved the health information technician (HIT) noticed that the results revealed a serious abnormality. Instead of releasing a copy of the report to the patient, the HIT explained to the patient that she should discuss the results of the brain scan with her primary care physician. The patient became very nervous and scared and could not be convinced to discuss the results with her primary care physician. The HIT then decided to escort the patient to the emergency department and explain the situation to the emergency physician, who agreed to review the results with the patient. That physician also contacted the patient's primary care physician to let him know about the situation.

Example 2
A health information department clerk responded to a request to carry patient records to a nursing floor. One of the patients was an employee of the health information department, and during transport the clerk read the record and asked the employee why she was on a particular medication. The employee reported the incident to the health information manager, who contacted Human Resources. The incident was investigated, and the clerk was terminated.

HIPAA is the first federal law that governs the privacy of health information nationwide. HIPAA legislation was organized according to five titles:

- Title I—Health Care Access, Portability, and Renewability
- Title II—Preventing Health Care Fraud and Abuse, Administrative Simplification, and Medical Liability Reform
- Title III—Tax-Related Health Provisions
- Title IV—Application and Enforcement of Group Health Plan Requirements
- Title V—Revenue Offsets

Note: Only HIPAA Title II content is discussed in this chapter because the remaining content covers health care reimbursement issues, which is discussed in Chapter 10. Title II legal aspects include medical liability, privacy, and security, discussed below.

HIPAA Made Simple

HIPAA resulted from Clinton administration and congressional efforts to reform health care by enabling workers of all professions to change jobs even if they (or family members) have pre-existing medical conditions, by reducing health care fraud and abuse, by reducing paperwork associated with health claims processing, and by guaranteeing the security and privacy of health information. The "portability" aspect of HIPAA protects health insurance coverage for workers and their families when they change or lose their jobs. The "accountability" aspect protects health data integrity, availability, and confidentiality and has the greatest impact on health care organizations.

Medical Liability

The threat of excessive awards in medical liability cases has increased providers' liability insurance premiums and resulted in increases in health care costs. As a result, some providers stop practicing medicine in areas of the country where liability insurance costs are highest, and the direct impact on individuals and communities across the country is reduced access to quality medical care. Although medical liability reform was included in HIPAA legislation, no final rule was published. While individual states, such as Ohio, have passed medical liability reform, the United States Congress is also formulating separate federal medical liability reform legislation. One early attempt to address medical liability occurred in 2003, when the House of Representatives (HR) passed HR 5 for medical liability reform. In addition, the Senate (S) introduced S 607, the *HEALTH Act,* a medical liability reform bill that includes a hard cap of $250,000 on non-economic damages. There have been numerous attempts to pass federal medical liability reforms. The American Medical Association strongly supports liability reforms at the federal and state levels. For the most current information on medical liability reform visit www.ama-assn.org and search on medical liability reform.

Privacy Rule

The HIPAA standards for privacy of individually iden-tifiable health information (or privacy rule) include provisions that protect the security and confidential-ity of health information. Because the use and disclo-sure of health information is inconsistently protected by state laws, patients' privacy and confidentiality is also inconsistently protected. The HIPAA privacy rule establishes standards to protect the confidentiality of individually identifiable health information main-tained or transmitted electronically in connection with certain administrative and financial transactions (e.g., electronic transfer of health insurance claims). The rule provides rights for individuals with respect to protected health information about themselves and mandates compliance by covered entities, which are private- and public-sector organizations that must fol-low HIPAA provisions. For the privacy rule, covered entities include health care providers that conduct certain transactions in electronic form, health plans, and health care clearinghouses.

Protected health information (PHI) is information that is identifiable to an individual (or individual identifiers) such as name, address, telephone numbers, date of birth, Medicaid ID number and other medical record numbers, social security number (SSN), and name of employer. In most instances, covered entities are required to obtain an individual's authorization prior to disclosing their health information, and HIPAA has established specific requirements for an authorization form.

All medical records and other individually identifiable health information used or disclosed by a covered entity in any form, whether electronically, paper-based, or verbal, are covered by the privacy rule. The provisions of the privacy rule, which are extensive, are summarized below.

Patients have the following specific rights:

- *Patient education on privacy protections.* Covered entities are required to provide patients with a clear, written explanation (Figure 9-4) of how the covered entity may use and disclose their health

PRIVACY NOTICE	Effective October 1, 2013

THIS NOTICE DESCRIBES HOW PERSONAL AND MEDICAL INFORMATION ABOUT YOU MAY BE USED AND DISCLOSED AND HOW YOU CAN GET ACCESS TO THIS INFORMATION. PLEASE REVIEW IT CAREFULLY.

Understanding the Type of Information We Have. We get information about you when you enroll in a health plan. It includes your date of birth, sex, ID number and other personal information. We also get bills, reports from your doctor and other data about your medical care.

Our Privacy Commitment To You. We care about your privacy. The information we collect about you is private. We are required to give you a notice of our privacy practices. Only people who have both the need and the legal right may see your information. Unless you give us permission in writing, we will only disclose your information for purposes of treatment, payment, business operations (TPO) or when we are required by law to do so.

- **Treatment.** We may disclose medical information about you to coordinate your health care. For example, we may notify your doctor about care you get in an emergency room.

- **Payment.** We may use and disclose information so the care you get can be properly billed and paid for. For example, we may ask an emergency room for details before we pay the bill for your care.

- **Business Operations.** We may need to use and disclose information for our business operations. For example, we may use information to review the quality of care you get.

- **Exceptions.** For certain kinds of records, your permission may be needed even for release for treatment, payment and business operations.

- **As Required By Law.** We will release information when we are required by law to do so. Examples of such releases would be for law enforcement or national security purposes, subpoenas or other court orders, communicable disease reporting, disaster relief, review of our activities by government agencies, to avert a serious threat to health or safety or in other kinds of emergencies.

With Your Permission. If you give us permission in writing, we may use and disclose your personal information. If you give us permission, you have the right to change your mind and revoke it. This must be in writing, too. We cannot take back any uses or disclosures already made with your permission.

Your Privacy Rights. You have the following rights regarding the health information that we have about you. Your requests must be made in writing to the Department of Health at the address below.

- **Your Right to Inspect and Copy.** In most cases, you have the right to look at or get copies of your records. You may be charged a fee for the cost of copying your records.

- **Your Right to Amend.** You may ask us to change your records if you feel that there is a mistake. We can deny your request for certain reasons, but we must give you a written reason for our denial.

- **Your Right to a List of Disclosures.** You have the right to ask for a list of disclosures made after April 14, 2003. This list will not include the times that information was disclosed for treatment, payment, or health care operations. The list will not include information provided directly to you or your family, or information that was sent with your authorization.

- **Your Right to Request Restrictions on Our Use or Disclosure of Information.** You have the right to ask for limits on how your information is used or disclosed. We are not required to agree to such requests.

- **Your Right to Request Confidential Communications.** You have the right to ask that we share information with you in a certain way or in a certain place. For example, you may ask us to send information to your work address instead of your home address. You do not have to explain the basis for your request.

Changes to this Notice. We reserve the right to revise this notice. A revised notice will be effective for medical information we already have about you as well as any information we may receive in the future. We are required by law to comply with whatever notice is currently in effect. Any changes to our notice will be published on our Web site. Go to www.medicaid.gov, click on Health Care Coverage, and look under Spotlight.If the changes are material, a new notice will be mailed to you before it takes effect.

How to Use Your Rights Under This Notice. If you want to use your rights under this notice, you may call us or write to us. If your request to us must be in writing, we will help you prepare your written request, if you wish.

Complaints to the Federal Government. If you believe that your privacy rights have been violated, you have the right to file a complaint with the federal government. You may write to: Office of Civil Rights, Dept. of Health and Human Services, 200 Independence Avenue, S.W., Washington, D.C. 20201, Phone: 866-627-7748, TTY: 886-788-4989, Email: ocrprivacy@hhs.gov. You will not be penalized for filing a complaint with the federal government.

Complaints and Communications to Us. If you want to exercise your rights under this notice or if you wish to communicate with us about privacy issues or if you wish to file a complaint, you can write to: Privacy Officer, Global Insurance Plan, 100 Main Street, Anywhere US 12345, (101) 555-1234, TDD: (101) 555-1111. You will not be penalized for filing a complaint.

Copies of this Notice. You have the right to receive an additional copy of this notice at any time. Even if you have agreed to receive this notice electronically, you are still entitled to a paper copy of this notice. Please call or write to us to request a copy. This notice is available in other languages and alternate formats that meet the guidelines for the Americans with Disabilities Act (ADA). Esta notificaci n est disponible en otras lenguas y formatos diferentes que satisfacen las normas del Acta de Americans with Disabilities (ADA).

FIGURE 9-4 Privacy Notice

information. When HIPAA rules are revised, such as those associated with the HITECH Act of 2009, the privacy notice must be revised and redistributed. (However, an inmate has no right to such a notice, and a correctional facility has no obligation to provide such a notice. Special rules and exceptions also apply to group health plans.) Patients must also be provided with an opportunity to object to disclosure of PHI.

Note: An individual may revoke an authorization at any time, provided that the revocation is in writing, except to the extent that (1) the covered entity has taken action in reliance thereon (e.g., facility has already released PHI based on previously executed authorization); or (2) if the authorization was obtained as a condition of obtaining insurance coverage, other law provides the insurer with the right to contest a claim under the policy.

- *Redisclosure of PHI.* The patient authorization to release PHI should include a general statement that the health information may no longer be protected by the privacy rule once it is disclosed by the covered entity. (Covered entities should inform recipients of PHI of their obligation to not redisclose PHI unless authorized to do so.)
- *Patient access to their records.* Patients will be allowed to obtain copies of their records and to request that amendments be made to documentation. In addition, non-routine disclosure must be communicated to patients. The HITECH Act of 2009 requires patient access to EPHI, and covered entities must provide an electronic copy of PHI that is maintained electronically and located in one or more designated record sets. The covered entity must produce a copy of the electronic record in the form and format requested by the patient. Fees for paper and electronic copies are defined, which means providers can charge for the cost of labor and materials used to copy PHI, whether in paper or electronic form. Labor costs can include a reasonable cost-based fee for skilled technical staff time spent creating and copying the electronic file. However, an entity cannot withhold copies of patient records due to a failure to pay for any services above the copying costs.

Note: HIPAA mandates a time limit of 60 days for covered entities to respond to requests for amendments and release of information requests.

- *Disclosures to business associates.* A covered entity may disclose PHI to a business associate (e.g., third-party payer) and may allow a business associate to create or receive PHI on its behalf if the entity obtains satisfactory assurance that the business associate will appropriately safeguard the information.
- *Patient care and notification.* A covered entity may disclose to a family member (or other personal representative) PHI directly related to that person's involvement with the patient's care or payment related to care. A covered entity may also disclose PHI to notify a family member (or other personal representative) of a patient's location, general condition, or death.
- *Disclosures about deceased patients.* Individually identifiable health information of a person deceased more than 50 years is not considered PHI under the HIPAA privacy rule. Health information of patients who have been dead less than 50 years is still considered PHI and is subject to protection. (Disclosures for research purposes are exempt from this standard.)
- *Fundraising activities.* Covered entities must provide the recipient of any fundraising communication with a clear and conspicuous opportunity to opt out of receiving any further fundraising communications.
- *Limited uses and disclosures when the patient is not available.* The covered entity may exercise professional judgment to determine whether disclosure of PHI is in the best interest of the patient and disclose only that PHI directly related to the person's involvement with the patient's health care. For example, a person could act on behalf of the patient to pick up filled prescriptions, medical supplies, x-rays, and so on.
- *Disclosures by whistleblowers and workforce member crime victims.* A covered entity is not considered to have violated this standard if a member of its workforce or a business associate discloses PHI as the result of good faith judgment that the covered entity (1) has engaged in conduct that is unlawful or otherwise violates professional or clinical standards; or (2) that the care, services, or conditions provided by the covered entity potentially endanger one or more patients, workers, or the public; and (3) the disclosure is to a health oversight agency, attorney, or law enforcement official involving a victim of a crime.
- *Obtaining patient authorization before information is disclosed.* Except for circumstances requiring patient authorization (e.g., psychotherapy notes), providers are not required to obtain patient authorization prior to disclosing information

for treatment, payment, and health care operations (TPO). A covered entity must comply with the *minimum* necessary privacy standard by making reasonable efforts not to use or disclose more than the minimum amount of PHI necessary to accomplish a task. **Treatment, payment, and health care operations (TPO)** activities are defined as follows:

○ *Treatment* generally means the provision, coordination, or management of health care and related services among health care providers or by a health care provider with a third party, consultation between health care providers regarding a patient, or the referral of a patient from one health care provider to another.

○ *Payment* encompasses the various activities of health care providers to obtain payment or be reimbursed for their services, and of a health plan to obtain premiums, fulfill coverage responsibilities and provide benefits under the plan, and obtain or provide reimbursement for the provision of health care.

○ *Health care operations* are certain administrative, financial, legal, and quality improvement activities of a covered entity that are necessary to run its business and support the core functions of treatment and payment.

Many providers opt to obtain authorization to disclose PHI for TPO purposes (Figure 9-5). Separate patient authorization *must* be obtained for non-routine disclosures and non-health care purposes (Figure 9-6), and patients have the right to request restrictions as to use and disclosure of their PHI. Do not confuse patient consent to TPO with patient authorization to disclose PHI. According to HIPAA, patients "consent to use and disclose information," which means they provide written permission to providers so that health information related to TPO can be used or disclosed. Patients are permitted to restrict health plan (third-party payer) access to medical records that pertain to treatment paid for by the patient out of pocket. Covered entities are permitted to disclose a decedent's PHI to family members and others who were involved in the care or payment for care of a decedent prior to death, unless doing so is inconsistent with any known prior expressed preference of the individual.

Example 1
Disclosure of PHI for TPO purposes

Patients routinely sign the consent form on the reverse of an inpatient face sheet, which allows the facility to communicate final diagnoses and procedures to third-party payers so that the facility can be reimbursed for care provided to the patient. In addition, patients routinely consent to medical treatment when they are admitted as a hospital inpatients. This consent form is usually located on the reverse of the face sheet. (HIPAA no longer requires covered entities to obtain consent to TPO; however, most covered entities continue to obtain consent from patients.)

Example 2
Disclosure of PHI for other than TPO purposes

Patients "authorize the use or disclosure of information" when they provide written permission to providers so that PHI can be released for purposes other than TPO. For example, when third-party payers request a copy of the patient's entire medical record to determine whether to reimburse the facility for services provided, the patient must sign a special authorization to release PHI.

● *Proof of immunization.* Covered entities can disclose proof of immunization to a school where state or other law requires it prior to admitting a student. Written authorization is no longer required, but an agreement must still be obtained, which can be oral.

● *Recourse if privacy protections are violated.* Patients have the right to file a formal complaint with a covered entity, or with HHS, when violations of privacy protections occur. For example, releasing information to an employer, without the patient's authorization, so that personnel decisions can be made is a violation.

Covered entities have the flexibility to establish their own policies and procedures to meet privacy rule standards. They should:

● *Create written privacy policies and procedures* that clarify who has the right to access protected information, how protected information will be used within the covered entity, and when protected information may be disclosed. Covered entities must ensure that their business associates also protect the privacy of health information (e.g., add HIPAA clause to business agreements).

● *Train employees* regarding HIPAA privacy policies and procedures.

● *Designate a privacy officer* who is responsible for ensuring that procedures are followed (e.g., health information manager).

Covered entities are required to take reasonable steps to limit the use or disclosure of, and requests for, PHI to the minimum necessary to accomplish the

Inform individual that PHI may be used and disclosed to carry out TPO.

Refer to privacy notice for additional information about uses and disclosures.

State that the individual has the right to review the privacy notice prior to signing the TPO consent form. If the covered entity reserves the right to change its privacy practices in its notice, indicate that terms of the notice may change and describe how the individual may obtain a copy of the updated Privacy Notice.

State that the individual has the right to revoke the consent in writing, to the extent the covered entity has not already acted in reliance upon it.

State that the individual has a right to request restrictions on uses and disclosures of PHI for TPO, and that the covered entity is not required to agree to an individual's request but, if covered entity agrees to restriction, covered entity is bound by it.

Alfred State Medical Center
100 Main Street
Anywhere NY 00000
(101) 555-1234

Patient Consent for Use and Disclosure of Protected Health Information (PHI) for Treatment, Payment, and Health Care Operations (TPO)

I hereby give my consent for Alfred State Medical Center to use and disclose protected health information (PHI) about me to carry out treatment, payment, and health care operations (TPO).

(The Privacy Notice provided by Alfred State Medical Center describes such uses and disclosures more completely.)

I have the right to review the Privacy Notice prior to signing this consent. Alfred State Medical Center reserves the right to revise its Privacy Notice at any time. A revised Privacy Notice may be obtained by forwarding a written request to Privacy Officer, Alfred State Medical Center, 100 Main Street, Anywhere NY 00000.

With this consent, Alfred State Medical Center may call my home or other alternative location and leave a message on voice mail or in person in reference to any items that assist the practice in carrying out TPO, such as appointment reminders, insurance items, and any calls pertaining to my clinical care, including laboratory test results, among others.

With this consent, Alfred State Medical Center may mail to my home or other alternative location any items that assist the practice in carrying out TPO, such as appointment reminder cards and patient statements as long as they are marked Personal and Confidential.

With this consent, Alfred State Medical Center may email to my home or other alternative location any items that assist the practice in carrying out TPO, such as appointment reminder cards and patient statements. I have the right to request that Alfred State Medical Center restrict how it uses or discloses my PHI to carry out TPO. The practice is not required to agree to my requested restrictions, but if it does, it is bound by this agreement.

By signing this form, I am consenting to allow Alfred State Medical Center to use and disclose my PHI to carry out TPO.

I may revoke my consent in writing except to the extent that the practice has already made disclosures in reliance upon my prior consent. If I do not sign this consent, or later revoke it, Alfred State Medical Center may decline to provide treatment to me.

_____
Signature of Patient or Legal Guardian

Be signed by the individual and dated.

_____   _____
Print Patient s Name   Date

_____
Print Name of Patient or Legal Guardian, if applicable

FIGURE 9-5 TPO Consent Form with HIPAA Content Requirements

intended purpose. The minimum necessary provisions do not apply to the following:

- Disclosures to or requests by a provider for treatment purposes
- Disclosures to the individual who is the subject of the information

- Uses or disclosures made pursuant to authorization by the individual
- Uses or disclosures required for compliance with HIPAA transactions

Must be written in plain language.

Name of person(s) or class of persons authorized to use or disclose PHI.

Description of information to be used or disclosed, with sufficient specificity.

Name of person(s) or class of persons to whom the covered entity is authorized to make use or disclosure.

Statement of the individual's right to revoke authorization in writing and exceptions thereto, with description on how to revoke.

Expiration date or an expiration event that relates to the individual or the purpose of the use or disclosure.

Statement that information used or disclosed may be subject to re-disclosure by recipient and may no longer be protected by this rule.

Signature of individual and date.

If signed by personal representative, a description of the representative's authority to act for the individual.

Alfred State Medical Center
100 Main Street
Anywhere NY 00000
(101) 555-1234

AUTHORIZATION FOR DISCLOSURE OF PROTECTED HEALTH INFORMATION (PHI)

(1) I hereby authorize Alfred State Medical Center to disclose/obtain information from the health records of:

_____   _____   _____
Patient Name   Date of Birth (mmddyyyy)   Telephone (w/ area code)

_____   _____
Patient Address   Medical Record Number

(2) Covering the period(s) of healthcare:

_____   _____   _____   _____
From (mmddyyyy)   To (mmddyyyy)   From (mmddyyyy)   To (mmddyyyy)

(3) I authorize the following information to be released by Alfred State Medical Center (check applicable reports):

❏ Face Sheet   ❏ Progress Notes   ❏ Pathology Report   ❏ Drug Abuse Care
❏ Discharge Summary   ❏ Lab Results   ❏ Nurses Notes   ❏ Other:
❏ History & Physical Exam ❏ X-ray Reports   ❏ HIV Testing Results   _____
❏ Consultation   ❏ Scan Results   ❏ Mental Health Care   _____
❏ Doctors Orders   ❏ Operative Report   ❏ Alcohol Abuse Care   _____

This information is to be disclosed to or obtained from:

_____   _____   _____
Name of Organization   Address of Organization   Telephone Number

for the purpose of: _____

(4) I understand that I have a right to revoke this authorization at any time. I understand that if I revoke this authorization I must do so in writing and present my written revocation to the Health Information Management Department. I understand that the revocation will not apply to information that has already been released in response to this authorization. I understand that the revocation will not apply to my insurance company when the law provides my insurer with the right to contest a claim under my policy. Unless otherwise revoked, this authorization will expire on the following date, event, or condition:

_____   _____   _____
Expiration Date   Expiration Event   Expiration Condition

If I fail to specify an expiration date, event, or condition, this authorization will expire within six (6) months.

(5) I understand that authorizing the disclosure of this health information is voluntary. I can refuse to sign this authorization. I need not sign this form in order to assure treatment. I understand that I may inspect or copy the information to be used or disclosed, provided in CFR 164.534. I understand that any disclosure of information carries with it the potential for an unauthorized re-disclosure and may not be protected by federalconfidentiality rules. If I have questions about disclosure of my health information, I can contact the Privacy Officer atAlfred State Medical Center.

Signed:

_____   _____
Signature of Patient or Legal Representative   Date

If signed by legal representative:

_____   _____
Relationship to Patient   Signature of Witness

FIGURE 9-6 Authorization Form for Disclosure of Protected Health Information

The following penalties apply when covered entities misuse personal health information:

- *Civil monetary penalties* of $100 per violation, up to $25,000 per person, per year for each requirement or prohibition violated.
- *Federal criminal penalties* of up to $50,000 and one year in prison for obtaining or disclosing protected health information; up to $100,000 and up to five years in prison for obtaining protected health information under "false pretenses"; and up to $250,000 and up to 10 years in prison for obtaining or disclosing protected health information with the intent to sell, transfer, or use it for commercial advantage, personal gain, or malicious harm.
- The HITECH Act of 2009 increased civil penalties for willful neglect up to $250,000, with repeat and/or uncorrected violations extending up to $1.5 million.

Note: Special protection exists for psychotherapy notes that are used only by a psychotherapist, do not become part of the patient's medical record, and are never intended to be shared with anyone else. In addition, when stronger state laws (e.g., disclosure of AIDS, HIV, and mental health records) exist, they preempt HIPAA privacy provisions. This means that, while the HIPAA privacy rule establishes a baseline for standards that protect the confidentiality and privacy of patient information, in some states patients will have additional protection. Many state health departments have developed documents that compare state law with HIPAA federal regulations. It should be noted that HIPAA also addresses disclosures for judicial and administrative proceedings.

Security Rule

The HIPAA security rule, published February 20, 2003, adopts standards and safeguards to protect health information that is collected, maintained, used, or transmitted *electronically*. Covered entities impacted by this rule include health plans, health care clearinghouses, and certain health care providers. Health care business associates and their subcontractors must also follow the HIPAA Security Rule for electronic protected health information (EPHI) as a result of the HITECH Act of 2009. This means that business associates must obtain HIPAA-compliant agreements with their subcontractors (instead of the business associate's covered entity, such as a hospital). CMS is responsible for overseeing compliance with and complaints about security rules.

Note: The proposed standard for electronic signature is digital, which applies a mathematical function to the electronic document resulting in a *unique bit string* (computer code) called a *message digest* that is encrypted and appended to the electronic document. (Encrypt means to encode a computer file, making it safe for electronic transmission so that unauthorized parties cannot read it.) The recipient of the transmitted electronic document decrypts (decodes) the message digest and compares the decoded digest with the transmitted version. If they are identical, the message is unaltered and the identity of the signer is proven.

The DHHS Medicare Program, other federal agencies operating health plans or providing health care, state Medicaid agencies, private health plans, health care providers, and health care clearinghouses must assure their customers (e.g., patients, insured individuals, providers, and health plans) that the integrity, confidentiality, and availability of electronic protected health information they collect, maintain, use, or transmit is protected. The confidentiality of health information is threatened not only by the risk of improper access to stored information, but also by the risk of interception during electronic transmission of the information. The purpose of the *security rule* is to adopt national standards for safeguards to protect the confidentiality, integrity, and availability of EPHI. Prior to publication of the security rule, no standard measures existed in the health care industry to address all aspects of the security of electronic health information while it is being stored or during the exchange of that information between entities. In general, security provisions should include the following policies and procedures:

- Define authorized users of patient information to control access
- Implement a tracking procedure to sign out records to authorized personnel
- Limit record storage access to authorized users
- Lock record storage areas at all times
- Require that all original medical records remain in the facility at all times

Note: It is usually acceptable to submit a copy of the medical record for legal proceedings. If the original record is required, obtain a receipt from the court clerk and retain a copy of the record in the storage area. Be sure to properly protect the original record when transporting it to court by placing it in a locked storage container. Make sure that the original record remains in the custody of health care personnel transporting the record until entered into evidence.

HIPAA's security rule standards include the following safeguards:

- Administrative (Table 9-1A)
- Physical (Table 9-1B)
- Technical (Table 9-1C)

Excerpt from HIPAA Regulation- 45 CFR §164.512(e) (Reprinted according to HHS Web reuse policy.)

(e) Standard: Disclosures for judicial and administrative proceedings

(1) Permitted disclosures. A covered entity may disclose protected health information in the course of any judicial or administrative proceeding:

(i) In response to an order of a court or administrative tribunal, provided that the covered entity discloses only the protected health information expressly authorized by such order; or

(ii) In response to a subpoena, discovery request, or other lawful process, that is not accompanied by an order of a court or administrative tribunal, if:

(A) The covered entity receives satisfactory assurance, as described in paragraph (e)(1)(iii) of this section, from the party seeking the information that reasonable efforts have been made by such party to ensure that the individual who is the subject of the protected health information that has been requested has been given notice of the request; or

(B) The covered entity receives satisfactory assurance, as described in paragraph (e)(1)(iv) of this section, from the party seeking the information that reasonable efforts have beevn made by such party to secure a qualified protective order that meets the requirements of paragraph (e)(1)(v) of this section.

(iii) For the purposes of paragraph (e)(1)(ii)(A) of this section, a covered entity receives satisfactory assurances from a party seeking protecting health information if the covered entity receives from such party a written statement and accompanying documentation demonstrating that:

(A) The party requesting such information has made a good faith attempt to provide written notice to the individual (or, if the individual's location is unknown, to mail a notice to the individual's last known address);

(B) The notice included sufficient information about the litigation or proceeding in which the protected health information is requested to permit the individual to raise an objection to the court or administrative tribunal; and

(C) The time for the individual to raise objections to the court or administrative tribunal has elapsed, and:

(1) No objections were filed; or

(2) All objections filed by the individual have been resolved by the court or the administrative tribunal, and the disclosures being sought are consistent with such resolution.

(iv) For the purposes of paragraph (e)(1)(ii)(B) of this section, a covered entity receives satisfactory assurances from a party seeking protected health information, if the covered entity receives from such party a written statement and accompanying documentation demonstrating that:

(A) The parties to the dispute giving rise to the request for information have agreed to a qualified protective order and have presented it to the court or administrative tribunal with jurisdiction over the dispute; or

(B) The party seeking the protected health information has requested a qualified protective order from such court or administrative tribunal.

(v) For purposes of paragraph (e)(1) of this section, a qualified protective order means, with respect to protected health information requested under paragraph (e)(1)(ii) of this section, an order of a court or of an administrative tribunal or a stipulation by the parties to the litigation or administrative proceeding that:

(A) Prohibits the parties from using or disclosing the protected health information for any purpose other than the litigation or proceeding for which such information was requested; and

(B) Requires the return to the covered entity or destruction of the protected health information (including all copies made) at the end of the litigation or proceeding.

(vi) Notwithstanding paragraph (e)(1)(ii) of this section, a covered entity may disclose protected health information in response to the lawful process described in paragraph (e)(1)(ii) of this section without receiving satisfactory assurance under paragraph (e)(1)(ii)(A) or (B) of this section, if the covered entity makes reasonable efforts to provide notice to the individual sufficient to meet the requirements of paragraph (e)(1)(iii) of this section or to seek a qualified protective order sufficient to meet the requirements of paragraph (e)(1)(iv) of this section.

(2) Other uses and disclosures under this section. The provisions of this paragraph do not supersede other provisions of this section that otherwise permit or restrict uses or disclosures of protected health information.

TABLE 9-1A HIPAA Security Rule—Administrative Safeguards and Implementation Specifications

Administrative Safeguards	Implementation Specifications for Covered Entities
Security management process	Policies and procedures to prevent, detect, contain, and correct security violations include: • *Risk analysis* (assess potential risks and vulnerabilities to the confidentiality, integrity, and availability of EPHI) • *Risk management* (implement security measures sufficient to reduce risks and vulnerabilities to a reasonable and appropriate level) • *Sanction policy* (apply appropriate penalties against workforce members who fail to comply with the security policies and procedures of the covered entity) • *Information system activity review* (implement procedures to regularly review records of information system activity such as audit logs, access reports, and security incident tracking reports)
Assigned security responsibility	Identify the security official responsible for development and implementation of security policies and procedures.
Workforce security	Ensure that all workforce members have appropriate access to EPHI, and prevent those workforce members who do not have access from obtaining access to EPHI: • *Authorization and/or supervision* of workforce members who work with EPHI or in locations where PHI might be accessed • *Workforce clearance* to determine that the access of a workforce member to EPHI is appropriate • *Terminating access* to EPHI when the employment of a workforce member ends
Information access management	Authorizing access to EPHI: • *Isolating health care clearinghouse functions* if a health care clearinghouse is part of a larger organization; the clearinghouse must implement policies and procedures that protect EPHI of the clearinghouse from unauthorized access by the larger organization • *Authorizing access* to EPHI (e.g., workstation) • *Establishing and modifying access* to a transaction, program, or process
Security awareness and training	Security awareness and training program for all workforce members: • *Security reminders* via periodic security updates and protection from malicious software to guard against, detect, and report malicious software • *Log-in monitoring* to investigate log-in attempts and report discrepancies • *Password management* to create, change, and safeguard passwords
Security incident procedures	Address security incidents through *response and reporting:* • *Identify and respond* to suspected or known security incidents • *Mitigate,* to the extent practicable, harmful effects of security incidents that are known to the covered entity • *Document* security incidents and their outcomes
Contingency plan	Respond to an emergency or other occurrence (e.g., fire, vandalism, system failure, natural disaster) that damages systems containing EPHI: • *Data backup plan* to create and maintain retrievable, exact copies of EPHI • *Disaster recovery plan* to restore any loss of data

(Continues)

TABLE 9-1A HIPAA Security Rule—Administrative Safeguards and Implementation Specifications (*Continued*)

Administrative Safeguards	Implementation Specifications for Covered Entities
	• *Emergency mode operation plan* to enable continuation of critical business processes for protection of the security of EPHI while operating in emergency mode • *Testing and revision procedures* for periodic testing and revision of contingency plans • *Applications and data criticality analysis* to assess the relative criticality of specific applications and data in support of other contingency plan components
Evaluation	Perform periodic technical and nontechnical evaluations, based initially upon the standards implemented under this rule, and, subsequently in response to environmental or operational changes affecting the security of EPHI, which establishes the extent to which an entity's security policies and procedures meet security requirements.
Associate contracts and other arrangements	Permit a business associate to create, receive, maintain, or transmit EPHI on the covered entity's behalf *only* if the covered entity obtains satisfactory assurances that the business associate will appropriately safeguard the information.

TABLE 9-1B HIPAA Security Rule—Physical Safeguards and Implementation Specifications

Physical Safeguards	Implementation Specifications for Covered Entities
Facility access controls	Limit physical access to electronic information systems, and the facility or facilities in which they are housed, while ensuring that properly authorized access is allowed: • *Contingency operations* to allow facility access in support of restoration of lost data under the disaster recovery plan and emergency mode operations plan in the event of an emergency • *Facility security plan* to safeguard the facility and the equipment therein from unauthorized physical access, tampering, and theft • *Access control and validation procedures* to control and validate a person's access to facilities based on their role or function, including visitor control and control of access to software programs for testing and revision • *Maintenance records* to document repairs and modifications to the physical components of a facility that are related to security (e.g., hardware, walls, doors, locks)
Workstation use	Specify proper functions to be performed, the manner in which those functions are to be performed, and the physical attributes of the surroundings of a specific workstation or class of workstation that can access EPHI.
Workstation security	Physical safeguards for all workstations that access EPHI to restrict access to authorized users.
Device and media controls	Govern the receipt and removal of hardware and electronic media that contain EPHI into and out of a facility, and the movement of these items within the facility: • *Disposal* of EPHI and/or the hardware or electronic media on which it is stored • *Media re-use* to remove EPHI from electronic media before the media are made available for re-use • *Accountability* to maintain a record of the movements of hardware and electronic media and any person responsible therefore • *Data backup and storage* to create a retrievable, exact copy of EPHI, when needed, before relocating equipment

TABLE 9-1C HIPAA Security Rule—Technical Safeguards and Implementation Specifications

Technical Safeguards	Implementation Specifications for Covered Entities
Access control	Maintain EPHI to allow access only to those persons or software programs that have been granted access rights: • *Unique user identification* to assign a unique name and/or number for identifying and tracking user identity • *Emergency access procedure* to obtain necessary EPHI during an emergency • *Automatic log-off* electronic procedures that terminate an electronic session after a predetermined time of inactivity • *Encryption and decryption* mechanism to encrypt and decrypt EPHI
Audit controls	Hardware, software, and/or procedural mechanisms that record and examine activity in information systems that contain or use EPHI.
Integrity	Protect EPHI from improper alteration or destruction: • *Mechanism to authenticate EPHI* to corroborate that information has not been altered or destroyed in an unauthorized manner
Person or entity authentication	Verify that a person or entity seeking access to EPHI is the one claimed.
Transmission security	Technical security measures to guard against unauthorized access to EPHI that is being transmitted over an electronic communications network: • *Integrity controls* to ensure that electronically transmitted EPHI is not improperly modified without detection until disposed of • *Encryption mechanism* to encrypt EPHI whenever deemed appropriate
Business associate contracts or other arrangements	• Contracts or other arrangements between the covered entity and its business associate must meet HIPAA requirements
Requirements for group health plans	Ensure that its plan documents provide that the plan sponsor will reasonably and appropriately safeguard EPHI created, received, maintained, or transmitted to or by the plan sponsor on behalf of the group health plan.
Policies and procedures	Comply with the standards, implementation specifications, or other requirements of the security rule.
Documentation	Comply in written (which may be electronic) form; and if an action, activity, or assessment is required to be documented, maintain a written (which may be electronic) record of the action, activity, or assessment: • *Time limit* to retain required documentation is for six years from the date of its creation or the date when it last was in effect, whichever is later • *Availability*—documentation must be made available to those persons responsible for implementing the procedures to which the documentation pertains • *Updates*—documentation must be reviewed periodically and updated as needed in response to environmental or operational changes affecting the security of the EPHI

Note: While *security* and *privacy* are linked, do not confuse the purpose of each rule. The *security rule* defines administrative, physical, and technical safeguards to protect the availability, confidentiality, and integrity of EPHI. The standards require covered entities to implement basic safeguards to protect EPHI from unauthorized access, alteration, deletion, and transmission. In contrast, the *privacy rule* establishes standards for how EPHI should be controlled; it also establishes what uses (e.g., continuity of care) and disclosures (e.g., third-party reimbursement) are authorized or required as well as what rights patients have with respect to their health information (e.g., patient access).

EXERCISE 9–3 Confidentiality of Information and HIPAA Privacy and Security Provisions

True/False: Indicate whether each statement is true (T) or false (F).

_____ 1. The "accountability" aspect of HIPAA protects health information coverage for workers and their families when they change or lose their jobs.

_____ 2. The HIPAA privacy rule established standards to protect the confidentiality of individually identifiable health information.

_____ 3. The HIPAA privacy rule preempts stricter state laws such as disclosure of mental health records.

_____ 4. Electronic transmission of protected health information is impacted by the HIPAA security rule.

_____ 5. National standards to protect the confidentiality and availability of EPHI were established by the HIPAA security rule.

LEGISLATION THAT IMPACTS HEALTH INFORMATION MANAGEMENT

In the United States, protection of health information is generally divided between coverage for record-keeping systems maintained by federal (Table 9-2) and state (Table 9-3) government agencies and those maintained by the private sector. Federal protection measures are found in constitutional law, the Privacy Act of 1974, and statutes that regulate narrow areas of data use. State laws generally define the types of health information considered confidential and the circumstances under which the information can be shared without patient authorization. Information maintained by the private sector is regulated by laws that address specific types of organizations.

Note: The HITECH Act extends certain HIPAA privacy and security requirements and increases enforcement. For the most current information on the impact of the HITECH Act visit www.ahima.org and search on HITECH Act.

EXERCISE 9–4 Legislation That Impacts Health Information Management

Short Answer: Identify the federal law or regulation described below.

1. Requires that drug and alcohol abuse patient records be kept confidential and are not subject to disclosure except as provided by law.

2. Federal law that established the National Practitioner Data Bank (NPDB).

3. Established the Nursing Home Reform Act to ensure that residents of nursing facilities receive quality care and established a Residents' Bill of Rights.

4. Created a data bank to combat fraud and abuse in the health care industry, alerting users to conduct a comprehensive review of health care providers' past actions.

5. Federal legislation that mandated administrative simplification regulations to govern privacy, security, and electronic transaction standards for health care information.

RELEASE OF PROTECTED HEALTH INFORMATION

Individuals who work in health care settings have the responsibility for maintaining confidentiality of PHI and appropriately disclosing (releasing) that information if requested to do so. The *medical record* generated and maintained in the process of patient treatment contains PHI, and it is important not only to appropriately release a patient's PHI but also to *not* include information about care related to another patient, peer review or quality management documents, correspondence or notes from attorneys, and aberrant or deviant statements.

- Filing documents in a patient's record related to care provided to another patient occurs when material is misfiled in the wrong record. If these records are released in error, the provider is subject to possible civil lawsuit for breach of confidentiality.
- Including peer review, quality management documents, and correspondence or notes from attorneys in the patient record creates a dangerous situation—health care facilities generate these documents as internal documents for administrative purposes. Mistakenly including them in a patient's record subjects them to disclosure upon a third party's (e.g., plaintiff's attorney) request for information.
- Aberrant or deviant statements about the patient do not belong in the record. (Author Michelle Green recalls a situation as director of medical records when a copy of a patient's record was appropriately released to the patient. Upon review of the record, it was discovered that a nurse documented ". . . what a son of a bitch . . ." the patient was to care for.

TABLE 9-2 Federal Legislation That Impacts Health Information Management

Federal Law or Regulation	Description
Conditions of Participation (CoP) and Conditions for Coverage (CfC)	Federal regulations that health care organizations must meet to participate in the Medicare and Medicaid programs. Organizations include: • Ambulatory surgery centers (ASCs) • Comprehensive outpatient rehabilitation facilities (CORFs) • Critical access hospitals (CAHs) • Diabetes self-management training services • End-stage renal disease (ESRD) facilities • Home health agencies (HHAs) • Hospice • Hospitals • Intermediate care facilities for persons with mental retardation (ICFMR) • Long-term care facilities • Organ procurement organizations (OPOs) • Outpatient physical therapy providers • Programs of all-inclusive care for the elderly (PACE) • Psychiatric hospitals and units • Rehabilitation hospitals and units • Religious nonmedical health care institutions • Rural health clinics (RHCs)/federally qualified health centers (FQHCs) • Transplant hospitals
Drug Abuse and Treatment Act of 1972	Federal law requiring that drug and alcohol abuse patient records be kept confidential and not subject to disclosure except as provided by law. Applies to federally assisted alcohol or drug abuse programs that provide diagnosis, treatment, or referral for treatment of drug and/or alcohol abuse.
Emergency Medical Treatment and Labor Act (EMTALA)	Federal statute that addressed the problem of hospitals failing to screen, treat, or appropriately transfer patients by establishing criteria for the discharge and transfer of Medicare and Medicaid patients. (EMTALA is called the "antidumping" statute.)
Federal Patient Self-Determination Act	Requires consumers to be provided with informed consent, information about their right to make advance health care decisions (or advance directives), and information about state laws that impact legal choices in making health care decisions.
Freedom of Information Act of 1966	Allows open access to federal agency records, except for those with specific exemptions.
Health Care Quality Improvement Act of 1986	Federal law that established the National Practitioner Data Base (NPDB), which contains information about practitioners' credentials, including previous medical malpractice payment and adverse action history.
Health Insurance Portability and Accountability Act of 1996 (HIPAA)	Federal legislation that mandated administrative simplification regulations that govern privacy, security, and electronic transactions standards for health care information.
Healthcare Integrity and Protection Data Bank (HIPDB)	The HIPDB was created to combat fraud and abuse in health insurance and health care delivery by alerting users to conduct a comprehensive review of a practitioner's, provider's, or supplier's past actions.

(Continues)

TABLE 9-2 Federal Legislation That Impacts Health Information Management (*Continued*)

Federal Law or Regulation	Description
Occupational Safety & Health Act of 1970 (OSH Act)	The OSH Act created the **Occupational Safety & Health Administration (OSHA)** in 1971. Since OSHA was established, workplace fatalities have been reduced from 38 fatal injuries a day in 1970 to 12 in 2012; this is the lowest total since the fatal injury census was first conducted in 1992. In 2013, 4,405 workers died on the job—a significant decline from the 14,000 yearly workplace fatalities prior to OSHA's creation. Workplace fatalities have been reduced by more than 65 percent, and occupational injury and illness rates have declined by 67 percent. At the same time, U.S. employment has almost doubled (www.osha.gov/oshstats/commonstats.html; accessed November 12, 2014).
Omnibus Budget Reconciliation Act of 1987	Federal legislation that created the Nursing Home Reform Act, which ensures that residents of nursing homes receive quality care, requires the provision of certain services to each resident, and establishes a Residents' Bill of Rights.
Omnibus Budget Reconciliation Act of 1990	Federal legislation that requires reporting of adverse actions by CMS to state medical boards and licensing agencies.
Patient Access to Records	The HIPAA Privacy Rule states that "an individual has the right to inspect and obtain a copy of the individual's protected health information (PHI) in a designated record set," except for: • Psychotherapy notes • Information compiled in anticipation of or use in a civil, criminal, or administrative action or proceeding • PHI subject to *Clinical Laboratory Improvements Amendments (CLIA)* of 1988, the federal law that delineates requirements for certification of clinical laboratories • PHI exempt from CLIA (e.g., information generated by facilities that perform forensic testing procedures) *Note:* Individual states (e.g., New York State) may have passed laws or established regulations for patient access to records; providers must follow these laws or regulations if they are stricter than HIPAA provisions.
Patient Safety and Quality Improvement Act of 2005	Federal legislation that amends Title IX of the Public Health Service Act encourages the confidential reporting of health care mistakes to **patient safety organizations (PSOs)**. Hospitals, doctors, and other health care providers can voluntarily report health care mistakes to a PSO. The PSO will analyze the reported information on a privileged and confidential basis. The legislation includes the following: • Confidential protections for information that is gathered during the review process • Requirements that entities must meet to become PSOs • Processes for the review and acceptance of PSO certifications
Privacy Act of 1974	Federal code of fair information practices that mandates how government agencies (e.g., military) shall maintain records about individuals. Applies to government records that: • Contain information on individuals • Are maintained by a government agency or its contractors • Are retrieved by a personal identifier (e.g., person's name, Social Security number, medical record number) *Note:* Individuals can request access to their own records in writing or in person, except when records contain information that could have an "adverse effect." In that case, the record is sent to a representative (e.g., family doctor) willing to review the record and inform the individual of its contents.

(*Continues*)

TABLE 9-2 Federal Legislation That Impacts Health Information Management (*Continued*)

Federal Law or Regulation	Description
Uniform Healthcare Information Act (UHIA)	Federal legislation that serves as a model for state adoption and provides rules about health information management. Includes the following provisions: • Providers are prohibited from disclosing information to a third party without patient authorization. • Providers are not required to provide patient information during a legal proceeding unless the patient has provided authorization in writing to the release, except in certain circumstances (e.g., *subpoena duces tecum*). • Patients can have access to their own records (but providers can deny access). • Patients can request providers to amend or correct patient information (but providers can refuse to amend or correct information). (Figure 9-7 is a reproduction of the form and instructions used by the Indian Health Service for patients to request a correction or amendment to their PHI.) *Note:* As of this writing, only Montana and Washington had enacted this model legislation. (This may explain HIPAA's privacy provisions.)

TABLE 9-3 State Legislation That Impacts Health Information Management

State Law or Regulation	Description
Mental Health Records	State laws govern patient access and restrictions on disclosure of mental health records. *Example:* California statutes specify that "no provider of health care, health care service plan, or contractor shall disclose medical information regarding a patient of the provider of health care or an enrollee or subscriber of a health care service plan without first obtaining an authorization . . . ."
Reportable Diseases	Each state establishes a list of reportable communicable and other diseases for which providers must submit patient information to appropriate state agencies. • *Local county public health department and the state department of health:* cancer, human immunodeficiency virus (HIV), infectious diseases including isolated cases as well as community and/or facility outbreaks (e.g., encephalitis), nursing facility elder abuse, rabies, and sexually transmitted diseases (e.g., syphilis). *Note:* Any infectious diseases involving military personnel are also reported to the local military base's office of preventive medicine (e.g., MacDill Air Force Base in Tampa, Florida).
Reportable Events	Each state establishes a list of reportable events for which providers must submit patient information to appropriate agencies. • *Local law enforcement agencies:* assault and battery, child abuse, child malnourishment, child neglect, dog bites, gunshot wounds, motor vehicle accidents, rape, sexual assault, stabbings, and any accidental injuries occurring on public property. (**Assault** is an unlawful threat or attempt to do bodily harm to another, such as threatening to withhold medication from a patient or to place the patient in restraints. **Battery** is unlawful touching, such as a surgeon performing a procedure on a patient without having obtained consent.) *Note:* State departments of health usually provide a toll-free number to report child abuse, child malnourishment, and child neglect.

(Continues)

TABLE 9-3 State Legislation That Impacts Health Information Management (*Continued*)

State Law or Regulation	Description
	• *State poison control centers:* any overdose, regardless of whether accidental or intentional. • *Organ and tissue donor agencies:* deaths and imminent deaths of patients who are initially screened (by telephone) for potential donation. If a patient meets initial screening criteria, further workup may lead to an eventual request to the family for organ donation. • *State department of health:* hospital-wide reportable events such as wrong patient, wrong site (surgical procedures), incorrect procedure or treatment, unintentionally retained foreign body due to inaccurate surgical count or break in procedural technique, cardiac and/or respiratory arrest requiring basic life support (BLS) or advanced cardiac life support (ACLS) intervention, errors of omission or delay in treatment resulting in death or serious injury related to the patient's underlying condition, malfunction of equipment during treatment or diagnosis, or a defective product causing death or serious injury. *Note:* Some states require adverse events to be reported using special software, such as the New York Patient Occurrence Reporting Tracking System (NYPORTS). The data is made available to the public. In addition a *root cause analysis* must be performed on any event assigned ICD-9-CM codes 900–963, which is a process intended to find out what happened, why it happened, and what the facility can do to prevent it from happening again.
Retention of Records	State laws govern retention of records. Refer to the Chapter 4 discussion of this topic.

The hospital administrator instructed Green to have the nurse remove the comment and rewrite that page of notes; Green refused to carry out this instruction, stating it would be considered tampering with the record, which is illegal.)

Note: Disclosure of PHI is related to the ownership and physical control of the medical record (including x-ray films, scans, and so on).

Remember! While the health care provider owns the medical record, the patient owns the information contained in the medical record. This means that third parties that have a legitimate interest in medical record content have the legal right to request access to PHI. The provider is responsible for ensuring that PHI is released in accordance with federal (e.g., HIPAA Privacy Rule) and state laws.

The Health Insurance Portability and Accountability Act (HIPAA) of 1996 and state confidentiality laws control the disclosure of information from patient records. The following must be considered:

- When an authorization to disclose PHI is required and when it is *not* required
- Special circumstances that impact disclosure of PHI (e.g., correctional facilities, HIV, military records)

- Patient access to records
- Accounting of disclosures of PHI
- Prohibition on redisclosure of PHI
- Use of release of information log to document disclosure of PHI

In most circumstances, the patient (or legal representative) controls the disclosure of PHI to third parties (e.g., insurance company) because an authorization for release of PHI must be obtained prior to disclosure. HIPAA and state laws establish standards for content of the authorization form, with state laws superseding HIPAA only if they contain stricter provisions.

Authorization to Disclose PHI Is Not Required

According to HIPAA, the following uses and disclosures of PHI do *not* require the covered entity (e.g., provider) to obtain consent or authorization from the patient, or to provide the opportunity for the patient to agree or object to disclosure:

- Health oversight activities
- Public health activities
- Law enforcement purposes
- Judicial and administrative proceedings

IHS-917 (4/09)   FRONT

FORM APPROVED: OMB NO. 0917-0030
Expiration Date: 4/30/2016
See OMB Statement on Reverse.

DEPARTMENT OF HEALTH AND HUMAN SERVICES
Indian Health Service

REQUEST FOR CORRECTION/AMENDMENT OF PROTECTED HEALTH INFORMATION

PATIENT NAME

DATE OF BIRTH

PATIENT RECORD NUMBER

PATIENT ADDRESS

DATE OF ENTRY TO BE CORRECTED/AMENDED

INFORMATION TO BE CORRECTED/AMENDED

Please explain how the entry is incorrect or incomplete. What should the entry say to be more accurate or complete? Use additional sheets if needed and attach to this form.

If you agree, IHS will make a reasonable effort to provide the amendment to other persons who IHS knows received the information in the past and who may have relied, or are likely to rely, on such information in a manner that may be detrimental to your health care.

☐ I agree to allow IHS to release any amended information to individuals or entities as described above.

Would you like this amendment sent to anyone else who received the information in the past?   ☐ Yes   ☐ No
If yes, please specify the name and address of the organization(s) or individual(s).

SIGNATURE OF PATIENT OR PERSONAL REPRESENTATIVE
(If Personal Representative, state relationship to patient)

DATE

SIGNATURE OF WITNESS *(If signature of patient is a thumbprint or mark)*

DATE

FOR IHS USE ONLY

DATE RECEIVED

AMENDMENT HAS BEEN

☐ Accepted   ☐ Denied

IF DENIED, CHECK REASON FOR DENIAL

☐ PHI is not part of the patient's designated record set

☐ Record is not available to the patient for inspection under Federal law

☐ IHS did not create record

☐ Record is accurate and complete

COMMENTS OF HEALTHCARE PROVIDER *(If applicable)*

SIGNATURE OF HEALTHCARE PROVIDER *(If applicable)*

TITLE

DATE

SIGNATURE OF CEO OR DESIGNEE

DATE

PSC Graphics (301) 443-1090   EF

FIGURE 9-7 Request to Correct/Amend PHI (Permission to reprint in accordance with IHS.gov Web reuse policy.)

IHS-917 (4/09) BACK

Instructions for Completing IHS Form 917 –
Request for Correction/Amendment of Protected Health Information (PHI)

1. Print legibly in all fields using dark permanent ink.

2. Sign and date the request.

3. Submit the completed and signed form to the Chief Executive Officer (CEO) or designee.

4. You will receive a photocopy of your completed form, as an acknowledgement of receipt of your request, no later than 10 business days after IHS receives your request.

5. You will be notified of the acceptance or denial of your request.

6. If you agree to allow IHS to release any amended information and if your request to amend is accepted:
   a. If you are a U.S. citizen or alien lawfully admitted for permanent residence, IHS is required by law to notify any previous recipient of the record in question of the corrective action taken, if IHS made an accounting of such disclosure.
   b. Regardless of your citizenship status, IHS will make reasonable efforts to send any amended or corrected information to anyone who IHS knows received this information in the past and who may have relied, or is likely to rely, on such information to your detriment.
   c. IHS will make reasonable efforts to send the correction or amendment to those individuals or entities/organizations you identify and who have a need for the correction or amendment.

7. If you are not a U.S. citizen or alien lawfully admitted for permanent residence, and your request is denied, you may do the following:
   a. Submit to the Service Unit CEO a one page written statement disagreeing with the denial and the basis of such disagreement.
   b. If you do not submit a statement of disagreement, you may request that IHS provide this request for correction or amendment (or summary) and the denial with any future disclosures.
   c. IHS has the right to prepare a written rebuttal to any statement of disagreement. You will be provided a copy of any rebuttal statement. Any written rebuttal prepared by IHS is not subject to correction or amendment.

8. If you are a U.S. citizen or alien lawfully admitted for permanent residence, and your request is denied, you may do the following:
   a. Appeal the refusal to correct or amend the requested information to the Area Director.
   b. In the event your appeal is ultimately denied, or if you elect not to appeal, you may submit a statement of disagreement or request as described in 7(a) and 7(b) above.
   c. IHS has the right to prepare a written rebuttal to any statement of disagreement. You will be provided a copy of any rebuttal statement. Any written rebuttal prepared by IHS is not subject to correction or amendment.
   d. In addition, if your appeal is denied, you may seek judicial review of the decision.

9. If you have a complaint about IHS' policies and procedures regarding health information, you may file such a complaint with the Service Unit CEO; Department of Health and Human Services, Office for Civil Rights; or with the Secretary, Department of Health and Human Services, Washington, DC 20201.

10. This form and subsequent information pertaining to this request will become part of your permanent health record.

FOR IHS CEO: Insert Service Unit address, CEO's name & Title, and Telephone # into area below.

OMB STATEMENT

Public reporting burden for this collection of information is estimated to average 15 minutes per response including time for reviewing instructions, searching existing data sources, gathering and maintaining the data needed, and completing and reviewing the collection of information. An agency may not conduct or sponsor, and a person is not required to respond to, a collection of information unless it displays a currently valid OMB control number. Send comments regarding this burden estimate or any other aspect of this collection of information, including suggestions for reducing this burden to: Indian Health Service, 801 Thompson Ave., TMP Suite 450, Rockville, MD 20852, RE: PRA 0917-0030. Please DO NOT SEND this form to this address.

FIGURE 9-7 Request to Correct/Amend PHI (*Continued*) (Permission to reprint in accordance with IHS.gov Web reuse policy.)

- Identification and location purposes
- Decedents who are deceased over 50 years
- Research purposes
- FDA
- Specialized government functions (e.g., military and veterans activities)
- Workers' compensation

Health Oversight Activities Authorized by Law

The covered entity (e.g., provider) may disclose PHI to health oversight agencies for activities authorized by law, including:

- Audits (e.g., quality improvement organization, QIO, studies)
- Civil, administrative, or criminal investigations (e.g., state office of professional misconduct)
- Inspections (e.g., state department of health on-site inspection, OSHA)
- Licensure or disciplinary actions (e.g., physician disciplinary action)
- Civil, administrative, or criminal proceedings or actions (e.g., *subpoena duces tecum* issued for records in a medical malpractice lawsuit)
- Other activities necessary for appropriate oversight of health care system (e.g., government benefit programs such as Medicare and Medicaid)

Note: If a covered entity is also a health oversight agency, the covered entity may use PHI for health oversight activities as outlined above.

Public Health Activities

The covered entity (e.g., provider) may disclose PHI for public health activities and purposes to:

- Public health authorities authorized by law to collect or receive reportable disease and/or event information (e.g., births, deaths, cancer cases)
- Public health authority or other government authority authorized by law to receive reports of child abuse or neglect (e.g., local law enforcement)
- FDA for the purpose of tracking products; enabling product recalls, repairs, or replacement; and conducting post-marketing surveillance (e.g., adverse events, product defects or problems, or biological product deviations)
- Person(s) who may have been exposed to a communicable disease or may otherwise be at risk of contracting or spreading a disease or condition (e.g., sexually transmitted disease)
- Employer, about an employee, to evaluate whether the individual has a work-related illness or injury (e.g., employee uses workers' compensation benefits to receive health care services)

Law Enforcement Agencies

A covered entity may disclose PHI about victims of abuse, neglect, or domestic violence to a governmental authority that is authorized to receive such reports. The covered entity must promptly inform the individual that a report has been or will be made unless the covered entity:

- Believes that notification would place the individual at risk of serious harm
- Would be notifying a personal representative who is responsible for the abuse, neglect, or other injury (and, as such, would not act in the individual's best interests)

A covered entity may also disclose PHI to law enforcement officials:

- When reporting certain types of wounds and injuries (e.g., gunshot wounds)
- In response to a law enforcement official's request to assist in identifying or locating a suspect, fugitive, material witness, or missing person; only the following information may be disclosed:
  - Name and address
  - Date and place of birth
  - SSN
  - ABO blood type and Rh factor
  - Type of injury
  - Date and time of treatment
  - Date and time of death
  - Distinguishing physical characteristics, including weight, gender, race, hair and eye color, presence or absence of facial hair, scars, and tattoos

Note: The covered entity may *not* disclose for identification or location purposes any PHI relating to DNA or DNA analysis; dental records; or typing, samples, or analysis of body fluids or tissues.

The covered entity may disclose PHI in response to a law enforcement official's request relating to an individual who is (or is suspected of being) a victim of a crime if the:

- Individual (alleged victim) agrees
- Covered entity is unable to obtain an individual's agreement because of incapacity or other emergency provided that the:
  - Law enforcement official needs the information to determine if someone else committed a crime, and the PHI will not be used against the victim
  - Immediate law enforcement activity that depends on disclosure of the PHI would be materially and adversely affected by waiting
  - Covered entity, exercising professional judgment, believes disclosure is in the best interest of the victim

The covered entity may disclose a decedent's (dead person's) PHI to law enforcement if the death is suspected as resulting from criminal conduct and/or there is possible evidence that a crime was committed on the premises of the covered entity. Typically, suspicious deaths become coroner or medical examiner cases. A coroner is a public officer who investigates deaths due to other than natural causes. A medical examiner is a physician officially authorized by a governmental agency to determine causes of deaths, especially those due to other than natural causes.

Note: A medical examiner is always a physician, but a coroner might not be a physician. Coroners are elected individuals who are interested in this field (e.g., funeral director, veterinarians, and even health care professors).

A covered entity that provides off-site emergency medical care may report PHI to alert law enforcement as to the commission and nature of a crime, location of the crime and of crime victim(s), and the identity, description, and location of the perpetrator. PHI may be disclosed to a correctional institution or to a law enforcement official with custody of the individual when PHI is necessary to provide care to the individual, or for the health and safety of the individual, other inmates, correctional employees, transport employees, law enforcement personnel at the location, and for the safety, security, and good order of the institution. Covered entities that are correctional institutions may use PHI for any purpose. *An individual is no longer an inmate once released on parole, probation or supervised release, or is otherwise no longer in lawful custody.*

Judicial or Administrative Proceedings

A covered entity may disclose PHI in the course of any judicial or administrative proceeding in response to a(n):

- Court order, but only the PHI expressly authorized for release by such order
- *Subpoena duces tecum,* if the covered entity has satisfactory assurance:
  - From the party seeking the PHI that reasonable efforts have been made to give the individual notice of the request
  - From the party seeking the PHI that reasonable efforts have been made to secure a qualified protective order
  - That the individual has been given notice. This condition may be met by provision of a written statement and accompanying documentation demonstrating that the
    - party requesting the PHI has made a good faith attempt to provide written notice to the individual
    - notice includes sufficient information about the litigation or proceeding to permit the individual to raise an objection in the tribunal, and
    - time to raise objections has lapsed and either no objection was filed or objections have been resolved in a manner consistent with disclosure
  - That reasonable efforts have been made to secure a qualified protective order. This may be met by provision of a written statement and accompanying documentation demonstrating that the parties to the dispute have agreed to a qualified protective order and presented it to the tribunal, or the party seeking the PHI has requested a qualified protective order from the tribunal.

A qualified protective order prohibits the use or disclosure of PHI for any purpose beyond the litigation at hand, and requires that the PHI, and all copies, be returned to the covered entity or destroyed when the litigation ends.

Identification and Location Purposes

Information for the identification and location of an individual is limited to the following:

- Name and address
- Date and place of birth
- SSN
- ABO blood type and Rh factor
- Type of injury
- Date and time of treatment
- Date and time of death
- Description of physical characteristics

Note: DNA, dental records, typing samples, or analysis of body fluids or tissue cannot be disclosed unless the request for information is accompanied by appropriate legal documents or the individual authorizes disclosure.

The de-identification of protected health information (PHI) contains no identification information about an individual; de-identified information can be disclosed (e.g., for research purposes) if nothing can individually identify the patient. The following identifiers are removed:

- Names
- Addresses and other geographic identifiers
- Relatives

- Employers or household members
- Zip codes
- All dates (except years) related to an individual
- Numbers
  - Telephone
  - Fax
  - SSN
  - Medical records
  - Beneficiary numbers
  - Account numbers
  - Certificate/license numbers
  - VIN numbers
  - License plate numbers
  - Device identifiers and serial numbers
  - URLs
  - IP address
  - Biometric identifiers
  - Photographic images and any other unique identifying number, characteristic, or code

Decedents

Covered entities are allowed to disclose PHI to the following in order to carry out their duties with respect to the deceased person:

- Coroners and medical examiners
- Funeral directors
- Cadaver organ, eye, or tissue donation purposes

Research Purposes

Most health care providers routinely allow medical professionals engaged in clinical or epidemiological research to access patient records, abstract individually identifiable information (e.g., date of birth, birthplace), and exchange that information with other researchers. A covered entity may use or disclose PHI without obtaining written authorization of the individual for activities and purposes associated with research *that has been approved by an institutional review board (IRB) or a privacy board.* While it is not practical to require researchers to obtain authorizations from patients, it is necessary to review and approve research projects so that patients' privacy is protected.

Note: An authorization for the use and disclosure of PHI *is* required when research includes the actual treatment of the individual.

Example 1
The search for the cause of Legionnaires' disease would have been almost impossible to conduct if researchers had been required to obtain patient authorizations before reviewing medical records. (Some victims were not located until months after the event.)

Example 2
A researcher conducting a follow-up study of individuals who had been enrolled in a methadone maintenance program had the name and address of one individual who had been enrolled several years previously. The researcher went to the individual's residence on a Saturday night, interrupting a party, and announced "Hi, I am so-and-so from such-and-such an organization, and we are doing a follow-up study of patients who had been enrolled in the methadone maintenance program."

Food and Drug Administration (FDA)

A covered entity may disclose PHI without obtaining authorization from the individual to the jurisdiction of the Food and Drug Administration regarding FDA-regulated products or activities related to quality, safety, or effectiveness of products or activities and to collect or report adverse events, product defects, or problems. Such disclosure allows for the tracking of FDA-regulated products to enable recalls, repairs, or replacements. Individuals can be located and notified about product defects or problems, and post-marketing surveillance can be conducted.

Specialized Government Functions

A covered entity may use or disclose protected health information (PHI) without obtaining authorization from the individual for the following:

- Medicare
- Medicaid
- Military and veterans activities
- Armed forces personnel
- National security and intelligence activities
- Protective services for the president and others
- Medical suitability determinations
- Correctional institutions for the provision of health care

Note: Proper procedure and appropriate documentation is required from the requesting source.

Example Army patients often transport their own medical records from one military location to another, and in the process soldiers occasionally discard their records accidentally. Many military bases release medical records in a "can" so that "garbage pickers" can go through dumpsters on a weekly basis to look for the cans and return them (with medical records inside) to the medical records department. Some soldiers place their medical records at the bottom of their duffel bag and forget about them. When the soldier cannot find the record, the Army gets blamed for the loss. Sometimes soldiers even remove reports from their records because they are afraid that such information will be held against them for promotion purposes. The Army recognizes these problems and is taking several steps to resolve them. The electronic medical record (EHR) is one such measure; another is ensuring that the permanent record does not deploy with the soldier. The Army piloted a smartcard program for identity authentication as an alternative to username/password login to Army and Department of Defence websites.

Workers' Compensation

A covered entity may disclose protected health information to comply with workers' compensation laws that provide benefits for work-related injuries or illness regardless of fault.

Note: Many state laws prohibit disclosure of PHI for workers' compensation purposes unless the patient has signed an authorization for release of information. In these circumstances, state law supersedes the HIPAA privacy standard. This means you must follow state law and obtain patient authorization to release information for workers' compensation purposes.

Authorization to Disclose PHI Is Required

The patient's authorization to disclose PHI must be obtained for the following circumstances:

- Attorney requests (*except* the provider's attorney when the PHI is released during a normal course of business, such as to prepare for a medical malpractice lawsuit)
- Compound authorizations for research, with certain rules attached.
- Employers (*except* when PHI is released to report work-related illnesses or injuries)
- Government agencies (e.g., Department of Social Services, Bureau of Disability Determinations, and so on)
- Health care providers that did not render care to the patient
- HIV-related information
- Internal Revenue Service (IRS)
- Law enforcement (e.g., police, FBI, CIA, *except* when no authorization is required by HIPAA)
- Marketing communications (e.g., reports to news media)
- Patient or patient representative (*except* when no authorization is required by HIPAA)
- Research that includes treatment of an individual
- Third-party payers (e.g., insurance companies, *except* in the course of TPO)
- Workers' compensation carriers (when required by state law)

Covered entities are allowed to maintain a directory of the following patient information (unless the patient objects): patient name, location in the facility, condition described in general terms that do not communicate specific medical information, and religious affiliation. Directory information can be disclosed to members of the clergy or to other persons who ask for the individual by name.

Note: Patients must authorize any health marketing they receive, though some exceptions apply, such as prescription refill reminders. Business associates must also obtain authorizations prior to marketing, and the sale of PHI by a covered entity or business associate is prohibited and defined by the HIPAA privacy rule.

Attorney Requests

The covered entity must obtain the patient's authorization to disclose PHI to all attorneys, *except* the provider's attorney when the PHI is released during a normal course of business, such as to prepare for a medical malpractice lawsuit. Prior to processing a request for the release of PHI to an attorney, notify your facility's risk manager to determine if a review of the record should be conducted. Such a review could alert appropriate facility personnel to the potential for a lawsuit where the facility is named as defendant.

Note: Upon review of the record, the risk manager will search for any incident reports completed on the patient.

Remember! Incident reports are *never* filed in the medical record because that would subject them to disclosure. Incident reports are internal administrative documents completed by health care personnel about the events of an incident. They allow those called to testify (e.g., primary care nurse) in a lawsuit to review the events of an incident prior to testimony.

Employers

The covered entity must obtain the patient's authorization to disclose PHI to all employers, *except* when PHI is released to report work-related illnesses or injuries. In addition, as permitted by state law, covered entities may release information to self-insured employers when PHI is needed to process payment for health care provided. In this situation, self-insured employers must agree to protect the individual's data from internal disclosure that would affect the individual.

Government Agencies

The covered entity must obtain the patient's authorization to disclose PHI to all government agencies, *except* as required by HIPAA. This means that government agencies such as the Department of Social Services and the Bureau of Disability Determinations must provide a patient authorization to release PHI before receiving that information.

Health Care Providers

The covered entity must obtain the patient's authorization to disclose PHI to all health care providers, *except* those involved in direct care of the patient.

Note: When a health care provider contacts you to request PHI during an emergency situation, be sure to implement the **call-back method**, which involves obtaining the requesting provider's main number from the phonebook or directory assistance. Call the main number and ask to be connected to the requesting provider to ensure that you are speaking with an individual authorized to obtain PHI. As a follow-up, require the requesting provider to obtain the patient's authorization to release PHI and mail or email it to your attention.

HIV-Related Information

Confidential human immunodeficiency virus (HIV) related information is any information indicating that a person had an HIV-related test; or has HIV infection, HIV-related illness, or acquired immunodeficiency syndrome (AIDS); or any information that could indicate a person has been potentially exposed to HIV. Many states have passed legislation governing the release of HIV-related information, including New York State, which states:

> [C]onfidential HIV related information can only be disclosed after the patient has signed a written release [Figure 9-8]. Exceptions to this disclosure law include those who need to know a patient's HIV status to provide medical care and services, including:

- Medical care providers
- Persons involved with foster care or adoption
- Parents and guardians who consent to care of minors
- Jail, prison, probation, and parole employees
- Emergency response workers
- Other workers in hospitals, other regulated settings, or medical offices, who are exposed to blood/body fluids in the course of their employment
- Organizations that review the services the patient received

State law also allows HIV information to be released under limited circumstances:

- Special court order
- Public health officials as required by law
- Insurers as necessary to pay for care and treatment

Under state law, anyone who illegally discloses HIV related information may be punished by a fine of up to $5,000 and a jail term of up to one year.

The covered entity must obtain the patient's authorization to disclose HIV-related PHI.

Internal Revenue Service (IRS)

The covered entity must obtain the patient's authorization to disclose PHI to the Internal Revenue Service.

Law Enforcement Agencies

The covered entity must obtain the patient's authorization to disclose PHI to all law enforcement agencies, *except* when no authorization is required by HIPAA.

Marketing Communications

The covered entity must obtain the patient's authorization to disclose PHI for all marketing communications, including reports to news media. This means that a provider cannot sell PHI to a company that wants to market its products and services.

Note: HIPAA does allow for the marketing of fund-raising activities if the only PHI used or disclosed is demographic information and dates of service. However, the facility's privacy notice must describe the use and/or disclosure of individually identifiable PHI for fund raising and include information on how an individual can opt out of fund-raising mailings.

Patient or Patient Representative

The covered entity must obtain the patient's authorization to disclose PHI to the patient or patient representative, *except* when no authorization is required by HIPAA.

If urgent or continuing care is required and the patient is incapacitated, state health information disclosure laws contain provisions for a patient representative to authorize the release of PHI. If a state law does not exist, AHIMA's practice brief on disclosure states, "Information may be disclosed without patient authorization as required for continued care." In emergency situations, case law recognizes exceptions to authorization to release PHI. In an emergency situation, follow the call-back method discussed earlier in this chapter.

Note: For additional information, refer to the discussion of patient access to records that follows.

Research That Includes Treatment of an Individual

The covered entity must obtain the patient's authorization to disclose PHI to all health care providers, *except* those involved in direct care of the patient.

Third-Party Payers

The covered entity must obtain the patient's authorization to disclose PHI to all third-party payers, *except* in the course of TPO.

Alfred State Medical Center
100 Main Street
Anywhere NY 00000
(101) 555-1234

Name and address of facility/provider obtaining release:

Name of person whose HIV related information will be released:

Name(s) and address(es) of person(s) signing this form (if other than above):

Relationship to person whose HIV information will be released:

Name(s) and address(es) of person(s) who will be given HIV related information:

Reason for release of HIV related information:

Time during which release is authorized:

From: To:

The Facility/Provider obtaining this release must complete the following:

Exceptions, if any, to the right to revoke consent for disclosure: (for example cannot revoke if disclosure has already been made.)

Description of the consequences, if any, of failing to consent to disclosure upon treatment, payment, enrollment, or eligibility for benefits:

(Note: Federal privacy regulations may restrict some consequences.)

My questions about this form have been answered. I know that I do not have to allow release of HIV related information, and that I can change my mind at any time and revoke my authorization by writing the facility/provider obtaining this release.

Date   Signature

FIGURE 9-8 Authorization for Release of Confidential HIV-Related Information. (This form, and any updates to it, is available to the public on the New York State Department of Health Website, www.health.state.ny.us.) (From New York State Department of Health, http://www.health.state.ny.us.)

Workers' Compensation Carriers

The covered entity must obtain the patient's authorization to disclose PHI to all workers' compensation carriers, when required by state law.

Patient Access to Records

An individual has the right to access his or her own PHI for the purpose of inspection and to obtain a copy, *except* for the following:

- Psychotherapy notes
- Information compiled for use in a civil, criminal, or administrative action

Note: An emancipated minor may authorize disclosure of PHI. State laws define emancipated minors as married, living away from home and self-supporting, declared legally emancipated by a court of law, pregnant and unmarried, on active duty with the United States Armed Forces, at least 16 years of age and living independently from parents or guardians. In addition, if state laws permit a minor to seek alcohol or drug abuse treatment, the minor can authorize disclosure of PHI.

A covered entity can deny an individual the right to access his or her PHI if the:

- PHI is exempt from the right of access (above)
- Individual's access to PHI was created or obtained by a covered entity during research—including treatment that may be suspended while the research is in progress, *if* the individual agreed to the denial of access when consenting to participate in the research *and* if the provider informed the individual that right of access would be reinstated upon completion of research
- Individual's access to PHI is contained in records subject to the Privacy Act, which may be denied in accordance with the requirements of the Act
- PHI was obtained from someone other than a covered entity under a promise of confidentiality *and* the access would likely reveal the source of the information
- Covered entity is a correctional institution or a covered health care provider acting under direction of a correctional institution

Note: Correctional institutions may deny an inmate's access to PHI if access would jeopardize the health, safety, security, custody, or rehabilitation of the inmate or of other inmates, or the safety of any officer, employee, or other person at the correctional institution or entity responsible for transporting the inmate.

The covered entity may deny an individual access to PHI, *provided the individual is given a right to have such denials reviewed,* in the following circumstances:

- A licensed health care professional has determined, in the exercise of professional judgment, that access is likely to endanger the life or physical safety of the individual or another person.
- The PHI makes reference to another person (not a health care provider) *and* a licensed health care professional has determined, in the exercise of professional judgment, that the access requested is reasonably likely to cause substantial harm to such other person.
- The request for access is made by the individual's personal representative *and* the PHI makes reference to another person (not a health care provider) *and* a licensed health care professional has determined, in the exercise of professional judgment, that the access requested is reasonably likely to cause substantial harm to the individual or another person.

Note: If patient access to PHI is denied and the individual has the right to have the denial reviewed, that review must be conducted by a licensed health care professional designated as a reviewing official and who did not participate in the original decision to deny access.

A covered entity may require individuals to request access to PHI in writing if it has informed individuals of this requirement. The covered entity must comply with a patient access request no later than 30 days after receipt of the request, as follows:

- If the covered entity grants the request, it must inform the individual that access is provided.
- If the covered entity denies the request, it must provide the individual with a written denial.
- If the request is for access to PHI that is not maintained or accessible to the covered entity on-site, the covered entity must act on the request no later than 60 days from receipt of the request.
- If the covered entity is unable to act on the request within the appropriate time limit (30 or 60 days, as applicable), it may extend the time for such actions by no more than 30 days (if the individual has been notified in writing about the delay).

Note: The covered entity may charge a reasonable cost-based fee for copying PHI, postage, and/or preparing an explanation or summary of the PHI, if agreed to by the individual. The covered entity may not charge a fee for retrieval of PHI or monitoring an individual's review of PHI.

Disclosure of Laboratory Test Results

On February 3, 2014 the Department of Health and Human Services announced the final rule that amended the Clinical Laboratory Improvement Amendments of 1988 (CLIA) regulations to allow laboratories to give a patient, or a person designated by the patient, his or her "personal representative," access to the patient's completed test reports on the patient's or patient's personal representative's request. Therefore patients can continue to access laboratory test results from their provider's office or obtain their test reports directly from the laboratory that performed the testing. The final rule is issued jointly by three agencies within HHS:

- Centers for Medicare & Medicaid Services (CMS). CMS is responsible for laboratory regulation under CLIA.
- Centers for Disease Control and Prevention (CDC). The CDC provides scientific and technical advice to CMS related to CLIA.
- Office for Civil Rights (OCR). OCR is responsible for enforcing the HIPAA Privacy Rule.

Prohibition on Redisclosure

When copies of PHI are appropriately released to a provider, they are usually filed in the patient's current medical record. That provider is prohibited from redisclosing another entity's copies of PHI unless authorized to do so, as follows:

- The Drug Abuse and Treatment Act of 1972 requires that the following notice accompany each disclosure of PHI:

  This information has been disclosed to you from records protected by federal confidentiality rules (42 CFR Part 2). The Federal rules prohibit you from making any further disclosure of this information unless further disclosure is expressly permitted by the written consent of the person to whom it pertains or as otherwise permitted by 42 CFR Part 2. A general authorization for the release of medical or other information is not sufficient for this purpose. The Federal rules restrict any use of the information to criminally investigate or prosecute any alcohol or drug abuse patient.

- The HIPAA Final Privacy Rule requires that the patient authorization to disclose PHI contain a general statement that

  PHI may no longer be protected by the Privacy Rule once it is disclosed by the covered entity.

This means a provider *is* allowed to redisclose PHI created by another party *if* disclosure is for a purpose permitted by the privacy rule (e.g., treatment).

When releasing copies of PHI from a patient's medical record, be sure to include a cover sheet that includes a statement prohibiting redisclosure unless authorized. The following language is suggested:

  This protected health information PHI has been disclosed to you from confidential records that are protected by federal and state law. You are prohibited from redisclosure of this PHI without the specific written authorization of the individual to whom it pertains (or his representative), or as permitted by state law, or as otherwise permitted by federal law (e.g., to provide urgent patient care). Any unauthorized redisclosure in violation of federal or state law may result in a fine or jail sentence or both.

Tracking Disclosures of PHI

Health information departments have traditionally maintained a release of information log to document patient information released to authorized requestors. Data was entered manually (e.g., three-ring binder) or using tracking software. The HIPAA privacy rule requires covered entities to track the release of PHI so that individuals can obtain an accounting of disclosures for the six years prior to the date of their request, retroactive to April 16, 2003. To respond to

this requirement, each covered entity must establish a tracking mechanism and reporting process that includes the following:

- Date of disclosure
- Name and address of the entity or person who received the PHI
- Description of the PHI disclosed
- Statement of reason for disclosure (or a copy of the written request for disclosure)

Note: If an entity releases PHI to the same entity for the same reason, the first disclosure is documented, along with the number of disclosures made during the accounting period and the date of the last disclosure in the accounting period.

An individual has the right to receive an accounting of all disclosures of PHI made by a covered entity during the six years prior to the date an accounting is requested, *except* for disclosures:

- To carry out TPO
- To individuals, themselves, of PHI
- Entered in the facility's directory
- To persons involved in the individual's care
- For other notification purposes such as:
  - National security or intelligence purposes
  - Correctional institutions or law enforcement officials
  - Those that occurred prior to the compliance date for the covered entity

Note: A covered entity must temporarily suspend an individual's right to an accounting of disclosures *if* a health oversight agency or law enforcement official notifies the covered entity *in writing* that such an accounting would be reasonably likely to impede the agency's activities. The temporary suspension *must* include an expiration date.

When an individual requests an accounting of disclosed PHI, the covered entity has 60 days to act on the request, and one 30-day extension is allowed. If there is a delay in responding to the individual's request for an accounting, the covered entity must inform the individual of the delay in writing and cite a reason for the delay and the date the accounting will be provided.

Covered entities should select a method for tracking disclosures that will work best for them such as a(n):

- Computerized tracking system (use database or spreadsheet software to collect required elements and to automate production of an individual's accounting report) (Figure 9-9, Figure 9-10, Figure 9-11)

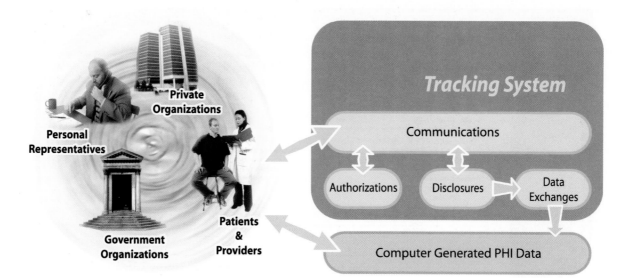

FIGURE 9-9 Flow of Released PHI Using Automated Tracking Software (Permission to reprint granted by IO Datasphere, Inc.)

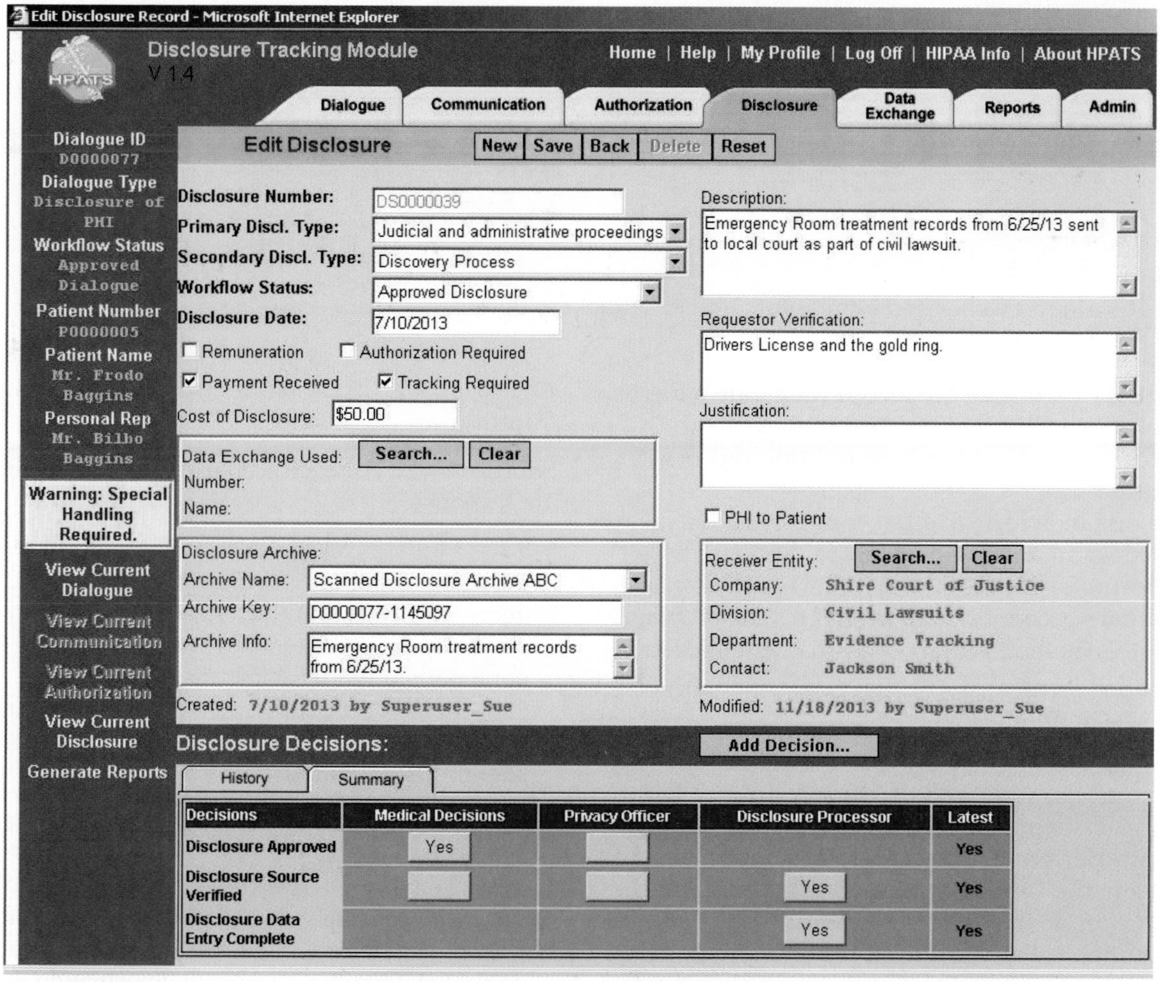

FIGURE 9-10 Disclosure Tracking Software Screen (Permission to reprint granted by IO Datasphere, Inc.)

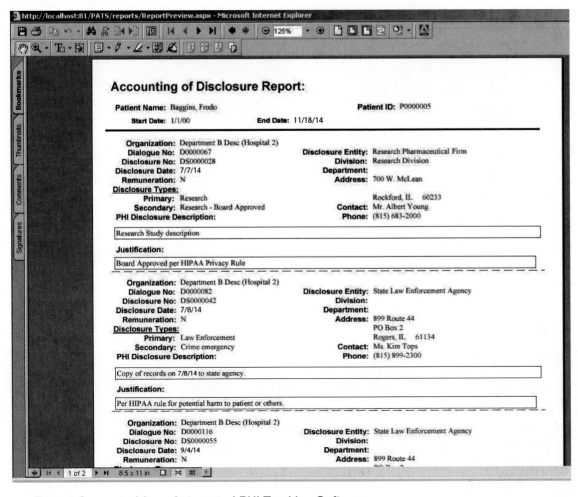

FIGURE 9-11 Report Generated from Automated PHI Tracking Software (Permission to reprint granted by IO Datasphere, Inc.)

- Manual PHI disclosure record (generate a log sheet for each individual, a copy of which serves as an individual's accounting report) (Figure 9-12)
- Authorization form (e.g., store authorization forms signed by an individual in one folder to track disclosure of PHI, copies of which serve as an individual's accounting report) (*Note:* The problem with this method is that not all disclosures require patient authorization, so this results in an incomplete accounting.)

A covered entity must provide an individual with one free accounting report during any 12-month period. Subsequent reports generated during the 12-month period can be assessed a reasonable fee (based on the entity's costs of providing the accounting report). The covered entity must inform an individual of any required fee and allow the individual an opportunity to amend his or her request to avoid or reduce the fee.

EXERCISE 9–5 Release of Protected Health Information

Short Answer: For each scenario, provide an appropriate response.

1. Miss Molly, a clerk with release of information responsibilities at New Directions Medical Center, received a call from the Pathway Drug and Alcohol Rehabilitation Center. Pathway is assuming care for a patient who is being discharged from New Directions today. Pathway is requesting that a copy of the patient's biopsychosocial report be faxed to them. What action should Miss Molly take?

2. Ms. Marie, a health information department staff member at New Directions Medical Center, received a call from the emergency department at St. John's Hospital requesting that all previous records for a patient named Sally Smith be faxed to them immediately. (Sally Smith was a health information department staff member at New Directions. She resigned

PROTECTED HEALTH INFORMATION (PHI) DISCLOSURE RECORD

Patient Name: ______________________ DOB: ____/____/____ (Month / Day / Year)

Authorized Methods of Communication (✔ Check all that apply)			
❑ *Residence Telephone*	❑ *Work Telephone*	❑ *Written Correspondence*	❑ *Other (Specify)*
Number: ( )	Number: ( )	❑ Mail/Delivery Service	
❑ Leave call back number only; do not leave message	❑ Leave call back number only; do not leave message	❑ Fax: ( )	
❑ Okay to leave detailed message with person	❑ Okay to leave detailed message with operator	❑ E-Mail @ Residence:	
❑ Okay to leave detailed message on answering machine	❑ Okay to leave detailed message on personal voice mail	❑ E-Mail @ Work:	

Patient Signature: ______________________ Date: ________

Record of Disclosures					
Date Of Disclosure	Disclosed to: Name & Address or Contact Number	Description of PHI Disclosed and Purpose of Disclosure (If a copy of the authorization or request is attached, check ❑ below.)	Type of Disclosure *Enter T, P, or O	Person Disclosing	Method of Disclosure **Enter M, P, F, E, or OT
		❑			
		❑			
		❑			
		❑			
		❑			
		❑			
		❑			
		❑			
		❑			
		❑			

*T = Treatment, P = Payment, O = Health Care Operations Activities
**M = Mail, P = Telephone, F = Fax, E = E-Mail, OT = Other (and specify mode of delivery)

ORDER #22-8404-01 · CHART ORGANIZING DIVIDERS · 2003 BIBBERO SYSTEMS, INC. · PETALUMA, CA
TO REORDER CALL TOLL FREE: (800) BIBBERO (800-242-2376) OR FAX (800) 242-9330 MFG IN U.S.A.

FIGURE 9-12 Manual PHI Disclosure Record (Reprinted with permission of Bibbero Systems, Inc., Petaluma, CA. 800 242-2376.www.bibbero.com.)

last year to return to college full-time.) Because of the urgency of her medical condition, Sally Smith is being taken to the surgery suite immediately. Ms. Marie knows Sally's family and is considering calling Sally's sister. What action should Ms. Marie take?

3. Pam Page, an office manager for Dr. Brown, receives an email from a patient requesting that she reply with his lab test results. Pam knows that the office's email system does not encrypt messages. What action should Pam take?

Internet Links

HIPAA
http://hipaa.yale.edu
DHHS Office for Civil Rights (OCR) privacy rule
http://www.hhs.gov
CMS Conditions of Participation (CoP) and Conditions for Coverage (CfC)
http://cms.hhs.gov
Electronic Privacy Information Center (EPIC)
https://epic.org

United States gateway to government information
http://www.usa.gov
Privacy Rights Clearinghouse
http://privacy.org
Federal regulatory clearinghouse
http://www.regulations.gov
Occupational Safety & Health Administration (OSHA)
https://www.osha.gov
HIMSS
http://www.himss.org

SUMMARY

Numerous sources of laws impact health care: the Constitution of the United States, individual state constitutions, administrative law, case law (or common law), and statutory law. The medical record is a legal business record that must be maintained according to accreditation standards, legal principles, professional practice standards, and regulations. The Health Insurance Portability and Accountability Act of 1996 established privacy and security provisions. Both federal and state legislation impacts health information management, and HIM professionals must manage health information according to the strictest legislation.

STUDY CHECKLIST

- Read the textbook chapter and highlight key concepts. (Use colored highlighter sparingly throughout the chapter.)
- Create an index card for each key term. (Write the key term on one side of the index card and the concept on the other. Learn the definition of each key term, and match the term to the concept.)
- Access chapter Internet links to learn more about concepts.
- Answer the chapter exercises and review questions, verifying answers with your instructor.
- Study content, view videos, and take practice tests online at www.CengageBrain.com.
- Complete lab manual assignments, verifying answers with your instructor.
- Form a study group with classmates to discuss chapter concepts in preparation for an exam.

CHAPTER REVIEW

True/False: Indicate whether the statement is true (T) or false (F).

_____ 1. The plaintiff is the individual who initiates a civil complaint and has the burden of proof.

_____ 2. *Res ipsa loquitur* is Latin for "things done," which means that something is self-evident.

_____ 3. Medical malpractice results when a physician acts in an improper manner and the patient is not satisfied with the care given.

_____ 4. The HIPAA security rule specifies that facilities implement workstation security measures, which establish physical safeguards for all workstations that access EPHI to restrict access to authorized users only.

_____ 5. A breach of confidentiality occurs when a health care provider releases patient information to others who do not have a right to access the information.

Multiple Choice: Select the most appropriate response.

6. A security management process that assesses potential risks and vulnerabilities to the confidentiality, integrity, and availability of EPHI is a(n)
   a. information system activity review.
   b. risk analysis.
   c. risk management review.
   d. security policy.

7. Public law deals with relationships between individuals and the government, and includes
   a. criminal law and torts.
   b. contracts and torts.
   c. criminal law and regulations.
   d. contracts and regulations.

8. The Latin phrase for "let the master answer," which means an employer is responsible for the legal consequences of an employee's actions, is called
   a. *res gestae.*
   b. *respondeat superior.*
   c. *stare decisis.*
   d. *subpoena ad testificandum.*

9. Safeguards that are implemented to ensure that facilities, equipment, and patient information are safe from damage, theft, or unauthorized access are known as _____ safeguards.
   a. administrative
   b. implementation
   c. privacy
   d. security

10. A technical safeguard that records and examines activity in information systems that contain or use electronic protected health information is called
    a. access control.
    b. audit control.
    c. security safeguard.
    d. security control.

Fill-in-the-Blank: Enter the appropriate term(s) to complete each statement.

11. The HIPAA privacy rule establishes standards for how _____ should be controlled.

12. Any information communicated by a patient to a health care provider is private and is also considered _____.

13. When patient information is released to individuals who do not have a right to access the information, _____ occurs.

14. The HIPAA privacy rule established provisions for all medical records and other individually identifiable health information used or disclosed by a covered entity in any form including electronic, _____, or _____.

15. Providers are required to obtain _____ before disclosing information for treatment, payment, and health care operations.

Short Answer: Briefly respond to each question.

16. Civil monetary and federal criminal penalties apply when covered entities misuse protected health information. Discuss the penalties.

17. Sources of law include administrative, case, and statutory law. Discuss each type of law.

18. For a medical record to be considered admissible as evidence, the records must be maintained according to four principles. Discuss the four principles.

19. Define protected health information (PHI).

20. Policies and procedures should be established by covered entities to meet the HIPAA privacy rule standards. Outline what covered entities should do to meet this standard.

Chapter 10

INTRODUCTION TO CODING AND REIMBURSEMENT

Key Terms

abuse
capitation payment
case mix
case-mix adjustment
case mix index (CMI)
chargemaster
check digit
Civil Monetary Penalties Act
classification system
clearinghouse
CMS-1450
CMS-1500
codes
coding system
compliance guidance
consumer-directed health plans (CDHPs)
copayment
critical pathway

disability income insurance
disability insurance
electronic data interchange (EDI)
elimination period
False Claims Act (FCA)
federal antikickback statute
fee-for-service
fraud
hospital-acquired conditions (HACs)
local coverage determination (LCD)
medical necessity
medical nomenclature
managed care
National Correct Coding Initiative (NCCI)
national coverage determination (NCD)
national employer identifier

national health plan identifier (PlanID)
national provider identifier (NPI)
never event
overpayment recovery
Payment Error and Prevention Program (PEPP)
personal identifier
physician self-referral law
Physicians at Teaching Hospitals (PATH) initiative
present on admission (POA)
prospective payment system (PPS)
Recovery Audit Contractor (RAC) program
revenue codes
safe harbor regulation
severity of illness

Social Security Disability
  Insurance
Stark I

Stark II
subscriber
Supplemental Security Income

third-party payer
UB-04
utilization management

Objectives

At the end of this chapter, the student should be able to:

- Define key terms
- Differentiate among classifications, taxonomies, nomenclatures, terminologies, and clinical vocabularies, and state uses of each

- List and explain differences among third-party payers
- List and define health care reimbursement methodologies

INTRODUCTION

Health care providers and third-party payers use nomenclatures and classification systems to collect, store, and process data for a variety of purposes (e.g., reimbursement processing). The Centers for Medicare & Medicaid Services (CMS), an administrative agency of the Department of Health & Human Services (DHHS), manages implementation of Medicare prospective payment systems (PPS), payment systems, fee schedules, and exclusions. Typically, third-party payers adopt payment systems, fee schedules, and exclusions after Medicare has implemented them; payers modify them to suit their needs. Hospitals use a chargemaster to record encounter data about ambulatory care, and the chargemaster review process is crucial to the recording of accurate data. Physician offices use an encounter form (or superbill) for the same purpose. Hospitals submit UB-04 claims to payers for inpatient and ambulatory care encounters, and physicians submit CMS-1500 claims for office encounters. Most health care settings participate in electronic data interchange (EDI) with third-party payers and clearinghouses.

For comprehensive coverage of coding and reimbursement, refer to Cengage Learning's *3-2-1 Code It!*, by Michelle A. Green, *Understanding ICD-9-CM*, by Mary Jo Bowie, *Understanding ICD-10-CM*, by Mary Jo Bowie, and *Understanding Procedural Coding*, by Mary Jo Bowie.

CLINICAL CLASSIFICATION SYSTEMS

When health care providers document patient care they use a medical nomenclature (Table 10-1), which is a vocabulary of clinical and medical terms (e.g.,

myocardial infarction, diabetes mellitus, appendectomy). A coding system (or classification system) (Table 10-2) organizes a medical nomenclature according to similar conditions, diseases, procedures, and services and establishes codes (numeric and alphanumeric characters) for each. Codes are reported to third-party payers for reimbursement, to external agencies for data collection, and internally for education and research.

Example ICD-9-CM codes are assigned to hospital inpatient diagnoses and procedures and entered into automated abstracting software. Codes are reported to the billing department and printed on inpatient bills. Diagnosis and procedure indexes are generated from abstracted data and later used to retrieve specific patient records and summary data for cancer research.

Administrative simplification provisions of the Health Insurance Portability and Accountability Act of 1996 (HIPAA) required adoption of two types of code sets for encoding data elements (e.g., diagnosis codes or procedure codes). Large code sets include coding systems for:

- Diseases, injuries, impairments, other health-related problems, and their manifestations
- Causes of injury, disease, impairment, or other health-related problems
- Actions taken to prevent, diagnose, treat, or manage diseases, injuries, and impairments and any substances, equipment, supplies, or other items used to perform these actions

TABLE 10-1 Nomenclatures (in order of development)

Nomenclature	Description

Basle Nomina Anatomica Standardized Nomenclature of Disease (SND)	• Developed in the late 1800s by the Anatomical Society
	• Initiated standardization of anatomical terms used in medicine
	• Developed in 1929 by the New York Academy of Medicine
	• First medical nomenclature to be universally accepted in the United States
	• Introduced the concept of multi-axial coding:
	  ○ Topology (anatomy)
	  ○ Etiology (cause of disease)
	    Note: Although entitled a nomenclature, SND is also a classification system.
	
	    Example: Prostate is assigned code 764. Adenocarcinoma is assigned code 8091. Adenocarcinoma of the prostate is coded as 764-8091.

Standardized Nomenclature of Diseases and Operations (SNDO)	• Developed in 1936 by the American Medical Association (AMA) • Based on SND, and added an axis for operations *Example:* Radical excision is assigned code 14. Prostate is assigned code 764. Radical prostatectomy is coded as 764-14.
Systematized Nomenclature of Pathology (SNOP)	• Published in 1965 by the College of American Pathologists (CAP) • Four-axis system of terms and related codes for use by pathologists interested • in storage and retrieval of medical data

Systematized Nomenclature of Medicine (SNOMED)	• Developed in 1974 by CAP, based on SNOP, and cross-referenced to ICD-9-CM
	• Codifies all activities within the patient record, including medical diagnoses and procedures, nursing diagnoses and procedures, patient signs and symptoms, occupational history, and the many causes and etiologies of diseases (e.g., infectious conditions, genetic and congenital conditions, physical causes of injury)
	• CAP published subsequent revisions:
	  ○ SNOMED II (1979) (hierarchy expanded to 6 modules)
	  ○ SNOMED III (1993) (hierarchy expanded to 11 modules)
	  ○ SNOMED DICOM Microglossary (SDM) (1996) (collaborative effort between CAP and the American College of Radiology and the National Equipment Manufacturers Association; developed as a subset of the Digital Imaging and Communications in Medicine [DICOM] standard)
	  ○ SNOMED RT® (2000) (collaborative reference terminology effort with the Kaiser Permanente Convergent Medical Technology [CMT] Project; integrated with Logical Observation Identifiers Names and Codes [LOINC®], a universal standard medical vocabulary for identifying laboratory and clinical observations)
	    Note: The laboratory section of LOINC covers chemistry, hematology, microbiology, serology, and toxicology. The clinical observation section contains entries for cardiac echocardiography, EKG, gastroendoscopic procedures, hemodynamics, intake/output, obstetric ultrasound, pulmonary ventilator management, urologic imaging, and vital signs.
	  ○ SNOMED CT® (2002) (combines content and structure of SNOMED RT with U.K. National Health Service's Clinical Terms Version 3) (formerly Read Codes, which were developed in the early 1980s by Dr. James Read to record and retrieve primary care data in a computer)
	    Note: Since 2004, the National Library of Medicine (NLM) provides free-of-charge access through its Unified Medical Language System® (UMLS®) Metathesaurus® to SNOMED CT core content and all version updates. Qualifying entities include U.S. federal agencies, state and local government agencies, territories, the District of Columbia, and any public, for-profit, and non-profit organization located, incorporated, and operating in the United States.

(Continues)

TABLE 10-1 Nomenclatures (in order of development) (*Continued*)

Nomenclature	Description
Current Medical Information & Terminology (CMIT)	• Published in 1981 by the AMA • Used for naming and describing diseases and conditions in practice and in areas related to medicine 　*Note:* No subsequent revisions were published.
Unified Medical Language System® (UMLS®)	• A set of software and files developed by the National Library of Medicine (NLM) that unites health and biomedical vocabularies and standards. • Purpose is to link medical terms, drug names, and billing codes across different computer systems to help health professionals and researchers retrieve and integrate electronic biomedical information from a variety of sources, making it easier for users to link disparate information systems, including computer-based patient records, bibliographic databases, factual databases, and expert systems

TABLE 10-2 Medical Classification and Coding Systems (in order of development)

Coding System	Description
London Bills of Mortality	• Developed during the latter part of the sixteenth century • Considered the first classification system • Bills were collected and collated by parish clerks (with no medical training)
Nosologia Methodica	• Medical classification system developed in the mid-1700s by François Bossier de Lacroix (Sauvages)
Bertillon International Statistical Classification of Causes of Death	• Classification of diseases by site, adopted in 1893 • Subsequent revisions were entitled *International List of Causes of Death* (ICD-1, ICD-2, ICD-3, and ICD-4) • Classifications of diseases for morbidity reporting purposes were integrated into subsequent revisions • ICD-5 added mental diseases and deficiency (mental deficiency, schizophrenia, manic depressive psychosis, and other mental diseases) • In 1946, the World Health Organization (WHO) revised ICD-6 and established an International List of Causes of Morbidity
Manual of the International Statistical Classification of Diseases, Injuries, and Causes of Death (ICD-6)	• ICD-6 is adopted internationally in 1948 by the First World Health Assembly • WHO reviews and revises ICD about every 10 years: 　○ ICD-7 (1955) 　○ ICD-8 (1965) 　○ ICD-9 (1975) 　○ ICD-10 (1989, with WHO member states adopting in 1994) • ICD-10 is entitled the *International Statistical Classification of Diseases and Related Health Problems (ICD-10)* and differs from ICD-9: 　○ More detailed (8,000 categories in ICD-10-CM vs. 4,000 in ICD-9-CM) 　○ Uses three-digit alphanumeric category codes (vs. three-digit numeric and alphanumeric category codes in ICD-9-CM disease tabular list and two-digit numeric category codes in ICD-9-CM procedure tabular list) 　○ ICD-10-CM contains three additional chapters, and other chapters have been reorganized (and ICD-10-PCS is an entirely separate procedure classification system)

TABLE 10-2 Medical Classification and Coding Systems (in order of development) (*Continued*)

Coding System	Description
	○ ICD-10 cause-of-death titles are modified and conditions reorganized ○ Some ICD-10-CM and ICD-10-PCS coding rules have changed ○ ICD-10-CM and ICD-10-PCS are each published in separate volumes that contain an index and tabular list or index and tables, respectively *Note:* It is anticipated that the United States will implement ICD-10-CM and ICD-10-PCS in 2015.
International Classification of Diseases, Adapted for Use in the US (ICDA)	• The United States adapted ICD-8 in 1966 to include additional detail for coding hospital and morbidity data, abbreviated ICDA-8. • In 1968, the Commission on Professional and Hospital Activities (CPHA) of Ann Arbor, Michigan, published a hospital adaptation of ICDA, H-ICDA, which was revised in 1973 as H-ICDA-2. *Note:* United States hospitals were divided in their use of ICDA-8 and H-ICDA. (Author recalls coding inpatient cases using ICD-9-CM in 1979, while her utilization review coordinator coded according to H-ICDA as required by the county Professional Standards Review Organization.) • In 1979, all hospitals were required to adopt the International Classification of Diseases, Ninth Revision, Clinical Modification (ICD-9-CM), which classifies diagnoses (Volumes 1 and 2) and procedures (Volume 3). All hospitals and ambulatory care settings use ICD-9-CM to report diagnoses; hospitals use ICD-9-CM procedure codes to report inpatient procedures and services. • It is anticipated that, on October 1, 2015, the United States will implement ICD-10-CM and ICD-10-PCS. The National Center for Health Statistics (NCHS) is the federal agency responsible for developing ICD-10-CM. The ICD-10-PCS (Procedure Coding System) was developed with support of the CMS under contract with 3M Health Information Systems. The National Committee on Vital Health and Statistics (NCVHS) serves as a public advisory body to the secretary of DHHS in the development of ICD-10-PCS.

Diagnostic and Statistical Manual of Mental Disorders (DSM)	• Published by the American Psychiatric Association as a standard classification of mental disorders used by mental health professionals in the United States
	○ DSM (1952)
	○ DSM-II (1968)
	○ DSM-III (1980); a multi-axial classification was added:
	  > Axis I—mental disorders or illnesses (e.g., substance abuse)
	  > Axis II—personality disorders or traits (e.g., mental retardation)
	  > Axis III—general medical illnesses (e.g., hypertension)
	  > Axis IV—life events or problems (e.g., divorce)
	  > Axis V—global assessment of functioning (GAF) (e.g., occupational)
	○ DSM-III-R (1987)
	○ DSM-IV (1994)
	○ DSM-IV-TR (2000) (text revision to correct DSM-IV errors, update codes according to ICD-9-CM annual revisions, and so on)
	○ DSM-V (2013). The DSM-5 was published on May 18, 2013, superseding the DSM-IV-TR
	• Derived from ICD-9-CM, designed for use in a variety of health care settings; consists of three major components:
	○ Diagnostic classification
	○ Diagnostic criteria sets
	○ Descriptive text

(Continues)

TABLE 10-2 Medical Classification and Coding Systems (in order of development) (*Continued*)

Coding System	Description
Current Procedural Terminology (CPT)	• Originally published by the AMA in 1966. • Subsequent editions were published about every five years, until the late 1980s, when the AMA began publishing annual revisions of CPT-4. • The CPT-5 Project was initiated by the AMA in 2000 to address challenges presented by emerging user needs, the HIPAA, and needed improvements in CPT. The primary goal of the CPT-5 Project was to have CPT chosen by the Secretary of Health and Human Services as the national standard procedure code set for physician services under HIPAA. A Final Rule, issued in the August 17, 2000, *Federal Register,* named CPT as the national standard code set for physician services. CPT-5 Project recommendations are implemented annually along with code additions/ deletions/revisions. • CPT classifies procedures and services; physicians and ambulatory care settings use CPT codes to report procedures and services. • CPT is level I of the Healthcare Common Procedure Coding System (HCPCS).
International Classification of Diseases for Oncology, third edition (ICD-O-3)	• First edition of ICD-O was published in 1976, and a revision (primarily of topography codes) was published in 1990. • ICD-O-3 was implemented in 2001. • Ten-digit code, which describes the tumor's primary site (four-characters) topography code, histology (four-digit cell type code), behavior (one-digit code for malignant, benign, and so on), and aggression (one-digit differentiation or grade code).
International Classification of Injuries, Disabilities, and Handicaps (ICIDH)	• Published in 1980, ICIDH classifies health and health-related domains that describe body functions and structures, activities, and participation. • In 2001, with publication of its second edition, the name changed to *International Classification of Functioning, Disability and Health* (ICF). • ICF complements ICD-10, expanding beyond mortality and disease.
HCPCS Level II (national codes)	• Published by a variety of vendors. The coding system is in the public domain, which means it is not copyrighted. • Managed by the CMS. • Classifies medical equipment, injectable drugs, transportation services, and other services not classified in CPT. Physicians and ambulatory care settings use HCPCS Level II to report procedures and services.
Current Dental Terminology (CDT)	• Published biannually by the American Dental Association (ADA). • Classifies dental procedures and services. • Dental providers and ambulatory care settings use CDT to report procedures and services. • CDT codes are also included in HCPCS Level II; they begin with the alpha-character D.
National Drug Codes (NDC)	• Published by a variety of vendors, the coding system is in the public domain. • Managed by the Food and Drug Administration (FDA). • Originally established as part of an out-of-hospital drug reimbursement program under Medicare. • Serves as a universal product identifier for human drugs. • Current edition is limited to prescription drugs and a few selected over-the-counter (OTC) products. • Retail pharmacies use NDC to report pharmacy transactions. • Some health care professionals also report NDC codes on claims.

(Continues)

TABLE 10-2 Medical Classification and Coding Systems (in order of development) (*Continued*)

Coding System	Description
Alternative Billing Codes (ABCcodes™)	• Alternative Billing Codes (ABCcodes™) classify services not included in the CPT manual to describe the service, supply, or therapy provided; they may also be assigned to report nursing services and alternative medicine professions. The codes are five characters in length, consisting of letters, and are supplemented by two-digit code modifiers to identify the practitioner performing the service. *Example:* During an office visit, an acupuncture physician assessed the health status of a new client and developed a treatment plan, a process that took 45 minutes. ABCcode assigned: ACAAC-1C. (The office visit is coded as ACAAC, and the acupuncture physician is assigned modifier 1C.) • HIPAA authorized the secretary of DHHS to permit exceptions from HIPAA transaction and code set standards to commercialize and evaluate proposed modifications to those standards. The ABCcodes system was granted that exception in 2003, and the codes were evaluated through 2005 for possible adoption. However, adoption was not approved.

Small code sets encode:

- Race/ethnicity
- Type of facility
- Type of unit

The code sets proposed by HIPAA are already in use by most health plans, clearinghouses, and providers, and include:

- International Classification of Diseases, Ninth Revision, Clinical Modification (ICD-9-CM)
- Current Procedural Terminology (CPT)
- HCPCS Level II (national codes)
- Current Dental Terminology (CDT)
- National Drug Codes (NDC)

Note: The intent of standard coding guidelines is to simplify claims submission for health care providers who deal with multiple third-party payers (or health plans) and to improve data quality. Payers that do not follow official coding guidelines will be required to modify their systems to accept all valid codes or to contract with a health care clearinghouse to process standard transactions. A clearinghouse is a public or private entity (e.g., billing service, repricing company) that processes or facilitates the processing of health information received from another entity (e.g., provider, third-party payer) from a nonstandard into a standard format.

EXERCISE 10–1 Clinical Classification Systems

Fill-in-the-Blank: Enter the appropriate term(s) to complete each of the following statements.

1. A public or private entity that processes or facilitates the processing of health information received from another entity from a(n) _____ format into a standard format is known as a(n) _____.

2. The _____ was developed during the latter part of the sixteenth century and is considered the first classification system.

3. Published in 1965, the _____ uses a four-axis system of terms and codes for use by pathologists interested in storage and retrieval of medical data.

4. The *Diagnostic and Statistical Manual of Mental Disorders* is published by the _____ as a standard classification of mental disorders.

5. CPT is the abbreviation for _____.

True/False: Indicate whether each statement is true (T) or false (F).

____ 6. The National Drug Codes are managed by the American Medical Association and serve as a universal product identifier for human drugs.

____ 7. The CDT is published by the American Dental Association and classifies dental procedures and services.

____ 8. The Centers for Medicare and Medicaid Services manage HCPCS Level II national codes that classify medical equipment, injectable drugs, transportation services, and other services.

_____ 9. CPT was last published in 1981 by the AMA to name and describe diseases and conditions in the practice of medicine.

_____ 10. CD-10 uses 3-digit alphanumeric category codes as compared to the 3-digit numeric category codes used in ICD-9.

THIRD-PARTY PAYERS

A third-party payer is an organization that processes claims for reimbursement covered by a health care plan. Payers serve as Medicare administrative contractors (MACs), formerly known as carriers and fiscal intermediaries (FI) and process Medicare claims for physicians (Part B) and health care facilities (Part A), respectively. Third-party payers (Table 10-3) include:

- BlueCross and BlueShield (BCBS)
- Commercial insurance companies
- Employer self-insurance plans
- Government-sponsored programs (e.g., Medicaid, Medicare, TRICARE)
- Managed care (e.g., health maintenance organization)
- Workers' compensation

TABLE 10-3 Third-Party Payers

Payer	Description
BlueCross and BlueShield (BCBS)	• Covers the costs of hospital care and physicians' services. • BlueCross initially covered just hospital care, and BlueShield covered just physicians' services. Today, both offer a full range of health care coverage. • While each independent BCBS plan serves its local community, its membership in the BCBS Association allows it to link with other local plans in order to serve regional and national employers (e.g., employee can receive health care services while traveling).
Commercial Payers	• Includes private health insurance and employer-based group health insurance. • Private health insurance usually consists of an indemnity plan, which covers individuals for certain health care expenses. The insurance company reimburses the patient or the provider, depending on the contract language. Individuals pay annual premiums (pre-determined rates). • Employer-based group health insurance is often provided as an employee benefit in which the employer typically pays 80 percent of insurance premiums (and the employee pays the remaining 20 percent), and the employer contracts with a commercial health insurance plan (e.g., Aetna).

Employer Self-Insurance Plans	• An employer that accepts direct responsibility (or the risk) for paying employees' health care without purchasing health insurance creates an employer self-insurance plan.
	• Usually, the plan contracts with a third-party administrator (TPA), an organization that provides the following services to employers (and insurance companies):
	  ○ Benefit design (medical services covered by the plan)
	  ○ Claims administration (processing claims to reimburse services)
	  ○ Utilization management (controls health care costs and quality by reviewing cases for appropriateness and medical necessity) (e.g., preadmission authorization)

Government-Sponsored Programs	• Civilian Health and Medical Program of the Department of Veterans Affairs (CHAMPVA) program provides health care benefits to dependents of veterans rated as 100 percent permanently and totally disabled as a result of service-connected conditions, veterans who died as a result of service-connected conditions, and veterans who died on duty with less than 30 days of active service.

(Continues)

TABLE 10-3 Third-Party Payers (*Continued*)

Payer	Description
Government-Sponsored Programs (*continued*)	• Federal Employee Health Benefits Program (FEHBP or FEP) is a voluntary health care program that covers federal employees, retirees, and their dependents and survivors. • Indian Health Service (IHS) is a DHHS agency that provides federal health care services to Native Americans and Alaska Natives. • Medicaid (Title XIX of the Social Security Act Amendments of 1965) is a joint federal and state program that provides health care coverage to low-income populations and certain aged and disabled individuals; it is an entitlement program that is jointly financed by state and federal governments, with federal spending levels determined by the number of participants and services provided. • Medicare (Title XVIII of the Social Security Act Amendments of 1965) provides health care coverage to elderly and disabled persons; federal spending is funded by the Medicare Trust Fund (payroll tax). • Military Health System (MHS) provides and maintains readiness to provide health care services and support to members of the uniformed services during military operations; it also provides health care services and support to members of the uniformed services, their family members, and others entitled to DoD health care. TRICARE is the military health plan that covers active duty and retired members of the uniformed services and their dependents; it combines military health care resources (e.g., military treatment facilities) and networks of civilian health care professionals. TRICARE was formerly called the Civilian Health and Medical Program of the United States (CHAMPUS). • Programs of All-inclusive Care for the Elderly (PACE) are community-based Medicare and Medicaid programs that provide integrated health care and long-term care services to elderly persons who require a nursing-facility level of care. • State Children's Health Insurance Program (SCHIP) was established to provide health assistance to uninsured, low-income children either through separate programs or through expanded eligibility under state Medicaid programs.
Managed Care	• Capitation of health care requires providers to manage and provide cost-effective, quality health care. The provider accepts a **capitation payment**, which is a predetermined payment for each **subscriber** (health plan enrollee) for a specific period of time (e.g., month). Appropriate health care services must be provided to the subscriber even if costs exceed capitation. • Managed care plans range from structured closed-panel staff model health maintenance organizations (HMOs) to less structured preferred provider organizations (PPOs). • Managed care is currently challenged by growth of **consumer-directed health plans (CDHPs)**, which define employer contributions and ask employees to be more responsible for health care decisions and cost sharing. They include customized sub-capitation plan (CSCP), flexible spending account (FSA), health savings account (HSA) (health savings security account, HSSA), health care reimbursement account (HCRA), and health reimbursement arrangement (HRA).
Workers' Compensation	• State-mandated insurance program that reimburses health care costs and lost wages if an employee suffers a work-related disease or injury; qualified employees and their dependents are eligible for reimbursement.

Note: Disability insurance (or disability income insurance) replaces 40 to 60 percent of an individual's gross income (tax free) if an illness or injury prevents the individual from earning an income. Policies usually require a 90-day waiting period from onset of disability before the individual can apply for disability benefits, which is called the elimination period. Social Security Disability Insurance pays benefits to the individual (and certain family members) if the individual worked long enough and paid Social Security taxes. Supplemental Security Income pays benefits based on financial need.

EXERCISE 10–2 Third-Party Payers

True/False: Indicate whether each statement is true (T) or false (F).

_____ 1. Medicare (Title XVIII of the Social Security Act of 1965) provides health care coverage to elderly and disabled persons.

_____ 2. Worker's compensation is a federally mandated insurance program that reimburses health care cost and lost wages if an employee suffers a work-related disease or injury.

_____ 3. Medicare Part B reimburses claims for physicians' services.

_____ 4. Blue Cross initially covered just physicians' services.

_____ 5. Commercial plans include private health insurance and employer-based group health insurance.

_____ 6. Employer-based group health insurance is often provided as an employee benefit in which the employer typically pays 80 percent of insurance premiums.

_____ 7. Utilization management is the process of reviewing medical care for appropriateness, necessity, and quality.

_____ 8. Medicare provides health care services and support to members of the uniformed services during military operations.

_____ 9. The Federal Employee Health Benefits Program is a voluntary health care program that covers federal employees, retirees, and their dependents and survivors.

_____ 10. TRICARE is the military health plan that covers only active duty members of the uniformed services and their families.

REIMBURSEMENT METHODOLOGIES

Prior to implementation of major government-sponsored health programs (e.g., Medicare, Medicaid) beginning in 1965, health care services were reimbursed as follows:

- BlueCross and BlueShield (private and group health plans)
- Commercial health insurance (private)
- Employer-based group health insurance and self-insurance plans
- Government-sponsored programs, limited to the following:
  - Indian Health Service (limited eligibility)
  - Dependents medical care program (health care for dependents of active military personnel)
- Prepaid health plans (forerunner of managed care)
- Self-pay (patients paid cash)
- Workers' compensation (limited eligibility)

Most payers (except prepaid or managed care plans) initially reimbursed providers according to fee-for-service, a *retrospective payment system* that billed payers after health care services were provided to the patient. Hospital reimbursement was generated as *per diem*, a retrospective payment system that issued payment based on daily charges.

> *Example* Payers paid providers 80 percent of charges submitted, and patients paid the remaining 20 percent (coinsurance). Thus, a provider who submitted a charge of $120 was paid $96 by the payer and $24 by the patient.

Health care costs increased dramatically with implementation of government-sponsored health programs, leading to the creation of prospective payment systems (PPS) (Table 10-4), which pre-establish reimbursement rates for health care services. In addition, Medicare has established a multitude of payment systems and fee schedules (Table 10-5).

> *Example* Prior to 1983, acute care hospitals generated invoices based on total charges for an inpatient stay. In 1982, an eight-day inpatient hospitalization at $225/day (including ancillary service charges) would be billed $1,800. This per diem reimbursement rate actually discouraged hospitals from limiting inpatient lengths of stay. In 1983, a PPS rate of $950 would be reimbursed for the same inpatient hospitalization, regardless of length of stay (unless the case qualified for additional reimbursement as an outlier, discussed in Table 10-4).

TABLE 10-4 Prospective Payment Systems (according to year implemented)

Prospective Payment System	Description
Diagnosis-Related Groups (1983)	The Tax Equity and Fiscal Responsibility Act of 1983 (TEFRA) legislated the inpatient prospective payment system (IPPS), which uses *diagnosis-related groups (DRGs)* to reimburse short-term hospitals a predetermined rate for Medicare inpatient services. (Other payers soon adopted the IPPS.) DRG grouper software is used to assign each DRG according to data input for each inpatient stay (e.g., principal diagnosis code, patient's discharge status).
	Note: The Medicare Severity DRG (MS-DRG) was implemented by CMS in 2007 to classify inpatient hospital cases into groups according to similar resource utilization.
	An inpatient case that qualifies for additional reimbursement is categorized as a cost outlier, which adjusts the DRG rate when a case results in unusually high costs when compared with other cases in the same DRG. (When DRGs were first implemented, cases could also be adjusted as day outliers. This adjustment was discontinued.)
	The IPPS three-day payment window (or 72-hour rule) requires that outpatient preadmission services provided by a hospital up to three days prior to a patient's inpatient admission be covered by the IPPS DRG payment for: • Diagnostic services (e.g., lab testing) • Therapeutic (or non-diagnostic) services for which the inpatient principal diagnosis code (ICD-9-CM or ICD-10-CM, when implemented) exactly matches that for preadmission services.
Resource Utilization Groups (RUGs) (1998)	The BBA legislated implementation of a Skilled Nursing Facility Prospective Payment System (SNF PPS) called Resource Utilization Groups (RUGs), which reimburse Medicare SNF services according to a per diem prospective rate adjusted for case mix. A resident assessment instrument (RAI) completed on each SNF patient captures the minimum data set (MDS) according to the following schedule: 5, 14, 30, 60, and 90 days after admission. Patients are assigned to one of 44 RUGs, for which a per diem prospective rate is established. Resident Assessment Validation and Entry (RAVEN) software, developed by CMS, is a data-entry system that allows SNFs to capture and transmit the MDS.
Home Health Resource Groups (HHRGs) (2000)	The Omnibus Consolidated and Emergency Supplemental Appropriations Act (OCESAA) of 1999 called for implementation of a Home Health Prospective Payment System (HH PPS) for Medicare home health services. Home Health Resource Groups (HHRGs) reimburse Medicare home health care services according to prospectively determined rates and require recertification every 60 days (or more frequently when there is a beneficiary-elected transfer, a significant change in condition resulting in a change in the case-mix assignment, or a discharge and return to the same home health agency during the 60-day episode) by the physician who reviews the plan of care.
	Home health agencies (HHAs) collect the Outcome and Assessment Information Set (OASIS) and enter the data set into Home Assessment Validation and Entry (HAVEN) data-entry software, which was developed by CMS.

(Continues)

TABLE 10-4 Prospective Payment Systems (according to year implemented) (*Continued*)

Prospective Payment System	Description
Ambulatory Payment Classifications (APCs) (2001)	The BBA also legislated implementation of an outpatient prospective payment system (OPPS), called ambulatory payment classifications (APCs), which organize similar health care services clinically and according to resources required. A payment rate is established for each APC, and depending on services provided hospitals can be paid for more than one APC per encounter, with second and subsequent APCs discounted at 50 percent. APC grouper software is used to assign an APC to each HCPCS/CPT code on an outpatient claim and to ICD-9-CM diagnosis codes as appropriate. *Note:* A Medicare patient's coinsurance amount is initially calculated for each APC based on 20 percent of the *national median charge* for services in the APC. The coinsurance amount for an APC does not change until the amount becomes 20 percent of the total APC payment, and no coinsurance amount can be greater than the hospital inpatient deductible in a given year. *Note:* New York State is scheduled to implement ambulatory payment groups (APGs) as an OPPS for Medicaid procedures and services.
Inpatient Rehabilitation Facility Prospective Payment System (IRF PPS) (2002)	The BBA authorized implementation of a per-discharge Inpatient Rehabilitation Facility Prospective Payment System (IRF PPS), which utilizes information from a patient assessment instrument (IRF PAI) to classify patients into distinct groups based on clinical characteristics and expected resource needs. Separate payments are calculated for each group, including the application of case and facility level adjustments. Each facility must demonstrate that during its most recent 12-month cost reporting period, it served an inpatient population of whom at least 75 percent required intensive rehabilitative services for the treatment of one or more of the following conditions: • Amputation • Brain injury • Burns • Congenital deformity • Hip fracture • Major multiple trauma • Neurological disorders • Polyarthritis • Stroke • Spinal cord injury The IRF PPS one-day payment window (or 24-hour rule) requires that outpatient preadmission services provided by an IRF up to one day prior to a patient's inpatient admission be covered by the IRF PPS payment.
Long-Term Care Diagnosis-Related Groups (LTC DRGs) (2001)	The Balanced Budget Refinement Act of 1999 (BBRA) mandates implementation of a long-term care prospective payment system (LTC PPS), which uses information from long-term care hospital (LTCH) patient records to classify patients into distinct long-term care diagnosis-related groups (LTC DRGs) based on clinical characteristics and expected resource needs. The LTCH PPS replaced the reasonable cost-based payment system authorized by TEFRA, which mandated DRGs (and exempted LTCHs from participation). The LTCF PPS one-day payment window (or 24-hour rule) requires that outpatient preadmission services provided by an LTCF up to one day prior to a patient's inpatient admission be covered by the LTCF PPS DRG payment.

TABLE 10-5 Payment Systems and Fee Schedules (according to year implemented)

Payment System	Description
Clinical Laboratory Fee Schedule (1985)	The Deficit Reduction Act of 1984 established the clinical laboratory fee schedule as a methodology for determining fees for existing tests, and one year later the Consolidated Omnibus Budget Reconciliation Act of 1985 established a national limitation amount (NLA), which serves as a payment ceiling or "cap" on the amount Medicare could pay for each test—originally set at 115 percent of the median of all carrier-set rates, it eventually dropped to 74 percent.
Durable Medical Equipment, Prosthetics/Orthotics, and Supplies (DMEPOS) Fee Schedule (1989)	The durable medical equipment, prosthetics, orthotics, and supplies(DMEPOS) fee schedule is a payment methodology mandated by the Omnibus Budget Reconciliation Act of 1987 (OBRA). The fee schedule was implemented in 1989 (except for the surgical dressings fee schedule that was implemented in 1994 and the parenteral and enteral nutrition [PEN] fee schedule that was implemented in 2002). The fee schedule is released annually and updated on a quarterly basis to implement fee schedule amounts for new codes and to revise any amounts for existing codes that were calculated in error.
Resource Based Relative Value Scale (RBRVS) System (1992)	The Omnibus Budget Reconciliation Act of 1989 implemented the Resource Based Relative Value Scale (RBRVS), which is used to reimburse physician services covered by Medicare Part B. RBRVS is now commonly called the Medicare Physician Fee Schedule or PFS.
Ambulatory Surgical Centers (ASCs) Payments (1994)	The Omnibus Budget Reconciliation Act of 1980 mandated that an ambulatory surgical center (ASC) could participate in Medicare if certain conditions were met (e.g., state licensed) and stated that the ASC payment rate is "expected to be calculated on a prospective basis . . . utilizing sample survey and similar techniques to establish reasonable estimated overhead allowances for each of the listed procedures which take account of volume (within reasonable limits)." In 2008, Medicare implemented use of the ambulatory payment classification (APC) OPPS and relative payment weights to reimburse ASCs for surgical procedures performed. (The payment weights are multiplied by an ASC conversion factor to calculate ASC payment rates.)
Ambulance Fee Schedule (2002)	The Balanced Budget Act of 1997 required implementation of an ambulance fee schedule, which reimburses ambulance service providers a pre-established fee for each service provided. Characteristics of the fee schedule include: • Seven categories of ground ambulance services, ranging from basic life support to specialty care transport, and two categories of air ambulance services are established. • Payment for each category is based on the relative value assigned to the service, adjusted to reflect wage differences in different parts of the country (mileage also will affect payment levels). • Ambulance providers will not be allowed to charge beneficiaries more than their deductible and 20 percent of Medicare's fee for the service (under the old payment system, providers could charge beneficiaries higher rates). • The fee schedule allows for increased payments when an ambulance service is provided in rural areas.
End-Stage Renal Disease (ESRD) Composite Payment Rate System (2005)	The Medicare Prescription Drug, Improvement, and Modernization Act Composite Payment Rate System (2005) (MMA) of 2003 established the ESRD composite payment rate system. The ESRD composite payment rate system for dialysis services is based on a case-mix adjusted composite rate. It is a single-payment fixed rate that does not vary according to the characteristics of the beneficiary treated (and includes the cost of some drugs, laboratory tests, and other items and services provided to Medicare beneficiaries receiving dialysis).

The PPS rate encourages hospitals to limit inpatient lengths of stay because any reimbursement received in excess of the actual cost of providing care can be retained by the facility. (In this example, if the $950 PPS rate had been paid in 1980, the hospital would have absorbed the loss.)

PROCESSING INSURANCE CLAIMS

For a physician's office, the processing of an insurance claim is initiated when the patient contacts a health care provider's office and schedules an appointment. The insurance claim used to report professional and technical services is the CMS-1500 claim form. For health care facilities (e.g., hospitals), processing of the claim begins when the patient is registered for care (e.g., inpatient, outpatient, emergency department), and the claim form UB-04 is used. The provider's claim for payment is generated from information located on the patient's encounter form (physician office) or chargemaster (hospital outpatient), and on the source document (e.g., patient record). Information from these documents is transferred to the CMS-1500 or the UB-04 claim form. Such information includes patient and insurance policy identification, codes and charges for procedures and/or services, and codes for diagnoses treated and/or managed during the encounter. The patient is responsible for paying any copayment, coinsurance, and/or deductible amounts.

A Brief History of Health Insurance in the United States

The Franklin Health Assurance Company of Massachusetts was the first United States commercial insurance company to provide private health care coverage for injuries that did not result in death. By 1880, approximately 60 additional insurance companies offered health plans that covered loss of income and a limited number of illnesses (e.g., scarlet fever, smallpox, typhoid).

Note: In the early 1900s, most patients paid cash (or bartered) for health care services (with some choosing not to seek health care).

In 1908, legislation to provide workers' compensation for certain *federal* employees in unusually hazardous jobs was enacted. That was replaced by the Federal Employees' Compensation Act (FECA) in 1916 to provide *civilian employees of the federal government* with medical care, survivors' benefits, and compensation for lost wages. The first prepaid health plans were introduced in 1920. The federal Indian Health Service was created in 1921. The first Blue Cross policy

was written in 1929, when an official at Baylor University in Dallas (Justin Ford Kimball) introduced a plan to guarantee school-teachers 21 days of hospital care for $6 a year. In 1939, the first Blue Shield plan was created in California; it was based on plans created for lumber and mining camp employees in the Pacific Northwest, where employers paid monthly fees to *medical service bureaus* comprised of groups of physicians. Group health insurance became available to full-time employees as a benefit during the 1940s; it was not subject to income or Social Security taxes. The *Hill-Burton Act of 1946* provided federal grant funds to modernize hospitals that had become obsolete because of a lack of capital investment during the Great Depression and WWII (1929 to 1945). In return, facilities were required to provide free or reduced-rate health care services to patients unable to pay for care. The *Taft-Hartley Act of 1947* created third-party administrators (TPAs), and by 1950, insurance companies began offering major medical insurance, which provided coverage for catastrophic or prolonged illnesses and injuries and included large deductibles and lifetime maximum amounts. (A *deductible* is the amount for which the patient is financially responsible before an insurance policy provides coverage. A *lifetime maximum amount* is the maximum benefit payable to a health plan participant.) Copayments and coinsurance were introduced in later years. A copayment (or copay) requires a specified dollar amount to be paid to a health care provider for each visit or medical service received. *Coinsurance* is the split the subscriber and plan share; for example, the plan pays 80 percent of health care costs and the patient pays 20 percent. The *Dependents Medical Care Act of 1956* provided health care to dependents of active military personnel, amendments to the SSA created Medicare and Medicaid in 1965, and the *Military Medical Benefits Amendments of 1966* created the *Civilian Health and Medical Program of the Uniformed Services (CHAMPUS,* now called *TRICARE* as a result of the *CHAMPUS Reform Initiative of 1988,* or *CRI*). The *Veterans Healthcare Expansion Act of 1973* authorized Veterans Affairs (VA) to establish the *Civilian Health and Medical Program of the Department of Veterans Affairs (CHAMPVA),* and the *Health Maintenance Organization Assistance Act of 1973* authorized federal grants and loans to private organizations that wished to develop HMOs. In 1977, the *Health Care Financing Administration (HCFA)* was created to manage the Medicare and Medicaid programs; its name was changed to the *Centers for Medicare & Medicaid Services (CMS)* in 2001. The *Balanced Budget Act of 1997 (BBA)* established the *State Children's Health Insurance Program (SCHIP).*

EXAMPLES OF RELATIVE WEIGHTS FOR CASE-MIX GROUPS (CMGs)

CMG	CMG description (M=motor, C=cognitive, A=age)	Relative weights				Average length of stay			
		Tier 1	Tier 2	Tier 3	None	Tier 1	Tier 2	Tier 3	None
0101	Stroke; M=69–84 and C=23–35	0.4778	0.4279	0.4078	0.3859	10	9	6	8
0102	Stroke; M=59–68 and C=23–35	0.6506	0.5827	0.5553	0.5255	11	12	10	10
0103	Stroke; M=59–84 and C=5–22	0.8296	0.7430	0.7080	0.6700	14	12	12	12
0104	Stroke; M=53–58	0.9007	0.8067	0.7687	0.7275	17	13	12	13
0105	Stroke; M=47–52	1.1339	1.0155	0.9677	0.9158	16	17	15	16

FIGURE 10-1 Case-Mix Groups (CMGs) (From http://www.cms.gov/)

Case-Mix Analysis and Severity of Illness Systems

Implementation of Medicare prospective payment systems resulted in health care facilities analyzing their case mix (types and categories of patients) (Figure 10-1) to forecast health care trends unique to their individual settings, ensure that they continue to provide appropriate services to their patient populations, and recognize that different patients require different resources for care. A case mix index (CMI) indicates the average weight of a hospital's diagnosis-related groups (DRGs); a high CMI means the hospital provides high cost services and thus receives increased reimbursement per patient. To calculate a CMI, select a time period (e.g., one month) add together all of the relative weights (RW) for all DRGs billed by the hospital; then, divide the total RW by the total number of DRGs. For example, during the month of January the hospital's relative weights totaled 14,902.59, and the total number of DRGs submitted for reimbursement was 950; thus, 14,902.59 divided by 950 equals a CMI of 15.686. In addition, Medicare and other payers are also interested in reviewing case-mix data because they recognize that some facilities may serve caseloads that include disproportionate shares of patients with above-average (or below-average) care needs. Multiple possible payment rates (e.g., RUG categories) based on patients' anticipated care needs allow payment systems to decrease the average difference between the pre-established payment and each patient's actual cost to the facility (called a case-mix adjustment). This results in a reduced risk to facilities and to payers, and facilities are willing to admit high-resource cases because higher payments can be anticipated. It also creates a disincentive for facilities to admit large volumes of low-need, low-cost patients, which will result in lower payments.

Health care facilities use case mix and severity of illness software to analyze and measure standards of patient care to assess quality, including:

- Acute Physiological and Chronic Health Evaluation (APACHE)
- Atlas Outcomes/MediQual Systems (formerly Medical Illness Severity Grouping System, or MEDISGRPS)
- Comprehensive Severity Index (CSI)
- Patient Management Categories (PMCs)
- Severity of Illness Index (SOII)

Severity of illness is the physiologic complexity that comprises the extent and interactions of a patient's disease(s) as presented to medical personnel. Severity of illness scores are based on physiologic measures (not just ICD-9-CM or ICD-10-CM/PCS codes) of the degree of abnormality of individual signs and symptoms of a patient's disease(s). The more abnormal the signs and symptoms, the higher the score.

Example 1
A Comprehensive Severity Index (CSI) score of level 4 indicates that signs and symptoms are catastrophic, life-threatening, or likely to result in organ failure.

Example 2
The National Institutes of Health (NIH) studied MEDISGRPS data from five hospitals that indicated severity level at admission is an important predictor of resource use, is essential for analysis of patients who deteriorate and/or respond poorly to therapy, and is useful to further specify DRGs.

Risk management tools that identify the risk of dying include:

- Acute Physiological and Chronic Health Evaluation (APACHE)
- Medicare Mortality Predictor System (MMPS)

Example The Health Data Institute created MMPS software to capture data on Medicare patients admitted with stroke, pneumonia, myocardial infarction, and congestive heart failure. The purpose was to predict death within 30 days of hospital admission because these conditions accounted for 13 percent of discharges and 31 percent of 30-day mortality for Medicare patients over age 64 previous to 1988. The MMPS system was "calibrated on a stratified, random sample of 5,888 discharges (about 1,470 for each condition) from seven states, with stratification by hospital type to make the sample nationally representative" and predictors were abstracted from the patient record. The organization determined that "risk-adjusted predicted group mortality rates may be useful in interpreting information on unadjusted mortality rates, and patient-specific predictions may be useful in identifying unexpected deaths for clinical review."

Source: Daley, J., Jencks, S., Draper, D., Lenhart, G., Thomas, N., & Walker, J. (1988, December 23). Predicting hospital-associated mortality for Medicare patients: a method for patients with stroke, pneumonia, acute myocardial infarction, and congestive heart failure. *Journal of the American Medical Association, 260(24).* Chicago: American Medical Association

Systems developed for payment purposes (based on CMS's DRG system) include:

- All-Patient Refined DRGs (APR-DRGs)
- International Refined-DRG System (IR-DRG)
- New York All Patient DRGs (AP-DRGs)
- Yale Refined Diagnosis-Related Groups (RDRGs)
- Medicare Severity DRGs (MS-DRGs)

Example All-Patient DRGs (AP-DRGs) were developed to classify the non-Medicare population (e.g., HIV patients, neonates, pediatric patients). The AP-DRG system was originally designed to classify the non-elderly population in New York State; other countries adapted it for their own use, resulting in the International Refined-DRG System (IR-DRG), which compares resource usage across health care facilities as well as regions and incorporates the concept of severity of illness adjustments by using multiple levels of comorbid and complication (CC) conditions.

Critical pathways are interdisciplinary guidelines developed by hospitals to facilitate management and delivery of quality clinical care in a time of constrained resources. They allow for the planning of provision of clinical services that have expected time frames and resources targeted to specific diagnoses and/or procedures. The targeted clinical services are frequently those that are high in volume and resource use and, therefore, costly. Critical pathways are usually interdisciplinary in focus, merging medical and nursing plans of care with other disciplines (e.g., physical therapy, nutrition, mental health). Critical pathways can essentially be viewed as interdisciplinary practice guidelines with predetermined standards of care. They provide opportunities for collaborative practice and team approaches that can maximize the expertise of multiple disciplines.

Note: Originally, critical pathways began with admission and ended with discharge from the hospital. Now that they are being implemented in other health care settings, there is potential for pathways to be focused more on the full range of an episode of care.

Chargemaster and Encounter Form

A chargemaster (Figure 10-2) lists all the procedures, services, and supplies provided to patients by a hospital; charges for each may also appear.

```
Alfred State Medical Center
Chargemaster
Issue Date: 09/30/YYYY                          Program-ID: CM12
Issue Time: 11:50:00                            Page Number: 1

Charge No.   Description      Relative      CPT Code   Revenue Cost   Charge
                             Value Scale                  Center

385-6765     Rubeola titer       0.85         86765        300      $   27.00

385-6787     Varicella titer     0.95         86787        300      $   20.00

385-6920     Clear outer canal   1.05         69200        982      $  110.00

385-6921     Removal ear wax     1.00         69210        982      $   70.00
```

FIGURE 10-2 Sample Portion of Chargemaster

Sunny Valley Physicians			Encounter # :	
One Feelbetter Blvd.	Patient Name:		Provider number:	Date of Service:
Binghamton, NY 13901	Address:		Primary Insurance:	
Patient Date of birth			Appointment time:	
Reason for encounter:				

Code	Description	Code	Description
Office Visits		**Laboratory**	
99201	☐ New Patient- level 1	81001	☐ Urinalysis with microscopy
99202	☐ New Patient- level 2	82044	☐ Urine-Microalbumin
99303	☐ New Patient- level 3	82947	☐ Blood Glucose
99204	☐ New Patient- level 4	85014	☐ Hematocrit
99205	☐ New Patient- level 5	85611	☐ Protime
99211	☐ Established Patient level 1	86580	☐ PPD
99212	☐ Established Patient level 2	87060	☐ Strep Screen
99213	☐ Established Patient level 3		
99214	☐ Established Patient level 4		
99215	☐ Established Patient level 5		

Procedures		**Common Diagnosis:**	
10060	☐ Incision and Drainage	401.9	☐ Hypertension, unspecified
36415	☐ Venipuncture	477.9	☐ Rhinitis, allergeric
94010	☐ Spirometry	486	☐ Pneumonia
		780.2	☐ Fainting
		783.21	☐ Weight loss
		786.2	☐ Cough

		Additional Diagnoses:	
Next Appointment:			
Provider Signature:			

FIGURE 10-3A Encounter Form with ICD-9-CM Diagnostic Codes (Superbill)

An encounter form (or superbill) lists procedures, services, and supplies provided to patients by a physician; charges may also appear. Figure 10-3A illustrates an encounter form with ICD-9-CM codes. Figure 10-3B illustrates an encounter form with ICD-10-CM codes. Chargemaster and encounter forms are usually developed using database software that allows for the entry of thousands of items and potential charges; each item includes an accounting code number, CPT/HCPCS code number, and brief narrative description.

Because they play a crucial role in data capture for hospital billing purposes, chargemasters should undergo routine (at least annual) review by one or two designated individual(s) who have knowledge of proper revenue and expense matching to the Medicare cost center report (e.g., revenue codes) and who are willing to spend the time necessary on an extremely detailed and time-consuming task. Because it results in the generation of gross revenue for the health care facility, all who use the chargemaster must be educated about its proper use and its impact on the facility's financial status. Similarly, the encounter form should be assigned to one individual in the physician's office who will take responsibility for reviewing and updating it annually.

| Sunny Valley Physicians | | | Encounter # : | |

One Feelbetter Blvd.
Binghamton, NY 13901

Patient Name:
Address:

Provider number:
Primary Insurance:

Date of Service:

Patient Date of birth

Appointment time:

Reason for encounter:

Code	Description	Code	Description
Office Visits		**Laboratory**	
99201	☐ New Patient- level 1	81001	☐ Urinalysis with microscopy
99302	☐ New Patient- level 2	82044	☐ Urine-Microalbumin
99203	☐ New Patient- level 3	82947	☐ Blood Glucose
99204	☐ New Patient- level 4	85014	☐ Hematocrit
99205	☐ New Patient- level 5	85611	☐ Protime
99211	☐ Established Patient level 1	86580	☐ PPD
99212	☐ Established Patient level 2	87060	☐ Strep Screen
99213	☐ Established Patient level 3		
99214	☐ Established Patient level 4		
99215	☐ Established Patient level 5		

Procedures		**Common Diagnosis:**	
10060	☐ Incision and Drainage	I10	☐ Hypertension, unspecified
36415	☐ Venipuncture	J30.9	☐ Rhinitis, allergeric
94010	☐ Spirometry	J18.9	☐ Pneumonia
		R55	☐ Fainting
		R63.4	☐ Weight loss
		R05	☐ Cough

		Additional Diagnoses:	
Next Appointment:			
Provider Signature:			

FIGURE 10-3B Encounter Form with ICD-10-CM Diagnostic Codes

CMS-1450 (or UB-04) and CMS-1500

A CMS-1450 (or UB-04) (Figure 10-4) is a standard institutional claim form submitted by hospitals, skilled nursing facilities, and other institutional-based providers to payers to obtain reimbursement for health care services provided to patients. It requires input of revenue codes, which classify hospital categories of service by revenue cost center (e.g., intensive care unit, emergency department, and so on). The CMS-1500 is a universal claim form developed by CMS and used by providers of services (e.g., physicians) to bill professional fees to health carriers. Figure 10-5 illustrates a completed CMS-1500 form using ICD-9-CM codes, while figure 10-6 illustrates a completed CMS-1500 form using ICD-10-CM codes.

HIPAA administrative simplification standards require the following national identifiers to be developed:

- National employer identifier. The IRS's federal tax employer identification number (EIN) was adopted as the national employer identifier, retaining the hyphen after the first two numbers (e.g., 12-3456789).

1 ALFRED STATE MEDICAL CENTER	2 ALFRED STATE MEDICAL CENTER	3a PAT. CNTL # 859451562987		4 TYPE OF BILL
548 N MAIN ST	548 N MAIN ST	b. MED. REC. # 987654		131
ALFRED NY 14802	ALFRED NY 14802	5 FED. TAX NO.	6 STATEMENT COVERS PERIOD FROM THROUGH	7
6075551234	USA 87 1349061	871349061	0505YY 0505YY	

8 PATIENT NAME a PUBLIC JOHN Q	9 PATIENT ADDRESS a 15 HILL ST ALFRED NY 14802 USA
b	b c d e

10 BIRTHDATE	11 SEX	12 DATE	ADMISSION 13 HR	14 TYPE	15 SRC	16 DHR	17 STAT	18	19	20	21	CONDITION CODES 22 23 24 25 26 27 28	29 ACDT STATE	30
08051970	M	0505YY	09	3	1									

31 OCCURRENCE CODE DATE	32 OCCURRENCE CODE DATE	33 OCCURRENCE CODE DATE	34 OCCURRENCE CODE DATE	35 OCCURRENCE SPAN CODE FROM THROUGH	36 OCCURRENCE SPAN CODE FROM THROUGH	37
a						

38		39 VALUE CODES CODE AMOUNT	40 VALUE CODES CODE AMOUNT	41 VALUE CODES CODE AMOUNT
PUBLIC JOHN Q 15 HILL ST ALFRED NY 14802	a b c d			

42 REV. CD.	43 DESCRIPTION	44 HCPCS / RATE / HIPPS CODE	45 SERV. DATE	46 SERV. UNITS	47 TOTAL CHARGES	48 NON-COVERED CHARGES	49
0324	CHEST XRAY SINGLE VIEW	71010	0505YY	1	74 50		

PAGE 001 OF 001 CREATION DATE 0505YY TOTALS ➡ 74 50

50 PAYER NAME	51 HEALTH PLAN ID	52 REL INFO	53 ASG BEN.	54 PRIOR PAYMENTS	55 EST. AMOUNT DUE	56 NPI
A AETNA	1265891895	Y	Y		74 50	57 OTHER PRV ID

58 INSURED'S NAME	59 P.REL	60 INSURED'S UNIQUE ID	61 GROUP NAME	62 INSURANCE GROUP NO.
PUBLIC JOHN Q	01	524856254	COMMERCIAL	495G

63 TREATMENT AUTHORIZATION CODES	64 DOCUMENT CONTROL NUMBER	65 EMPLOYER NAME

66 DX 67 496	A	B	C	D	E	F	G	H	68
I	J	K	L	M	N	O	P	Q	

69 ADMIT DX 496	70 PATIENT REASON DX a 496 b c	71 PPS CODE 496	72 ECI a b c	73

74 PRINCIPAL PROCEDURE CODE DATE	a. OTHER PROCEDURE CODE DATE	b. OTHER PROCEDURE CODE DATE	75	76 ATTENDING NPI 1265891895 QUAL
71010 0505YY				LAST SMITH FIRST JOHN
c. OTHER PROCEDURE CODE DATE	d. OTHER PROCEDURE CODE DATE	e. OTHER PROCEDURE CODE DATE		77 OPERATING NPI QUAL
				LAST FIRST

80 REMARKS	81CC a	78 OTHER NPI QUAL
AETNA	b	LAST FIRST
PO BOX 650	c	79 OTHER NPI QUAL
CANANDAIGUA NY 14424	d	LAST FIRST

UB-04 CMS-1450   APPROVED OMB NO.   NUBC National Uniform Billing Committee LIC9213257   THE CERTIFICATIONS ON THE REVERSE APPLY TO THIS BILL AND ARE MADE A PART HEREOF

FIGURE 10-4 Completed UB-04 (CMS-1450) Claim Form (From http://www.cms.gov/)

HEALTH INSURANCE CLAIM FORM

APPROVED BY NATIONAL UNIFORM CLAIM COMMITTEE (NUCC) 02/12

| | | PICA | | | | | | | | | PICA | | |

CARRIER

1. MEDICARE MEDICAID TRICARE CHAMPVA GROUP HEALTH PLAN FECA BLK LUNG OTHER	1a. INSURED'S I.D. NUMBER (For Program in Item 1)
☐ (Medicare#) ☐ (Medicaid#) ☐ (ID#/DoD#) ☐ (Member ID#) ☒ (ID#) ☐ (ID#) ☐ (ID#)	WW123456

2. PATIENT'S NAME (Last Name, First Name, Middle Initial)	3. PATIENT'S BIRTH DATE SEX	4. INSURED'S NAME (Last Name, First Name, Middle Initial)
PUBLIC, JOHN, Q	03 09 1945 M ☒ F ☐	PUBLIC, JOHN, Q

5. PATIENT'S ADDRESS (No., Street)	6. PATIENT RELATIONSHIP TO INSURED	7. INSURED'S ADDRESS (No., Street)
10A SENATE AVENUE	Self ☒ Spouse ☐ Child ☐ Other ☐	10A SENATE AVENUE

CITY STATE	8. RESERVED FOR NUCC USE	CITY STATE
ANYWHERE NY		ANYWHERE NY

ZIP CODE TELEPHONE (Include Area Code)		ZIP CODE TELEPHONE (Include Area Code)
12345-1234 (101) 2017891		12345-1234 (101) 2017891

PATIENT AND INSURED INFORMATION

9. OTHER INSURED'S NAME (Last Name, First Name, Middle Initial)	10. IS PATIENT'S CONDITION RELATED TO:	11. INSURED'S POLICY GROUP OR FECA NUMBER
		50698

a. OTHER INSURED'S POLICY OR GROUP NUMBER	a. EMPLOYMENT? (Current or Previous) ☐ YES ☒ NO	a. INSURED'S DATE OF BIRTH SEX
		03 09 1945 M ☒ F ☐

| b. RESERVED FOR NUCC USE | b. AUTO ACCIDENT?   PLACE (State) ☐ YES ☒ NO | b. OTHER CLAIM ID (Designated by NUCC) |

| c. RESERVED FOR NUCC USE | c. OTHER ACCIDENT? ☐ YES ☒ NO | c. INSURANCE PLAN NAME OR PROGRAM NAME BLUECROSS BLUESHIELD |

| d. INSURANCE PLAN NAME OR PROGRAM NAME | 10d. CLAIM CODES (Designated by NUCC) | d. IS THERE ANOTHER HEALTH BENEFIT PLAN? ☐ YES ☒ NO If yes, complete items 9, 9a, and 9d. |

READ BACK OF FORM BEFORE COMPLETING & SIGNING THIS FORM.

12. PATIENT'S OR AUTHORIZED PERSON'S SIGNATURE I authorize the release of any medical or other information necessary to process this claim. I also request payment of government benefits either to myself or to the party who accepts assignment below.

SIGNED SIGNATURE ON FILE   DATE _____

13. INSURED'S OR AUTHORIZED PERSON'S SIGNATURE I authorize payment of medical benefits to the undersigned physician or supplier for services described below.

SIGNED _____

14. DATE OF CURRENT ILLNESS, INJURY, or PREGNANCY (LMP)	15. OTHER DATE	16. DATES PATIENT UNABLE TO WORK IN CURRENT OCCUPATION
01 12 YYYY QUAL. 431	QUAL. ___ MM DD YY	FROM ___ TO ___

17. NAME OF REFERRING PROVIDER OR OTHER SOURCE	17a.	18. HOSPITALIZATION DATES RELATED TO CURRENT SERVICES
DN IVAN GOODDOC MD	17b. NPI 3456789012	FROM ___ TO ___

| 19. ADDITIONAL CLAIM INFORMATION (Designated by NUCC) | 20. OUTSIDE LAB? $ CHARGES ☐ YES ☒ NO |

21. DIAGNOSIS OR NATURE OF ILLNESS OR INJURY Relate A-L to service line below (24E) ICD Ind. 0	22. RESUBMISSION CODE ___ ORIGINAL REF. NO.

A. 485   B. 788.41   C. ___   D. ___

E. ___   F. ___   G. ___   H. ___

I. ___   J. ___   K. ___   L. ___

23. PRIOR AUTHORIZATION NUMBER

PHYSICIAN OR SUPPLIER INFORMATION

24. A. DATE(S) OF SERVICE		B. PLACE OF SERVICE	C. EMG	D. PROCEDURES, SERVICES, OR SUPPLIES (Explain Unusual Circumstances) CPT/HCPCS MODIFIER	E. DIAGNOSIS POINTER	F. $ CHARGES	G. DAYS OR UNITS	H. EPSDT Family Plan	I. ID. QUAL.	J. RENDERING PROVIDER ID. #
From MM DD YY	To MM DD YY									
1 01 12 YY		11		99213	A	75 00	1		NPI	
2 01 12 YY		11		81001	B	10 00	1		NPI	
3 01 12 YY		11		71020	A	50 00	1		NPI	
4									NPI	
5									NPI	
6									NPI	

25. FEDERAL TAX I.D. NUMBER SSN EIN	26. PATIENT'S ACCOUNT NO.	27. ACCEPT ASSIGNMENT? (For govt. claims, see back)	28. TOTAL CHARGE	29. AMOUNT PAID	30. Rsvd for NUCC Use
111234523 ☐ ☒	13-1	☒ YES ☐ NO	$ 135 00	$	

31. SIGNATURE OF PHYSICIAN OR SUPPLIER INCLUDING DEGREES OR CREDENTIALS (I certify that the statements on the reverse apply to this bill and are made a part thereof.)	32. SERVICE FACILITY LOCATION INFORMATION	33. BILLING PROVIDER INFO & PH # (101) 1111234
		ERIN A HELPER MD 101 MEDIC DRIVE ANYWHERE NY 12345
ERIN A HELPER MD MMDDYYYY SIGNED DATE	a. NPI b.	a. 1234567890 b.

FIGURE 10-5 Completed CMS-1500 Claim Form Using ICD-9-CM Codes (From http://www.cms.gov/)

HEALTH INSURANCE CLAIM FORM

APPROVED BY NATIONAL UNIFORM CLAIM COMMITTEE (NUCC) 02/12

| | PICA | | | | | | | | PICA | |

1. MEDICARE (Medicare#) **MEDICAID** (Medicaid#) **TRICARE** (ID#/DoD#) **CHAMPVA** (Member ID#) **GROUP HEALTH PLAN** (ID#) [X] **FECA BLK LUNG** (ID#) **OTHER** (ID#)

1a. INSURED'S I.D. NUMBER (For Program in Item 1)
WW123456

2. PATIENT'S NAME (Last Name, First Name, Middle Initial)
PUBLIC, JOHN, Q

3. PATIENT'S BIRTH DATE MM 03 DD 09 YY 1945 **SEX** M [X] F

4. INSURED'S NAME (Last Name, First Name, Middle Initial)
PUBLIC, JOHN, Q

5. PATIENT'S ADDRESS (No., Street)
10A SENATE AVENUE

6. PATIENT RELATIONSHIP TO INSURED
Self [X] Spouse Child Other

7. INSURED'S ADDRESS (No., Street)
10A SENATE AVENUE

CITY ANYWHERE **STATE** NY

8. RESERVED FOR NUCC USE

CITY ANYWHERE **STATE** NY

ZIP CODE 12345-1234 **TELEPHONE (Include Area Code)** (101) 2017891

ZIP CODE 12345-1234 **TELEPHONE (Include Area Code)** (101) 2017891

9. OTHER INSURED'S NAME (Last Name, First Name, Middle Initial)

10. IS PATIENT'S CONDITION RELATED TO:

11. INSURED'S POLICY GROUP OR FECA NUMBER
50698

a. OTHER INSURED'S POLICY OR GROUP NUMBER

a. EMPLOYMENT? (Current or Previous)
YES [X] NO

a. INSURED'S DATE OF BIRTH MM 03 DD 09 YY 1945 **SEX** M [X] F

b. RESERVED FOR NUCC USE

b. AUTO ACCIDENT? PLACE (State)
YES [X] NO

b. OTHER CLAIM ID (Designated by NUCC)

c. RESERVED FOR NUCC USE

c. OTHER ACCIDENT?
YES [X] NO

c. INSURANCE PLAN NAME OR PROGRAM NAME
BLUECROSS BLUESHIELD

d. INSURANCE PLAN NAME OR PROGRAM NAME

10d. CLAIM CODES (Designated by NUCC)

d. IS THERE ANOTHER HEALTH BENEFIT PLAN?
YES [X] NO *If yes,* complete items 9, 9a, and 9d.

READ BACK OF FORM BEFORE COMPLETING & SIGNING THIS FORM.
12. PATIENT'S OR AUTHORIZED PERSON'S SIGNATURE I authorize the release of any medical or other information necessary to process this claim. I also request payment of government benefits either to myself or to the party who accepts assignment below.

SIGNED SIGNATURE ON FILE DATE

13. INSURED'S OR AUTHORIZED PERSON'S SIGNATURE I authorize payment of medical benefits to the undersigned physician or supplier for services described below.

SIGNED

14. DATE OF CURRENT ILLNESS, INJURY, or PREGNANCY (LMP) MM 01 DD 12 YY YYYY QUAL. 431

15. OTHER DATE QUAL. MM DD YY

16. DATES PATIENT UNABLE TO WORK IN CURRENT OCCUPATION FROM MM DD YY TO MM DD YY

17. NAME OF REFERRING PROVIDER OR OTHER SOURCE
DN IVAN GOODDOC MD

17a.
17b. NPI 3456789012

18. HOSPITALIZATION DATES RELATED TO CURRENT SERVICES FROM MM DD YY TO MM DD YY

19. ADDITIONAL CLAIM INFORMATION (Designated by NUCC)

20. OUTSIDE LAB? YES [X] NO **$ CHARGES**

21. DIAGNOSIS OR NATURE OF ILLNESS OR INJURY Relate A-L to service line below (24E) **ICD Ind.** 0

A. J18.0 B. R35.0 C. D.
E. F. G. H.
I. J. K. L.

22. RESUBMISSION CODE ORIGINAL REF. NO.

23. PRIOR AUTHORIZATION NUMBER

24. A. DATE(S) OF SERVICE						B. PLACE OF SERVICE	C. EMG	D. PROCEDURES, SERVICES, OR SUPPLIES (Explain Unusual Circumstances) CPT/HCPCS | MODIFIER	E. DIAGNOSIS POINTER	F. $ CHARGES	G. DAYS OR UNITS	H. EPSDT Family Plan	I. ID. QUAL.	J. RENDERING PROVIDER ID. #
From MM	DD	YY	To MM	DD	YY									
1 01	12	YY				11		99213	A	75 00	1		NPI	
2 01	12	YY				11		81001	B	10 00	1		NPI	
3 01	12	YY				11		71020	A	50 00	1		NPI	
4													NPI	
5													NPI	
6													NPI	

25. FEDERAL TAX I.D. NUMBER SSN EIN [X]
111234523

26. PATIENT'S ACCOUNT NO.
13-1

27. ACCEPT ASSIGNMENT? (For govt. claims, see back)
[X] YES NO

28. TOTAL CHARGE $ 135 00

29. AMOUNT PAID $

30. Rsvd for NUCC Use

31. SIGNATURE OF PHYSICIAN OR SUPPLIER INCLUDING DEGREES OR CREDENTIALS (I certify that the statements on the reverse apply to this bill and are made a part thereof.)

ERIN A HELPER MD MMDDYYYY
SIGNED DATE

32. SERVICE FACILITY LOCATION INFORMATION

a. NPI b.

33. BILLING PROVIDER INFO & PH # (101) 1111234
ERIN A HELPER MD
101 MEDIC DRIVE
ANYWHERE NY 12345

a. 1234567890 b.

NUCC Instruction Manual available at: www.nucc.org **PLEASE PRINT OR TYPE**

FIGURE 10-6 Completed CMS-1500 Claim Form Using ICD-10-CM Codes (From http://www.cms.gov/)

- National provider identifier (NPI). HIPAA standard that requires hospitals, doctors, nursing homes, and other health care providers to obtain a unique identifier consisting of 10 numeric digits for filing electronic claims with public and private insurance programs. Providers apply for an identifier once and keep it if they relocate or change specialties. Health care providers were assigned different ID numbers by each health plan, which resulted in slower payments, increased costs, and a lack of coordination.
- National health plan identifier (PlanID). The PlanID is assigned to third-party payers. It contains 10 numeric positions including a check digit in the 10th position (e.g., 1234567890). (The PlanID was formerly called the PAYERID.)

Note: A check digit is a one-digit character, alphabetic or numeric, that is used to verify the validity of a unique identifier.

- Personal identifier. This HIPAA requirement has been withdrawn. Although HIPAA included a requirement for a unique personal health care identifier, HHS and Congress have put the development of such a standard on hold indefinitely. In 1998, HHS delayed any work on this standard until after comprehensive privacy protections were in place. Since 1999, Congress has adopted budget language to ensure that no such standard is adopted without Congress's approval. HHS has no plans to develop such an identifier.

Electronic Data Interchange

Electronic data interchange (EDI) is the computer-to-computer transfer of data between provider and payer (or clearinghouse) via a data format agreed upon by the sending and receiving parties. Administrative simplification provisions of HIPAA directed the federal government to adopt national electronic standards for automated transfer of certain health care data between health care payers (e.g., carriers and fiscal intermediaries), plans (e.g., BCBS), and providers (e.g., hospitals and physicians). This enables the entire health care industry to communicate electronic data using a single set of standards, thereby eliminating all nonstandard formats currently in use. Thus a health care provider is able to submit a standard transaction for eligibility, authorization, referrals, claims, or attachments containing the same standard data content to any health plan. This "simplifies" many clinical, billing, and other financial applications and reduce costs.

Note: HHS has adopted *X12 Version 5010* (health care claims) and *NCPDP Version D.0* (pharmacy claims) for HIPAA transactions to accommodate reporting of ICD-10-CM and ICD-10-PCS codes.

Electronic claims will not be processed if they are in a format other than the HIPAA format. Providers who are not small providers (institutional organizations with fewer than 25 full-time employees, or physicians with fewer than 10 full-time employees) must send all claims electronically in the HIPAA format. Advantages of EDI include:

- Claim status and eligibility information in 24 hours or less
- Cost-effectiveness and reduction in opportunity for error
- Electronic funds transfer of accounts receivable into provider's bank
- Electronic remittances sent to a provider-preferred location
- Faster payment of electronic claims
- Lower administrative, postage, and handling costs
- On-line receipt or acknowledgment
- Standardized electronic claims submission, coordination of benefits exchange, and remittance receipt to reduce system costs

Fraud and Abuse

Fraud is an act that represents a crime against payers or other health care programs (e.g., Medicare), or an attempt or conspiracy to commit those crimes. Abuse is a pattern of practice that is inconsistent with sound business, fiscal, or health service practices and which results in unnecessary costs to payers and government programs (e.g., Medicare), reimbursement for services not medically necessary, or failure to meet professionally recognized standards for health services.

Examples of Fraud:

- Billing Medicare for services or supplies not provided
- Entering another person's Medicare number on a claim to obtain reimbursement for a patient not eligible for Medicare
- Unbundling codes reported on claims. This involves assigning separate codes for component services instead of a combination code for the services provided
- Upcoding claims submitted to payers. This involves reporting codes not supported by documentation in the patient record to increase reimbursement

Examples of Abuse:

- Billing a Medicare patient using a higher fee schedule rate than used for non-Medicare patients
- Submitting claims to Medicare when Medicare is not the beneficiary's primary payer
- Submitting excessive charges for services or supplies or claims for services that are not medically necessary
- Violating Medicare participation or assignment agreements

Note: Medical necessity requires the documentation of services or supplies that are proper and needed for the diagnosis or treatment of a medical condition; are provided for the diagnosis, direct care, and treatment of a medical condition; meet the standards of good medical practice in the local area; and are not mainly for the convenience of a patient or a physician.

CMS employs a four-part strategy to deter fraud and abuse that focuses on prevention, early detection, coordination, and enforcement.

- *Prevention* involves paying the claim correctly the first time, and it is the most desirable approach. It is also the best way to guarantee initial accuracy of claims and payments, and it avoids the requirement to "pay and chase" providers, which is a lengthy, uncertain, and expensive process.
- *Early detection* identifies patterns of fraudulent activity early by using data to monitor unusual billing patterns and other indicators of the integrity and financial status of providers, promptly identifying and collecting overpayments, and making appropriate referrals to law enforcement. If CMS finds errors, repayment is pursued and further action may be warranted depending on the facts and circumstances of each case.
- *Coordination* with partners is another important way CMS maximizes its success in preventing fraud. Information and tactics for fighting fraud and abuse are shared with individual states, the Department of Justice (e.g., FBI), and the private sector.
- *Enforcement* action (e.g., suspension of payment, referral to OIG for potential exclusion from Medicare program, disenrollment, collection of overpayments, imposition of civil monetary penalties) is taken against fraudulent providers. Investing in prevention, early detection, and enforcement has a proven record of returns to the Medicare Trust Fund. The Medicare Integrity Program prevents inappropriate payments through audits, medical reviews, and ensuring that Medicare does not pay

for claims owed by private insurers. The Correct Coding Initiative (CCI) was implemented to reduce Medicare program expenditures by detecting inappropriate coding on claims and denying payment for them.

- Waivers of patient deductibles (21 percent)
- Other (2 percent)

In 2000, the AMA found that "one in three physicians stated patients have asked them to deceive third-party payers to help obtain coverage for health care services," and "one of ten physicians have reported signs or symptoms a patient did not have in order to secure coverage for services provided." The federal False Claims Act imposes stiff fines for health care providers who commit fraud, including $10,000 per claim *plus* three times the charges submitted on the claim.

> *Example* A provider bills Medicare for services provided to a patient that are not documented in the patient record. The charges submitted on the claim total $54.00. If found guilty of fraud, the provider would be required to pay a fine in the amount of $10,162.00.

Medicare fraudulent practices are regulated by the following legislation.

The Civil Monetary Penalties Act imposes a maximum penalty of up to $10,000 plus a maximum assessment of up to three times the amount claimed by providers who knew that a procedure/service was not rendered as submitted on the claim. Violators can also be excluded from participation in government programs (e.g., Medicaid, Medicare).

The Department of Health and Human Services (DHHS) Office of the Inspector General (OIG) developed a series of provider-specific compliance guidances, which identify risk areas and offer concrete suggestions to improve and enhance an organization's internal controls so that its billing practices and other business arrangements are in compliance with Medicare's rules and regulations. Voluntary compliance guidances have been established for the following:

- Ambulance industry
- Ambulance suppliers
- Clinical laboratories
- Durable medical equipment prosthetics, orthotics, and supply industry
- Home health agencies
- Hospices
- Hospital industry
- Hospitals
- Individual and small group physician practices

- Nursing facilities
- Medicare+Choice organizations
- Pharmaceutical manufacturers
- Third-party medical billing companies

The National Correct Coding Initiative (NCCI) was developed by CMS promote national correct coding methodologies and to eliminate improper coding. NCCI edits are based on coding conventions defined in CPT along with current standards of medical and surgical coding practice, input from specialty societies, and analysis of current coding practice.

The federal False Claims Act (FCA) was enacted in 1863 in response to widespread abuses by government contractors during the Civil War, and it was amended in 1986 to strengthen the law and increase monetary awards (e.g., up to $11,000 per false claim, plus three times the amount of damages that the government sustains). It imposes civil liability on those who submit false/fraudulent claims to the government for payment and can exclude violators from participation in government programs (e.g., Medicaid, Medicare).

Note: Qui tam provisions of the FCA encourage and reward private individuals (sometimes called whistleblowers) who are aware of fraud being committed against the government to report that information.

The federal antikickback statute prohibits the offer, payment, receipt, or solicitation of compensation for referring Medicaid/Medicare patients and imposes a $25,000 fine per violation, plus imprisonment for up to five years. Civil penalties may also be imposed, and violators can be excluded from participation in government programs (e.g., Medicaid, Medicare). Safe harbor regulations were also implemented, specifing various payment and business practices that, although potentially capable of inducing referrals of business reimbursable under the federal health care programs, would not be treated as criminal offenses under the antikickback statute.

Example DHHS implemented a safe harbor for the waiver or reduction of coinsurance or deductible amounts (cost-sharing amounts) for inpatient hospital services reimbursed under the prospective payment system. For full or partial waivers to be protected, three standards had to be met:

1. The hospital could not claim waived amounts as bad debt or otherwise shift the cost of the waivers.
2. The hospital could not discriminate in offering waivers or reductions based on the patient's reason for admission.

3. The waivers or reductions could not result from an agreement between the hospital and a third-party payer.

The Department concluded that waivers of cost-sharing amounts for inpatient hospital services that complied with these standards would not increase costs to the Medicare program, shift costs to other payers, or increase patient demand for inpatient hospital services.

Subtitle A of HIPAA authorized implementation of a fraud and abuse control program, which coordinates federal, state, and local law enforcement programs to control fraud and abuse with respect to health plans; conducts investigations, audits, evaluations, and inspections relating to delivery of and payment for health care in the United States; facilitates enforcement of health care fraud and abuse provisions; provides for modification and establishment of safe harbors; and issues advisory opinions and special fraud alerts to provide for reporting and disclosure of certain final, adverse actions against health care providers, suppliers, or practitioners.

The Payment Error and Prevention Program (PEPP) identifies and reduces improper Medicare payments, resulting in a reduction in the Medicare payment error rate. It also participates in overpayment recovery by collecting overpayments made by Medicare, Medicaid, and other payers.

A physician self-referral law (or Stark I), enacted as part of the Omnibus Budget Reconciliation Act of 1989, prohibits a physician from referring Medicare patients to *clinical laboratory services* where they or a member of their family have a financial interest. (The financial interest includes both ownership/investment interests and compensation arrangements.) By 1994, because some providers routinely waived coinsurance and copayments, the DHHS Office of Inspector General (OIG) issued the following fraud alert:

Routine waiver of deductibles and copayments by charge-based providers, practitioners or suppliers is unlawful because it results in (1) false claims, (2) violations of the anti-kickback statute, and (3) excessive utilization of items and services paid for by Medicare.

(The only exception to the alert is waiving deductibles and copayments for financial hardship cases, but this *cannot be done on a routine basis*.)

In 1995, the Stark II physician self-referral law expanded the Stark I by including referrals of Medicare *and Medicaid* patients for the following DHCS:

1. Clinical laboratory services
2. Durable medical equipment and supplies

3. Home health services
4. Inpatient and outpatient hospitalization services
5. Occupational therapy services
6. Outpatient prescription drugs
7. Parenteral and enteral nutrients, equipment, and supplies
8. Physical therapy services
9. Prosthetics, orthotics, and prosthetic devices and supplies
10. Radiation therapy services and supplies
11. Radiology services, including MRIs, CAT scans, and ultrasound services

Medicare Part A reimburses health care facilities for costs associated with training residents. The Physicians at Teaching Hospitals (PATH) initiative resulted from the discovery that some health care organizations were billing Medicare Part B for services that were already paid under Part A. PATH requires a national review of teaching hospitals' compliance with reimbursement rules and training of physicians who provide services at teaching facilities.

The Recovery Audit Contractor (RAC) program is mandated by the Medicare Prescription Drug, Improvement, and Modernization Act of 2003 (MMA) to find and correct improper Medicare payments paid to health care providers participating in fee-for-service Medicare. The goal of the RAC program is to identify improper payments made on claims of health care services provided to Medicare beneficiaries. *Improper payments* include:

- *Overpayments*, which occur when health care providers submit claims that do not meet Medicare's NCCI or medical necessity policies.
- *Underpayments*, which occur when health care providers submit claims for a simple procedure, but upon review of the patient record a more complicated procedure was documented as actually being performed.

Health care providers to be reviewed include hospitals, physician practices, nursing homes, home health agencies, durable medical equipment suppliers, and any other provider or supplier who bills Medicare Parts A and B.

Note: Medicare processes more than 1.2 billion Medicare claims annually, submitted by more than one million health care providers, including hospitals, skilled nursing facilities, physicians, and medical equipment suppliers. Errors in claims submitted by these health care providers for services provided to Medicare beneficiaries can account for billions of dollars in improper payments each year.

Local Coverage Determinations and National Coverage Determinations

Local coverage determinations (LCDs) and national coverage determinations (NCDs) specify the clinical circumstances under which a service is covered (including which clinical circumstances are considered reasonable and necessary) and correctly coded. They assist providers (e.g., facilities, physicians, and suppliers) in submitting correct claims for payment. LCDs outline how contractors (e.g., Medicare carriers) will review claims to ensure that they meet Medicare coverage requirements. Contractors publish LCDs to provide guidance to the public and medical community within a specified geographic area. CMS publishes NCDs and requires that LCDs be consistent with national guidance (although they can be more detailed or specific), developed with scientific evidence and clinical practice, and developed through specified federal guidelines. If a contractor develops an LCD, it applies only within the area it services. While another contractor may come to a similar decision, CMS does not require it to do so.

Never Events

Never events are errors in medical care that are clearly identifiable, preventable, and serious in their consequences for patients. They indicate a real problem in the safety and credibility of a health care facility. Examples of never events include surgery performed on the wrong body part, foreign body left in a patient after surgery, mismatched blood transfusion, major medication error, severe "pressure ulcer" acquired in the hospital, and preventable postoperative deaths. Medicare has generally paid for services without regard to quality, outcomes, or overall costs of care. However, during recent years, CMS began working with provider groups to identify quality standards that can serve as a basis for public reporting and payment (e.g., Hospital Quality Alliance, which developed an expanding set of quality measures). Federal legislation (e.g., Medicare Modernization Act, 2005 Deficit Reduction Act of 2005, or DRA) provides increased reimbursement to hospitals that publicly report quality measures. Paying for *never events* is not consistent with the goals of Medicare payment reforms, and reducing or eliminating payments for "never events" will result in additional resources being directed toward preventing such events (rather than paying more when they occur). The DRA also allows CMS to adjust payments for hospital-acquired infections, and CMS continues to review its administrative authority to reduce payments for "never events" and to provide more reliable information to the public when they occur.

Hospital-Acquired Conditions and Present on Admission Indicator Reporting

The DRA resulted in a quality adjustment in MS-DRG payments to hospitals eligible for reimbursement under the inpatient prospective payment system for certain hospital-acquired conditions (HACs), which include foreign objects retained after surgery, air embolism, blood incompatibility, falls and trauma, manifestations of poor glycemic control, catheter-associated urinary tract infection, vascular catheter-associated infection, and surgical site infection following certain procedures. HACs include those that (1) are high cost or high volume, or both; (2) result in the assignment of a case to an MS-DRG that has a higher payment when present as a secondary diagnosis; and (3) could reasonably have been prevented through the application of evidence-based guidelines. IPPS hospitals are not reimbursed additional amounts when one of the selected conditions is acquired during a patient's hospitalization (e.g., was not present on admission). This means that the case is reimbursed as if the reported secondary diagnosis was not present. CMS also required hospitals to report present on admission (POA) indicators for principal and secondary diagnoses, including external cause of injuries, that are present at the time the order for inpatient admission occurs. POA conditions include those that develop during an outpatient encounter (e.g., emergency department, observation, outpatient surgery). Inpatient coders determine the POA indicator to be reported based on review of the patient record and coding of the principal and secondary diagnoses.

EXERCISE 10–3 Health Care Reimbursement Systems

True/False: Indicate whether each statement is true (T) or false (F).

_____ 1. Historically, most payers initially reimbursed providers according to a fee-for-service payment system that billed payers after health care services were rendered.

_____ 2. Prepaid health plans are considered the forerunner of managed care programs.

_____ 3. Health care costs in the United States decreased dramatically with implementation of government sponsored health programs.

_____ 4. Retrospective payment systems establish predetermined rates for health care services prior to delivery of care.

_____ 5. Paying cash or bartering for health care services was the most common method of payment for services in the early 1900s.

_____ 6. The first prepaid health plans (now called managed care) were introduced in the United States in 1960.

_____ 7. The first Blue Cross policy was based on 1939 California plans created for lumber and mining camp employees in the Pacific Northwest.

_____ 8. Grouper software is used to assign each DRG according to data input for skilled nursing home admissions.

_____ 9. Health care abuse is defined as a pattern of practice that constitutes a crime against payers or other health care programs, or an attempt or conspiracy to commit those crimes.

_____ 10. The clinical laboratory fee schedule was established as a methodology for determining fees for existing laboratory tests in 1984 by the Deficit Reduction Act.

Fill-in-the-Blank: Enter the appropriate term(s) to complete each statement.

11. RBRVS is used to reimburse _____ covered by Medicare Part B and was established as part of OBRA of 1989.

12. The BBA of 1997 legislated implementation of a(n) _____, which uses APCs to reimburse services.

13. Interdisciplinary guidelines, also called _____, are developed by acute care hospitals to facilitate management and delivery of quality clinical care in a time of constrained resources.

14. Hospital categories of service classifed by revenue cost center are called _____.

15. HIPAA administrative simplification standards require that the IRS federal tax employer identification number be adopted as the _____.

Internet Links

BCBS Association
http://www.bcbs.com

CMS Medicare Learning Network
https://cms.meridianksi.com

DHHS Office of Inspector General
http://www.oig.hhs.gov

HIPAA
http://hipaa.yale.edu

Indian Health Service
http://www.ihs.gov

Managed Care Magazine
http://managedcaremag.com

Medicaid and Medicare
http://www.cms.gov

Medicare
http://medicare.gov

MediQual
http://mediqual.com

National Uniform Billing Committee
http://www.nubc.org

National Uniform Claims Committee
http://nucc.org

TRICARE
http://tricare.mil

Workers' Compensation
http://workerscompensation.com

SUMMARY

A medical nomenclature is a vocabulary of clinical and medical terms. A classification system (or coding system) organizes a medical nomenclature according to similar conditions, diseases, procedures, and services. Codes consist of numeric and alphanumeric characters. A third-party payer is an organization that processes claims for reimbursement covered by a health care plan. Health care reimbursement systems include (1) fee-for-service *retrospective* payment systems that base payment on health care services provided to the patient and (2) prospective payment systems that reimburse facilities based on pre-established rates for health care services.

STUDY CHECKLIST

- Read the textbook chapter and highlight key concepts. (Use colored highlighter sparingly throughout the chapter.)
- Create an index card for each key term. (Write the key term on one side of the index card and the concept on the other. Learn the definition of each key term, and match the term to the concept.)
- Access chapter Internet links to learn more about concepts.
- Answer the chapter exercises and review questions, verifying answers with your instructor.

- Study content, view videos, and take practice tests online at www.CengageBrain.com.
- Complete lab manual assignments, verifying answers with your instructor.
- Form a study group with classmates to discuss chapter concepts in preparation for an exam.

CHAPTER REVIEW

Multiple Choice: Select the most appropriate response.

1. The organization that reviews and revises ICD is
   a. ADA.
   b. AMA.
   c. CMS.
   d. WHO.

2. In 1980, DSM-III was expanded to include a multi-axial classification containing _____ axes.
   a. three
   b. four
   c. five
   d. six

3. The AMA publishes this coding system that classifies procedures and services performed by physicians.
   a. CMIT
   b. CDT
   c. CPT
   d. CMT

4. Retail pharmacies use _____ to report pharmacy transactions.
   a. CPT
   b. HCPCS
   c. ICD-9
   d. NDC

5. Which was developed to help health professionals and researchers retrieve and integrate electronic biomedical information from a variety of sources?
   a. DSM-III
   b. ICD-9
   c. NDC
   d. UMLS

True/False: Indicate whether each statement is true (T) or false (F).

_____ 6. The BBA of 1997 legislated implementation of a SNF PPS called RUGs, which reimburse Medicare SNF services according to a per diem prospective rate.

_____ 7. The HHRGs, which reimburse Medicare HHA services according to prospectively determined rates, require recertification every 30 days (or more frequently when there is a beneficiary-elected transfer, a significant change in condition resulting in a change in the case-mix assignment, or a discharge and return to the same home health agency during the 30-day episode) by a physician.

_____ 8. The BBA of 1997 legislated implementation of an outpatient PPS (OPPS) called ambulatory patient groups, which organize similar health care services clinically and according to resources required.

_____ 9. Hospitals can be paid for more than one APC per encounter per patient visit.

_____ 10. The NLA serves as a payment ceiling or "cap on the amount Medicare could pay for each laboratory test."

Fill-in-the-Blank: Enter the appropriate term(s) to complete each statement.

11. A third-party administrator is an organization that provides benefit design, _____, and _____ services to employers and insurance companies.

12. Title XIX of the Social Security Act of 1965, also known as _____, is a joint federal and state program that provides health care coverage to low-income populations and certain aged and disabled individuals.

13. TRICARE is the military health plan that covers active duty and retired members of the uniformed services and their families. TRICARE was previously called _____.

14. The _____ Insurance Program was established to provide health assistance to uninsured, low-income children either through separate programs or through expanded eligibility under state Medicaid programs.

15. The processing of claims to reimburse for medical services provided is known as _____.

16. Health plan enrollees are also known as _____.

17. An employer _____ plan is created by employers who accept direct responsibility for paying employees' health care without purchasing health insurance.

18. Community-based Medicare and Medicaid programs that provide integrated health care and long-term care services to elderly persons who require a nursing-facility level of care are known as _____.

19. State-mandated insurance programs, known as _____, reimburse health care costs and lost wages if an employee suffers a work-related disease or injury; qualified employees and their dependents are eligible for reimbursement.

20. The DHHS agency that provides federal health care services to Native Americans and Alaska Natives is the _____.

21. Abuse is a pattern of practice that is inconsistent with sound business, fiscal, or health practices, and can result in _____ to payers and government-based programs.

22. Acts that constitute crimes against payers and other health care programs, or attempts or conspiracies to commit those crimes, are called _____.

23. HIPAA administrative simplification provisions direct the federal government to adopt _____ for automated transfer of certain health care data between payers, plans, and providers.

24. The creation of PPS for Medicare resulted in implementation of _____ reimbursement rates for health care services.

25. Previous to the inpatient PPS, acute care hospital reimbursement was generated on a per diem basis, which was a type of _____ payment system that issued payment based on daily charges.

26. The FECA of 1916 provided federal _____ with medical care, survivor's benefits, and compensation for lost wages.

27. A copayment, or _____, requires that a specified dollar amount be paid to a provider for each visit or service provided.

28. The amount for which the patient is financially responsible before an insurance policy provides coverage is called the _____.

29. Federal grants and loans to private organizations that wished to develop HMOs were authorized by the _____.

30. An inpatient case that qualifies for additional reimbursement is categorized as a(n) _____.

Short Answer: Respond in paragraph format to each of the following.

31. Describe the differences between the terms *medical nomenclature* and *coding system*.

32. Discuss the purpose of the standard coding guidelines.

33. Explain the term *public domain*.

34. Describe the characteristics of the ICD-10 coding system.

35. Summarize the purpose of the SNOMED.

36. List and discuss the health care plans that paid for services prior to implementation of major government health programs.

37. Differentiate between prospective and retrospective payment systems.

38. Discuss the purpose of a chargemaster.

39. List and discuss the HIPAA national identifiers.

40. Discuss the purpose of local coverage determinations.

Glossary

A

abbreviation list (4) Includes medical staff–approved abbreviations and symbols (and their meanings) that can be documented in patient records. When more than one meaning exists for an abbreviation, the facility should choose one meaning or identify the context in which the abbreviation is to be documented; The Joint Commission standards have not explicitly required an approved list of abbreviations since 1991; however, its National Patient Safety Goals prohibit the use of "dangerous" abbreviations, acronyms, and symbols in patient records, which include those that could be misinterpreted (e.g., D/C could be interpreted as discharge *or* discontinue).

abstracting (1) Data entry of codes and other pertinent information (e.g., patient identification data, admission/discharge dates) utilizing computer software.

abuse (10) Pattern of practice that is inconsistent with sound business, fiscal, or health service practices, and which results in unnecessary costs to payers and government programs, reimbursement for services not medically necessary, or failure to meet professionally recognized standards for health services.

accreditation (1) Voluntary process that a health care facility or organization undergoes to demonstrate that it has met standards beyond those required by law.

Accreditation Council for Graduate Medical Education (ACGME) (1) Professional organization responsible for accrediting medical training programs in the United States through a peer review process that is based on established standards and guidelines.

active (1) Medical staff member who delivers most hospital medical services and performs significant organizational and administrative medical staff duties.

activities of daily living (ADL) (3) Bathing, dressing, eating, toileting, walking, and so on.

acute care facility (ACF) (3) Hospital that provides health care services to patients who have serious, sudden, or acute illnesses or injuries and/or who need certain surgeries.

addendum (4) Amending a patient record entry to *clarify* (avoid incorrect interpretation of information) or add additional information about previous documentation or to enter a *late entry* (out of sequence). Its purpose is to provide additional information, *not to change documentation*. The addendum should be documented as soon after the original entry as possible.

addressograph machine (6) Plastic card containing patient identification; used to imprint information on each report in the patient record.

Administration for Children and Families (ACF) (3) DHHS programs that provide services and assistance to needy children and families, including Temporary Assistance to Needy Families (TANF).

Administration on Aging (AoA) (3) DHHS program that supports a nationwide aging network, providing services to the elderly to enable them to remain independent.

administrative data (4) Demographic, socioeconomic, and financial information.

administrative law (9) Regulations created by administrative agencies of government.

admission/discharge record (6) *See* face sheet.

admission/discharge/transfer (ADT) system (8) Used to input patient registration information, which results in creation of an automated master patient index database that allows for the storage and retrieval of the information.

admission note (6) Progress note *documented by the attending physician* at the time of patient admission. The note features reason for admission, including description of patient's condition, brief history of present illness, patient care plan, method/mode of arrival, patient's response to admission, and physical assessment.

admission register (8) Record usually maintained by the admissions office, which is organized by admission date; contents include patient's name, patient number, admitting physician, admission date, admission diagnosis, and room number.

admitting diagnosis (6) *See* provisional diagnosis.

adult day care (3) Provides care and supervision in a structured environment to seniors with physical or mental limitations.

advance directive (6) Legal document that provides instructions as to how patients want to be treated in the event they become very ill and there is no reasonable hope for recovery. Written instructions direct a health care provider regarding a patient's preferences for care before the need for medical treatment.

advance directive notification form (6) Signed by patients as proof they were notified of their right to have an advance directive.

against medical advice (AMA) (6) Patients who sign themselves out of a facility and sign a release from responsibility for discharge.

Agency for Healthcare Research and Quality (AHRQ) (3) DHHS agency that supports research designed to improve the outcomes and quality of health care, reduce its costs, address patient safety and medical errors, and broaden access to effective services.

Agency for Toxic Substances and Disease Registry (ATSDR) (3) DHHS agency that works with states and other federal agencies to prevent exposure to hazardous substances from waste sites.

agenda (1) Listing of all items of business to be discussed at a committee meeting.

age of consent (4) State-mandated age of emancipation. Facilities must retain records for that state-mandated time period (such as 18 years) *in addition to* the retention law; also called age of majority.

age of majority (4) *See* age of consent.

aggregate data (8) Category of health care data based on performance, utilization, and resource management.

alias (6) An assumed name.

alphabetic filing system (7) Patient's last name, first name, and middle initial are used to file patient records (when no numbering system is selected for use by the facility) and to file master patient index cards (when a numbering system is used by the facility).

alternate care facilities (4) Provide behavioral health, home health, hospice, outpatient, skilled nursing, and other forms of care. Also serve as the documentation source for patient care information.

alternative storage method (4) System for locating storage for patient records other than at the health care facility such as off-site storage, microfilm, or optical imaging.

Alzheimer's treatment facilities (3) Long-term care facility that specializes in the care of patients diagnosed with Alzheimer's disease.

ambulance report (6) Generated by emergency medical technicians to document clinical information such as vital signs, level of consciousness, appearance of the patient, and so on. A copy of the ambulance report is placed in the emergency department record; the original ambulance report is the property of the ambulance company.

ambulatory care (3) Outpatient care that allows patients to receive care in one day without the need for inpatient hospitalization; also called outpatient care.

ambulatory infusion center (AIC) (3) *See* infusion center.

ambulatory patients (3) Patients who are treated and released the same day and do not stay overnight in the hospital; length of stay is a maximum of 23 hours, 59 minutes, and 59 seconds; also called outpatients.

ambulatory record (6) *See* hospital outpatient record.

ambulatory surgery patient (3) Certain procedures can be performed on an outpatient basis, with the patient treated and released the same day. Length of stay is a maximum of 23 hours, 59 minutes, and 59 seconds; if patients require a longer stay, they must be admitted to the facility as inpatients.

ambulatory surgical center (ASC) (3) Surgery is performed on an outpatient basis at a free-standing ambulatory surgical center. Patients arrive on the day of procedure, undergo surgery in an operating room, and recover under the care of nursing staff.

amending the patient record (4) Correction of an incorrect patient record entry by the author of the original entry. To amend an entry in a manual patient record system, the provider should draw a single line through the incorrect information, document a reason for the error, and enter the correct information. To amend an entry in an electronic health record system, the basic principles for correcting documentation errors are followed, and the electronic health record system should store both the original *and* the corrected entry as well as a record of who documented each entry.

American Recovery and Reinvestment Act (1) Legislation that authorized an expenditure of $1.5 billion in grants for construction, renovation, and equipment, and for the acquisition of health information technology systems; Health Information Technology for Economic and Clinical Health Act (HITECH Act) was included in American Recovery and Reinvestment Act of 2009 and amended the Public Health Service Act to establish an Office of National Coordinator for Health Information Technology within HHS to improve health care quality, safety, and efficiency.

ancillary reports (6) Documented by such departments as laboratory, radiology, and nuclear medicine to assist physicians in diagnosis and treatment of patients.

ancillary services (3) Diagnostic and therapeutic services provided to inpatients and outpatients.

ancillary service visit (6) Appearance of an outpatient to a hospital department to receive an ordered service, test, or procedure; also called occasion of service.

anesthesia report (6) Required when a patient receives an anesthetic other than a local anesthetic to document patient monitoring during administration of anesthetic agents and other activities related to the surgical episode.

antepartum record (6) Generated in the physician's office and includes health history of the mother, family and social history, pregnancy risk factors, care during pregnancy including tests performed, and medications administered; also called prenatal record.

anti-dumping legislation (6) *See* Emergency Medical Treatment and Labor Act (EMTALA).

APGAR score (6) Measures a baby's appearance (A) (e.g., skin color), pulse (P), grimace (G) (e.g., irritability), activity (A) (e.g., muscle tone and motion), and respirations (R) on a scale of 1 to 10 (with up to 2 points assigned for each measurement and 10 being the maximum score).

Application software (5) Computer programs that allow the user to perform a particular task or function.

archived records (4) Records that are placed in storage and rarely accessed; also called inactive records.

arithmetic mean (8) Mathematical average.

assault (9) An unlawful threat or attempt to do bodily harm to another, such as threatening to withhold medication from a patient or to place the patient in restraints.

assessment (A) (4) Portion of the POR progress note that documents judgment, opinion, or evaluation made by the health care provider.

assisted-living facility (ALF) (3) Combination of housing and supportive services including personal care and household management for seniors. Residents pay monthly rent and additional fees for services they require.

associate (1) Medical staff member whose advancement to active category is being considered.

ASTM E 1762–Standard Guide for Authentication of Healthcare Information (4) Document intended to complement standards developed by other organizations and define a document structure for use by electronic signature mechanisms, the characteristics of an electronic signature process, minimum requirements for different electronic signature mechanisms, signature attributes for use with electronic signature mechanisms, acceptable electronic signature mechanisms and technologies, minimum requirements for user identification, access control, and other security requirements for electronic signatures, and technical details for all electronic signature mechanisms in sufficient detail to allow interoperability between systems supporting the same signature mechanism.

attestation statement (6) Signed by the attending physician to verify diagnoses and procedures documented and coded at discharge of a hospital patient; discontinued in 1995.

audit trail (4) List of all changes made to patient documentation in an electronic health record system, including all transactions and activities, date, time, and user who performed the transaction.

authentication (4) A patient record entry signed by the author (e.g., provider).

auto-authentication (4) Authentication of a dictated report by a provider prior to its transcription. This practice is not consistent with proper authentication procedures because providers must authenticate the document *after* it was transcribed.

automated case abstracting systems (8) Methods that allow health care facilities to calculate PPS reimbursement, create and maintain patient abstracts within the software system, generate case abstract statistics, generate reports and statistics for case mix analysis, generate special reports according to user-defined criteria, review patient charges concurrently (while patients are being treated), and submit mandatory reporting data to appropriate state and federal agencies.

automated chart tracking system (7) A method that allows providers to request records using a computer; the health information department clerk references a computer screen to process all requests.

automated MPI (8) Resides on a computer and consists of a database of identification data about patients who have received health care services from a facility.

automatic stop order (6) *See* stop order.

autopsy (6) An examination of a body after death. Includes the macroscopic and microscopic examination of vital organs and tissue specimens to assist in determining a cause of death and the character or extent of changes produced by disease; also called necropsy.

autopsy report (6) Contains summary of patient's clinical history including diseases, surgical history, and treatment; detailed results of the macroscopic and microscopic findings, including external appearance of the body and internal examination by body system; contributing factors that led to death; clinical-pathologic correlation; and authentication by pathologist.

average daily census (8) Average number of inpatients treated during a given time period. It is calculated for varying time periods, such as weekly, monthly, and annually.

average length of stay (8) Total LOS divided by the number of patients discharged.

B

bar code reader (5) An input device that reads a bar code and identifies a document as belonging to a specific patient.

bar codes (5) Machine-generated identification codes.

bar code scanner (5) See bar code reader.

bar coding (7) Preprinted scanning code located on a file folder.

bar graph (8) Displays data along an X-axis and a Y-axis.

batched (8) Predetermined groups; in health care, batched abstracting forms are submitted for data entry and report generation.

battery (9) Unlawful touching, such as a surgeon performing a procedure on a patient without having obtained consent.

bed count (3) *See* bed size.

bedside terminal system (6) Computer system located at the patient's bedside. Used to automate nursing documentation; patient information can be entered, stored, retrieved, and displayed.

bed size (3) Total number of inpatient beds for which the facility is licensed by the state; also called bed count.

behavioral health care hospital (3) Specializes in treating individuals with mental health diagnoses.

binders (7) Store records for hospital patients who are currently receiving care.

biometrics (1) An identifier that measures a borrower's unique physical characteristic or behavior and compares it to a stored digital template to authenticate the identity of the borrower, such as fingerprints, hand or face geometry, a retinal scan, or handwritten signature.

birth history (6) Documents summary of pregnancy, labor and delivery, and newborn's condition at birth.

board of directors (1) *See* governing board.

board of governors (1) *See* governing board.

board of trustees (1) *See* governing board.

breach of confidentiality (9) Occurs when patient information is disclosed to other(s) who do not have a right to access the information.

burden of proof (9) "Proving harm" is the responsibility of the individual who initiates a civil complaint.

Bureau of Prisons (BOP) (3) Federal program that provides necessary medical, dental, and mental health services to inmates by a professional staff and consistent with acceptable community standards. It consists of 82 institutions, each of which provides inmate ambulatory care.

bylaws (1) Rules that delineate medical staff responsibilities.

C

call-back method (9) Used in an emergency situation to release protected health information (PHI) by obtaining the requesting provider's main number from the phone book or directory assistance, calling the main number, and asking to be connected to the requesting provider to ensure that you are speaking with an individual authorized to obtain PHI. As a follow-up, require the requesting provider to obtain the patient's authorization to release PHI and mail it to your attention.

cancer registrar (2) Collects cancer data from a variety of sources and reports cancer statistics to government and health care agencies (e.g., state cancer registries); also called tumor registrar.

Capitation payment (10) A predetermined payment for each health plan enrollee.

case abstracting (8) An automated or manual process performed by health information department staff to collect patient information to determine prospective payment system (PPS) status, generate indexes, and to report data to quality improvement organizations and state and federal agencies.

case law (9) Based on judicial decisions and precedent rather than on statutes; also called common law.

case management note (6) Progress note *documented by a case manager*. Outlines a discharge plan that includes case management/social services provided and patient education.

case manager (2) *See* utilization manager.

case mix (1) Types and categories of patients treated by a health care facility.

case mix adjustment (10) Multiple possible payment rates based on patients' anticipated care needs that allow payment systems to decrease the average difference between the pre-established payment and each patient's actual cost to the facility.

case mix analysis (8) Study of types of patients treated by the facility.

case mix index (CMI) (10) Indicates the average weight of a hospital's diagnosis-related groups (DRGs); calculated by adding together all relative weights (RW) for all DRGs billed by the hospital during a selected time period, and dividing the total RW by the total number of DRGs.

case report forms (8) Submitted by health care facilities and providers to report data to sponsoring agencies, facilities, and organizations.

Centers for Disease Control and Prevention (CDC) (3) DHHS agency that provides a system of health surveillance to monitor and prevent the outbreak of diseases.

Centers for Medicare & Medicaid Services (CMS) (1) DHHS agency that administers Medicare, Medicaid, and the Children's Health Insurance Program (CHIP); formerly called the Health Care Financing Administration (HCFA).

centralized filing system (7) Organizes patient records in one central location under the control of the facility's health information department.

central processing unit (CPU) (5) Controls the processing of information throughout a computer system and includes the control unit, arithmetic/logic unit, and primary storage unit.

certificate of birth (6) Record of birth information about the newborn patient and the parents, which identifies medical information regarding the pregnancy and birth of the newborn; also called birth certificate.

certificate of death (6) Contains a record of information regarding the decedent, his or her family, cause of death, and the disposition of the body; also called death certificate.

Certified Documentation Improvement Practitioner (CDIP) (2) Credential validating an individual's knowledge and competency in ensuring that health record documentation captures the clinical information necessary to fully document patients' health care diagnoses and treatments.

Certified Healthcare Technology Specialist (CHTS) (2) Credential validating an individual's understanding of technologies and procedures relevant to information technology in the health care industry.

Certified Health Data Analyst (CHDA) (2) Credential validating an individual's expertise in health data analysis.

Certified in Healthcare Privacy and Security (CHPS) (2) Credential validating an individual's competency in health care data and information privacy and security issues.

character (5) Lowercase and uppercase letters, numeric digits, and special characters.

chargemaster (10) Lists all the procedures, services, and supplies provided to patients by a hospital; charges for each may also appear.

charge-out system (7) Controls the movement of records in and out of the file area and accounts for the location of each record removed.

chart deficiencies (4) Missing reports, documentation, and signatures as determined upon patient record analysis.

chart tracking system (7) Controls the release and return of patient records and uses record requisition forms to retrieve and track requests for patient records.

check digit (10) A one-digit character, alphabetic or numeric, used to verify the validity of a unique identifier.

chemical dependency program (3) Provides 24-hour medically directed evaluation and withdrawal management in an acute care inpatient setting. Treatment services usually include detoxification and withdrawal management, chemical dependency/substance abuse assessment, and therapy.

chemotherapy (3) Intravenous administration of chemical agents that have specific and toxic effects upon a disease-causing cell or organism.

chief complaint (CC) (6) Patient's description of medical condition, stated in the patient's own words.

Chief Information Officer (CIO) (2) Person responsible for the overall technological direction of an organization.

Chief Knowledge Officer (CKO) (2) Person who leads the development, management and sharing of knowledge within an organization.

chief resident (1) Position held by a physician in the final year of residency (e.g., surgery) or in the year after the residency has been completed (e.g., pediatrics); plays a significant administrative or teaching role in guiding new residents.

chronological date order (4) Oldest information is filed first in a section of a discharged patient record. With integrated records, the order of reports is in strict date order, allowing the record to read like a diary.

circulation system (7) Transports records from one location in the facility to another (as well as to locations outside of the facility).

civil law (9) Deals with legal rights and relationships of private individuals; includes torts and contracts.

Civil Monetary Penalties Act (10) Imposes a maximum penalty of up to $10,000 plus a maximum assessment of up to three times the amount claimed by providers who knew that a procedure/service was not rendered as submitted on the claim; violators can also be excluded from participation in government programs.

claims examiner (2) See health insurance specialist.

classification system (10) See coding system.

clearinghouse (10) Public or private entity (e.g., billing service, repricing company, and so on) that processes or facilitates the processing of health information received from another entity (e.g., provider, third-party payer, and so on) from a nonstandard into a standard format.

clinical data (4) Health information obtained throughout treatment and care of patient. Includes health care information obtained about a patient's care and treatment, which is documented on numerous forms in the patient record.

clinical data repository (5) Allows for the collection of all clinical data in one centralized database, and provides easy access to data in electronic or printed form to the patient's clinical history.

clinical documentation improvement (CDI) program (2) Helps health care facilities comply with government programs and other initiatives with the goal of improving health care quality.

clinical laboratory (3) Performs testing in microbiology, clinical chemistry, and toxicology; directed by a pathologist; and testing is performed by certified, professional technologists and technicians.

Clinical Laboratory Improvements Amendments (CLIA) (9) Federal law that delineates requirements for certification of clinical laboratories.

clinical résumé (6) *See* discharge summary.

clinic outpatient (3) Hospital ambulatory care patient who receives scheduled diagnostic and therapeutic care.

CMS-1450 (10) Standard institutional claim form submitted by hospitals, skilled nursing facilities, and other institutional-based providers to payers to obtain reimbursement for health care services provided to patients, also called UB-04.

CMS-1500 (10) Universal claim form developed by the Centers for Medicare & Medicaid Services and used by providers (e.g., physicians) to bill payers for professional fees and office procedures and services.

Code of Federal Regulations (CFR) (1) Codification of the general and permanent rules published in the *Federal Register* by the executive departments and agencies of the federal government.

codes (10) Numeric and alphanumeric characters.

coding (1) Assigning numeric and alphanumeric codes to diagnoses, procedures, and services; this function is usually performed by credentialed individuals (e.g., certified coding specialists).

coding and reimbursement specialist (2) Acquires a working knowledge of CPT and ICD-9-CM coding principles, governmental regulations, and third-party payer requirements to ensure that all diagnoses, services, and procedures documented in patient records are coded accurately for reimbursement, research, and statistical purposes; also called coding specialist.

coding specialist (2) *See* coding and reimbursement specialist.

coding system (10) Organizes a medical nomenclature according to similar conditions, diseases, procedures and services, and established codes; also called classification system.

color-coding (7) Assignment of color to primary and secondary patient numbers or letters used for filing patient records. Color bars are placed on the sides/edges of file folders so that when filed, all records with the same primary and secondary numbers have the same color pattern; this allows misfiles to be easily identified.

combination centralized/decentralized filing system (7) Establishes the health information department manager as responsible for facility records management. This individual manages the record storage plan and ensures that established procedures are followed.

common law (9) *See* case law.

comorbidities (6) Pre-existing conditions that will, because of its presence with a specific principal diagnosis, cause an increase in the patient's length of stay by at least one day in 75 percent of cases.

comparative data (8) Category of health care data used for health service outcomes measurement and research.

compliance guidance (10) Guidelines that identify risk areas and offer concrete suggestions to improve and enhance an organization's internal controls so that its billing practices and other business arrangements are in compliance with Medicare's rules and regulations.

complications (6) Additional diagnoses that describe conditions arising *after* the beginning of hospital observation and treatment and that modify the course of the patient's illness or the medical care required; they prolong the patient's length of stay by at least one day in 75 percent of the cases.

compressible files (7) *See* movable files.

computer-based patient record (CPR) (5) Multidisciplinary and multi-enterprise software that has the ability to link patient information at different locations according to a unique patient identifier.

computer interface (8) Exchange of data among multiple software products.

computerized medical records (5) Term used in 1970–1980 to describe early medical record automation attempts.

computers (7) Devices that allow for rapid circulation of patient information. Access to all patient information contained in the automated record is possible for authorized users via a computer terminal, an intranet, and/or the Internet.

conditions of admission (6) *See* consent to admission.

confidentiality (9) The process of keeping privileged communication secret, which means that information cannot be disclosed without the patient's authorization.

consecutive numeric filing (7) *See* straight numeric filing.

consent to admission (6) A generalized consent that documents a patient's consent to receive medical treatment at the facility; also called conditions of admission.

consultant (2) One who practices a profession. A general term that can be applied to any number of individuals with a wide variety of educational backgrounds, knowledge, and skills.

consultation (6) Provision of health care services by a consulting physician whose opinion or advice is requested by another physician.

consultation report (6) Documented by the consultant and includes the consultant's opinion and findings based on a physical examination and review of patient records.

consulting (1) Label used to describe highly qualified practitioner who is available as a consultant when needed.

consumer-directed health plans (CDHPs) (10) Defines employer contributions and asks employees to be more responsible for health care decisions and cost sharing; includes customized sub-capitation plan (CSCP), flexible spending account (FSA), health savings account (HSA) (health savings security account, HSSA), health care reimbursement account (HCRA), and health reimbursement arrangement (HRA).

contempt of court (9) Failure to obey a subpoena; punishable by fine or imprisonment.

continuing care retirement community (CCRC) (3) Provides different levels of care based on the residents' needs from independent living apartments to skilled nursing care in an affiliated nursing facility.

continuous quality improvement (CQI) (8) Emphasizes the organization and systems; focuses on process rather than on individuals; promotes the need for objective data to analyze and improve processes.

continuum of care (1) Complete range of programs and services, with the *type of health care* indicating the *health care services provided*.

contracts (9) Binding agreements between two or more parties.

contract services (1) Arranging with outside agencies to perform certain functions, such as health information services, housekeeping, medical waste disposal, and clinical services; the purpose of contracting out these services is to improve quality while containing costs.

conveyor belt (7) Device similar to a pneumatic tube, except it uses a belt instead of a tube, and records are clipped to the belt for transport from one area to another.

copayment (10) A specified dollar amount to be paid to a health care provider for each visit or medical service received.

coroner (9) Public officer who investigates deaths due to other than natural causes.

correctional facilities (3) Provide inmates with a secure housing environment that also offers vocational and educational advancement. Medical, dental, and mental health care services are provided to inmates according to a standard of care imposed by court decisions, legislation, accepted correctional and health care standards, and department policies and procedures.

countersignature (4) Authentication performed by an individual (e.g., attending physician) in addition to the signature by the original author of an entry (e.g., resident).

courtesy (1) Medical staff member who admits an occasional patient to the hospital.

court order (9) Written command or direction ordered by a court or judge.

covered entities (9) Private and public sector organizations that must follow HIPAA provisions; include health care providers that conduct certain transactions in electronic form, health plans, and health care clearinghouses.

criminal law (9) A type of public law that deals with crimes and their punishments.

crisis service (3) Provides short-term (usually fewer than 15 days) crisis intervention and treatment; patients receive 24-hour-per-day supervision.

critical access hospital (CAH) (3) Located more than 35 miles from any other hospital or another CAH, or they are state certified as being a necessary provider of health care to area residents.

critical pathways (10) Interdisciplinary guidelines developed by hospitals to facilitate management and delivery of quality clinical care in a time of constrained resources.

curative care (3) Therapeutic.

Current Procedural Terminology (CPT) (1) Published annually by the American Medical Association; codes are five-digit numbers assigned to ambulatory procedures and services.

D

daily census count (8) Number of inpatients present at census–taking time. Census-taking time is usually midnight.

daily inpatient census (8) Official count of inpatients pres-ent at midnight which is calculated each day.

data (5) Raw facts that are not interpreted or processed (e.g., numbers, letters, images, symbols, and sounds).

data accessibility (8) Involves the ease with which data can be obtained.

data accuracy (8) Data that is error free and correct.

data analysis (8) Process of translating data into information utilized for an application.

data application (8) Purpose for which data is collected.

database (4) Documentation in the POR of a minimum set of data collected on every patient, such as chief complaint; present conditions and diagnoses; social data; past, personal, medical, and social history; review of systems; physical examination; and baseline laboratory data. Serves as an overview of patient information.

data collection (8) Processes by which data elements are accumulated.

data comprehensiveness (8) All required data elements are present in the patient record.

data consistency (8) Ensures reliability of data regardless of the way in which data are stored, displayed, or processed.

data currency (8) *See* data timeliness.

data definition (8) Data elements should have defined meanings and values so all present and future users understand the data. Facilities create a *data dictionary* to facilitate this process.

data dictionary (8) A collection of data element definitions.

data granularity (8) Each attribute and value of data is defined at the correct level of detail.

data integrity (8) Data has integrity if it is accurate, complete, consistent, up-to-date, and the same no matter where the data is recorded.

data mining (8) Technique that uses software to search for patterns and trends and to produce data content relationships.

data precision (8) Yields accurate data collection by defining expected data values.

data relevancy (8) Data that is valuable for the performance of a process or activity.

data reliability (8) Data is reliable if it is consistent throughout all systems in which it is stored, processed, and/or retrieved.

data set (8) Establishing a standard method for collecting and reporting individual data elements so data can be easily compared.

data timeliness (8) Data must be collected and available to the user within a reasonable amount of time; data must also be up-to-date. Also called data currency.

data validity (8) Data is valid if it conforms to an expected range of values.

data warehousing (8) Processes and systems used to archive data and data journals.

day treatment program (3) Intensive treatment program provided to patients who live in the community but come to the facility up to five days per week.

death certificate (6) *See* certificate of death.

death register (8) Usually maintained by the health information department; organized according to date of death; contents include patient's name, patient number, attending physician, admission date, date of death, and service (e.g., medical, surgical, obstetrics, and so on).

decentralized filing system (7) Organizes patient records throughout the facility in patient care areas under the control of the department that creates them.

decrypt (9) Recipient of transmitted electronic document decodes the *message digest* and compares the decoded digest with the transmitted version; if identical, the message is unaltered and the identity of the signer is proven.

deemed status (1) Hospitals that are accredited by approved accreditation organizations (e.g., The Joint Commission) are determined to have met or exceeded *Conditions of Participation* to participate in the Medicare and Medicaid programs.

deeming authority (1) When an accrediting organization's standards have met or exceeded CMS's Conditions of Participation for Medicare certification, accredited facilities are eligible for reimbursement under Medicare and Medicaid, and CMS is less likely to conduct an on-site survey of its own.

defendant (9) Individual against whom the complaint is brought; there is a defendant in criminal law.

deficiency slip (4) Form or software completed by the health information analysis clerk and attached to the patient record, which is used to record or enter chart deficiencies that are noted in the patient's record (e.g., missing physician signatures).

Deficit Reduction Act of 2005 (1) Created the Medicaid Integrity Program (MIP), which is a fraud and abuse detection program.

de-identification of protected health information (9) Contains no identification information about an individual; de-identified information can be disclosed if nothing can individually identify the patient.

delinquent record rate (4) Statistic calculated by dividing total number of delinquent records by the number of discharges in the period.

delinquent records (4) Records that remain incomplete 30 days after patient discharge (The Joint Commission standard).

dementia care facilities (3) Long-term care facilities that specialize in the care of patients diagnosed with dementia.

demographic data (4) Patient identification information collected according to facility policy that includes the patient's name and other information, such as date of birth, place of birth, mother's maiden name, and social security number.

deposition (9) Form of discovery used to learn answers to certain questions, obtain a sworn statement from the deponent, observe a witness's behavior and ability to testify, and discover weaknesses and strengths in each party's case.

descriptive statistics (8) Summarize a set of data using charts, graphs, and tables.

developmentally disabled/mentally retarded facilities (3) Sometimes categorized as an intermediate care facility (ICF), these facilities provide residential care and day programming, including academic training, clinical and technical assistance, health care services, and diagnosis and evaluation of individuals with developmental disabilities.

diagnosis-related groups (DRGs) (3) Inpatient hospital cases classified into groups that are expected to consume similar hospital resources. Hospital inpatients are discharged once the acute phase of illness has passed, and they are often transferred to other types of health care, such as outpatient care, skilled care facilities, rehabilitation hospitals, home health care, and so on.

diagnostic/management plans (4) Category of POR's initial plan that documents the patient's condition and management of the condition.

dietary progress note (6) Progress note *documented by the dietitian (or authorized designee).* Includes patient's dietary needs and any dietary observations made by staff.

differential diagnosis (6) Indicates that several diagnoses are being considered as possible.

digital (9) Proposed standard for electronic signatures, which applies a mathematical function to the electronic document resulting in a *unique bit string* (computer code) called a *message digest* that is encrypted and appended to the electronic document.

digital archive (4) Storage solution that consolidates electronic records on a computer server for management and retrieval.

digital signature (1) Type of electronic signature that uses public key cryptography. Created using *public key cryptography* to authenticate a document or message.

disability income insurance (10) *See* disability insurance.

disability insurance (10) Replaces 40 to 60 percent of an individual's gross income (tax free) if an illness or injury prevents the individual from earning an income; also called disability income insurance.

disaster recovery plan (1) Ensures an appropriate response to internal and external disasters (e.g., explosion) that may affect hospital staff, patients, visitors, and the community. The plan identifies responsibilities of individuals and departments during the management of a disaster situation.

discharge data statistics (8) Measure health status and outcomes, health care utilization, and access to health care; often reported to federal and state agencies.

discharge note (6) Final progress note *documented by the attending physician.* Includes patient's discharge destination, discharge medications, activity level allowed, and follow-up plan.

discharge order (6) Final physician order documented to release a patient from a facility.

discharge register (8) Usually maintained by the health information department, this record is organized according to discharge date; contents include the patient's name, patient number, attending physician, admission date, discharge date, disposition, and service (e.g., medical, surgical, obstetrics, and so on); used by the health information department to account for records of patients discharged on a particular date to ensure that all have been processed (assembled, analyzed, coded, and abstracted).

discharge summary (6) Provides information for continuity of care and facilitates medical staff committee review; documents the patient's hospitalization, including reason(s) for hospitalization, course of treatment, and condition at discharge; also called clinical résumé.

disclosed (9) Released.

discovery (9) Legal process lawyers use to obtain information about all aspects of a case; goal is to find information that will help prepare a case for trial or settlement.

disease index (8) Organized according to ICD-9-CM disease codes.

doctors orders (6) *See* physician orders.

document imaging (5) *See* optical disk imaging.

do not resuscitate (DNR) (1) An order documented in the patient's medical record by the physician, which instructs medical and nursing staff to not try to revive the patient if breathing or heartbeat stops.

DRG Creep (6) *See* upcoding.

drug therapy (3) Intravenous administration of other drugs including antibiotics, antivirals, and so on.

dumbwaiter (7) Small elevator that transports records from one floor to another.

durable medical equipment (DME) (3) Includes canes, crutches, IV supplies, hospital beds, ostomy supplies, oxygen, prostheses, walkers, wheelchairs, and so on.

durable power of attorney (6) *See* health care proxy.

E

electronic data interchange (EDI) (10) Computer-to-computer transfer of data between provider and payer (or clearinghouse) using a data format agreed upon by the sending and receiving parties.

electronic health record (EHR) (1, 4) Automated record system that contains a collection of information documented by a number of providers at different facilities regarding one patient; has the ability to link patient information created at different locations according to a unique patient identifier; provides access to complete and accurate health problems, status, and treatment data; and contains alerts (e.g., drug interaction) and reminders (e.g., prescription renewal notice) for health care providers.

electronic medical record (EMR) (5) Automated record system that documents patient care using a computer with a keyboard, mouse, optical pen device, voice recognition system, scanner, or touch screen. Records are often created using vendor software, which also assists in provider decision making and is most commonly associated with office practices that need practice management solutions.

electronic protected health information (EPHI) (9) Protected health information that is in electronic format.

electronic signature (1) Encompasses all technology options available that can be used to authenticate a document. Generic term that refers to the various methods an electronic document can be authenticated, including name typed at the end of an email message by the sender, digitized image of a handwritten signature that is inserted (or attached) to an electronic document, secret code or PIN (personal identification number) to identify the sender to the recipient, unique biometrics-based identifier, or digital signature.

elimination period (10) A 90-day waiting period from onset of disability policies usually require before the individual can apply for disability benefits.

emancipated minor (9) Individual who is married, living away from home and self-supporting, declared legally emancipated by a court of law, pregnant and unmarried, on active duty with the U.S. Armed Forces, or at least 16 years of age and living independently from parents or guardians. If state laws permit a minor to seek alcohol or drug abuse treatment, the minor can authorize disclosure of PHI.

emergency care center (3) *See* urgent care center.

emergency care patient (3) One treated for urgent problems and either released the same day or admitted to the hospital as an inpatient.

Emergency Medical Treatment and Labor Act (EMTALA) (1) Addressed the problem of hospitals failing to screen, treat, or appropriately transfer patients (patient dumping) by establishing criteria for the discharge and transfer of Medicare and Medicaid patients; also called the anti-dumping statute.

emergency record (6) Documents the evaluation and treatment of patients seen in the facility's emergency department for immediate attention of urgent medical conditions or traumatic injuries.

emergency requisition (7) *See* non-routine requisition.

encounter (6) Professional contact between a patient and a provider who delivers services or is professionally responsible for services delivered to a patient.

encounter form (6) Commonly used in physician offices to capture charges generated during an office visit and consists of a single page that contains a list of common services provided in the office. Initiated when the patient registers at the front desk and is completed by providers as the patient receives care; also called superbill or fee slip.

encrypt (9) To encode a computer file, making it safe for electronic transmission so that unauthorized parties cannot read it.

envelopes (7) *See* jackets.

ethics (2) Judgments about what is right and wrong.

F

face sheet (6) Contains patient identification (or demographic), financial, and clinical information (or data). Usually filed as the first page of the patient record because it is frequently referenced; also called admission/ discharge record.

facility identification (6) Name of the facility, mailing address, and a telephone number; included on each report in the record so that an individual or health care facility in receipt of copies of the record can contact the facility for clarification of record content.

facsimile machines (7) Computer devices that transmit a document's image via telephone lines.

False Claims Act (FCA) (10) Enacted in 1863 in response to widespread abuses by government contractors during the Civil War and amended in 1986 to strengthen the law and increase monetary awards (e.g., up to $11,000 per false claim, plus three times the amount of damages that the government sustains). Imposes civil liability on those who submit false/fraudulent claims to the government for payment and can exclude violators from participation in government programs.

family history (6) Review of the medical events in the patient's family, including diseases which may be hereditary or present a risk to the patient.

family numbering (7) Adaptation of unit numbering system in which each household is assigned a unique patient number and each family member is assigned a two-digit modifier number that serves as a prefix to the patient number.

family practitioners (3) Provide care for the entire family and focus on general medicine, obstetrics, pediatrics, and geriatrics.

family support services (3) Services provided to assist families in caring for the patient.

fax (7) *See* facsimile machines.

federal antikickback statute (10) Prohibits the offer, payment, receipt, or solicitation of compensation for referring Medicaid/Medicare patients and imposes a $25,000 fine per violation, plus imprisonment for up to five years. Civil penalties may also be imposed, and violators can be excluded from participation in government programs.

federal certification (3) Measures ability of health care facilities to deliver care that is safe and adequate, in accordance with *federal* law and regulation.

federal medical centers (FMCs) (3) Provide major medical care to federal correctional facility inmates.

Federal Register (1) Legal newspaper published every business day by the National Archives and Records Administration (NARA); available in paper form, on microfiche, and online.

fee-for-service (10) A *retrospective payment system* that billed payers after health care services were provided to the patient; hospital reimbursement was generated as *per diem*, a retrospective payment system that issued payment based on daily charges.

fee slip (6) *See* encounter form.

field (5) Group of characters.

file (5) Collection of related records.

file folders (7) Store paper-based records; are color-coded, durable, come in a variety of sizes and weights, and can be customized by vendors.

filing controls (7) Established to ensure accurate filing and timely retrieval of patient records, including chart tracking system (manual or computerized), file guides, and periodic audit of file system.

final diagnosis (6) Diagnosis determined after evaluation and documented by the attending physician upon discharge of the patient from the facility.

first-listed diagnosis (6) Reason for which the patient sought treatment during that encounter; reflects the current, most significant reason for services provided or procedures performed.

follow-up progress note (6) Daily progress notes *documented by the responsible physicians.* Include patient's condition, findings on examination, significant changes in condition and/or diagnosis, response to medications administered, response to clinical treatment, abnormal test findings, and treatment plan related to each.

Food and Drug Administration (FDA) (3) DHHS agency that assures the safety of foods and cosmetics, and the safety and efficacy of pharmaceuticals, biological products, and medical devices.

forms committee (6) Established to oversee the process of adding, deleting, and changing forms and to approve forms used in the record.

for-profit (1) Business in which excess income is distributed to shareholders and owners.

fraud (10) An act that represents a crime against payers or other health care programs, or attempts or conspiracies to commit those crimes.

G

general hospitals (3) Provide emergency care, perform general surgery, and admit patients for a range of problems from fractures to heart disease, based on licensing by the state.

Genetic Information Nondiscrimination Act of 2008 (1) Prohibits group health plans and health insurance companies from denying coverage to a healthy individual or charging higher premiums based solely on a genetic predisposition to development of a disease in the future; also bars employers from using genetic information when making hiring, firing, job placement, and promotion decisions.

given name (7) First name.

governing board (1) Membership serves without pay and is represented by professionals from the business community; has ultimate legal authority and responsibility for the hospital's operation and is responsible for the quality of care administered to patients; also called board of trustees, board of governors, board of directors.

government-supported hospitals (1) Not-for-profit, supported by local, regional, or federal taxes, and operated by local, state, or federal governments; also called public hospitals.

graphic sheet (6) Documents patient's vital signs (e.g., temperature, pulse, respiration, blood pressure, and so on) using a graph for easy interpretation of data.

H

Hardware (5) The physical equipment is used by a computer system, including the central processing unit, storage devices, input and output devices, and networking equipment.

HCPCS Level II (national) codes (1) Developed by the Centers for Medicare & Medicaid Services (CMS) and used to classify report procedures and services. Codes are reported to third-party payers (e.g., insurance companies) for reimbursement purposes.

Healthcare Integrity and Protection Data Bank (HIP-DB) (1) Created as part of HIPAA to combat fraud and abuse in health insurance and health care delivery by alerting users to conduct a comprehensive review of a practitioner's, provider's, or supplier's past actions.

Health Care Procedure Coding System (HCPCS) (1) Comprised of Level I (CPT) and Level II (National) codes.

health care proxy (1) Legal document (recognized by New York State) in which the patient chooses another person to make treatment decisions in the event the patient becomes incapable of making these decisions.

health data (5) Health facts that are collected about a patient or group of patients that describe a health issue.

health data analyst (2) Obtains employment in a variety of health care settings and is also employed by data warehousing companies to conduct research data management and clinical trials management.

health information (5) Health data that has meaning and has been processed or organized in a manner that is useful for decision making.

health information exchange (5) Exchange and access to patient information generated by other facilities.

health information manager (2) Expert in managing patient health information and medical records, administering computer information systems, and coding diagnoses and procedures for health care services provided to patients.

Health Information Technology for Economic and Clinical Health Act (HITECH) (5) Provides incentives through the Medicare and Medicaid EHR Incentive program.

Health Insurance Portability and Accountability Act (HIPAA) (1) Mandated administrative simplification regulations that govern privacy, security, and electronic transactions standards for health care information; also protects health insurance coverage for workers and their families when they change or lose their jobs.

health insurance specialist (2) Reviews health-related claims to determine whether the costs are reasonable and medically necessary, based on the patient's diagnosis; also called claims examiner.

Health Level Seven (HL7) (5) Standards development organization that develops electronic health record (EHR) standards under the direction of the U.S. Department of Health and Human Services.

Health Plan Employer Data and Information Set (HEDIS) (1) The National Committee for Quality Assurance (NCQA) "tool used by health plans to collect data about the quality of care and service they provide."

Health Resources and Services Administration (HRSA) (3) DHHS agency that provides health resources for medically underserved populations, works to build the health care workforce, maintains the National Health Service Corps, oversees the nation's organ transplantation system, works to decrease infant mortality and improve child health, and provides services to people with AIDS through the Ryan White CARE Act programs.

health services manager (2) Plan, direct, coordinate, and supervise the delivery of health care; includes specialists who direct clinical departments or services and generalists who manage an entire facility or system.

heart and vascular center (3) Provides ambulatory cardiovascular services to include diagnosis and treatment, disease prevention, research, education, and cardiac rehabilitation.

Hill-Burton Act (1) Provided federal grants to modernize hospitals that had become obsolete due to lack of capital investment throughout the period of the Great Depression and World War II (1929 to 1945); in return for federal funds, facilities agreed to provide free or reduced charge medical services to persons unable to pay.

HIPAA standards for privacy of individually identifiable health information (9) Provisions that protect the security and confidentiality of health information; also called the privacy rule.

Hippocrates (1) First physician to consider medicine a science and art separate from the practice of religion.

Hippocratic Oath (1) Adopted as an expression of early medical ethics and reflected high ideals.

history (6) Documents the patient's chief complaint, history of present illness (HPI), past/family/social history (PFSH), and review of systems (ROS). Individual responsible for documenting the history should obtain the information directly from the patient and should document only the facts regarding the patient's case; source of history should also be documented, especially when the individual providing the information is someone other than the patient.

history of present illness (HPI) (6) Chronological description of patient's present condition from time of onset to present; should include location, quality, severity, duration of the condition, and associated signs and symptoms.

home care (3) Allows people who are seriously ill or dying to remain at home and receive treatment from nurses, social workers, therapists, and other licensed health care professionals who provide skilled care in the home.

home infusion care (3) Provided by home health care agencies when intravenous administration of medication is medically appropriate for the patient's condition, and treatment is administered in the home instead of on an inpatient hospital basis.

honorary (1) Retired medical staff member who is honored with emeritus status; also includes outstanding practitioners whom the medical staff wish to honor.

hospice care (3) Provides comprehensive medical and supportive social, emotional, and spiritual care to terminally ill patients and their families. Goal is palliative rather than curative.

hospital-acquired conditions (HACs) (10) Conditions that are considered reasonably preventable that develop/occur to a patient while being treated in hospital, that were not present at the time of admission.

hospital administration (1) Serves as liaison between the medical staff and governing board and is responsible for developing a strategic plan for supporting the mission and goals of the organization.

hospital ambulatory care record (4) *See* hospital outpatient record.

hospital departments (1) Provide direct patient care as well as ancillary (e.g., clinical laboratory) and support services (e.g., health information department).

hospital inpatient record (4) Documents the care and treatment received by a patient admitted to the hospital.

hospitalist (1) Physician who spends most of his or her time in a hospital setting admitting patients to inpatient services from local primary care providers.

hospital outpatient record (4) Documents services received by a patient who has not been admitted to the hospital overnight, and includes ancillary services, emergency department services, and outpatient (or ambulatory) surgery; also called hospital ambulatory care record.

hospital-owned physician practice (3) Practices that are at least partially owned by the hospital, and physicians participate in a compensation plan provided by the hospital.

Human Genome Project (1) Nationally coordinated effort to characterize all human genetic material by determining the complete sequence of the DNA in the human genome; in 2000, the human genome sequencing was published.

hybrid record (1) Combination of paper reports and digital files.

hydration therapy (3) Intravenous administration of fluids, electrolytes, and other additives.

I

imaging center (3) Freestanding facility that provides radiographic and other imaging services to ambulatory patients. Some centers also provide training and participate in national research projects.

impeach (9) If an answer to a trial question is different from that given to the same question in interrogatory format, the judge could doubt the party's honesty.

inactive records (4) *See* archived records.

incident report (4) Collects information about a potentially compensable event (PCE); it is generated on patients and visits and provides a summary of the PCE in case the patient or visit files a lawsuit.

incomplete record processing (1) Includes the assembly and analysis of discharged patient records.

independent database (4) Contains clinical information created by researchers, typically in academic medical centers.

index (8) In health care, serves as a reference to an alphabetized list of names.

indexed (5) Identification of scanned pages according to a unique identification number, making it unnecessary to scan documents for the same patient at the time; each scanned page is indexed so the complete patient record can be retrieved even if a patient's reports are scanned at different times.

Indian Health Service (IHS) (3) DHHS agency that supports a network of 37 hospitals, 60 health centers, 3 school health centers, 46 health stations, and 34 urban Indian health centers to provide services to nearly 1.5 million American Indians and Alaska Natives of 557 federally recognized tribes.

industrial health clinic (3) Located in a business setting, the emphasis is on employee health and safety.

information (5) Data that has meaning and is useful in decision making.

information capture (4) Process of recording representations of human thought, perceptions, or actions in documenting patient care, as well as device-generated information that is gathered and/or computed about a patient as part of health care.

informed consent (6) Process of advising a patient about treatment options; depending on state laws, the provider may be obligated to disclose a patient's diagnosis, proposed treatment/surgery, reason for the treatment/ surgery, possible complications, likelihood of success, alternative treatment options, and risks if the patient does not undergo treatment/surgery.

infusion center (3) Freestanding center that dispenses and administers prescribed medications by continuous or intermittent infusion to ambulatory patients. Infusion is supervised by a licensed health care professional; also called ambulatory infusion center (AIC).

initial plan (4) Documentation in the POR that describes actions that will be taken to learn more about the patient's condition and to treat and educate the patient according to three categories: diagnostic/ management plans, therapeutic plans, and patient education plans.

inpatients (3) Those who remain overnight in the facility for 24 or more hours and are provided with room and board and nursing services.

Input device (5) Equipment that allows users to enter information into the computer system, including the keyboard, the mouse, scanners, microphones, and cameras.

integrated progress notes (6) Progress notes documented by physicians, nurses, physical therapists, occupational therapists, and other professional staff members are organized in the same section of the record. Allow the patient's course of treatment to be easily followed because a chronological "picture" of patient information is presented.

integrated record (4) Patient record format that usually arranges reports in strict chronological date order. The record could also be arranged in reverse date order.

intensive case management (3) Specially trained individuals coordinate and/or provide mental health, financial, legal, and medical services to help the patient live successfully at home and in the community.

intermediate care facility (ICF) (3) Provides developmentally disabled people with medical care and supervision, nursing services, occupational and physical therapies, activity programs, educational and recreational services, and psychological services.

intern (1) Historical term used to designate physicians in the first year of graduate medical education (GME); since 1975, the Accreditation Council for Graduate Medical Education (ACGME) has referred to individuals in their first year of GME as residents.

internal medicine physicians (3) Specialize in the care of adults.

International Classification of Diseases, Ninth Revision, Clinical Modification (ICD-9-CM) (1) Used in the United States to collect information about diseases and injuries and to classify diagnoses and procedures. ICD-9-CM is in use until October 1, 2013, when ICD-10-CM and ICD-10-PCS will be implemented.

interrogatory (9) Form of discovery that includes a list of written questions that must be answered by the party upon whom it is served (either defendant or plaintiff), and that party must swear, under oath, that the answers provided are accurate to the best of his or her knowledge.

interval history (6) Documents a patient's history of pres-ent illness and any pertinent changes and physical findings that occurred *since a previous inpatient admission if the patient is readmitted within 30 days after discharge for the same condition.* Original history and physical examination must also be made available to the attending physician. In this situation, it would be appropriate for the attending physician to document an interval note that documents the patient's present complaint, pertinent changes, and physical findings since the last admission.

intranet (1) Private network that utilizes Internet protocols and technology and allows users to immediately and simultaneously access health care information with complete security and an audit trail, regardless of where users are located.

J

jackets (7) Store x-rays and other oversized materials; open at the top and closed on three sides; also called envelopes.

L

labor and delivery record (6) Records progress of the mother from time of admission through time of de- livery; information includes time of onset of contractions, severity of contractions, medications administered, patient and fetal vital signs, and progression of labor.

lateral file (7) Two- to eight-shelf unit with retractable doors (and lock system if desired).

law (9) A rule of conduct passed by a legislative body that is enforced by the government and results in penalties when violated; also called a statute.

length of stay (LOS) data (8) Represents the number of calendar days that a patient was an inpatient.

licensed practitioner (6) One who is required to have a public license/certification to deliver care to patients.

licensure (1) Obtaining a license to operate.

line diagram (8) Displays data over a period of time; also called a run chart.

listserv (2) Internet-based or email discussion forum that covers a variety of topics and issues.

living will (1) Contains the patient's instructions about the use of life-sustaining treatment.

local coverage determination (LCD) (10) Local payers specify clinical circumstances for which a service is covered by a Medicare payer (including under what clinical circumstances it is considered to be reasonable and necessary) and correctly coded.

longitudinal patient record (5) Records from different episodes of care, providers, and facilities that are

linked to form a view, over time, of a patient's health care encounters. It facilitates clinical decision support and analysis of diagnoses, treatments, and illnesses.

long-term care (3) Includes a range of nursing, social, and rehabilitative services for people who need ongoing assistance. Lengths of stay typically average greater than 30 days.

long-term care hospital (LTCH) (3) Defined in Medicare law as hospitals that have an average inpatient length of stay greater than 25 days. These hospitals typically provide extended medical and rehabilitative care for patients who are clinically complex and may suffer from multiple acute or chronic conditions.

long-term hospital classification (3) *See* long-term care hospital (LTCH).

loose filing (7) Individual reports that must be filed in the patient record after discharge from the facility.

M

macroscopic (6) Gross examination of tissue; visible to the naked eye.

magnetic degaussing (4) Destruction of electronic records by altering magnetic fields on a computer medium.

magnetic stripe card (8) Contains an electromagnetic surface capable of holding a small amount of information.

malpractice insurance (9) *See* medical liability insurance.

managed care (10) Originally referred to the prepaid health care sector, such as HMOs, which combined health care delivery with the financing of health care services; increasingly used to refer to preferred provider organizations (PPOs) and some forms of indemnity coverage that incorporate utilization management activities.

manual case abstracting systems (8) Require health information department staff to enter patient data on a case abstract form and submit batched forms to a vendor for data entry and report generation.

manual master patient index (MPI) (8) Requires typing or hand posting of patient identification information on preprinted index cards; limited information can be retrieved as compared with an automated master patient index.

manual record (4) Maintenance of patient records in paper format. It includes the source oriented record (SOR), problem oriented record (POR), and integrated record.

master patient index (MPI) (8) Links a patient's medical record number with common identification data elements; also called master person index (MPI).

master person index (MPI) (8) *See* master patient index (MPI).

maximizing codes (6) *See* upcoding.

meaningful use (5) Term used as part of the HITECH legislation that outlines the requirements providers must meet in order to receive incentives for using electronic health records.

Medicaid (Title 19) (1) Joint federal and state program that helps with medical costs for some people with low incomes and limited resources. Medicaid programs vary from state to state, but most health care costs are covered for those who qualify for both Medicare and Medicaid.

medical assistant (2) Performs routine administrative and clinical tasks to keep the offices and clinics of physicians, podiatrists, chiropractors, and optometrists running smoothly. Do not confuse medical assistants with physician assistants who examine, diagnose, and treat patients under the direct supervision of a physician.

medical examiner (9) Physician officially authorized by a governmental agency to determine causes of deaths, especially those due to other than natural causes.

medical liability insurance (9) Pays a lawsuit's covered damages or settlement amount and defense costs; also called malpractice insurance.

medical malpractice (9) Results when a health care provider acts in an improper or negligent manner and the patient's result is injury, damage, or loss.

medical necessity (10) Requires the documentation of services or supplies that are proper and needed for the diagnosis or treatment of a medical condition; are provided for the diagnosis, direct care, and treatment of a medical condition; meet the standards of good medical practice in the local area; and are not mainly for the convenience of the patient or physician.

medical nomenclature (10) Vocabulary of clinical and medical terms.

medical office administrator (2) *See* medical office manager.

medical office manager (2) Coordinates the communication, contract, data, financial, human resource, health information, insurance, marketing, and risk management operations of a provider's office; also called medical office administrator.

medical staff (1) Licensed physicians and other licensed providers as permitted by law (e.g., nurse practitioners and physician assistants) who are granted clinical privileges.

medical staff coordinator (2) Responsible for managing the medical staff office functions and assisting with physician credentialing process.

medical transcription (1) Accurate and timely transcription of dictated reports (e.g., history, physical examination, discharge summary).

medical transcriptionist (2) Transcribes prerecorded dictation, creating medical reports, correspondence, and other administrative documents. Uses a special headset to listen to dictation and a foot pedal to pause dictation while keying text into a personal computer (editing grammar as necessary).

Medicare (Title 18) (1) Health program for people 65 years of age or older, certain younger people with disabilities, and people with End-Stage Renal Disease (ESRD, which is permanent kidney failure treated with dialysis or a transplant).

Medicare Prescription Drug, Improvement, and Modernization Act of 2003 (MMA) (1) Provides Medicare recipients with prescription drug savings and additional health care plan choices (other than traditional Medicare); modernizes Medicare by allowing private health plans to compete; and requires the Medicare Trustees to analyze the combined fiscal status of the Medicare Trust Funds and warn Congress and the President when Medicare's general fund subsidy exceeds 45 percent.

medication administration record (MAR) (6) Documents medications administered, date and time of administration, name of drug, dosage, route of administration, and initials of nurse administering medication.

Medieval medicine (1) Developed during the Middle Ages (or Dark Ages), its most significant event was the construction of hospitals to care for the sick (e.g., bubonic plague).

mHealth (4) Refers to use of wireless technology to enable health care professionals to make better-quality decisions while reducing the cost of care and improving convenience to caregivers.

microfilm (4) Photographic process that records the original paper record on film, with the film image appearing similar to a photograph negative.

Middle Ages (1) Characterized by a lack of education except among nobility and the most wealthy; also called Dark Ages.

middle-digit filing (7) A variation of *terminal-digit filing*, which assigns the middle digits as primary, digits on the left as secondary, and digits on the right as tertiary.

Military Health System (MHS) (3) Administers health care for active members of the uniformed services (and their dependents) as provided by military treatment facilities and networks of civilian health care professionals.

Military Medical Support Office (MMSO) (3) Coordinates civilian health care services when military treatment facility (MTF) services are unavailable.

military treatment facility (MTF) (3) Clinic and/or hospital located on a U.S. military base.

minutes (1) Concise, accurate records of actions taken and decisions made during a meeting.

mirrored processing (7) The simultaneous entry and storage of data into a primary and secondary server.

modern medicine (1) Characterized by the implementation of standards for sanitation, ventilation, hygiene, and nutrition; in addition, choosing health care as a profession became more acceptable, hospitals were reformed, and training of physicians and nurses improved.

movable files (7) Include both manual and power types. Manual movable files are mounted on tracks that are secured to the floor and are "moved" by using a handle or crank; power movable files are motorized systems that move when the file clerk "touches a button." Also called compressible files.

multi-hospital systems (3) Category of hospitals where two or more hospitals are owned, managed, or leased by a single organization; these may include acute, long-term, pediatric, rehabilitation, and/or psychiatric care facilities.

multispecialty group physician practices (3) Offer various types of medical specialty care in one organization, and they may be located in more than one location.

N

National Center for Health Statistics (NCHS) (8) Federal agency responsible for maintaining official vital statistics, while registration of vital events is a state function.

National Commission on Correctional Health Care (NCCHC) (3) Provides an external peer review process for correctional institutions that wish to meet its nationally accepted Standards for Health Services.

National Correct Coding Initiative (NCCI) (10) Developed by CMS to promote national correct coding methodologies and to eliminate improper coding. NCCI edits are based on coding conventions defined in CPT along with current standards of medical and surgical coding practice, input from specialty societies, and analysis of current coding practice.

national coverage determination (NCD) (10) Issued by CMS to specify clinical circumstances for which a service is covered.

national employer identifier (10) IRS federal tax identification number (EIN) adopted as the national employer identifier, retaining the hyphen after the first two numbers.

national health plan identifier (PlanID) (10) Assigned to third-party payers; contains 10 numeric positions including a check digit in the 10th position (e.g., 1234567890); formerly called the PAYERID.

National Institutes of Health (NIH) (3) DHHS research center, with 17 separate institutes, is the world's premier medical research organization, supporting some 35,000 research projects nationwide in diseases like cancer, Alzheimer's disease, diabetes, arthritis, heart ailments, and AIDS.

National Practitioner Data Bank (NPDB) (1) Established by the federal Health Care Quality Improvement Act of 1986. It contains information about practitioners' credentials, including previous medical malpractice payment and adverse action history; state licensing boards, hospitals, and other health care facilities access the NPDB to identify and discipline practitioners who engage in unprofessional behavior.

national provider identifier (NPI) (10) HIPAA standard that would require hospitals, doctors, nursing homes, and other health care providers to obtain a unique identifier consisting of 10 numeric digits for filing electronic claims with public and private insurance programs.

natural or man-made disaster record destruction corroboration process (7) Confirms allegations that patient records were destroyed during a natural or man-made disaster.

necropsy (6) *See* autopsy.

necropsy report (6) *See* autopsy report.

negligence (9) Failure to exercise the degree of care considered reasonable under the circumstances, resulting in an unintended injury to another party (*American Heritage® Dictionary of the English Language*).

neighborhood health center (3) Health care is provided to economically disadvantaged people, and treatment is family-centered because illnesses may result indirectly from crowded living conditions, unsanitary facilities, and other socioeconomic factors. Family care team consisting of a physician, nurse, and social worker provides continuity of care to families.

neonatal record (6) Newborn's record that contains a birth history, newborn identification, physical examination, and progress notes.

Networking equipment (5) The wires, modems, routers, and cables that are used to connect an information system.

never events (10) Errors in medical care that are clearly identifiable, preventable, and serious in their consequences for patients.

newborn identification (6) Immediately following birth, footprints and fingerprints of the newborn are created, and a wrist or ankle band is placed on the newborn (with an identical band placed on the mother). Within 12 hours of birth, an identification form is also used to document information about the newborn and mother.

newborn patients (3) Those who receive infant care upon birth, and if necessary they receive neonatal intensive care either within the hospital or as the result of transfer to another hospital.

newborn physical examination (6) An assessment of the newborn's condition immediately after birth, including time and date of birth, vital signs, birth weight and length, head and chest measurements, general appearance and physical findings.

newborn progress notes (6) Documents information gathered by nurses in the nursery and includes vital signs, skin color, intake and output, weight, medications and treatments, and observations.

non-licensed practitioner (6) Does not have a public license/certification and is supervised by a licensed/certified professional in the delivery of care to patients.

non-routine requisition (7) Occurs when a patient record is needed for an unscheduled service, such as an emergency room visit; also called emergency requisition.

not-for-profit (1) Excess income is reinvested in the facility.

numbering systems (7) Identify and file patient records according to preassigned numbers, including serial, unit, or serial-unit.

numeric filing (7) Uses number to file patient records.

nurses notes (6) Documents daily observation about patients, including an initial history of the patient, patient's reactions to treatments, and treatments rendered.

nursing assessment (4) Documents patient's history, current medications, and vital signs on a variety of nursing forms, including nurses notes and graphic charts.

nursing care plan (6) Documents nursing diagnoses as well as interventions used to care for the patient.

nursing discharge summary (6) Documents patient discharge plans and instructions.

nursing documentation (6) Crucial to patient care because the majority of care delivered to inpatients is performed by nursing staff.

nursing facility (NF) (3) *See* skilled nursing facility (SNF).

O

objective (O) (4) Portion of the POR progress note that documents observations about the patient, such as physical findings or lab or x-ray results (e.g., chest x-ray negative).

observation patients (3) Receive services furnished on a hospital's premises that are ordered by a physician or other authorized individual, including use of a bed and periodic monitoring by nursing or other staff, which are reasonable and necessary to evaluate an outpatient's condition or determine the need for a possible admission as an inpatient.

obstetrical record (6) Mother's record that contains an antepartum record, labor and delivery record, and postpartum record.

occasion of service (6) *See* ancillary service visit.

Occupational Safety & Health Administration (OSHA) (9) Ensures safe and healthful workplaces in America.

off-site storage (4) Location separate from the facility used to store records; also called remote storage.

online analytical processing (OLAP) servers (8) Store data in multiple dimensions and facilitate trend analysis and forecasting, allowing health care organizations to make informed, proactive decisions.

open-shelf file (7) Six- to eight-shelf unit, which resembles a bookshelf, provides twice as much filing space as a standard drawer file cabinet, and requires less than 10 percent additional floor space.

Operating software (5) A set of computer programs that control hardware and interface with application software.

operative record (6) Describes gross findings, organs examined (visually or palpated), and techniques associated with the performance of surgery.

optical disk imaging (5) Provides an alternative to traditional microfilm or remote storage systems because patient records are converted to an electronic image and saved on storage media; also called document imaging.

ORYX® initiative (1) Introduced by The Joint Commission to integrate outcomes and other performance measurement data into the accreditation process.

outguide (7) Replaces the record in the file area to indicate it has been removed and to identify its current location.

outpatient care (3) *See* ambulatory care.

outpatient clinic (3) Facility where patients receive follow-up care. Visits are usually under one hour. The number of weekly visits depends on the patient's needs.

outpatients (3) *See* ambulatory patients.

outpatient visit (6) Visit of a patient on one calendar day to one or more hospital departments for the purpose of receiving outpatient health care services.

Output device (5) Equipment that allows users to print or display information produced by a computer system, including printers and computer screens.

overpayment recovery (10) Collecting overpayments made by Medicare, Medicaid, and other payers.

P

pain management (3) Intravenous administration of narcotics and other drugs designed to relieve pain.

pain management center (3) Specializes in treatment of acute and chronic pain syndromes using proven medications and procedures. Usually a multidisciplinary approach is used, involving participating specialists such as physiatrists, psychiatrists, neurologists, neurosurgeons, internists, and physical and occupational therapists.

paleopathology (1) Study of human remains.

palliative care (3) Comfort management.

papyrus (1) Loose-textured, porous, white paper used as a writing material and made from the papyrus water plant.

partial hospitalization program (3) Program for hospital patients who regularly use the hospital facilities for a substantial number of either daytime or nighttime hours.

past history (6) Summary of past illnesses, operations, injuries, treatments, and known allergies.

pathology report (6) Assists in the diagnosis and treatment of patients by documenting the analysis of tissue removed surgically or diagnostically, or that is expelled by the patient; also called tissue report.

patient-centric data (8) Category of health care data directly related to patients.

patient education plans (4) Category of POR's initial plan that documents patient teaching about conditions and treatments.

patient identification (6) Patient's name and some other piece of identifying information such as medical record number, date of birth, or social security number; every report in the patient record and every screen in an automated record system must include patient identification.

patient monitoring system (5) System that collects and monitors patient physiological data and records the information.

Patient portal (5) Special application that provides patients with secure access to their electronic health information and patient-provider communication tools.

patient property form (6) Records items patients bring with them to the hospital.

patient record (4) Serves as the business record for a patient encounter, contains documentation of all health care services provided to a patient, and is a repository of information that includes demographic data, and documentation to support diagnoses, justify treatment, and record treatment results.

patient record documentation committee (6) *See* forms committee.

Patient Safety and Quality Improvement Act of 2005 (1) Amends Title IX of the Public Health Service Act to provide improved patient safety and reduced incidence of events adversely affecting patient safety.

patient safety organizations (PSOs) (9) A federally established organization where health care providers can confidentially report health care mistakes.

Patient Self-Determination Act (1) Requires consumers to be provided with informed consent, information about their right to make advance health care decisions (called advance directives), and information about state laws that impact legal choices in making health care decisions.

patient's representative (4) Person who has legal responsibility for the patient and signs an admission consent form to document consent to treatment.

Payment Error and Prevention Program (PEPP) (10) Identifies and reduces improper Medicare payments, resulting in a reduction in the Medicare payment error rate; also participates in overpayment recovery.

pediatricians (3) Provide comprehensive services for infants, children, and adolescents.

periodic audit of file area (7) Review of charged-out records to ensure that all records removed from the file area are returned in a timely fashion.

personal care and support services (3) Provide assistance in performing daily living activities, such as bathing, dressing, grooming, going to the toilet, mealtime assistance, travel training, and accessing recreation services.

personal health record (PHR) (5) Electronic or paper medical record maintained and updated by an individual for his or her own personal use.

personal identifier (10) HIPAA requirement for a unique personal health care identifier has been withdrawn although originally included; HHS and Congress have put the development of such a standard on hold indefinitely.

physical examination (6) Assessment of the patient's body systems to assist in determining a diagnosis, documenting a *provisional diagnosis,* which may include differential diagnoses.

physician index (8) Organized according to numbers assigned by the facility to physicians who treat inpatients and outpatients.

physician office records (6) Documents patient health care services received in a physician's office. Should contain patient registration information, a problem list, a medication record, progress notes (including patient's history and physical examination), and results of ancillary reports.

physician orders (6) Direct the diagnostic and therapeutic patient care activities; also called doctors orders.

Physician Quality Reporting Initiative (PQRI) (1) The Tax Relief and Health Care Act of 2006 (TRHCA) authorized implementation to establish a financial incentive for eligible professionals who participate in a voluntary quality reporting program.

Physicians at Teaching Hospitals (PATH) initiative (10) Resulted from the discovery that some health care organizations were billing Medicare Part B for services that were already paid under Part A; requires a national review of teaching hospitals' compliance with reimbursement rules and training of physicians who provide services at teaching facilities.

physician self-referral law (10) Enacted as part of the Omnibus Budget Reconciliation Act of 1989.

Prohibits a physician from referring Medicare patients to *clinical laboratory services* where they or a member of their family have a financial interest; financial interest includes both ownership/investment interests and compensation arrangements. 1994 DHHS OIG alert stated "routine waiver of deductibles and copayments by charge-based providers, practitioners, or suppliers is unlawful because it results in (1) false claims, (2) violations of the anti-kickback statute, and (3) excessive utilization of items and services paid for by Medicare." The only exception to the alert is waiving deductibles and copayments for financial hardship cases, but this *cannot be done on a routine basis*. See also Stark I.

pie chart (8) Displays component parts of data as it relates to the whole.

plaintiff (9) The individual who initiates a civil complaint; there is no plaintiff in criminal law.

plan (P) (4) Portion of the POR progress note that documents diagnostic, therapeutic, and educational plans to resolve the problems.

planned requisition (7) Request of a patient record for a scheduled service.

pneumatic tube (7) Transports a single record in a tube through a tunnel.

postanesthesia care unit (PACU) record (6) Delineates care administered to the patient from the time of arrival until the patient is moved to a nursing unit or discharged home.

postanesthesia evaluation note (6) Progress note *documented by any individual qualified to administer anesthesia*. Includes patient's general condition following surgery, description of presence/absence of anesthesia-related complications and/or postoperative abnormalities, blood pressure, pulse, presence/absence of swallowing reflex and cyanosis; sometimes documented on a special form located on the reverse of the anesthesia record.

postmortem report (6) *See* autopsy report.

postoperative note (6) Progress note *documented by the surgeon* after surgery.

postpartum record (6) Documents information concerning the mother's condition after delivery.

potentially compensable event (PCE) (4) An accident or medical error that results in personal injury or loss of property.

power filing machines (7) Equipment designed to utilize ceiling height rather than floor space; clerks quickly access records without bending, lifting, or stretching.

preadmission testing (PAT) (4) Incorporates patient registration, testing, and other services into one visit prior to inpatient admission (or scheduled outpatient surgery) with the results incorporated into the patient's record.

preanesthesia evaluation note (6) Progress note *documented by any individual qualified to administer anesthesia* prior to the induction of anesthesia. Includes evidence of patient interview to verify past and present medical and drug history and previous anesthesia experience(s), evaluation of the patient's physical status, review of the results of relevant diagnostic studies, discussion of preanesthesia medications and choice of anesthesia to be administered, surgical and/or obstetrical procedure to be performed, and potential anesthetic problems and risks; sometimes documented on a special form located on the reverse of the anesthesia record.

Prehistoric medicine and ancient medicine (1) Characterized by the belief that illness was caused by the supernatural; an attempt to explain changes in body functions that were not understood (e.g., evil spirits were said to have invaded the body of the sick person).

prenatal record (6) *See* antepartum record.

preoperative note (6) Progress note *documented by the surgeon* prior to surgery. Summarizes the patient's condition and documents a preoperative diagnosis.

present on admission (10) Principal and secondary diagnoses, including external cause of injuries, that are present at the time the order for inpatient admission occurs.

primary care (1) Services include preventive and acute care that are referred to as the *point of first contact* and are provided by a general practitioner or other health professional (e.g., nurse practitioner) who has first contact with a patient seeking medical treatment, including general dental, ophthalmic, and pharmaceutical services.

primary care center (3) Offers adult and family care medicine in internal medicine, pediatrics, and family practice.

primary memory (7) A computer's built-in microchip that stores data and information.

primary sources (4) Records that document patient care provided by health care professionals and include original patient record, x-rays, scans, EKGs, and other documents of clinical findings.

primary storage (7) *See* primary memory.

principal diagnosis (6) Condition established after study to be chiefly responsible for occasioning the admission of the patient to the hospital for care.

principal procedure (6) Procedure performed for definitive or therapeutic reasons, rather than diagnostic purposes, or to treat a complication, or that procedure which is most closely related to the principal diagnosis.

privacy (9) Information cannot be disclosed without patient authorization.

privacy officer (2) Oversees all ongoing activities related to the development, implementation, maintenance of, and adherence to the organization's policies and procedures covering the privacy of, and access to, patient health information in compliance with federal and state laws and the health care organization's information privacy practices.

privacy rule (9) *See* HIPAA standards for privacy of individually identifiable health information.

privileged communication (9) Any information communicated by a patient to a health care provider.

problem list (4) Documentation in the POR that acts as a table of contents for the patient record because it is filed at the beginning of the record and contains a list of the patient's problems. Each problem is numbered, which helps to index documentation throughout the record.

problem oriented medical record (POMR) (4) *See* problem oriented record (POR).

problem oriented record (POR) (4) Systematic method of documentation, which consists of four components: database, problem list, initial plan, and progress notes. Also called problem oriented medical record (POMR).

procedure index (8) Organized according to ICD-9-CM and/or CPT/HCPCS procedure/service codes.

professional practice experience (2) Externship or internship.

professional practice experience supervisor (2) Individual to whom the student reports while completing the professional practice experience at a health care facility.

progress notes (6) Contain statements related to the course of the patient's illness, response to treatment, and status at discharge. They facilitate health care team member communication because progress notes provide a chronological picture and analysis of the patient's clinical course; they document continuity of care, which is crucial to quality care.

proprietary hospitals (1) For-profit hospitals owned by corporations (e.g., Humana), partnerships (e.g., physicians), or private foundations (e.g., Tarpon Springs Hospital Foundation, Inc., which does business as Helen Ellis Memorial Hospital in Tarpon Springs, Florida).

prospective payment system (PPS) (10) Pre-establishes reimbursement rates for health care services.

protected health information (PHI) (9) Information that is identifiable to an individual (or individual identifiers) such as name, address, telephone numbers, date of birth, Medicaid ID number and other medical record numbers, social security number (SSN), or name of employer.

provisional diagnosis (4) Working, tentative, admission, and preliminary diagnosis obtained from the attending physician; it is the diagnosis upon which inpatient care is initially based.

pseudonumber (7) Assigned to patients who do not have a social security number; used in association with social security numbering.

public health department (3) Provides preventive medicine services such as well baby clinics, which include immunizations and routine checkups.

Public Health Service (PHS) (3) Uniformed Service of the Department of Health and Human Services. Leadership is provided by the U.S. Surgeon General. It provides highly trained and mobile health professionals who carry out programs to promote the nation's health, understand and prevent disease and injury, assure safe and effective drugs and medical devices, deliver health services to federal beneficiaries, and furnish health expertise in time of war or other national or international emergencies.

public hospitals (1) *See* government-supported hospitals.

public key cryptography (1) Attaches an alphanumeric number to a document that is unique to the document and to the person signing the document. Uses an algorithm of two keys, one for creating the digital signature by transforming data into a seemingly unintelligible form and the other to verify a digital signature and return the message to its original form.

public law (9) Deals with relationships between individuals and government and includes criminal law and regulations.

purge (4) Remove inactive paper-based records from a file system for the purpose of converting them to microfilm or optical disk or destroying them.

Q

qualified protective order (9) Prohibits the use or disclosure of PHI for any purpose beyond the litigation at hand, and requires that the PHI, and all copies, be returned to the covered entity or destroyed when the litigation is over.

quality improvement organization (QIO) (1) New name for peer review organizations (PROs); QIOs continue to perform quality control and utilization review of health care furnished to Medicare beneficiaries.

quality manager (2) Coordinates a health care facility's quality improvement program to ensure quality patient care, improve patient outcomes, confirm accreditation/ regulatory compliance, and prepare for surveys.

quaternary care (1) Considered as an extension of "tertiary care" and includes advanced levels of medicine that are highly specialized, not widely used (e.g., experimental medicine), and very costly; it is typically provided by tertiary care centers.

R

read and verified (RAV) (6) Abbreviation entered by staff member who documents a telephone order to document that the telephone order call-back policy was followed.

reciprocity (2) Recognition of credentials by other entities.

record (5) Collection of related fields.

record circulation (1) Includes the retrieval of patient records for the purpose of inpatient readmission, scheduled and unscheduled outpatient clinic visits, authorized quality management studies, and education and research.

record destruction methods (4) Paper records are usually dissolved in acid, incinerated (burned), pulped or pulverized (crushing into powder), or shredded.

record retention schedule (4) Outlines patient information that will be maintained, time period for retention, and manner in which information will be stored. Records are stored on paper, microfilm, magnetic tape, optical disk, or as part of an electronic (or computer) system.

record transitional template (5) A document that delineates the various sources of the component parts of the patient's record and assists in the transition from paper to electronic formats.

Recovery Audit Contractor (RAC) program (10) Mandated by the Medicare Prescription Drug, Improvement, and Modernization Act of 2003 (MMA) to find and correct improper Medicare payments paid to health care providers participating in the fee-for-service Medicare health plan.

recovery room record (6) See postanesthesia care unit (PACU) record.

referred outpatient (3) Hospital ambulatory care patient who receives diagnostic or therapeutic care because such care is unavailable in the primary care provider's office. Follow-up is done at the primary care provider's office.

regional health information organization (RHIO) (5) Electronic network of medical information about patients, which was gathered from multiple health care organizations in a geographic region.

register (8) In health care, a record of admissions, discharges, births, deaths, operations, and other events.

registration-admission-discharge-transfer system (RADT) (5) Centralized database of patient demographic information that is used during processing of inpatient admissions and discharges.

registry (8) An organized system for the collection, storage, retrieval, analysis, and dissemination of information on individuals who have either a particular disease, a condition that predisposes to the occurrence of a health-related event, or prior exposure to substances or circumstances known or suspected to cause adverse health effects.

regulation (1) Interpretation of a law; written by a responsible regulatory agency such as Centers for Medicare & Medicaid Services (CMS).

rehabilitation facility (outpatient) (3) Provides occupational, physical, and speech therapy to patients with various injuries and various neurological and neuromuscular conditions.

rehabilitation hospital (inpatient) (3) Admits patients who are diagnosed with trauma or disease and who need to learn how to function.

rehabilitation therapy progress note (6) Progress notes *documented by various rehabilitation therapists* that demonstrate the patient's progress (or lack thereof) toward established therapy goals.

relational database (8) Contains a limited two-dimensional structure that does not allow for complete trend analysis.

release of information log (9) Document of patient information released to authorized requestors; data is entered manually (e.g., 3-ring binder) or by using tracking software.

remote storage (4) *See* off-site storage.

Renaissance medicine (1) Mostly associated with Europe; was characterized by a renewed interest in the arts, sciences, and philosophy. This was the beginning of modern medicine, based on education instead of spiritual beliefs.

report generation (4) Consists of formatting and/or structuring captured information. A process of analyzing, organizing, and presenting recorded patient information for authentication and inclusion in the patient's health care record.

requisition form (7) Submitted to the health information department to retrieve the record and track its return.

res gestae **(9)** Latin for "things done," which means that hearsay statements made during an incident are admissible as evidence.

resident (1) Physician who has completed an internship and is engaged in a program of training designed to increase his or her knowledge of the clinical disciplines of medicine, surgery, or any of the other special fields that provide advanced training in preparation for the practice of a specialty.

residential care facility (RCF) (3) Provides non-medical custodial care, which can be provided in a single family residence, a retirement residence, or in any appropriate care facility including a nursing home.

residential treatment facility (3) Seriously disturbed patients receive intensive and comprehensive psychiatric treatment on a long-term basis.

res ipsa loquitur **(9)** Latin for "the thing speaks for itself," which means that something is self-evident.

res judicata **(9)** Latin for "the thing is decided," which means that the final judgment of a competent court is conclusive. It prevents a plaintiff from suing on a claim that has already been decided, and it prevents a defendant from raising any new defense to defeat enforcement of an earlier judgment.

respiratory therapy progress note (6) Progress notes *documented by respiratory therapists.* Include therapy administered, machines used, medication(s) added to machines, type of therapy, dates/times of administration, specifications of the prescription, effects of therapy including any adverse reactions, and reassessment of duration/ frequency of respiratory therapy.

respite care (3) Care provided by specially trained individuals at a setting other than the patient's home to offer relief and rest to primary caregivers.

respondeat superior (9) Latin for "let the master answer," which means that an employer is responsible for the legal consequences of an employee's actions.

retention period (4) Length of time a facility will maintain an archived record, based on federal and state laws.

revenue codes (10) Codes that classify hospital categories of service by revenue cost center; reported on the CMS 1450 (UB-04).

reverse chronological date order (4) Most current document is filed first in a section of the inpatient record.

reverse numeric filing (7) *See* terminal-digit filing.

review of systems (ROS) (6) Inventory by systems to reveal subjective symptoms stated by the patient; provides an opportunity to gather information that the patient may have forgotten to mention or that may have seemed unimportant.

risk manager (2) Responsible for gathering information and recommending settlements concerning professional and general liability incidents, claims, and lawsuits.

root cause analysis (9) Performed on any event assigned ICD-9-CM codes 900–963, it is a process intended to determine what happened, why it happened, and what the facility can do to prevent it from happening again.

routine order (6) Physician orders preapproved by the medical staff, which are preprinted and placed on a patient's record. Include standard admitting orders for a surgical patient, discharge orders following surgery, and so on.

rules and regulations (1) procedures based on federal and state regulations, and accreditation standards, which clarify medical staff bylaws.

run chart (8) *See* line diagram.

S

safe harbor regulations (10) Specify various payment and business practices that, although potentially capable of inducing referrals of business reimbursable under the federal health care programs, would not be treated as criminal offenses under the antikickback statute.

satellite clinics (3) Ambulatory care centers established remotely from the hospital. Primary care is provided by an on-duty physician (usually salaried).

scanner (5) Used to capture paper record images onto the storage media and allows for rapid automated retrieval of records.

secondary care (1) Services provided by medical specialists or hospital staff members to a patient whose primary care was provided by a general practitioner who first diagnosed or treated the patient (the primary care provider refers the patient to the specialist).

secondary device (7) Physical equipment that stores data and programs.

secondary diagnoses (6) Additional conditions for which the patient received treatment and/or impacted the inpatient care.

secondary procedure(s) (6) Additional procedure(s) performed during inpatient admission.

secondary sources (4) Patient information that contains data abstracted (selected) from primary sources of patient information such as indexes and registers, committee minutes, and incident reports.

secondary storage (7) Auxiliary, external, or permanent storage on devices or servers.

sectionalized record (4) Each source of data in the inpatient record has a section that is labeled.

security (9) Keeping facilities, equipment, and patient information safe from damage, loss, tampering, theft, or unauthorized access.

security rule (9) Adopts standards and safeguards to protect health information that is collected, maintained, used, or transmitted *electronically.*

serial numbering system (7) Each time the patient is registered, a new patient number is assigned by the provider and a new patient record is created. A patient who has had multiple admissions to the facility also has multiple patient numbers. Patient records are filed in multiple locations in the permanent file system. Usually selected by facilities that do not use computerized registration/ admission/discharge/ transfer (RADT) software.

serial-unit numbering (7) Patients receive a new number each time they are registered by the facility, and records from a previous admission or encounter are reassigned the new number. All patient records are filed in the most current folder in one location.

severity of illness (10) Physiologic complexity that comprises the extent and interactions of a patient's disease(s) as presented to medical personnel.

shadow record (4) Paper record that contains copies of original records and is maintained separately from the primary record.

Shared Visions—New Pathways™ (1) Introduced by The Joint Commission in 2003 to radically change the survey process so it focuses on whether the organization is making improvements system-wide. Facilities will adopt a continuous survey process starting in 2004, which means survey preparation will be an ongoing process (instead of the traditional once-every-three-years labor-intensive preparation that proved not to impact on improving patient care).

short stay (6) An uncomplicated hospital stay of less than 48 hours.

short stay record (6) Allows providers to record the patient's history, physical examination, progress notes, physician orders, and nursing documentation on one double-sided form.

short-term (acute) hospital classification (3) Patients have an average LOS of 4–5 days and a total LOS of less than 25 days; also called acute hospital classification.

signature legend (4) Document maintained by the health information department to identify the author by full signature when initials are used to authenti-cate entries. Initials are typically used to authenticate entries on nursing flow sheets, such as medication administration records.

signature stamp (4) When authorized for use in a facility, the provider whose signature the stamp represents must sign a statement that the provider alone will use the stamp to authenticate documents. The statement is maintained on file in the facility's administrative offices.

single hospitals (3) Category of hospitals that are selfcontained and not part of a larger organization.

single-specialty group physician practices (3) Single- specialty practices that consist of two or more physicians who provide patients with one specific type of care.

skilled care (3) Includes services that are ordered by a physician and provided under the supervision of a reg- istered nurse, or physical, occupational, or speech therapist.

skilled nursing facility (SNF) (3) Provides medically necessary care to inpatients on a daily basis that is performed by, or under the supervision of, skilled medical personnel. SNFs provide IV therapy, rehabilitation, and wound care services; also called nursing facility (NF).

smart card (1) Plastic card that contains a small central processing unit, some memory, and a small rectan-gular gold-colored contact area that interacts with a smart-card reader.

social history (6) Age-appropriate review of past and current activities such as daily routine, dietary habits, exercise routine, marital status, occupation, sleeping patterns, smoking, use of alcohol and other drugs, sexual activities, and so on.

Social Security Disability Insurance (10) Pays benefits to the individual (and certain family members) if the individual worked long enough and paid Social Security taxes.

social security numbering (7) Adaptation of unit numbering system in which a patient's social security number (SSN) is assigned as the patient number; used in Veterans Affairs medical centers (VAMCs) because each veteran has a SSN, and the Social Security Administration (SSA) assists VAMCs in locating social security numbers as needed.

software (5) Program used to operate a computer and perform functions.

solo physician practices (3) Organizations that do not have physician partners or employment affiliations with other practice organizations.

solo practitioner (4) *See* solo physician practices.

Soundex (7) Phonetic indexing system that allows surnames that sound alike, but are spelled differently, to be filed together. Developed so that a surname could be located easily even though Should be though it might have been filed under various spellings.

source oriented record (SOR) (4) Traditional patient record format that maintains reports according to source of documentation.

sources of law (9) Constitution of the United States, individual state constitutions, administrative law, case law (or common law), and statutory law.

specialty hospitals (3) Concentrate on a particular population of patients or disease.

speech recognition software (4) Software that translates speech into text; sometimes called "talk to text."

standards (1) Measurements developed by an accreditation organization to evaluate a health care organization's level of performance in specific areas (usually more rigorous than regulations).

standing order (6) Physician orders preapproved by the medical staff that direct the continual administra-tion of specific activities for a specific period of time as a part of diagnostic or therapeutic care.

stare decisis (9) Latin for "to stand by things decided," which means it is a doctrine of precedent and courts adhere to the previous ruling.

Stark I (10) *See* physician self-referral law (Stark I).

Stark II (10) Physician self-referral law expanded to include referrals of Medicare *and Medicaid* patients for designated health care services (DHCS).

State Children's Health Insurance Program (SCHIP) (1) Health insurance program for infants, children, and teens that covers health care services such as doctor visits, prescription medicines, and hospitalizations; also called Title XXI of the Balanced Budget Act of 1997.

state department of health (1) Departments estab-lished by state governments to oversee health concerns within a state.

statute (9) *See* law.

statute of limitations (9) Refers to the time period after which a lawsuit cannot be filed. Statutes of limitations vary state to state, and the statute of limitations for medical malpractice cases varies from 1 to 3 years.

statutory law (9) Passed by a legislative body, and it can be amended, repealed, or expanded by the legislative body.

stop order (6) As a patient safety mechanism, state law mandates, and in the absence of state law facilities decide, for which circumstances preapproved standing physician orders are automatically discontinued (stopped), requiring the physician to document a new order.

Storage device (5) Used to save, retrieve, and use data, such as computer chips, CDs, DVDs, hard drives, and magnetic tape.

straight numeric filing (7) Records are filed in strict chronologic order according to patient number, from lowest to highest; also called consecutive numeric filing.

student health center (3) Provides health care to full- and part-time students who become ill or injured.

subacute care (3) Provided in hospitals that provide specialized long-term acute care such as chemotherapy, injury rehabilitation, ventilator support, wound care, and other types of health care services provided to seriously ill patients.

subjective (S) (4) Portion of the POR progress note that documents the patient's statement about how he or she feels, including symptomatic information.

subpoena ad testificandum (9) Court order that requires an individual to appear in court to testify.

subpoena duces tecum (9) Written command or direction that requires an individual to appear in court with documents; a *subpoena duces tecum* is signed by the clerk of the court.

subscriber (10) A health plan enrollee.

Substance Abuse and Mental Health Services Administration (SAMHSA) (3) DHHS agency that works to improve the quality and availability of substance abuse prevention, addiction treatment, and mental health services.

superbill (6) *See* encounter form.

Supplemental Security Income (10) Pays benefits based on financial need.

surname (7) Last name.

survey (1) Evaluation process conducted off-site and on-site to determine whether the facility complies with standards.

swing bed (3) Allows a rural hospital to admit a nonacute care patient.

T

Tax Equity and Fiscal Responsibility Act of 1982 (TEFRA) (1) Established the first Medicare prospective payment system, called Diagnosis Related Groups (DRGs), which was implemented in 1983.

teaching hospitals (1) Government (not-for-profit), proprietary (for-profit), or voluntary (non-profit) hospitals that are affiliated with a medical school.

telephone order (T.O.) (4) A verbal order taken over the telephone by a qualified professional (e.g., registered nurse) from a physician.

telephone order call-back policy (6) Requires the authorized staff member to read back and verify what the physician dictated to ensure that the order is entered accurately.

Temporary Assistance to Needy Families (TANF) (3) State-federal welfare program.

terminal-digit filing (7) Commonly used in health care facilities that assign six-digit (or longer) patient numbers because the number can be easily subdivided into three parts: primary, secondary, and tertiary digits. Also called reverse numeric filing.

tertiary care (1) Services provided by specialized hospitals equipped with diagnostic and treatment facilities not generally available at hospitals other than primary teaching hospitals or Level I, II, III, or IV trauma centers.

therapeutic group home (3) Six to 10 individuals are provided with supervised housing that may be linked with a day treatment program.

therapeutic plans (4) Category of POR's initial plan that specifies medications, goals, procedures, therapies, and treatments used to care for the patient.

third-party payer (10) An organization that processes claims for reimbursement covered by a health care plan.

tissue report (6) *See* pathology report.

Title XXI of the Balanced Budget Act of 1997 (1) *See* State Children's Health Insurance Program.

torts (9) Wrongful acts for which a civil suit can be brought.

total length of stay (8) Calculated for all discharged patients for a given time period.

total parenteral nutrition (TPN) (3) Administration of nutritional substances by peripheral or central intravenous infusion to patients who are either already malnourished or have the potential for developing malnutrition.

transfer note (4) Documented when a patient is being transferred to another facility. It summarizes the reason for admission, current diagnoses and medical information, and reason for transfer.

transfer order (6) Physician order documented to transfer a patient from one facility to another.

transformed-based data (8) Category of health care data used for clinical and management decision support, and planning.

treatment, payment, and health care operations (TPO) (9) *Treatment* generally means the provision, coordination, or management of health care and related services among health care providers or by a health care provider with a third party, consultation between health care providers regarding a patient, or the referral of a patient from one health care provider to another. *Payment* encompasses the various activities of health care providers to obtain payment or be reimbursed for their services and of a health plan to obtain premiums, to fulfill their coverage responsibilities and provide benefits under the plan, and to obtain or provide reimbursement for the provision of health care. *Health care operations* are certain administrative, financial, legal, and quality improvement activities of a covered entity that are necessary to run its business and to support the core functions of treatment and payment.

triage (1) An organized method of identifying and treating patients according to urgency of care required.

tumor registrar (2) *See* cancer registrar.

U

UB-04 (10) *See* CMS-1450.

Uniform Ambulatory Care Data Set (UACDS) (6) Minimum core data set collected on Medicare and Medicaid outpatients.

Uniform Hospital Discharge Data Set (UHDDS) (6) Minimum core data set collected on individual hospital discharges for the Medicare and Medicaid programs; much of this information is located on the face sheet.

unit numbering system (7) Patient is assigned a patient number the first time he or she is registered, and the patient is reassigned that same number for all subsequent admissions and encounters. Facilities that adopt the unit numbering system use admission/discharge/transfer software to manage patient number assignment, and all patient records are filed in one folder (as a unit) in the file system.

universal chart order (1) Discharged patient record is organized in the same order as when the patient was on the nursing floor; eliminates the time-consuming assembly task performed by the health information department.

upcoding (6) Documentation of diagnoses and procedures that result in higher payment for a facility; also called maximizing codes or DRG Creep.

urgent care center (3) Immediate care is provided by an on-duty physician (usually salaried). The center is usually owned by private corporations in states where permitted or non-profit facilities; also called emergency care center.

utilization management (10) Controls health care costs and the quality of health care by reviewing cases for appropriateness and medical necessity.

utilization manager (2) Responsible for coordinating patient care to ensure the appropriate utilization of resources, delivery of health care services, and timely discharge or transfer; also called case manager.

V

vendor salesperson (2) Manages a company's sales for a given territory, provides information about available consulting services, and demonstrates products to potential customers.

verbal order (6) Orders dictated to an authorized facility staff member because the responsible physician is unable to personally document the order.

vertical file (7) Resembles a file cabinet in which records are stored in a drawer.

veterans (1) Individuals who have served in the United States military and who are eligible to receive care at VA Medical Centers (VAMCs) located throughout the United States.

Veterans Health Administration (VHA) (3) An agency in the Department of Veterans Affairs that provides medical, surgical, and rehabilitative care to veterans of the armed services.

Veterans Integrated Service Network (VISN) (3) Administers and provides health care services at VA Medical Centers (VAMCs) and community-based outpatient clinics.

visible file (7) File system that allows user to easily view contents of a file drawer.

vital statistics (8) Compiled for events, including births, deaths, fetal deaths, marriages, and divorces.

voice order (V.O.) (4) Physician dictates an order in the presence of a responsible person; this is no longer accepted as standard practice by health care facilities and is documented in emergencies only.

voice recognition software (4) *See* speech recognition software.

voluntary hospitals (1) Not-for-profit hospitals operated by religious or other voluntary groups (e.g., Shriners).

W

written order (6) Orders that are handwritten in a paper-based record or entered into an electronic health record by the responsible physician.

Bibliography

Books

Abdelhak, M. (2011). *Health information: Management of a strategic resource* (4th ed.). Philadelphia, PA: Elsevier.

Ciampa, M., & Revels, M. (2012). *Introduction to healthcare information technology.* Clifton Park, NY: Cengage Learning.

Claeys, T. (1997). *Medical filing* (2nd ed.). Clifton Park, NY: Cengage Learning.

CPT (Standard Version). (2014). Salt Lake City, UT: Optum.

Damp, D. V. (2006). *Health care job explosion: High growth health careers and job locator.* Moon Township, PA: Bookhaven Press.

DeVore, A. (2012). *The Electronic Health Record for the Physician's Office.* St. Louis, MO: Elsevier.

Documentation for ambulatory care (Rev. ed.). (2001). Chicago, IL: American Health Information Management Association.

Green, M. A. *3-2-1 Code it!* (3rd ed.). (2012). Clifton Park, NY: Cengage Learning.

Green, M. A., & Rowell, J. (2015). *Understanding health insurance: A guide to professional billing* (12th ed.). Clifton Park, NY: Cengage Learning.

HCPCS Level II professional. (2014). Salt Lake City, UT: Optum.

ICD-9-CM Professional for Hospitals (Volumes 1, 2, & 3). (2014). Salt Lake City, UT: Optum.

James, E. (2009). *Documentation and reimbursement for long-term care* (2nd ed.). Chicago, IL: American Health Information Management Association.

Koch, G. (2015). *Basic allied health statistics and analysis* (4th ed.). Clifton Park, NY: Cengage Learning.

LaTour, K. M., & Eichenwald, S. (2012). *Health information management: Concepts, principles, and practice* (4th ed.). Chicago, IL: American Health Information Management Association.

Marrelli, T. M. (2012). *Handbook of home health standards and documentation guidelines for reimbursement* (5th ed.). St. Louis, MO: Elsevier.

McWay, D. (2010). *Legal aspects of health information* (3rd ed.). Clifton Park, NY: Cengage Learning.

McWay, D. (2014). *Today's health information management: An integrated approach* (2nd ed.). Clifton Park, NY: Cengage Learning.

Mitchel, J., & Haroun, L. (2012). *Introduction to health care* (3rd ed.). Clifton Park, NY: Cengage Learning.

Odum-Wesley, B., & Meyers, C. (2009). *Documentation for medical records.* Chicago, IL: American Health Information Management Association.

Peden, A. (2012). *Comparative records for health information management* (3rd ed.). Clifton Park, NY: Cengage Learning.

Pozgar, G. (2011). *Legal aspects of health care administration* (11th ed.). Sudbury, MA: Jones and Bartlett Publishers.

Sayles, N. (2013). *Health information management technology: An applied approach* (4th ed.). Chicago, IL: American Health Information Management Association.

Sayles, N. (2013). *Introduction to computer systems for health information technology* (2nd ed.). American Health Information Management Association.

Shaw, P., Elliott, C., Isaacson, P., & Murphy, E. (2012). *Quality and performance improvement* (5th ed.). Chicago, IL: American Health Information Management Association.

Simmers, L. (2014). *Diversified health occupations* (8th ed.). Clifton Park, NY: Cengage Learning.

Brochures, Bulletins, and Handbooks

Comprehensive accreditation manual for hospital (CAMH): The official handbook. (2010). Oakbrook Terrace, IL: The Joint Commission.

Medicare & you. (2009). Baltimore, MD: Centers for Medicare and Medicaid Services.

PRG quick notes: HIPAA privacy basics. (2003). Clifton Park, NY: Cengage Learning.

Journals, E-Newsletters, and Newsmagazines

Advance for health information professionals. King of Prussia, PA: Merion Publications.

Briefings on coding compliance strategies. (2009). Opus Communications. Marblehead, MA: HCPro.

For the record. (2009). Spring City, PA: Great Valley Publishing Company.

iHealthBeat. (2009). Oakland, CA: California HealthCare Foundation.

Journal of AHIMA. (2009). Chicago, IL: American Health Information Management Association.

Internet References

http://access.gpo.gov. Free electronic access to Government Printing Office (GPO) products produced by the federal government, including the *Code of Federal Regulations (CFR)* or *Federal Register*.

http://www.bibbero.com. A resource for color-coded file organizing systems and custom printing.

http://www.bls.gov. U.S. Department of Labor, Bureau of Labor Statistics.

http://training.seer.cancer.gov. U.S. National Cancer Institute's Surveillance, Epidemiology, and End Results (SEER) Program Training Web site. SEER's training Web site provides Web-based training modules for cancer registration and surveillance.

http://www.usa.gov. U.S. government's official portal for online information, services, and resources.

Software

Encoder Pro Expert. (2014). Salt Lake City, UT: Optum.

SimClaim. (2014). Clifton Park, NY: Cengage Learning.

Index